Baseball's Best

D1409390

150th Anniversary Edition

Stat Geek Baseball's Best Ever Book
from statgeekbaseball.com

Edited by J.D. Peterman

150th Anniversary Edition: Paperback and Ebook, 2020, 2021

Cover and other book graphics Copyright © 2020, 2021 JDP ECON Publications, statgeekbaseball.com, and its licensors. All rights reserved.

Printed/Digital Copy in the United States of America by JDP ECON Publications & Books, 2217 Bruce Drive, Pottstown, Pa., U.S.A. 19464-1514

Paperback ISBN: 9798556144521

About the Baseball's Best @150 Book

This 150th Anniversary Edition of Stat Geek Baseball's Best Ever Book series is, in essence, a book of lists and comparisons of Major League baseball players over the first 150 years of baseball. From 1871, with the first year of the National Association, through the initial campaigns of the National League in 1876 and the American League in 1901, and also includes leagues such as the Union Association, Federal League, and Pacific League, to today's most recent season of the shortened variety of 2020.

There will be lists of the Best Batters of All-Time, the Best Pitchers of All-Time, and for the first time included in the general Best Ever Book, the Best Fielders of All-Time. But not only will there be one hundred and fifty, or more, of the best in those overall categories, there will be lists and ranks of Baseball's Best from every current Major League Team, plus those of the distant past. Yes, so if you're a fan of Major League baseball when it was in Buffalo, they'll be here, too. We've compiled the Best Ever list of the Top Players by every Team and Franchise in baseball history.

Not only will there be ranks of the Best Careers in all those categories and for all those teams, but there will also be lists of the Best Seasons Ever.

For a better understanding of what's included in ...

Baseball's Best @ 150

Best Batting Seasons	Best Ever Postseason Years for Batters
Best Pitching Seasons (Pitchers/Relief Pitchers)	Best Ever Postseason Years for Pitchers
Best Seasons Ranked by Every Team	Best Ever Postseason Batting Careers
Best Batting Careers	Best Ever Postseason Pitching Careers
Best Pitching Careers	Hall of Fame Ranks
Best Fielding Careers	Best Batting, Pitching, Overall Teams Ever
Best Careers by Every Team for Batters, Pitchers, and Fielders	

How are These Rankings Compiled?

Using our unique system of Player Rankings that can compare players of different eras, all developed around the Stat called PEVA. The Stat Geek Baseball Player Rating decision model, a research study that took five thousand hours to complete, rated every player in baseball history, using millions of traditional counting stats, and developed circa two million new ones of our own. It tracks correlations between how baseball statistics of all eras compare and are valued by real baseball.

For more on the details of PEVA, check out our ABOUT OUR STATS section at the end of the book, but for a quick look, let's talk PEVA. PEVA is a player performance grade for every player in history for every season of their career. It accounts for each era and can be used to rather accurately compare a player or pitcher or fielder no matter whether they played in a time of limited or expanded home runs or offense in general. PEVA is ranked on a scale of 0.200 to 64.000.

How can it do that?

It tracks domination. How well the player dominated his time and season.

That's the interior of the matter of how and why, but perhaps we shouldn't dwell on the weeds and mechanics. Now it's time to see how your favorite player compares to others.

Track how your current favorites are moving up the career list for their team or baseball as a whole and what that means to their Hall of Fame potential.

See who makes it onto the All-Time team for your favorite franchise, then debate whether you would have other players there instead.

We hope you enjoy our take on Baseball's Best over the first one hundred and fifty years of the Major Leagues.

Thanks for taking a look.

PEVA Player Ratings Boxscore

PEVA	One Word	Description
64.000	Maximum	Maximum Player Rating
32.000	Fantastic	MVP/Cy Young Award Candidate
20.000	Great	All-League
15.000	Very Good	All-Star Caliber
10.000	Good	Plus Starter
3.500	Average	Bench Player
0.200	Minimum	Minimum Player Rating

Chapter Index

1. Babe Ruth, New York Yankees, 1923
58.931 PEVA RATING

There was no player in baseball history as dominant as Babe Ruth. Just look at the list of the best two hundred seasons by a position player, and you'll see just what domination is. He takes six of the Top Ten seasons of All-Time, including the Top Two. There's that stadium basically constructed, the House That Ruth Built, in the Bronx, even if it's now supplanted by a newer edition. His 1923 season was the first played in that stadium. The season itself was phenomenal; Ruth walked 170 times, 69 more than the batter in second place. His OPS was 1.309. Some baseball historians point to the 1927 season as being more dominant, and that's an understandable quibble. But for us, 1923, that first season in the house that was constructed because of the skill of Babe Ruth and the fervor he brought to New York City and the baseball world, ranks as the Best Season of All-Time.

How Dominant was Babe Ruth in 1923?

He was 1st in baseball for Runs Scored (151). 1st in RBI (131). And his Run Production (Runs Plus RBI) at 282 was 525.4% higher than baseball's average for that year of 53.67.

His On Base Percentage of 0.545 was 1st, 157.1% higher than baseball's average of 0.347.

His Slugging Percentage of 0.764 was 1st, 195.4% higher than baseball's average of 0.391.

His Field Value was 1.57 (the Maximum FV for an Outfielder is 1.70).

2. Babe Ruth, New York Yankees, 1920
55.754 PEVA RATING

For those that don't consider 1927 as Babe Ruth's best, many think that his 1920 season ranks ahead of both that year and 1923. This first season of Ruth after the trade from the Boston Red Sox to the Yankees, when he was no longer a rotation pitcher, may rank as his best offensively. Ruth hit 54 home runs; second place was 19. Ruth had a slugging percentage of 0.847; the MLB average in 1920 was 0.372. So why doesn't 1920 rank ahead of 1923 for us. Ruth played less games, and had fewer plate appearances, lowering his durability factor. Three years into full-time Outfield play, and Ruth was also a better defensive player in 1923 than 1920 as well, with his Field Value in 1920 at 1.29 (out of a maximum of 1.70) lower than that in 1923, 1.57. So for those two reasons, Ruth in 1920 was not quite as great, to us, as his season in 1923. But boy, it was sure great.

How Dominant was Babe Ruth in 1920?

He was 1st in baseball for Runs Scored (158). 1st in RBI (137). And his Run Production (Runs Plus RBI) at 295 was 600.3% higher than baseball's average for that year of 49.14.

His On Base Percentage of 0.532 was 1st, 158.8% higher than baseball's average of 0.335.

His Slugging Percentage of 0.847 was 1st, 227.7% higher than baseball's average of 0.372.

His Field Value was 1.29 (the Maximum FV for an Outfielder is 1.70).

3. Barry Bonds, San Francisco Giants, 2001
55.207 PEVA RATING

For anyone who watched baseball in the more current era, there's no doubting that the most Ruthian player years of the era of prodigious offense came from Barry Bonds. Yes, there were likely reasons for that beyond beer, i.e. steroids, so any diminution you would like to do concerning this entry is up to you. But per pure statistical measure, there's no doubting what Bonds did in 2001. He walked 177 times. He hit 73 home runs, even if the record does deserve some punctuation, an asterisk, denoting the differentials of era. He had an OPS of 1.378, still far ahead of Sammy Sosa at 1.174. So why isn't Bonds ranked higher than Ruth. In part due to his lack of games played, only 153 of 162. In other parts due to the fact that Bonds did not lead baseball in 2001 in Run Production, only 4th in Runs and 6th in RBI, which we and the PEVA system considers important.

How Dominant was Barry Bonds in 2001?

He was 4th in baseball for Runs Scored (129). 6th in RBI (137). And his Run Production (Runs Plus RBI) at 266 was 441.1% higher than baseball's average for that year of 59.9.

His On Base Percentage of 0.515 was 1st, 155.1% higher than baseball's average of 0.332.

His Slugging Percentage of 0.863 was 1st, 202.1% higher than baseball's average of 0.427.

His Field Value was 1.31 (the Maximum FV for an Outfielder is 1.70).

4. Babe Ruth, New York Yankees, 1921
54.876 PEVA RATING

The 1921 season saw Ruth plying his trade at the Polo Grounds, a fact the Giants, the National League tenant, did not prefer. They suggested the Yankees move, which they started to do, with construction of a sixty thousand seat stadium, double the average seat capacity for a stadium at that time. They knew Ruth would fill it. In the 1921 season, Ruth scored 177 runs and batted in 171. He was six times as likely to produce a run as the average Major League Player. 1921 was the first year the Yanks won the pennant, eventually losing the World Series to the Giants, their co-tenant at those Polo Grounds.

How Dominant was Babe Ruth in 1921?

He was 1st in baseball for Runs Scored (177). 1st in RBI (171). And his Run Production (Runs Plus RBI) at 348 was 616.8% higher than baseball's average for that year of 56.42.

His On Base Percentage of 0.512 was 1st, 147.1% higher than baseball's average of 0.348.

His Slugging Percentage of 0.846 was 1st, 209.9% higher than baseball's average of 0.403.

His Field Value was 1.47 (the Maximum FV for an Outfielder is 1.70).

5. Barry Bonds, San Francisco Giants, 2002
54.848 PEVA RATING

Barry Bonds would set a record for On Base Percentage in 2002 at 0.582, although it would only stand for two years when he would break it again. They walked him 198 times, another record, to be broken two years later by Barry Bonds again, with 232. The reasons for him ranking below Ruth again were due to the fact that his use, or durability, was lower than the maximum, playing only 143 games. Durability is an important factor in the PEVA system. It's impossible to help your team if you don't play. A lack of Run Production also lowered Bonds PEVA ranking, only #8 in Runs Scored and #14 in Runs Batted In for the season.

How Dominant was Barry Bonds in 2002?

He was 8th in baseball for Runs Scored (117). 14th in RBI (110). And his Run Production (Runs Plus RBI) at 227 was 379.9% higher than baseball's average for that year of 59.75.

His On Base Percentage of 0.582 was 1st, 175.8% higher than baseball's average of 0.331.

His Slugging Percentage of 0.799 was 1st, 191.6% higher than baseball's average of 0.417.

His Field Value was 1.19 (the Maximum FV for an Outfielder is 1.70).

6. Ted Williams, Boston Red Sox, 1942
52.075 PEVA RATING

Williams, unlike Bonds, was a Run Producing Machine, first in Major League Baseball in 1942 in both Runs Scored and Runs Batted In, and he was an On Base Machine at the same time, at the clip of 0.499. The Number Six position of All-Time seasons also included a Fielding Percentage of 1.55, and a Slugging Percentage of 0.648. And this would be the last season for Ted Williams until 1946 due to his service in World War II. Imagine how high those intervening years would be on the list, after his #6 1942 season coming after the #8 season of 1941. When you consider that his returning season in 1946 comes in at #26, it's not hard to imagine the Splendid Splinter with more entries in the Top Ten.

How Dominant was Ted Williams in 1942?

He was 1st in baseball for Runs Scored (141). 1st in RBI (137). And his Run Production (Runs Plus RBI) at 278 was 647.9% higher than baseball's average for that year of 42.91.

His On Base Percentage of 0.499 was 1st, 154.5% higher than baseball's average of 0.323.

His Slugging Percentage of 0.648 was 1st, 185.1% higher than baseball's average of 0.350.

His Field Value was 1.55 (the Maximum FV for an Outfielder is 1.70).

7. Babe Ruth, New York Yankees, 1927
51.850 PEVA RATING

Yes, if you asked most ardent baseball fans what was the best Position Player year in history, it's more than likely Babe Ruth's season of 1927 would head many lists. And there's good reasons why. Babe Ruth hit sixty home runs in 1927 in a 154 game season, powering the Yankees to 110 wins. But Ruth's On Base Percentage had begun to drop, from its high of 0.545 in 1923 to the rate of 0.486. He wouldn't have an OBP above 0.500 for the rest of his career. But whether it ranks #7 or #1, is not particularly important to Yankee fans of yesterday or today. They won the World Series in four straight games over the Pittsburgh Pirates.

How Dominant was Babe Ruth in 1927?

He was 1st in baseball for Runs Scored (158). 2nd in RBI (164). And his Run Production (Runs Plus RBI) at 322 was 639.5% higher than baseball's average for that year of 50.35.

His On Base Percentage of 0.486 was 1st, 140.9% higher than baseball's average of 0.345.

His Slugging Percentage of 0.772 was 1st, 196.4% higher than baseball's average of 0.393.

His Field Value was 1.43 (the Maximum FV for an Outfielder is 1.70).

8. Ted Williams, Boston Red Sox, 1941
51.730 PEVA RATING

The position of the United States was effectively neutral in World War II during the summer when Ted Williams had the #8 best season in baseball history. What the sport could not contemplate was that by December 7, 1941, the United States would be attacked at Pearl Harbor, and eventually lose Williams for several years (1943-1945) to the service. But for that one last season of innocence prior to the attack, Williams was marvelous, battling Joe DiMaggio for attention. This was the year Joe hit in 56 straight, still a MLB record. In 1941, Ted Williams hit for average, 0.406, the last man to hit 0.400. He hit for power, 37 homers, and knocked in 120.

How Dominant was Ted Williams in 1941?

He was 1st in baseball for Runs Scored (135). 4th in RBI (120). And his Run Production (Runs Plus RBI) at 255 was 535.0% higher than baseball's average for that year of 47.66.

His On Base Percentage of 0.533 was 1st, 165.6% higher than baseball's average of 0.334.

His Slugging Percentage of 0.735 was 1st, 196.0% higher than baseball's average of 0.375.

His Field Value was 1.33 (the Maximum FV for an Outfielder is 1.70).

9. Babe Ruth, New York Yankees, 1926
51.603 PEVA RATING

Just another year at the new ballpark for Ruth, leading baseball in Runs Scored, Runs Batted In, On Base and Slugging Percentage, all while leading his team to the World Series, although the Yankees would lose to the Cardinals there. Ruth hit 47 Home Runs in 1926, knocked in 146 Runs Batted In, and had a Slugging Percentage of 0.737, all adding up to the 9th Best Season in Baseball History, even though it was only his 5th Best.

How Dominant was Babe Ruth in 1926?

He was 1st in baseball for Runs Scored (139). 1st in RBI (146). And his Run Production (Runs Plus RBI) at 285 was 552.1% higher than baseball's average for that year of 51.62.

His On Base Percentage of 0.516 was 1st, 149.6% higher than baseball's average of 0.345.

His Slugging Percentage of 0.737 was 1st, 189.5% higher than baseball's average of 0.389.

His Field Value was 1.47 (the Maximum FV for an Outfielder is 1.70).

10. Babe Ruth, New York Yankees, 1924
51.324 PEVA RATING

Ruth's season in 1924 proved that Ruth was not only a prodigious Run Producer, but that he could get a basic hit when needed, too. Ruth hit 0.378 in 1924, with 108 singles, 39 doubles, 7 triples, and 46 home runs, to the total of 200 hits. He also walked 142 times. That's 342 times on base without even counting his 4 Hit By Pitch. Coming in as the 6th entrant of Babe Ruth on the all-time best seasons list, it may bring up the rear, however, it once again added to the legacy of the man who built a Yankee Stadium, filled it to the rafters each night, and charmed the public and media throughout his career.

How Dominant was Babe Ruth in 1924?

He was 1st in baseball for Runs Scored (143). 3rd in RBI (121). And his Run Production (Runs

Plus RBI) at 264 was 522.3% higher than baseball's average for that year of 50.55.

His On Base Percentage of 0.513 was 1st, 147.4% higher than baseball's average of 0.348.

His Slugging Percentage of 0.739 was 1st, 187.6% higher than baseball's average of 0.394.

His Field Value was 1.53 (the Maximum FV for an Outfielder is 1.70).

Top 200 Best Seasons Ever

Best Position Players Ever (1871-2020) – Regular Season

Rank	Name	First	Year	Team	Lg	HR	RBI	AVG	Age	PEVA-B
1	Ruth	Babe	1923	NYA	AL	41	131	0.393	28	58.931
2	Ruth	Babe	1920	NYA	AL	54	137	0.376	25	55.754
3	Bonds	Barry	2001	SFN	NL	73	137	0.328	37	55.207
4	Ruth	Babe	1921	NYA	AL	59	171	0.378	26	54.876
5	Bonds	Barry	2002	SFN	NL	46	110	0.370	38	54.848
6	Williams	Ted	1942	BOS	AL	36	137	0.356	24	52.075
7	Ruth	Babe	1927	NYA	AL	60	164	0.356	32	51.850
8	Williams	Ted	1941	BOS	AL	37	120	0.406	23	51.730
9	Ruth	Babe	1926	NYA	AL	47	146	0.372	31	51.603
10	Ruth	Babe	1924	NYA	AL	46	121	0.378	29	51.324
11	Gehrig	Lou	1927	NYA	AL	47	175	0.373	24	50.953
12	Shaffer	Orator	1878	IN1	NL	0	30	0.338	27	50.240
13	Gehrig	Lou	1934	NYA	AL	49	165	0.363	31	50.136
14	Cobb	Ty	1917	DET	AL	6	102	0.383	31	48.911
15	Wagner	Honus	1908	PIT	NL	10	109	0.354	34	48.837
16	Bonds	Barry	2004	SFN	NL	45	101	0.362	40	48.632
17	Rosen	Al	1953	CLE	AL	43	145	0.336	29	48.401
18	Mantle	Mickey	1956	NYA	AL	52	130	0.353	25	47.236
19	Barnes	Ross	1876	CHN	NL	1	59	0.429	26	46.554
20	Gehrig	Lou	1936	NYA	AL	49	152	0.354	33	45.995
21	Yount	Robin	1982	ML4	AL	29	114	0.331	27	45.717
22	Ruth	Babe	1919	BOS	AL	29	114	0.322	24	45.484
23	Hornsby	Rogers	1922	SLN	NL	42	152	0.401	26	45.149
24	Robinson	Frank	1962	CIN	NL	39	136	0.342	27	44.982
25	Jones	Charley	1879	BSN	NL	9	62	0.315	29	44.728
26	Williams	Ted	1946	BOS	AL	38	123	0.342	28	44.043
27	Pujols	Albert	2009	SLN	NL	47	135	0.327	29	43.955
28	Hines	Paul	1879	PRO	NL	2	52	0.357	24	43.731
29	Cobb	Ty	1915	DET	AL	3	99	0.369	29	43.671
30	Bonds	Barry	1993	SFN	NL	46	123	0.336	29	43.404
31	Speaker	Tris	1912	BOS	AL	10	90	0.383	24	43.198
32	Mays	Willie	1965	SFN	NL	52	112	0.317	34	43.109
33	Robinson	Frank	1966	BAL	AL	49	122	0.316	31	42.918
34	Stone	George	1906	SLA	AL	6	71	0.358	30	42.914
35	Barnes	Ross	1873	BS1	NA	2	62	0.425	23	42.762
36	Delahanty	Ed	1899	PHI	NL	9	137	0.410	32	42.557
37	Foxx	Jimmie	1933	PHA	AL	48	163	0.356	26	42.539
38	Cobb	Ty	1911	DET	AL	8	127	0.420	25	42.464
39	Mantle	Mickey	1961	NYA	AL	54	128	0.317	30	42.398
40	Mantle	Mickey	1960	NYA	AL	40	94	0.275	29	42.394

Rank	Name	First	Year	Team	Lg	HR	RBI	AVG	Age	PEVA-B
41	Speaker	Tris	1916	CLE	AL	2	79	0.386	28	42.388
42	Bench	Johnny	1972	CIN	NL	40	125	0.270	25	42.271
43	Brouthers	Dan	1892	BRO	NL	5	124	0.335	34	42.196
44	Ruth	Babe	1931	NYA	AL	46	163	0.373	36	41.968
45	Hornsby	Rogers	1929	CHN	NL	39	149	0.380	33	41.923
46	Aaron	Hank	1959	ML1	NL	39	123	0.355	25	41.920
47	Williams	Ted	1949	BOS	AL	43	159	0.343	31	41.778
48	Mathews	Eddie	1953	ML1	NL	47	135	0.302	22	41.677
49	Mathews	Eddie	1960	ML1	NL	39	124	0.277	29	41.382
50	Musial	Stan	1943	SLN	NL	13	81	0.357	23	41.278
51	Thomas	Frank	1994	CHA	AL	38	101	0.353	26	41.278
52	Foxx	Jimmie	1932	PHA	AL	58	169	0.364	25	41.252
53	Piazza	Mike	1997	LAN	NL	40	124	0.362	29	41.108
54	Trout	Mike	2014	LAA	AL	36	111	0.287	23	41.098
55	Schmidt	Mike	1981	PHI	NL	31	91	0.316	32	40.963
56	Mays	Willie	1962	SFN	NL	49	141	0.304	31	40.947
57	McGwire	Mark	1998	SLN	NL	70	147	0.299	35	40.809
58	Rodriguez	Alex	2007	NYA	AL	54	156	0.314	32	40.717
59	Mantle	Mickey	1957	NYA	AL	34	94	0.365	26	40.637
60	Musial	Stan	1953	SLN	NL	30	113	0.337	33	40.502
61	Yastrzemski	Carl	1967	BOS	AL	44	121	0.326	28	40.383
62	Delahanty	Ed	1896	PHI	NL	13	126	0.397	29	40.317
63	Aaron	Hank	1963	ML1	NL	44	130	0.319	29	40.268
64	Trout	Mike	2016	LAA	AL	29	100	0.315	25	40.170
65	Gehrig	Lou	1931	NYA	AL	46	184	0.341	28	40.131
66	Holmes	Tommy	1945	BSN	NL	28	117	0.352	28	40.065
67	Ruth	Babe	1928	NYA	AL	54	142	0.323	33	40.061
68	Gehrig	Lou	1930	NYA	AL	41	174	0.379	27	39.839
69	Cobb	Ty	1909	DET	AL	9	107	0.377	23	39.724
70	Trout	Mike	2013	LAA	AL	27	97	0.323	22	39.602
71	Brouthers	Dan	1883	BFN	NL	3	97	0.374	25	39.597
72	Posey	Buster	2012	SFN	NL	24	103	0.336	25	39.507
73	Mays	Willie	1955	NY1	NL	51	127	0.319	24	39.404
74	Brett	George	1985	KCA	AL	30	112	0.335	32	39.324
75	Cabrera	Miguel	2012	DET	AL	44	139	0.330	29	39.160
76	Pujols	Albert	2010	SLN	NL	42	118	0.312	30	39.067
77	Ruth	Babe	1930	NYA	AL	49	153	0.359	35	39.019
78	Sosa	Sammy	2001	CHN	NL	64	160	0.328	33	38.918
79	Mays	Willie	1960	SFN	NL	29	103	0.319	29	38.898
80	Musial	Stan	1944	SLN	NL	12	94	0.347	24	38.717
81	Snider	Duke	1953	BRO	NL	42	126	0.336	27	38.655
82	McCutchen	Andrew	2012	PIT	NL	31	96	0.327	26	38.647
83	Lajoie	Nap	1901	PHA	AL	14	125	0.426	27	38.604
84	Mathews	Eddie	1959	ML1	NL	46	114	0.306	28	38.592
85	Hines	Paul	1878	PRO	NL	4	50	0.358	23	38.405
86	Campanella	Roy	1953	BRO	NL	41	142	0.312	32	38.348
87	Anson	Cap	1881	CHN	NL	1	82	0.399	29	38.143
88	Bagwell	Jeff	1994	HOU	NL	39	116	0.368	26	38.044
89	Jackson	Joe	1912	CLE	AL	3	90	0.395	23	37.904
90	Musial	Stan	1952	SLN	NL	21	91	0.336	32	37.889

Rank	Name	First	Year	Team	Lg	HR	RBI	AVG	Age	PEVA-B
91	Stanton	Giancarlo	2017	MIA	AL	59	132	0.289	28	37.866
92	DiMaggio	Joe	1941	NYA	AL	30	125	0.357	27	37.809
93	Gehrig	Lou	1937	NYA	AL	37	159	0.351	34	37.760
94	Cobb	Ty	1918	DET	AL	3	64	0.382	32	37.701
95	Flick	Elmer	1900	PHI	NL	11	110	0.367	24	37.675
96	Hornsby	Rogers	1925	SLN	NL	39	143	0.403	29	37.655
97	Foxx	Jimmie	1938	BOS	AL	50	175	0.349	31	37.579
98	Dunlap	Fred	1884	SLU	UA	13	NA	0.412	25	37.571
99	Murray	Eddie	1984	BAL	AL	29	110	0.306	28	37.406
100	Musial	Stan	1951	SLN	NL	32	108	0.355	31	37.339
101	Speaker	Tris	1914	BOS	AL	4	90	0.338	26	37.327
102	Aaron	Hank	1962	ML1	NL	45	128	0.323	28	37.264
103	Kiner	Ralph	1951	PIT	NL	42	109	0.309	29	37.003
104	Kelley	Joe	1896	BLN	NL	8	100	0.364	25	36.936
105	McCovey	Willie	1969	SFN	NL	45	126	0.320	31	36.924
106	Delahanty	Ed	1893	PHI	NL	19	146	0.368	26	36.872
107	Gehrig	Lou	1933	NYA	AL	32	139	0.334	30	36.863
108	Mantle	Mickey	1955	NYA	AL	37	99	0.306	24	36.784
109	Mays	Willie	1958	SFN	NL	29	96	0.347	27	36.606
110	Baker	Frank	1912	PHA	AL	10	130	0.347	26	36.589
111	Ott	Mel	1929	NY1	NL	42	151	0.328	20	36.437
112	Mantle	Mickey	1958	NYA	AL	42	97	0.304	27	36.436
113	Williams	Ted	1947	BOS	AL	32	114	0.343	29	36.436
114	Pujols	Albert	2006	SLN	NL	49	137	0.331	26	36.422
115	Mays	Willie	1964	SFN	NL	47	111	0.296	33	36.258
116	Magee	Sherry	1910	PHI	NL	6	123	0.331	26	36.256
117	Cash	Norm	1961	DET	AL	41	132	0.361	27	36.206
118	Cobb	Ty	1912	DET	AL	7	83	0.409	26	36.188
119	White	Deacon	1877	BSN	NL	2	49	0.387	30	36.179
120	Canseco	Jose	1988	OAK	AL	42	124	0.307	24	36.135
121	Bonds	Barry	1990	PIT	NL	33	114	0.301	26	36.095
122	Cabrera	Miguel	2010	DET	AL	38	126	0.328	27	36.079
123	Sheckard	Jimmy	1903	BRO	NL	9	75	0.332	25	36.040
124	Thomas	Frank	1991	CHA	AL	32	109	0.318	23	36.023
125	Bagwell	Jeff	1999	HOU	NL	42	126	0.304	31	35.960
126	Ripken, Jr.	Cal	1984	BAL	AL	27	86	0.304	24	35.874
127	Seymour	Cy	1905	CIN	NL	8	121	0.377	33	35.870
128	Ripken, Jr.	Cal	1991	BAL	AL	34	114	0.323	31	35.853
129	Evans	Dwight	1984	BOS	AL	32	104	0.295	33	35.847
130	Wagner	Honus	1907	PIT	NL	6	82	0.350	33	35.816
131	Musial	Stan	1948	SLN	NL	39	131	0.376	28	35.811
132	DiMaggio	Joe	1937	NYA	AL	46	167	0.346	23	35.806
133	Wilson	Hack	1930	CHN	NL	56	191	0.356	30	35.799
134	Kemp	Matt	2011	LAN	NL	39	126	0.324	26	35.783
135	Browning	Pete	1885	LS2	AA	9	73	0.362	24	35.668
136	McVey	Cal	1875	BS1	NA	3	87	0.355	26	35.627
137	Trout	Mike	2018	LAA	AL	39	79	0.312	27	35.599
138	Santo	Ron	1964	CHN	NL	30	114	0.313	24	35.556
139	Howard	Ryan	2006	PHI	NL	58	149	0.313	27	35.507
140	Wagner	Honus	1905	PIT	NL	6	101	0.363	31	35.473

Rank	Name	First	Year	Team	Lg	HR	RBI	AVG	Age	PEVA-B
141	Trout	Mike	2015	LAA	AL	41	90	0.299	24	35.459
142	Duffy	Hugh	1894	BSN	NL	18	145	0.440	28	35.452
143	Bonds	Barry	1992	PIT	NL	34	103	0.311	28	35.418
144	Kauff	Benny	1914	IND	FL	8	95	0.370	24	35.356
145	Delahanty	Ed	1897	PHI	NL	5	96	0.377	30	35.320
146	Mattingly	Don	1986	NYA	AL	31	113	0.352	25	35.246
147	Speaker	Tris	1923	CLE	AL	17	130	0.380	35	35.232
148	Nicholson	Bill	1943	CHN	NL	29	128	0.309	29	35.190
149	Greenberg	Hank	1937	DET	AL	40	183	0.337	26	35.096
150	White	Deacon	1875	BS1	NA	1	60	0.367	28	35.065
151	Speaker	Tris	1920	CLE	AL	8	107	0.388	32	35.002
152	Hamilton	Billy	1894	PHI	NL	4	87	0.404	28	34.987
153	Doby	Larry	1952	CLE	AL	32	104	0.276	29	34.855
154	Brouthers	Dan	1891	BS2	AA	5	109	0.350	33	34.762
155	Nicholson	Bill	1944	CHN	NL	33	122	0.287	30	34.757
156	Snider	Duke	1955	BRO	NL	42	136	0.309	29	34.757
157	Allen	Dick	1972	CHA	AL	37	113	0.308	30	34.744
158	Johnson	Bob	1944	BOS	AL	17	106	0.324	39	34.713
159	Delahanty	Ed	1902	WS1	AL	10	93	0.376	35	34.689
160	Cabrera	Miguel	2013	DET	AL	44	137	0.348	30	34.680
161	Giambi	Jason	2000	OAK	AL	43	137	0.333	29	34.676
162	Martinez	Edgar	1995	SEA	AL	29	113	0.356	32	34.622
163	Boggs	Wade	1987	BOS	AL	24	89	0.363	29	34.592
164	Rodriguez	Alex	2000	SEA	AL	41	132	0.316	25	34.588
165	Banks	Ernie	1959	CHN	NL	45	143	0.304	28	34.546
166	Torre	Joe	1971	SLN	NL	24	137	0.363	31	34.530
167	Cobb	Ty	1916	DET	AL	5	68	0.371	30	34.488
168	Keeler	Willie	1897	BLN	NL	0	74	0.424	25	34.488
169	Mays	Willie	1963	SFN	NL	38	103	0.314	32	34.477
170	Brouthers	Dan	1882	BFN	NL	6	63	0.368	24	34.359
171	Hornsby	Rogers	1924	SLN	NL	25	94	0.424	28	34.349
172	Stovey	Harry	1889	PH4	AA	19	119	0.308	33	34.320
173	Lajoie	Nap	1906	CLE	AL	0	91	0.355	32	34.293
174	Gehrig	Lou	1928	NYA	AL	27	142	0.374	25	34.257
175	Foster	George	1977	CIN	NL	52	149	0.320	29	34.233
176	Rodriguez	Alex	2005	NYA	AL	48	130	0.321	30	34.230
177	Jackson	Joe	1911	CLE	AL	7	83	0.408	22	34.179
178	Delgado	Carlos	2000	TOR	AL	41	137	0.344	28	34.143
179	Jennings	Hughie	1896	BLN	NL	0	121	0.401	27	34.143
180	Gehrig	Lou	1932	NYA	AL	34	151	0.349	29	34.089
181	Fielder	Prince	2009	MIL	NL	46	141	0.299	25	34.062
182	Lajoie	Nap	1904	CLE	AL	6	102	0.376	30	34.027
183	Schmidt	Mike	1974	PHI	NL	36	116	0.282	25	34.027
184	Votto	Joey	2010	CIN	NL	37	113	0.324	26	33.995
185	Mays	Willie	1954	NY1	NL	41	110	0.345	23	33.994
186	Foxx	Jimmie	1934	PHA	AL	44	130	0.334	27	33.948
187	Bonds	Barry	1996	SFN	NL	42	129	0.308	32	33.905
188	Harper	Bryce	2015	WAS	NL	42	99	0.330	23	33.903
189	Jackson	Reggie	1969	OAK	AL	47	118	0.275	23	33.898
190	Bellinger	Cody	2019	LAN	NL	47	115	0.305	24	33.859

Rank	Name	First	Year	Team	Lg	HR	RBI	AVG	Age	PEVA-B
191	Freeman	Freddie	2020	ATL	NL	13	53	0.341	31	**33.816**
192	Thomas	Frank	1992	CHA	AL	24	115	0.323	24	**33.764**
193	Killebrew	Harmon	1969	MIN	AL	49	140	0.276	33	**33.634**
194	Banks	Ernie	1958	CHN	NL	47	129	0.313	27	**33.578**
195	Stargell	Willie	1973	PIT	NL	44	119	0.299	33	**33.533**
196	Aaron	Hank	1960	ML1	NL	40	126	0.292	26	**33.522**
197	Carter	Gary	1982	MON	NL	29	97	0.293	28	**33.521**
198	Pujols	Albert	2003	SLN	NL	43	124	0.359	23	**33.510**
199	Trout	Mike	2012	LAA	AL	30	83	0.326	21	**33.502**
200	Jeter	Derek	1999	NYA	AL	24	102	0.349	25	**33.492**

Note: Age = Player age at the end of the year.

1. Greg Maddux, Atlanta Braves, 1994
57.974 PEVA RATING

Yes, this is a surprise, as the 1994 season of Greg Maddux would not head the top of Best Pitching Seasons for most baseball fans or baseball stat aficionados. Part of that, of course, is that it was the year baseball went on strike, and lost a World Series, and thus, the counting stats do not look particularly great, and the memories from that season not its most stellar. However, that should not take away from the historic season Greg Maddux had. For two years, including the next shortened season, 1995, due to the strike continuation, Maddux had what is likely the best two year stretch in baseball history for a pitcher. In 1994, Maddux only gave up 0.18 HR for every 9 innings he pitched compared to the average in baseball that year of 1.04. His ERA, in a hitter's park, was 34.6% of the average ERA in baseball. That leading ERA was over 1 run better than the man in second place in 1994. He only walked 31 batters all season. So, whether the year was short and the World Series canceled, it should not take away from the fact that Maddux had one of the best pitching seasons in history, whether you agree or not with the #1 rank. And what would his stats had looked like if you would prorate them to a full 162 game schedule. 23 wins, 9 losses, 1.56 ERA, 222 SO, 287 IP. Pretty darn good.

How Dominant was Great Maddux in 1994?

He was 2nd in baseball for Wins (16), 470.6% higher than baseball's average for that year of 3.40.

He was 1st in IP (202.0), 332.1% higher than baseball's average of 60.82.

His ERA of 1.56 was 1st, 34.6% of baseball's average of 4.51.

His Walks/Hits per 9 Innings Pitched (WHIP9) of 8.06 was 1st, 62.6% of baseball's average of 12.87.

His SO/W Ratio of 5.03 was 3rd, 282.6% of baseball's average of 1.78.

2. Silver King, St. Louis Browns, 1888
56.728 PEVA RATING

Most baseball fans likely don't even recall his name. He played a long time ago when the Cardinals were known as the Browns, who played in Sportmen's Park and the league of the American Association (no not American League). They won their league that year with a 92-43 record, with Silver King winning 45 games of those games over 485.7 innings pitched in a two or three man rotation. King started 65 of the 135 games the Browns played that year. All this, and the rate stats noted below, rise Silver King to the Second Best Pitching Season of All-Time to us. For his career, King did not have any year like this again, although he did win 203 games over 10 seasons, but for that one season, Silver King was nearly the best ever of the best.

How Dominant was Silver King in 1888?

He was 1st in baseball for Wins (45), 492.3% higher than baseball's average for that year of 9.14.

He was 1st in IP (585.7), 355.8% higher than baseball's average of 164.63.

His ERA of 1.64 was 1st, 55.6% of baseball's average of 2.95.

His Walks/Hits per 9 Innings Pitched (WHIP9) of 7.88 was 1st, 74.2% of baseball's average of

10.62.

His SO/W Ratio of 3.39 was 5th, 194.8% of baseball's average of 1.74.

3. Amos Rusie, New York Giants, 1894
55.357 PEVA RATING

Another pitcher unknown to most fans today, even though he is in the Hall of Fame, Amos Rusie was a New York Giants pitcher, who just prior to the turn of the century, had the 3rd Best Season in Baseball History for a pitcher. Baseball had turned to offense during the 1890s. In only the six years since King's great performance, the major league average ERA had risen from 2.95 to 5.31 and the WHIP9 from 10.62 to 15.38. Home Runs were growing, but still accounted for only 0.41 per game. The increased offense did not matter to Rusie, whose ERA of 2.78 was 52.4% of the league average during the season. Rusie was not a strikeout pitcher, with only 195 in 444 innings, but then again, the era was so odd compared to today (he walked 200 batters). A walk had only been considered four balls since 1889, before then it was more, and the mound had been moved back from 50 feet to 60 feet 6 inches only in 1893. I guess they were still getting used to that. But all in all, comparing apples to apples in the decade of the 1890s, Amos Rusie dominated this season just as King and Maddux had theirs. He finished in the Top 2 pitchers in Wins, Innings Pitched, ERA, WHIP9, and Strike Out to Walk Ratio.

How Dominant was Amos Rusie in 1894?

He was 1st in baseball for Wins (36), 525.5% higher than baseball's average for that year of 6.85.

He was 2nd in IP (444.0), 368.6% higher than baseball's average of 120.45.

His ERA of 2.78 was 1st, 52.4% of baseball's average of 5.31.

His Walks/Hits per 9 Innings Pitched (WHIP9) of 12.69 was 2nd, 82.5% of baseball's average of 15.38.

His SO/W Ratio of 0.98 was 2nd, 171.9% of baseball's average of 0.57.

4. Bret Saberhagen, Kansas City Royals, 1989
53.447 PEVA RATING

Saberhagen pitched in a season that was not one hundred years ago, but his exploits are lesser known outside the Kansas City metro where he pitched. However, for a couple seasons in the late 1980s, Saberhagen was one of the most dominant pitchers in the game, no more so than in 1989 when he ranked #1 in all five of the major stat categories below. He won the most games, 23, pitched the most innings, 262.3, had the lowest ERA, 2.16, allowed the fewest Walks and Hits, 8.65 per 9 innings, and had the best SO/W Ratio at 4.49. Now those numbers weren't quite as dominant as those of the three seasons ranked above him, but they were enough to push Saberhagen into the #4 pitching season of all pitching seasons in baseball history.

How Dominant was Bret Saberhagen in 1989?

He was 1st in baseball for Wins (23), 491.5% higher than baseball's average for that year of 4.68.

He was 1st in IP (262.3), 312.3% higher than baseball's average of 84.00.

His ERA of 2.16 was 1st, 58.2% of baseball's average of 3.71.

His Walks/Hits per 9 Innings Pitched (WHIP9) of 8.65 was 1st, 72.8% of baseball's average of 11.89.

His SO/W Ratio of 4.49 was 1st, 256.6% of baseball's average of 1.75.

5. Walter Johnson, Washington Senators, 1912
52.347 PEVA RATING

In 1912, Walter Johnson ran through batters like an express train. He struck out 303 batters, barely over 8 batters reached base each nine IP, and pitched to an ERA so minuscule, you had to look a long time before finding any crooked innings. And while that ERA and the WHIP numbers weren't quite as good in comparison to major league averages of the season as Greg Maddux was in 1994 (ERA at 41.2% for Johnson while Maddux was at 34.2%; WHIP at 67.0% for Johnson while Maddux was at 62.6%), it was quite fantastic enough to raise him to the #5 pitching season of all-time. And 1912 would not be the last time Johnson would dominate. Before the end of his Hall of Fame career, he would win 20 games 12 times and amass 417 total victories.

How Dominant was Walter Johnson in 1912?

He was 2nd in baseball for Wins (33), 644.5% higher than baseball's average for that year of 5.12.

He was 2nd in IP (369.0), 401.4% higher than baseball's average of 91.93.

His ERA of 1.39 was 1st, 41.2% of baseball's average of 3.37.

His Walks/Hits per 9 Innings Pitched (WHIP9) of 8.17 was 1st, 67.0% of baseball's average of 12.20.

His SO/W Ratio of 3.99 was 1st, 311.7% of baseball's average of 1.28.

6. Lefty Grove, Philadelphia Athletics, 1930
52.344 PEVA RATING

Fans at Philly's Shibe Park, 721,663 of them, knew what was coming each time Lefty Grove took the mound in 1930. He would win 28 of their first place 102 victories. Grove led all of baseball that year in Wins, ERA, WHIP, and SO/W Ratio, just falling short of the 5 tool sweep by pitching a 5th place total of innings, but it was in the dominance over the league average where Grove really stood out. The A's would be the toast of the Philadelphia town for a couple more decades before they took their traveling show to Kansas City and then Oakland in baseball's migration west, but for the season of 1930 when their team led by Grove took the field, they witnessed a stellar pitching season, one which would propel him to Cooperstown.

How Dominant was Lefty Grove in 1930?

He was 1st in baseball for Wins (28), 452.3% higher than baseball's average for that year of 6.19.

He was 4th in IP (291.0), 264.9% higher than baseball's average of 109.86.

His ERA of 2.54 was 1st, 52.8% of baseball's average of 4.81.

His Walks/Hits per 9 Innings Pitched (WHIP9) of 10.30 was 1st, 75.2% of baseball's average of 13.69.

His SO/W Ratio of 3.48 was 1st, 334.6% of baseball's average of 1.04.

7. Pete (Grover Cleveland) Alexander
Philadelphia Phillies, 1915
52.205 PEVA RATING

There wasn't a whole lot to cheer about for the Phillies franchise in their first one hundred years of existence. By 1915, they still hadn't won a World Series, and wouldn't for 65 more years. But in 1915, they had one of their best seasons ever with a 90-62 record and first place finish, led by the man known as Grover Cleveland Alexander. Alexander took the ball and mound for 31 of their victories with an ERA of 1.22, at 42.1% of the baseball average. It would be a very long time before the fans in the stands of a Philly park would witness a pitching season anywhere near the caliber of Alexander again. But in the summer of 1915 in the Bowl they called Baker, Alexander dominated the competition.

How Dominant was Pete Alexander in 1915?

He was 1st in baseball for Wins (31), 482.1% higher than baseball's average for that year of 6.43.

He was 2nd in IP (376.3), 321.8% higher than baseball's average of 116.93.

His ERA of 1.22 was 1st, 42.1% of baseball's average of 2.90.

His Walks/Hits per 9 Innings Pitched (WHIP9) of 7.58 was 1st, 67.5% of baseball's average of 11.23.

His SO/W Ratio of 3.77 was 1st, 296.9% of baseball's average of 1.27.

8. Greg Maddux, Atlanta Braves, 1995
52.118 PEVA RATING

In the second of the strike shortened seasons of the mid-1990's, Maddux continued his dominance. Greg Maddux kept up his mastery from 1994, in 1995 he'd win 19 games, fashion an ERA of 1.63, and all without a mid 90's MPH fastball. The ERA of 1.63 was just 36.6% of the league average, just above the 34.6% level of 1994. Can you imagine pitching almost 210 innings and walking only 23, plus once again, this non-strikeout oriented pitcher had 181 strikeouts in 1995, 7.76 per 9 innings pitched? So let's prorate those stats to the full 162 game schedule again as we did for the 1994 season just for fun. 21 wins, 2 losses, 1.63 ERA, 204 SO, 236 IP, plus those dizzy WHIP and SO/W ratio numbers.

How Dominant was Greg Maddux in 1995?

He was 1st in baseball for Wins (19), 520.5% higher than baseball's average for that year of 3.65.

He was 6th in IP (209.7), 321.3% higher than baseball's average of 65.27.

His ERA of 1.63 was 1st, 36.6% of baseball's average of 4.45.

His Walks/Hits per 9 Innings Pitched (WHIP9) of 7.30 was 1st, 57.1% of baseball's average of 12.79.

His SO/W Ratio of 7.87 was 1st, 439.7% of baseball's average of 1.79.

9. Randy Johnson, Arizona Diamondbacks, 2001
52.009 PEVA RATING

As office accountant as Greg Maddux looked on the mound with his average stature and below average fastball, Randy Johnson looked just the opposite. He was a gangly wild west outlaw standing sixty feet away. But what made Johnson special, particularly in this 2001 season, was not only the fastball in the high 90s or that towering presence, but the fact that he had both of those things plus an ability to control his balls and strikes. Power and precision, it's the best combination you can have in this game. He led baseball in ERA and WHIP with an ERA of 2.49 in a hitter's ballpark, Bank One, at only 56.3% of the average ERA of the season.

How Dominant was Randy Johnson in 2001?

He was 3rd in baseball for Wins (21), 510.9% higher than baseball's average for that year of 4.11.

He was 2nd in IP (249.7), 340.9% higher than baseball's average of 73.24.

His ERA of 2.49 was 1st, 56.3% of baseball's average of 4.42.

His Walks/Hits per 9 Innings Pitched (WHIP9) of 9.08 was 1st, 73.2% of baseball's average of 12.41.

His SO/W Ratio of 5.24 was 4th, 255.6% of baseball's average of 2.05.

10. Carl Hubbell, New York Giants, 1933
52.001 PEVA RATING

It doesn't take much more than the listing of one fact, Hubbell, in 1933, pitched to an ERA less than half of the average, at 43.6%. Add in baseball bests in WHIP and SO/W ratio and you cement your position. A Hall of Fame career would follow this great season after his days on the mound were done, and while many Giants fans remember the exploits of Mathewson, Marichal, even Lincecum, more than they might Carl Hubbell, it's his 1933 season that was better, only behind Amos Rusie in Giants history, and #10 of All-Time.

How Dominant was Carl Hubbell in 1933?

He was 3rd in baseball for Wins (23), 348.0% higher than baseball's average for that year of 6.61.

He was 2nd in IP (308.7), 259.4% higher than baseball's average of 119.02.

His ERA of 1.66 was 1st, 43.6% of baseball's average of 3.81.

His Walks/Hits per 9 Innings Pitched (WHIP9) of 8.84 was 1st, 70.9% of baseball's average of 12.46.

His SO/W Ratio of 3.32 was 1st, 328.7% of baseball's average of 1.01.

Top 200 Best Seasons Ever

Best Pitching Years Ever (1871-2020) – Regular Season

Rank	Name	First	Year	Team	Lg	W	L	SV	IP	ERA	Age	PEVA-P
1	Maddux	Greg	1994	ATL	NL	16	6	0	202.0	1.56	28	**57.974**
2	King	Silver	1888	SL4	AA	45	21	0	585.7	1.64	20	**56.728**
3	Rusie	Amos	1894	NY1	NL	36	13	1	444.0	2.78	23	**55.357**
4	Saberhagen	Bret	1989	KCA	AL	23	6	0	262.3	2.16	25	**53.447**
5	Johnson	Walter	1912	WS1	AL	33	12	2	369.0	1.39	25	**52.347**
6	Grove	Lefty	1930	PHA	AL	28	5	9	291.0	2.54	30	**52.344**
7	Alexander	Pete	1915	PHI	NL	31	10	3	376.3	1.22	28	**52.205**
8	Maddux	Greg	1995	ATL	NL	19	2	0	209.7	1.63	29	**52.118**
9	Johnson	Randy	2001	ARI	NL	21	6	0	249.7	2.49	38	**52.009**
10	Hubbell	Carl	1933	NY1	NL	23	12	5	308.7	1.66	30	**52.001**

Rank	Name	First	Year	Team	Lg	W	L	SV	IP	ERA	Age	PEVA-P
11	Maddux	Greg	1993	ATL	NL	20	10	0	267.0	2.36	27	50.920
12	Koufax	Sandy	1963	LAN	NL	25	5	0	311.0	1.88	28	50.345
13	Arrieta	Jake	2015	CHN	NL	22	6	0	229.0	1.77	29	50.219
14	Maddux	Greg	1992	CHN	NL	20	11	0	268.0	2.18	26	49.969
15	Hubbell	Carl	1936	NY1	NL	26	6	3	304.0	2.31	33	48.808
16	Young	Cy	1901	BOS	AL	33	10	0	371.3	1.62	34	48.628
17	Carlton	Steve	1980	PHI	NL	24	9	0	304.0	2.34	36	48.494
18	Newhouser	Hal	1945	DET	AL	25	9	2	313.3	1.81	24	48.483
19	Kluber	Corey	2017	CLE	AL	18	4	0	203.7	2.25	31	48.424
20	Verlander	Justin	2019	HOU	AL	21	6	0	223.0	2.58	36	47.983
21	Cooper	Mort	1942	SLN	NL	22	7	0	278.7	1.78	29	47.763
22	Alexander	Pete	1916	PHI	NL	33	12	3	389.0	1.55	29	47.561
23	Nichols	Kid	1897	BSN	NL	31	11	3	368.0	2.64	28	47.498
24	Lee	Cliff	2008	CLE	AL	22	3	0	223.3	2.54	30	47.417
25	Maddux	Greg	1997	ATL	NL	19	4	0	232.7	2.20	31	47.132
26	Clemens	Roger	1997	TOR	AL	21	7	0	264.0	2.05	35	47.079
27	Maddux	Greg	1998	ATL	NL	18	9	0	251.0	2.22	32	46.792
28	Santana	Johan	2006	MIN	AL	19	6	0	233.7	2.77	27	46.748
29	Blackwell	Ewell	1947	CIN	NL	22	8	0	273.0	2.47	25	46.689
30	Feller	Bob	1940	CLE	AL	27	11	4	320.3	2.61	22	46.643
31	Grove	Lefty	1931	PHA	AL	31	4	5	288.7	2.06	31	46.335
32	Koufax	Sandy	1965	LAN	NL	26	8	2	335.7	2.04	30	46.321
33	Walsh	Ed	1908	CHA	AL	40	15	6	464.0	1.42	27	46.136
34	Halladay	Roy	2008	TOR	AL	20	11	0	246.0	2.78	31	46.107
35	Martinez	Pedro	1999	BOS	AL	23	4	0	213.3	2.07	28	45.790
36	Johnson	Walter	1910	WS1	AL	25	17	1	370.0	1.36	23	45.752
37	Gooden	Dwight	1985	NYN	NL	24	4	0	276.7	1.53	21	45.645
38	Johnson	Randy	2004	ARI	NL	16	14	0	245.7	2.60	41	44.961
39	Scott	Mike	1986	HOU	NL	18	10	0	275.3	2.22	31	44.955
40	Vance	Dazzy	1924	BRO	NL	28	6	0	308.3	2.16	33	44.534
41	Cole	Gerrit	2019	HOU	AL	20	5	0	212.3	2.50	29	44.051
42	Verlander	Justin	2011	DET	AL	24	5	0	251.0	2.40	28	43.997
43	Hubbell	Carl	1934	NY1	NL	21	12	8	313.0	2.30	31	43.860
44	Johnson	Walter	1913	WS1	AL	36	7	2	346.0	1.14	26	43.737
45	Young	Cy	1893	CL4	NL	34	16	1	422.7	3.36	26	43.542
46	Halladay	Roy	2010	PHI	NL	21	10	0	251.7	2.44	33	43.316
47	Johnson	Randy	2002	ARI	NL	24	5	0	260.0	2.32	39	43.254
48	Johnson	Walter	1918	WS1	AL	23	13	3	326.0	1.27	31	43.252
49	Clemens	Roger	1987	BOS	AL	20	9	0	281.7	2.97	25	43.210
50	Clemens	Roger	1991	BOS	AL	18	10	0	271.3	2.62	29	43.004
51	Wyatt	Whit	1941	BRO	NL	22	10	1	288.3	2.34	34	42.854
52	Brown	Kevin	1998	SDN	NL	18	7	0	257.0	2.38	33	42.712
53	Luque	Dolf	1923	CIN	NL	27	8	2	322.0	1.93	33	42.654
54	Marichal	Juan	1969	SFN	NL	21	11	0	299.7	2.10	32	42.465
55	Chandler	Spud	1943	NYA	AL	20	4	0	253.0	1.64	36	42.384
56	Greinke	Zack	2009	KCA	AL	16	8	0	229.3	2.16	26	42.305
57	Clarkson	John	1885	CHN	NL	53	16	0	623.0	1.85	24	42.218
58	Halladay	Roy	2011	PHI	NL	19	6	0	233.7	2.35	34	42.170
59	Donohue	Pete	1925	CIN	NL	21	14	2	301.0	3.08	25	42.024
60	Bond	Tommy	1879	BSN	NL	43	19	0	555.3	1.96	23	41.857

Rank	Name	First	Year	Team	Lg	W	L	SV	IP	ERA	Age	PEVA-P
61	Kershaw	Clayton	2013	LAN	NL	16	9	42	236.0	1.83	25	41.458
62	Clemens	Roger	1990	BOS	AL	21	6	0	228.3	1.93	28	41.426
63	Devlin	Jim	1877	LS1	NL	35	25	0	559.0	2.25	28	41.423
64	Walters	Bucky	1939	CIN	NL	27	11	0	319.0	2.29	30	41.246
65	Chesbro	Jack	1904	NYA	AL	41	12	0	454.7	1.82	30	41.233
66	Smoltz	John	1996	ATL	NL	24	8	0	253.7	2.94	29	41.196
67	Greinke	Zack	2015	LAN	NL	19	3	0	222.7	1.66	32	41.995
68	Peavy	Jake	2007	SDN	NL	19	6	0	223.3	2.54	26	41.129
69	Young	Cy	1899	SLN	NL	26	16	1	369.3	2.58	32	40.907
70	Bieber	Shane	2020	CLE	AL	8	1	0	77.3	1.63	25	40.664
71	Brown	Mordecai	1909	CHN	NL	27	9	7	342.7	1.31	33	40.455
72	Porcello	Rick	2016	BOS	AL	22	4	0	223.0	3.15	28	40.336
73	Martinez	Pedro	2000	BOS	AL	18	6	0	217.0	1.74	29	40.251
74	Alexander	Pete	1920	CHN	NL	27	14	5	363.3	1.91	33	40.230
75	Brown	Kevin	1996	FLO	NL	17	11	0	233.0	1.89	31	40.004
76	Alexander	Pete	1917	PHI	NL	30	13	0	388.0	1.83	30	39.958
77	Kershaw	Clayton	2014	LAN	NL	22	3	0	198.3	1.77	26	39.635
78	Spahn	Warren	1947	BSN	NL	21	10	3	289.7	2.33	26	39.610
79	Sale	Chris	2017	BOS	AL	17	8	0	214.3	2.90	26	39.592
80	Guidry	Ron	1978	NYA	AL	25	3	0	273.7	1.74	28	39.576
81	Sabathia	C.C.	2008	CLE/ MIL	AL/ NL	17	10	0	253.0	2.70	28	39.539
82	Kershaw	Clayton	2011	LAN	NL	21	5	0	233.3	2.28	23	39.502
83	Sabathia	C.C.	2007	CLE	AL	19	7	0	241.0	3.21	27	39.488
84	Trout	Dizzy	1944	DET	AL	27	14	0	352.3	2.12	29	39.350
85	Hecker	Guy	1884	LS2	AA	52	20	0	670.7	1.80	28	39.319
86	Carlton	Steve	1972	PHI	NL	27	10	0	346.3	1.97	28	39.105
87	Santana	Johan	2004	MIN	AL	20	6	0	228.0	2.61	25	39.021
88	Newhouser	Hal	1946	DET	AL	26	9	1	292.7	1.94	25	38.936
89	Tudor	John	1985	SLN	NL	21	8	0	275.0	1.93	31	38.832
90	Roberts	Robin	1951	PHI	NL	21	15	2	315.0	3.03	25	38.640
91	Schilling	Curt	2001	ARI	NL	22	6	0	256.7	2.98	35	38.613
92	Martinez	Pedro	1997	MON	NL	17	8	0	241.3	1.90	26	38.574
93	Friend	Bob	1960	PIT	NL	18	12	1	275.7	3.00	30	38.546
94	Grove	Lefty	1929	PHA	AL	20	6	4	275.3	2.81	29	38.544
95	Young	Cy	1896	CL4	NL	28	15	3	414.3	3.24	29	38.520
96	Roberts	Robin	1952	PHI	NL	28	7	2	330.0	2.59	26	38.501
97	Roberts	Robin	1953	PHI	NL	23	16	2	346.7	2.75	27	38.372
98	Radbourn	Charley	1883	PRO	NL	48	25	1	632.3	2.05	29	38.272
99	Nichols	Kid	1898	BSN	NL	31	12	4	388.0	2.13	29	38.155
100	Wood	Joe	1912	BOS	AL	34	5	1	344.0	1.91	23	38.082
101	Kershaw	Clayton	2015	LAN	NL	16	7	0	232.7	2.13	27	38.045
102	Greinke	Zack	2019	ARI/ HOU	NL/ AL	18	5	0	208.7	2.93	36	38.011
103	Gooden	Dwight	1984	NYN	NL	17	9	0	218.0	2.60	20	37.956
104	Rusie	Amos	1893	NY1	NL	33	21	1	482.0	3.23	22	37.905
105	Brecheen	Harry	1948	SLN	NL	20	7	1	233.3	2.24	34	37.896
106	Martinez	Pedro	2002	BOS	AL	20	4	0	199.3	2.26	31	37.759
107	Lincecum	Tim	2009	SFN	NL	15	7	0	225.3	2.48	25	37.546
108	Darvish	Yu	2020	CHN	NL	8	3	0	76.0	2.01	34	37.335

Rank	Name	First	Year	Team	Lg	W	L	SV	IP	ERA	Age	PEVA-P
109	Koufax	Sandy	1966	LAN	NL	27	9	0	323.0	1.73	31	37.199
110	Schilling	Curt	2002	ARI	NL	23	7	0	259.3	3.23	36	37.153
111	Willis	Vic	1899	BSN	NL	27	8	2	342.7	2.50	23	37.022
112	Faber	Red	1921	CHA	AL	25	15	1	330.7	2.48	33	37.013
113	Johnson	Walter	1914	WS1	AL	28	18	1	371.7	1.72	27	36.936
114	Rogers	Steve	1982	MON	NL	19	8	0	277.0	2.40	33	36.926
115	Johnson	Walter	1915	WS1	AL	27	13	4	336.7	1.55	28	36.871
116	Halladay	Roy	2003	TOR	AL	22	7	0	266.0	3.25	26	36.858
117	Radbourn	Charley	1884	PRO	NL	59	12	1	678.7	1.38	30	36.790
118	Bradley	George	1876	SL3	NL	45	19	0	573.0	1.23	24	36.677
119	Walters	Bucky	1940	CIN	NL	22	10	0	305.0	2.48	31	36.538
120	Gibson	Bob	1968	SLN	NL	22	9	0	304.7	1.12	33	36.485
121	Appier	Kevin	1993	KCA	AL	18	8	0	238.7	2.56	26	36.409
122	Walsh	Ed	1911	CHA	AL	27	18	4	368.7	2.22	30	36.402
123	Palmer	Jim	1975	BAL	AL	23	11	1	323.0	2.09	30	36.388
124	Verlander	Justin	2012	DET	NL	17	8	0	238.3	2.64	29	36.365
125	Faber	Red	1922	CHA	AL	21	17	2	352.0	2.81	34	36.363
126	Shocker	Urban	1922	SLA	AL	24	17	3	348.0	2.97	32	36.261
127	Webb	Brandon	2006	ARI	NL	16	8	0	235.0	3.10	27	36.142
128	Scherzer	Max	2017	WAS	NL	16	6	0	200.7	2.51	33	36.052
129	Key	Jimmy	1987	TOR	AL	17	8	0	261.0	2.76	26	36.007
130	Hunter	Catfish	1974	OAK	AL	25	12	0	318.3	2.49	28	35.949
131	Cicotte	Eddie	1917	CHA	AL	28	12	4	346.7	1.53	33	35.909
132	Maddux	Greg	2001	ATL	NL	17	11	0	233.0	3.05	35	35.904
133	Luque	Dolf	1925	CIN	NL	16	18	0	291.0	2.63	35	35.862
134	Gomez	Lefty	1937	NYA	AL	21	11	0	278.3	2.33	29	35.814
135	Passeau	Claude	1940	CHN	NL	20	13	5	280.7	2.50	31	35.806
136	Roberts	Robin	1954	PHI	NL	23	15	4	336.7	2.97	28	35.774
137	Wainwright	Adam	2010	SLN	NL	20	11	0	230.3	2.42	29	35.716
138	Dean	Dizzy	1934	SLN	NL	30	7	7	311.7	2.66	24	35.666
139	Maglie	Sal	1951	NY1	NL	23	6	4	298.0	2.93	34	35.603
140	Dickey	R.A.	2012	NYN	NL	20	6	0	233.7	2.73	38	35.214
141	Webb	Brandon	2007	ARI	NL	18	10	0	236.3	3.01	28	35.177
142	Richard	J.R.	1979	HOU	NL	18	13	0	292.3	2.71	29	35.177
143	Maddux	Greg	1996	ATL	NL	15	11	0	245.0	2.72	30	35.136
144	Glavine	Tom	1991	ATL	NL	20	11	0	246.7	2.55	25	35.128
145	Carpenter	Chris	2009	SLN	NL	17	4	0	192.7	2.24	34	35.125
146	Scherzer	Max	2018	WAS	NL	18	7	0	220.7	2.53	34	35.063
147	Wood	Wilbur	1971	CHA	AL	22	13	1	334.0	1.91	30	35.043
148	Clemens	Roger	1986	BOS	AL	24	4	0	254.0	2.48	24	35.030
149	Carlton	Steve	1982	PHI	NL	23	11	0	295.7	3.10	38	35.010
150	Johnson	Randy	1999	ARI	NL	17	9	0	271.7	2.48	36	34.970
151	Feller	Bob	1946	CLE	AL	26	15	4	371.3	2.18	28	34.939
152	Vance	Dazzy	1928	BRO	NL	22	10	2	280.3	2.09	37	34.912
153	Lincecum	Tim	2008	SFN	NL	18	5	0	227.0	2.62	24	34.883
154	Lee	Bill	1938	CHN	NL	22	9	2	291.0	2.66	29	34.833
155	Mathewson	Christy	1909	NY1	NL	25	6	2	275.3	1.14	29	34.761
156	Clemens	Roger	1992	BOS	AL	18	11	0	246.7	2.41	30	34.707
157	Jenkins	Fergie	1970	CHN	NL	22	16	0	313.0	3.39	28	34.695
158	Walsh	Ed	1910	CHA	AL	18	20	5	369.7	1.27	29	34.646

Rank	Name	First	Year	Team	Lg	W	L	SV	IP	ERA	Age	PEVA-P
159	Rixey	Eppa	1925	CIN	NL	21	11	1	287.3	2.88	34	34.428
160	Derringer	Paul	1939	CIN	NL	25	7	0	301.0	2.93	33	34.402
161	Jenkins	Fergie	1974	TEX	AL	25	12	0	328.3	2.82	32	34.395
162	Andujar	Joaquin	1982	SLN	NL	15	10	0	265.7	2.47	30	34.352
163	Dierker	Larry	1969	HOU	NL	20	13	0	305.3	2.33	23	34.302
164	McGinnity	Joe	1899	BLN	NL	28	16	2	366.3	2.68	28	34.184
165	Blue	Vida	1971	OAK	AL	24	8	0	312.0	1.82	22	34.160
166	Derringer	Paul	1938	CIN	NL	21	14	3	307.0	2.93	32	34.132
167	Johnson	Randy	1995	SEA	AL	18	2	0	214.3	2.48	32	34.064
168	Hunter	Catfish	1975	NYA	AL	23	14	0	328.0	2.58	29	34.002
169	Hernandez	Felix	2009	SEA	AL	19	5	0	238.7	2.49	23	33.947
170	Marberry	Firpo	1929	WS1	AL	19	12	11	250.3	3.06	31	33.863
171	McGinnity	Joe	1904	NY1	NL	35	8	5	408.0	1.61	33	33.860
172	Marichal	Juan	1966	SFN	NL	25	6	0	307.3	2.23	29	33.441
173	Singer	Bill	1969	LAN	NL	20	12	1	315.7	2.34	25	33.351
174	Lee	Cliff	2011	PHI	NL	17	8	0	232.7	2.40	33	33.297
175	Hahn	Noodles	1899	CIN	NL	23	8	0	309.0	2.68	20	33.291
176	Morris	Ed	1886	PT1	AA	41	20	1	555.3	2.45	24	33.289
177	Scherzer	Max	2016	WAS	NL	20	7	0	228.3	2.96	32	33.220
178	Hutchison	Bill	1890	CHN	NL	42	25	2	603.0	2.70	31	33.191
179	Clemens	Roger	1998	TOR	AL	20	6	0	234.7	2.65	36	33.173
180	Cueto	Johnny	2014	CIN	NL	20	9	0	243.7	2.25	28	33.132
181	Drysdale	Don	1962	LAN	NL	25	9	1	314.3	2.83	26	33.051
182	Perry	Gaylord	1972	CLE	AL	24	16	1	342.7	1.92	34	33.015
183	Coombs	Jack	1910	PHA	AL	31	9	1	353.0	1.30	28	32.981
184	Ramsey	Toad	1886	LS2	AA	38	27	0	588.7	2.45	22	32.963
185	Clarkson	John	1889	BSN	NL	49	19	1	620.0	2.73	28	32.959
186	Young	Cy	1895	CL4	NL	35	10	0	369.7	3.26	28	32.941
187	Spahn	Warren	1953	ML1	NL	23	7	3	265.7	2.10	32	32.929
188	Melton	Cliff	1937	NY1	NL	20	9	7	248.0	2.61	25	32.906
189	Blanton	Cy	1935	PIT	NL	18	13	1	254.3	2.58	27	32.884
190	Mathewson	Christy	1905	NY1	NL	31	9	2	338.7	1.28	25	32.837
191	deGrom	Jacob	2018	NYN	NL	10	9	0	217.0	1.70	30	32.813
192	Nichols	Kid	1893	BSN	NL	34	14	1	425.0	3.52	24	32.804
193	Rijo	Jose	1993	CIN	NL	14	9	0	257.3	2.48	28	32.798
194	Stratton	Scott	1890	LS2	AA	34	14	0	431.0	2.36	21	32.787
195	Marichal	Juan	1965	SFN	NL	22	13	1	295.3	2.13	28	32.690
196	Palmer	Jim	1976	BAL	AL	22	13	0	315.0	2.51	31	32.669
197	Tewksbury	Bob	1992	SLN	NL	16	5	0	233.0	2.16	32	32.658
198	Haines	Jesse	1927	SLN	NL	24	10	1	300.7	2.72	34	32.652
199	Gibson	Bob	1969	SLN	NL	20	13	0	314.0	2.18	34	32.616
200	Meekin	Jouett	1894	NY1	NL	33	9	2	409.0	3.70	27	32.597

Best Relief Pitching Seasons Ever (1871-2020) – Regular Season

Rank	Name	First	Year	Team	Lg	W	L	SV	IP	ERA	Age	PEVA-P
1	Quisenberry	Dan	1983	KCA	AL	5	3	45	139.0	1.94	30	24.535
2	Gagne	Eric	2003	LAN	NL	2	3	55	82.3	1.20	27	23.161
3	McDaniel	Lindy	1960	SLN	NL	12	4	26	116.3	2.09	25	22.970
4	Moore	Wilcy	1927	NYA	AL	19	7	13	213.0	2.28	30	22.864
5	Jansen	Kenley	2016	LAN	NL	3	2	47	68.7	1.83	29	22.072

Rank	Name	First	Year	Team	Lg	W	L	SV	IP	ERA	Age	PEVA-P
6	Melancon	Mark	2016	MULT	NL	2	2	47	71.3	1.64	31	22.036
7	Jansen	Kenley	2017	LAN	NL	5	0	41	68.3	1.32	30	22.019
8	Hernandez	Willie	1984	DET	AL	9	3	32	140.3	1.92	30	21.765
9	Rivera	Mariano	2001	NYA	AL	4	6	50	80.7	2.34	32	21.526
10	Diaz	Edwin	2018	SEA	AL	0	4	57	73.3	1.96	24	20.848
11	Yates	Kirby	2019	SDN	NL	0	5	41	60.7	1.19	32	20.633
12	Konstanty	Jim	1950	PHI	NL	16	7	22	152.0	2.66	33	20.439
13	Sutter	Bruce	1979	CHN	NL	6	6	37	101.3	2.22	26	20.400
14	Hendriks	Liam	2020	OAK	AL	3	1	14	25.3	1.78	31	20.393
15	Gagne	Eric	2002	LAN	NL	4	1	52	82.3	1.97	26	20.362
16	Rodney	Fernando	2012	TBA	AL	2	2	48	74.7	0.60	35	20.284
17	Fingers	Rollie	1981	ML4	AL	6	3	28	78.0	1.04	35	20.222
18	Wetteland	John	1993	MON	NL	9	3	43	85.3	1.37	27	20.171
19	Rivera	Mariano	2005	NYA	AL	7	4	43	78.3	1.38	36	20.171
20	Sutter	Bruce	1977	CHN	NL	7	3	31	107.3	1.34	24	19.860
21	Kimbrel	Craig	2017	BOS	AL	5	0	35	69.0	1.43	29	19.704
22	Jones	Doug	1992	HOU	NL	11	8	36	111.7	1.85	35	19.538
23	Putz	J.J.	2006	SEA	AL	4	1	36	78.3	2.30	29	19.452
24	Holland	Greg	2013	KCA	AL	2	1	47	67.0	1.21	28	19.447
25	Radatz	Dick	1962	BOS	AL	9	6	24	124.7	2.24	25	19.399
26	Hand	Brad	2020	CLE	AL	2	1	16	22.0	2.05	30	19.113
27	Britton	Zach	2016	BAL	AL	2	1	47	67.0	0.54	29	18.823
28	Treinen	Blake	2018	OAK	AL	9	2	38	80.3	0.78	30	18.930
29	Eckersley	Dennis	1990	OAK	AL	4	2	48	73.3	0.61	36	18.752
30	Gagne	Eric	2004	LAN	NL	7	3	45	82.3	2.19	28	18.671
31	Gossage	Rich	1977	PIT	NL	11	9	26	133.0	1.62	26	18.589
32	Nathan	Joe	2006	MIN	AL	7	0	36	68.3	1.58	32	18.535
33	Kimbrel	Craig	2012	ATL	NL	3	1	42	62.7	1.01	24	18.504
34	Quisenberry	Dan	1984	KCA	AL	6	3	44	129.3	2.64	31	18.502
35	Jones	Doug	1997	ML4	AL	6	6	36	80.3	2.02	40	18.476
36	Montgomery	Jeff	1993	KCA	AL	7	5	45	87.3	2.27	31	18.356
37	Hiller	John	1973	DET	AL	10	5	38	125.3	1.44	30	18.324
38	Rivera	Mariano	2011	NYA	AL	1	2	44	61.3	1.91	42	18.288
39	Sutter	Bruce	1984	SLN	NL	5	7	45	122.7	1.54	31	18.275
40	Hoffman	Trevor	1998	SDN	NL	4	2	53	73.0	1.48	31	18.234

Note: Relief pitchers defined as those with three times the amount of
Games Pitched vs. Games Started.

Note: Age = Player age at the end of the year.

CHAPTER THREE
BEST CAREERS EVER
POSITION PLAYER (1871-2020)

1. Babe Ruth (1914-1935)
641.539 PEVA RATING

Domination of the game for the entire decade of the 1920's when many seasons rank in the Top Ten of All-Time, then add in more great seasons the next decade and you have a career that most baseball historians rank as the Best of All-Time. We concur. Now, we acknowledge there are others in the conversation. Willie Mays to some. Hank Aaron to others. Ted Williams, with his lost years added back, to more. But Babe Ruth was, and is, the Tiger Woods and Jack Nicklaus of golf, combined to baseball, and we're not even adding in the fact that Babe Ruth, prior to turning into a full time position player, was an All-Star level pitcher, winning 94 games with an ERA of 2.28. If you add his pitching rating to the Batting PEVA, it would rise by nearly 50 points.

But it would be with that big stick where Ruth would amaze the crowds of folks who filled the seats at Yankee Stadium. His Slugging Percentage is the highest in baseball history, at 0.690 over 56 points higher than the man in second place, Ted Williams, at 0.634. He had 17 seasons with more than 20 home runs and hit 0.342 for his entire career. So when the passion subsides and the newsreel footage rolls, it is Babe Ruth who accumulated statistics that almost defy logic. In a career of 154 game seasons, he hit 714 Home Runs, one per every 11.6 At Bats. All with a glass of beer and no PED allegations.

Where Ruth Ranks

Category	Stats	Rank	Category	Stats	Rank
HR	714	3	SLG	0.690	1
RBI	2213	2	HITS	2873	45
AVE	0.342	10	RUNS	2174	4
OBP	0.474	2			

2. Barry Bonds (1986-2007)
606.700 PEVA RATING

Barry Bonds played in the steroid era, and some of the statistics, as well as the PEVA ratings, may be elevated due to that fact. And while there's no doubt that Bonds dominated among his peers, some of which did similar things, some of these numbers, well, they're inflated. But, there's also little doubt that Bonds was one of the best players of his era, and likely any era. So, we'll stop there and let you decide what matters. Bonds had speed, power, defensive ability in his early years with Pittsburgh, and was a complete player from the start of his career. By the end of it, Bonds had stolen 514 bases to go along with those Home Runs and RBIs. To get an idea of just how great a player Bonds was in his early years, just take a look at the last three years he played for the Pirates. 33, 116, 0.301 in 1990 followed by 25, 116, 0.292 in 1991 then 34, 103, 0.311 in 1992.

Where Bonds Ranks

Category	Stats	Rank	Category	Stats	Rank
HR	762	1	SLG	0.607	5
RBI	1996	6	HITS	2935	37
AVE	0.298	230	RUNS	2227	3
OBP	0.444	6			

3. Ty Cobb (1905-1928)
569.252 PEVA RATING

Gritty, tough, not particularly nice from the reports. Ty Cobb has the best Batting Average ever, plus the 2nd most Hits and Runs Scored. He was a phenom from the time he was 19, and had longevity in his game as well, batting 0.357 and knocking in 93 runs in 1927 at the age of 41. Cobb had no season between the ages of 20 and 42 when he hit less than 0.300 with three seasons over 0.400. There hasn't been a lot of chatter about Ty Cobb lately, with Ruth, Mays, Williams, and Aaron getting more publicity in the debates about best players ever. Could be because he was dissed by Joe Jackson in the movie Field of Dreams. But Ty Cobb, diss or not, is our Third Best Position Player in history.

Where Cobb Ranks

Category	Stats	Rank	Category	Stats	Rank
HR	117	763	SLG	0.512	78
RBI	1937	9	HITS	4189	2
AVE	0.366	1	RUNS	2246	2
OBP	0.433	9			

4. Hank Aaron (1954-1976)
535.808 PEVA RATING

During his playing career there was always the debate of whether Hank or Willie was the best player? And while Mays was the more flashy player, Aaron was more consistent, and it's not beyond us in the irony that the debate continues today, with the two men standing next to each other in this list of the Best Ever. Yes, Aaron gets the slight nod. And it was slight, only 15 PEVA points apart. When Hank Aaron hit the Home Run that bested the record of Ruth, it was national news, and news that surpassed the game itself. For most fans of baseball, Hank Aaron not only has the record for most Runs Batted In All-Time, actually the better record if you think about it, but he still has the Home Run Record, taking in consideration of the asterisk behind the man who actually holds it. Aaron was durable and spectacular, all the way to Cooperstown.

Where Aaron Ranks

Category	Stats	Rank	Category	Stats	Rank
HR	755	2	SLG	0.555	20
RBI	2297	1	HITS	3771	3
AVE	0.305	143	RUNS	2174	4
OBP	0.374	228			

5. Willie Mays (1951-1973)
520.998 PEVA RATING

More than fifty years later, perhaps the most highlighted clip in baseball history is that remarkable over the shoulder catch. But after a slow career start, by the age of 23, Mays was knocking out 40 home run seasons and batting 0.345. Mays had 660 home runs in his career and he stole 338 bases. He was the ultimate 5 tool baseball player. He could field, hit, hit for power, run, and throw all the way from the Polo Grounds of New York City to Candlestick Park along San Francisco Bay.

Where Mays Ranks

Category	Stats	Rank	Category	Stats	Rank
HR	660	6	SLG	0.558	17
RBI	1903	12	HITS	3283	12
AVE	0.302	187	RUNS	2062	7
OBP	0.384	140			

6. Ted Williams (1939-1960)
493.074 PEVA RATING

Ted Williams was the best player prior to World War II and the best player after it was over and he returned from losing three of his potentially productive seasons to service. Just imagine how great the numbers would be had those three seasons been added to his counting stats. If you just do a little quick math, during the three seasons before his first missed season in 1943, Ted averaged 32 Home Runs, 123 RBI, and a PEVA Rating of 44. For the three seasons after returning, Williams averaged 32 HR, 121 RBI, and PEVA of 37. Add those averages in to the already gaudy numbers and that raises Ted Williams to 617 HR, 2205 RBI, and a Career PEVA Rating of 614.5, good for #2. But we know, that's only projection, and there really is no need anyway, because Ted Williams was one of the Top Ten position players in baseball with or without them, and it doesn't really matter whether that's at #2 or #6.

Where Williams Ranks

Category	Stats	Rank	Category	Stats	Rank
HR	521	20	SLG	0.634	2
RBI	1839	15	HITS	2654	77
AVE	0.344	7	RUNS	1798	20
OBP	0.482	1			

7. Stan Musial (1941-1963)
481.182 PEVA RATING

Stan Musial began his career in 1941 and played until he was in his 43rd year. He was the consummate hitter, hitting for average, with patience at the plate, and the ability to slug. There aren't a whole lot of 0.300/0.400/0.500 players in AVE/OBP/SLG in baseball history; even three of the batters ranked above him could not accomplish that. Musial also missed time for service in World War II, losing the season of 1945 due to Naval service. But Musial became even better once the war years were over, adding power to his game.

Where Musial Ranks

Category	Stats	Rank	Category	Stats	Rank
HR	475	32	SLG	0.559	16
RBI	1951	8	HITS	3630	4
AVE	0.331	30	RUNS	1949	10
OBP	0.417	23			

8. Tris Speaker (1907-1928)
479.577 PEVA RATING

There is way too little discussion around baseball about how great Tris Speaker was. However, that doesn't take away his fantastic accomplishments. His career with Boston, Cleveland, Washington, and the Philadelphia Athletics, was played during an era when his comparison to Ty Cobb often pushed him below the Detroit Tiger. He had six seasons when his PEVA Rating was above 30.000, beginning with the 1912 season when he hit 0.383. Speaker played at a high level until he was 38 years old with only two seasons at the end of his career when he didn't reach the 10.000 PEVA Rating level of an above average starting player.

Where Speaker Ranks

Category	Stats	Rank	Category	Stats	Rank
HR	117	763	SLG	0.500	103
RBI	1529	51	HITS	3514	5
AVE	0.345	6	RUNS	1882	13
OBP	0.428	11			

9. Lou Gehrig (1923-1939)
479.522 PEVA RATING

Try to imagine pitching to a lineup that included Lou Gehrig and Babe Ruth. Lou Gehrig complimented the exploits of Babe Ruth in a tandem that would never be duplicated. Now it certainly helped both men to have the other surrounding them in the batting order, but with those rate stats, Gehrig and Ruth could have batted for today's worst team and still knocked in 100 runs. Gehrig and Ruth had themselves to be compared to; each did it well. Well enough to be the only teammates present within the Best Ever Top Ten.

Where Gehrig Ranks

Category	Stats	Rank	Category	Stats	Rank
HR	493	28	SLG	0.632	3
RBI	1995	7	HITS	2721	64
AVE	0.340	16	RUNS	1888	12
OBP	0.447	5			

10. Mickey Mantle (1951-1968)
455.611 PEVA RATING

So the argument in New York City during the three team era was whether you were a Mantle, Mays, or Duke Snider fan. Why choose? Mantle played with reckless abandon, and his body did not hold up as well as Mays. Yes, injuries caused more than a few seasons for Mantle when his ability couldn't overcome them. By the time Mantle was 33, his career was over as a premier player. Mantle was only 21 years old when he burst onto the scene of his sophomore season and took the league by storm, batting 0.311 with 87 RBI's and a PEVA Rating of 31.043. By the time he was 25, he had hit 52 homers, knocked in 130, and batted 0.353, all grading out to the tune of 47.236. Mickey Mantle comes in at #10 in the Best Ever list of position players, because, at his peak, he was the best player in baseball. The fact that he does not rank higher comes because his peak just didn't last quite long enough.

Where Mantle Ranks

Category	Stats	Rank	Category	Stats	Rank
HR	536	18	SLG	0.557	18
RBI	1509	56	HITS	2415	123
AVE	0.298	230	RUNS	1677	30
OBP	0.421	17			

Note: Career Stat Ranks as of September 23, 2020, Minimum 3,000 Plate Appearances.

Top 500 Batting Careers
(1871-2020)

RANK	NAME	FIRST	LYEAR	PEVAB	YRS	PPYR	HR	RBI	HITS	AVE
1	Ruth	Babe	1935	641.539	22	29.161	714	2217	2873	0.342
2	Bonds	Barry	2007	606.700	22	27.577	762	1996	2935	0.298
3	Cobb	Ty	1928	569.252	24	23.719	117	1937	4189	0.366
4	Aaron	Hank	1976	535.808	23	23.296	755	2297	3771	0.305
5	Mays	Willie	1973	520.998	22	23.682	660	1903	3283	0.302
6	Williams	Ted	1960	493.074	19	25.951	521	1839	2654	0.344
7	Musial	Stan	1963	481.182	22	21.872	475	1951	3630	0.331
8	Speaker	Tris	1928	479.577	22	21.799	117	1529	3514	0.345
9	Gehrig	Lou	1939	479.522	17	28.207	493	1995	2721	0.340
10	Mantle	Mickey	1968	455.611	18	25.312	536	1509	2415	0.298
11	Wagner	Honus	1917	451.473	21	21.499	101	1732	3415	0.327
12	Anson	Cap	1897	432.886	27	16.033	97	2076	3418	0.333
13	Pujols	Albert	2020	414.037	20	20.702	662	2100	3236	0.299
14	Robinson	Frank	1976	411.403	21	19.591	586	1812	2943	0.294
15	Schmidt	Mike	1989	383.574	18	21.310	548	1595	2234	0.267
16	Rodriguez	Alex	2016	373.185	22	16.963	696	2086	3115	0.295
17	Ott	Mel	1947	369.518	22	16.796	511	1860	2876	0.304
18	Hornsby	Rogers	1937	361.117	23	15.701	301	1584	2930	0.358
19	Mathews	Eddie	1968	360.187	17	21.187	512	1453	2315	0.271
20	Foxx	Jimmie	1945	359.936	20	17.997	534	1922	2646	0.325
21	Delahanty	Ed	1903	351.660	16	21.979	101	1464	2596	0.346
22	Cabrera	Miguel	2019	350.883	18	19.494	487	1729	2866	0.313
23	Collins	Eddie	1930	349.132	25	13.965	47	1300	3315	0.333
24	Rose	Pete	1986	349.020	24	14.543	160	1314	4256	0.303
25	Brouthers	Dan	1904	348.085	19	18.320	106	1296	2296	0.342
26	Yastrzemski	Carl	1983	339.141	23	14.745	452	1844	3419	0.285
27	Lajoie	Nap	1916	337.934	21	16.092	83	1599	3242	0.338
28	Connor	Roger	1897	336.978	18	18.721	138	1322	2467	0.317
29	Thomas	Frank	2008	333.924	19	17.575	521	1704	2468	0.301
30	Henderson	Rickey	2003	331.490	25	13.260	297	1115	3055	0.279

RANK	NAME	FIRST	LYEAR	PEVAB	YRS	PPYR	HR	RBI	HITS	AVE
31	O'Rourke	Jim	1904	329.813	23	14.340	62	1203	2643	0.311
32	Winfield	Dave	1995	327.767	22	14.899	465	1833	3110	0.283
33	Murray	Eddie	1997	324.361	21	15.446	504	1917	3255	0.287
34	Ripken	Cal	2001	320.189	21	15.247	431	1695	3184	0.276
35	Trout	Mike	2020	304.881	10	30.488	302	798	1380	0.304
36	Brett	George	1993	301.897	21	14.376	317	1595	3154	0.305
37	Jackson	Reggie	1987	301.318	21	14.348	563	1702	2584	0.262
38	DiMaggio	Joe	1951	297.630	13	22.895	361	1537	2214	0.325
39	Kaline	Al	1974	297.259	22	13.512	399	1583	3007	0.297
40	Crawford	Sam	1917	295.985	19	15.578	97	1525	2961	0.309
41	Bagwell	Jeff	2005	293.606	15	19.574	449	1529	2314	0.297
42	Boggs	Wade	1999	293.035	18	16.280	118	1014	3010	0.328
43	Yount	Robin	1993	291.977	20	14.599	251	1406	3142	0.285
44	Ramirez	Manny	2011	289.016	19	15.211	555	1831	2574	0.312
45	Morgan	Joe	1984	287.829	22	13.083	268	1133	2517	0.271
46	Griffey	Ken	2010	286.056	22	13.003	630	1836	2781	0.284
47	Jones	Chipper	2012	277.793	19	14.621	468	1623	2726	0.303
48	Burkett	Jesse	1905	276.152	16	17.259	75	952	2850	0.338
49	Williams	Billy	1976	275.511	18	15.306	426	1475	2711	0.290
50	White	Deacon	1890	274.719	20	13.736	23	977	2066	0.312
51	Hines	Paul	1891	274.652	20	13.733	57	855	2134	0.302
52	Killebrew	Harmon	1975	270.652	22	12.302	573	1584	2086	0.256
53	Sheffield	Gary	2009	267.943	22	12.179	509	1676	2689	0.292
54	Banks	Ernie	1971	264.788	19	13.936	512	1636	2583	0.274
55	Clemente	Roberto	1972	264.635	18	14.702	240	1305	3000	0.317
56	Evans	Dwight	1991	264.273	20	13.214	385	1384	2446	0.272
57	McGwire	Mark	2001	261.187	16	16.324	583	1414	1626	0.263
58	McCovey	Willie	1980	261.038	22	11.865	521	1555	2211	0.270
59	Palmeiro	Rafael	2005	260.423	20	13.021	569	1835	3020	0.288
60	Santo	Ron	1974	259.712	15	17.314	342	1331	2254	0.277
61	Jeter	Derek	2014	259.537	20	12.977	260	1311	3465	0.310
62	Thome	Jim	2012	257.862	22	11.721	612	1699	2328	0.276
63	Bench	Johnny	1983	256.662	17	15.098	389	1376	2048	0.267
64	Piazza	Mike	2007	255.855	16	15.991	427	1335	2127	0.308
65	Clarke	Fred	1915	255.011	21	12.143	67	1015	2672	0.312
66	Snider	Duke	1964	253.178	18	14.065	407	1333	2116	0.295
67	Berra	Yogi	1965	251.624	19	13.243	358	1430	2150	0.285
68	Heilmann	Harry	1932	249.516	17	14.677	183	1539	2660	0.342
69	Ortiz	David	2016	246.658	20	12.333	541	1768	2472	0.286
70	Davis	George	1909	245.441	20	12.272	73	1437	2660	0.295
71	Beltre	Adrian	2018	243.600	21	11.600	477	1707	3166	0.286
72	Waner	Paul	1945	242.637	20	12.132	113	1309	3152	0.333
73	Molitor	Paul	1998	242.403	21	11.543	234	1307	3319	0.306

RANK	NAME	FIRST	LYEAR	PEVAB	YRS	PPYR	HR	RBI	HITS	AVE
74	Magee	Sherry	1919	242.236	16	15.140	83	1176	2169	0.291
75	Stargell	Willie	1982	241.847	21	11.517	475	1540	2232	0.282
76	Simmons	Ted	1988	239.550	21	11.407	248	1389	2472	0.285
77	Gwynn	Tony	2001	238.944	20	11.947	135	1138	3141	0.338
78	Johnson	Bob	1945	237.767	13	18.290	288	1283	2051	0.296
79	Simmons	Al	1944	237.604	20	11.880	307	1827	2927	0.334
80	Allen	Dick	1977	237.460	15	15.831	351	1119	1848	0.292
81	Stovey	Harry	1893	236.465	14	16.890	122	908	1771	0.289
82	Jackson	Joe	1920	235.944	13	18.150	54	785	1772	0.356
83	Kelly	King	1893	235.100	16	14.694	69	950	1813	0.308
84	Staub	Rusty	1985	234.389	23	10.191	292	1466	2716	0.279
85	Carter	Gary	1992	233.612	19	12.295	324	1225	2092	0.262
86	Gehringer	Charlie	1942	233.202	19	12.274	184	1427	2839	0.320
87	Robinson	Brooks	1977	232.882	23	10.125	268	1357	2848	0.267
88	Sosa	Sammy	2007	232.724	18	12.929	609	1667	2408	0.273
89	Hamilton	Billy	1901	231.802	14	16.557	40	736	2158	0.344
90	Dawson	Andre	1996	230.234	21	10.964	438	1591	2774	0.279
91	Murphy	Dale	1993	228.942	18	12.719	398	1266	2111	0.265
92	Abreu	Bobby	2014	228.123	18	12.673	288	1363	2470	0.291
93	Beltran	Carlos	2017	227.895	20	11.395	435	1587	2725	0.279
94	Biggio	Craig	2007	226.358	20	11.318	291	1175	3060	0.281
95	Raines	Tim	2002	226.257	23	9.837	170	980	2605	0.294
96	Kelley	Joe	1908	226.052	17	13.297	65	1194	2220	0.317
97	Martinez	Edgar	2004	225.436	18	12.524	309	1261	2247	0.312
98	Wynn	Jimmy	1977	224.886	15	14.992	291	964	1665	0.250
99	McGriff	Fred	2004	224.159	19	11.798	493	1550	2490	0.284
100	Rice	Jim	1989	224.083	16	14.005	382	1451	2452	0.298
101	Votto	Joey	2020	223.308	14	15.951	295	966	1908	0.304
102	Goslin	Goose	1938	220.227	18	12.235	248	1609	2735	0.316
103	Keeler	Willie	1910	220.111	19	11.585	33	810	2932	0.341
104	Dahlen	Bill	1911	216.119	21	10.291	84	1233	2457	0.272
105	Perez	Tony	1986	215.662	23	9.377	379	1652	2732	0.279
106	Singleton	Ken	1984	215.555	15	14.370	246	1065	2029	0.282
107	Duffy	Hugh	1906	215.369	17	12.669	106	1302	2282	0.324
108	Greenberg	Hank	1947	215.163	13	16.551	331	1276	1628	0.313
109	Fisk	Carlton	1993	214.953	24	8.956	376	1330	2356	0.269
110	Torre	Joe	1977	214.765	18	11.931	252	1185	2342	0.297
111	Guerrero	Vladimir	2011	214.609	16	13.413	449	1496	2590	0.318
112	Evans	Darrell	1989	214.577	21	10.218	414	1354	2223	0.248
113	Giambi	Jason	2014	214.039	20	10.702	440	1441	2010	0.277
114	Jones	Charley	1888	213.948	12	17.829	56	552	1114	0.298
115	Wheat	Zack	1927	213.679	19	11.246	132	1248	2884	0.317
116	Beckley	Jake	1907	213.234	20	10.662	86	1575	2930	0.308

RANK	NAME	FIRST	LYEAR	PEVAB	YRS	PPYR	HR	RBI	HITS	AVE
117	Van Haltren	George	1903	210.974	17	12.410	69	1014	2532	0.316
118	Barnes	Ross	1881	210.856	9	23.428	6	350	859	0.359
119	Appling	Luke	1950	210.671	20	10.534	45	1116	2749	0.310
120	Cepeda	Orlando	1974	209.487	17	12.323	379	1365	2351	0.297
121	Kiner	Ralph	1955	208.610	10	20.861	369	1015	1451	0.279
122	Cano	Robinson	2020	208.176	16	13.011	334	1302	2624	0.303
123	Carew	Rod	1985	208.083	19	10.952	92	1015	3053	0.328
124	Flick	Elmer	1910	207.666	13	15.974	48	756	1752	0.313
125	Ashburn	Richie	1962	207.541	15	13.836	29	586	2574	0.308
126	Belle	Albert	2000	206.268	12	17.189	381	1239	1726	0.295
127	Thompson	Sam	1906	206.208	15	13.747	127	1299	1979	0.331
128	Sheckard	Jimmy	1913	205.718	17	12.101	56	813	2084	0.274
129	Colavito	Rocky	1968	204.838	14	14.631	374	1159	1730	0.266
130	Berkman	Lance	2013	204.814	15	13.654	366	1234	1905	0.293
131	Baker	Frank	1922	204.500	13	15.731	96	987	1838	0.307
132	Gore	George	1892	204.244	14	14.589	46	618	1612	0.301
133	Puckett	Kirby	1995	204.074	12	17.006	207	1085	2304	0.318
134	Delgado	Carlos	2009	203.096	17	11.947	473	1512	2038	0.280
135	Minoso	Minnie	1980	202.978	17	11.940	186	1023	1963	0.298
136	McCutchen	Andrew	2020	202.747	12	16.896	243	853	1719	0.285
137	Dickey	Bill	1946	202.680	17	11.922	202	1209	1969	0.313
138	Ryan	Jimmy	1903	202.409	18	11.245	118	1093	2502	0.306
139	Parker	Dave	1991	202.393	19	10.652	339	1493	2712	0.290
140	Williams	Bernie	2006	201.883	16	12.618	287	1257	2336	0.297
141	Pinson	Vada	1975	201.635	18	11.202	256	1170	2757	0.286
142	Hernandez	Keith	1990	199.518	17	11.736	162	1071	2182	0.296
143	Veach	Bobby	1925	199.427	14	14.245	64	1166	2063	0.310
144	Bonds	Bobby	1981	199.147	14	14.225	332	1024	1886	0.268
145	Cronin	Joe	1945	196.868	20	9.843	170	1424	2285	0.301
146	Gonzalez	Luis	2008	196.581	19	10.346	354	1439	2591	0.283
147	Gonzalez	Adrian	2018	195.853	15	13.057	317	1202	2050	0.287
148	Helton	Todd	2013	195.680	17	11.511	369	1406	2519	0.316
149	Oliver	Al	1985	195.039	18	10.836	219	1326	2743	0.303
150	Clark	Will	2000	194.626	15	12.975	284	1205	2176	0.303
151	Carey	Max	1929	194.330	20	9.717	70	800	2665	0.285
152	Clark	Jack	1992	193.774	18	10.765	340	1180	1826	0.267
153	Mattingly	Don	1995	193.054	14	13.790	222	1099	2153	0.307
154	Edmonds	Jim	2010	192.783	17	11.340	393	1199	1949	0.284
155	Holliday	Matt	2018	192.665	15	12.844	316	1220	2096	0.299
156	Sisler	George	1930	192.406	15	12.827	102	1175	2812	0.340
157	Rodriguez	Ivan	2011	192.302	21	9.157	311	1332	2844	0.296
158	Howard	Frank	1973	192.157	16	12.010	382	1119	1774	0.273
159	Foster	George	1986	191.583	18	10.643	348	1239	1925	0.274

RANK	NAME	FIRST	LYEAR	PEVAB	YRS	PPYR	HR	RBI	HITS	AVE
160	Mize	Johnny	1953	191.547	15	12.770	359	1337	2011	0.312
161	Vaughan	Arky	1948	191.280	14	13.663	96	926	2103	0.318
162	Hooper	Harry	1925	191.097	17	11.241	75	817	2466	0.281
163	Lynn	Fred	1990	190.089	17	11.182	306	1111	1960	0.283
164	Bando	Sal	1981	189.399	16	11.837	242	1039	1790	0.254
165	Trammell	Alan	1996	189.324	20	9.466	185	1003	2365	0.285
166	Downing	Brian	1992	189.089	20	9.454	275	1073	2099	0.267
167	Mauer	Joe	2018	188.930	15	12.595	143	923	2123	0.306
168	Baines	Harold	2001	188.522	22	8.569	384	1628	2866	0.289
169	Smith	Reggie	1982	188.012	17	11.060	314	1092	2020	0.287
170	Averill	Earl	1941	187.958	13	14.458	238	1164	2019	0.318
171	Braun	Ryan	2020	187.723	14	13.409	352	1154	1963	0.296
172	Suzuki	Ichiro	2019	187.346	19	9.860	117	780	3089	0.311
173	Bell	Buddy	1989	187.015	18	10.390	201	1106	2514	0.279
174	Cey	Ron	1987	186.886	17	10.993	316	1139	1868	0.261
175	Medwick	Joe	1948	186.522	17	10.972	205	1383	2471	0.324
176	Yost	Eddie	1962	185.716	18	10.318	139	683	1863	0.254
177	Giles	Brian	2009	185.683	15	12.379	287	1078	1897	0.291
178	Butler	Brett	1997	185.209	17	10.895	54	578	2375	0.290
179	Nettles	Graig	1988	185.124	22	8.415	390	1314	2225	0.248
180	Canseco	Jose	2001	184.776	17	10.869	462	1407	1877	0.266
181	Alomar	Roberto	2004	184.493	17	10.853	210	1134	2724	0.300
182	Browning	Pete	1894	184.248	13	14.173	46	659	1646	0.341
183	Wright	David	2018	183.995	14	13.143	242	970	1777	0.296
184	Cruz	Jose	1988	183.794	19	9.673	165	1077	2251	0.284
185	Doby	Larry	1959	183.611	13	14.124	253	970	1515	0.283
186	Rice	Sam	1934	182.577	20	9.129	34	1078	2987	0.322
187	Elliott	Bob	1953	180.955	15	12.064	170	1195	2061	0.289
188	Garvey	Steve	1987	180.570	19	9.504	272	1308	2599	0.294
189	Olerud	John	2005	180.484	17	10.617	255	1230	2239	0.295
190	Slaughter	Enos	1959	180.421	19	9.496	169	1304	2383	0.300
191	Rolen	Scott	2012	180.033	17	10.590	316	1287	2077	0.281
192	Tiernan	Mike	1899	180.026	13	13.848	106	851	1834	0.311
193	Fielder	Prince	2016	179.819	12	14.985	319	1028	1645	0.283
194	Walker	Larry	2005	179.516	17	10.560	383	1311	2160	0.313
195	Brock	Lou	1979	179.216	19	9.432	149	900	3023	0.293
196	Wallace	Bobby	1918	179.183	25	7.167	34	1121	2309	0.268
197	Freeman	Freddie	2020	179.151	11	16.286	240	858	1524	0.295
198	Glasscock	Jack	1895	178.962	17	10.527	27	825	2040	0.290
199	Boyer	Ken	1969	178.433	15	11.896	282	1141	2143	0.287
200	Davis	Chili	1999	177.938	19	9.365	350	1372	2380	0.274
201	Murcer	Bobby	1983	177.477	17	10.440	252	1043	1862	0.277
202	Kent	Jeff	2008	177.365	17	10.433	377	1518	2461	0.290

RANK	NAME	FIRST	LYEAR	PEVAB	YRS	PPYR	HR	RBI	HITS	AVE
203	Sandberg	Ryne	1997	177.296	16	11.081	282	1061	2386	0.285
204	Tejada	Miguel	2013	176.202	16	11.013	307	1302	2407	0.285
205	Carter	Joe	1998	175.685	16	10.980	396	1445	2184	0.259
206	Bonilla	Bobby	2001	175.138	16	10.946	287	1173	2010	0.279
207	Cash	Norm	1974	174.984	17	10.293	377	1103	1820	0.271
208	Griffin	Mike	1898	174.674	12	14.556	42	719	1753	0.296
209	Cedeno	Cesar	1986	173.719	17	10.219	199	976	2087	0.285
210	Cochrane	Mickey	1937	173.444	13	13.342	119	832	1652	0.320
211	Roush	Edd	1931	173.402	18	9.633	68	981	2376	0.323
212	Markakis	Nick	2020	171.933	15	11.462	189	1046	2388	0.288
213	Bautista	Jose	2018	171.515	15	11.434	344	975	1496	0.247
214	Hunter	Torii	2015	170.999	19	9.000	353	1391	2452	0.277
215	Jones	Andruw	2012	170.851	17	10.050	434	1289	1933	0.254
216	Burns	George	1925	170.571	15	11.371	41	611	2077	0.287
217	Davis	Willie	1979	170.488	18	9.472	182	1053	2561	0.279
218	Harrah	Toby	1986	170.485	17	10.029	195	918	1954	0.264
219	Whitaker	Lou	1995	170.423	19	8.970	244	1084	2369	0.276
220	McVey	Cal	1879	170.048	9	18.894	11	448	869	0.346
221	Luzinski	Greg	1984	169.911	15	11.327	307	1128	1795	0.276
222	Klein	Chuck	1944	169.818	17	9.989	300	1201	2076	0.320
223	Hodges	Gil	1963	169.363	18	9.409	370	1274	1921	0.273
224	Damon	Johnny	2012	169.350	18	9.408	235	1139	2769	0.284
225	Finley	Steve	2007	169.123	19	8.901	304	1167	2548	0.271
226	Vernon	Mickey	1960	168.790	20	8.440	172	1311	2495	0.286
227	Boudreau	Lou	1952	168.772	15	11.251	68	789	1779	0.295
228	Konetchy	Ed	1921	168.590	15	11.239	74	992	2150	0.281
229	Teixeira	Mark	2016	168.207	14	12.015	409	1298	1862	0.268
230	Jones	Fielder	1915	167.891	15	11.193	21	631	1920	0.285
231	O'Neill	Paul	2001	167.694	17	9.864	281	1269	2105	0.288
232	Baylor	Don	1988	167.552	19	8.819	338	1276	2135	0.260
233	Cruz	Nelson	2020	167.328	16	10.458	417	1152	1777	0.278
234	Collins	Jimmy	1908	167.223	14	11.944	65	983	1999	0.294
235	York	Tom	1885	167.187	15	11.146	15	502	1095	0.274
236	Powell	Boog	1977	167.003	17	9.824	339	1187	1776	0.266
237	Reese	Pee Wee	1958	166.689	16	10.418	126	885	2170	0.269
238	Longoria	Evan	2020	166.502	13	12.808	304	1043	1752	0.266
239	McPhee	Bid	1899	166.066	18	9.226	53	1067	2250	0.271
240	Larkin	Barry	2004	165.994	19	8.737	198	960	2340	0.295
241	Thomas	Roy	1911	165.829	13	12.756	7	299	1537	0.290
242	Grich	Bobby	1986	165.495	17	9.735	224	864	1833	0.266
243	Ventura	Robin	2004	164.910	16	10.307	294	1182	1885	0.267
244	White	Roy	1979	164.619	15	10.975	160	758	1803	0.271
245	Start	Joe	1886	164.544	16	10.284	15	544	1418	0.299

RANK	NAME	FIRST	LYEAR	PEVAB	YRS	PPYR	HR	RBI	HITS	AVE
246	Leach	Tommy	1918	164.542	19	8.660	63	810	2143	0.269
247	Cross	Lave	1907	164.121	21	7.815	47	1371	2645	0.292
248	Goldschmidt	Paul	2020	164.099	10	16.410	249	828	1395	0.293
249	Ennis	Del	1959	163.943	14	11.710	288	1284	2063	0.284
250	Nicholson	Bill	1953	163.304	16	10.207	235	948	1484	0.268
251	Hoy	Dummy	1902	163.266	14	11.662	40	726	2044	0.287
252	Campanella	Roy	1957	162.658	10	16.266	242	856	1161	0.276
253	Otis	Amos	1984	162.237	17	9.543	193	1007	2020	0.277
254	Smith	Ozzie	1996	162.053	19	8.529	28	793	2460	0.262
255	Clift	Harlond	1945	161.666	12	13.472	178	829	1558	0.272
256	Cuyler	Kiki	1938	161.663	18	8.981	128	1065	2299	0.321
257	Sutton	Ezra	1888	160.676	18	8.926	25	671	1574	0.294
258	Martinez	Victor	2018	160.668	16	10.042	246	1178	2153	0.295
259	Richardson	Hardy	1892	160.021	14	11.430	70	822	1688	0.299
260	Gaetti	Gary	2000	159.980	20	7.999	360	1341	2280	0.255
261	Lemon	Chet	1990	159.807	16	9.988	215	884	1875	0.273
262	Franco	Julio	2007	159.393	23	6.930	173	1194	2586	0.298
263	Hack	Stan	1947	159.139	16	9.946	57	642	2193	0.301
264	Posada	Jorge	2011	159.103	17	9.359	275	1065	1664	0.273
265	Sewell	Joe	1933	159.049	14	11.361	49	1055	2226	0.312
266	Stephens	Vern	1955	158.794	15	10.586	247	1174	1859	0.286
267	Granderson	Curtis	2019	158.638	16	9.915	344	937	1800	0.249
268	Ordonez	Magglio	2011	158.550	15	10.570	294	1236	2156	0.309
269	Parrish	Lance	1995	158.477	19	8.341	324	1070	1782	0.252
270	Selbach	Kip	1906	157.811	13	12.139	44	779	1803	0.293
271	Cooper	Cecil	1987	157.313	17	9.254	241	1125	2192	0.298
272	Terry	Bill	1936	157.227	14	11.231	154	1078	2193	0.341
273	Rollins	Jimmy	2016	157.125	17	9.243	231	936	2455	0.264
274	Ramirez	Aramis	2015	157.092	18	8.727	386	1417	2303	0.283
275	Doerr	Bobby	1951	157.073	14	11.219	223	1247	2042	0.288
276	McKean	Ed	1899	156.981	13	12.075	66	1124	2083	0.302
277	Walker	Dixie	1949	156.832	18	8.713	105	1023	2064	0.306
278	Grace	Mark	2003	156.827	16	9.802	173	1146	2445	0.303
279	Aparicio	Luis	1973	156.787	18	8.710	83	791	2677	0.262
280	Brown	Tom	1898	156.353	17	9.197	64	736	1951	0.265
281	Strawberry	Darryl	1999	156.264	17	9.192	335	1000	1401	0.259
282	Manush	Heinie	1939	156.227	17	9.190	110	1183	2524	0.330
283	Oliva	Tony	1976	155.849	15	10.390	220	947	1917	0.304
284	Kemp	Matt	2020	155.776	15	10.385	287	1031	1808	0.284
285	Wright	George	1882	155.731	12	12.978	11	330	867	0.302
286	Fox	Nellie	1965	155.463	19	8.182	35	790	2663	0.288
287	Hartnett	Gabby	1941	155.361	20	7.768	236	1179	1912	0.297
288	Rosen	Al	1956	154.897	10	15.490	192	717	1063	0.285

RANK	NAME	FIRST	LYEAR	PEVAB	YRS	PPYR	HR	RBI	HITS	AVE
289	Green	Shawn	2007	154.634	15	10.309	328	1070	2003	0.283
290	Gonzalez	Juan	2005	154.558	17	9.092	434	1404	1936	0.295
291	Encarnacion	Edwin	2020	154.190	16	9.637	424	1261	1832	0.260
292	Lofton	Kenny	2007	152.858	17	8.992	130	781	2428	0.299
293	Wallach	Tim	1996	152.755	17	8.986	260	1125	2085	0.257
294	Jennings	Hughie	1918	152.306	17	8.959	18	840	1527	0.311
295	Guerrero	Pedro	1992	152.252	15	10.150	215	898	1618	0.300
296	Konerko	Paul	2014	152.064	18	8.448	439	1412	2340	0.279
297	Callison	Johnny	1973	152.023	16	9.501	226	840	1757	0.264
298	Larkin	Henry	1893	151.769	10	15.177	53	836	1429	0.303
299	Dunn	Adam	2014	151.215	14	10.801	462	1168	1631	0.237
300	Bush	Donie	1923	150.871	16	9.429	9	436	1804	0.250
301	Baker	Dusty	1986	150.737	19	7.934	242	1013	1981	0.278
302	Salmon	Tim	2006	150.732	14	10.767	299	1016	1674	0.282
303	Williams	Matt	2003	149.950	17	8.821	378	1218	1878	0.268
304	Posey	Buster	2019	149.898	11	13.627	140	673	1380	0.302
305	Wilson	Hack	1934	149.587	12	12.466	244	1063	1461	0.307
306	Alou	Moises	2008	149.281	17	8.781	332	1287	2134	0.303
307	Galan	Augie	1949	148.693	16	9.293	100	830	1706	0.287
308	Maranville	Rabbit	1935	148.551	23	6.459	28	884	2605	0.258
309	Lee	Carlos	2012	147.615	14	10.544	358	1363	2273	0.285
310	Keller	Charlie	1952	146.592	13	11.276	189	760	1085	0.286
311	Vizquel	Omar	2012	146.273	24	6.095	80	951	2877	0.272
312	Ewing	Buck	1897	146.265	18	8.126	71	883	1625	0.303
313	Robinson	Jackie	1956	146.208	10	14.621	137	734	1518	0.311
314	Sierra	Ruben	2006	145.729	20	7.286	306	1322	2152	0.268
315	Bottomley	Jim	1937	145.525	16	9.095	219	1422	2313	0.310
316	Groh	Heinie	1927	145.428	16	9.089	26	566	1774	0.292
317	Freehan	Bill	1976	145.340	15	9.689	200	758	1591	0.262
318	York	Rudy	1948	145.003	13	11.154	277	1152	1621	0.275
319	Chapman	Ben	1946	144.921	15	9.661	90	977	1958	0.302
320	Kendall	Jason	2010	144.913	15	9.661	75	744	2195	0.288
321	Dalrymple	Abner	1891	144.723	12	12.060	43	407	1202	0.288
322	Hendrick	George	1988	144.471	18	8.026	267	1111	1980	0.278
323	Ramirez	Hanley	2019	144.429	15	9.629	271	917	1834	0.289
324	Sievers	Roy	1965	143.958	17	8.468	318	1147	1703	0.267
325	Williamson	Ned	1890	143.762	13	11.059	64	667	1159	0.255
326	Burks	Ellis	2004	143.485	18	7.971	352	1206	2107	0.291
327	Howard	Ryan	2016	143.152	13	11.012	382	1194	1475	0.258
328	Lansford	Carney	1992	143.016	15	9.534	151	874	2074	0.290
329	Shaffer	Orator	1890	142.759	13	10.981	11	317	1000	0.282
330	May	Lee	1982	142.473	18	7.915	354	1244	2031	0.267
331	Anderson	Garret	2010	142.217	17	8.366	287	1365	2529	0.293

RANK	NAME	FIRST	LYEAR	PEVAB	YRS	PPYR	HR	RBI	HITS	AVE
332	Frisch	Frankie	1937	141.796	19	7.463	105	1244	2880	0.316
333	Traynor	Pie	1937	141.423	17	8.319	58	1273	2416	0.320
334	Childs	Cupid	1901	141.383	13	10.876	20	743	1720	0.306
335	Galarraga	Andres	2004	140.938	19	7.418	399	1425	2333	0.288
336	Ward	John	1894	140.851	17	8.285	26	867	2104	0.275
337	Long	Herman	1904	140.840	16	8.803	91	1055	2127	0.277
338	Matthews	Gary	1987	140.782	16	8.799	234	978	2011	0.281
339	Young	Michael	2013	140.352	14	10.025	185	1030	2375	0.300
340	Beaumont	Ginger	1910	140.093	12	11.674	39	617	1759	0.311
341	Lee	Derrek	2011	139.798	15	9.320	331	1078	1959	0.281
342	Milan	Clyde	1922	139.763	16	8.735	17	617	2100	0.285
343	Williams	Cy	1930	139.688	19	7.352	251	1005	1981	0.292
344	Seymour	Cy	1913	139.378	16	8.711	52	799	1723	0.303
345	Molina	Yadier	2020	139.280	17	8.193	160	932	2001	0.281
346	Soriano	Rafael	2015	139.004	17	8.177	412	1159	2095	0.270
347	Caminiti	Ken	2001	138.421	15	9.228	239	983	1710	0.272
348	Maris	Roger	1968	138.127	12	11.511	275	851	1325	0.260
349	Lyons	Denny	1897	137.809	13	10.601	62	755	1333	0.310
350	Harper	Bryce	2020	137.661	9	15.296	232	668	1122	0.276
351	Watson	Bob	1984	137.414	19	7.232	184	989	1826	0.295
352	Phillips	Tony	1999	137.398	18	7.633	160	819	2023	0.266
353	Stanton	Giancarlo	2020	137.199	11	12.473	312	796	1160	0.268
354	Pafko	Andy	1959	136.514	17	8.030	213	976	1796	0.285
355	Gardner	Larry	1924	136.459	17	8.027	27	934	1931	0.289
356	O'Neill	Tip	1892	136.175	10	13.618	52	757	1386	0.326
357	Thomson	Bobby	1960	135.796	15	9.053	264	1026	1705	0.270
358	Allison	Bob	1970	135.670	13	10.436	256	796	1281	0.255
359	Kluszewski	Ted	1961	135.572	15	9.038	279	1028	1766	0.298
360	Bell	Jay	2003	135.350	18	7.519	195	860	1963	0.265
361	Kell	George	1957	134.828	15	8.989	78	870	2054	0.306
362	Choo	Shin-Soo	2020	134.792	16	8.424	218	782	1671	0.275
363	Cramer	Doc	1948	134.475	20	6.724	37	842	2705	0.296
364	Munson	Thurman	1979	134.322	11	12.211	113	701	1558	0.292
365	Cravath	Gavvy	1920	134.238	11	12.203	119	719	1134	0.287
366	Hrbek	Kent	1994	134.078	14	9.577	293	1086	1749	0.282
367	Fregosi	Jim	1978	133.839	18	7.435	151	706	1726	0.265
368	Scott	George	1979	133.684	14	9.549	271	1051	1992	0.268
369	Herman	Babe	1945	133.641	13	10.280	181	997	1818	0.324
370	Alou	Felipe	1974	133.359	17	7.845	206	852	2101	0.286
371	Fernandez	Tony	2001	133.085	17	7.829	94	844	2276	0.288
372	McCann	Brian	2019	132.851	15	8.857	282	1018	1590	0.262
373	Anderson	Brady	2002	132.779	15	8.852	210	761	1661	0.256
374	Gordon	Sid	1955	132.470	13	10.190	202	805	1415	0.283

RANK	NAME	FIRST	LYEAR	PEVAB	YRS	PPYR	HR	RBI	HITS	AVE
375	Vaughn	Mo	2003	132.139	12	11.012	328	1064	1620	0.293
376	Bell	George	1993	131.710	12	10.976	265	1002	1702	0.278
377	Randolph	Willie	1992	131.449	18	7.303	54	687	2210	0.276
378	Griffey	Ken	1991	131.432	19	6.917	152	859	2143	0.296
379	Combs	Earle	1935	131.405	12	10.950	58	632	1866	0.325
380	Schoendienst	Red	1963	131.156	19	6.903	84	773	2449	0.289
381	Donaldson	Josh	2020	131.129	10	13.113	225	656	1066	0.272
382	Pratt	Del	1924	131.097	13	10.084	43	970	1996	0.292
383	Herman	Billy	1947	131.084	15	8.739	47	839	2345	0.304
384	Monday	Rick	1984	131.076	19	6.899	241	775	1619	0.264
385	Jones	Adam	2019	131.027	14	9.359	282	945	1939	0.277
386	McRae	Hal	1987	131.020	19	6.896	191	1097	2091	0.290
387	Zimmerman	Ryan	2019	130.664	15	8.711	270	1015	1784	0.279
388	Doyle	Larry	1920	130.652	14	9.332	74	793	1887	0.290
389	Woodling	Gene	1962	130.339	17	7.667	147	830	1585	0.284
390	Joyner	Wally	2001	130.181	16	8.136	204	1106	2060	0.289
391	Tenace	Gene	1983	130.074	15	8.672	201	674	1060	0.241
392	Keltner	Ken	1950	130.026	13	10.002	163	852	1570	0.276
393	Concepcion	Dave	1988	130.003	19	6.842	101	950	2326	0.267
394	Titus	John	1913	129.978	11	11.816	38	561	1401	0.282
395	Corcoran	Tommy	1907	129.562	18	7.198	34	1135	2252	0.256
396	Upton	Justin	2020	129.381	14	9.241	307	959	1681	0.265
397	Jensen	Jackie	1961	129.098	11	11.736	199	929	1463	0.279
398	Daubert	Jake	1924	129.093	15	8.606	56	722	2326	0.303
399	Porter	Darrell	1987	129.013	17	7.589	188	826	1369	0.247
400	Utley	Chase	2018	128.981	16	8.061	259	1025	1885	0.275
401	Pence	Hunter	2020	128.478	14	9.177	244	942	1791	0.279
402	Schulte	Frank	1918	128.351	15	8.557	92	792	1766	0.270
403	Rizzo	Anthony	2020	128.276	10	12.828	229	753	1249	0.271
404	Wood	George	1892	128.191	13	9.861	68	601	1467	0.273
405	Madlock	Bill	1987	128.170	15	8.545	163	860	2008	0.305
406	Reilly	John	1891	128.016	10	12.802	69	740	1352	0.289
407	Dark	Alvin	1960	127.973	14	9.141	126	757	2089	0.289
408	Machado	Manny	2020	127.949	9	14.217	223	645	1268	0.280
409	Davis	Harry	1917	127.900	22	5.814	75	951	1841	0.277
410	Gordon	Joe	1950	127.893	11	11.627	253	975	1530	0.268
411	Kuhel	Joe	1947	127.834	18	7.102	131	1049	2212	0.277
412	Trosky	Hal	1946	127.735	11	11.612	228	1012	1561	0.302
413	Holmes	Tommy	1952	127.603	11	11.600	88	581	1507	0.302
414	Fairly	Ron	1978	127.559	21	6.074	215	1044	1913	0.266
415	Grissom	Marquis	2005	127.400	17	7.494	227	967	2251	0.272
416	Van Slyke	Andy	1995	127.394	13	9.800	164	792	1562	0.274
417	DeCinces	Doug	1987	127.103	15	8.474	237	879	1505	0.259

RANK	NAME	FIRST	LYEAR	PEVAB	YRS	PPYR	HR	RBI	HITS	AVE
418	DiMaggio	Dom	1953	127.048	11	11.550	87	618	1680	0.298
419	Lombardi	Ernie	1947	126.894	17	7.464	190	990	1792	0.306
420	Dunlap	Fred	1891	126.889	12	10.574	41	366	1159	0.292
421	Lazzeri	Tony	1939	126.796	14	9.057	178	1191	1840	0.292
422	Kauff	Benny	1920	126.714	8	15.839	49	454	961	0.311
423	Williams	Ken	1929	126.510	14	9.036	196	913	1552	0.319
424	Tenney	Fred	1911	126.468	17	7.439	22	688	2231	0.294
425	McInnis	Stuffy	1927	126.365	19	6.651	20	1063	2405	0.307
426	Fryman	Travis	2002	126.328	13	9.718	223	1022	1776	0.274
427	Lankford	Ray	2004	126.135	14	9.010	238	874	1561	0.272
428	Buckner	Bill	1990	125.901	22	5.723	174	1208	2715	0.289
429	Moses	Wally	1951	125.890	17	7.405	89	679	2138	0.291
430	Furillo	Carl	1960	125.828	15	8.389	192	1058	1910	0.299
431	Heath	Jeff	1949	125.783	14	8.985	194	887	1447	0.293
432	Mayberry	John	1982	125.747	15	8.383	255	879	1379	0.253
433	Wertz	Vic	1963	125.654	17	7.391	266	1178	1692	0.277
434	Ibanez	Raul	2014	125.636	19	6.612	305	1207	2034	0.272
435	Higgins	Pinky	1946	125.489	14	8.964	140	1075	1941	0.292
436	Cavarretta	Phil	1955	125.119	22	5.687	95	920	1977	0.293
437	Stahl	Chick	1906	124.305	10	12.431	36	622	1546	0.305
438	Zeile	Todd	2004	124.223	16	7.764	253	1110	2004	0.265
439	Santana	Carlos	2020	124.030	11	11.275	240	796	1325	0.248
440	Campaneris	Bert	1983	123.969	19	6.525	79	646	2249	0.259
441	Renteria	Edgar	2011	123.424	16	7.714	140	923	2327	0.286
442	Tartabull	Danny	1997	123.346	14	8.810	262	925	1366	0.273
443	Burns	Oyster	1895	123.319	11	11.211	65	832	1389	0.300
444	Smith	Elmer	1901	123.216	14	8.801	37	663	1454	0.310
445	Berger	Wally	1940	123.076	11	11.189	242	898	1550	0.300
446	Adcock	Joe	1966	122.934	17	7.231	336	1122	1832	0.277
447	Judge	Joe	1934	122.894	20	6.145	71	1034	2352	0.298
448	Myer	Buddy	1941	122.894	17	7.229	38	850	2131	0.303
449	Seager	Kyle	2020	122.851	10	12.285	207	706	1267	0.256
450	Bancroft	Dave	1930	122.761	16	7.673	32	591	2004	0.279
451	Nash	Billy	1898	122.428	15	8.162	60	977	1606	0.275
452	Surhoff	B.J.	2005	122.382	19	6.441	188	1153	2326	0.282
453	Peckinpaugh	Roger	1927	122.295	17	7.194	48	740	1876	0.259
454	Paskert	Dode	1921	122.199	15	8.147	42	577	1613	0.268
455	Horton	Willie	1980	122.172	18	6.787	325	1163	1993	0.273
456	Gibson	Kirk	1995	122.078	17	7.181	255	870	1553	0.268
457	Bell	Gus	1964	122.017	15	8.134	206	942	1823	0.281
458	Latham	Arlie	1909	122.015	17	7.177	27	563	1833	0.269
459	Groat	Dick	1967	121.479	14	8.677	39	707	2138	0.286
460	Flood	Curt	1971	121.336	15	8.089	85	636	1861	0.293

RANK	NAME	FIRST	LYEAR	PEVAB	YRS	PPYR	HR	RBI	HITS	AVE
461	Camilli	Dolph	1945	121.287	12	10.107	239	950	1482	0.277
462	Pendleton	Terry	1998	121.273	15	8.085	140	946	1897	0.270
463	Bradley	Bill	1915	120.886	14	8.635	33	552	1471	0.271
464	Garciaparra	Nomar	2009	120.880	14	8.634	229	936	1747	0.313
465	Kuenn	Harvey	1966	120.870	15	8.058	87	671	2092	0.303
466	Burroughs	Jeff	1985	120.741	16	7.546	240	882	1443	0.261
467	Chase	Hal	1919	120.683	15	8.046	57	941	2158	0.291
468	Fournier	Jack	1927	120.401	15	8.027	136	859	1631	0.313
469	Wills	Maury	1972	120.339	14	8.596	20	458	2134	0.281
470	Justice	David	2002	120.261	14	8.590	305	1017	1571	0.279
471	Schang	Wally	1931	120.176	19	6.325	59	710	1506	0.284
472	Abreu	Jose	2020	120.112	7	17.159	198	671	1114	0.294
473	Arenado	Nolan	2020	120.060	8	15.008	235	760	1206	0.293
474	Betts	Mookie	2020	119.833	7	17.119	155	509	1029	0.301
475	Wells	Vernon	2013	119.750	15	7.983	270	958	1794	0.270
476	Knoblauch	Chuck	2002	119.682	12	9.973	98	615	1839	0.289
477	Bresnahan	Roger	1915	119.654	17	7.038	26	530	1252	0.279
478	Tinker	Joe	1916	119.628	15	7.975	31	782	1687	0.262
479	Kingman	Dave	1986	119.486	16	7.468	442	1210	1575	0.236
480	Martinez	Tino	2005	119.460	16	7.466	339	1271	1925	0.271
481	Fielder	Cecil	1998	118.951	13	9.150	319	1008	1313	0.255
482	Pipp	Wally	1928	118.827	15	7.922	90	998	1941	0.281
483	Tettleton	Mickey	1997	118.622	14	8.473	245	732	1132	0.241
484	Davis	Tommy	1976	118.537	18	6.585	153	1052	2121	0.294
485	Glaus	Troy	2010	118.499	13	9.115	320	950	1375	0.254
486	Vaughn	Greg	2003	118.488	15	7.899	355	1072	1475	0.242
487	Thornton	Andre	1987	118.475	14	8.463	253	895	1342	0.254
488	Cameron	Mike	2011	118.228	17	6.955	278	968	1700	0.249
489	White	Devon	2001	118.194	17	6.953	208	846	1934	0.263
490	Carty	Rico	1979	118.157	15	7.877	204	890	1677	0.299
491	Gordon	Alex	2020	118.012	14	8.429	190	749	1643	0.257
492	Altuve	Jose	2020	118.010	10	11.801	133	556	1610	0.311
493	Yelich	Christian	2020	117.852	8	14.732	151	522	1108	0.296
494	Gant	Ron	2003	117.848	16	7.365	321	1008	1651	0.256
495	Cabrera	Melky	2019	117.130	15	7.809	144	854	1962	0.285
496	Williams	Jimmy	1909	117.083	11	10.644	49	796	1507	0.275
497	Buhner	Jay	2001	117.017	15	7.801	310	965	1273	0.254
498	Pike	Lip	1887	116.787	10	11.679	20	332	637	0.321
499	Jones	Willie	1961	116.648	15	7.777	190	812	1502	0.258
500	Morrill	John	1890	116.595	15	7.773	43	643	1275	0.260

Note: PEVA-B represents Batting PEVA for all regular seasons. It does not include Pitching PEVA values.

Note: LYEAR represents last year of player's career.

CHAPTER FOUR
BEST CAREERS EVER
PITCHING (1871-2020)

1. Greg Maddux (1986-2008)
594.209 PEVA RATING

For many, Greg Maddux is the most consistent pitcher in Major League history. His twenty straight seasons of fifteen wins, even with two strike shortened seasons in the middle, are a remarkable achievement in a time when pitchers no longer manned three or four pitcher rotations. Now some think Maddux is below the level of being #1 on a Best Ever list. We respect that. They would choose historic pitchers like Cy Young, or Christy Mathewson, or Walter Johnson, who are high on this list as well. There's those who think a pitcher who didn't dominant a game with a high 90's fastball, or strike out ten per game should be this high in a ranking. We respect that as well. A surprise might be that Maddux actually did strike out more than you'd think, #10 on the All-Time strikeout list. And we shouldn't forget that most of the pitchers who rank higher in ERA or WHIP9 pitched in eras when people did not get lots of hits or score many runs. But we'll stop our defense and let you form your own opinion about just where Maddux should rank. At the top, in the Top Ten, or perhaps even lower. For us, he's the #1 regular season pitcher in history.

Where Maddux Ranks

Category	Stats	Rank	Category	Stats	Rank
WINS	355	8	WHIP9	10.29	64
SO	3371	10	SO/W	3.37	39
ERA	3.16	233	IP	5008.3	13

2. Cy Young (1890-1911)
504.145 PEVA RATING

Cy Young was the best pitcher at the turn of the century and many think the best pitcher in the game. There's that award named after him. There's the fact that he won 511 games and pitched over 400 innings five times. Now that's not what would happen today, although it's hard to imagine a manager heading out to the mound in the fifth inning and pulling him as he approached one hundred pitches. Only one season in a span of 19 years from 1891 to 1909 did Cy Young fail to win 15 games, including over 30 wins in four separate seasons. There were six seasons with an ERA south of the pitcher's Mendoza line of 2.00.

Where Young Ranks

Category	Stats	Rank	Category	Stats	Rank
WINS	511	1	WHIP9	10.17	45
SO	2803	22	SO/W	2.30	214
ERA	2.63	61	IP	7356	1

3. Roger Clemens (1984-2007)
487.448 PEVA RATING

While Maddux was stellar season after season, contemporary Clemens was dominant game after game. Whether rumors of other substances change that calculation, or influence where he should rank, we'll stick to the statistical facts. Why would Clemens rank below Maddux? One simple word, durability. He logged five seasons below 200 innings from the age of 24-40 while Maddux had only one. Yes, you may pick Clemens for that one game you'd have to win over Maddux, but if you were counting on a whole season of work, Maddux would have been available more often. That said, it is hard to choose. And no matter that choice, Roger Clemens, from a statistical standpoint, is a Top Ten pitcher in baseball history.

Where Clemens Ranks

Category	Stats	Rank	Category	Stats	Rank
WINS	354	9	WHIP9	10.55	102
SO	4672	3	SO/W	2.96	69
ERA	3.13	216	IP	4916.7	16

4. Walter Johnson (1907-1927)
479.881 PEVA RATING

Should the Big Train rank even higher; there are many who think that's accurate. Johnson was really the first pitcher in history to dominate the game with the strikeout. He was the pitching version of Babe Ruth. He ranks #2 in All-Time Wins, #3 in Innings Pitched, and #7 in ERA plus adjusted. Johnson had eleven seasons with a regular, non adjusted ERA under 2.00. Oh, my. And it might be hard to imagine, but think about how many more wins Johnson would have had if he pitched for a traditional power team, instead of the old Washington Senators, today's Minnesota Twins, ... his 0.599 winning percentage is the 2nd lowest of the Top Ten on this list. Maybe he'd even approach Cy for the #1 Win Total.

Where Walter Johnson Ranks

Category	Stats	Rank	Category	Stats	Rank
WINS	417	2	WHIP9	9.55	11
SO	3509	9	SO/W	2.57	126
ERA	2.17	12	IP	5914.7	3

5. Randy Johnson (1988-2009)
408.708 PEVA RATING

He pitched from angles most pitchers can not. It looked as if he was handing the ball to the catcher at times from his 6'10 inch frame. Many think Johnson will be the last pitcher to win 300 games, and that feat for Johnson is even more remarkable considering the fact that he got a rather late career start to being great. It wasn't until Johnson pitched for Seattle in 1993, his seventh season when he turned 30 years old, that Randy had a stellar, All-Star caliber season. Johnson struck more men out than everyone but Nolan Ryan and his Strikeout to Walk ratio was amazing for a pitcher with that many K's. And for four consecutive years from 1999 to 2002, the Cy Young Award was his.

Where Randy Johnson Ranks

Category	Stats	Rank	Category	Stats	Rank
WINS	303	22	WHIP9	10.54	99
SO	4875	2	SO/W	3.26	49
ERA	3.29	296	IP	4135.3	38

6. Grover Cleveland Alexander (1911-1930)
386.297 PEVA RATING

In the first third of the 20th Century, the trio of Cy Young, Walter Johnson, and Grover Cleveland Alexander dominated the discussion of who was the best pitcher of not only that era, but All-Time. Grover Cleveland Alexander started with a splash, winning 28 games in his rookie season in Baker Bowl for the Philadelphia Phillies. Unlike Walter Johnson, Alexander won more with control and not the strikeout, but that added up to the stat that mattered most, at least until recent years, the Win. He won 373 games, 3rd most All-Time for the Phils, Cubs, and Cardinals over a twenty year career at a winning percentage clip of 0.642. Like some of the World War II era players like Ted Williams, there were some in the World War I time that lost baseball time to military service. Alexander lost most of the 1918 season, serving in France.

Where Alexander Ranks

Category	Stats	Rank	Category	Stats	Rank
WINS	373	3	WHIP9	10.09	42
SO	2198	66	SO/W	2.31	212
ERA	2.56	51	IP	5190.0	10

7. Warren Spahn (1942-1965)
370.496 PEVA RATING

Warren Spahn pitched for the Braves in their Boston and Milwaukee days and won 363 games, the most by a left-handed pitcher in the history of baseball. It was not until Spahn was 26 that he had his breakout year, winning 21 games in 1947 over 289.7 innings with an ERA of just 2.33. Spahn was a remarkably durable player once his career took off, pitching over 240 innings every year from the age of 26 to 44. At the age of 42, Spahn went 23-7 with a 2.60 ERA. His one flaw to some statistical types was his SO/W ratio at 1.80, low compared to other great pitchers. But that minor flaw did not limit victory, and that's what Spahn did so well after all.

Where Spahn Ranks

Category	Stats	Rank	Category	Stats	Rank
WINS	363	6	WHIP9	10.75	140
SO	2583	29	SO/W	1.80	482
ERA	3.09	195	IP	5243.7	8

8. Lefty Grove (1925-1941)
342.625 PEVA RATING

Lefty Grove won 68% of his games for #8 on the Career List and his adjusted ERA plus ranks as #6. On those two stats alone, it's understood why Lefty Grove comes into the Top Ten Career list for pitchers at #8. Lefty Grove reached the Major Leagues late, not reaching the Philadelphia Athletics until the year he turned 25 because his minor league team, which was not affiliated with a Major League club, had refused offers for Grove's service until the price was right. By 1924, Grove was sold to Philadelphia for $100,500, the most ever at the time. Once Grove reached the major leagues, it didn't take him long to make an impact. In his second year, he won his first ERA title and won 20 games, starting a streak of twenty win seasons that would last seven years. Grove was particularly stingy giving up runs, winning eight more ERA titles in his career after the first in 1926.

Where Grove Ranks

Category	Stats	Rank	Category	Stats	Rank
WINS	300	23	WHIP9	11.43	415
SO	2266	59	SO/W	1.91	408
ERA	3.06	183	IP	3940.7	44

9. Tom Seaver (1967-1986)
336.016 PEVA RATING

Tom Seaver was a strikeout pitcher, tough, stout, and strong, with 311 wins to his credit over his twenty year career and a #6 ranking in Strikeouts ever and an Innings Pitched rank of #19, that's even greater when you consider he pitched in the second half of the century, not the first. He won the Rookie of the Year Award and three Cy Youngs. All hail, Tom Terrific, for leading the Mets from the wilderness to the World Series podium in 1969 and for all the great years of his career.

Where Seaver Ranks

Category	Stats	Rank	Category	Stats	Rank
WINS	311	18	WHIP9	10.09	41
SO	3640	6	SO/W	2.62	114
ERA	2.86	126	IP	4783.0	19

10. Pedro Martinez (1992-2009)
328.493 PEVA RATING

Pedro did not give up hits or walks or runs. His adjusted ERA plus ranks #3 on the All-Time Career list, he is #5 in WHIP and #3 in Strikeout to Walk Ratio. He won 68.7% of his games, #7 All-Time. So there's no doubt that Pedro Martinez belongs in the list of Top Ten pitchers of All-Time, even with a lower total of wins or games or even innings pitched. Because in the games he pitched, he won. He pitched with power that belied his lean 5'11" frame, style, guile, and moxie. He beguiled the crowds, infuriated opponents, and won baseball games.

Where Martinez Ranks

Category	Stats	Rank	Category	Stats	Rank
WINS	219	80	WHIP9	9.49	8
SO	3154	13	SO/W	4.15	12
ERA	2.93	148	IP	2827.3	168

Note: Career Stat Ranks as of September 24, 2020 .
Rate stats rankings based on players with at least 1,000 IP.

Top 250 Pitching Careers
(1871-2020)

RANK	NAME	FIRST	LYEAR	PEVAP	YRS	PPYR	WINS	LOSS	SV	ERA
1	Maddux	Greg	2008	**594.209**	23	25.835	355	227	0	3.16
2	Young	Cy	1911	**504.145**	22	22.916	511	316	17	2.63

RANK	NAME	FIRST	LYEAR	PEVAP	YRS	PPYR	WINS	LOSS	SV	ERA
3	Clemens	Roger	2007	487.448	24	20.310	354	184	0	3.12
4	Johnson	Walter	1927	479.881	21	22.851	417	279	34	2.17
5	Johnson	Randy	2009	408.708	22	18.578	303	166	2	3.29
6	Alexander	Pete	1930	386.297	20	19.315	373	208	32	2.56
7	Spahn	Warren	1965	370.496	21	17.643	363	245	29	3.09
8	Grove	Lefty	1941	342.625	17	20.154	300	141	55	3.06
9	Seaver	Tom	1986	336.016	20	16.801	311	205	1	2.86
10	Martinez	Pedro	2009	328.493	18	18.250	219	100	3	2.93
11	Carlton	Steve	1988	328.364	24	13.682	329	244	2	3.22
12	Glavine	Tom	2008	325.047	22	14.775	305	203	0	3.54
13	Kershaw	Clayton	2020	322.730	13	24.825	175	76	0	2.43
14	Verlander	Justin	2020	322.278	16	20.142	226	129	0	3.33
15	Nichols	Kid	1906	315.802	15	21.053	361	208	17	2.95
16	Roberts	Robin	1966	307.347	19	16.176	286	245	25	3.41
17	Halladay	Roy	2013	304.746	16	19.047	203	105	1	3.38
18	Hubbell	Carl	1943	301.955	16	18.872	253	154	33	2.98
19	Smoltz	John	2009	301.456	21	14.355	213	155	154	3.33
20	Mathewson	Christy	1916	290.943	17	17.114	373	188	28	2.13
21	Perry	Gaylord	1983	286.287	22	13.013	314	265	11	3.11
22	Schilling	Curt	2007	282.056	20	14.103	216	146	22	3.46
23	Mussina	Mike	2008	276.995	18	15.389	270	153	0	3.68
24	Greinke	Zack	2020	276.028	17	16.237	208	126	1	3.37
25	Blyleven	Bert	1992	271.050	22	12.320	287	250	0	3.31
26	Ryan	Nolan	1993	270.518	27	10.019	324	292	3	3.19
27	Niekro	Phil	1987	269.835	24	11.243	318	274	29	3.35
28	Sutton	Don	1988	266.168	23	11.573	324	256	5	3.26
29	Brown	Kevin	2005	263.325	19	13.859	211	144	0	3.28
30	Sabathia	CC	2017	258.875	17	15.228	237	146	0	3.70
31	Scherzer	Max	2019	252.387	13	19.414	175	93	0	3.21
32	Jenkins	Fergie	1983	250.554	19	13.187	284	226	7	3.34
33	Feller	Bob	1956	246.330	18	13.685	266	162	21	3.25
34	Rivera	Mariano	2013	245.654	19	12.929	82	60	652	2.21
35	Palmer	Jim	1984	240.163	19	12.640	268	152	4	2.86
36	Bunning	Jim	1971	232.747	17	13.691	224	184	16	3.27
37	Marichal	Juan	1975	231.714	16	14.482	243	142	2	2.89
38	Drysdale	Don	1969	228.992	14	16.357	209	166	6	2.95
39	Gibson	Bob	1975	225.768	17	13.280	251	174	6	2.91
40	Wynn	Early	1963	220.535	23	9.588	300	244	15	3.54
41	Newhouser	Hal	1955	218.723	17	12.866	207	150	26	3.06
42	Eckersley	Dennis	1998	217.107	24	9.046	197	171	390	3.50
43	Walsh	Ed	1917	213.766	14	15.269	195	126	34	1.82
44	Vance	Dazzy	1935	212.748	16	13.297	197	140	11	3.24

RANK	NAME	FIRST	LYEAR	PEVAP	YRS	PPYR	WINS	LOSS	SV	ERA
45	Hudson	Tim	2015	211.222	17	12.425	222	133	0	3.49
46	Pettitte	Andy	2013	210.009	18	11.667	256	153	0	3.85
47	Martinez	Dennis	1998	209.456	23	9.107	245	193	8	3.70
48	Rusie	Amos	1901	208.983	10	20.898	245	174	5	3.07
49	Santana	Johan	2012	207.195	12	17.266	139	78	1	3.20
50	Koufax	Sandy	1966	206.787	12	17.232	165	87	9	2.76
51	Saberhagen	Bret	2001	204.005	16	12.750	167	117	1	3.34
52	Hershiser	Orel	2000	203.300	18	11.294	204	150	5	3.48
53	Derringer	Paul	1945	202.808	15	13.521	223	212	29	3.46
54	Buehrle	Mark	2015	202.522	16	12.658	214	160	0	3.81
55	Rixey	Eppa	1933	202.000	21	9.619	266	251	14	3.15
56	Ford	Whitey	1967	200.553	16	12.535	236	106	10	2.75
57	Wainwright	Adam	2020	198.362	15	13.224	167	98	3	3.38
58	Hernandez	Felix	2019	197.663	15	13.178	169	136	0	3.42
59	Lee	Cliff	2014	195.319	13	15.025	143	91	0	3.52
60	Morris	Jack	1994	194.913	18	10.829	254	186	0	3.90
61	Clarkson	John	1894	194.134	12	16.178	328	178	5	2.81
62	Oswalt	Roy	2013	193.498	13	14.884	163	102	0	3.36
63	Lester	Jon	2020	193.007	15	12.867	193	111	0	3.60
64	Moyer	Jamie	2012	191.907	25	7.676	269	209	0	4.25
65	Hamels	Cole	2020	191.355	15	12.757	163	122	0	3.43
66	Gooden	Dwight	2000	189.771	16	11.861	194	112	3	3.51
67	Reuschel	Rick	1991	187.186	19	9.852	214	191	5	3.37
68	Grimes	Burleigh	1934	185.950	19	9.787	270	212	18	3.53
69	Cone	David	2003	185.152	17	10.891	194	126	1	3.46
70	Kaat	Jim	1983	184.824	25	7.393	283	237	18	3.45
71	Walters	Bucky	1950	182.990	15	12.199	198	160	4	3.30
72	John	Tommy	1989	182.842	26	7.032	288	231	4	3.34
73	Lowe	Derek	2013	180.817	17	10.636	176	157	86	4.03
74	Colon	Bartolo	2018	180.463	21	8.593	247	188	0	4.12
75	Lyons	Ted	1946	178.627	21	8.506	260	230	23	3.67
76	Viola	Frank	1996	178.435	15	11.896	176	150	0	3.73
77	Tanana	Frank	1993	177.300	21	8.443	240	236	1	3.66
78	Faber	Red	1933	177.153	20	8.858	254	213	28	3.15
79	Friend	Bob	1966	176.919	16	11.057	197	230	11	3.58
80	Haren	Dan	2015	176.009	13	13.539	153	131	1	3.75
81	McGinnity	Joe	1908	175.944	10	17.594	246	142	24	2.66
82	Coveleski	Stan	1928	175.862	14	12.562	215	142	21	2.89
83	Pierce	Billy	1964	175.777	18	9.765	211	169	32	3.27
84	Stieb	Dave	1998	174.001	16	10.875	176	137	3	3.44
85	Wells	David	2007	173.846	21	8.278	239	157	13	4.13
86	Key	Jimmy	1998	173.444	15	11.563	186	117	10	3.51
87	Keefe	Tim	1893	173.362	14	12.383	342	225	2	2.62

RANK	NAME	FIRST	LYEAR	PEVAP	YRS	PPYR	WINS	LOSS	SV	ERA
88	Plank	Eddie	1917	173.294	17	10.194	326	194	23	2.35
89	Vazquez	Javier	2011	172.439	14	12.317	165	160	0	4.22
90	Hunter	Catfish	1979	171.445	15	11.430	224	166	1	3.26
91	Blue	Vida	1986	171.111	17	10.065	209	161	2	3.27
92	Leonard	Dutch	1953	170.527	20	8.526	191	181	44	3.25
93	Carpenter	Chris	2012	167.841	15	11.189	144	94	0	3.76
94	Wilhelm	Hoyt	1972	167.483	21	7.975	143	122	227	2.52
95	Brown	Mordecai	1916	167.406	14	11.958	239	130	49	2.06
96	Spalding	Al	1877	167.275	7	23.896	253	65	11	2.14
97	Hoffman	Trevor	2010	166.371	18	9.243	61	75	601	2.87
98	Lemon	Bob	1958	165.840	13	12.757	207	128	22	3.23
99	Sale	Chris	2019	164.883	10	16.488	109	73	12	3.03
100	Cooper	Wilbur	1926	164.114	15	10.941	216	178	14	2.89
101	Lackey	John	2017	163.379	15	10.892	188	147	0	3.92
102	Appier	Kevin	2004	163.015	16	10.188	169	137	0	3.74
103	Dean	Dizzy	1947	162.809	12	13.567	150	83	30	3.02
104	Finley	Chuck	2002	162.129	17	9.537	200	173	0	3.85
105	Valenzuela	Fernando	1997	162.020	17	9.531	173	153	2	3.54
106	Rogers	Kenny	2008	161.713	20	8.086	219	156	28	4.27
107	Luque	Dolf	1935	159.395	20	7.970	194	179	28	3.24
108	Willis	Vic	1910	159.260	13	12.251	249	205	11	2.63
109	Rogers	Steve	1985	159.201	13	12.246	158	152	2	3.17
110	Adams	Babe	1926	158.436	19	8.339	194	140	15	2.76
111	Ruffing	Red	1947	157.733	22	7.170	273	225	16	3.80
112	Welch	Bob	1994	157.692	17	9.276	211	146	8	3.47
113	Warneke	Lon	1945	157.469	15	10.498	192	121	13	3.18
114	Jackson	Larry	1968	153.706	14	10.979	194	183	20	3.40
115	Cueto	Johnny	2020	153.666	13	11.820	128	90	0	3.41
116	Price	David	2019	152.590	12	12.716	150	80	0	3.31
117	Langston	Mark	1999	152.005	16	9.500	179	158	0	3.97
118	Reuss	Jerry	1990	151.558	22	6.889	220	191	11	3.64
119	Peavy	Jake	2016	151.536	15	10.102	152	126	0	3.63
120	Koosman	Jerry	1985	151.117	19	7.954	222	209	17	3.36
121	Zito	Barry	2013	150.880	14	10.777	165	143	0	4.02
122	Shields	James	2018	150.857	13	11.604	145	139	0	4.01
123	Kluber	Corey	2020	150.813	10	15.081	98	58	0	3.16
124	Hough	Charlie	1994	150.721	25	6.029	216	216	61	3.75
125	Hoyt	Waite	1938	150.378	21	7.161	237	182	52	3.59
126	Weaver	Jered	2017	150.142	12	12.512	150	98	0	3.63
127	Mays	Carl	1929	149.606	15	9.974	207	126	31	2.92
128	Passeau	Claude	1947	148.781	13	11.445	162	150	21	3.32
129	Niekro	Joe	1988	147.104	22	6.687	221	204	16	3.59

RANK	NAME	FIRST	LYEAR	PEVAP	YRS	PPYR	WINS	LOSS	SV	ERA
130	Tiant	Luis	1982	**147.094**	19	7.742	229	172	15	3.30
131	Galvin	Pud	1892	**146.925**	15	9.795	364	310	2	2.86
132	Drabek	Doug	1998	**146.466**	13	11.267	155	134	0	3.73
133	French	Larry	1942	**146.144**	14	10.439	197	171	17	3.44
134	Wagner	Billy	2010	**146.055**	16	9.128	47	40	422	2.31
135	Newsom	Bobo	1953	**145.446**	20	7.272	211	222	21	3.98
136	Guidry	Ron	1988	**144.658**	14	10.333	170	91	4	3.29
137	Root	Charley	1941	**144.582**	17	8.505	201	160	40	3.59
138	Hernandez	Livan	2012	**143.854**	17	8.462	178	177	1	4.44
139	Wood	Wilbur	1978	**143.431**	17	8.437	164	156	57	3.24
140	Webb	Brandon	2009	**142.694**	7	20.385	87	62	0	3.27
141	Bond	Tommy	1884	**141.227**	10	14.123	234	163	0	2.31
142	Cicotte	Eddie	1920	**140.807**	14	10.058	208	149	25	2.38
143	Quinn	Jack	1933	**140.371**	23	6.103	247	218	57	3.29
144	Newcombe	Don	1960	**140.056**	10	14.006	149	90	7	3.56
145	Bumgarner	Madison	2020	**140.046**	12	11.671	120	96	0	3.20
146	Scott	Mike	1991	**138.503**	13	10.654	124	108	3	3.54
147	Fitzsimmons	Freddie	1943	**138.188**	19	7.273	217	146	13	3.51
148	Gossage	Rich	1994	**138.013**	22	6.273	124	107	310	3.01
149	Nathan	Joe	2016	**137.790**	16	8.612	64	34	377	2.87
150	Millwood	Kevin	2012	**137.685**	16	8.605	169	152	0	4.11
151	Lolich	Mickey	1979	**137.305**	16	8.582	217	191	11	3.44
152	Radbourn	Charley	1891	**136.077**	11	12.371	309	195	2	2.67
153	Cuellar	Mike	1977	**135.827**	15	9.055	185	130	11	3.14
154	Shocker	Urban	1928	**135.739**	13	10.441	187	117	25	3.17
155	Rijo	Jose	2002	**135.731**	14	9.695	116	91	3	3.24
156	Gomez	Lefty	1943	**135.569**	14	9.683	189	102	9	3.34
157	Cole	Gerrit	2020	**133.554**	8	16.694	101	55	0	3.19
158	Griffith	Clark	1914	**133.483**	20	6.674	237	146	6	3.31
159	Burdette	Lew	1967	**133.345**	18	7.408	203	144	31	3.66
160	Candelaria	John	1993	**131.995**	19	6.947	177	122	29	3.33
161	Lee	Bill	1947	**130.593**	14	9.328	169	157	13	3.54
162	Fingers	Rollie	1985	**130.458**	17	7.674	114	118	341	2.90
163	Vaughn	Hippo	1921	**130.329**	13	10.025	178	137	5	2.49
164	Radke	Brad	2006	**130.309**	12	10.859	148	139	0	4.22
165	Cooper	Mort	1949	**129.805**	11	11.800	128	75	14	2.97
166	Lincecum	Tim	2016	**129.312**	10	12.931	110	89	1	3.74
167	Santana	Ervin	2019	**129.015**	15	8.601	149	127	0	4.09
168	Ferrell	Wes	1941	**128.949**	15	8.597	193	128	13	4.04
169	Cain	Matt	2017	**128.865**	13	9.913	104	118	0	3.68
170	Trout	Dizzy	1957	**128.842**	15	8.589	170	161	35	3.23
171	Gonzalez	Gio	2020	**128.770**	13	9.905	131	101	0	3.70

RANK	NAME	FIRST	LYEAR	PEVAP	YRS	PPYR	WINS	LOSS	SV	ERA
172	deGrom	Jacob	2020	128.750	7	18.393	70	51	0	2.61
173	Perry	Jim	1975	128.689	17	7.570	215	174	10	3.45
174	Waddell	Rube	1910	128.642	13	9.896	193	143	5	2.16
175	Arroyo	Bronson	2017	128.630	16	8.039	148	137	1	4.28
176	Strasburg	Stephen	2020	127.798	11	11.618	112	59	0	3.19
177	Burnett	A.J.	2015	127.450	17	7.497	164	157	0	3.99
178	Benes	Andy	2002	127.349	14	9.096	155	139	1	3.97
179	Porcello	Rick	2020	125.997	12	10.500	150	125	0	4.40
180	Leiter	Al	2005	125.172	19	6.588	162	132	2	3.80
181	Alexander	Doyle	1989	124.644	19	6.560	194	174	3	3.76
182	Pennock	Herb	1934	124.016	22	5.637	240	162	32	3.60
183	Beckett	Josh	2014	123.897	14	8.850	138	106	0	3.88
184	Garcia	Mike	1961	123.707	14	8.836	142	97	23	3.27
185	Osteen	Claude	1975	122.918	18	6.829	196	195	1	3.30
186	Wakefield	Tim	2011	122.453	19	6.445	200	180	22	4.41
187	Simmons	Curt	1967	121.668	20	6.083	193	183	5	3.54
188	Mathews	Bobby	1887	121.473	15	8.098	297	248	3	2.89
189	Burkett	John	2003	121.463	15	8.098	166	136	1	4.31
190	Stewart	Dave	1995	121.446	16	7.590	168	129	19	3.95
191	Joss	Addie	1910	121.395	9	13.488	160	97	5	1.89
192	Pascual	Camilo	1971	121.302	18	6.739	174	170	10	3.63
193	Candiotti	Tom	1999	120.634	16	7.540	151	164	0	3.73
194	Chesbro	Jack	1909	120.549	11	10.959	198	132	5	2.68
195	Dempster	Ryan	2013	119.920	16	7.495	132	133	87	4.35
196	Schmidt	Jason	2009	119.909	14	8.565	130	96	0	3.96
197	Papelbon	Jonathan	2016	119.863	12	9.989	41	36	368	2.44
198	Arrieta	Jake	2020	119.754	11	10.887	110	79	0	3.76
199	Zambrano	Carlos	2012	119.710	12	9.976	132	91	0	3.66
200	Jansen	Larry	1956	118.922	9	13.214	122	89	10	3.58
201	King	Silver	1897	118.857	10	11.886	203	154	6	3.18
202	Lary	Frank	1965	118.731	12	9.894	128	116	11	3.49
203	Jansen	Kenley	2020	117.627	11	10.693	33	22	312	2.39
204	Lynn	Lance	2020	117.333	9	13.037	104	71	1	3.57
205	Bridges	Tommy	1946	117.328	16	7.333	194	138	10	3.57
206	Trucks	Virgil	1958	117.186	17	6.893	177	135	30	3.39
207	Powell	Jack	1912	116.822	16	7.301	245	254	15	2.97
208	Darwin	Danny	1998	116.591	21	5.552	171	182	32	3.84
209	Haines	Jesse	1937	116.440	19	6.128	210	158	10	3.64
210	Harder	Mel	1947	116.071	20	5.804	223	186	23	3.80
211	Lohse	Kyle	2016	115.799	16	7.237	147	143	2	4.40
212	Messersmith	Andy	1979	115.459	12	9.622	130	99	15	2.86
213	Belcher	Tim	2000	114.914	14	8.208	146	140	5	4.16
214	Uhle	George	1936	114.370	17	6.728	200	166	25	3.99

RANK	NAME	FIRST	LYEAR	PEVAP	YRS	PPYR	WINS	LOSS	SV	ERA
215	Gullickson	Bill	1994	**114.091**	14	8.149	162	136	0	3.93
216	Phillippe	Deacon	1911	**114.075**	13	8.775	189	109	12	2.59
217	Moore	Mike	1995	**113.959**	14	8.140	161	176	2	4.39
218	Jones	Sam	1935	**113.860**	22	5.175	229	217	31	3.84
219	Smith	Lee	1997	**113.816**	18	6.323	71	92	478	3.03
220	Schumacher	Hal	1946	**113.603**	13	8.739	158	121	7	3.36
221	Kimbrel	Craig	2020	**112.980**	11	10.271	31	24	348	2.17
222	Antonelli	Johnny	1961	**112.813**	12	9.401	126	110	21	3.34
223	Hahn	Noodles	1906	**112.516**	8	14.064	130	94	0	2.55
224	Jones	Doug	2000	**112.347**	16	7.022	69	79	303	3.30
225	Lilly	Ted	2013	**112.337**	15	7.489	130	113	0	4.14
226	Hampton	Mike	2010	**112.163**	16	7.010	148	115	1	4.06
227	Marberry	Firpo	1936	**111.823**	14	7.987	148	88	101	3.63
228	Rodriguez	Francisco	2017	**111.804**	16	6.988	52	53	437	2.86
229	Donohue	Pete	1932	**111.741**	12	9.312	134	118	12	3.87
230	Hutchison	Bill	1897	**111.227**	9	12.359	183	163	4	3.59
231	McNally	Dave	1975	**111.184**	14	7.942	184	119	2	3.24
232	Brecheen	Harry	1953	**111.170**	12	9.264	133	92	18	2.92
233	Gordon	Tom	2009	**110.831**	21	5.278	138	126	158	3.96
234	Garcia	Freddy	2013	**110.482**	15	7.365	156	108	0	4.15
235	Knepper	Bob	1990	**110.426**	15	7.362	146	155	1	3.68
236	Sain	Johnny	1955	**110.416**	11	10.038	139	116	51	3.49
237	White	Will	1886	**110.286**	10	11.029	229	166	0	2.28
238	Pappas	Milt	1973	**110.110**	17	6.477	209	164	4	3.40
239	Hooton	Burt	1985	**109.906**	15	7.327	151	136	7	3.38
240	McDowell	Sam	1975	**109.730**	15	7.315	141	134	14	3.17
241	Mullane	Tony	1894	**109.564**	13	8.428	284	220	15	3.05
242	Kile	Darryl	2002	**109.549**	12	9.129	133	119	0	4.12
243	Soto	Mario	1988	**109.458**	12	9.121	100	92	4	3.47
244	Lopat	Ed	1955	**109.148**	12	9.096	166	112	3	3.21
245	Sutter	Bruce	1988	**108.819**	12	9.068	68	71	300	2.83
246	Trachsel	Steve	2008	**108.447**	16	6.778	143	159	0	4.39
247	Harang	Aaron	2015	**108.400**	14	7.743	128	143	0	4.26
248	McCormick	Jim	1887	**108.323**	10	10.832	265	214	1	2.43
249	Fassero	Jeff	2006	**107.708**	16	6.732	121	124	25	4.11
250	Rommel	Eddie	1932	**107.495**	13	8.269	171	119	29	3.54

Note: PEVA-P represents Pitching PEVA for all regular seasons.
It does not include Batting PEVA values.

Note: LYEAR represents last year of player's career.

Top 150 Fielding First Basemen

1B RANK	NAME	FIRST	PosFV	LYEAR	GP	PO	A	E	PCT	RF(pg)
1	Banks	Ernie	**1.3398**	1971	1259	12005	809	80	0.994	10.18
2	Garvey	Steve	**1.3352**	1987	2059	18844	1026	81	0.996	9.65
3	Goldschmidt	Paul	**1.3284**	2020	1281	10985	856	44	0.996	9.24
4	McCormick	Frank	**1.3278**	1948	1448	13798	1001	78	0.995	10.22
5	Helton	Todd	**1.3230**	2013	2178	18891	1721	79	0.996	9.46
6	Terry	Bill	**1.3118**	1936	1579	15972	1108	138	0.992	10.82
7	Grace	Mark	**1.2887**	2003	2162	18503	1665	110	0.995	9.33
8	Hernandez	Keith	**1.2838**	1990	2014	17909	1682	115	0.994	9.73
9	Donahue	Jiggs	**1.2811**	1909	745	8151	556	112	0.987	11.69
10	Parker	Wes	**1.2788**	1972	1108	9640	695	45	0.996	9.33
11	LaChance	Candy	**1.2766**	1905	1176	12320	457	207	0.984	10.86
12	Mattingly	Don	**1.2701**	1995	1634	14148	1104	64	0.996	9.33
13	Fletcher	Elbie	**1.2657**	1949	1380	13237	975	107	0.993	10.30
14	Konetchy	Ed	**1.2609**	1921	2073	21361	1292	224	0.990	10.93
15	Isbell	Frank	**1.2543**	1909	619	6663	455	99	0.986	11.50
16	Murray	Eddie	**1.2507**	1996	2413	21255	1865	167	0.993	9.58
17	Todt	Phil	**1.2479**	1931	904	9079	623	80	0.992	10.73
18	Pipp	Wally	**1.2473**	1928	1819	18779	1152	168	0.992	10.96
19	McInnis	Stuffy	**1.2466**	1927	1995	19962	1238	160	0.993	10.63
20	Chambliss	Chris	**1.2395**	1986	1962	17771	1351	130	0.993	9.75
21	Kelly	George	**1.2394**	1932	1373	14232	861	121	0.992	10.99
22	White	Bill	**1.2380**	1969	1477	12735	960	105	0.992	9.27
23	Lupien	Tony	**1.2364**	1948	602	5633	399	45	0.993	10.02
24	Pujols	Albert	**1.2329**	2020	1928	16498	1582	113	0.994	9.38
25	Start	Joe	**1.2304**	1886	1070	11209	229	435	0.963	10.69
26	Kotchman	Casey	**1.2298**	2013	870	6767	545	18	0.998	8.40
27	Colbert	Nate	**1.2282**	1976	890	7754	568	74	0.991	9.35
28	Brogna	Rico	**1.2234**	2001	817	6282	609	33	0.995	8.43
29	Young	Kevin	**1.2230**	2003	1049	8604	590	74	0.992	8.76
30	Olerud	John	**1.2225**	2005	2053	16166	1419	82	0.995	8.57
31	McGann	Dan	**1.2217**	1908	1377	13682	798	168	0.989	10.52
32	Gonzalez	Adrian	**1.2219**	2018	1836	14960	1390	76	0.995	8.91
33	Lee	Travis	**1.2214**	2006	1018	8107	585	29	0.997	8.54
34	Sheely	Earl	**1.2194**	1931	1220	12067	744	113	0.991	10.50
35	Clendenon	Donn	**1.2190**	1972	1200	10913	819	146	0.988	9.78
36	O'Brien	Pete	**1.2180**	1993	1377	11651	1064	79	0.994	9.23

IB RANK	NAME	FIRST	PosFV	LYEAR	GP	PO	A	E	PCT	RF(pg)
37	Hodges	Gil	1.2178	1963	1908	15344	1281	126	0.992	8.71
38	Power	Vic	1.2175	1965	1304	10141	1078	66	0.994	8.60
39	Joyner	Wally	1.2166	2001	1913	16081	1469	99	0.994	9.17
40	Phillips	Bill	1.2165	1888	1032	10540	305	324	0.971	10.51
41	Durham	Leon	1.2149	1989	618	5308	377	37	0.994	9.20
42	May	Lee	1.2143	1982	1507	12885	894	88	0.994	9.14
43	Bagwell	Jeff	1.2138	2005	2111	17543	1703	129	0.993	9.12
44	Rizzo	Anthony	1.2129	2020	1256	9983	1054	51	0.995	8.79
45	Mayberry	John	1.2129	1982	1478	13169	827	88	0.994	9.47
46	Karros	Eric	1.2119	2004	1698	14055	1359	111	0.993	9.08
47	Teixeira	Mark	1.2093	2016	1769	14943	966	55	0.997	8.99
48	Connor	Roger	1.2085	1897	1758	17605	856	419	0.978	10.50
49	Adcock	Joe	1.2069	1966	1501	13006	879	83	0.994	9.25
50	Clark	Will	1.2052	2000	1889	16696	1293	136	0.992	9.52
51	Freeman	Freddie	1.2046	2020	1380	11165	787	60	0.995	8.66
52	Waitkus	Eddie	1.2019	1955	1049	9150	716	72	0.993	9.41
53	Martinez	Tino	1.2004	2005	1869	15001	1158	80	0.995	8.65
54	Anderson	John	1.1979	1908	599	6224	332	117	0.982	10.94
55	McGriff	Fred	1.1960	2004	2239	18981	1447	167	0.992	9.12
56	Ganzel	John	1.1950	1908	726	7430	416	102	0.987	10.81
57	Gandil	Chick	1.1945	1919	1138	11118	754	99	0.992	10.43
58	Buckner	Bill	1.1942	1990	1555	13901	1351	128	0.992	9.81
59	Rose	Pete	1.1938	1986	939	7881	665	51	0.994	9.10
60	Jones	Tom	1.1932	1910	1033	10872	698	183	0.984	11.20
61	Thompson	Jason	1.1930	1986	1314	11818	819	97	0.992	9.62
62	Palmeiro	Rafael	1.1916	2005	2139	17737	1587	111	0.994	9.03
63	Cooper	Cecil	1.1913	1986	1475	13361	1000	121	0.992	9.74
64	Werden	Perry	1.1905	1897	667	6579	416	158	0.978	10.49
65	Pepitone	Joe	1.1888	1973	953	8172	627	61	0.993	9.23
66	Davis	Alvin	1.1868	1992	887	7803	572	67	0.992	9.44
67	Galarraga	Andres	1.1847	2004	2106	18242	1376	176	0.991	9.32
68	Davis	Glenn	1.1843	1993	870	7431	617	69	0.991	9.25
69	Cepeda	Orlando	1.1839	1972	1683	14459	1012	162	0.990	9.19
70	Bonura	Zeke	1.1835	1940	900	8808	595	72	0.992	10.45
71	Kluszewski	Ted	1.1806	1961	1481	12652	799	97	0.993	9.08
72	Holke	Walter	1.1768	1925	1193	12158	665	96	0.993	10.75
73	Hrbek	Kent	1.1768	1994	1609	13725	1049	87	0.994	9.18
74	Anson	Cap	1.1755	1897	2151	21695	983	657	0.972	10.54
75	Snow	J.T.	1.1746	2008	1658	12853	1015	63	0.995	8.36
76	Driessen	Dan	1.1726	1987	1375	10863	732	58	0.995	8.43
77	Scott	George	1.1709	1979	1773	15405	1132	165	0.990	9.33

IB RANK	NAME	FIRST	PosFV	LYEAR	GP	PO	A	E	PCT	RF(pg)
78	Beckley	Jake	1.1708	1907	2377	23709	1315	481	0.981	10.53
79	Montanez	Willie	1.1704	1982	1164	10006	714	87	0.992	9.21
80	Comiskey	Charlie	1.1703	1894	1363	13821	508	403	0.973	10.51
81	Musial	Stan	1.1692	1960	1016	8709	688	78	0.992	9.25
82	McGwire	Mark	1.1691	2001	1763	14451	1042	103	0.993	8.79
83	Grimm	Charlie	1.1681	1936	2131	20711	1214	162	0.993	10.29
84	Morneau	Justin	1.1680	2015	1324	11237	921	49	0.996	9.18
85	Fondy	Dee	1.1673	1958	874	7434	641	98	0.988	9.24
86	Sanchez	Gaby	1.1672	2014	610	4347	339	25	0.995	7.68
87	Tebeau	Patsy	1.1672	1899	595	6007	290	100	0.984	10.58
88	Balboni	Steve	1.1652	1990	630	5579	386	64	0.989	9.47
89	Daubert	Jake	1.1647	1924	2002	19634	1128	181	0.991	10.37
90	Overbay	Lyle	1.1628	2014	1435	11752	1001	68	0.995	8.89
91	Farrar	Sid	1.1608	1890	943	9550	358	262	0.974	10.51
92	Skowron	Bill	1.1606	1967	1463	12043	903	102	0.992	8.85
93	Stovall	George	1.1590	1915	1217	12709	846	194	0.986	11.14
94	Vernon	Mickey	1.1584	1959	2237	19808	1448	211	0.990	9.50
95	Lockman	Whitey	1.1567	1960	771	6716	510	80	0.989	9.37
96	Long	Dale	1.1562	1963	819	6960	550	88	0.988	9.17
97	Upshaw	Willie	1.1553	1988	1094	8939	799	98	0.990	8.90
98	Luderus	Fred	1.1552	1920	1326	13126	843	201	0.986	10.53
99	Spencer	Jim	1.1549	1982	1221	9898	797	55	0.995	8.76
100	Carew	Rod	1.1540	1985	1184	10930	774	106	0.991	9.89
101	York	Rudy	1.1533	1948	1263	11359	963	122	0.990	9.76
102	Suhr	Gus	1.1501	1940	1406	13103	766	116	0.992	9.86
103	Walker	Greg	1.1499	1990	689	5828	363	45	0.993	8.99
104	Delgado	Carlos	1.1483	2009	1767	15146	1062	129	0.992	9.17
105	Tenney	Fred	1.1480	1911	1810	17903	1363	327	0.983	10.64
106	Sexson	Richie	1.1451	2008	1198	9685	942	61	0.994	8.87
107	Hosmer	Eric	1.1438	2020	1374	10837	872	69	0.994	8.52
108	Siebern	Norm	1.1429	1968	827	6905	571	61	0.992	9.04
109	Robinson	Eddie	1.1426	1957	1126	9832	636	109	0.990	9.30
110	Mientkiewicz	Doug	1.1421	2009	959	7535	447	30	0.996	8.32
111	Mize	Johnny	1.1403	1953	1667	14850	1032	133	0.992	9.53
112	Segui	David	1.1374	2004	1121	8479	768	43	0.995	8.25
113	Orr	Dave	1.1334	1890	787	7923	254	227	0.973	10.39
114	Blue	Lu	1.1331	1933	1571	15644	1016	191	0.989	10.60
115	Gehrig	Lou	1.1330	1939	2137	19510	1087	193	0.991	9.64
116	Hargrove	Mike	1.1329	1985	1378	11274	1022	115	0.991	8.92
117	Casey	Sean	1.1325	2008	1313	10872	559	53	0.995	8.71
118	Bissonette	Del	1.1306	1933	598	5760	281	75	0.988	10.10

IB RANK	NAME	FIRST	PosFV	LYEAR	GP	PO	A	E	PCT	RF(pg)
119	Perez	Tony	1.1300	1986	1778	14481	936	117	0.992	8.67
120	Robertson	Bob	1.1290	1979	602	4915	453	32	0.994	8.92
121	Votto	Joey	1.1263	2020	1724	13081	1593	97	0.993	8.51
122	Hauser	Joe	1.1261	1929	547	5430	316	57	0.990	10.50
123	Kuhel	Joe	1.1259	1946	2057	19386	1163	173	0.992	9.99
124	Mauer	Joe	1.1243	2018	603	4873	376	19	0.996	8.70
125	Dahlgren	Babe	1.1243	1946	1030	9619	587	102	0.990	9.91
126	Reilly	John	1.1240	1891	1075	10875	286	316	0.972	10.38
127	Burns	Jack	1.1232	1936	879	8063	525	66	0.992	9.77
128	Clark	Tony	1.1218	2009	1211	9347	710	75	0.993	8.30
129	Thornton	Andre	1.1204	1984	729	6223	501	51	0.992	9.22
130	LaRoche	Adam	1.1203	2015	1468	12070	934	70	0.995	8.86
131	Runnels	Pete	1.1193	1964	644	4876	346	30	0.994	8.11
132	Yastrzemski	Carl	1.1190	1983	765	6459	512	41	0.994	9.11
133	Tucker	Tommy	1.1186	1899	1669	16393	749	393	0.978	10.27
134	Powell	Boog	1.1169	1977	1479	12130	859	116	0.991	8.78
135	Erstad	Darin	1.1167	2009	628	4784	320	23	0.996	8.13
136	Fielder	Prince	1.1166	2016	1324	10721	743	95	0.992	8.66
137	Thome	Jim	1.1166	2012	1105	9160	709	64	0.994	8.93
138	Bream	Sid	1.1136	1994	954	7437	786	69	0.992	8.62
139	Trosky	Hal	1.1136	1946	1321	12124	752	121	0.991	9.75
140	Perry	Gerald	1.1132	1995	656	5532	382	73	0.988	9.02
141	Lee	Derrek	1.1124	2011	1901	14910	1370	98	0.994	8.56
142	Merkle	Fred	1.1121	1926	1547	15419	847	252	0.985	10.51
143	Greenberg	Hank	1.1117	1947	1138	10564	724	104	0.991	9.92
144	Camilli	Dolph	1.1116	1945	1476	13724	957	141	0.990	9.95
145	Saier	Vic	1.1102	1919	838	8392	378	129	0.986	10.47
146	Smoak	Justin	1.1102	2020	1163	8972	510	39	0.996	8.15
147	Gentile	Jim	1.1097	1966	854	6725	564	73	0.990	8.54
148	Cash	Norm	1.1087	1974	1943	15157	1317	131	0.992	8.48
149	Konerko	Paul	1.1084	2014	1904	15931	1112	83	0.995	8.95
150	Giambi	Jason	1.1077	2012	1307	10759	513	91	0.992	8.62

Notes: Career Field Value possible maximum for 1st Basemen is 1.4000.
Minimum 500 Adjusted Games Played.

Top 150 Fielding Second Basemen

2B RANK	NAME	FIRST	PosFV	LYEAR	GP	PO	A	E	PCT	RF(pg)
1	McPhee	Bid	1.4438	1899	2126	6545	6905	791	0.944	6.33
2	Fox	Nellie	1.4281	1965	2295	6090	6373	209	0.984	5.43
3	Sandberg	Ryne	1.4233	1997	1995	3807	6363	109	0.989	5.10
4	LeMahieu	DJ	1.4189	2020	1004	1751	2869	44	0.991	4.60
5	Doerr	Bobby	1.4133	1951	1852	4928	5710	214	0.980	5.74
6	Clarke	Horace	1.4098	1974	1102	2682	3179	104	0.983	5.32
7	Mazeroski	Bill	1.4054	1972	2094	4974	6685	204	0.983	5.57
8	Wills	Bump	1.4023	1982	800	1815	2582	94	0.979	5.50
9	Lind	Jose	1.3964	1995	1038	2183	3094	62	0.988	5.08
10	Lajoie	Nap	1.3892	1916	2035	5496	6262	451	0.963	5.78
11	Collins	Eddie	1.3881	1928	2650	6526	7630	435	0.970	5.34
12	Grich	Bobby	1.3870	1986	1765	4217	5381	156	0.984	5.44
13	Melillo	Ski	1.3851	1937	1316	3437	4448	215	0.973	5.99
14	Ferris	Hobe	1.3781	1909	1019	2503	3152	271	0.954	5.55
15	Reed	Jody	1.3775	1997	1050	2135	3187	65	0.988	5.07
16	Cash	Dave	1.3766	1980	1330	3185	3841	117	0.984	5.28
17	Polanco	Placido	1.3702	2011	1027	2130	2794	36	0.993	4.79
18	Maguire	Freddie	1.3697	1931	589	1528	1959	103	0.971	5.92
19	Schoendienst	Red	1.3691	1962	1834	4616	5243	170	0.983	5.38
20	Knoop	Bobby	1.3615	1972	1116	2566	3218	119	0.980	5.18
21	Cutshaw	George	1.3613	1923	1486	3762	4473	299	0.965	5.54
22	Trillo	Manny	1.3612	1989	1518	3403	4699	157	0.981	5.34
23	Helms	Tommy	1.3528	1977	1129	2688	3237	101	0.983	5.25
24	Rath	Morrie	1.3492	1920	510	1167	1565	85	0.970	5.36
25	Gehringer	Charlie	1.3477	1942	2206	5369	7068	309	0.976	5.64
26	Lowe	Bobby	1.3476	1906	1313	3332	4161	388	0.951	5.71
27	Lansing	Mike	1.3473	2001	893	1849	2343	59	0.986	4.69
28	White	Frank	1.3457	1990	2150	4740	6250	178	0.984	5.11
29	Dozier	Brian	1.3444	2020	1038	1753	2813	60	0.987	4.40
30	Dunlap	Fred	1.3424	1891	963	3027	3331	523	0.924	6.60
31	Alomar	Roberto	1.3407	2004	2320	4459	6525	181	0.984	4.73
32	Hubbard	Glenn	1.3380	1989	1332	2795	4444	127	0.983	5.43
33	Critz	Hughie	1.3364	1935	1453	3446	5138	231	0.974	5.91
34	Hudson	Orlando	1.3362	2012	1279	2635	3807	88	0.987	5.04
35	Ellis	Mark	1.3359	2014	1364	2673	3908	60	0.991	4.82
36	Robinson	Jackie	1.3349	1956	748	1877	2047	68	0.983	5.25
37	Ritchey	Claude	1.3336	1909	1478	3440	4474	355	0.957	5.35
38	Barrett	Marty	1.3307	1991	908	1827	2631	63	0.986	4.91
39	Bierbauer	Lou	1.3295	1898	1364	3724	4555	574	0.935	6.07
40	Frey	Lonny	1.3280	1948	966	2369	2986	151	0.973	5.54

2B RANK	NAME	FIRST	PosFV	LYEAR	GP	PO	A	E	PCT	RF(pg)
41	Maranville	Rabbit	1.3278	1935	513	1268	1608	80	0.973	5.61
42	Herr	Tom	1.3274	1991	1416	2932	3999	77	0.989	4.89
43	Biggio	Craig	1.3273	2007	1989	3992	5450	156	0.984	4.75
44	Herman	Billy	1.3261	1947	1813	4780	5681	354	0.967	5.77
45	Oquendo	Jose	1.3253	1995	649	1284	1765	25	0.992	4.70
46	Huggins	Miller	1.3250	1916	1530	3425	4697	376	0.956	5.31
47	Shean	Dave	1.3243	1919	554	1323	1693	123	0.961	5.44
48	Whitehead	Burgess	1.3236	1946	718	1847	2297	118	0.972	5.77
49	Priddy	Jerry	1.3233	1953	1179	3226	3567	190	0.973	5.76
50	Sweeney	Bill	1.3220	1914	566	1448	1717	169	0.949	5.59
51	Knoblauch	Chuck	1.3171	2000	1381	2530	3821	119	0.982	4.60
52	Cano	Robinson	1.3152	2020	2158	4040	5833	124	0.988	4.58
53	Pratt	Del	1.3148	1924	1688	4069	5075	381	0.960	5.42
54	Boone	Bret	1.3143	2005	1763	3442	4591	117	0.986	4.56
55	Gerhardt	Joe	1.3137	1891	893	2794	2978	558	0.912	6.46
56	Ray	Johnny	1.3136	1990	1277	2682	3836	118	0.982	5.10
57	Morgan	Joe	1.3131	1984	2527	5742	6967	244	0.981	5.03
58	Stirnweiss	Snuffy	1.3108	1951	787	1978	2224	84	0.980	5.34
59	Reynolds	Harold	1.3106	1994	1339	2749	3932	141	0.979	4.99
60	Johnson	Davey	1.3106	1978	1198	2837	3153	123	0.980	5.00
61	Pfeffer	Fred	1.3095	1897	1537	4713	5104	857	0.920	6.39
62	Whitaker	Lou	1.3093	1995	2308	4771	6653	189	0.984	4.95
63	Cruz	Julio	1.3086	1986	1123	2393	3435	103	0.983	5.19
64	Williams	Jimmy	1.3071	1909	1176	2759	3509	292	0.955	5.33
65	Schilling	Chuck	1.3070	1965	502	1119	1366	37	0.985	4.95
66	Millan	Felix	1.3069	1977	1450	3495	3846	151	0.980	5.06
67	Lumpe	Jerry	1.3047	1967	1100	2469	2845	88	0.984	4.83
68	Cuccinello	Tony	1.3045	1944	1205	2883	3891	190	0.973	5.62
69	Frisch	Frankie	1.3044	1937	1762	4348	6026	280	0.974	5.89
70	Gedeon	Joe	1.3036	1920	549	1283	1605	92	0.969	5.26
71	Gantner	Jim	1.2993	1992	1449	3139	4347	115	0.985	5.17
72	Sax	Steve	1.2982	1994	1679	3574	4805	187	0.978	4.99
73	Pedroia	Dustin	1.2973	2019	1492	2574	4004	57	0.991	4.41
74	Randolph	Willie	1.2951	1992	2152	4859	6336	234	0.980	5.20
75	Barkley	Sam	1.2949	1889	504	1509	1545	235	0.929	6.06
76	Harris	Bucky	1.2949	1931	1253	3412	3842	263	0.965	5.79
77	Vina	Fernando	1.2935	2004	1049	2281	2856	86	0.984	4.90
78	Morandini	Mickey	1.2933	2000	1245	2383	3202	64	0.989	4.49
79	Veras	Quilvio	1.2929	2001	729	1554	2055	55	0.985	4.95
80	Thompson	Robby	1.2883	1996	1279	2611	3704	110	0.983	4.94
81	Egan	Dick	1.2880	1916	686	1460	2022	160	0.956	5.08

2B

RANK	NAME	FIRST	PosFV	LYEAR	GP	PO	A	E	PCT	RF(pg)
82	Phillips	Brandon	1.2880	2018	1831	3548	4925	107	0.988	4.63
83	Adams	Sparky	1.2879	1934	551	1321	1888	85	0.974	5.82
84	Fuentes	Tito	1.2876	1978	1275	3046	3654	182	0.974	5.25
85	Counsell	Craig	1.2874	2011	574	1079	1526	23	0.991	4.54
86	Stennett	Rennie	1.2869	1981	1049	2568	3100	129	0.978	5.40
87	Sizemore	Ted	1.2864	1980	1288	2928	3761	143	0.979	5.19
88	Stanky	Eddie	1.2859	1953	1152	3030	3215	162	0.975	5.42
89	Mayo	Eddie	1.2840	1948	544	1334	1564	65	0.978	5.33
90	Remy	Jerry	1.2829	1984	1117	2292	3241	110	0.981	4.95
91	Baerga	Carlos	1.2828	2005	1063	2177	3101	130	0.976	4.97
92	Ford	Hod	1.2825	1932	589	1338	2009	88	0.974	5.68
93	Beckert	Glenn	1.2817	1974	1242	2710	3712	179	0.973	5.17
94	Loretta	Mark	1.2807	2009	829	1475	2134	40	0.989	4.35
95	Gordon	Joe	1.2794	1950	1519	3600	4706	260	0.970	5.47
96	Ward	Aaron	1.2789	1928	809	1846	2546	134	0.970	5.43
97	Reitz	Heinie	1.2775	1899	687	1646	2189	180	0.955	5.58
98	Young	Bobby	1.2768	1958	661	1610	1754	70	0.980	5.09
99	Adair	Jerry	1.2763	1970	810	1860	2008	58	0.985	4.78
100	Bolling	Frank	1.2755	1966	1518	3423	4019	136	0.982	4.90
101	Avila	Bobby	1.2748	1959	1168	2820	3126	130	0.979	5.09
102	Hill	Aaron	1.2730	2017	1210	2065	3620	64	0.989	4.70
103	Richardson	Bobby	1.2723	1966	1339	3125	3445	143	0.979	4.91
104	Rojas	Cookie	1.2697	1977	1447	3100	3819	115	0.984	4.78
105	Thompson	Fresco	1.2696	1931	622	1625	2044	145	0.962	5.90
106	Richardson	Danny	1.2688	1894	644	1697	2140	245	0.940	5.96
107	Kuiper	Duane	1.2687	1984	920	2000	2466	76	0.983	4.85
108	Gardner	Billy	1.2679	1963	839	1923	2173	91	0.978	4.88
109	Myer	Buddy	1.2668	1941	1340	3487	4068	200	0.974	5.64
110	Wong	Kolten	1.2664	2020	785	1327	2105	67	0.981	4.37
111	Crooks	Jack	1.2656	1898	627	1742	1826	204	0.946	5.69
112	Fletcher	Scott	1.2649	1995	729	1382	2002	35	0.990	4.64
113	Gleason	Kid	1.2639	1912	1583	3883	4768	571	0.938	5.46
114	Ripken	Billy	1.2638	1998	769	1516	2146	50	0.987	4.76
115	Schoop	Jonathan	1.2634	2020	805	1376	2166	68	0.981	4.40
116	Burdock	Jack	1.2634	1891	1086	3075	3322	665	0.906	5.89
117	Walker	Neil	1.2633	2020	1050	1895	2796	56	0.988	4.47
118	Bloodworth	Jimmy	1.2622	1951	867	2257	2498	123	0.975	5.48
119	Womack	Tony	1.2606	2006	529	1015	1501	59	0.977	4.76
120	Blasingame	Don	1.2575	1966	1310	3065	3550	144	0.979	5.05
121	Easley	Damion	1.2569	2008	1172	2168	3321	91	0.984	4.68
122	Runnels	Pete	1.2558	1963	642	1583	1675	67	0.980	5.07
123	Green	Dick	1.2541	1974	1158	2518	3063	96	0.983	4.82

2B RANK	NAME	FIRST	PosFV	LYEAR	GP	PO	A	E	PCT	RF(pg)
124	Alomar Sr.	Sandy	1.2522	1978	1156	2572	2988	128	0.977	4.81
125	Alfonzo	Edgardo	1.2517	2006	549	1021	1362	33	0.986	4.34
126	Quinn	Joe	1.2514	1901	1303	3315	3805	408	0.946	5.46
127	O'Connell	Danny	1.2510	1962	713	1657	2049	74	0.980	5.20
128	Evers	Johnny	1.2499	1929	1735	3758	5124	423	0.955	5.12
129	Childs	Cupid	1.2491	1901	1454	3859	4678	646	0.930	5.87
130	Kinsler	Ian	1.2491	2019	1828	3397	5219	168	0.981	4.71
131	Franco	Julio	1.2490	1997	663	1300	1845	69	0.979	4.74
132	Bernazard	Tony	1.2485	1991	1000	2100	2901	114	0.978	5.00
133	Hummel	John	1.2468	1918	548	1218	1541	105	0.963	5.03
134	Barney	Darwin	1.2456	2017	648	1066	1596	31	0.988	4.11
135	Strange-Gordon	Dee	1.2443	2020	728	1335	1845	58	0.982	4.37
136	Kent	Jeff	1.2440	2008	2034	4015	5575	194	0.980	4.71
137	Knabe	Otto	1.2436	1916	1239	2743	3583	287	0.957	5.11
138	Verban	Emil	1.2428	1950	802	1994	2179	123	0.971	5.20
139	Panik	Joe	1.2425	2020	662	1164	1666	36	0.987	4.27
140	Lopes	Davey	1.2419	1985	1418	3142	3829	162	0.977	4.92
141	Oester	Ron	1.2382	1990	1171	2591	3197	116	0.980	4.94
142	Doran	Bill	1.2368	1993	1359	2619	3651	108	0.983	4.61
143	Grudzielanek	Mark	1.2364	2010	1135	2058	3140	72	0.986	4.58
144	Flynn	Doug	1.2360	1985	961	1920	2415	61	0.986	4.51
145	Samuel	Juan	1.2344	1998	1190	2580	3228	164	0.973	4.88
146	Rose	Pete	1.2340	1979	628	1470	1502	75	0.975	4.73
147	Lemke	Mark	1.2324	1998	965	1737	2579	70	0.984	4.47
148	Richardson	Hardy	1.2321	1892	585	1756	1986	349	0.915	6.40
149	Young	Ralph	1.2318	1922	993	2356	2954	228	0.959	5.35
150	Hayes	Jackie	1.2316	1940	904	2189	2983	126	0.976	5.72

Notes: Career Field Value maximum for 2nd Basemen is 1.5000.
Minimum 500 Adjusted Games Played.

Top 150 Fielding Third Basemen

3B Rank	Player	First	PosFV	LYear	GP	PO	A	E	PCT	RF(pg)
1	Arenado	Nolan	1.6700	2020	1069	725	2429	91	0.972	2.95
2	Kamm	Willie	1.6683	1935	1674	2151	3345	185	0.967	3.28
3	Robinson	Brooks	1.6397	1977	2870	2697	6205	263	0.971	3.10
4	Bell	Buddy	1.6138	1989	2183	1798	4925	254	0.964	3.08
5	Pendleton	Terry	1.6064	1998	1785	1386	3891	238	0.957	2.96
6	Inge	Brandon	1.6021	2013	1083	850	2188	121	0.962	2.81
7	Seager	Kyle	1.5985	2020	1278	846	2639	121	0.966	2.73
8	Boyer	Clete	1.5965	1971	1439	1470	3218	168	0.965	3.26
9	Jones	Willie	1.5914	1961	1614	2045	2934	192	0.963	3.08
10	Polanco	Placido	1.5872	2013	752	475	1420	32	0.983	2.52
11	May	Pinky	1.5815	1943	646	737	1391	84	0.962	3.29
12	Nettles	Graig	1.5806	1988	2412	1898	5279	295	0.961	2.98
13	Gaetti	Gary	1.5787	1999	2282	1699	4531	224	0.965	2.73
14	Wallach	Tim	1.5780	1996	2054	1662	3992	240	0.959	2.75
15	Schmidt	Mike	1.5777	1989	2212	1591	5045	313	0.955	3.00
16	Williamson	Ned	1.5755	1890	716	878	1719	401	0.866	3.63
17	Keltner	Ken	1.5750	1950	1500	1576	3070	171	0.965	3.10
18	Rolen	Scott	1.5748	2012	2023	1478	4080	186	0.968	2.75
19	Boone	Ray	1.5728	1959	510	576	1058	72	0.958	3.20
20	Collins	Jimmy	1.5702	1908	1544	2229	3445	418	0.931	3.67
21	Santo	Ron	1.5697	1974	2130	1955	4581	317	0.954	3.07
22	Lowell	Mike	1.5678	2010	1474	1140	2686	101	0.974	2.60
23	Ventura	Robin	1.5630	2004	1887	1469	3551	220	0.958	2.66
24	Baker	Frank	1.5623	1922	1548	2154	3155	322	0.943	3.43
25	Cey	Ron	1.5614	1987	1989	1500	4018	223	0.961	2.77
26	Machado	Manny	1.5600	2020	906	689	1827	81	0.969	2.78
27	Kell	George	1.5560	1957	1692	1825	3303	166	0.969	3.03
28	Clift	Harlond	1.5558	1945	1550	1777	3262	279	0.948	3.25
29	Whitney	Pinky	1.5547	1939	1358	1455	2640	164	0.961	3.02
30	Chavez	Eric	1.5529	2014	1402	1035	2731	116	0.970	2.69
31	Nash	Billy	1.5527	1898	1464	2219	3119	614	0.897	3.65
32	Malzone	Frank	1.5525	1966	1370	1308	2884	196	0.955	3.06
33	Reitz	Ken	1.5512	1982	1321	996	2477	109	0.970	2.63
34	Castilla	Vinny	1.5483	2006	1656	1156	3261	161	0.965	2.67
35	Williams	Matt	1.5478	2003	1743	1293	3366	177	0.963	2.67
36	Groh	Heinie	1.5473	1927	1299	1456	2554	136	0.967	3.09
37	Boggs	Wade	1.5461	1999	2215	1550	4246	229	0.962	2.62
38	Cross	Lave	1.5458	1907	1721	2306	3706	394	0.936	3.49
39	Denny	Jerry	1.5454	1894	1109	1777	2338	552	0.882	3.71
40	McMullen	Ken	1.5427	1977	1318	1259	2731	162	0.961	3.03

3B Rank	Player	First	PosFV	LYear	GP	PO	A	E	PCT	RF(pg)
41	Tannehill	Lee	1.5408	1912	668	753	1624	156	0.938	3.56
42	Rodriguez	Aurelio	1.5406	1983	1983	1529	4150	215	0.964	2.86
43	Vitt	Ossie	1.5379	1921	833	1026	1846	119	0.960	3.45
44	Wert	Don	1.5379	1971	1043	914	1987	97	0.968	2.78
45	Rolfe	Red	1.5376	1942	1084	1220	2128	155	0.956	3.09
46	Cirillo	Jeff	1.5352	2007	1403	942	2546	119	0.967	2.49
47	Sewell	Joe	1.5340	1933	643	644	1253	72	0.963	2.95
48	Buechele	Steve	1.5318	1995	1269	895	2281	104	0.968	2.50
49	Shindle	Billy	1.5318	1898	1272	1815	2886	568	0.892	3.70
50	Burns	Tom	1.5306	1892	704	1043	1494	327	0.886	3.60
51	Bando	Sal	1.5305	1981	1896	1647	3720	228	0.959	2.83
52	Rader	Doug	1.5295	1977	1349	1138	2887	187	0.956	2.98
53	DeCinces	Doug	1.5279	1987	1543	1256	3215	198	0.958	2.90
54	Beltre	Adrian	1.5276	2018	2759	2194	5182	311	0.960	2.67
55	Majeski	Hank	1.5273	1955	861	911	1750	89	0.968	3.09
56	Mathews	Eddie	1.5252	1968	2181	2049	4322	293	0.956	2.92
57	Longoria	Evan	1.5223	2020	1639	1193	2969	147	0.966	2.54
58	Brett	George	1.5220	1992	1692	1372	3674	261	0.951	2.98
59	Bradley	Bill	1.5207	1915	1390	1755	2943	336	0.933	3.38
60	Hoak	Don	1.5205	1963	1199	1219	2331	153	0.959	2.96
61	Yost	Eddie	1.5198	1962	2008	2356	3659	270	0.957	3.00
62	Devlin	Art	1.5186	1913	1192	1399	2481	257	0.938	3.26
63	McKechnie	Bill	1.5175	1920	553	700	1086	91	0.952	3.23
64	Austin	Jimmy	1.5174	1929	1431	2042	2949	358	0.933	3.49
65	Traynor	Pie	1.5164	1937	1863	2289	3521	324	0.947	3.12
66	Boyer	Ken	1.5156	1968	1785	1567	3652	264	0.952	2.92
67	Bluege	Ossie	1.5154	1939	1487	1551	3040	208	0.957	3.09
68	Pinelli	Babe	1.5142	1927	677	814	1514	131	0.947	3.44
69	Owen	Marv	1.5142	1940	921	1032	1695	135	0.953	2.96
70	Zimmerman	Ryan	1.5141	2014	1133	853	2181	137	0.957	2.68
71	Gardner	Larry	1.5113	1924	1656	1789	3408	287	0.948	3.14
72	Gruber	Kelly	1.5095	1993	846	619	1651	107	0.955	2.68
73	Petrocelli	Rico	1.5083	1976	727	581	1453	63	0.970	2.80
74	Evans	Darrell	1.5067	1989	1442	1273	3123	253	0.946	3.05
75	Fryman	Travis	1.5054	2002	1359	872	2530	123	0.965	2.50
76	Rendon	Anthony	1.5048	2020	811	571	1324	56	0.971	2.34
77	Rosen	Al	1.5048	1956	932	970	1773	112	0.961	2.94
78	Hankinson	Frank	1.5024	1888	764	1029	1579	373	0.875	3.41
79	Money	Don	1.5019	1983	1025	897	2061	97	0.968	2.89
80	Jacoby	Brook	1.5007	1992	1166	776	2058	123	0.958	2.43
81	Lansford	Carney	1.4996	1992	1720	1382	2799	148	0.966	2.43

3B Rank	Player	First	PosFV	LYear	GP	PO	A	E	PCT	RF(pg)
82	Mora	Melvin	1.4963	2011	908	644	1773	99	0.961	2.66
83	Hayes	Charlie	1.4947	2001	1328	882	2480	162	0.954	2.53
84	Byrne	Bobby	1.4923	1917	1147	1456	2221	258	0.934	3.21
85	Hack	Stan	1.4921	1947	1836	1944	3494	246	0.957	2.96
86	Donaldson	Josh	1.4906	2020	979	774	1856	114	0.958	2.69
87	Latham	Arlie	1.4893	1896	1571	1975	3545	822	0.870	3.51
88	Presley	Jim	1.4880	1991	911	633	1709	127	0.949	2.57
89	Irwin	Charlie	1.4876	1902	865	1228	1441	217	0.920	3.40
90	Randa	Joe	1.4866	2006	1362	1005	2489	137	0.962	2.57
91	Melton	Bill	1.4841	1977	901	700	2045	147	0.949	3.05
92	Brosius	Scott	1.4834	2001	934	661	1733	110	0.956	2.56
93	Molitor	Paul	1.4829	1990	791	642	1639	121	0.950	2.88
94	Oberkfell	Ken	1.4826	1991	1046	627	1996	96	0.965	2.51
95	Koskie	Corey	1.4816	2006	908	624	1703	81	0.966	2.56
96	Headley	Chase	1.4816	2018	1123	703	2078	107	0.963	2.48
97	Feliz	Pedro	1.4810	2010	1001	610	1788	92	0.963	2.40
98	Phillips	Bubba	1.4800	1964	762	808	1416	92	0.960	2.92
99	Sabo	Chris	1.4790	1996	831	453	1514	76	0.963	2.37
100	Caminiti	Ken	1.4780	2001	1676	1251	3127	249	0.946	2.61
101	Werber	Billy	1.4777	1942	1143	1264	2415	220	0.944	3.22
102	King	Jeff	1.4771	1998	586	347	1179	75	0.953	2.60
103	Glaus	Troy	1.4767	2010	1337	893	2502	171	0.952	2.54
104	Jackson	Randy	1.4757	1959	844	868	1725	123	0.955	3.07
105	Deal	Charlie	1.4757	1921	823	956	1705	117	0.958	3.23
106	Alfonzo	Edgardo	1.4749	2006	889	599	1612	73	0.968	2.49
107	Soderholm	Eric	1.4745	1980	759	620	1589	88	0.962	2.91
108	Perez	Tony	1.4736	1971	760	644	1496	123	0.946	2.82
109	McManus	Marty	1.4731	1934	725	866	1450	103	0.957	3.19
110	Charles	Ed	1.4727	1969	942	879	1833	122	0.957	2.88
111	Ripken Jr.	Cal	1.4725	2001	675	461	1237	69	0.961	2.52
112	Coughlin	Bill	1.4702	1908	863	1121	1634	205	0.931	3.19
113	Mowrey	Mike	1.4700	1917	1196	1363	2363	221	0.944	3.12
114	Steinfeldt	Harry	1.4664	1911	1386	1774	2799	365	0.926	3.30
115	Moustakas	Mike	1.4663	2020	1044	763	1871	110	0.960	2.52
116	Kurowski	Whitey	1.4659	1949	868	1025	1569	116	0.957	2.99
117	Alvis	Max	1.4658	1970	971	962	1693	123	0.956	2.73
118	Seitzer	Kevin	1.4628	1997	1051	696	1920	142	0.949	2.49
119	Lutzke	Rube	1.4620	1927	553	676	1222	110	0.945	3.43
120	Baird	Doug	1.4618	1920	522	624	1125	103	0.944	3.35
121	Lindstrom	Freddie	1.4599	1935	809	835	1536	102	0.959	2.93
122	Wright	David	1.4598	2018	1572	1087	2947	190	0.955	2.57

3B Rank	Player	First	PosFV	LYear	GP	PO	A	E	PCT	RF(pg)
123	Rose	Pete	**1.4591**	1979	634	464	1083	63	0.961	2.44
124	Aspromonte	Bob	**1.4587**	1971	1094	1025	1879	121	0.960	2.65
125	Gomez	Leo	**1.4575**	1996	570	373	978	53	0.962	2.37
126	Pinkney	George	**1.4569**	1893	1061	1343	2042	387	0.897	3.19
127	Kouzmanoff	Kevin	**1.4562**	2014	657	453	1122	64	0.961	2.40
128	Gilbert	Wally	**1.4556**	1932	587	512	1157	94	0.947	2.84
129	Frazier	Todd	**1.4545**	2020	1066	683	1884	96	0.964	2.41
130	Batista	Tony	**1.4511**	2007	807	527	1550	96	0.956	2.57
131	Suarez	Eugenio	**1.4506**	2020	665	454	1110	73	0.955	2.35
132	Crede	Joe	**1.4501**	2009	875	616	1678	83	0.965	2.62
133	Hatton	Grady	**1.4487**	1956	956	979	1844	129	0.956	2.95
134	Reilly	Charlie	**1.4483**	1897	556	814	1307	263	0.890	3.81
135	Smith	Red	**1.4472**	1919	1050	1210	2136	244	0.932	3.19
136	Casey	Doc	**1.4381**	1907	1100	1312	2184	325	0.915	3.18
137	Harrah	Toby	**1.4466**	1984	1099	781	1942	106	0.963	2.48
138	Rodriguez	Alex	**1.4465**	2016	1194	750	2075	103	0.965	2.37
139	Elliott	Bob	**1.4449**	1953	1365	1448	2744	236	0.947	3.07
140	Davis	George	**1.4448**	1901	527	730	1158	210	0.900	3.58
141	Pagliarulo	Mike	**1.4441**	1995	1179	693	2119	133	0.955	2.39
142	Lewis	Buddy	**1.4409**	1941	671	679	1415	164	0.927	3.12
143	Jones	Bob	**1.4409**	1925	774	917	1600	124	0.953	3.25
144	Ward	Pete	**1.4393**	1969	562	470	1182	97	0.945	2.94
145	Stripp	Joe	**1.4385**	1938	914	956	1665	106	0.961	2.87
146	Carey	Andy	**1.4462**	1962	882	847	1692	111	0.958	2.88
147	Grant	Eddie	**1.4376**	1915	769	962	1423	148	0.942	3.10
148	Dykes	Jimmie	**1.4367**	1939	1257	1361	2403	188	0.952	2.99
149	Leach	Tommy	**1.4337**	1914	955	1323	2127	344	0.909	3.61
150	Knight	Ray	**1.4334**	1988	1021	694	1653	105	0.957	2.30

Note: Career Field Value maximum for 3rd Basemen is 1.7000.
Minimum 500 Adjusted Games Played.

Top 150 Fielding Shortstops

SS Rank	Player	First	PosFV	LYear	GP	PO	A	E	PCT	RF(pg)
1	Smith	Ozzie	**1.6876**	1996	2511	4249	8375	281	0.978	5.03
2	Ripken Jr.	Cal	**1.6822**	1997	2302	3651	6977	225	0.979	4.62
3	Allen	Bob	**1.6732**	1900	604	1399	2169	330	0.915	5.91
4	Maranville	Rabbit	**1.6682**	1931	2153	5139	7354	631	0.952	5.80
5	Jennings	Hughie	**1.6586**	1907	899	2390	3147	470	0.922	6.16
6	Simmons	Andrelton	**1.6580**	2020	1057	1582	3004	88	0.981	4.34
7	Miller	Eddie	**1.6572**	1950	1395	2976	4500	217	0.972	5.36
8	Glasscock	Jack	**1.6561**	1895	1628	2821	5630	832	0.910	5.19
9	Wright	George	**1.6556**	1882	530	714	1878	395	0.868	4.89
10	Banks	Ernie	**1.6542**	1961	1125	2087	3441	174	0.969	4.91
11	Aparicio	Luis	**1.6530**	1973	2583	4548	8016	366	0.972	4.86
12	McMillan	Roy	**1.6520**	1966	2028	3705	6191	290	0.972	4.88
13	Tulowitzki	Troy	**1.6513**	2019	1268	1946	3889	91	0.985	4.60
14	Story	Trevor	**1.6492**	2020	595	797	1694	52	0.980	4.19
15	Fernandez	Tony	**1.6469**	1997	1573	2708	4511	151	0.980	4.59
16	Davis	George	**1.6457**	1908	1372	3231	4787	511	0.940	5.84
17	Bowa	Larry	**1.6449**	1985	2222	3314	6857	211	0.980	4.58
18	Bell	Jay	**1.6348**	2003	1515	2309	4595	176	0.975	4.56
19	Burleson	Rick	**1.6341**	1986	1192	2151	3871	179	0.971	5.05
20	McBride	George	**1.6340**	1920	1626	3585	5274	484	0.948	5.45
21	Boudreau	Lou	**1.6327**	1952	1539	3132	4760	223	0.973	5.13
22	Galvis	Freddy	**1.6302**	2020	801	1077	2084	51	0.984	3.95
23	Wallace	Bobby	**1.6301**	1918	1826	4142	6303	685	0.938	5.72
24	Logan	Johnny	**1.6276**	1963	1380	2612	4397	256	0.965	5.08
25	Vizquel	Omar	**1.6255**	2012	2709	4102	7678	183	0.985	4.35
26	Scott	Everett	**1.6232**	1926	1691	3445	5179	317	0.965	5.10
27	Bartell	Dick	**1.6216**	1943	1679	3872	5590	471	0.953	5.64
28	Bancroft	Dave	**1.6210**	1930	1873	4623	6561	660	0.944	5.97
29	Dent	Bucky	**1.6188**	1984	1382	2116	4332	156	0.976	4.67
30	Hansen	Ron	**1.6166**	1972	1143	2011	3503	185	0.968	4.82
31	Marion	Marty	**1.6161**	1952	1547	2986	4829	252	0.969	5.05
32	Rodriguez	Alex	**1.6121**	2005	1272	2014	3604	131	0.977	4.42
33	Bordick	Mike	**1.6121**	2003	1577	2606	4410	128	0.982	4.45
34	Sewell	Joe	**1.6089**	1928	1216	2591	3933	333	0.951	5.37
35	Doolan	Mickey	**1.6076**	1916	1625	3578	5290	570	0.940	5.46
36	Jackson	Travis	**1.6075**	1936	1326	2878	4636	381	0.952	5.67
37	Groat	Dick	**1.6058**	1967	1877	3505	5811	374	0.961	4.96
38	Lanier	Hal	**1.6055**	1973	655	1091	2083	96	0.971	4.85
39	Jurges	Billy	**1.6034**	1947	1540	3133	4959	305	0.964	5.25

SS Rank	Player	First	PosFV	LYear	GP	PO	A	E	PCT	RF(pg)
40	Force	Davy	1.6033	1886	716	916	2471	392	0.896	4.73
41	Foli	Tim	1.6016	1985	1524	2687	4804	210	0.973	4.92
42	DiSarcina	Gary	1.6003	2000	1069	1631	3172	131	0.973	4.49
43	Belanger	Mark	1.5999	1982	1942	3005	5786	210	0.977	4.53
44	Brinkman	Ed	1.5989	1975	1795	2924	5466	259	0.970	4.67
45	Cardenas	Leo	1.5957	1975	1843	3218	5303	259	0.971	4.62
46	Tinker	Joe	1.5932	1916	1743	3758	5848	635	0.938	5.51
47	Wagner	Honus	1.5922	1917	1887	4576	6041	676	0.940	5.63
48	Kerr	Buddy	1.5917	1951	1038	2045	3297	185	0.967	5.15
49	Schofield	Dick	1.5904	1996	1348	2140	3873	146	0.976	4.46
50	Yount	Robin	1.5896	1984	1479	2588	4794	272	0.964	4.99
51	Metzger	Roger	1.5889	1980	1173	1845	3535	135	0.976	4.59
52	Reese	Pee Wee	1.5879	1958	2014	4040	5891	388	0.962	4.93
53	Rizzuto	Phil	1.5868	1956	1647	3219	4666	263	0.968	4.79
54	Bush	Donie	1.5857	1921	1867	4038	6119	689	0.936	5.44
55	Concepcion	Dave	1.5849	1988	2178	3670	6594	311	0.971	4.71
56	Wilson	Jack	1.5846	2012	1274	1814	4059	136	0.977	4.61
57	Kessinger	Don	1.5833	1979	1955	3151	6212	334	0.966	4.79
58	Ramirez	Alexei	1.5832	2016	1228	1720	3513	136	0.975	4.26
59	Kuenn	Harvey	1.5826	1961	748	1343	2116	129	0.964	4.62
60	Fregosi	Jim	1.5826	1973	1396	2397	4169	251	0.963	4.70
61	Andrus	Elvis	1.5822	2020	1628	2529	4487	194	0.973	4.31
62	Corcoran	Tommy	1.5805	1906	2073	4550	7106	956	0.924	5.62
63	Pesky	Johnny	1.5801	1954	591	1175	1810	111	0.964	5.05
64	Carrasquel	Chico	1.5796	1959	1241	2131	3619	185	0.969	4.63
65	Dahlen	Bill	1.5774	1911	2132	4850	7500	975	0.927	5.79
66	Rogell	Billy	1.5770	1940	1235	2362	3886	287	0.956	5.06
67	Duffy	Frank	1.5746	1978	839	1292	2445	87	0.977	4.45
68	Trammell	Alan	1.5744	1996	2139	3391	6172	227	0.977	4.47
69	Petrocelli	Rico	1.5735	1976	774	1283	2283	113	0.969	4.61
70	Alley	Gene	1.5728	1973	977	1609	3198	149	0.970	4.92
71	Guillen	Ozzie	1.5715	2000	1896	2911	5335	222	0.974	4.35
72	Crawford	Brandon	1.5681	2020	1274	1711	3516	135	0.975	4.10
73	Fletcher	Art	1.5673	1922	1448	2836	5134	521	0.939	5.50
74	Peters	John	1.5672	1884	557	758	1868	377	0.874	4.71
75	Young	Michael	1.5655	2013	793	1122	2278	81	0.977	4.29
76	Hollocher	Charlie	1.5649	1924	751	1587	2569	202	0.954	5.53
77	Ahmed	Nick	1.5649	2020	646	803	1786	59	0.978	4.01
78	Semien	Marcus	1.5645	2020	775	1024	2182	104	0.969	4.14
79	Smith	Germany	1.5645	1898	1665	2813	6154	971	0.902	5.39
80	Rollins	Jimmy	1.5643	1989	2227	2982	6139	154	0.983	4.10

SS Rank	Player	First	PosFV	LYear	GP	PO	A	E	PCT	RF(pg)
81	Speier	Chris	1.5638	1989	1900	3057	5781	275	0.970	4.65
82	Lary	Lyn	1.5614	1940	1138	2373	3388	268	0.956	5.06
83	Valentin	John	1.5611	2002	580	914	1707	76	0.972	4.52
84	Perez	Neifi	1.5610	2007	1115	1784	3282	117	0.977	4.54
85	Wagner	Heinie	1.5605	1916	822	1950	2629	356	0.928	5.57
86	Dark	Alvin	1.5604	1959	1404	2672	4168	286	0.960	4.87
87	Vaughan	Arky	1.5601	1943	1485	2995	4780	397	0.951	5.24
88	Stephens	Vern	1.5598	1953	1330	2385	4150	269	0.960	4.91
89	Turner	Terry	1.5590	1919	741	1376	2452	191	0.952	5.17
90	Cronin	Joe	1.5589	1942	1843	3696	5814	485	0.951	5.16
91	Tejada	Miguel	1.5582	2011	1946	2896	5803	255	0.972	4.47
92	Lindor	Francisco	1.5568	2020	763	984	1908	57	0.981	3.79
93	DeJesus	Ivan	1.5564	1988	1303	1839	4036	228	0.963	4.51
94	Gagne	Greg	1.5560	1997	1765	2559	4930	214	0.972	4.24
95	Peralta	Jhonny	1.5556	2017	1459	2097	4123	124	0.980	4.26
96	Long	Herman	1.5550	1903	1795	4229	6137	1070	0.906	5.77
97	Wills	Maury	1.5543	1972	1555	2550	4804	284	0.963	4.73
98	Owen	Spike	1.5535	1995	1373	2087	3814	139	0.977	4.30
99	Durocher	Leo	1.5527	1943	1509	3097	4431	307	0.961	4.99
100	Joost	Eddie	1.5509	1955	1297	2755	3844	291	0.958	5.09
101	Escobar	Alcides	1.5498	2018	1386	1950	3708	140	0.976	4.08
102	Hardy	J.J.	1.5488	2017	1544	2089	4339	110	0.983	4.16
103	Peckinpaugh	Roger	1.5488	1927	1982	3919	6337	553	0.949	5.17
104	Kubek	Tony	1.5474	1965	882	1544	2734	144	0.967	4.85
105	Ryan	Brendan	1.5465	2016	721	944	2082	69	0.978	4.20
106	Sand	Heinie	1.5436	1928	772	1811	2443	258	0.943	5.51
107	Templeton	Garry	1.5426	1991	1964	3393	6041	384	0.961	4.80
108	Mercer	Jordy	1.5391	2020	837	999	2239	67	0.980	3.87
109	Cruz	Deivi	1.5369	2005	1124	1541	3200	107	0.978	4.22
110	Gonzalez	Alex	1.5354	2006	1262	2011	3543	143	0.975	4.40
111	Bridwell	Al	1.5351	1914	1094	2267	3351	366	0.939	5.14
112	Santana	Rafael	1.5340	1990	639	1014	1697	87	0.969	4.24
113	Clayton	Royce	1.5336	2007	2053	3095	5902	242	0.974	4.38
114	Ordonez	Rey	1.5332	2004	963	1457	2643	102	0.976	4.26
115	Cozart	Zack	1.5325	2019	741	1094	1929	64	0.979	4.08
116	Campaneris	Bert	1.5322	1981	2097	3608	6160	365	0.964	4.66
117	Chapman	Ray	1.5288	1920	957	2204	2950	336	0.939	5.39
118	Larkin	Barry	1.5267	2004	2085	3148	5858	235	0.975	4.32
119	Franco	Julio	1.5254	1987	715	1161	2020	134	0.960	4.45
120	Iglesias	Jose	1.5249	2020	778	957	1967	46	0.985	3.76
121	Cross	Monte	1.5247	1907	1676	3975	5369	810	0.920	5.58

SS Rank	Player	First	PosFV	LYear	GP	PO	A	E	PCT	RF(pg)
122	Smalley	Roy	1.5241	1987	1069	1688	3274	174	0.966	4.64
123	Irwin	Arthur	1.5239	1894	947	1301	3093	594	0.881	4.64
124	Maxvill	Dal	1.5239	1975	1207	1759	3405	145	0.973	4.28
125	Ward	John	1.5233	1891	826	1422	2641	530	0.885	4.92
126	Appling	Luke	1.5217	1950	2218	4398	7218	643	0.948	5.24
127	Patek	Freddie	1.5206	1981	1588	2690	4786	293	0.962	4.71
128	DeMaestri	Joe	1.5185	1961	1029	1689	2852	156	0.967	4.41
129	Russell	Bill	1.5173	1986	1746	2536	5546	339	0.960	4.63
130	Ely	Bones	1.5155	1902	1238	2585	4328	578	0.923	5.58
131	Cabrera	Orlando	1.5158	2011	1843	2823	5097	188	0.977	4.30
132	Wine	Bobby	1.5153	1972	1067	1754	2974	141	0.971	4.43
133	Griffin	Alfredo	1.5140	1993	1861	3207	5186	340	0.961	4.51
134	Gelbert	Charlie	1.5113	1940	680	1405	2125	182	0.951	5.19
135	Versalles	Zoilo	1.5083	1971	1265	2126	3645	268	0.956	4.56
136	Stallcup	Virgil	1.5081	1952	556	968	1608	94	0.965	4.63
137	Tavener	Jackie	1.5076	1929	626	1238	1908	163	0.951	5.03
138	Izturis	Cesar	1.5075	2013	1149	1514	3078	90	0.981	4.00
139	Uribe	Juan	1.5073	2012	917	1480	2621	104	0.975	4.47
140	Weaver	Buck	1.5064	1920	822	1878	2570	311	0.935	5.41
141	Knickerbocker	Bill	1.5056	1942	649	1205	2043	152	0.955	5.00
142	Harrelson	Bud	1.5056	1980	1400	2387	3975	203	0.969	4.54
143	Dunston	Shawon	1.5052	2002	1363	2287	3731	205	0.967	4.42
144	Ford	Hod	1.5035	1933	846	1821	2644	185	0.960	5.28
145	Uribe	Jose	1.5030	1993	1015	1436	2821	136	0.969	4.19
146	O'Leary	Charley	1.5027	1913	737	1709	2241	273	0.935	5.36
147	Meares	Pat	1.5016	2000	884	1432	2469	142	0.965	4.41
148	Sanchez	Rey	1.5007	2005	984	1496	2865	83	0.981	4.43
149	Urbanski	Billy	1.5002	1936	653	1386	2001	182	0.949	5.19
150	Wright	Glenn	1.4997	1933	1051	2156	3473	351	0.941	5.36

Notes: Career Field Value possible maximum for Shortstops is 1.7500.
Minimum 500 Adjusted Games Played.

Top 150 Fielding Catchers

C Rank	Player	First	PosFV	LYear	GP	PO	A	E	PCT	RF(pg)	CS%
1	Campanella	Roy	2.0572	1957	1183	6520	550	85	0.988	5.98	0.574
2	Schalk	Ray	2.0053	1929	1727	7168	1811	175	0.981	5.20	0.512
3	Hartnett	Gabby	2.0010	1941	1793	7292	1254	139	0.984	4.77	0.561
4	Sundberg	Jim	1.9878	1989	1927	9767	1007	81	0.993	5.59	0.407
5	Dickey	Bill	1.9752	1946	1708	7965	954	108	0.988	5.22	0.466
6	Freehan	Bill	1.9724	1976	1581	9941	721	72	0.993	6.74	0.368
7	Bench	Johnny	1.9703	1983	1742	9249	850	97	0.990	5.80	0.432
8	Berra	Yogi	1.9692	1965	1699	8738	798	110	0.989	5.61	0.486
9	Carter	Gary	1.9686	1992	2056	11785	1203	121	0.991	6.32	0.347
10	Ausmus	Brad	1.9659	2010	1938	12844	954	79	0.994	7.12	0.355
11	Killefer	Bill	1.9631	1921	1005	4830	1319	148	0.976	6.12	0.482
12	Miller	Damian	1.9546	2007	958	6697	509	35	0.995	7.52	0.365
13	Cochrane	Mickey	1.9532	1937	1451	6414	840	111	0.985	5.00	0.394
14	Pena	Tony	1.9532	1997	1950	11212	1045	117	0.991	6.29	0.345
15	Zimmer	Chief	1.9507	1903	1239	4883	1580	328	0.952	5.22	0.436
16	Molina	Yadier	1.9501	2020	1989	13741	988	77	0.995	7.41	0.403
17	Roseboro	Johnny	1.9455	1970	1476	9291	675	107	0.989	6.75	0.418
18	Scioscia	Mike	1.9411	1992	1395	8335	737	114	0.988	6.50	0.339
19	Parrish	Lance	1.9394	1995	1818	9647	980	94	0.991	5.85	0.382
20	Rosar	Buddy	1.9367	1951	934	3845	511	36	0.992	4.66	0.548
21	Hegan	Jim	1.9356	1960	1629	7506	695	86	0.990	5.03	0.498
22	Edwards	Johnny	1.9349	1974	1392	8925	703	82	0.992	6.92	0.389
23	Bennett	Charlie	1.9344	1893	954	5123	1048	379	0.942	6.47	0.373
24	Rodriguez	Ivan	1.9288	2011	2427	14864	1227	142	0.991	6.63	0.457
25	Kling	Johnny	1.9279	1913	1168	5468	1552	210	0.971	6.01	0.478
26	Meyers	Chief	1.9278	1917	911	4537	996	146	0.974	6.07	0.469
27	Battey	Earl	1.9272	1967	1087	6176	501	69	0.990	6.14	0.436
28	Ruel	Muddy	1.9245	1934	1410	5347	1136	116	0.982	4.60	0.454
29	Ewing	Buck	1.9242	1893	636	3301	1017	322	0.931	6.79	0.379
30	Hundley	Randy	1.9189	1977	1026	5765	493	61	0.990	6.10	0.420
31	Azcue	Joe	1.9123	1972	868	5329	452	44	0.992	6.66	0.449
32	Schreckengost	Ossee	1.9114	1908	751	4321	969	166	0.970	7.04	0.437
33	Criger	Lou	1.9099	1912	984	4354	1342	170	0.971	5.79	0.480
34	Lollar	Sherm	1.9089	1963	1571	7059	688	62	0.992	4.93	0.468
35	Boone	Bob	1.9077	1990	2225	11260	1174	178	0.986	5.59	0.392
36	Johnson	Charles	1.9064	2005	1160	7218	568	51	0.993	6.71	0.395
37	Howard	Elston	1.9049	1968	1138	6447	479	51	0.993	6.09	0.437
38	Ellis	A.J.	1.9047	2018	620	4622	393	16	0.997	8.09	0.329
39	Wynegar	Butch	1.9030	1988	1247	6281	583	75	0.989	5.50	0.398

C Rank	Player	First	PosFV	LYear	GP	PO	A	E	PCT	RF(pg)	CS%
40	Wilson	Dan	1.9018	2005	1281	8109	468	45	0.995	6.70	0.341
41	Bushong	Doc	1.9015	1890	668	3481	1001	412	0.916	6.71	0.240
42	Danning	Harry	1.9003	1942	801	3257	455	57	0.985	4.63	0.469
43	Snyder	Chris	1.8970	2013	690	4565	366	12	0.998	7.15	0.291
44	Bassler	Johnny	1.8961	1927	756	2607	708	67	0.980	4.38	0.467
45	Gibson	George	1.8948	1918	1194	5214	1386	153	0.977	5.53	0.463
46	Sullivan	Billy	1.8938	1916	1122	4776	1314	148	0.976	5.43	0.477
47	Henry	John	1.8926	1918	629	3055	826	87	0.978	6.17	0.460
48	Taylor	Zack	1.8924	1935	856	2880	752	86	0.977	4.24	0.496
49	Crandall	Del	1.8882	1966	1479	7352	759	89	0.989	5.48	0.455
50	Lopez	Al	1.8880	1947	1918	6644	1115	122	0.985	4.05	0.541
51	Dalrymple	Clay	1.8866	1971	1003	5557	566	78	0.987	6.10	0.487
52	Bergen	Bill	1.8857	1911	941	4233	1444	161	0.972	6.03	0.473
53	Grote	Jerry	1.8852	1981	1348	8081	635	78	0.991	6.47	0.372
54	Martin	Russell	1.8823	2019	1579	11613	940	89	0.993	7.95	0.303
55	Munson	Thurman	1.8822	1979	1278	6253	742	127	0.982	5.47	0.441
56	Davis	Jody	1.8811	1990	1039	5520	640	81	0.987	5.93	0.349
57	Warner	John	1.8798	1908	1032	4498	1309	205	0.966	5.63	0.453
58	Molina	Jose	1.8807	2014	915	6037	438	39	0.994	7.08	0.367
59	Barnhart	Tucker	1.8766	2020	567	4306	333	14	0.997	8.18	0.327
60	Milligan	Jocko	1.8764	1893	585	3230	825	304	0.930	6.93	0.364
61	Schmidt	Walter	1.8735	1925	734	2598	858	69	0.980	4.71	0.498
62	Blanco	Henry	1.8717	2013	914	5659	475	38	0.994	6.71	0.428
63	Valle	Dave	1.8709	1996	902	4898	407	44	0.992	5.88	0.360
64	Ferrell	Rick	1.8694	1947	1806	7248	1127	135	0.984	4.64	0.445
65	Gomes	Yan	1.8674	2020	721	6038	393	47	0.993	8.92	0.333
66	Perez	Salvador	1.8669	2020	908	6511	505	36	0.995	7.73	0.351
67	Owen	Mickey	1.8666	1954	1175	4527	581	96	0.982	4.35	0.502
68	Perkins	Cy	1.8656	1931	1111	3809	1037	109	0.978	4.36	0.483
69	Molina	Bengie	1.8655	2010	1285	8125	657	52	0.994	6.83	0.311
70	Archer	Jimmy	1.8640	1918	736	3293	979	127	0.971	5.80	0.492
71	Flint	Silver	1.8627	1889	743	3592	1071	456	0.911	6.28	NA
72	Posey	Buster	1.8608	2019	987	7475	509	41	0.995	8.09	0.331
73	Moran	Pat	1.8598	1914	697	3384	990	109	0.976	6.28	0.461
74	Snyder	Pop	1.8596	1891	877	4208	1444	679	0.893	6.44	0.328
75	Mauer	Joe	1.8570	2018	921	5832	323	30	0.995	6.68	0.332
76	Grandal	Yasmani	1.8570	2020	800	6583	350	42	0.994	8.67	0.264
77	Severeid	Hank	1.8537	1926	1225	4657	1112	131	0.978	4.71	0.434
78	Varitek	Jason	1.8536	2011	1488	10166	542	69	0.994	7.20	0.231
79	Lopez	Javy	1.8536	2006	1351	8990	633	73	0.992	7.12	0.276
80	Rodgers	Buck	1.8534	1969	895	4750	472	63	0.988	5.83	0.433

Rank	Player	First	PosFV	LYear	GP	PO	A	E	PCT	RF(pg)	CS%
81	Haller	Tom	1.8531	1972	1199	7012	508	64	0.992	6.27	0.344
82	Maldonado	Martin	1.8529	2020	708	5391	353	43	0.993	8.11	0.360
83	Gonzalez	Mike	1.8505	1932	868	3050	838	79	0.980	4.48	0.469
84	Foote	Barry	1.8498	1982	637	3263	326	53	0.985	5.63	0.378
85	Downing	Brian	1.8495	1981	675	3383	325	40	0.989	5.49	0.333
86	Simmons	Ted	1.8485	1988	1771	8906	915	130	0.987	5.55	0.336
87	Pytlak	Frankie	1.8476	1946	699	2958	395	29	0.991	4.80	0.432
88	Schneider	Brian	1.8466	2012	992	5991	433	39	0.994	6.48	0.356
89	Hoiles	Chris	1.8456	1998	819	4830	320	29	0.994	6.29	0.266
90	Ruiz	Carlos	1.8453	2017	1085	7669	588	53	0.994	7.61	0.273
91	Soto	Geovany	1.8449	2017	667	4961	333	41	0.992	7.94	0.268
92	Stearns	John	1.8447	1984	699	3712	446	63	0.985	5.95	0.369
93	Mack	Connie	1.8445	1896	609	2698	863	281	0.927	5.85	0.380
94	Lieberthal	Mike	1.8428	2007	1170	7829	490	72	0.991	7.11	0.296
95	Whitt	Ernie	1.8424	1991	1246	6091	497	59	0.991	5.29	0.332
96	Bowerman	Frank	1.8422	1909	826	3659	1072	182	0.963	5.73	0.477
97	Farrell	Duke	1.8411	1905	1003	4101	1417	365	0.938	5.50	0.441
98	McFarland	Ed	1.8408	1908	830	3139	1024	144	0.967	5.03	0.443
99	Snyder	Frank	1.8403	1927	1247	4308	1332	112	0.981	4.52	0.476
100	Hogan	Shanty	1.8397	1937	908	3190	493	56	0.985	4.06	0.471
101	Cerone	Rick	1.8394	1992	1279	6548	536	70	0.990	5.54	0.367
102	Fosse	Ray	1.8390	1979	889	4831	438	78	0.985	5.93	0.391
103	Triandos	Gus	1.8389	1965	992	5123	448	72	0.987	5.62	0.465
104	Kittridge	Malachi	1.8388	1906	1196	5121	1363	264	0.961	5.42	0.394
105	Hanigan	Ryan	1.8387	2017	656	4440	291	20	0.996	7.21	0.363
106	Sanguillen	Manny	1.8380	1979	1114	5996	540	94	0.986	5.87	0.381
107	McCann	James	1.8380	2020	570	4227	229	22	0.995	7.82	0.359
108	O'Neill	Steve	1.8377	1928	1532	5967	1698	217	0.972	5.00	0.462
109	Santiago	Benito	1.8363	2005	1917	10817	960	151	0.987	6.14	0.344
110	Matheny	Mike	1.8355	2006	1285	7119	611	44	0.994	6.02	0.346
111	McCarver	Tim	1.8343	1979	1387	8206	588	91	0.990	6.34	0.336
112	Spencer	Roy	1.8340	1938	585	2138	275	40	0.984	4.12	0.497
113	Zunino	Mike	1.8329	2020	692	5364	316	28	0.995	8.21	0.294
114	Peitz	Heinie	1.8328	1913	960	3723	1094	187	0.963	5.02	0.433
115	Ramos	Wilson	1.8325	2020	894	7019	454	45	0.994	8.36	0.273
116	White	Sammy	1.8320	1962	1027	4738	506	84	0.984	5.11	0.472
117	Diaz	Bo	1.8311	1989	965	5294	525	82	0.986	6.03	0.334
118	Mueller	Ray	1.8310	1951	917	3095	503	43	0.988	3.92	0.519
119	Wilson	Jimmie	1.8301	1940	1351	4916	931	136	0.977	4.33	0.479
120	Piazza	Mike	1.8282	2006	1629	10846	731	124	0.989	7.11	0.230
121	Smith	Hal	1.8278	1965	548	2810	247	33	0.989	5.58	0.418
122	Wilkins	Rick	1.8271	2001	650	3608	373	31	0.992	6.12	0.382

Rank	Player	First	PosFV	LYear	GP	PO	A	E	PCT	RF(pg)	CS%
123	McCann	Brian	1.8267	2019	1612	12049	728	95	0.993	7.93	0.249
124	Holbert	Bill	1.8264	1888	538	2840	1013	393	0.907	7.16	NA
125	Tresh	Mike	1.8261	1949	1019	3961	575	78	0.983	4.45	0.450
126	Romano	Johnny	1.8259	1967	810	4415	343	47	0.990	5.87	0.345
127	Boyle	Jack	1.8254	1898	544	2430	681	237	0.929	5.72	0.369
128	Kendall	Jason	1.8251	2010	2025	13019	989	144	0.990	6.92	0.290
129	Fisk	Carlton	1.8246	1993	2226	11369	1048	155	0.988	5.58	0.335
130	Avila	Alex	1.8244	2020	902	6423	398	37	0.995	7.56	0.299
131	Robinson	Aaron	1.8237	1951	577	2259	271	25	0.990	4.38	0.467
132	Daulton	Darren	1.8235	1995	965	5417	445	66	0.989	6.07	0.292
133	Rodriguez	Ellie	1.8230	1976	737	3713	360	45	0.989	5.53	0.411
134	Pagnozzi	Tom	1.8230	1998	827	4124	389	38	0.992	5.46	0.367
135	Karkovice	Ron	1.8227	1997	918	4757	404	42	0.992	5.62	0.401
136	DeBerry	Hank	1.8221	1930	569	2701	444	59	0.982	5.53	0.380
137	Girardi	Joe	1.8220	2003	1247	7619	605	77	0.991	6.60	0.320
138	Mancuso	Gus	1.8199	1945	1360	5613	803	148	0.977	4.72	0.507
139	Pierzynski	A.J.	1.8198	2016	1936	12604	820	68	0.995	6.93	0.244
140	Berres	Ray	1.8180	1945	551	1704	278	23	0.989	3.60	0.490
141	Wieters	Matt	1.8171	2020	1075	7697	428	58	0.993	7.56	0.324
142	Sewell	Luke	1.8163	1942	1562	5444	1084	150	0.978	4.18	0.462
143	Rice	Del	1.8157	1961	1249	5353	537	75	0.987	4.72	0.421
144	Ryan	Mike	1.8152	1974	632	3473	325	34	0.991	6.01	0.433
145	Gowdy	Hank	1.8152	1930	893	3149	1000	105	0.975	4.65	0.522
146	LaValliere	Mike	1.8151	1995	850	4138	416	35	0.992	5.36	0.365
147	Schlei	Admiral	1.8145	1910	561	2527	792	111	0.968	5.92	0.482
148	Rariden	Bill	1.8137	1920	948	4127	1231	150	0.973	5.65	0.436
149	Realmuto	J.T.	1.8136	2020	663	5105	337	41	0.993	8.21	0.358
150	Mitterwald	George	1.8135	1977	796	4289	434	64	0.987	5.93	0.394

Note: Career Field Value possible maximum for Catchers is 2.1000.
Minimum 500 Adjusted Games Played.

Top 450 Fielding Outfielders

OF Rank	Player	First	PosFV	Year	GP	PO	A	E	PCT	RF(pg)	APG
1	Griffin	Mike	1.6182	1898	1478	3535	243	173	0.956	2.56	0.164
2	Speaker	Tris	1.6169	1928	2698	6788	449	222	0.970	2.68	0.166
3	Hamilton	Billy	1.6124	2020	803	1792	57	10	0.995	2.30	0.071
4	Puckett	Kirby	1.6107	1995	1696	4392	142	51	0.989	2.67	0.084
5	Fogarty	Jim	1.6099	1890	685	1540	171	110	0.940	2.50	0.250
6	Oliver	Tom	1.6097	1933	504	1425	45	21	0.986	2.92	0.089
7	Ashburn	Richie	1.6038	1962	2104	6089	178	110	0.983	2.98	0.085
8	DiMaggio	Dom	1.5997	1952	1373	3859	147	89	0.978	2.92	0.107
9	Thomas	Roy	1.5941	1911	1434	3291	188	102	0.972	2.43	0.131
10	Corkhill	Pop	1.5927	1892	1041	2158	224	134	0.947	2.29	0.215
11	Otis	Amos	1.5909	1984	1928	4936	126	47	0.991	2.63	0.065
12	Welch	Curt	1.5902	1893	1075	2366	210	185	0.933	2.40	0.195
13	Felsch	Happy	1.5882	1920	741	1921	116	53	0.975	2.75	0.157
14	Carey	Max	1.5839	1929	2421	6363	339	235	0.966	2.77	0.140
15	Flood	Curt	1.5825	1971	1697	4021	114	54	0.987	2.44	0.067
16	DiMaggio	Vince	1.5818	1946	1081	2840	125	57	0.981	2.74	0.116
17	Butler	Brett	1.5788	1997	2164	5296	122	41	0.992	2.50	0.056
18	Lange	Bill	1.5770	1899	716	1732	136	116	0.942	2.61	0.190
19	Jones	Andruw	1.5717	2012	2060	4956	125	50	0.990	2.47	0.061
20	West	Sam	1.5696	1942	1573	4300	151	76	0.983	2.83	0.096
21	Rose	Pete	1.5640	1984	1327	2579	99	24	0.991	2.02	0.075
22	Yount	Robin	1.5595	1993	1218	3202	54	32	0.990	2.67	0.044
23	Trout	Mike	1.5590	2020	1235	2888	38	20	0.993	2.37	0.031
24	Mostil	Johnny	1.5586	1929	907	2561	101	79	0.971	2.93	0.111
25	Remsen	Jack	1.5585	1884	566	1173	83	176	0.877	2.22	0.147
26	Betts	Mookie	1.5571	2020	827	1859	51	19	0.990	2.31	0.062
27	Victorino	Shane	1.5567	2015	1242	2613	76	15	0.994	2.17	0.061
28	Eggler	Dave	1.5553	1885	575	1204	87	144	0.900	2.25	0.151
29	Judnich	Wally	1.5546	1949	604	1636	33	20	0.988	2.76	0.055
30	Barrett	Jimmy	1.5545	1908	855	1814	143	95	0.954	2.29	0.167
31	Brodie	Steve	1.5545	1902	1420	3139	208	142	0.959	2.36	0.146
32	Spence	Stan	1.5528	1949	990	2582	96	44	0.984	2.71	0.097
33	Murphy	Dwayne	1.5526	1989	1272	3579	80	47	0.987	2.88	0.063
34	Kreevich	Mike	1.5516	1945	1177	3304	93	64	0.982	2.89	0.079
35	Holmes	Tommy	1.5461	1952	1231	2823	115	33	0.989	2.39	0.093
36	Craft	Harry	1.5459	1942	552	1394	46	21	0.986	2.61	0.083
37	DiMaggio	Joe	1.5447	1951	1721	4516	153	105	0.978	2.71	0.089
38	Statz	Jigger	1.5417	1928	638	1770	85	59	0.969	2.91	0.133
39	Mays	Willie	1.5415	1973	2842	7095	195	141	0.981	2.57	0.069
40	Delahanty	Ed	1.5413	1903	1344	2951	243	166	0.951	2.38	0.181

OF Rank	Player	First	PosFV	Year	GP	PO	A	E	PCT	RF(pg)	APG
41	Martin	Leonys	1.5399	2019	755	1818	63	21	0.989	2.49	0.083
42	Bradley, Jr.	Jackie	1.5396	2020	876	1936	59	20	0.990	2.28	0.067
43	Glanville	Doug	1.5392	2004	1050	2300	68	22	0.991	2.26	0.065
44	Bostock	Lyman	1.5378	1978	511	1223	30	15	0.988	2.45	0.059
45	Blair	Paul	1.5378	1980	1878	4343	111	54	0.988	2.37	0.059
46	Moreno	Omar	1.5367	1986	1323	3405	93	63	0.982	2.64	0.070
47	Landis	Jim	1.5360	1967	1265	2927	72	32	0.989	2.37	0.057
48	Berry	Ken	1.5355	1975	1311	2722	85	30	0.989	2.14	0.065
49	Virdon	Bill	1.5353	1968	1542	3777	100	73	0.982	2.51	0.065
50	Markakis	Nick	1.5352	2020	2128	4129	122	27	0.994	2.00	0.057
51	Moore	Terry	1.5343	1948	1189	3117	102	48	0.985	2.71	0.086
52	Gordon	Alex	1.5328	2020	1392	2753	102	18	0.994	2.05	0.073
53	Paskert	Dode	1.5311	1921	1633	3734	223	125	0.969	2.42	0.137
54	Erstad	Darin	1.5310	2009	912	2180	50	10	0.996	2.45	0.055
55	Jones	Fielder	1.5304	1915	1770	3580	225	144	0.964	2.15	0.127
56	Welsh	Jimmy	1.5304	1930	687	1756	100	55	0.971	2.70	0.146
57	Jones	Charley	1.5298	1888	885	1697	163	252	0.881	2.10	0.184
58	Bruton	Bill	1.5295	1964	1561	3905	105	77	0.981	2.57	0.067
59	McAleer	Jimmy	1.5292	1902	1015	2464	151	154	0.944	2.58	0.149
60	Winn	Randy	1.5289	2010	1720	3686	78	31	0.992	2.19	0.045
61	Inciarte	Ender	1.5279	2020	810	1874	50	25	0.987	2.38	0.062
62	Wells	Vernon	1.5270	2013	1673	3726	74	25	0.993	2.27	0.044
63	Johnston	Dick	1.5252	1891	743	1621	172	193	0.903	2.41	0.231
64	Waner	Lloyd	1.5248	1945	1818	4860	151	87	0.983	2.76	0.083
65	Callison	Johnny	1.5243	1973	1777	3349	175	57	0.984	1.98	0.098
66	Lemon	Chet	1.5236	1990	1925	4993	115	81	0.984	2.65	0.060
67	Kepler	Max	1.5233	2020	627	1195	29	11	0.991	1.95	0.046
68	Myers	Hy	1.5228	1925	1182	2898	151	87	0.972	2.58	0.128
69	Shafer	Orator	1.5221	1890	854	1309	290	259	0.861	1.87	0.340
70	Suzuki	Ichiro	1.5207	2019	2404	5022	122	38	0.993	2.14	0.051
71	Lynn	Fred	1.5202	1990	1825	4556	114	55	0.988	2.56	0.062
72	York	Tom	1.5189	1885	963	1946	130	291	0.877	2.16	0.135
73	Cramer	Doc	1.5186	1948	2142	5412	172	118	0.979	2.61	0.080
74	Oakes	Rebel	1.5184	1915	970	2154	119	93	0.961	2.34	0.123
75	Pinson	Vada	1.5183	1975	2403	5097	172	101	0.981	2.19	0.072
76	Ellsbury	Jacoby	1.5160	2017	1228	2784	33	15	0.995	2.29	0.027
77	Wilson	Chief	1.5159	1916	1269	2430	181	85	0.968	2.06	0.143
78	Unser	Del	1.5150	1982	1407	3123	112	52	0.984	2.30	0.080
79	Barfield	Jesse	1.5150	1992	1387	2951	162	62	0.980	2.24	0.117
80	Douthit	Taylor	1.5144	1933	1036	3109	70	91	0.972	3.07	0.068
81	Edmonds	Jim	1.5137	2010	1872	4533	129	58	0.988	2.49	0.069

Rank	Player	First	PosFV	Year	GP	PO	A	E	PCT	RF(pg)	APG
82	Leach	Tommy	1.5135	1918	1079	2548	133	70	0.975	2.48	0.123
83	Upton	B. J.	1.5129	2014	1070	2585	64	35	0.987	2.48	0.060
84	Finley	Steve	1.5122	2007	2488	5663	134	72	0.988	2.33	0.054
85	Chapman	Sam	1.5115	1951	1309	3579	115	107	0.972	2.82	0.088
86	Wright	George	1.5098	1986	566	1355	35	22	0.984	2.46	0.062
87	Piersall	Jim	1.5096	1967	1614	3851	95	39	0.990	2.44	0.059
88	Hunter	Torii	1.5092	2015	2264	5262	131	52	0.990	2.38	0.058
89	Murphy	Dale	1.5089	1993	1853	4053	113	71	0.983	2.25	0.061
90	White	Devon	1.5085	2001	1869	4737	97	71	0.986	2.59	0.052
91	Bourn	Michael	1.5079	2016	1333	2844	61	29	0.990	2.18	0.046
92	Wynn	Jimmy	1.5075	1977	1810	3912	139	80	0.981	2.24	0.077
93	Grissom	Marquis	1.5073	2005	2097	4880	99	61	0.988	2.37	0.047
94	Granderson	Curtis	1.5073	2019	1956	4183	80	31	0.993	2.18	0.041
95	Tuttle	Bill	1.5073	1963	1191	2698	97	48	0.983	2.35	0.081
96	Davis	Willie	1.5068	1979	2323	5449	143	127	0.978	2.41	0.062
97	Jones	Adam	1.5062	2019	1787	4272	102	64	0.986	2.45	0.057
98	Mitchell	Mike	1.5056	1914	1107	2107	180	97	0.959	2.07	0.163
99	Sheckard	Jimmy	1.5045	1913	2071	4203	307	197	0.958	2.18	0.148
100	Lofton	Kenny	1.5041	2007	2045	4856	141	79	0.984	2.44	0.069
101	Kiermaier	Kevin	1.5019	2020	719	1723	49	23	0.987	2.46	0.068
102	Kaline	Al	1.5011	1973	2488	5035	170	73	0.986	2.09	0.068
103	Tucker	Thurman	1.5007	1950	574	1617	52	21	0.988	2.91	0.091
104	Maddox	Garry	1.5007	1986	1687	4449	94	78	0.983	2.69	0.056
105	Williams	Bernie	1.5005	2006	1926	4709	65	48	0.990	2.48	0.034
106	McRae	Brian	1.4996	1999	1307	3081	37	33	0.990	2.39	0.028
107	Manning	Rick	1.4995	1987	1508	3831	71	58	0.985	2.59	0.047
108	Heidrick	Emmet	1.4991	1908	748	1562	133	97	0.946	2.27	0.178
109	Moseby	Lloyd	1.4991	1991	1529	3765	73	62	0.984	2.51	0.048
110	Rivers	Mickey	1.4990	1984	1253	3150	95	61	0.982	2.59	0.076
111	DeJesus	David	1.4990	2015	1389	2903	67	24	0.992	2.14	0.048
112	Pettis	Gary	1.4987	1992	1128	2948	63	44	0.986	2.67	0.056
113	Cedeno	Cesar	1.4987	1986	1718	4131	102	64	0.985	2.46	0.059
114	Dykstra	Lenny	1.4979	1996	1221	3108	58	41	0.987	2.59	0.048
115	Span	Denard	1.4977	2018	1388	3198	46	30	0.991	2.34	0.033
116	Van Slyke	Andy	1.4976	1995	1499	3336	107	43	0.988	2.30	0.071
117	Jones	Ruppert	1.4972	1987	1205	3051	75	43	0.986	2.59	0.062
118	Herrera	Odubel	1.4971	2019	609	1416	24	19	0.987	2.36	0.039
119	Jacobson	Baby Doll	1.4969	1927	1378	3477	113	99	0.973	2.61	0.082
120	McReynolds	Kevin	1.4965	1994	1469	3120	104	44	0.987	2.19	0.071
121	Dawson	Andre	1.4964	1996	2323	5158	157	93	0.983	2.29	0.068
122	Simmons	Al	1.4956	1944	2142	4988	169	94	0.982	2.41	0.079
123	Snodgrass	Fred	1.4949	1916	818	1757	134	69	0.965	2.31	0.164

OF Rank	Player	First	PosFV	Year	GP	PO	A	E	PCT	RF(pg)	APG
124	Kotsay	Mark	1.4943	2013	1538	3301	124	45	0.987	2.23	0.081
125	Williams	Cy	1.4940	1930	1818	4180	226	123	0.973	2.42	0.124
126	Uhlaender	Ted	1.4937	1972	793	1588	36	15	0.991	2.05	0.045
127	Busby	Jim	1.4932	1962	1280	3284	68	42	0.988	2.62	0.053
128	Rowand	Aaron	1.4923	2011	1344	2836	62	31	0.989	2.16	0.046
129	White	Roy	1.4921	1979	1625	3356	86	43	0.988	2.12	0.053
130	Hanlon	Ned	1.4920	1892	1251	2653	208	350	0.891	2.29	0.166
131	Thomas	Gorman	1.4915	1984	1159	2905	53	49	0.984	2.55	0.046
132	Roush	Edd	1.4912	1931	1848	4537	222	137	0.972	2.58	0.120
133	Burns	George	1.4909	1925	1844	3918	197	128	0.970	2.23	0.107
134	Cain	Lorenzo	1.4908	2020	1042	2585	52	39	0.985	2.53	0.050
135	Hornung	Joe	1.4903	1890	1054	1925	176	178	0.922	1.99	0.167
136	Flagstead	Ira	1.4903	1930	1036	2482	159	71	0.974	2.55	0.153
137	Kauff	Benny	1.4903	1920	853	1881	136	85	0.960	2.36	0.159
138	Yastrzemski	Carl	1.4899	1983	2076	3941	195	82	0.981	1.99	0.094
139	Clarke	Fred	1.4898	1915	2189	4790	254	256	0.952	2.30	0.116
140	Murcer	Bobby	1.4897	1980	1644	3269	125	65	0.981	2.06	0.076
141	Bell	Gus	1.4897	1962	1642	3500	133	54	0.985	2.21	0.081
142	Hunter	Brian	1.4892	2003	930	1926	69	40	0.980	2.15	0.074
143	Duffy	Hugh	1.4880	1905	1681	3392	240	220	0.943	2.16	0.143
144	Schulte	Fred	1.4865	1937	1060	2853	81	72	0.976	2.77	0.076
145	Hoy	Dummy	1.4864	1902	1795	3958	273	394	0.915	2.36	0.152
146	Cameron	Mike	1.4861	2011	1957	4952	78	71	0.986	2.57	0.040
147	Aaron	Hank	1.4856	1976	2760	5539	201	117	0.980	2.08	0.073
148	Milner	Eddie	1.4848	1988	719	1690	44	23	0.987	2.41	0.061
149	Wilson	Willie	1.4847	1994	2031	5060	76	67	0.987	2.53	0.037
150	Gutierrez	Franklin	1.4832	2017	756	1792	25	16	0.991	2.40	0.033
151	Clemente	Roberto	1.4832	1972	2370	4696	266	140	0.973	2.09	0.112
152	Seymour	Cy	1.4832	1913	1333	2855	188	177	0.945	2.28	0.141
153	McTamany	Jim	1.4827	1891	813	1542	151	161	0.913	2.08	0.186
154	Hamilton	Darryl	1.4815	2001	1238	2711	46	14	0.995	2.23	0.037
155	Evans	Dwight	1.4813	1991	2146	4371	157	59	0.987	2.11	0.073
156	Johnson	Lance	1.4812	2000	1387	3508	68	62	0.983	2.58	0.049
157	McCutchen	Andrew	1.4812	2020	1588	3379	74	40	0.989	2.17	0.047
158	Stahl	Chick	1.4812	1906	1295	2435	162	105	0.961	2.01	0.125
159	Selbach	Kip	1.4811	1906	1568	3392	197	214	0.944	2.29	0.126
160	North	Billy	1.4802	1981	1066	2820	63	57	0.981	2.70	0.059
161	Sizemore	Grady	1.4798	2015	1015	2390	24	19	0.992	2.38	0.024
162	Brunansky	Tom	1.4792	1994	1679	3506	117	60	0.984	2.16	0.070
163	Almada	Mel	1.4790	1939	607	1466	71	47	0.970	2.53	0.117
164	Lewis	Darren	1.4785	2002	1315	2778	42	16	0.994	2.14	0.032

Rank	Player	First	PosFV	Year	GP	PO	A	E	PCT	RF(pg)	APG
165	Stanley	Mickey	1.4785	1978	1290	2819	61	27	0.991	2.23	0.047
166	Henderson	Dave	1.4783	1994	1388	3334	99	55	0.984	2.47	0.071
167	Doby	Larry	1.4776	1959	1440	3616	68	63	0.983	2.57	0.061
168	Beltran	Carlos	1.4774	2017	2218	5153	144	75	0.986	2.39	0.065
169	Griffey	Ken	1.4772	2009	2386	5602	155	89	0.985	2.41	0.065
170	Maloney	Billy	1.4769	1908	596	1248	73	63	0.954	2.22	0.122
171	Gwynn	Tony	1.4768	2001	2326	4512	160	62	0.987	2.01	0.069
172	Bradley	Phil	1.4761	1990	996	1931	60	24	0.988	2.00	0.060
173	Tovar	Cesar	1.4759	1976	945	2043	71	44	0.980	2.24	0.075
174	Shannon	Spike	1.4754	1908	890	1303	86	36	0.974	1.98	0.096
175	Downing	Brian	1.4752	1987	777	1491	39	7	0.995	1.97	0.050
176	Bumbry	Al	1.4746	1985	1241	2975	68	44	0.986	2.45	0.055
177	Milan	Clyde	1.4744	1922	1903	4095	294	216	0.953	2.31	0.154
178	Wolf	Jimmy	1.4743	1892	1042	1642	229	168	0.918	1.80	0.220
179	Hines	Paul	1.4735	1891	1376	2694	237	385	0.884	2.13	0.172
180	Hidalgo	Richard	1.4735	2005	1091	2058	82	28	0.987	1.96	0.075
181	Birmingham	Joe	1.4720	1914	712	1478	129	70	0.958	2.26	0.181
182	Nicol	Hugh	1.4717	1890	823	1290	226	146	0.912	1.84	0.275
183	McBride	Bake	1.4713	1983	963	2163	59	25	0.989	2.31	0.061
184	Averill	Earl	1.4693	1941	1589	3969	115	126	0.970	2.57	0.072
185	Allen	Ethan	1.4690	1938	1123	2746	103	56	0.981	2.54	0.092
186	Philley	Dave	1.4689	1962	1454	3242	137	64	0.981	2.32	0.094
187	Ward	Gary	1.4679	1990	1094	2436	81	41	0.984	2.30	0.074
188	McIntyre	Matty	1.4677	1912	1039	2037	133	81	0.964	2.09	0.128
189	Arnovich	Morrie	1.4674	1946	544	1260	52	25	0.981	2.41	0.096
190	Singleton	Chris	1.4673	2005	697	1556	32	21	0.987	2.28	0.046
191	Brown	Tom	1.4672	1898	1783	3623	348	490	0.890	2.23	0.195
192	Johnson	Bob	1.4667	1945	1769	4003	208	141	0.968	2.38	0.118
193	Geronimo	Cesar	1.4664	1983	1376	2901	81	35	0.988	2.17	0.059
194	Rice	Harry	1.4664	1933	911	2160	114	80	0.966	2.50	0.125
195	Anderson	Garret	1.4660	2010	1952	4056	111	48	0.989	2.13	0.057
196	O'Neill	Paul	1.4657	2001	1932	3725	110	46	0.988	1.98	0.057
197	Jackson	Austin	1.4656	2018	1104	2519	42	30	0.988	2.32	0.038
198	Berger	Wally	1.4653	1940	1296	3324	87	91	0.974	2.63	0.067
199	Baker	Dusty	1.4653	1986	1842	3663	110	56	0.985	2.05	0.060
200	Gardner	Brett	1.4648	2020	1557	2864	76	24	0.992	1.89	0.049
201	Cromartie	Warren	1.4638	1991	780	1615	74	39	0.977	2.17	0.095
202	Slagle	Jimmy	1.4638	1908	1292	2692	168	150	0.950	2.21	0.130
203	Cobb	Ty	1.4637	1928	2934	6361	392	271	0.961	2.30	0.134
204	Colavito	Rocky	1.4637	1968	1774	3323	123	70	0.980	1.94	0.069
205	Phillips	Adolfo	1.4633	1972	593	1241	43	26	0.980	2.17	0.073
206	Damon	Johnny	1.4631	2012	2128	4716	80	56	0.988	2.25	0.038

Rank	Player	First	PosFV	Year	GP	PO	A	E	PCT	RF(pg)	APG
207	McCosky	Barney	1.4624	1952	1036	2490	48	41	0.984	2.45	0.046
208	Mantle	Mickey	1.4620	1966	2019	4438	117	82	0.982	2.26	0.058
209	Neale	Greasy	1.4611	1924	736	1569	87	48	0.972	2.25	0.118
210	Goodwin	Tom	1.4610	2004	1125	2347	34	22	0.991	2.12	0.030
211	Ott	Mel	1.4610	1946	2313	4511	256	98	0.980	2.06	0.111
212	Haas	Mule	1.4609	1938	1022	2486	68	42	0.984	2.50	0.067
213	Young	Chris	1.4608	2018	1364	2895	48	29	0.990	2.16	0.035
214	Hotaling	Pete	1.4598	1888	825	1476	163	246	0.869	1.99	0.198
215	Gilkey	Bernard	1.4598	2001	1085	1955	107	36	0.983	1.90	0.099
216	Bay	Harry	1.4595	1907	665	1391	72	48	0.968	2.20	0.108
217	Winfield	Dave	1.4594	1994	2469	4975	166	95	0.982	2.08	0.067
218	Chapman	Ben	1.4593	1945	1495	3476	156	125	0.967	2.43	0.104
219	Waner	Paul	1.4591	1944	2288	4872	241	132	0.975	2.23	0.105
220	Taveras	Willy	1.4588	2010	624	1445	40	23	0.985	2.38	0.064
221	Cardenal	Jose	1.4585	1980	1778	3565	143	90	0.976	2.09	0.080
222	Cowens	Al	1.4582	1986	1477	2854	112	46	0.985	2.01	0.076
223	Strunk	Amos	1.4581	1924	1327	2830	159	61	0.980	2.25	0.120
224	Devereaux	Mike	1.4578	1998	1059	2410	44	29	0.988	2.32	0.042
225	Oliva	Tony	1.4573	1972	1178	2332	71	61	0.975	2.04	0.060
226	Medwick	Joe	1.4571	1948	1852	3994	139	84	0.980	2.23	0.075
227	Veach	Bobby	1.4571	1925	1740	3754	207	150	0.964	2.28	0.119
228	Bescher	Bob	1.4570	1918	1188	2493	137	109	0.960	2.21	0.115
229	Raines	Tim	1.4569	2002	2125	4198	134	54	0.988	2.04	0.063
230	Robinson	Frank	1.4558	1976	2132	3978	135	68	0.984	1.93	0.063
231	Gonzalez	Tony	1.4558	1971	1447	2783	73	39	0.987	1.97	0.050
232	Foster	George	1.4554	1986	1880	3809	119	62	0.984	2.09	0.063
233	Pillar	Kevin	1.4549	2020	895	2025	45	21	0.990	2.31	0.050
234	Gladden	Dan	1.4545	1993	1137	2520	81	43	0.984	2.29	0.071
235	Kelley	Joe	1.4540	1908	1465	2864	212	144	0.955	2.10	0.145
236	Smoot	Homer	1.4537	1906	678	1363	81	71	0.95	2.13	0.119
237	Anderson	Brady	1.4526	2002	1705	3714	59	42	0.989	2.21	0.035
238	Smith	Reggie	1.4526	1980	1668	3676	127	94	0.976	2.28	0.076
239	Powell	Ray	1.4524	1924	826	2020	124	91	0.959	2.60	0.150
240	Thomson	Bobby	1.4524	1960	1508	3563	111	74	0.980	2.44	0.074
241	Vosmik	Joe	1.4524	1944	1370	2958	107	66	0.979	2.24	0.078
242	Curtis	Chad	1.4521	2001	1202	2503	75	48	0.982	2.14	0.062
243	Hooper	Harry	1.4520	1925	2284	3981	344	151	0.966	1.89	0.151
244	Bonds	Bobby	1.4516	1981	1736	3659	128	89	0.977	2.18	0.074
245	Rice	Sam	1.4513	1934	2270	4774	278	184	0.965	2.23	0.122
246	Young	Gerald	1.4512	1994	568	1194	38	12	0.990	2.17	0.067
247	Payton	Jay	1.4509	2010	1249	2532	61	33	0.987	2.08	0.049
248	Thompson	Sam	1.4508	1906	1406	2165	283	171	0.935	1.74	0.201

OF Rank	Player	First	PosFV	Year	GP	PO	A	E	PCT	RF(pg)	APG
249	Van Haltren	George	1.4507	1903	1827	3490	348	358	0.915	2.10	0.190
250	Rios	Alex	1.4505	2015	1678	3503	94	48	0.987	2.14	0.056
251	Pierre	Juan	1.4503	2013	1846	3879	45	40	0.990	2.13	0.024
252	Revere	Ben	1.4502	2017	824	1733	31	19	0.989	2.14	0.038
253	Hatcher	Billy	1.4501	1995	1143	2289	67	33	0.986	2.06	0.059
254	Lock	Don	1.4499	1969	831	1789	59	45	0.976	2.22	0.071
255	Andrews	Ed	1.4493	1891	652	1257	129	134	0.912	2.13	0.198
256	Groth	Johnny	1.4492	1960	1155	2566	82	36	0.987	2.29	0.071
257	Puhl	Terry	1.4490	1991	1300	2576	57	18	0.993	2.03	0.044
258	Calhoun	Kole	1.4484	2020	1000	1956	59	31	0.985	2.02	0.059
259	Gillespie	Pete	1.4484	1887	714	1229	90	142	0.903	1.85	0.126
260	Beaumont	Ginger	1.4483	1910	1407	2845	167	139	0.956	2.14	0.119
261	Magee	Sherry	1.4480	1919	1861	3800	176	123	0.970	2.14	0.095
262	Jensen	Jackie	1.4479	1961	1391	2739	124	68	0.977	2.06	0.089
263	Maddox	Elliott	1.4476	1980	719	1493	61	18	0.989	2.16	0.085
264	Snider	Duke	1.4475	1964	1918	4099	123	66	0.985	2.20	0.064
265	Frederick	Johnny	1.4464	1934	733	1813	60	50	0.974	2.56	0.082
266	Wheat	Zack	1.4457	1927	2337	4996	232	183	0.966	2.24	0.099
267	Cuyler	Kiki	1.4456	1938	1807	4034	191	121	0.972	2.34	0.106
268	Rice	Jim	1.4453	1988	1543	3103	137	66	0.980	2.10	0.089
269	Snyder	Cory	1.4449	1994	877	1674	89	31	0.983	2.01	0.101
270	Brandt	Jackie	1.4445	1967	1100	2131	76	44	0.980	2.01	0.069
271	Wilson	Mookie	1.4445	1991	1273	3084	54	58	0.982	2.47	0.042
272	Buhner	Jay	1.4443	2001	1397	2527	101	33	0.988	1.88	0.072
273	Hendrick	George	1.4443	1988	1813	3751	114	57	0.985	2.13	0.063
274	Mazzilli	Lee	1.4440	1989	868	1933	48	28	0.986	2.28	0.055
275	Sweeney	Darnell	1.4437	2015	698	1275	37	9	0.993	1.88	0.053
276	Becker	Rich	1.4429	2000	739	1481	55	27	0.983	2.08	0.074
277	Surhoff	B.J.	1.4427	2005	995	1796	74	20	0.989	1.88	0.074
278	Weaver	Farmer	1.4422	1894	651	1206	135	106	0.927	2.06	0.207
279	Cruz	Jose	1.4422	2008	1397	2882	81	43	0.986	2.12	0.058
280	McDowell	Oddibe	1.4412	1994	746	1687	40	22	0.987	2.32	0.054
281	Wilson	Glenn	1.4410	1993	1131	2225	109	55	0.977	2.06	0.096
282	Brantley	Michael	1.4410	2020	1170	2112	61	15	0.993	1.86	0.052
283	Bigbee	Carson	1.4408	1926	1031	2302	142	86	0.966	2.37	0.138
284	Springer	George	1.4408	2020	833	1461	42	16	0.989	1.80	0.050
285	Duncan	Pat	1.4406	1924	707	1466	70	47	0.970	2.17	0.099
286	Armas	Tony	1.4403	1989	1306	3091	78	60	0.981	2.43	0.060
287	Walker	Larry	1.4402	2005	1814	3314	155	48	0.986	1.91	0.085
288	Lindstrom	Freddie	1.4399	1936	551	1311	49	24	0.983	2.47	0.089
289	Pollock	AJ	1.4397	2020	718	1451	34	11	0.993	2.07	0.047
290	Ellis	Rube	1.4395	1912	510	1070	84	70	0.943	2.26	0.165

OF Rank	Player	First	PosFV	Year	GP	PO	A	E	PCT	RF(pg)	APG
291	Agee	Tommie	1.4395	1973	1073	2371	53	61	0.975	2.26	0.049
292	Lewis	Duffy	1.4371	1921	1432	2657	210	123	0.959	2.00	0.147
293	Hisle	Larry	1.4360	1979	1017	2213	70	52	0.978	2.24	0.069
294	Kelly	Roberto	1.4354	2000	1312	2898	57	44	0.985	2.25	0.043
295	Noren	Irv	1.4353	1960	801	1778	76	31	0.984	2.31	0.095
296	Maxwell	Charlie	1.4348	1963	834	1665	44	21	0.988	2.05	0.053
297	Tresh	Tom	1.4348	1969	727	1380	50	31	0.979	1.97	0.069
298	LeFlore	Ron	1.4346	1982	1040	2521	89	86	0.968	2.51	0.086
299	Crisp	Coco	1.4344	2016	1498	3410	43	30	0.991	2.31	0.029
300	Staub	Rusty	1.4340	1985	1675	3018	165	103	0.969	1.90	0.099
301	Buford	Don	1.4336	1972	555	983	37	12	0.988	1.84	0.067
302	Bonds	Barry	1.4331	2007	2877	5638	174	97	0.984	2.02	0.060
303	Magee	Lee	1.4323	1919	519	1123	83	38	0.969	2.32	0.160
304	Gomez	Carlos	1.4320	2019	1401	3141	74	53	0.984	2.29	0.053
305	O'Brien	Darby	1.4313	1892	703	1331	90	101	0.934	2.02	0.128
306	Bates	Johnny	1.4311	1914	1080	2078	162	106	0.955	2.07	0.150
307	Cooney	Johnny	1.4310	1944	794	1791	56	22	0.988	2.33	0.071
308	Pence	Hunter	1.4306	2020	1580	3263	96	48	0.986	2.13	0.061
309	Lagares	Juan	1.4305	2020	676	1324	35	19	0.986	2.01	0.052
310	Marshall	Willard	1.4304	1955	1145	2184	125	50	0.979	2.02	0.109
311	Jordan	Brian	1.4301	2006	1366	2712	85	33	0.988	2.05	0.062
312	Jennings	Desmond	1.4299	2016	554	1145	17	6	0.995	2.10	0.031
313	Yelich	Christian	1.4299	2020	1020	1822	31	18	0.990	1.82	0.030
314	Cordova	Marty	1.4297	2003	761	1576	51	26	0.984	2.14	0.067
315	Jackson	Joe	1.4297	1920	1289	2362	183	100	0.962	1.97	0.142
316	Salmon	Tim	1.4296	2006	1267	2694	99	64	0.978	2.20	0.078
317	Heyward	Jason	1.4295	2020	1497	2743	69	33	0.988	1.88	0.046
318	Blackmon	Charlie	1.4293	2020	1078	2111	41	26	0.988	2.00	0.038
319	Oliver	Al	1.4284	1985	1376	3136	65	64	0.980	2.33	0.047
320	Del Greco	Bobby	1.4272	1965	665	1456	49	29	0.981	2.26	0.074
321	Williams	Billy	1.4268	1976	2088	3562	143	101	0.973	1.77	0.068
322	Hamilton	Billy	1.4267	1901	1584	3444	182	288	0.926	2.29	0.115
323	Wood	George	1.4262	1892	1232	2139	203	276	0.895	1.90	0.165
324	Hershberger	Mike	1.4261	1971	1037	1763	84	38	0.980	1.78	0.081
325	Dalrymple	Abner	1.4260	1891	951	1655	146	285	0.863	1.89	0.154
326	Mumphrey	Jerry	1.4258	1988	1386	3057	74	60	0.981	2.26	0.053
327	Ryan	Jimmy	1.4257	1903	1943	3698	375	365	0.918	2.10	0.193
328	Cabrera	Melky	1.4255	2019	1878	3232	123	38	0.989	1.79	0.065
329	Hofman	Solly	1.4253	1916	702	1478	113	55	0.967	2.27	0.161
330	Burke	Eddie	1.4252	1897	789	1673	119	153	0.921	2.27	0.151
331	Bourjos	Peter	1.4244	2019	803	1466	28	11	0.993	1.86	0.035
332	Geiger	Gary	1.4243	1970	749	1464	58	21	0.986	2.03	0.077

Rank	Player	First	PosFV	Year	GP	PO	A	E	PCT	RF(pg)	APG
333	Ross	Cody	1.4237	2015	1081	1823	59	21	0.989	1.74	0.055
334	Furillo	Carl	1.4236	1960	1739	3322	151	74	0.979	2.00	0.087
335	McGeachy	Jack	1.4234	1891	602	1053	131	118	0.909	1.97	0.218
336	Mazara	Nomar	1.4234	2020	547	1012	27	11	0.990	1.90	0.049
337	Burks	Ellis	1.4232	2003	1695	3436	83	60	0.983	2.08	0.049
338	Russell	Jim	1.4228	1951	942	2255	67	45	0.981	2.46	0.071
339	Tasby	Willie	1.4227	1963	543	1133	26	24	0.980	2.13	0.048
340	Belle	Albert	1.4225	2000	1311	2639	91	66	0.976	2.08	0.069
341	Davalillo	Vic	1.4221	1979	1066	2121	58	31	0.986	2.04	0.054
342	May	Carlos	1.4221	1977	677	1083	60	18	0.984	1.69	0.089
343	Heathcote	Cliff	1.4216	1931	1157	2620	157	82	0.971	2.40	0.136
344	Stenzel	Jake	1.4215	1899	741	1569	93	131	0.927	2.24	0.126
345	Eaton	Adam	1.4215	2020	818	1767	50	29	0.984	2.22	0.061
346	Ganley	Bob	1.4213	1909	564	1013	64	42	0.962	1.91	0.113
347	Hall	Jimmie	1.4209	1970	806	1507	48	29	0.982	1.93	0.060
348	Carroll	Cliff	1.4205	1893	991	1683	156	194	0.905	1.86	0.157
349	Lezcano	Sixto	1.4205	1985	1196	2401	106	51	0.980	2.10	0.089
350	Rudi	Joe	1.4204	1982	1195	2294	60	22	0.991	1.97	0.050
351	Brown	Eddie	1.4202	1928	731	1867	38	59	0.970	2.61	0.052
352	Evers	Hoot	1.4199	1956	1051	2440	71	43	0.983	2.39	0.068
353	Dyson	Jarrod	1.4196	2020	822	1671	62	29	0.984	2.11	0.075
354	Maris	Roger	1.4193	1968	1383	2649	76	49	0.982	1.97	0.055
355	Bodie	Ping	1.4192	1921	995	1893	139	73	0.965	2.04	0.140
356	Pafko	Andy	1.4191	1959	1570	3199	130	54	0.984	2.12	0.083
357	Seery	Emmett	1.4187	1892	914	1567	173	203	0.896	1.90	0.189
358	Scott	Tony	1.4183	1984	853	1803	53	27	0.986	2.18	0.062
359	Clark	Jack	1.4183	1989	1039	2004	96	48	0.978	2.02	0.092
360	Mack	Shane	1.4181	1998	832	1788	39	27	0.985	2.20	0.047
361	May	Dave	1.4177	1978	1021	2177	68	50	0.978	2.20	0.067
362	Cooley	Duff	1.4173	1905	1094	2388	96	145	0.945	2.27	0.088
363	Jones	Jacque	1.4171	2008	1248	2586	68	40	0.985	2.13	0.054
364	Combs	Earle	1.4168	1935	1387	3449	69	95	0.974	2.54	0.050
365	Shotton	Burt	1.4160	1922	1279	2816	173	184	0.942	2.34	0.135
366	Moore	Gene	1.4159	1945	914	1892	109	52	0.975	2.19	0.119
367	Baines	Harold	1.4156	1997	1061	2031	69	47	0.978	1.98	0.065
368	Bragg	Darren	1.4152	2004	835	1390	49	18	0.988	1.72	0.059
369	Lankford	Ray	1.4151	2004	1593	3528	72	63	0.983	2.26	0.045
370	Miller	Rick	1.4147	1985	1248	2786	69	42	0.986	2.29	0.055
371	Byrd	Marlon	1.4144	2016	1555	3224	75	43	0.987	2.12	0.048
372	Crawford	Sam	1.4141	1917	2299	3626	268	143	0.965	1.69	0.117
373	Martinez	Dave	1.4139	2001	1638	3024	101	43	0.986	1.91	0.062
374	Minoso	Minnie	1.4136	1964	1665	3276	139	91	0.974	2.05	0.083

OF Rank	Player	First	PosFV	Year	GP	PO	A	E	PCT	RF(pg)	APG
375	Gore	George	1.4134	1892	1297	2359	243	368	0.876	2.01	0.187
376	Gonzalez	Luis	1.4134	2008	2445	4483	110	64	0.986	1.88	0.045
377	Jamieson	Charlie	1.4133	1932	1638	3423	196	122	0.967	2.21	0.120
378	Bruce	Jay	1.4130	2020	1532	2994	104	51	0.984	2.02	0.068
379	Brye	Steve	1.4130	1978	623	1219	45	12	0.991	2.03	0.072
380	Deer	Rob	1.4129	1996	1053	2260	76	56	0.977	2.22	0.072
381	Greenwell	Mike	1.4128	1996	1165	2091	85	42	0.981	1.87	0.073
382	Holliday	Bug	1.4125	1898	891	1690	125	127	0.935	2.04	0.140
383	McCarthy	Tommy	1.4121	1896	1189	2019	268	263	0.897	1.92	0.225
384	Adams	Buster	1.4119	1947	527	1339	35	29	0.979	2.61	0.066
385	Law	Rudy	1.4119	1986	665	1446	27	21	0.986	2.22	0.041
386	Gallagher	Dave	1.4118	1995	699	1336	38	9	0.993	1.97	0.054
387	Delsing	Jim	1.4117	1960	698	1606	41	19	0.989	2.36	0.059
388	Cassidy	John	1.4113	1885	571	745	148	168	0.842	1.56	0.259
389	Crawford	Carl	1.4111	2016	1649	3319	56	36	0.989	2.05	0.034
390	Walker	Tilly	1.4110	1923	1348	2904	221	167	0.949	2.32	0.164
391	Musial	Stan	1.4108	1963	1890	3730	130	64	0.984	2.04	0.069
392	Dobbs	John	1.4106	1905	563	1181	59	60	0.954	2.20	0.105
393	Conigliaro	Tony	1.4104	1971	839	1483	48	33	0.979	1.82	0.057
394	Burch	Al	1.4101	1911	555	1088	98	62	0.950	2.14	0.177
395	Wilson	Preston	1.4096	2007	1077	2283	57	43	0.982	2.17	0.053
396	Buford	Damon	1.4093	2001	631	1254	28	14	0.989	2.03	0.044
397	Pearson	Albie	1.4093	1966	833	1725	40	36	0.980	2.12	0.048
398	Higginson	Bobby	1.4091	2005	1311	2590	124	64	0.977	2.07	0.095
399	Marisnick	Jake	1.4088	2020	652	1190	33	11	0.991	1.88	0.051
400	Bay	Jason	1.4086	2013	1275	2302	68	27	0.989	1.86	0.053
401	Witt	Whitey	1.4085	1926	729	1601	59	50	0.971	2.28	0.081
402	Walker	Curt	1.4084	1930	1310	2776	144	112	0.963	2.23	0.110
403	Falk	Bibb	1.4083	1931	1222	2520	136	92	0.967	2.17	0.111
404	Zisk	Richie	1.4081	1980	905	1680	68	33	0.981	1.93	0.075
405	Sommer	Joe	1.4073	1890	713	1326	109	157	0.901	2.01	0.153
406	Green	Shawn	1.4072	2007	1762	3301	88	48	0.986	1.92	0.050
407	Stone	George	1.4066	1910	837	1490	76	68	0.958	1.87	0.091
408	Saunders	Michael	1.4062	2017	593	1219	26	11	0.991	2.10	0.044
409	Patterson	Corey	1.4059	2011	1164	2333	48	32	0.987	2.05	0.041
410	Sievers	Roy	1.4058	1962	838	1790	56	35	0.981	2.20	0.067
411	McHenry	Austin	1.4058	1922	529	1128	81	51	0.960	2.29	0.153
412	Williams	Ken	1.4052	1929	1298	2948	167	137	0.958	2.40	0.129
413	Stubbs	Drew	1.4040	2017	872	1722	39	27	0.985	2.02	0.045
414	Jay	Jon	1.4038	2020	1128	2088	34	9	0.996	1.88	0.030
415	Diering	Chuck	1.4036	1956	631	1274	50	18	0.987	2.10	0.079
416	Harper	Tommy	1.4035	1976	1227	2168	51	31	0.986	1.81	0.042

OF Rank	Player	First	PosFV	Year	GP	PO	A	E	PCT	RF(pg)	APG
417	Conforto	Michael	1.4035	2020	622	1076	34	12	0.989	1.78	0.055
418	Lee	Hal	1.4033	1936	718	1696	40	49	0.973	2.42	0.056
419	Nicholson	Bill	1.4024	1953	1471	2954	118	67	0.979	2.09	0.080
420	Carter	Joe	1.4023	1998	1731	3669	111	89	0.977	2.18	0.064
421	Coleman	John	1.4020	1890	510	833	110	137	0.873	1.85	0.216
422	Radford	Paul	1.4016	1894	902	1404	217	179	0.901	1.80	0.241
423	Whitted	Possum	1.4014	1921	651	1391	69	38	0.975	2.24	0.106
424	Goslin	Goose	1.4012	1938	2188	4792	221	209	0.960	2.29	0.101
425	Monday	Rick	1.4011	1984	1688	3534	86	76	0.979	2.14	0.051
426	Hayes	Von	1.4007	1992	1040	2247	56	41	0.983	2.21	0.054
427	Burkett	Jesse	1.4006	1905	2053	3961	270	383	0.917	2.06	0.132
428	Henderson	Rickey	1.4006	2003	2850	6466	131	141	0.979	2.31	0.046
429	Jose	Felix	1.4006	2003	689	1300	48	27	0.980	1.96	0.070
430	Benard	Marvin	1.4005	2003	797	1410	36	21	0.986	1.81	0.045
431	Allison	Bob	1.4005	1970	1320	2486	82	67	0.975	1.95	0.062
432	McGee	Willie	1.3996	1999	2008	4259	129	108	0.976	2.19	0.064
433	Jackson	Darrin	1.3993	1999	908	1797	50	21	0.989	2.03	0.055
434	Kemp	Steve	1.3993	1988	1004	1962	55	37	0.982	2.01	0.055
435	Shanks	Howie	1.3988	1925	702	1423	99	45	0.971	2.17	0.141
436	Gonzalez	Juan	1.3987	2005	1312	2594	91	46	0.983	2.05	0.069
437	Case	George	1.3984	1947	1187	2805	88	90	0.970	2.44	0.074
438	Slaughter	Enos	1.3984	1959	2064	3925	152	82	0.980	1.98	0.074
439	Leach	Freddy	1.3974	1932	875	1940	76	51	0.975	2.30	0.087
440	Davis	Chili	1.3973	1994	1184	2565	77	80	0.971	2.23	0.065
441	Pickering	Ollie	1.3969	1908	859	1628	109	94	0.949	2.02	0.127
442	Chavez	Endy	1.3964	2014	1052	1780	60	19	0.990	1.75	0.057
443	Orsulak	Joe	1.3963	1997	1257	2284	105	43	0.982	1.90	0.084
444	Ordonez	Magglio	1.3962	2011	1740	3209	108	44	0.987	1.91	0.062
445	Demaree	Frank	1.3960	1944	1076	2124	97	51	0.978	2.06	0.090
446	Galan	Augie	1.3959	1949	1359	2996	88	61	0.981	2.27	0.065
447	Stovey	Harry	1.3959	1893	944	1801	165	229	0.896	2.08	0.175
448	Alou	Matty	1.3957	1974	1312	2346	88	51	0.979	1.86	0.067
449	Hockett	Oris	1.3957	1945	520	1206	40	33	0.974	2.40	0.077
450	Richardson	Hardy	1.3954	1892	544	1029	110	89	0.928	2.09	0.202

Note: Career Field Value possible maximum for Outfielders is 1.7000.
Minimum 500 Adjusted Games Played.
Games played for outfielders from 2000 forward contains total amount of games played for all positions combined and may reflect higher than individual games played and thus a minimally lower Range Factor and Assists Per Game.

Top 150 Fielding Pitchers

P Rank	Player	First	PosFV	LYear	IP	PO	A	E	PCT	RF (p9IP)
1	Spalding	Al	1.1340	1877	2891	215	654	118	0.880	2.71
2	Bond	Tommy	1.1314	1884	3629	218	896	109	0.911	2.76
3	Lemon	Bob	1.1103	1958	2850	263	709	31	0.969	3.07
4	Devlin	Jim	1.1096	1877	1405	89	262	30	0.921	2.25
5	Morton	Carl	1.1093	1976	1649	182	249	11	0.975	2.35
6	Joss	Addie	1.1074	1910	2327	144	846	36	0.965	3.83
7	Owen	Frank	1.1070	1909	1368	92	527	14	0.978	4.07
8	Mathewson	Christy	1.1058	1916	4781	281	1503	52	0.972	3.36
9	Ward	John	1.1058	1884	2462	169	574	54	0.932	2.72
10	Stottlemyre	Mel	1.1015	1974	2661	242	570	26	0.969	2.75
11	Maddux	Greg	1.1010	2008	5008	546	1194	53	0.970	3.13
12	Walsh	Ed	1.1007	1917	2964	233	1207	56	0.963	4.37
13	Breitenstein	Ted	1.0986	1901	2964	244	690	57	0.942	2.84
14	Altrock	Nick	1.0973	1924	1514	167	610	29	0.964	4.62
15	Alexander	Pete	1.0941	1930	5190	189	1419	25	0.985	2.79
16	Corcoran	Larry	1.0915	1887	2392	182	498	67	0.910	2.56
17	Buehrle	Mark	1.0914	2015	3283	182	608	22	0.973	2.17
18	Jansen	Larry	1.0911	1956	1766	138	335	11	0.977	2.41
19	Glavine	Tom	1.0898	2008	4413	262	856	26	0.977	2.28
20	Suggs	George	1.0893	1915	1652	74	521	17	0.972	3.24
21	Coveleski	Stan	1.0881	1928	3082	174	851	29	0.972	2.99
22	Mays	Carl	1.0881	1929	3021	174	1138	44	0.968	3.91
23	Coveleski	Harry	1.0849	1918	1248	46	461	28	0.948	3.66
24	Hernandez	Livan	1.0843	2012	3189	211	600	15	0.982	2.29
25	Walters	Bucky	1.0839	1950	3105	153	746	24	0.974	2.61
26	Hecker	Guy	1.0838	1890	2906	216	639	60	0.934	2.65
27	Foutz	Dave	1.0828	1894	1997	195	408	49	0.925	2.72
28	Wainwright	Adam	1.0822	2020	2169	191	280	8	0.983	1.95
29	Rudolph	Dick	1.0815	1927	2049	79	624	22	0.970	3.09
30	Fitzsimmons	Freddie	1.0815	1943	3224	237	942	28	0.977	3.29
31	Ruth	Babe	1.0800	1933	1221	95	354	15	0.968	3.31
32	Halladay	Roy	1.0797	2013	2749	228	391	15	0.976	2.03
33	Burdette	Lew	1.0797	1967	3067	245	622	27	0.970	2.54
34	Mullane	Tony	1.0786	1894	4531	328	1041	123	0.918	2.72
35	Reuschel	Rick	1.0786	1991	3548	328	667	29	0.972	2.52
36	Dauss	Hooks	1.0782	1926	3391	99	1128	41	0.968	3.26
37	Ferguson	Charlie	1.0781	1887	1515	99	310	36	0.919	2.43
38	Sweeney	Charlie	1.0781	1887	1031	73	246	32	0.909	2.79
39	Radke	Brad	1.0776	2006	2451	213	314	7	0.987	1.94
40	Stieb	Dave	1.0771	1998	2895	272	493	22	0.972	2.38

P Rank	Player	First	PosFV	LYear	IP	PO	A	E	PCT	RF (p9IP)
41	Galvin	Pud	1.0764	1892	6003	325	1404	163	0.914	2.59
42	Passeau	Claude	1.0759	1947	2720	130	583	17	0.977	2.36
43	Petry	Dan	1.0758	1991	2080	255	336	12	0.980	2.56
44	Bradley	George	1.0755	1884	2940	216	630	98	0.896	2.59
45	Barnes	Jesse	1.0740	1927	2570	138	748	22	0.976	3.10
46	McBride	Dick	1.0739	1876	2082	125	319	69	0.865	1.92
47	Mullin	George	1.0736	1915	3687	229	1244	82	0.947	3.60
48	Howell	Harry	1.0735	1910	2568	209	965	51	0.958	4.12
49	Jones	Randy	1.0734	1982	1933	114	465	18	0.970	2.70
50	Willis	Vic	1.0733	1910	3996	271	1124	67	0.954	3.14
51	Mulcahy	Hugh	1.0731	1947	1162	75	285	15	0.960	2.79
52	Schumacher	Hal	1.0731	1946	2482	154	646	24	0.971	2.90
53	Greinke	Zack	1.0728	2020	2939	292	425	9	0.988	2.20
54	Niekro	Phil	1.0717	1987	5404	386	878	37	0.972	2.10
55	Osteen	Claude	1.0713	1975	3460	159	699	26	0.971	2.23
56	Buffinton	Charlie	1.0713	1892	3404	172	851	94	0.916	2.70
57	Chandler	Spud	1.0710	1947	1485	106	385	10	0.980	2.98
58	Davis	Curt	1.0709	1946	2325	146	616	21	0.973	2.95
59	Tobin	Jim	1.0694	1945	1900	96	479	21	0.965	2.72
60	Stratton	Scott	1.0688	1895	1883	119	483	40	0.938	2.88
61	Taylor	Jack	1.0687	1907	2617	127	738	42	0.954	2.97
62	Kennedy	Brickyard	1.0682	1903	3021	123	767	57	0.940	2.65
63	Perry	Gaylord	1.0678	1983	5350	349	877	38	0.970	2.06
64	McCormick	Jim	1.0677	1887	4276	263	922	99	0.923	2.49
65	Langford	Rick	1.0673	1986	1491	145	211	6	0.983	2.15
66	Kluber	Corey	1.0672	2020	1343	104	114	3	0.986	1.46
67	Rommel	Eddie	1.0671	1932	2556	159	810	32	0.968	3.41
68	Weaver	Sam	1.0670	1886	1326	81	311	39	0.910	2.66
69	Gumbert	Harry	1.0667	1950	2156	129	670	17	0.979	3.34
70	Ferrell	Wes	1.0667	1941	2623	122	532	17	0.975	2.24
71	Webb	Brandon	1.0664	2009	1320	100	268	20	0.948	2.51
72	Wood	Wilbur	1.0663	1978	2684	84	523	14	0.977	2.04
73	Ehmke	Howard	1.0656	1930	2821	143	853	44	0.958	3.18
74	Hart	Bill	1.0653	1901	1582	90	461	46	0.923	3.13
75	Dickson	Murry	1.0645	1959	3052	236	668	30	0.968	2.67
76	Smith	Frank	1.0644	1915	2273	167	782	37	0.962	3.76
77	Harmon	Bob	1.0639	1918	2054	88	620	26	0.965	3.10
78	Friend	Bob	1.0638	1966	3611	228	630	27	0.969	2.14
79	Martinez	Dennis	1.0637	1998	4000	319	763	42	0.963	2.43
80	Jackson	Larry	1.0633	1968	3263	257	656	38	0.960	2.52
81	Valenzuela	Fernando	1.0631	1997	2930	200	586	30	0.963	2.41
82	Barrett	Red	1.0629	1949	1263	98	261	11	0.970	2.56

P Rank	Player	First	PosFV	LYear	IP	PO	A	E	PCT	RF (p9IP)
83	Young	Cy	1.0628	1911	7355	229	2014	146	0.939	2.74
84	Clarkson	John	1.0627	1894	4536	221	1143	162	0.894	2.71
85	McMahon	Sadie	1.0625	1897	2634	101	664	70	0.916	2.61
86	Nagy	Charles	1.0622	2003	1955	185	335	12	0.977	2.39
87	Patterson	Roy	1.0618	1907	1365	75	432	23	0.957	3.34
88	Nichols	Kid	1.0618	1906	5056	311	1031	67	0.952	2.39
89	Radbourn	Charley	1.0615	1891	4535	230	942	111	0.913	2.33
90	Hendricks	Kyle	1.0611	2020	1047	84	177	4	0.985	2.24
91	Morgan	Cy	1.0607	1913	1445	53	508	33	0.944	3.49
92	Purkey	Bob	1.0607	1966	2115	184	464	23	0.966	2.76
93	Nehf	Art	1.0604	1929	2708	142	749	22	0.976	2.96
94	Rogers	Steve	1.0604	1985	2838	237	462	31	0.958	2.22
95	Callahan	Nixey	1.0603	1903	1603	127	506	43	0.936	3.55
96	Stein	Ed	1.0601	1898	1656	110	353	28	0.943	2.52
97	Donahue	Red	1.0601	1906	2975	127	903	51	0.953	3.12
98	Terrell	Walt	1.0601	1992	1987	194	285	10	0.980	2.17
99	Frey	Benny	1.0598	1936	1160	54	354	15	0.965	3.17
100	Bush	Joe	1.0597	1928	3087	208	839	34	0.969	3.05
101	Smith	Bob	1.0595	1937	2246	118	539	13	0.981	2.63
102	deGrom	Jacob	1.0595	2020	1170	95	146	5	0.980	1.85
103	Sudhoff	Willie	1.0590	1906	2086	106	762	56	0.939	3.74
104	Moore	Mike	1.0586	1995	2832	278	444	33	0.956	2.29
105	Rixey	Eppa	1.0586	1933	4495	131	1195	30	0.978	2.66
106	Warneke	Lon	1.0583	1945	2782	126	538	8	0.988	2.15
107	Gura	Larry	1.0579	1985	2047	107	369	7	0.986	2.09
108	Grimes	Burleigh	1.0578	1934	4180	225	1252	71	0.954	3.18
109	Kilroy	Matt	1.0573	1898	2436	156	599	91	0.892	2.79
110	Wright	Clyde	1.0569	1975	1729	108	344	18	0.962	2.35
111	Caldwell	Mike	1.0567	1984	2409	116	499	15	0.976	2.30
112	Wood	Joe	1.0565	1920	1436	123	409	17	0.969	3.33
113	Mahler	Rick	1.0562	1991	1951	160	338	21	0.960	2.30
114	Hubbell	Carl	1.0561	1943	3590	155	824	33	0.967	2.45
115	Auker	Elden	1.0560	1942	1963	120	460	20	0.967	2.66
116	Christopher	Russ	1.0557	1948	1000	93	314	9	0.978	3.66
117	Willett	Ed	1.0554	1915	1773	72	695	41	0.949	3.89
118	Ortiz	Russ	1.0553	2010	1661	106	267	5	0.987	2.02
119	Garcia	Mike	1.0547	1961	2175	134	359	14	0.972	2.04
120	Caruthers	Bob	1.0546	1892	2829	192	580	61	0.927	2.46
121	Candiotti	Tom	1.0542	1999	2725	230	437	18	0.974	2.20
122	Arroyo	Bronson	1.0541	2017	2436	221	325	16	0.972	2.02
123	Keuchel	Dallas	1.0538	2020	1365	82	260	9	0.974	2.25
124	Dunn	Jack	1.0532	1904	1077	77	278	23	0.939	2.97

P Rank	Player	First	PosFV	LYear	IP	PO	A	E	PCT	RF (p9IP)
125	White	Doc	1.0531	1913	3041	236	963	50	0.960	3.55
126	Taylor	Jack	1.0531	1899	2079	101	579	77	0.898	2.94
127	Minner	Paul	1.0526	1956	1310	75	310	13	0.967	2.64
128	Brewer	Tom	1.0524	1961	1509	125	343	16	0.967	2.79
129	Hudson	Tim	1.0524	2015	3126	258	493	24	0.969	2.16
130	Bickford	Vern	1.0522	1954	1076	68	202	6	0.978	2.26
131	Seaver	Tom	1.0515	1986	4783	328	692	42	0.960	1.92
132	Rueter	Kirk	1.0512	2005	1918	135	441	7	0.988	2.70
133	Baldwin	Lady	1.0510	1890	1017	34	222	18	0.934	2.27
134	Shocker	Urban	1.0509	1928	2682	155	599	15	0.980	2.53
135	Teheran	Julio	1.0503	2020	1391	85	221	6	0.981	1.98
136	Erickson	Scott	1.0502	2006	2361	223	400	29	0.956	2.38
137	Shantz	Bobby	1.0498	1964	1936	174	468	16	0.976	2.99
138	Corbin	Patrick	1.0498	2020	1213	53	191	5	0.980	1.81
139	Hutchinson	Fred	1.0498	1953	1464	108	310	13	0.970	2.57
140	Brandt	Ed	1.0497	1938	2268	78	512	14	0.977	2.34
141	Westbrook	Jake	1.0495	2013	1748	193	377	18	0.969	2.94
142	Dickey	R.A.	1.0492	2016	1884	104	342	14	0.970	2.13
143	Dubuc	Jean	1.0492	1919	1444	79	537	31	0.952	3.84
144	Brown	Clint	1.0492	1942	1486	75	387	12	0.975	2.80
145	Palmer	Jim	1.0492	1984	3948	292	577	34	0.962	1.98
146	Oswalt	Roy	1.0491	2013	2245	168	310	9	0.982	1.92
147	Wyse	Hank	1.0487	1951	1258	56	291	15	0.959	2.48
148	Garver	Ned	1.0486	1961	2477	203	469	27	0.961	2.44
149	Quinn	Jack	1.0486	1933	3920	139	1240	45	0.968	3.17
150	Sutcliffe	Rick	1.0486	1994	2698	211	404	17	0.973	2.05

Notes: Career Field Value possible maximum for Pitchers is 1.1500.
Minimum 1000 Innings Pitched.
Range Factor is listed as per 9 Innings Pitched, not Games Played.

ARIZONA DIAMONDBACKS
Best Seasons and Careers of All-Time

For a young franchise, the accumulation of stats and the crafting of an All-Time team seem both a bit premature, but also ever changing. Yes, it's still true that Arizona is looking for its seminal player. It almost had one in Paul Goldschmidt, but sent him off when free agency dollars were about to come calling. It has had more than a few pitchers make great splashes, however, in Zach Grienke, Curt Schilling, and Randy Johnson, and that's where this All-Time team, if put on the field, would shine. Just imagine having those three pitchers in some of their best years pitching in a short series. It would be a daunting experience. The offense might be a bit lacking compared to that of the Yankees, but even in these few decades of existence, that pitching might even pass the Bronx Bombers.

Reserves

Bench - Justin Upton (OF), David Peralta (OF), A.J. Pollock (OF), Matt Williams (3B), Jake Lamb (3B, 1B), Tony Womack (2B, SS, OF), Chris Snyder (CATCHER).

Bullpen - Jose Valverde (CL), Brad Ziegler (SU), Patrick Corbin, J.J. Putz, Ian Kennedy, Wade Miley.

Arizona Diamondbacks - Best Position Player Years

Rank	Name	First	Year	Team	Lg	HR	RBI	AVG	Age	PEVA-B
1	Gonzalez	Luis	2001	ARI	NL	57	142	0.325	34	30.146
2	Goldschmidt	Paul	2015	ARI	NL	33	110	0.321	28	28.649
3	Goldschmidt	Paul	2013	ARI	NL	36	125	0.302	26	26.428
4	Goldschmidt	Paul	2017	ARI	NL	36	120	0.297	30	21.231
5	Gonzalez	Luis	1999	ARI	NL	26	111	0.336	32	20.603
6	Goldschmidt	Paul	2016	ARI	NL	24	95	0.297	29	19.659
7	Marte	Ketel	2019	ARI	NL	32	92	0.329	26	18.551
8	Williams	Matt	1999	ARI	NL	35	142	0.303	34	17.667
9	Gonzalez	Luis	2000	ARI	NL	31	114	0.311	33	17.155
10	Pollack	A.J.	2015	ARI	NL	20	76	0.315	28	16.951
11	Hill	Aaron	2012	ARI	NL	26	85	0.302	30	16.872
12	Montero	Miguel	2012	ARI	NL	15	88	0.286	28	16.756
13	Bell	Jay	1999	ARI	NL	38	112	0.289	34	16.663
14	Goldschmidt	Paul	2018	ARI	NL	33	83	0.290	31	16.239
15	Upton	Justin	2011	ARI	NL	31	88	0.289	23	16.045
16	Escobar	Eduardo	2019	ARI	NL	35	118	0.269	30	15.109
17	Finley	Steve	1999	ARI	NL	34	103	0.264	34	14.535
18	Gonzalez	Luis	2003	ARI	NL	26	104	0.304	36	14.087
19	Finley	Steve	2000	ARI	NL	35	96	0.280	35	13.458
20	Young	Chris	2010	ARI	NL	27	91	0.257	27	13.293

Arizona Diamondbacks - Best Pitcher Years

Rank	Name	First	Year	Team	Lg	W	L	SV	IP	ERA	Age	PEVA-P
1	Johnson	Randy	2001	ARI	NL	21	6	0	249.7	2.49	38	52.009
2	Johnson	Randy	2004	ARI	NL	16	14	0	245.7	2.60	41	44.961
3	Johnson	Randy	2002	ARI	NL	24	5	0	260.0	2.32	39	43.254
4	Schilling	Curt	2001	ARI	NL	22	6	0	256.7	2.98	35	38.613
5	Schilling	Curt	2002	ARI	NL	23	7	0	259.3	3.23	36	37.153
6	Webb	Brandon	2006	ARI	NL	16	8	0	235.0	3.10	27	36.142
7	Webb	Brandon	2007	ARI	NL	18	10	0	236.3	3.01	28	35.177
8	Johnson	Randy	1999	ARI	NL	17	9	0	271.7	2.48	36	34.970
9	Webb	Brandon	2008	ARI	NL	22	7	0	226.7	3.30	29	31.968
10	Johnson	Randy	2000	ARI	NL	19	7	0	248.7	2.64	37	31.544
11	Haren	Danny	2009	ARI	NL	14	10	0	229.3	3.14	29	29.954
12	Haren	Danny	2008	ARI	NL	16	8	0	216.0	3.33	28	29.540
13	Greinke	Zack	2017	ARI	NL	17	7	0	202.3	3.20	34	27.376
14	Greinke	Zack	2019	ARI	NL	10	4	0	146.0	2.90	36	26.595
15	Kennedy	Ian	2011	ARI	NL	21	4	0	222.0	2.88	26	26.292
16	Corbin	Patrick	2018	ARI	NL	11	7	0	200.0	3.15	29	20.329
17	Greinke	Zack	2018	ARI	NL	15	11	0	207.7	3.21	35	20.118
18	Miley	Wade	2012	ARI	NL	16	11	0	194.7	3.33	26	18.150
19	Ray	Robbie	2017	ARI	NL	15	5	0	162.0	2.89	26	17.993
20	Putz	J.J.	2011	ARI	NL	2	2	45	58.0	2.17	34	15.180

Arizona Diamondbacks - Top Career Batters

RANK	NAME	FIRST	LYR	TEAM	LG	PEVA-B	YRS	PPYR	HR	RBI	H	AVE
1	Goldschmidt	Paul	2018	ARI	NL	138.530	8	17.316	209	710	1182	0.297
2	Gonzalez	Luis	2006	ARI	NL	118.928	8	14.866	224	774	1337	0.298

RANK	NAME	FIRST	LYR	TEAM	LG	PEVA-B	YRS	PPYR	HR	RBI	H	AVE
3	Finley	Steve	2004	ARI	NL	61.202	6	10.200	153	479	847	0.278
4	Montero	Miguel	2014	ARI	NL	55.686	9	6.187	97	448	795	0.264
5	Young	Chris	2012	ARI	NL	50.480	7	7.211	132	408	758	0.239
6	Upton	Justin	2012	ARI	NL	47.543	6	7.924	108	363	739	0.278
7	Peralta	David	2020	ARI	NL	43.861	7	6.266	90	364	765	0.291
8	Drew	Stephen	2012	ARI	NL	39.975	7	5.711	72	333	776	0.266
9	Pollock	A.J.	2018	ARI	NL	39.850	7	5.693	74	264	640	0.281
10	Bell	Jay	2002	ARI	NL	36.706	5	7.341	91	304	573	0.263
11	Reynolds	Mark	2010	ARI	NL	35.402	4	8.850	121	346	480	0.242
12	Williams	Matt	2003	ARI	NL	34.312	6	5.719	99	381	629	0.278
13	Ahmed	Nick	2020	ARI	NL	33.220	7	4.746	60	260	528	0.239
14	Parra	Gerardo	2014	ARI	NL	31.738	6	5.290	39	250	728	0.274
15	Marte	Ketel	2020	ARI	NL	30.027	4	7.507	53	186	432	0.289
16	Hill	Aaron	2015	ARI	NL	29.548	5	5.910	55	241	512	0.273
17	Lamb	Jake	2020	ARI	NL	28.856	7	4.122	81	303	471	0.239
18	Womack	Tony	2003	ARI	NL	26.177	5	5.235	21	200	677	0.269
19	Tracy	Chad	2009	ARI	NL	26.100	6	4.350	78	318	654	0.280
20	Counsell	Craig	2006	ARI	NL	23.861	6	3.977	24	193	611	0.266
21	Escobar	Eduardo	2020	ARI	NL	23.293	3	7.764	47	159	267	0.257
22	Byrnes	Eric	2009	ARI	NL	20.545	4	5.136	61	216	426	0.261
23	Snyder	Chris	2010	ARI	NL	20.522	7	2.932	62	240	379	0.233
24	Jackson	Conor	2010	ARI	NL	19.269	6	3.211	46	247	492	0.277
25	Miller	Damian	2002	ARI	NL	18.873	5	3.775	48	194	394	0.269
26	Hudson	Orlando	2008	ARI	NL	18.610	3	6.203	33	171	442	0.294
27	Johnson	Kelly	2011	ARI	NL	17.854	2	8.927	44	120	256	0.252
28	Walker	Christian	2020	ARI	NL	16.467	4	4.117	41	115	207	0.256
29	Green	Shawn	2006	ARI	NL	16.093	2	8.047	33	124	284	0.285
30	Bautista	Danny	2004	ARI	NL	14.781	5	2.956	33	197	432	0.296
31	Owings	Chris	2018	ARI	NL	14.715	6	2.452	31	196	490	0.250
32	Prado	Martin	2014	ARI	NL	14.596	2	7.298	19	124	281	0.278
33	Glaus	Troy	2005	ARI	NL	13.277	1	13.277	37	97	139	0.258
34	Cintron	Alex	2005	ARI	NL	13.169	5	2.634	25	152	398	0.279
35	Roberts	Ryan	2012	ARI	NL	13.094	4	3.273	34	133	281	0.254
36	Kubel	Jason	2013	ARI	NL	12.914	2	6.457	35	122	181	0.242
37	Spivey	Junior	2003	ARI	NL	12.753	3	4.251	34	149	297	0.279
38	Lee	Travis	2000	ARI	NL	12.472	3	4.157	39	162	292	0.252
39	Segura	Jean	2016	ARI	NL	12.207	1	12.207	20	64	203	0.319
40	Tomas	Yasmany	2019	ARI	NL	11.812	4	2.953	48	163	295	0.266
41	Dellucci	David	2003	ARI	NL	11.276	6	1.879	25	156	322	0.272
42	Calhoun	Kole	2020	ARI	NL	11.066	1	11.066	16	40	43	0.226
43	Clark	Tony	2009	ARI	NL	10.396	5	2.079	59	178	212	0.255
44	Inciarte	Ender	2015	ARI	NL	10.336	2	5.168	10	72	275	0.292
45	Colbrunn	Greg	2004	ARI	NL	10.174	5	2.035	34	127	235	0.310

RANK	NAME	FIRST	LYR	TEAM	LG	PEVA-B	YRS	PPYR	HR	RBI	H	AVE
46	Hillenbrand	Shea	2004	ARI	NL	9.966	2	4.983	32	139	262	0.294
47	Durazo	Erubiel	2002	ARI	NL	9.736	4	2.434	47	149	208	0.278
48	LaRoche	Adam	2010	ARI	NL	9.717	1	9.717	25	100	146	0.261
49	Castillo	Welington	2016	ARI	NL	9.522	2	4.761	31	118	180	0.261
50	Grace	Mark	2003	ARI	NL	9.142	3	3.047	25	142	244	0.268

Arizona Diamondbacks - Top Career Pitchers

RANK	NAME	FIRST	LYEAR	LTEAM	LG	PEVA	YRS	PPYR	W	L	SV	IP	ERA
1	Johnson	Randy	2008	ARI	NL	223.198	8	27.900	118	62	0	1630.3	2.83
2	Webb	Brandon	2009	ARI	NL	142.694	7	20.385	87	62	0	1319.7	3.27
3	Schilling	Curt	2003	ARI	NL	94.007	4	23.502	58	28	0	781.7	3.14
4	Greinke	Zack	2019	ARI	NL	79.886	4	19.972	55	29	0	714.7	3.40
5	Haren	Danny	2010	ARI	NL	67.057	3	22.352	37	26	0	586.3	3.56
6	Corbin	Patrick	2018	ARI	NL	54.846	6	9.141	56	54	2	945.7	3.91
7	Kennedy	Ian	2013	ARI	NL	53.969	4	13.492	48	34	0	748.3	3.82
8	Ray	Robbie	2019	ARI	NL	46.665	6	7.778	47	46	0	793.0	4.11
9	Miley	Wade	2014	ARI	NL	36.086	4	9.021	38	35	0	638.7	3.79
10	Ziegler	Brad	2018	ARI	NL	35.355	7	5.051	22	12	62	357.3	2.57
11	Batista	Miguel	2006	ARI	NL	31.261	4	7.815	40	34	0	723.7	3.99
12	Valverde	Jose	2007	ARI	NL	29.829	5	5.966	9	14	98	260.0	3.29
13	Kim	Byung-Hyun	2007	ARI	NL	28.739	6	4.790	21	23	70	325.7	3.43
14	Putz	J. J.	2014	ARI	NL	28.670	4	7.168	7	9	83	160.3	2.81
15	Anderson	Brian	2002	ARI	NL	27.527	5	5.505	41	42	1	840.7	4.52
16	Davis	Doug	2009	ARI	NL	26.069	3	8.690	28	34	0	542.0	4.22
17	Hudson	Daniel	2016	ARI	NL	24.831	6	4.138	33	21	9	477.7	3.88
18	Bradley	Archie	2020	ARI	NL	24.455	6	4.076	22	25	28	404.3	3.96
19	Collmenter	Josh	2016	ARI	NL	24.331	6	4.055	36	33	2	659.3	3.54
20	Godley	Zack	2019	ARI	NL	22.988	5	4.598	36	30	2	520.7	4.70
21	Daal	Omar	2000	ARI	NL	22.872	3	7.624	26	31	0	473.3	4.11
22	Benes	Andy	1999	ARI	NL	20.332	2	10.166	27	25	0	429.7	4.36
23	Saunders	Joe	2012	ARI	NL	18.759	3	6.253	21	30	0	424.7	3.96
24	Hernandez	David	2017	ARI	NL	17.290	5	3.458	15	18	18	252.3	3.64
25	Cahill	Trevor	2014	ARI	NL	17.233	3	5.744	24	34	1	457.3	4.29
26	Qualls	Chad	2010	ARI	NL	17.153	3	5.718	7	14	45	163.7	4.34
27	Kelly	Merrill	2020	ARI	NL	16.574	2	8.287	16	16	0	214.7	4.15
28	Chafin	Andrew	2020	ARI	NL	14.716	7	2.102	10	12	2	271.7	3.68
29	Gallen	Zac	2020	ARI	NL	14.207	2	7.103	5	5	0	115.7	2.80
30	Mantei	Matt	2004	ARI	NL	14.014	6	2.336	8	11	74	173.7	4.04
31	Lyon	Brandon	2008	ARI	NL	12.502	4	3.126	11	15	42	232.0	4.03
32	Cruz	Juan	2008	ARI	NL	12.096	3	4.032	15	7	0	207.3	3.47
33	Koplove	Mike	2006	ARI	NL	12.042	6	2.007	15	7	2	248.7	3.76
34	Delgado	Randall	2018	ARI	NL	11.948	6	1.991	25	19	2	415.0	4.14

RANK	NAME	FIRST	LYEAR	LTEAM	LG	PEVA	YRS	PPYR	W	L	SV	IP	ERA
35	Swindell	Greg	2002	ARI	NL	11.394	4	2.848	8	14	4	227.3	3.76
36	Pena	Tony	2009	ARI	NL	11.368	4	2.842	16	13	7	222.7	4.08
37	Reynoso	Armando	2002	ARI	NL	11.311	4	2.828	22	24	0	386.0	4.99
38	Hernandez	Livan	2007	ARI	NL	10.904	2	5.452	15	16	0	273.7	4.64
39	Scherzer	Max	2009	ARI	NL	10.513	2	5.257	9	15	0	226.3	3.86
40	Owings	Micah	2011	ARI	NL	10.331	3	3.444	22	17	0	320.3	4.69

Arizona Diamondbacks – Top Fielders

Rank	FIRST BASE		FV	Lyear	G	FPCT	RF
1	Goldschmidt	Paul	1.3174	2018	1070	0.996	9.41
2	Lee	Travis	1.2641	2000	283	0.997	8.31
3	Jackson	Conor	1.0333	2010	334	0.989	8.72

Rank	SECOND BASE		FV	Lyear	G	FPCT	RF
1	Hill	Aaron	1.2914	2015	443	0.992	4.68
2	Hudson	Orlando	1.2382	2008	399	0.984	4.89
3	Bell	Jay	1.2067	2002	390	0.981	4.32
4	Spivey	Junior	1.0911	2003	307	0.980	4.18

Rank	SHORTSTOP		FV	Lyear	G	FPCT	RF
1	Ahmed	Nick	1.5649	2020	646	0.978	4.01
2	Drew	Stephen	1.4529	2012	753	0.978	4.00
3	Womack	Tony	1.2798	2003	487	0.964	3.78

Rank	THIRD BASE		FV	Lyear	G	FPCT	RF
1	Williams	Matt	1.4960	2003	581	0.969	2.56
2	Lamb	Jack	1.3948	2020	506	0.963	2.35
3	Tracy	Chad	1.3307	2009	340	0.940	2.48
4	Reynolds	Mark	1.3090	2010	526	0.937	2.31

Rank	CATCHER		FV	Lyear	G	FPCT	RF	CS%
1	Snyder	Chris	1.9605	2010	537	0.998	7.15	0.304
2	Miller	Damian	1.9406	2002	450	0.993	7.78	0.368
3	Montero	Miguel	1.8003	2014	837	0.991	7.37	0.313
4	Stinnett	Kelly	1.7034	2005	302	0.987	6.33	0.319

Rank	OUTFIELD		FV	Lyear	G	FPCT	RF	ApG
1	Finley	Steve	1.5216	2004	821	0.992	2.28	0.048
2	Young	Chris	1.5174	2012	851	0.989	2.50	0.039
3	Pollack	A.J.	1.4966	2018	595	0.994	2.19	0.052
4	Byrnes	Eric	1.4242	2009	438	0.989	1.97	0.048
5	Gonzalez	Luis	1.4009	2006	1177	0.988	1.77	0.041
6	Green	Shawn	1.3937	2006	276	0.996	1.74	0.018
7	Parra	Gerardo	1.3822	2014	766	0.983	1.98	0.081
8	Peralta	David	1.3174	2020	679	0.987	1.82	0.031
9	Bautista	Danny	1.2920	2004	413	0.984	1.75	0.046
10	Upton	Justin	1.2639	2012	715	0.967	2.06	0.032
11	Dellucci	David	1.2151	2003	361	0.984	1.50	0.019

Rank	PITCHING		FV	Lyear	IP	FPCT	RF
1	Greinke	Zack	1.1389	2019	715	0.991	2.67
2	Haren	Danny	1.0683	2010	586	1.000	1.44
3	Webb	Brandon	1.0664	2009	1320	0.948	2.51
4	Corbin	Josh	1.0454	2018	946	0.980	1.84
5	Anderson	Brian	1.0347	2002	841	0.965	2.62
6	Kennedy	Ian	1.0156	2013	748	0.960	1.46
7	Collmenter	Josh	1.0062	2016	659	1.000	1.75
8	Miley	Wade	0.9971	2014	638	0.955	1.51
9	Schilling	Curt	0.9599	2003	782	0.942	1.13
10	Davis	Doug	0.9689	2009	542	0.935	1.68

Franchise When and Where
Arizona Diamondbacks (1998 to Present)

ATLANTA BRAVES
Best Seasons and Careers of All-Time

Let's start off with the apparent. Who does Hank Aaron want flanking him on the Braves All-Time team? First off, there's Eddie Matthews, Chipper Jones (yes, he might be playing the Outfield), Dale Murphy, and Freddie Freeman. And what power in that outfield, although I'm sure some might think that a better center fielder defensively might be in order. Perhaps Andruw Jones. You make that call. And that starting rotation. You won't have to worry about getting a quality start or going to the bullpen early. There's Greg Maddux, Warren Spahn, and somebody many won't know too much about, Kid Nichols, who only won three hundred and twenty-nine games around the turn of the century, last year 1901 for the Braves, just to name the Top Three. Add in Hall of Fame pitchers on the back end in Glavine and Niekro, and I think Hank might be okay with his pitchers on the mound.

Reserves

Bench - Andruw Jones (OF), Hugh Duffy (OF), Tommy Holmes (OF), Ezra Sutton (IF/OF), Billy Nash (3B), Brian McCann (C), Fred Tenney (1B/OF/C).

Bullpen - John Smoltz (CL), Craig Kimbrel (SU), Lew Burdette, Vic Willis, Tommy Bond, Johnny Sain.

Atlanta Braves - Best Position Player Years

Rank	Name	First	Year	Team	Lg	HR	RBI	AVG	Age	PEVA-B
1	Jones	Charley	1879	BSN	NL	9	62	0.315	29	44.728
2	Aaron	Hank	1959	ML1	NL	39	123	0.355	25	41.920
3	Mathews	Eddie	1953	ML1	NL	47	135	0.302	22	41.677
4	Mathews	Eddie	1960	ML1	NL	39	124	0.277	29	41.382
5	Aaron	Hank	1963	ML1	NL	44	130	0.319	29	40.268
6	Holmes	Tommy	1945	BSN	NL	28	117	0.352	28	40.065
7	Mathews	Eddie	1959	ML1	NL	46	114	0.306	28	38.592
8	Aaron	Hank	1962	ML1	NL	45	128	0.323	28	37.264
9	White	Deacon	1877	BSN	NL	2	49	0.387	30	36.179
10	Duffy	Hugh	1894	BSN	NL	18	145	0.440	28	35.452
11	Freeman	Freddie	2020	ATL	NL	13	53	0.341	31	33.816
12	Aaron	Hank	1960	ML1	NL	40	126	0.292	26	33.522
13	Jones	Chipper	1999	ATL	NL	45	110	0.319	27	32.668
14	Mathews	Eddie	1955	ML1	NL	41	101	0.289	24	32.143
15	Aaron	Hank	1967	ATL	NL	39	109	0.307	33	32.133
16	Murphy	Dale	1983	ATL	NL	36	121	0.302	27	31.161
17	O'Rourke	Jim	1877	BSN	NL	0	23	0.362	27	29.542
18	Murphy	Dale	1987	ATL	NL	44	105	0.295	31	29.525
19	Aaron	Hank	1957	ML1	NL	44	132	0.322	23	29.093
20	Evans	Darrell	1973	ATL	NL	41	104	0.281	26	28.985

Atlanta Braves - Best Pitcher Years

Rank	Name	First	Year	Team	Lg	W	L	SV	IP	ERA	Age	PEVA-P
1	Maddux	Greg	1994	ATL	NL	16	6	0	202.0	1.56	28	57.974
2	Maddux	Greg	1995	ATL	NL	19	2	0	209.7	1.63	29	52.118
3	Maddux	Greg	1993	ATL	NL	20	10	0	267.0	2.36	27	50.920
4	Nichols	Kid	1897	BSN	NL	31	11	3	368.0	2.64	28	47.498
5	Maddux	Greg	1997	ATL	NL	19	4	0	232.7	2.20	31	47.132
6	Maddux	Greg	1998	ATL	NL	18	9	0	251.0	2.22	32	46.792
7	Bond	Tommy	1879	BSN	NL	43	19	0	555.3	1.96	23	41.857
8	Smoltz	John	1996	ATL	NL	24	8	0	253.7	2.94	29	41.196
9	Spahn	Warren	1947	BSN	NL	21	10	3	289.7	2.33	26	39.610
10	Nichols	Kid	1898	BSN	NL	31	12	4	388.0	2.13	29	38.155
11	Willis	Vic	1899	BSN	NL	27	8	2	342.7	2.50	23	37.022
12	Maddux	Greg	2001	ATL	NL	17	11	0	233.0	3.05	35	35.904
13	Maddux	Greg	1996	ATL	NL	15	11	0	245.0	2.72	30	35.136
14	Glavine	Tom	1991	ATL	NL	20	11	0	246.7	2.55	25	35.128
15	Clarkson	John	1889	BSN	NL	49	19	1	620.0	2.73	28	32.959
16	Spahn	Warren	1953	ML1	NL	23	7	3	265.7	2.10	32	32.929
17	Nichols	Kid	1893	BSN	NL	34	14	1	425.0	3.52	24	32.804
18	Bond	Tommy	1877	BSN	NL	40	17	0	521.0	2.11	21	32.408
19	Maddux	Greg	2000	ATL	NL	19	9	0	249.3	3.00	34	32.027
20	Sain	Johnny	1948	BSN	NL	24	15	1	314.7	2.60	31	31.497

Atlanta Braves (ATL, BSN, ML1) - Top Career Batters

RANK	NAME	FIRST	LYR	TEAM	LG	PEVA-B	YRS	PPYR	HR	RBI	H	AVE
1	Aaron	Hank	1974	ATL	NL	529.862	21	25.232	733	2202	3600	0.310
2	Mathews	Eddie	1966	ATL	NL	353.724	15	23.582	493	1388	2201	0.273

RANK	NAME	FIRST	LYR	TEAM	LG	PEVA-B	YRS	PPYR	HR	RBI	H	AVE
3	Jones	Chipper	2012	ATL	NL	277.793	19	14.621	468	1623	2726	0.303
4	Murphy	Dale	1990	ATL	NL	215.974	15	14.398	371	1143	1901	0.268
5	Freeman	Freddie	2020	ATL	NL	179.151	11	16.286	240	858	1524	0.295
6	Jones	Andruw	2007	ATL	NL	160.694	12	13.391	368	1117	1683	0.263
7	Duffy	Hugh	1900	BSN	NL	146.888	9	16.321	69	927	1544	0.332
8	Holmes	Tommy	1951	BSN	NL	127.403	10	12.740	88	580	1503	0.303
9	Long	Herman	1902	BSN	NL	125.822	13	9.679	88	964	1900	0.280
10	Sutton	Ezra	1888	BSN	NL	116.138	12	9.678	20	487	1161	0.287
11	Morrill	John	1888	BSN	NL	116.103	13	8.931	41	625	1247	0.262
12	Berger	Wally	1937	BSN	NL	111.484	8	13.936	199	746	1263	0.304
13	Tenney	Fred	1911	BSN	NL	109.435	15	7.296	17	609	1994	0.300
14	Torre	Joe	1968	ATL	NL	107.109	9	11.901	142	552	1087	0.294
15	Maranville	Rabbit	1935	BSN	NL	103.680	15	6.912	23	558	1696	0.252
16	Nash	Billy	1895	BSN	NL	103.383	10	10.338	51	809	1283	0.281
17	McCann	Brian	2019	ATL	NL	96.768	10	9.677	188	706	1139	0.275
18	Crandall	Del	1963	ML1	NL	93.077	13	7.160	170	628	1176	0.257
19	Logan	Johnny	1961	ML1	NL	92.375	11	8.398	92	521	1329	0.270
20	Adcock	Joe	1962	ML1	NL	91.345	10	9.135	239	760	1206	0.285
21	O'Rourke	Jim	1880	BSN	NL	86.924	4	21.731	9	140	369	0.309
22	Elliott	Bob	1951	BSN	NL	83.856	5	16.771	101	466	763	0.295
23	Lopez	Javy	2003	ATL	NL	83.795	12	6.983	214	694	1148	0.287
24	Lowe	Bobby	1901	BSN	NL	82.739	12	6.895	70	872	1606	0.286
25	Hamilton	Billy	1901	BSN	NL	81.780	6	13.630	14	281	884	0.338
26	Evans	Darrell	1989	ATL	NL	79.105	9	8.789	131	424	712	0.246
27	Collins	Jimmy	1900	BSN	NL	78.307	6	13.051	34	484	821	0.309
28	Carty	Rico	1972	ATL	NL	75.530	8	9.441	109	451	871	0.317
29	Gordon	Sid	1953	ML1	NL	75.292	4	18.823	100	362	582	0.289
30	Hornung	Joe	1888	BSN	NL	73.029	8	9.129	29	341	810	0.263
31	Horner	Bob	1986	ATL	NL	69.934	9	7.770	215	652	994	0.278
32	Alou	Felipe	1969	ATL	NL	68.863	6	11.477	94	335	989	0.295
33	Gant	Ron	1993	ATL	NL	67.509	7	9.644	147	480	836	0.262
34	Justice	David	1996	ATL	NL	66.736	8	8.342	160	522	786	0.275
35	Bruton	Bill	1960	ML1	NL	66.662	8	8.333	48	327	1126	0.276
36	Burdock	Jack	1888	BSN	NL	62.948	11	5.723	14	349	761	0.251
37	Blauser	Jeff	1997	ATL	NL	61.741	11	5.613	109	461	1060	0.268
38	Wise	Sam	1888	BSN	NL	59.181	7	8.454	33	383	755	0.267
39	Torgeson	Earl	1952	BSN	NL	59.012	6	9.835	82	377	657	0.265
40	Markakis	Nick	2019	ATL	NL	58.789	6	9.798	48	388	841	0.283
41	Smith	Red	1919	BSN	NL	58.172	6	9.695	13	314	678	0.278
42	Sweeney	Bill	1913	BSN	NL	56.981	7	8.140	10	350	902	0.280
43	Jones	Charley	1880	BSN	NL	56.466	2	28.233	14	99	196	0.309
44	Garr	Ralph	1975	ATL	NL	55.811	8	6.976	49	247	1022	0.317
45	McGriff	Fred	1997	ATL	NL	54.543	5	10.909	130	446	700	0.293

RANK	NAME	FIRST	LYR	TEAM	LG	PEVA-B	YRS	PPYR	HR	RBI	H	AVE
46	Pendleton	Terry	1996	ATL	NL	52.455	5	10.491	71	322	669	0.287
47	Baker	Dusty	1975	ATL	NL	52.053	8	6.507	77	324	616	0.278
48	Stahl	Chick	1900	BSN	NL	51.376	4	12.844	19	283	675	0.327
49	Furcal	Rafael	2005	ATL	NL	49.942	6	8.324	57	292	924	0.284
50	Heyward	Jason	2014	ATL	NL	48.805	5	9.761	84	292	644	0.262

Atlanta Braves - Top Career Pitchers

RANK	NAME	FIRST	LYEAR	LTEAM	LG	PEVA	YRS	PPYR	W	L	SV	IP	ERA
1	Maddux	Greg	2003	ATL	NL	408.394	11	37.127	194	88	0	2526.7	2.63
2	Spahn	Warren	1964	ML1	NL	367.584	20	18.379	356	229	29	5046.0	3.05
3	Nichols	Kid	1901	BSN	NL	302.820	12	25.235	329	183	16	4538.0	3.00
4	Smoltz	John	2008	ATL	NL	300.465	20	15.023	210	147	154	3395.0	3.26
5	Glavine	Tom	2008	ATL	NL	269.702	17	15.865	244	147	0	3408.0	3.41
6	Niekro	Phil	1987	ATL	NL	242.904	21	11.567	268	230	29	4622.7	3.20
7	Burdette	Lew	1963	ML1	NL	126.672	13	9.744	179	120	23	2638.0	3.53
8	Willis	Vic	1905	BSN	NL	107.648	8	13.456	151	147	5	2575.0	2.82
9	Hudson	Tim	2013	ATL	NL	107.217	9	11.913	113	72	0	1573.0	3.56
10	Bond	Tommy	1881	BSN	NL	102.049	5	20.410	149	87	0	2127.3	2.21
11	Sain	Johnny	1951	BSN	NL	92.311	7	13.187	104	91	11	1624.3	3.49
12	Teheran	Julio	2019	ATL	NL	81.110	9	9.012	77	73	0	1360.0	3.67
13	Clarkson	John	1892	BSN	NL	78.099	5	15.620	149	82	4	2092.7	2.82
14	Avery	Steve	1996	ATL	NL	75.914	7	10.845	72	62	0	1222.3	3.83
15	Rudolph	Dick	1927	BSN	NL	71.596	11	6.509	121	107	6	2035.0	2.62
16	Kimbrel	Craig	2014	ATL	NL	68.760	5	13.752	15	10	186	289.0	1.43
17	Millwood	Kevin	2002	ATL	NL	66.793	6	11.132	75	46	0	1004.3	3.73
18	Whitney	Jim	1885	BSN	NL	66.051	5	13.210	133	121	2	2263.7	2.49
19	Buhl	Bob	1962	ML1	NL	65.199	10	6.520	109	72	5	1599.7	3.27
20	Mahler	Rick	1991	ATL	NL	59.898	11	5.445	79	89	2	1558.7	4.00
21	Brandt	Ed	1935	BSN	NL	56.593	8	7.074	94	119	13	1761.7	4.01
22	MacFayden	Danny	1943	BSN	NL	53.591	6	8.932	60	64	2	1097.0	3.45
23	Garber	Gene	1987	ATL	NL	52.373	10	5.237	53	73	141	856.0	3.34
24	Tobin	Jim	1945	BSN	NL	49.392	6	8.232	72	83	3	1368.0	3.34
25	Stivetts	Jack	1898	BSN	NL	48.632	7	6.947	131	78	2	1798.7	4.12
26	Turner	Jim	1939	BSN	NL	44.638	3	14.879	38	40	1	682.3	3.24
27	Neagle	Denny	1998	ATL	NL	43.037	3	14.346	38	19	0	482.3	3.43
28	Smith	Bob	1937	BSN	NL	42.912	11	3.901	83	120	36	1813.3	4.06
29	Bickford	Vern	1953	ML1	NL	42.780	6	7.130	66	56	2	1072.3	3.69
30	Jurrjens	Jair	2012	ATL	NL	42.237	5	8.447	50	36	0	720.0	3.58
31	Camp	Rick	1985	ATL	NL	40.621	9	4.513	56	49	57	942.3	3.37
32	Cantwell	Ben	1936	BSN	NL	40.062	9	4.451	74	106	20	1464.7	3.87
33	Jarvis	Pat	1972	ATL	NL	38.760	7	5.537	83	72	3	1244.7	3.59
34	Javery	Al	1946	BSN	NL	38.126	7	5.447	53	74	5	1142.7	3.80
35	Fette	Lou	1945	BSN	NL	37.320	5	7.464	41	40	1	688.0	3.17

RANK	NAME	FIRST	LYEAR	LTEAM	LG	PEVA	YRS	PPYR	W	L	SV	IP	ERA
36	Leibrandt	Charlie	1992	ATL	NL	37.316	3	12.439	39	31	0	585.0	3.35
37	Tyler	Lefty	1917	BSN	NL	36.895	8	4.612	92	92	6	1687.7	3.06
38	Bedrosian	Steve	1995	ATL	NL	35.505	8	4.438	40	45	41	696.0	3.26
39	Morton	Carl	1976	ATL	NL	34.952	4	8.738	52	47	0	949.0	3.47
40	Pittinger	Togie	1904	BSN	NL	34.385	5	6.877	75	84	1	1471.7	3.08
41	Cloninger	Tony	1968	ATL	NL	34.279	8	4.285	86	62	5	1215.3	3.94
42	Fried	Max	2020	ATL	NL	34.214	4	8.553	26	11	0	281.3	3.52
43	Medlen	Kris	2013	ATL	NL	33.856	5	6.771	34	20	1	512.7	2.95
44	Wohlers	Mark	1999	ATL	NL	33.815	9	3.757	31	22	112	386.3	3.73
45	Hanson	Tommy	2012	ATL	NL	32.566	4	8.142	45	32	0	635.0	3.61
46	Lewis	Ted	1900	BSN	NL	32.390	5	6.478	78	47	3	1088.7	3.53
47	Reed	Ron	1975	ATL	NL	31.712	10	3.171	80	88	1	1419.7	3.74
48	Foltynewicz	Mike	2020	ATL	NL	30.873	6	5.146	44	41	0	667.3	4.30
49	Vazquez	Javier	2009	ATL	NL	30.398	1	30.398	15	10	0	219.3	2.87
50	Buffinton	Charlie	1886	BSN	NL	30.383	5	6.077	104	70	1	1547.3	2.83

Atlanta Braves – Top Fielders

Rank	FIRST BASE		FV	Lyear	G	FPCT	RF
1	Horner	Bob	1.3286	1986	273	0.995	10.53
2	Chambliss	Chris	1.2615	1986	710	0.994	9.96
3	Adcock	Joe	1.2554	1962	1109	0.994	9.46
4	McGriff	Fred	1.2501	1997	629	0.993	9.36
5	Konetchy	Ed	1.2456	1918	399	0.992	11.10
6	Fletcher	Elbie	1.2046	1949	486	0.991	10.31
7	Freeman	Freddie	1.2046	2020	1380	0.995	8.66
8	Holke	Walter	1.2013	1922	534	0.994	10.85
9	McInnis	Stuffy	1.1892	1924	300	0.992	10.40
10	Cepeda	Orlando	1.1816	1972	386	0.993	9.42

Rank	SECOND BASE		FV	Lyear	G	FPCT	RF
1	Ritchey	Claude	1.3722	1909	289	0.968	5.57
2	Hubbard	Glenn	1.3666	1987	1180	0.983	5.56
3	Millan	Felix	1.3496	1972	776	0.980	5.18
4	Lowe	Bobby	1.3451	1901	1011	0.948	5.72
5	Maguire	Freddie	1.3443	1931	432	0.972	5.75
6	Sweeney	Bill	1.3320	1913	432	0.948	5.64
7	Cuccinello	Tony	1.3307	1943	544	0.971	5.69
8	O'Connell	Danny	1.3255	1957	403	0.982	5.39
9	Albies	Ozzie	1.3093	2020	401	0.989	4.07
10	Maranville	Rabbit	1.2776	1935	323	0.972	5.40

Rank	SHORTSTOP		FV	Lyear	G	FPCT	RF
1	Miller	Eddie	1.7382	1942	524	0.972	5.55
3	Simmons	Andrelton	1.7038	2015	498	0.983	4.56
4	Maranville	Rabbit	1.6880	1931	1466	0.948	5.86
4	McMillan	Roy	1.6662	1964	391	0.975	4.76
5	Logan	Johnny	1.6470	1961	1330	0.966	5.10
6	Bancroft	Dave	1.5843	1927	431	0.950	5.85
7	Escobar	Yunel	1.5711	2010	392	0.976	4.36
8	Long	Herman	1.5613	1902	1606	0.910	5.75
9	Bridwell	Al	1.5217	1912	341	0.938	5.38
10	Warstler	Rabbit	1.5056	1940	408	0.942	5.34

Rank	THIRD BASE		FV	Lyear	G	FPCT	RF
1	Gremminger	Ed	1.7000	1903	280	0.943	3.65
2	Collins	Jimmy	1.6609	1900	658	0.929	3.96
3	Brain	Dave	1.6593	1907	269	0.917	3.88
4	Pendleton	Terry	1.6175	1996	585	0.954	2.87
5	Nash	Billy	1.5912	1895	1126	0.901	3.65

			FV	Lyear	G	FPCT	RF	
6	Whitney	Pinky	1.5409	1936	280	0.966	3.06	
7	Evans	Darrell	1.5378	1989	710	0.945	3.19	
8	Mathews	Eddie	1.5347	1966	2130	0.956	2.94	
9	Boyer	Clete	1.5315	1971	511	0.966	2.99	
10	Oberkfell	Ken	1.5193	1988	531	0.967	2.51	

Rank	CATCHER		FV	Lyear	G	FPCT	RF	CS%
1	Taylor	Zack	1.9575	1929	305	0.983	4.16	0.482
2	Lopez	Al	1.9444	1940	465	0.983	4.11	0.622
3	Crandall	Del	1.9015	1963	1305	0.989	5.43	0.460
4	Bergen	Marty	1.8999	1899	337	0.954	4.87	0.444
5	Bennett	Charlie	1.8736	1893	337	0.956	5.74	0.373
6	Lopez	Javy	1.8681	2003	1106	0.992	7.20	0.284
7	Hogan	Shanty	1.8526	1935	306	0.987	3.83	0.545
8	Moran	Pat	1.8484	1905	356	0.972	6.36	0.446
9	Olson	Greg	1.8463	1993	399	0.992	5.91	0.300
10	Gowdy	Hank	1.8332	1930	731	0.973	4.91	0.526

Rank	OUTFIELD		FV	Lyear	G	FPCT	RF	ApG
1	DiMaggio	Vince	1.6786	1938	279	0.977	2.89	0.143
2	Jones	Andruw	1.6184	2007	1758	0.991	2.62	0.064
3	Grissom	Marquis	1.5993	1996	294	0.996	2.27	0.065
4	Inciarte	Ender	1.5890	2020	550	0.990	2.52	0.055
5	Johnston	Dick	1.5691	1889	529	0.908	2.45	0.233
6	Beaumont	Ginger	1.5622	1909	381	0.965	2.23	0.163
7	Welsh	Jimmy	1.5554	1930	535	0.970	2.79	0.164
8	Holmes	Tommy	1.5469	1951	1225	0.989	2.39	0.093
9	Baker	Dusty	1.5451	1975	598	0.984	2.44	0.067
10	Duffy	Hugh	1.5395	1900	1128	0.953	2.35	0.122
11	Moore	Gene	1.5339	1941	550	0.977	2.29	0.147
12	Berger	Wally	1.5285	1937	1031	0.975	2.80	0.068
13	Hornung	Joe	1.5273	1888	699	0.937	2.03	0.155
14	Murphy	Dale	1.5242	1990	1622	0.983	2.29	0.063
15	Brodie	Steve	1.5202	1891	265	0.952	2.03	0.166
16	Markakis	Nick	1.5115	2020	768	0.994	1.93	0.038
17	Bruton	Bill	1.5109	1960	1042	0.978	2.59	0.080
18	Jordan	Brian	1.5041	2006	493	0.992	2.14	0.067
19	Stahl	Chick	1.4905	1900	519	0.960	1.87	0.152
20	Workman	Chuck	1.4865	1946	288	0.983	2.03	0.135
21	Aaron	Hank	1.4862	1974	2756	0.980	2.08	0.073
22	Jethroe	Sam	1.4760	1952	432	0.971	2.71	0.104
23	Magee	Sherry	1.4645	1917	320	0.975	2.29	0.091
24	Butler	Brett	1.4583	1983	257	0.990	1.97	0.066
25	Powell	Ray	1.4530	1924	825	0.959	2.60	0.150
26	Southworth	Billy	1.4497	1923	333	0.958	2.31	0.162
27	Francoeur	Jeff	1.4420	2016	688	0.981	1.99	0.105
28	James	Dion	1.4405	1989	292	0.993	1.99	0.031
29	Nixon	Otis	1.4247	1999	397	0.989	2.34	0.040
30	Gordon	Sid	1.4219	1953	524	0.987	2.03	0.059

Rank	PITCHING		FV	Lyear	IP	FPCT	RF	
1	Bond	Tommy	1.1490	1881	2127	0.945	2.69	
2	Morton	Carl	1.1215	1976	949	0.975	2.24	
3	Maddux	Greg	1.1064	2003	2527	0.968	3.16	
4	Glavine	Tom	1.0995	2008	3408	0.980	2.30	
5	Andrews	Nate	1.0982	1945	679	0.974	2.48	
6	Burdette	Lew	1.0968	1963	2638	0.971	2.58	
7	Tobin	Jim	1.0886	1945	1368	0.960	3.03	
8	Niekro	Phil	1.0834	1987	4623	0.972	2.17	
9	Rudolph	Dick	1.0825	1927	2032	0.970	3.10	
10	Barnes	Jesse	1.0816	1925	1183	0.983	3.01	

Franchise When and Where
Atlanta Braves (1966 to Present)
Milwaukee Braves (1953-1965)
Boston Braves (1912-1935); (1941-1952)
Boston Bees (1936-1940)
Boston Rustlers (1911); Boston Doves (1907-1910)
Boston Beaneaters (1883-1906); Boston Red Stockings (1876-1882)

BALTIMORE ORIOLES
Best Seasons and Careers of All-Time

There's the Robinsons, of course, Frank and Brooks, plus Cal, just to start and pitchers so stellar they'd even hold down the opposition if they all pitched in Camden Yards. It's another team so powerful, you might have to play with an outfield somewhat on the offensive side, but one could always DH a game or two, and allow a Brady Anderson to roam. Pitching starts with Palmer as the ace and his actual teammates McNally and Cuellar in the All-Time rotation just as they were in their heyday. Boy that was an awesome rotation. Now there might be some disagreement on just who should fill out the back of the bullpen, or whether Paul Blair should be on the team instead of someone else because they need his defensive presence, but there's no doubt that the All-Time team of the Orioles will play out just well against their counterparts. Wouldn't it be interesting to see that.

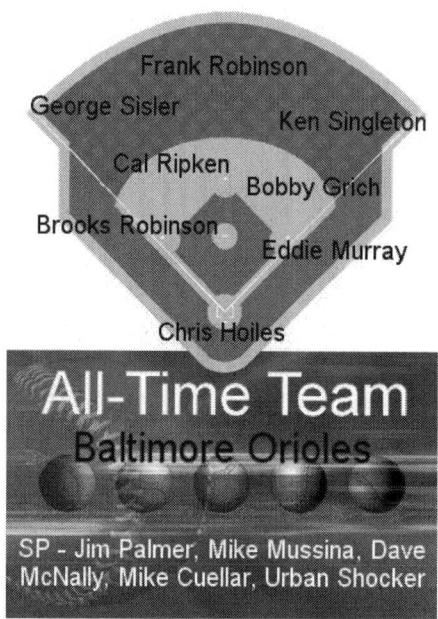

Reserves

Bench - Brady Anderson (OF), Ken Williams (OF), Adam Jones (OF), Harlond Clift (3B), Boog Powell (1B), Bobby Wallace (SS/3B), Hank Severeid (CATCHER).

Bullpen - Gregg Olson (CL), Milt Pappas (SU), Scott McGregor, Mike Flanagan, Mike Boddicker, Hoyt Wilhelm.

Baltimore Orioles - Best Position Player Years

Rank	Name	First	Year	Team	Lg	HR	RBI	AVG	Age	PEVA-B
1	Robinson	Frank	1966	BAL	AL	49	122	0.316	31	42.918
2	Stone	George	1906	SLA	AL	6	71	0.358	30	42.914
3	Murray	Eddie	1984	BAL	AL	29	110	0.306	28	37.406
4	Ripken, Jr.	Cal	1984	BAL	AL	27	86	0.304	24	35.874
5	Ripken, Jr.	Cal	1991	BAL	AL	34	114	0.323	31	35.853
6	Ripken, Jr.	Cal	1983	BAL	AL	27	102	0.318	23	31.713
7	Sisler	George	1920	SLA	AL	19	122	0.407	27	31.637
8	Murray	Eddie	1983	BAL	AL	33	111	0.306	27	28.889
9	Robinson	Brooks	1964	BAL	AL	28	118	0.317	27	28.302
10	Williams	Ken	1922	SLA	AL	39	155	0.332	32	27.478
11	Singleton	Ken	1979	BAL	AL	35	111	0.295	32	26.973
12	Singleton	Ken	1977	BAL	AL	24	99	0.328	30	26.828
13	Murray	Eddie	1982	BAL	AL	32	110	0.316	26	26.525
14	Davis	Chris	2013	BAL	AL	53	138	0.286	27	26.428
15	Clift	Harlond	1938	SLA	AL	34	118	0.290	26	26.044
16	Gentile	Jim	1961	BAL	AL	46	141	0.302	27	25.625
17	Murray	Eddie	1985	BAL	AL	31	124	0.297	29	24.922
18	Anderson	Brady	1996	BAL	AL	50	110	0.297	32	24.626
19	Robinson	Frank	1967	BAL	AL	30	94	0.311	32	24.064
20	Clift	Harlond	1937	SLA	AL	29	118	0.306	25	23.969

Baltimore Orioles - Best Pitcher Years

Rank	Name	First	Year	Team	Lg	W	L	SV	IP	ERA	Age	PEVA-P
1	Palmer	Jim	1975	BAL	AL	23	11	1	323.0	2.09	30	36.388
2	Shocker	Urban	1922	SLA	AL	24	17	3	348.0	2.97	32	36.261
3	Palmer	Jim	1976	BAL	AL	22	13	0	315.0	2.51	31	32.669
4	Cuellar	Mike	1969	BAL	AL	23	11	0	290.7	2.38	32	32.370
5	Boddicker	Mike	1984	BAL	AL	20	11	0	261.3	2.79	27	29.576
6	Palmer	Jim	1970	BAL	AL	20	10	0	305.0	2.71	25	26.828
7	Mussina	Mike	1992	BAL	AL	18	5	0	241.0	2.54	24	25.430
8	Mussina	Mike	1995	BAL	AL	19	9	0	221.7	3.29	27	25.181
9	McNally	Dave	1970	BAL	AL	24	9	0	296.0	3.22	28	23.420
10	Palmer	Jim	1977	BAL	AL	20	11	0	319.0	2.91	32	22.845
11	Cuellar	Mike	1970	BAL	AL	24	8	0	297.7	3.48	33	22.342
12	Flanagan	Mike	1979	BAL	AL	23	9	0	265.7	3.08	28	21.747
13	Mussina	Mike	1994	BAL	AL	16	5	0	176.3	3.06	26	21.206
14	Shocker	Urban	1921	SLA	AL	27	12	4	326.7	3.55	31	20.956
15	Palmer	Jim	1973	BAL	AL	22	9	1	296.3	2.40	28	20.679
16	McNally	Dave	1968	BAL	AL	22	10	0	273.0	1.95	26	20.047
17	O'Dell	Billy	1958	BAL	AL	14	11	8	221.3	2.97	26	19.683
18	Stewart	Lefty	1930	SLA	AL	20	12	0	271.0	3.45	30	19.662
19	Gray	Dolly	1929	SLA	AL	18	15	1	305.0	3.72	32	19.648
20	Potter	Nels	1945	SLA	AL	15	11	0	255.3	2.47	34	19.161

Baltimore Orioles (BAL, MLA, SLA) - Top Career Batters

RANK	NAME	FIRST	LYR	TEAM	LG	PEVA-B	YRS	PPYR	HR	RBI	H	AVE
1	Ripken	Cal	2001	BAL	AL	320.188	21	15.247	431	1695	3184	0.276
2	Murray	Eddie	1996	BAL	AL	239.660	13	18.435	343	1224	2080	0.294

RANK	NAME	FIRST	LYR	TEAM	LG	PEVA-B	YRS	PPYR	HR	RBI	H	AVE
3	Robinson	Brooks	1977	BAL	AL	232.881	23	10.125	268	1357	2848	0.267
4	Sisler	George	1927	SLA	AL	175.399	12	14.617	93	959	2295	0.344
5	Singleton	Ken	1984	BAL	AL	159.850	10	15.985	182	766	1455	0.284
6	Clift	Harlond	1943	SLA	AL	155.325	10	15.532	170	769	1463	0.277
7	Powell	Boog	1974	BAL	AL	151.843	14	10.846	303	1063	1574	0.266
8	Robinson	Frank	1971	BAL	AL	135.352	6	22.559	179	545	882	0.300
9	Anderson	Brady	2001	BAL	AL	131.590	14	9.399	209	744	1614	0.257
10	Jones	Adam	2018	BAL	AL	125.237	11	11.385	263	866	1781	0.279
11	Williams	Ken	1927	SLA	AL	116.736	10	11.674	185	808	1308	0.326
12	Markakis	Nick	2014	BAL	AL	113.144	9	12.572	141	658	1547	0.290
13	Wallace	Bobby	1916	SLA	AL	106.262	15	7.084	8	607	1424	0.258
14	Stone	George	1910	SLA	AL	106.169	6	17.695	23	268	986	0.301
15	Jacobson	Baby Doll	1926	SLA	AL	103.894	10	10.389	76	706	1508	0.317
16	Blair	Paul	1976	BAL	AL	97.931	13	7.533	126	567	1426	0.254
17	Palmeiro	Rafael	2005	BAL	AL	90.214	7	12.888	223	701	1071	0.284
18	Shotton	Burt	1917	SLA	AL	87.173	8	10.897	6	228	1070	0.274
19	Mora	Melvin	2009	BAL	AL	85.180	10	8.518	158	662	1323	0.280
20	Stephens	Vern	1955	BAL	AL	84.426	10	8.443	121	591	1100	0.292
21	Bumbry	Al	1984	BAL	AL	82.275	13	6.329	53	392	1403	0.283
22	Machado	Manny	2018	BAL	AL	80.594	7	11.513	162	471	977	0.283
23	Davis	Chris	2020	BAL	AL	80.309	10	8.031	253	656	941	0.230
24	Tobin	Jack	1925	SLA	AL	79.114	9	8.790	48	438	1399	0.318
25	McQuinn	George	1945	SLA	AL	73.372	8	9.171	108	625	1220	0.283
26	Roberts	Brian	2013	BAL	AL	73.093	13	5.623	92	521	1452	0.278
27	Pratt	Del	1917	SLA	AL	72.533	6	12.089	21	455	957	0.282
28	Tejada	Miguel	2010	BAL	AL	70.571	5	14.114	109	468	876	0.305
29	Grich	Bobby	1976	BAL	AL	70.110	7	10.016	70	307	730	0.262
30	Belanger	Mark	1981	BAL	AL	68.737	17	4.043	20	385	1304	0.227
31	Austin	Jimmy	1929	SLA	AL	67.192	16	4.199	10	315	1133	0.251
32	Hoiles	Chris	1998	BAL	AL	65.945	10	6.595	151	449	739	0.262
33	Gentile	Jim	1963	BAL	AL	65.350	4	16.338	124	398	519	0.272
34	Severeid	Hank	1925	SLA	AL	62.838	11	5.713	17	485	1121	0.290
35	Judnich	Wally	1947	SLA	AL	61.006	5	12.201	88	390	718	0.283
36	Triandos	Gus	1962	BAL	AL	59.758	8	7.470	142	517	794	0.249
37	Buford	Don	1972	BAL	AL	58.505	5	11.701	67	252	632	0.270
38	Surhoff	B.J.	2005	BAL	AL	56.629	8	7.079	120	551	1072	0.291
39	DeCinces	Doug	1981	BAL	AL	55.658	9	6.184	107	397	738	0.253
40	Gerber	Wally	1928	SLA	AL	53.900	12	4.492	7	431	1189	0.264
41	Wieters	Matt	2016	BAL	AL	53.730	8	6.716	117	437	802	0.256
42	West	Sam	1938	SLA	AL	52.826	6	8.804	45	328	819	0.305
43	Laabs	Chet	1946	SLA	AL	51.559	8	6.445	101	428	693	0.266
44	Johnson	Davey	1972	BAL	AL	50.901	8	6.363	66	391	904	0.259
45	McManus	Marty	1926	SLA	AL	50.507	7	7.215	56	509	949	0.298

RANK	NAME	FIRST	LYR	TEAM	LG	PEVA-B	YRS	PPYR	HR	RBI	H	AVE
46	Kress	Red	1939	SLA	AL	50.356	8	6.295	54	513	902	0.299
47	Roenicke	Gary	1985	BAL	AL	49.895	8	6.237	106	352	555	0.250
48	Devereaux	Mike	1996	BAL	AL	49.344	7	7.049	94	403	797	0.251
49	Hardy	J.J.	2017	BAL	AL	49.063	7	7.009	107	385	854	0.252
50	Nieman	Bob	1959	BAL	AL	49.004	6	8.167	82	336	626	0.301

Baltimore Orioles (BAL, MLA, SLA) - Top Career Pitchers

RANK	NAME	FIRST	LYEAR	LTEAM	LG	PEVA	YRS	PPYR	W	L	SV	IP	ERA
1	Palmer	Jim	1984	BAL	AL	240.163	19	12.640	268	152	4	3948.0	2.86
2	Mussina	Mike	2000	BAL	AL	152.295	10	15.230	147	81	0	2009.7	3.53
3	McNally	Dave	1974	BAL	AL	110.675	13	8.513	181	113	2	2652.7	3.18
4	Cuellar	Mike	1976	BAL	AL	109.565	8	13.696	143	88	1	2028.3	3.18
5	Shocker	Urban	1924	SLA	AL	102.739	7	14.677	126	80	20	1749.7	3.19
6	McGregor	Scott	1988	BAL	AL	85.930	13	6.610	138	108	5	2140.7	3.99
7	Flanagan	Mike	1992	BAL	AL	85.686	15	5.712	141	116	4	2317.7	3.89
8	Boddicker	Mike	1988	BAL	AL	68.578	9	7.620	79	73	0	1273.7	3.73
9	Pappas	Milt	1965	BAL	AL	66.639	9	7.404	110	74	4	1632.0	3.24
10	Martinez	Dennis	1986	BAL	AL	60.275	11	5.480	108	93	5	1775.0	4.16
11	Erickson	Scott	2002	BAL	AL	56.698	7	8.100	79	68	0	1287.7	4.73
12	Barber	Steve	1967	BAL	AL	56.276	8	7.034	95	75	4	1414.7	3.12
13	Tillman	Chris	2018	BAL	AL	53.565	10	5.356	74	60	0	1145.0	4.57
14	Wilhelm	Hoyt	1962	BAL	AL	50.330	5	10.066	43	39	40	616.3	2.42
15	Powell	Jack	1912	SLA	AL	48.970	10	4.897	117	143	11	2229.7	2.63
16	Hall	Dick	1971	BAL	AL	47.719	9	5.302	65	40	58	770.0	2.89
17	Gray	Dolly	1933	SLA	AL	46.693	6	7.782	67	82	14	1312.0	4.37
18	Howell	Harry	1910	SLA	AL	45.638	7	6.520	78	91	5	1580.7	2.06
19	Guthrie	Jeremy	2011	BAL	AL	45.137	5	9.027	47	65	0	983.3	4.12
20	McDonald	Ben	1995	BAL	AL	44.919	7	6.417	58	53	0	937.0	3.89
21	Blaeholder	George	1935	SLA	AL	44.049	10	4.405	90	111	12	1631.0	4.55
22	Stewart	Lefty	1932	SLA	AL	43.384	6	7.231	73	74	5	1236.7	4.11
23	Weilman	Carl	1920	SLA	AL	42.770	8	5.346	85	95	10	1521.0	2.67
24	Miller	Stu	1967	BAL	AL	42.468	5	8.494	38	36	100	502.0	2.37
25	Ponson	Sidney	2005	BAL	AL	42.450	8	5.306	73	85	1	1375.3	4.86
26	Vangilder	Elam	1927	SLA	AL	42.351	9	4.706	88	91	14	1548.0	4.30
27	Britton	Zach	2018	BAL	AL	41.718	7	5.960	26	21	103	451.0	3.41
28	Bedard	Erik	2007	BAL	AL	41.667	5	8.333	40	34	0	658.0	3.83
29	Johnson	Jim	2013	BAL	AL	40.887	8	5.111	18	26	122	400.0	3.11
30	Olson	Gregg	1993	BAL	AL	40.040	6	6.673	17	21	160	350.3	2.26
31	Garver	Ned	1952	SLA	AL	40.029	5	8.006	59	68	8	1076.3	3.64
32	Potter	Nels	1948	SLA	AL	39.296	6	6.549	57	43	3	933.7	3.05
33	Kramer	Jack	1947	SLA	AL	38.600	8	4.825	67	81	5	1188.7	4.13
34	O'Day	Darren	2018	BAL	AL	36.993	7	5.285	28	14	19	374.3	2.40
35	Lopez	Rodrigo	2006	BAL	AL	35.914	5	7.183	60	58	0	912.7	4.72

RANK	NAME	FIRST	LYEAR	LTEAM	LG	PEVA	YRS	PPYR	W	L	SV	IP	ERA
36	Pelty	Barney	1912	SLA	AL	35.902	10	3.590	91	113	4	1864.3	2.62
37	Martinez	Tippy	1986	BAL	AL	35.821	11	3.256	52	40	105	752.3	3.46
38	O'Dell	Billy	1959	BAL	AL	35.285	5	7.057	29	34	13	585.3	2.86
39	Chen	Wei-Yin	2015	BAL	AL	34.222	4	8.556	46	32	0	706.7	3.72
40	Watt	Eddie	1973	BAL	AL	33.550	8	4.194	37	34	74	615.3	2.74
41	Davis	Storm	1992	BAL	AL	32.331	6	5.389	61	43	5	944.3	3.63
42	Sothoron	Allen	1921	SLA	AL	31.771	7	4.539	55	62	9	1011.3	2.98
43	Muncrief	Bob	1947	SLA	AL	31.395	9	3.488	69	67	4	1215.3	3.66
44	Brown	Hal	1962	BAL	AL	31.328	8	3.916	62	48	9	1030.7	3.61
45	Crowder	Alvin	1930	SLA	AL	31.086	4	7.771	44	32	10	661.7	4.04
46	Gausman	Kevin	2018	BAL	AL	29.450	6	4.908	39	51	0	763.7	4.22
47	Roberts	Robin	1965	BAL	AL	27.747	4	6.937	42	36	0	761.3	3.09
48	Newsom	Bobo	1943	SLA	AL	27.335	5	5.467	40	49	7	732.7	4.83
49	Grimsley	Ross	1982	BAL	AL	26.473	5	5.295	51	45	1	907.7	3.78
50	Davis	Dixie	1926	SLA	AL	26.437	7	3.777	75	68	2	1242.0	4.04

Baltimore Orioles – Top Fielders

Rank	FIRST BASE		FV	Lyear	G	FPCT	RF
1	Anderson	John	1.2941	1903	384	0.984	11.17
2	Murray	Eddie	1.2822	1988	1602	0.993	9.78
3	Palmeiro	Rafael	1.2567	2005	949	0.995	9.26
4	Jones	Tom	1.2048	1909	817	0.986	11.32
5	Gentile	Jim	1.1620	1963	561	0.991	8.69
6	May	Lee	1.1586	1980	361	0.994	9.09
7	Blue	Lu	1.1567	1930	416	0.990	10.42
8	Burns	Jack	1.1331	1936	741	0.992	9.76
9	McQuinn	George	1.1291	1945	1125	0.993	9.69
10	Powell	Boog	1.1157	1974	1265	0.991	8.81

Rank	SECOND BASE		FV	Lyear	G	FPCT	RF
1	Grich	Bobby	1.4554	1976	668	0.984	5.77
2	Melillo	Ski	1.4131	1935	1099	0.973	6.08
3	Alomar	Roberto	1.3739	1998	394	0.986	4.89
4	Adair	Jerry	1.3422	1966	582	0.986	5.00
5	Pratt	Del	1.3414	1917	855	0.955	5.42
6	Johnson	Davey	1.3407	1972	947	0.983	5.01
7	Gedeon	Joe	1.3368	1920	394	0.972	5.43
8	Gardner	Billy	1.3187	1959	570	0.981	4.99
9	Priddy	Jerry	1.3153	1949	291	0.968	5.84
10	Williams	Jimmy	1.2906	1909	257	0.962	5.05

Rank	SHORTSTOP		FV	Lyear	G	FPCT	RF
1	Ripken Jr.	Cal	1.6822	1997	2302	0.979	4.62
2	Aparicio	Luis	1.6523	1967	713	0.974	4.70
3	Bordick	Mike	1.6446	2002	737	0.987	4.55
4	Lary	Lyn	1.6325	1940	260	0.959	5.60
5	Wallace	Bobby	1.6290	1916	1452	0.942	5.59
6	Izturis	Cesar	1.6187	2011	274	0.985	4.20
7	Belanger	Mark	1.6115	1981	1898	0.977	4.59
8	Hardy	J.J.	1.6066	2017	887	0.987	4.28
9	Hunter	Billy	1.5817	1954	276	0.960	4.99
10	Tejada	Miguel	1.5552	2007	596	0.971	4.51

Rank	THIRD BASE		FV	Lyear	G	FPCT	RF
1	Robinson	Brooks	1.6397	1977	2870	0.971	3.10
2	Machado	Manny	1.5900	2017	715	0.968	2.86
3	Clift	Harlond	1.5793	1943	1419	0.949	3.28
4	Ferris	Hobe	1.5782	1909	262	0.946	3.58
5	Mora	Melvin	1.5299	2009	807	0.961	2.75

			FV	Lyear	G	FPCT	RF	
6	Christman	Mark	1.5262	1946	336	0.975	3.13	
7	DeCinces	Doug	1.5214	1981	792	0.957	2.96	
8	Austin	Jimmy	1.5060	1929	1187	0.933	3.45	
9	Ripken Jr.	Cal	1.4725	2001	675	0.961	2.52	
10	Worthington	Craig	1.4654	1991	332	0.952	2.55	

Rank	CATCHER		FV	Lyear	G	FPCT	RF	CS%
1	Severeid	Hank	1.8774	1925	1090	0.979	4.82	0.439
2	Triandos	Gus	1.8716	1962	784	0.987	5.50	0.496
3	Dempsey	Rick	1.8662	1992	1230	0.989	5.06	0.402
4	Courtney	Clint	1.8594	1961	401	0.988	4.94	0.477
5	Hoiles	Chris	1.8456	1998	819	0.994	6.29	0.266
6	Ferrell	Rick	1.8325	1943	658	0.983	4.45	0.446
7	Wieters	Matt	1.8228	2016	812	0.992	7.32	0.327
8	Sugden	Joe	1.8174	1905	282	0.980	5.83	0.453
9	Schang	Wally	1.7847	1929	324	0.979	3.76	0.463
10	Etchebarren	Andy	1.7699	1975	714	0.989	5.81	0.408

Rank	OUTFIELD		FV	Lyear	G	FPCT	RF	ApG
1	West	Sam	1.6125	1938	676	0.984	2.93	0.092
2	Judnich	Wally	1.5962	1947	547	0.989	2.82	0.053
3	Blair	Paul	1.5842	1976	1654	0.988	2.48	0.063
4	Markakis	Nick	1.5486	2014	1360	0.994	2.04	0.068
5	Jones	Adam	1.5406	2018	1591	0.987	2.55	0.058
6	Walker	Tilly	1.5336	1915	307	0.953	2.42	0.202
7	Jacobson	Baby Doll	1.5278	1926	1189	0.973	2.69	0.084
8	Schulte	Fred	1.5038	1932	669	0.973	2.84	0.094
9	Solters	Moose	1.5021	1939	304	0.968	2.60	0.118
10	Byrnes	Milt	1.4979	1945	361	0.987	2.55	0.089
11	Heidrick	Emmet	1.4954	1908	383	0.953	2.37	0.151
12	Orsulak	Joe	1.4927	1992	577	0.987	2.25	0.090
13	Rice	Harry	1.4898	1927	350	0.961	2.33	0.177
14	Manush	Heinie	1.4874	1930	343	0.990	2.23	0.064
15	Devereaux	Mike	1.4857	1996	861	0.988	2.46	0.044
16	Diering	Chuck	1.4813	1956	266	0.982	2.53	0.102
17	Bumbry	Al	1.4808	1984	1224	0.986	2.46	0.056
18	Brandt	Jackie	1.4783	1965	768	0.978	2.21	0.070
19	Surhoff	B.J.	1.4649	2005	728	0.991	1.91	0.070
20	Belle	Albert	1.4624	2000	264	0.986	1.85	0.095
21	Anderson	Brady	1.4586	2001	1632	0.989	2.22	0.034
22	Shotton	Burt	1.4557	1917	1025	0.942	2.40	0.134
23	Lynn	Fred	1.4401	1988	414	0.990	2.45	0.027
24	Patterson	Corey	1.4395	2010	333	0.985	2.35	0.057
25	Buford	Don	1.4374	1972	543	0.988	1.85	0.066
26	Matos	Luis	1.4373	2006	491	0.989	2.36	0.041
27	Williams	Ken	1.4356	1927	1060	0.957	2.48	0.133
28	Bigbie	Larry	1.4318	2005	344	0.996	1.93	0.038
29	Bell	Beau	1.4255	1939	451	0.974	2.02	0.104
30	Singleton	Ken	1.4224	1982	950	0.985	1.85	0.042

Rank	PITCHING		FV	Lyear	IP	FPCT	RF	
1	Howell	Harry	1.1162	1910	1581	0.963	4.64	
2	Auker	Elden	1.0860	1942	729	0.972	2.53	
3	Sudhoff	Willie	1.0710	1905	980	0.954	4.04	
4	Martinez	Dennis	1.0646	1986	1775	0.972	2.44	
5	Erickson	Scott	1.0639	2002	1288	0.948	2.53	
6	Mussina	Mike	1.0619	2000	2010	0.986	1.85	
7	Boddicker	Mike	1.0578	1988	1274	0.947	2.76	
8	Palmer	Jim	1.0492	1984	3948	0.962	1.98	
9	Shocker	Urban	1.0483	1924	1750	0.980	2.51	
10	Stewart	Lefty	1.0462	1932	1237	0.979	2.34	

Franchise When and Where
Baltimore Orioles (1954 to Present)
St. Louis Browns (1902-1953)
Milwaukee Brewers (1901)

BOSTON RED SOX
Best Seasons and Careers of All-Time

It's Roger Clemens, Pedro Martinez, and Cy Young to start off any series, and a lineup so awesome, trying to pick out the order is a treat. We'd probably lead off with Speaker, follow him with Garciaparra, then go Yaz, Ted, and Big Poppy. Of course, you could push the Designated Hitter you chose from among Jim Rice or Jimmy Foxx ahead of one or the other. Now that's a dilemma any manager would love to have. Now, the back end of the rotation on some other teams might be better, the former Boston now Atlanta Braves does have five Hall of Famers, but boy would this team mash up the Green Monster of Fenway, or over it so many times, it might not even matter. And it's pretty good if you have Lefty Grove in the bullpen and want to start him in the rotation instead. That might be a really good alternative plan.

Reserves

Bench - Dwight Evans (OF), Jim Rice (OF), Harry Hooper (OF), Jimmie Foxx (1B/3B/C/OF), Joe Cronin (SS), Dustin Pedroia (2B), Jason Varitek (CATCHER).

Bullpen - Jonathan Papelbon (CL), Luis Tiant (SU), Josh Beckett, Lefty Grove, Joe Wood, Tex Hughson.

Boston Red Sox - Best Position Player Years

Rank	Name	First	Year	Team	Lg	HR	RBI	AVG	Age	PEVA-B
1	Williams	Ted	1942	BOS	AL	36	137	0.356	24	52.075
2	Williams	Ted	1941	BOS	AL	37	120	0.406	23	51.730
3	Ruth	Babe	1919	BOS	AL	29	114	0.322	24	45.484
4	Williams	Ted	1946	BOS	AL	38	123	0.342	28	44.043
5	Speaker	Tris	1912	BOS	AL	10	90	0.383	24	43.198
6	Williams	Ted	1949	BOS	AL	43	159	0.343	31	41.778
7	Yastrzemski	Carl	1967	BOS	AL	44	121	0.326	28	40.383
8	Foxx	Jimmie	1938	BOS	AL	50	175	0.349	31	37.579
9	Speaker	Tris	1914	BOS	AL	4	90	0.338	26	37.327
10	Williams	Ted	1947	BOS	AL	32	114	0.343	29	36.436
11	Evans	Dwight	1984	BOS	AL	32	104	0.295	33	35.847
12	Johnson	Bob	1944	BOS	AL	17	106	0.324	39	34.713
13	Boggs	Wade	1987	BOS	AL	24	89	0.363	29	34.592
14	Lynn	Fred	1979	BOS	AL	39	122	0.333	27	33.455
15	Williams	Ted	1957	BOS	AL	38	87	0.388	39	32.674
16	Evans	Dwight	1982	BOS	AL	32	98	0.292	31	31.949
17	Boggs	Wade	1988	BOS	AL	5	58	0.366	30	31.802
18	Yastrzemski	Carl	1968	BOS	AL	23	74	0.301	29	31.561
19	Yastrzemski	Carl	1970	BOS	AL	40	102	0.329	31	30.942
20	Williams	Ted	1951	BOS	AL	30	126	0.318	33	30.939

Boston Red Sox - Best Pitcher Years

Rank	Name	First	Year	Team	Lg	W	L	SV	IP	ERA	Age	PEVA-P
1	Young	Cy	1901	BOS	AL	33	10	0	371.3	1.62	34	48.628
2	Martinez	Pedro	1999	BOS	AL	23	4	0	213.3	2.07	28	45.790
3	Clemens	Roger	1987	BOS	AL	20	9	0	281.7	2.97	25	43.210
4	Clemens	Roger	1991	BOS	AL	18	10	0	271.3	2.62	29	43.004
5	Clemens	Roger	1990	BOS	AL	21	6	0	228.3	1.93	28	41.426
6	Porcello	Rick	2016	BOS	AL	22	4	0	223.0	3.15	28	40.336
7	Martinez	Pedro	2000	BOS	AL	18	6	0	217.0	1.74	29	40.251
8	Sale	Chris	2017	BOS	AL	17	8	0	214.3	2.90	28	39.592
9	Wood	Joe	1912	BOS	AL	34	5	1	344.0	1.91	23	38.082
10	Martinez	Pedro	2002	BOS	AL	20	4	0	199.3	2.26	31	37.759
11	Clemens	Roger	1986	BOS	AL	24	4	0	254.0	2.48	24	35.030
12	Clemens	Roger	1992	BOS	AL	18	11	0	246.7	2.41	30	34.707
13	Schilling	Curt	2004	BOS	AL	21	6	0	226.7	3.26	38	31.192
14	Lowe	Derek	2002	BOS	AL	21	8	0	219.7	2.58	29	31.179
15	Beckett	Josh	2007	BOS	AL	20	7	0	200.7	3.27	27	30.976
16	Clemens	Roger	1988	BOS	AL	18	12	0	264.0	2.93	26	28.435
17	Young	Cy	1902	BOS	AL	32	11	0	384.7	2.15	35	28.273
18	Sullivan	Frank	1957	BOS	AL	14	11	0	240.7	2.73	27	28.105
19	Wood	Joe	1911	BOS	AL	23	17	3	275.7	2.02	22	28.038
20	Parnell	Mel	1949	BOS	AL	25	7	2	295.3	2.77	27	27.333

Boston Red Sox - Top Career Batters

RANK	NAME	FIRST	LYR	TEAM	LG	PEVA-B	YRS	PPYR	HR	RBI	H	AVE
1	Williams	Ted	1960	BOS	AL	493.074	19	25.951	521	1839	2654	0.344
2	Yastrzemski	Carl	1983	BOS	AL	339.140	23	14.745	452	1844	3419	0.285

RANK	NAME	FIRST	LYR	TEAM	LG	PEVA-B	YRS	PPYR	HR	RBI	H	AVE
3	Evans	Dwight	1990	BOS	AL	260.131	19	13.691	379	1346	2373	0.272
4	Boggs	Wade	1992	BOS	AL	238.122	11	21.647	85	687	2098	0.338
5	Ortiz	David	2016	BOS	AL	232.357	14	16.597	483	1530	2079	0.290
6	Rice	Jim	1989	BOS	AL	224.084	16	14.005	382	1451	2452	0.298
7	Speaker	Tris	1915	BOS	AL	200.107	9	22.234	39	542	1327	0.337
8	Doerr	Bobby	1951	BOS	AL	157.073	14	11.219	223	1247	2042	0.288
9	Hooper	Harry	1920	BOS	AL	142.344	12	11.862	30	497	1707	0.272
10	Foxx	Jimmie	1942	BOS	AL	140.084	7	20.012	222	788	1051	0.320
11	Ramirez	Manny	2008	BOS	AL	139.989	8	17.499	274	868	1232	0.312
12	DiMaggio	Dom	1953	BOS	AL	127.048	11	11.550	87	618	1680	0.298
13	Vaughn	Mo	1998	BOS	AL	106.452	8	13.306	230	752	1165	0.304
14	Petrocelli	Rico	1976	BOS	AL	106.231	13	8.172	210	773	1352	0.251
15	Garciaparra	Nomar	2004	BOS	AL	106.002	9	11.778	178	690	1281	0.323
16	Lynn	Fred	1980	BOS	AL	103.569	7	14.796	124	521	944	0.308
17	Betts	Mookie	2019	BOS	AL	103.330	6	17.222	139	470	965	0.301
18	Cronin	Joe	1945	BOS	AL	102.213	11	9.292	119	737	1168	0.300
19	Pedroia	Dustin	2019	BOS	AL	102.046	14	7.289	140	725	1805	0.299
20	Greenwell	Mike	1996	BOS	AL	100.166	12	8.347	130	726	1400	0.303
21	Jensen	Jackie	1961	BOS	AL	100.047	7	14.292	170	733	1089	0.282
22	Fisk	Carlton	1980	BOS	AL	98.875	11	8.989	162	568	1097	0.284
23	Smith	Reggie	1973	BOS	AL	96.164	8	12.020	149	536	1064	0.281
24	Pesky	Johnny	1952	BOS	AL	93.667	8	11.708	13	361	1277	0.313
25	Malzone	Frank	1965	BOS	AL	92.281	11	8.389	131	716	1454	0.276
26	Lewis	Duffy	1917	BOS	AL	91.930	8	11.491	27	629	1248	0.289
27	Bogaerts	Xander	2020	BOS	AL	85.738	8	10.717	118	531	1083	0.289
28	Varitek	Jason	2011	BOS	AL	85.704	15	5.714	193	757	1307	0.256
29	Freeman	Buck	1907	BOS	AL	78.925	7	11.275	48	504	879	0.286
30	Parent	Freddy	1907	BOS	AL	77.084	7	11.012	19	386	1051	0.273
31	Gardner	Larry	1917	BOS	AL	75.819	10	7.582	16	481	1106	0.282
32	Collins	Jimmy	1907	BOS	AL	75.758	7	10.823	25	385	881	0.296
33	Ruth	Babe	1919	BOS	AL	73.928	6	12.321	49	230	342	0.308
34	Stahl	Chick	1906	BOS	AL	72.930	6	12.155	17	339	871	0.290
35	Stephens	Vern	1952	BOS	AL	72.572	5	14.514	122	562	721	0.283
36	Valentin	John	2001	BOS	AL	72.429	10	7.243	121	528	1043	0.281
37	Youkilis	Kevin	2010	BOS	AL	60.677	7	8.668	112	470	816	0.294
38	Goodman	Billy	1957	BOS	AL	60.352	11	5.487	14	464	1344	0.306
39	Conigliaro	Tony	1975	BOS	AL	59.890	7	8.556	162	501	790	0.267
40	Scott	George	1979	BOS	AL	59.681	9	6.631	154	562	1088	0.257
41	Ellsbury	Jacoby	2013	BOS	AL	59.639	7	8.520	65	314	865	0.297
142	Burleson	Rick	1980	BOS	AL	58.805	7	8.401	38	360	1114	0.274
43	Runnels	Pete	1962	BOS	AL	55.924	5	11.185	29	249	825	0.320
44	Piersall	Jim	1958	BOS	AL	55.848	8	6.981	66	366	919	0.273
45	Burks	Ellis	2004	BOS	AL	55.304	7	7.901	94	388	791	0.280

RANK	NAME	FIRST	LYR	TEAM	LG	PEVA-B	YRS	PPYR	HR	RBI	H	AVE
46	Scott	Everett	1921	BOS	AL	54.813	8	6.852	7	346	956	0.246
47	Nixon	Trot	2006	BOS	AL	54.795	10	5.480	133	523	912	0.278
48	Damon	Johnny	2005	BOS	AL	50.929	4	12.732	56	299	730	0.295
49	O'Leary	Troy	2001	BOS	AL	50.824	7	7.261	117	516	954	0.276
50	Flagstead	Ira	1929	BOS	AL	50.346	7	7.192	27	299	867	0.295

Boston Red Sox - Top Career Pitchers

RANK	NAME	FIRST	LYEAR	LTEAM	LG	PEVA	YRS	PPYR	W	L	SV	IP	ERA
1	Clemens	Roger	1996	BOS	AL	287.594	13	22.123	192	111	0	2776.0	3.06
2	Martinez	Pedro	2004	BOS	AL	205.515	7	29.359	117	37	0	1383.7	2.52
3	Young	Cy	1908	BOS	AL	191.940	8	23.992	192	112	9	2728.3	2.00
4	Wakefield	Tim	2011	BOS	AL	116.699	17	6.865	186	168	22	3006.0	4.43
5	Lester	Jon	2014	BOS	AL	102.515	9	11.391	110	63	0	1519.3	3.64
6	Beckett	Josh	2012	BOS	AL	92.654	7	13.236	89	58	0	1240.0	4.17
7	Grove	Lefty	1941	BOS	AL	91.139	8	11.392	105	62	4	1539.7	3.34
8	Tiant	Luis	1978	BOS	AL	89.502	8	11.188	122	81	3	1774.7	3.36
9	Parnell	Mel	1956	BOS	AL	89.418	10	8.942	123	75	10	1752.7	3.50
10	Wood	Joe	1915	BOS	AL	89.336	8	11.167	117	56	9	1418.0	1.99
11	Hughson	Tex	1949	BOS	AL	88.733	8	11.092	96	54	17	1375.7	2.94
12	Sullivan	Frank	1960	BOS	AL	84.612	8	10.576	90	80	6	1505.3	3.47
13	Lowe	Derek	2004	BOS	AL	79.777	8	9.972	70	55	85	1037.0	3.72
14	Papelbon	Jonathan	2011	BOS	AL	78.095	7	11.156	23	19	219	429.3	2.33
15	Kinder	Ellis	1955	BOS	AL	76.624	8	9.578	86	52	91	1142.3	3.28
16	Porcello	Rick	2019	BOS	AL	76.272	5	15.254	73	55	0	964.0	4.43
17	Sale	Chris	2019	BOS	AL	73.354	3	24.451	35	23	0	519.7	3.08
18	Eckersley	Dennis	1998	BOS	AL	61.819	8	7.727	88	71	1	1371.7	3.92
19	Dobson	Joe	1954	BOS	AL	58.959	9	6.551	106	72	9	1544.0	3.57
20	Schilling	Curt	2007	BOS	AL	55.818	4	13.955	53	29	9	675.0	3.95
21	Stanley	Bob	1989	BOS	AL	54.531	13	4.195	115	97	132	1707.0	3.64
22	Monbouquette	Bill	1965	BOS	AL	54.268	8	6.784	96	91	1	1622.0	3.69
23	Radatz	Dick	1966	BOS	AL	52.827	5	10.565	49	34	104	557.3	2.65
24	Buchholz	Clay	2016	BOS	AL	52.172	10	5.217	81	61	0	1167.7	3.96
25	Mays	Carl	1919	BOS	AL	51.610	5	10.322	72	51	12	1105.0	2.21
26	Leonard	Dutch	1918	BOS	AL	50.447	6	8.408	90	64	11	1361.3	2.13
27	Brewer	Tom	1961	BOS	AL	50.152	8	6.269	91	82	3	1509.3	4.00
28	Ruth	Babe	1919	BOS	AL	50.038	6	8.340	89	46	4	1190.3	2.19
29	Ferrell	Wes	1937	BOS	AL	46.871	4	11.718	62	40	1	877.7	4.11
30	Hurst	Bruce	1988	BOS	AL	45.809	9	5.090	88	73	0	1459.0	4.23
31	Collins	Ray	1915	BOS	AL	44.553	7	6.365	84	62	4	1336.0	2.51
32	Lee	Bill	1978	BOS	AL	41.741	10	4.174	94	68	13	1503.3	3.64
33	Ehmke	Howard	1926	BOS	AL	40.775	4	10.194	51	64	8	989.7	3.83
34	Dineen	Bill	1907	BOS	AL	40.214	6	6.702	85	85	3	1501.0	2.81
35	Price	David	2019	BOS	AL	38.536	4	9.634	46	24	0	588.0	3.84

RANK	NAME	FIRST	LYEAR	LTEAM	LG	PEVA	YRS	PPYR	W	L	SV	IP	ERA
36	Jones	Sam	1921	BOS	AL	37.347	6	6.225	64	59	4	1045.0	3.39
37	Culp	Ray	1973	BOS	AL	37.100	6	6.183	71	58	0	1092.3	3.50
38	Kimbrel	Craig	2018	BOS	AL	36.249	3	12.083	12	7	108	184.3	2.44
39	Ferriss	Dave	1950	BOS	AL	36.113	6	6.019	65	30	8	880.0	3.64
40	Uehara	Koji	2016	BOS	AL	34.861	4	8.715	14	13	79	226.0	2.19
41	Matsuzaka	Daisuke	2012	BOS	AL	32.041	6	5.340	50	37	0	668.3	4.52
42	Quinn	Jack	1925	BOS	AL	31.799	4	7.950	45	54	14	832.7	3.65
43	Lonborg	Jim	1971	BOS	AL	31.678	7	4.525	68	65	2	1099.0	3.94
44	Rodriguez	Eduardo	2019	BOS	AL	31.545	3	10.515	38	18	0	470.3	3.92
45	MacFayden	Danny	1932	BOS	AL	30.601	7	4.372	52	78	4	1167.0	4.23
46	Nixon	Willard	1958	BOS	AL	29.659	9	3.295	69	72	3	1234.0	4.39
47	Lackey	John	2014	BOS	AL	29.260	4	7.315	47	43	0	701.7	4.46
48	Darwin	Danny	1994	BOS	AL	28.969	4	7.242	34	31	3	534.3	4.14
49	Torrez	Mike	1982	BOS	AL	28.771	5	5.754	60	54	0	1012.7	4.51
50	Burgmeier	Tom	1982	BOS	AL	28.731	5	5.746	21	12	40	411.0	2.72

Boston Red Sox – Top Fielders

Rank	FIRST BASE		FV	Lyear	G	FPCT	RF
1	LaChance	Candy	1.3469	1905	448	0.987	11.23
2	McInnis	Stuffy	1.3417	1921	512	0.996	11.29
3	Todt	Phil	1.2630	1930	852	0.992	10.90
4	Goodman	Billy	1.1610	1955	392	0.991	9.53
5	Runnels	Pete	1.1498	1962	407	0.995	7.64
6	Scott	George	1.1443	1979	988	0.989	9.26
7	Lupien	Tony	1.1416	1943	282	0.993	9.94
8	Stapleton	Dave	1.1403	1986	318	0.993	8.79
9	Burns	George	1.1366	1923	286	0.988	10.78
10	Buckner	Bill	1.1345	1990	502	0.990	9.18

Rank	SECOND BASE		FV	Lyear	G	FPCT	RF
1	Doerr	Bobby	1.4133	1951	1852	0.980	5.74
2	Ferris	Hobe	1.3874	1907	985	0.954	5.56
3	Runnels	Pete	1.3343	1961	343	0.985	5.20
4	Barrett	Marty	1.3307	1990	906	0.986	4.91
5	Reed	Jody	1.3139	1992	496	0.984	5.12
6	Schilling	Chuck	1.3070	1965	502	0.985	4.95
7	Pedroia	Dustin	1.2973	2019	1492	0.991	4.41
8	Andrews	Mike	1.2608	1970	551	0.975	4.91
9	Remy	Jerry	1.2605	1984	685	0.982	4.90
10	Wambsganss	Bill	1.2588	1925	259	0.961	5.93

Rank	SHORTSTOP		FV	Lyear	G	FPCT	RF
1	Scott	Everett	1.6461	1921	1093	0.966	5.22
2	Burleson	Rick	1.6415	1980	1004	0.970	5.05
3	Stephens	Vern	1.6398	1952	511	0.971	4.91
4	Pesky	Johnny	1.6108	1952	549	0.965	5.11
5	Petrocelli	Rico	1.5735	1976	774	0.969	4.61
6	Valentin	John	1.5715	2001	556	0.972	4.59
7	Wagner	Heinie	1.5702	1916	805	0.929	5.60
8	Bressoud	Eddie	1.5241	1965	534	0.966	4.47
9	Cronin	Joe	1.5060	1942	897	0.953	4.97
10	Buddin	Don	1.5060	1961	632	0.953	4.79

Rank	THIRD BASE		FV	Lyear	G	FPCT	RF
1	Pesky	Johnny	1.5851	1952	457	0.963	3.28
2	Collins	Jimmy	1.5806	1906	735	0.932	3.46
3	Boggs	Wade	1.5702	1992	1520	0.959	2.71
4	Malzone	Frank	1.5652	1965	1335	0.956	3.07
5	Lowell	Mike	1.5562	2010	528	0.972	2.63

			FV	Lyear	G	FPCT	RF	
6	Vitt	Ossie	1.5184	1921	268	0.972	3.31	
7	Petrocelli	Rico	1.5083	1976	727	0.970	2.80	
8	Valentin	John	1.4860	2001	353	0.957	2.61	
9	Gardner	Larry	1.4782	1917	929	0.940	3.05	
10	Cooper	Scott	1.4477	1994	318	0.944	2.46	

Rank	CATCHER		FV	Lyear	G	FPCT	RF	CS%
1	Pena	Tony	2.0255	1993	539	0.994	6.41	0.332
2	Criger	Lou	1.9656	1908	613	0.975	6.12	0.503
3	Ferrell	Rick	1.9297	1937	514	0.987	4.85	0.444
4	Leon	Sandy	1.9078	2019	347	0.996	8.84	0.339
5	Vazquez	Christian	1.8986	2020	441	0.995	8.59	0.391
6	Desautels	Gene	1.8976	1940	345	0.991	4.99	0.424
7	Varitek	Jason	1.8536	2011	1488	0.994	7.20	0.231
8	White	Sammy	1.8495	1959	967	0.985	5.11	0.478
9	Gedman	Rich	1.8233	1990	857	0.984	5.90	0.350
10	Fisk	Carlton	1.8090	1980	990	0.983	5.65	0.356

Rank	OUTFIELD		FV	Lyear	G	FPCT	RF	ApG
1	Speaker	Tris	1.6594	1915	1053	0.962	2.63	0.197
2	Oliver	Tom	1.6097	1933	504	0.986	2.92	0.089
3	DiMaggio	Dom	1.5997	1952	1373	0.978	2.92	0.107
4	Lynn	Fred	1.5995	1980	811	0.987	2.81	0.080
5	Cramer	Doc	1.5943	1940	719	0.977	2.76	0.097
6	Flagstead	Ira	1.5811	1929	765	0.976	2.74	0.150
7	Betts	Mookie	1.5773	2019	774	0.992	2.32	0.065
8	Piersall	Jim	1.5719	1958	879	0.989	2.62	0.074
9	Damon	Johnny	1.5603	2005	590	0.991	2.51	0.041
10	Ellsbury	Jacoby	1.5472	2013	732	0.995	2.36	0.026
11	Crisp	Coco	1.5442	2008	361	0.996	2.50	0.039
12	Bradley, Jr.	Jackie	1.5396	2020	876	0.990	2.28	0.067
13	Geiger	Gary	1.5218	1965	542	0.988	2.25	0.083
14	Bragg	Darren	1.5196	1998	374	0.989	1.98	0.059
15	Smith	Reggie	1.5083	1973	981	0.976	2.45	0.073
16	Burks	Ellis	1.5072	1992	701	0.986	2.43	0.061
17	Yastrzemski	Carl	1.4899	1983	2076	0.981	1.99	0.094
18	Evans	Dwight	1.4865	1989	2079	0.987	2.12	0.073
19	Stahl	Chick	1.4749	1906	776	0.962	2.09	0.107
20	Almada	Mel	1.4716	1937	293	0.973	2.19	0.126
21	Jensen	Jackie	1.4684	1961	1026	0.977	2.07	0.090
22	Lewis	Darren	1.4560	2001	479	0.992	2.01	0.040
23	Johnson	Bob	1.4551	1945	282	0.976	2.14	0.135
24	Lewis	Duffy	1.4531	1917	1165	0.955	2.02	0.155
25	Hooper	Harry	1.4528	1920	1637	0.964	1.84	0.159
26	Rice	Jim	1.4453	1988	1543	0.980	2.10	0.089
27	Vosmik	Joe	1.4452	1939	290	0.976	2.14	0.079
28	Harper	Tommy	1.4445	1974	348	0.984	2.00	0.055
29	O'Leary	Troy	1.4176	2001	985	0.985	1.77	0.053
30	Greenwell	Mike	1.4128	1996	1165	0.981	1.87	0.073

Rank	PITCHING		FV	Lyear	IP	FPCT	RF
1	Wingfield	Ted	1.0971	1927	545	0.970	3.76
2	Mays	Carl	1.0910	1919	1105	0.965	4.23
3	Bush	Joe	1.0896	1921	780	0.974	3.07
4	Ehmke	Howard	1.0886	1926	990	0.955	3.07
5	Ruth	Babe	1.0819	1919	1190	0.967	3.32
6	Ferriss	Dave	1.0797	1950	880	0.979	2.40
7	Quinn	Jack	1.0742	1925	833	0.971	3.21
8	Wood	Joe	1.0566	1915	1418	0.969	3.32
9	Brewer	Tom	1.0524	1961	1509	0.967	2.79
10	Monbouquette	Bill	1.0480	1965	1622	0.985	1.88

Franchise When and Where
Boston Red Sox (1908 to Present)
Boston Americans (1901-1907)

CHICAGO WHITE SOX
Best Seasons and Careers of All-Time

There's a Frank Thomas sighting at the top of the list, and Carlton Fisk is starting for his second team. Now there's a different take on the Let's Play Two saying. The bullpen's solid with Hoyt Wilhelm and Wilbur Wood at the back of the game and there's a player from the current era that might just make a solid contribution to the team in Chris Sale. For most of the All-Time Chicago White Sox team, we're reaching back a few generations with players such as Luke Appling and Eddie Collins, Minnie Minoso and Fielder Jones. So for fans of the past twenty-five years or so of the South Side squad, you're gonna have to make do with the Big Hurt leading the way, a Mark Buehrle in the back end of the rotation, and Magglio Ordonez on the bench.

Reserves

Bench - Joe Jackson (OF), Magglio Ordonez (OF), Happy Felsch (OF), Paul Konerko (1B), Nellie Fox (2B), Luis Aparicio (IF), Ray Schalk (CATCHER).

Bullpen - Hoyt Wilhelm (CL), Wilbur Wood (SU), Eddie Cicotte, Jack McDowell, Chris Sale, Jack McDowell.

Chicago White Sox - Best Position Player Years

Rank	Name	First	Year	Team	Lg	HR	RBI	AVG	Age	PEVA-B
1	Thomas	Frank	1994	CHA	AL	38	101	0.353	26	41.278
2	Thomas	Frank	1991	CHA	AL	32	109	0.318	23	36.023
3	Allen	Dick	1972	CHA	AL	37	113	0.308	30	34.744
4	Thomas	Frank	1992	CHA	AL	24	115	0.323	24	33.764
5	Thomas	Frank	1995	CHA	AL	40	111	0.308	27	31.426
6	Jackson	Joe	1916	CHA	AL	3	78	0.341	27	30.605
7	Thomas	Frank	1997	CHA	AL	35	125	0.347	29	29.480
8	Thomas	Frank	1996	CHA	AL	40	134	0.349	28	29.396
9	Collins	Eddie	1915	CHA	AL	4	77	0.332	28	29.073
10	Thomas	Frank	1993	CHA	AL	41	128	0.317	25	27.858
11	Belle	Albert	1998	CHA	AL	49	152	0.328	32	27.673
12	Jackson	Joe	1920	CHA	AL	12	121	0.382	31	27.623
13	Abreu	Jose	2014	CHA	AL	36	107	0.317	27	26.970
14	Jackson	Joe	1919	CHA	AL	7	96	0.351	30	26.577
15	Thomas	Frank	2000	CHA	AL	43	143	0.328	32	25.624
16	Abreu	Jose	2020	CHA	AL	19	60	0.317	33	25.343
17	Minoso	Minnie	1960	CHA	AL	20	105	0.311	35	24.110
18	Minoso	Minnie	1954	CHA	AL	19	116	0.320	29	23.962
19	Appling	Luke	1943	CHA	AL	3	80	0.328	36	23.511
20	Collins	Eddie	1920	CHA	AL	3	76	0.372	33	22.630

Chicago White Sox - Best Pitcher Years

Rank	Name	First	Year	Team	Lg	W	L	SV	IP	ERA	Age	PEVA-P
1	Walsh	Ed	1908	CHA	AL	40	15	6	464.0	1.42	27	46.136
2	Faber	Red	1921	CHA	AL	25	15	1	330.7	2.48	33	37.013
3	Walsh	Ed	1911	CHA	AL	27	18	4	368.7	2.22	30	36.402
4	Faber	Red	1922	CHA	AL	21	17	2	352.0	2.81	34	36.363
5	Cicotte	Eddie	1917	CHA	AL	28	12	4	346.7	1.53	33	35.909
6	Wood	Wilbur	1971	CHA	AL	22	13	1	334.0	1.91	30	35.043
7	Walsh	Ed	1910	CHA	AL	18	20	5	369.7	1.27	29	34.646
8	Cicotte	Eddie	1919	CHA	AL	29	7	1	306.7	1.82	35	31.775
9	Walsh	Ed	1907	CHA	AL	24	18	4	422.3	1.60	26	28.794
10	Walsh	Ed	1912	CHA	AL	27	17	10	393.0	2.15	31	28.368
11	Horlen	Joe	1967	CHA	AL	19	7	0	258.0	2.06	30	28.268
12	Lyons	Ted	1927	CHA	AL	22	14	2	307.7	2.84	27	27.787
13	Smith	Frank	1909	CHA	AL	25	17	1	365.0	1.80	30	27.566
14	Loaiza	Esteban	2003	CHA	AL	21	9	0	226.3	2.90	32	27.439
15	Lee	Thornton	1941	CHA	AL	22	11	1	300.3	2.37	35	26.776
16	Wood	Wilbur	1972	CHA	AL	24	17	0	376.7	2.51	31	25.752
17	Thomas	Tommy	1927	CHA	AL	19	16	1	307.7	2.98	28	24.131
18	Pierce	Billy	1957	CHA	AL	20	12	2	257.0	3.26	30	23.698
19	Hoyt	La Marr	1983	CHA	AL	24	10	0	260.7	3.66	28	23.565
20	Buehrle	Mark	2001	CHA	AL	16	8	0	221.3	3.29	22	22.701

Chicago White Sox - Top Career Batters

RANK	NAME	FIRST	LYR	TEAM	LG	PEVA-B	YRS	PPYR	HR	RBI	H	AVE
1	Thomas	Frank	2005	CHA	AL	309.515	16	19.345	448	1465	2136	0.307
2	Appling	Luke	1950	CHA	AL	210.671	20	10.534	45	1116	2749	0.310

RANK	NAME	FIRST	LYR	TEAM	LG	PEVA-B	YRS	PPYR	HR	RBI	H	AVE
3	Collins	Eddie	1926	CHA	AL	187.849	12	15.654	31	804	2007	0.331
4	Minoso	Minnie	1980	CHA	AL	162.367	12	13.531	135	808	1523	0.304
5	Konerko	Paul	2014	CHA	AL	151.258	16	9.454	432	1383	2292	0.281
6	Fox	Nellie	1963	CHA	AL	148.794	14	10.628	35	740	2470	0.291
7	Baines	Harold	2001	CHA	AL	124.121	14	8.866	221	981	1773	0.288
8	Abreu	Jose	2020	CHA	AL	120.122	7	17.159	198	671	1114	0.294
9	Fisk	Carlton	1993	CHA	AL	116.078	13	8.929	214	762	1259	0.257
10	Jones	Fielder	1908	CHA	AL	115.066	8	14.383	10	375	1151	0.269
11	Ventura	Robin	1998	CHA	AL	113.229	10	11.323	171	741	1244	0.274
12	Jackson	Joe	1920	CHA	AL	111.528	6	18.588	30	426	829	0.340
13	Schalk	Ray	1928	CHA	AL	102.042	17	6.002	11	594	1345	0.254
14	Aparicio	Luis	1970	CHA	AL	98.124	10	9.812	43	464	1576	0.269
15	Lollar	Sherm	1963	CHA	AL	93.775	12	7.815	124	631	1122	0.265
16	Ordonez	Magglio	2004	CHA	AL	89.760	8	11.220	187	703	1167	0.307
17	Kamm	Willie	1931	CHA	AL	81.731	9	9.081	25	587	1136	0.279
18	Falk	Bibb	1928	CHA	AL	79.810	9	8.868	50	627	1219	0.315
19	Felsch	Happy	1920	CHA	AL	77.735	6	12.956	38	446	825	0.293
20	Weaver	Buck	1920	CHA	AL	77.322	9	8.591	21	421	1308	0.272
21	Robinson	Floyd	1966	CHA	AL	74.771	7	10.682	65	400	875	0.287
22	Mostil	Johnny	1929	CHA	AL	74.755	10	7.476	23	376	1054	0.301
23	Davis	George	1909	CHA	AL	73.995	7	10.571	6	377	785	0.259
24	Guillen	Ozzie	1997	CHA	AL	73.394	13	5.646	24	565	1608	0.265
25	Melton	Bill	1975	CHA	AL	70.821	8	8.853	154	535	901	0.258
26	Landis	Jim	1964	CHA	AL	70.608	8	8.826	83	398	892	0.250
27	May	Carlos	1976	CHA	AL	70.123	9	7.791	85	479	1000	0.275
28	Lemon	Chet	1981	CHA	AL	69.916	7	9.988	73	348	804	0.288
29	Collins	Shano	1920	CHA	AL	67.278	11	6.116	17	541	1254	0.262
30	Durham	Ray	2002	CHA	AL	66.728	8	8.341	106	484	1246	0.278
31	Sheely	Earl	1927	CHA	AL	66.116	7	9.445	41	582	1051	0.305
32	Ramirez	Alexei	2014	CHA	AL	64.660	7	9.237	99	480	1127	0.277
33	Ward	Pete	1969	CHA	AL	61.012	7	8.716	97	407	753	0.254
34	Pierzynski	A.J.	2012	CHA	AL	59.113	8	7.389	118	460	1087	0.279
35	Lee	Carlos	2004	CHA	AL	58.647	6	9.775	152	552	957	0.288
36	Dye	Jermaine	2009	CHA	AL	57.402	5	11.480	164	461	742	0.278
37	Johnson	Lance	1995	CHA	AL	54.926	8	6.866	17	327	1018	0.286
38	Raines	Tim	1995	CHA	AL	54.771	5	10.954	50	277	697	0.283
39	Allen	Dick	1974	CHA	AL	54.595	3	18.198	85	242	374	0.307
40	Kreevich	Mike	1941	CHA	AL	54.202	7	7.743	36	386	930	0.290
41	Kuhel	Joe	1947	CHA	AL	51.363	8	6.420	75	382	874	0.261
42	Carrasquel	Chico	1955	CHA	AL	50.880	6	8.480	32	307	825	0.265
43	Isbell	Frank	1909	CHA	AL	50.389	9	5.599	13	447	1019	0.251
44	Hooper	Harry	1925	CHA	AL	48.753	5	9.751	45	320	759	0.302
45	Wright	Taffy	1948	CHA	AL	48.666	6	8.111	30	399	834	0.312

RANK	NAME	FIRST	LYR	TEAM	LG	PEVA-B	YRS	PPYR	HR	RBI	H	AVE
46	Hansen	Ron	1969	CHA	AL	48.478	7	6.925	55	282	594	0.239
47	Orta	Jorge	1979	CHA	AL	48.311	8	6.039	79	456	1002	0.281
48	Robinson	Eddie	1952	CHA	AL	48.095	3	16.032	71	294	468	0.296
49	Smith	Al	1962	CHA	AL	48.027	5	9.605	85	360	699	0.276
50	Bonura	Zeke	1937	CHA	AL	47.936	4	11.984	79	440	664	0.317

Chicago White Sox - Top Career Pitchers

RANK	NAME	FIRST	LYEAR	LTEAM	LG	PEVA	YRS	PPYR	W	L	SV	IP	ERA
1	Walsh	Ed	1916	CHA	AL	213.566	13	16.428	195	125	34	2946.3	1.81
2	Lyons	Ted	1946	CHA	AL	178.627	21	8.506	260	230	23	4161.0	3.67
3	Faber	Red	1933	CHA	AL	177.153	20	8.858	254	213	28	4086.7	3.15
4	Pierce	Billy	1961	CHA	AL	163.992	13	12.615	186	152	19	2931.0	3.19
5	Buehrle	Mark	2011	CHA	AL	158.669	12	13.222	161	119	0	2476.7	3.83
6	Wood	Wilbur	1978	CHA	AL	140.663	12	11.722	163	148	57	2524.3	3.18
7	Cicotte	Eddie	1920	CHA	AL	122.749	9	13.639	156	102	21	2322.3	2.25
8	Sale	Chris	2016	CHA	AL	91.528	7	13.075	74	50	12	1110.0	3.00
9	McDowell	Jack	1994	CHA	AL	85.815	7	12.259	91	58	0	1343.7	3.50
10	Horlen	Joe	1971	CHA	AL	79.961	11	7.269	113	113	3	1918.0	3.11
11	Lee	Thornton	1947	CHA	AL	78.583	11	7.144	104	104	6	1888.0	3.33
12	White	Doc	1913	CHA	AL	76.793	11	6.981	159	123	4	2498.3	2.30
13	Peters	Gary	1969	CHA	AL	73.793	11	6.708	91	78	3	1560.0	2.92
14	Thomas	Tommy	1932	CHA	AL	72.167	7	10.310	83	92	8	1557.3	3.77
15	Fernandez	Alex	1996	CHA	AL	72.104	7	10.301	79	63	0	1346.3	3.78
16	Garland	Jon	2007	CHA	AL	65.908	8	8.238	92	81	1	1428.7	4.41
17	Danks	John	2016	CHA	AL	65.144	10	6.514	79	104	0	1503.3	4.38
18	Wilhelm	Hoyt	1968	CHA	AL	62.366	6	10.394	41	33	98	675.7	1.92
19	Smith	Frank	1910	CHA	AL	60.157	7	8.594	108	80	3	1717.3	2.18
20	Dotson	Richard	1989	CHA	AL	59.722	10	5.972	97	95	0	1606.0	4.02
21	Scott	Jim	1917	CHA	AL	58.515	9	6.502	107	113	9	1892.0	2.30
22	Donovan	Dick	1960	CHA	AL	57.898	6	9.650	73	50	3	1148.7	3.41
23	Quintana	Jose	2017	CHA	AL	55.467	6	9.245	50	54	0	1055.3	3.51
24	Alvarez	Wilson	1997	CHA	AL	55.096	7	7.871	67	50	1	1064.0	3.76
25	John	Tommy	1971	CHA	AL	51.819	7	7.403	82	80	3	1493.3	2.95
26	Hoyt	La Marr	1984	CHA	AL	49.336	6	8.223	74	49	10	942.0	3.92
27	Russell	Reb	1919	CHA	AL	49.303	7	7.043	81	59	13	1291.7	2.33
28	Bannister	Floyd	1987	CHA	AL	48.059	5	9.612	66	60	0	1040.0	4.05
29	Foulke	Keith	2002	CHA	AL	46.927	6	7.821	18	19	100	446.0	2.87
30	Floyd	Gavin	2013	CHA	AL	46.889	7	6.698	63	65	0	1042.7	4.22
31	Burns	Britt	1985	CHA	AL	45.659	8	5.707	70	60	3	1094.3	3.66
32	Rigney	Johnny	1947	CHA	AL	43.886	8	5.486	63	64	5	1186.3	3.59
33	Wynn	Early	1962	CHA	AL	43.299	5	8.660	64	55	3	1010.7	3.72
34	Thigpen	Bobby	1993	CHA	AL	42.763	8	5.345	28	33	201	541.7	3.26
35	Jenks	Bobby	2010	CHA	AL	42.399	6	7.067	14	18	173	341.7	3.40

RANK	NAME	FIRST	LYEAR	LTEAM	LG	PEVA	YRS	PPYR	W	L	SV	IP	ERA
36	Staley	Gerry	1961	CHA	AL	42.193	6	7.032	38	25	39	541.7	2.61
37	Pizarro	Juan	1966	CHA	AL	41.914	6	6.986	75	47	7	1037.3	3.05
38	Hernandez	Roberto	1997	CHA	AL	41.541	7	5.934	29	24	161	404.7	2.87
39	Owen	Frank	1909	CHA	AL	40.186	7	5.741	81	64	2	1312.3	240
40	Giolito	Lucas	2020	CHA	AL	38.971	4	9.743	31	28	0	467.7	4.33
41	Kaat	Jim	1975	CHA	AL	38.218	3	12.739	45	28	0	623.7	3.10
42	Garcia	Freddy	2010	CHA	AL	37.401	5	7.480	55	31	0	760.3	4.33
43	Benz	Joe	1919	CHA	AL	37.369	9	4.152	76	75	3	1359.7	2.43
44	Thornton	Matt	2013	CHA	AL	37.306	8	4.663	31	35	23	463.3	3.28
45	Vazquez	Javier	2008	CHA	AL	36.600	3	12.200	38	36	0	627.7	4.40
46	Contreras	Jose	2009	CHA	AL	36.061	6	6.010	55	56	0	900.0	4.66
47	Trucks	Virgil	1955	CHA	AL	35.622	3	11.874	47	26	4	616.0	3.14
48	Lopat	Ed	1947	CHA	AL	35.552	4	8.888	50	49	1	893.0	3.18
49	Williams	Lefty	1920	CHA	AL	34.927	5	6.985	81	44	4	1156.0	3.09
50	Smith	Eddie	1947	CHA	AL	34.016	7	4.859	63	82	3	1228.7	3.55

Chicago White Sox – Top Fielders

Rank	FIRST BASE		FV	Lyear	G	FPCT	RF
1	Donahue	Jiggs	1.3242	1909	646	0.989	11.99
2	Isbell	Frank	1.2543	1909	619	0.986	11.50
3	Bonura	Zeke	1.2461	1937	526	0.994	10.65
4	Sheely	Earl	1.2400	1927	938	0.990	10.65
5	Gandil	Chick	1.2089	1919	452	0.994	10.52
6	Skowron	Bill	1.1808	1966	313	0.994	8.99
7	Walker	Greg	1.1499	1990	689	0.993	8.99
8	Spencer	Jim	1.1481	1977	268	0.995	8.90
9	Allen	Dick	1.1470	1974	335	0.991	8.92
10	Kuhel	Joe	1.1465	1946	881	0.992	10.13

Rank	SECOND BASE		FV	Lyear	G	FPCT	RF
1	Fox	Nellie	1.4538	1963	2098	0.984	5.48
2	Collins	Eddie	1.3849	1926	1654	0.973	5.44
3	Bernazard	Tony	1.3770	1983	300	0.984	5.43
4	Kerr	John	1.3109	1931	291	0.971	5.93
5	Schalk	Roy	1.3022	1945	275	0.971	5.53
6	Hayes	Jackie	1.2670	1940	758	0.977	5.79
7	Durham	Ray	1.2609	2002	1124	0.977	4.62
8	Fletcher	Scott	1.2568	1991	367	0.990	4.39
9	Beckham	Gordon	1.2377	2015	638	0.984	4.79
10	Michaels	Cass	1.2213	1954	373	0.972	5.64

Rank	SHORTSTOP		FV	Lyear	G	FPCT	RF
1	Hansen	Ron	1.7004	1969	658	0.971	4.93
2	Aparicio	Luis	1.6919	1970	1508	0.971	5.04
3	Dent	Bucky	1.6624	1976	505	0.975	4.95
4	Carrasquel	Chico	1.6426	1955	835	0.971	4.85
5	Davis	George	1.6344	1908	716	0.945	5.54
6	Ramirez	Alexei	1.6034	2015	1101	0.975	4.32
7	Guillen	Ozzie	1.5998	1997	1724	0.974	4.46
8	Uribe	Juan	1.5503	2008	470	0.977	4.52
9	Tannehill	Lee	1.5385	1912	367	0.933	5.65
10	Appling	Luke	1.5217	1950	2218	0.948	5.24

Rank	THIRD BASE		FV	Lyear	G	FPCT	RF
1	Kamm	Willie	1.6652	1931	1159	0.967	3.42
2	Ventura	Robin	1.5725	1998	1220	0.957	2.69
3	Tannehill	Lee	1.5408	1912	668	0.938	3.56
4	Soderholm	Eric	1.5328	1979	310	0.974	3.00
5	Frazier	Todd	1.5081	2017	216	0.968	2.51

6	Melton	Bill	1.5009	1975	867	0.949	3.10	
7	Baker	Floyd	1.4556	1951	455	0.972	2.96	
8	Law	Vance	1.4491	1984	315	0.959	2.39	
9	Ward	Pete	1.4393	1969	562	0.945	2.94	
10	Crede	Joe	1.4382	2008	791	0.963	2.61	

Rank	CATCHER		FV	Lyear	G	FPCT	RF	CS%
1	Schalk	Ray	2.0064	1928	1722	0.981	5.21	0.512
2	Lollar	Sherm	1.9540	1963	1241	0.993	5.17	0.475
3	Sullivan	Billy	1.9040	1914	1033	0.977	5.49	0.483
4	Downing	Brian	1.8564	1977	365	0.989	5.50	0.360
5	Pierzynski	A.J.	1.8551	2012	1025	0.995	7.05	0.227
6	Fisk	Carlton	1.8370	1993	1236	0.992	5.52	0.320
7	Tresh	Mike	1.8306	1948	981	0.983	4.54	0.450
8	Sewell	Luke	1.8287	1938	421	0.985	4.43	0.408
9	Karkovice	Ron	1.8227	1997	918	0.992	5.62	0.401
10	Herrmann	Ed	1.7942	1974	612	0.988	5.85	0.366

Rank	OUTFIELD		FV	Lyear	G	FPCT	RF	ApG
1	Kreevich	Mike	1.6058	1941	794	0.980	2.90	0.093
2	Singleton	Chris	1.6023	2001	438	0.991	2.48	0.062
3	Jones	Fielder	1.5975	1908	1153	0.973	2.24	0.130
4	Felsch	Happy	1.5882	1920	741	0.975	2.75	0.157
5	Simmons	Al	1.5757	1935	409	0.986	2.55	0.083
6	Eaton	Adam	1.5748	2016	436	0.988	2.54	0.080
7	Landis	Jim	1.5709	1964	1035	0.990	2.49	0.062
8	Tucker	Thurman	1.5661	1947	432	0.987	3.03	0.100
9	Henderson	Ken	1.5595	1975	343	0.987	2.84	0.044
10	Mostil	Johnny	1.5586	1929	907	0.971	2.93	0.111
11	Lemon	Chet	1.5531	1981	755	0.982	2.92	0.073
12	Johnson	Lance	1.5408	1995	927	0.987	2.71	0.047
13	Philley	Dave	1.5386	1950	631	0.981	2.56	0.113
14	Berry	Ken	1.5262	1970	865	0.987	2.02	0.061
15	Agee	Tommie	1.5132	1967	320	0.976	2.33	0.056
16	Rios	Alexis	1.5106	2013	592	0.986	2.40	0.047
17	Gallagher	Dave	1.4943	1990	292	0.994	2.34	0.048
18	Raines	Tim	1.4824	1995	577	0.989	2.12	0.068
19	Ordonez	Magglio	1.4647	2004	989	0.988	2.05	0.063
20	Rowand	Aaron	1.4624	2005	596	0.986	1.95	0.045
21	Falk	Bibb	1.4544	1928	1027	0.969	2.22	0.113
22	Cameron	Mike	1.4530	1998	316	0.987	2.21	0.035
23	Jackson	Joe	1.4512	1920	646	0.972	2.15	0.110
24	Hooper	Harry	1.4498	1925	647	0.971	2.02	.0130
25	Moses	Wally	1.4458	1946	602	0.979	2.36	0.078
26	De Aza	Alejandro	1.4335	2014	510	0.987	2.08	0.031
27	Law	Rudy	1.4327	1985	476	0.985	2.28	0.040
28	Baines	Harold	1.4314	1989	1022	0.979	2.01	0.067
29	May	Carlos	1.4280	1976	666	0.985	1.68	0.090
30	Bodie	Ping	1.4214	1914	472	0.967	1.97	0.133

Rank	PITCHING		FV	Lyear	IP	FPCT	RF	
1	Altrock	Nick	1.1101	1909	1349	0.969	4.66	
2	Owen	Frank	1.1098	1909	1312	0.978	4.03	
3	Walsh	Ed	1.1016	1916	2946	0.963	4.37	
4	Buehrle	Mark	1.0960	2011	2477	0.974	2.19	
5	Herbert	Ray	1.0871	1964	711	0.985	2.48	
6	Seaver	Tom	1.0841	1986	547	0.984	2.06	
7	Smith	Frank	1.0790	1910	1717	0.964	3.80	
8	Wood	Wilbur	1.0757	1978	2524	0.978	2.06	
9	Callahan	Nixey	1.0619	1903	526	0.942	4.18	
10	Patterson	Roy	1.0618	1907	1365	0.957	3.34	

Franchise When and Where
Chicago White Sox (1901 to Present)

CHICAGO CUBS
Best Seasons and Careers of All-Time

Now here's the team with the player that made "Let's Play Two" famous, it's Ernie Banks playing shortstop with Ryne Sandberg as his double play partner on the All-Time Team of the Chicago Cubs at Wrigley Field. With Cap Anson playing first base from his pre-1900 perch, Sammy Sosa knocking them through the wind, and Billy Williams knocking them all over, the Cubs might just do pretty well against its competition despite that long drought between World Series championships. Add in Ferguson Jenkins and Greg Maddux to the top of the pitching rotation, with Grover Cleveland Alexander in the mix as well, and you might just have the ingredients for an All-Time team that could compete against the best of all franchises, even the Yankees. It's time for one of those "Let's Play Two" doubleheaders. Might as well play the Yanks and see where they stand.

Reserves

Bench - George Gore (OF), Bill Nicholson (OF), Hack Wilson (OF), Stan Hack (3B), Mark Grace (1B), King Kelly (IF/C), Ned Williamson (3B/SS).

Bullpen - Lee Smith (CL), Bruce Sutter (SU), Hippo Vaughn, John Clarkson, Jake Arrieta, Claude Passeau.

Chicago Cubs - Best Position Player Years

Rank	Name	First	Year	Team	Lg	HR	RBI	AVG	Age	PEVA-B
1	Barnes	Ross	1876	CHN	NL	1	59	0.429	26	46.554
2	Hornsby	Rogers	1929	CHN	NL	39	149	0.380	33	41.923
3	Sosa	Sammy	2001	CHN	NL	64	160	0.328	33	38.918
4	Anson	Cap	1881	CHN	NL	1	82	0.399	29	38.143
5	Wilson	Hack	1930	CHN	NL	56	191	0.356	30	35.799
6	Santo	Ron	1964	CHN	NL	30	114	0.313	24	35.556
7	Nicholson	Bill	1943	CHN	NL	29	128	0.309	29	35.190
8	Nicholson	Bill	1944	CHN	NL	33	122	0.287	30	34.757
9	Banks	Ernie	1959	CHN	NL	45	143	0.304	28	34.546
10	Banks	Ernie	1958	CHN	NL	47	129	0.313	27	33.578
11	Santo	Ron	1966	CHN	NL	30	94	0.312	26	33.049
12	Kelly	King	1884	CHN	NL	13	95	0.354	27	32.756
13	Dalrymple	Abner	1880	CHN	NL	0	36	0.330	23	32.143
14	Gore	George	1880	CHN	NL	2	47	0.360	23	31.318
15	Lee	Derrek	2005	CHN	NL	46	107	0.335	30	31.180
16	Williams	Billy	1965	CHN	NL	34	108	0.315	27	31.123
17	Anson	Cap	1882	CHN	NL	1	83	0.362	30	31.001
18	Santo	Ron	1967	CHN	NL	31	98	0.300	27	30.153
19	Williams	Billy	1972	CHN	NL	37	122	0.333	34	29.912
20	Wilson	Hack	1929	CHN	NL	39	159	0.345	29	29.897

Chicago Cubs - Best Pitcher Years

Rank	Name	First	Year	Team	Lg	W	L	SV	IP	ERA	Age	PEVA-P
1	Arrieta	Jake	2015	CHN	NL	22	6	0	229.0	1.77	29	50.219
2	Maddux	Greg	1992	CHN	NL	20	11	0	268.0	2.18	26	49.969
3	Clarkson	John	1885	CHN	NL	53	16	0	623.0	1.85	24	42.218
4	Brown	Mordecai	1909	CHN	NL	27	9	7	342.7	1.31	33	40.455
5	Alexander	Pete	1920	CHN	NL	27	14	5	363.3	1.91	33	40.230
6	Darvish	Yu	2020	CHN	NL	8	3	0	76.0	2.01	34	37.335
7	Passeau	Claude	1940	CHN	NL	20	13	5	280.7	2.50	31	35.806
8	Lee	Bill	1938	CHN	NL	22	9	2	291.0	2.66	29	34.833
9	Jenkins	Fergie	1970	CHN	NL	22	16	0	313.0	3.39	28	34.695
10	Hutchison	Bill	1890	CHN	NL	42	25	2	603.0	2.70	31	33.191
11	Clarkson	John	1887	CHN	NL	38	21	0	523.0	3.08	26	32.014
12	Hutchison	Bill	1891	CHN	NL	44	19	1	561.0	2.81	32	31.786
13	Brown	Mordecai	1906	CHN	NL	26	6	3	277.3	1.04	30	30.326
14	Hendricks	Kyle	2016	CHN	NL	16	8	0	190.0	2.13	27	30.303
15	Ellsworth	Dick	1963	CHN	NL	22	10	0	290.7	2.11	23	30.293
16	Hands	Bill	1969	CHN	NL	20	14	0	300.0	2.49	29	29.345
17	Vaughn	Hippo	1918	CHN	NL	22	10	0	290.3	1.74	30	28.883
18	Lester	Jon	2016	CHN	NL	19	5	0	202.7	2.44	32	28.284
19	Hutchison	Bill	1892	CHN	NL	36	36	1	622.0	2.76	33	28.107
20	Jenkins	Fergie	1971	CHN	NL	24	13	0	325.0	2.77	29	27.507

Chicago Cubs - Top Career Batters

RANK	NAME	FIRST	LYR	TEAM	LG	PEVA-B	YRS	PPYR	HR	RBI	H	AVE
1	Anson	Cap	1897	CHN	NL	374.385	22	17.017	97	1879	2995	0.329
2	Banks	Ernie	1971	CHN	NL	264.788	19	13.936	512	1636	2583	0.274
3	Williams	Billy	1974	CHN	NL	262.803	16	16.425	392	1353	2510	0.296
4	Santo	Ron	1973	CHN	NL	257.426	14	18.388	337	1290	2171	0.279
5	Sosa	Sammy	2004	CHN	NL	214.891	13	16.530	545	1414	1985	0.284
6	Sandberg	Ryne	1997	CHN	NL	177.095	15	11.806	282	1061	2385	0.285
7	Ryan	Jimmy	1900	CHN	NL	165.018	15	11.001	99	914	2073	0.307
8	Hack	Stan	1947	CHN	NL	159.139	16	9.946	57	642	2193	0.301
9	Gore	George	1886	CHN	NL	157.398	8	19.675	24	380	933	0.315
10	Nicholson	Bill	1948	CHN	NL	153.688	10	15.369	205	833	1323	0.272
11	Hartnett	Gabby	1940	CHN	NL	152.886	19	8.047	231	1153	1867	0.297
12	Grace	Mark	2000	CHN	NL	147.685	13	11.360	148	1004	2201	0.308
13	Kelly	King	1886	CHN	NL	142.521	7	20.360	33	480	899	0.316
14	Williamson	Ned	1889	CHN	NL	136.810	11	12.437	61	622	1050	0.260
15	Rizzo	Anthony	2020	CHN	NL	127.949	9	14.220	228	744	1231	0.274
16	Wilson	Hack	1931	CHN	NL	126.233	6	21.039	190	769	1017	0.322
17	Cavarretta	Phil	1953	CHN	NL	123.104	20	6.155	92	896	1927	0.292
18	Dalrymple	Abner	1886	CHN	NL	118.974	8	14.872	40	325	938	0.295
19	Schulte	Frank	1916	CHN	NL	115.881	13	8.914	91	712	1590	0.272
20	Dahlen	Bill	1898	CHN	NL	109.804	8	13.725	57	560	1166	0.299
21	Chance	Frank	1912	CHN	NL	108.446	15	7.230	20	590	1268	0.297
22	Tinker	Joe	1916	CHN	NL	103.088	12	8.591	28	670	1436	0.259
23	Burns	Tom	1891	CHN	NL	94.008	12	7.834	39	679	1291	0.264
24	Ramirez	Aramis	2011	CHN	NL	93.576	9	10.397	239	806	1246	0.294
25	Kessinger	Don	1975	CHN	NL	89.732	12	7.478	11	431	1619	0.255
26	Herman	Billy	1941	CHN	NL	89.590	11	8.145	37	577	1710	0.309
27	Pafko	Andy	1951	CHN	NL	89.307	9	9.923	126	584	1048	0.294
28	Cuyler	Kiki	1935	CHN	NL	88.743	8	11.093	79	602	1199	0.325
29	Sheckard	Jimmy	1912	CHN	NL	88.051	7	12.579	17	294	907	0.257
30	Lange	Bill	1899	CHN	NL	86.829	7	12.404	39	578	1055	0.330
31	Lee	Derrek	2010	CHN	NL	86.073	7	12.296	179	574	1046	0.298
32	Evers	Johnny	1913	CHN	NL	85.572	12	7.131	9	448	1340	0.276
33	Sauer	Hank	1955	CHN	NL	82.843	7	11.835	198	587	852	0.269
34	Bryant	Kris	2020	CHN	NL	82.579	6	13.763	142	414	778	0.280
35	Zimmerman	Heinie	1916	CHN	NL	81.170	10	8.117	48	561	1112	0.304
36	Pfeffer	Fred	1897	CHN	NL	79.904	10	7.990	78	677	1080	0.252
37	Dawson	Andre	1992	CHN	NL	78.398	6	13.066	174	587	929	0.285
38	Stephenson	Riggs	1934	CHN	NL	73.783	9	8.198	49	589	1167	0.336
39	Kling	Johnny	1911	CHN	NL	73.250	11	6.659	16	436	960	0.271
40	Durham	Leon	1988	CHN	NL	67.382	8	8.423	138	485	898	0.279
41	Slagle	Jimmy	1908	CHN	NL	65.148	7	9.307	1	231	906	0.268

RANK	NAME	FIRST	LYR	TEAM	LG	PEVA-B	YRS	PPYR	HR	RBI	H	AVE
42	English	Woody	1936	CHN	NL	64.770	10	6.477	31	373	1248	0.291
43	Steinfeldt	Harry	1910	CHN	NL	63.864	5	12.773	9	332	696	0.268
44	Monday	Rick	1976	CHN	NL	60.004	5	12.001	106	293	690	0.270
45	Saier	Vic	1917	CHN	NL	58.723	7	8.389	53	378	738	0.265
46	Soriano	Rafael	2015	CHN	NL	58.330	8	7.291	181	526	898	0.264
47	Dunston	Shawon	1997	CHN	NL	58.080	12	4.840	107	489	1219	0.267
48	Beckert	Glenn	1973	CHN	NL	57.500	9	6.389	22	353	1423	0.283
49	Davis	Jody	1988	CHN	NL	57.415	8	7.177	122	467	834	0.251
50	Hollocher	Charlie	1924	CHN	NL	56.715	7	8.102	14	241	894	0.304

Chicago Cubs - Top Career Pitchers

RANK	NAME	FIRST	LYEAR	LTEAM	LG	PEVA	YRS	PPYR	W	L	SV	IP	ERA
1	Jenkins	Fergie	1983	CHN	NL	163.228	10	16.323	167	132	6	2673.7	3.20
2	Maddux	Greg	2006	CHN	NL	159.849	10	15.985	133	112	0	2016.0	3.61
3	Brown	Mordecai	1916	CHN	NL	151.146	10	15.115	188	86	39	2329.0	1.80
4	Root	Charley	1941	CHN	NL	143.727	16	8.983	201	156	40	3137.3	3.55
5	Alexander	Pete	1926	CHN	NL	130.911	9	14.546	128	83	10	1884.3	2.84
6	Vaughn	Hippo	1921	CHN	NL	118.611	9	13.179	151	105	4	2216.3	2.33
7	Lee	Bill	1947	CHN	NL	118.275	11	10.752	139	123	9	2271.3	3.51
8	Passeau	Claude	1947	CHN	NL	118.148	9	13.128	124	94	15	1914.7	2.96
9	Zambrano	Carlos	2011	CHN	NL	117.304	11	10.664	125	81	0	1826.7	3.60
10	Hutchison	Bill	1895	CHN	NL	110.650	7	15.807	181	158	4	3021.0	3.56
11	Griffith	Clark	1900	CHN	NL	107.861	8	13.483	152	96	1	2188.7	3.40
12	Hendricks	Kyle	2020	CHN	NL	106.421	7	15.203	69	48	0	1047.3	3.12
13	Warneke	Lon	1945	CHN	NL	106.352	10	10.635	109	72	11	1624.7	2.84
14	Reuschel	Rick	1984	CHN	NL	104.862	12	8.738	135	127	3	2290.0	3.50
15	Clarkson	John	1887	CHN	NL	100.405	4	25.101	137	57	0	1730.7	2.39
16	Arrieta	Jake	2017	CHN	NL	97.040	5	19.408	68	31	0	803.0	2.73
17	Lester	Jon	2020	CHN	NL	83.735	6	13.956	77	44	0	1002.7	3.64
18	Rush	Bob	1957	CHN	NL	80.867	10	8.087	110	140	7	2132.7	3.71
19	Dempster	Ryan	2012	CHN	NL	76.136	9	8.460	67	66	87	1182.7	3.74
20	Bush	Guy	1934	CHN	NL	75.071	12	6.256	152	101	27	2201.7	3.81
21	Hands	Bill	1972	CHN	NL	71.330	7	10.190	92	86	9	1564.0	3.18
22	Wood	Kerry	2012	CHN	NL	67.745	12	5.645	80	68	35	1279.0	3.67
23	Malone	Pat	1934	CHN	NL	66.936	7	9.562	115	79	8	1632.0	3.57
24	Taylor	Jack	1907	CHN	NL	66.889	8	8.361	109	90	3	1801.0	2.66
25	French	Larry	1941	CHN	NL	65.000	7	9.286	95	84	8	1486.0	3.54
26	Corcoran	Larry	1885	CHN	NL	64.119	6	10.686	175	85	2	2338.3	2.26
27	Sutter	Bruce	1980	CHN	NL	63.700	5	12.740	32	30	133	493.3	2.39
28	Ellsworth	Dick	1966	CHN	NL	63.075	8	7.884	84	110	2	1613.3	3.70
29	Reulbach	Ed	1913	CHN	NL	61.639	9	6.849	136	65	9	1864.7	2.24
30	Lilly	Ted	2010	CHN	NL	59.723	4	14.931	47	34	0	705.7	3.70
31	Smith	Lee	1987	CHN	NL	55.939	8	6.992	40	51	180	681.3	2.92

RANK	NAME	FIRST	LYEAR	LTEAM	LG	PEVA	YRS	PPYR	W	L	SV	IP	ERA
32	Sutcliffe	Rick	1991	CHN	NL	54.479	8	6.810	82	65	0	1267.3	3.74
33	Trachsel	Steve	2007	CHN	NL	51.920	8	6.490	61	72	0	1163.7	4.41
34	Darvish	Yu	2020	CHN	NL	48.787	3	16.262	15	14	0	294.7	3.60
35	Lieber	Jon	2008	CHN	NL	47.441	5	9.488	50	39	0	874.3	4.04
36	Jackson	Larry	1966	CHN	NL	46.540	4	11.635	52	52	0	838.0	3.26
37	Schmitz	Johnny	1951	CHN	NL	46.224	8	5.778	69	80	12	1198.7	3.52
38	Holtzman	Ken	1979	CHN	NL	45.242	9	5.027	80	81	3	1447.0	3.76
39	Overall	Orval	1913	CHN	NL	44.101	6	7.350	86	43	12	1135.0	1.91
40	Prior	Mark	2006	CHN	NL	42.219	5	8.444	42	29	0	657.0	3.51
41	Wyse	Hank	1947	CHN	NL	42.107	6	7.018	69	54	8	1063.0	3.03
42	Blake	Sheriff	1931	CHN	NL	41.872	8	5.234	81	92	6	1455.3	3.95
43	Cheney	Larry	1915	CHN	NL	41.856	5	8.371	76	51	16	1061.0	2.74
44	Marmol	Carlos	2013	CHN	NL	41.500	8	5.187	23	32	117	542.3	3.50
45	Pfiester	Jack	1911	CHN	NL	37.448	6	6.241	70	40	0	1028.3	1.85
46	Castillo	Frank	1997	CHN	NL	35.014	7	5.002	47	62	0	949.7	4.29
47	Elston	Don	1964	CHN	NL	32.528	9	3.614	49	54	63	754.7	3.70
48	Burris	Ray	1979	CHN	NL	31.756	7	4.537	55	58	2	1068.3	4.27
49	Morgan	Mike	1998	CHN	NL	31.700	5	6.340	30	35	0	575.7	3.83
50	Hobbie	Glen	1964	CHN	NL	31.164	8	3.896	61	79	5	1218.7	4.20

Chicago Cubs – Top Fielders

Rank	FIRST BASE		FV	Lyear	G	FPCT	RF
1	Banks	Ernie	1.3398	1971	1259	0.994	10.18
2	Grace	Mark	1.3184	2000	1890	0.995	9.60
3	Everitt	Bill	1.2589	1900	308	0.973	11.20
4	Waitkus	Eddie	1.2506	1948	357	0.993	9.99
5	Buckner	Bill	1.2386	1984	855	0.992	10.34
6	Durham	Leon	1.2310	1988	575	0.994	9.48
7	Long	Dale	1.2284	1959	326	0.991	9.25
8	Rizzo	Anthony	1.2206	2020	1211	0.995	8.83
9	Anson	Cap	1.1834	1897	2058	0.974	10.57
10	Fondy	Dee	1.1778	1957	765	0.989	9.38

Rank	SECOND BASE		FV	Lyear	G	FPCT	RF
1	Sandberg	Ryne	1.4234	1997	1994	0.989	5.10
2	Trillo	Manny	1.3862	1988	636	0.974	5.46
3	Herman	Billy	1.3805	1941	1340	0.966	6.05
4	Morandini	Mickey	1.3582	1999	284	0.992	4.33
5	Adams	Sparky	1.3581	1927	370	0.976	6.03
6	Pfeffer	Fred	1.3437	1897	1073	0.916	6.48
7	Hubbs	Ken	1.3353	1963	319	0.979	5.36
8	Baker	Gene	1.3105	1956	434	0.967	5.59
9	Beckert	Glenn	1.2901	1973	1206	0.974	5.20
10	Barney	Darwin	1.2794	2014	508	0.990	4.31

Rank	SHORTSTOP		FV	Lyear	G	FPCT	RF
1	Banks	Ernie	1.6542	1961	1125	0.969	4.91
2	DeJesus	Ivan	1.6289	1981	736	0.963	5.00
3	Jurges	Billy	1.6185	1947	965	0.963	5.28
4	Kessinger	Don	1.6167	1975	1618	0.964	4.94
5	Tinker	Joe	1.5942	1916	1501	0.936	5.55
6	Bowa	Larry	1.5803	1985	483	0.976	4.52
7	Hollocher	Charlie	1.5649	1924	751	0.954	5.53
8	Rodgers	Andre	1.5503	1964	433	0.960	4.96
9	Dahlen	Bill	1.5477	1898	712	0.909	6.21

| 10 | Dunston | Shawon | 1.5353 | 1997 | 1228 | 0.968 | 4.50 |

Rank	THIRD BASE		FV	Lyear	G	FPCT	RF
1	Williamson	Ned	1.6384	1885	601	0.870	3.72
2	Santo	Ron	1.5734	1973	2102	0.954	3.07
3	Burns	Tom	1.5361	1891	696	0.888	3.62
4	Deal	Charlie	1.5179	1921	606	0.964	3.22
5	Steinfeldt	Harry	1.5175	1910	730	0.949	3.00
6	Buechele	Steve	1.4954	1995	323	0.968	2.33
7	Hack	Stan	1.4921	1947	1836	0.957	2.96
8	Jackson	Randy	1.4836	1959	687	0.951	3.07
9	Friberg	Bernie	1.4815	1925	319	0.950	3.02
10	Cey	Ron	1.4605	1986	518	0.954	2.31

Rank	CATCHER		FV	Lyear	G	FPCT	RF	CS%
1	Hartnett	Gabby	2.0074	1940	1759	0.984	4.77	0.565
2	Killefer	Bill	2.0044	1921	307	0.981	5.78	0.494
3	Kling	Johnny	1.9691	1911	960	0.973	6.07	0.489
4	Hundley	Randy	1.9471	1977	939	0.992	6.17	0.423
5	Gonzalez	Mike	1.9430	1929	269	0.989	4.42	0.542
6	Barrett	Michael	1.9036	2007	409	0.993	7.77	0.215
7	Davis	Jody	1.8911	1988	961	0.987	5.95	0.347
8	Wilkins	Rick	1.8883	1995	432	0.993	5.99	0.398
9	Soto	Geovany	1.8766	2012	533	0.992	7.87	0.266
10	Archer	Jimmy	1.8745	1916	677	0.971	5.92	0.489

Rank	OUTFIELD		FV	Lyear	G	FPCT	RF	ApG
1	Statz	Jigger	1.6009	1925	432	0.964	3.01	0.155
2	Lange	Bill	1.5770	1899	716	0.942	2.61	0.190
3	Leach	Tommy	1.5671	1914	330	0.977	2.47	0.127
4	Phillips	Adolfo	1.5482	1969	418	0.978	2.37	0.091
5	Thomson	Bobby	1.5317	1959	264	0.988	2.27	0.083
6	Sheckard	Jimmy	1.5224	1912	999	0.969	2.07	0.136
7	Pafko	Andy	1.5217	1951	757	0.986	2.62	0.110
8	Gore	George	1.5086	1886	706	0.870	2.06	0.227
9	McRae	Brian	1.4975	1997	399	0.991	2.36	0.023
10	Lowrey	Peanuts	1.4861	1949	555	0.982	2.41	0.106
11	Paskert	Dode	1.4822	1920	338	0.968	2.31	0.139
12	Byrd	Marlon	1.4807	2012	282	0.990	2.46	0.050
13	Monday	Rick	1.4773	1976	655	0.983	2.31	0.053
14	Dawson	Andre	1.4576	1992	826	0.987	1.85	0.062
15	Cuyler	Kiki	1.4529	1935	927	0.975	2.32	0.101
16	Carroll	Cliff	1.4525	1891	266	0.928	1.79	0.162
17	Hofman	Solly	1.4493	1916	552	0.965	2.33	0.149
18	Heathcote	Cliff	1.4461	1930	698	0.981	2.34	0.136
19	Dalrymple	Abner	1.4442	1886	709	0.857	1.87	0.150
20	Galan	Augie	1.4384	1941	772	0.980	2.30	0.070
21	Slagle	Jimmy	1.4364	1908	891	0.957	2.10	0.116
22	Wilson	Hack	1.4356	1931	837	0.966	2.49	0.080
23	Martin	Jerry	1.4316	1980	273	0.980	2.12	0.070
24	Heyward	Jason	1.4316	2020	670	0.989	1.66	0.039
25	Murcer	Bobby	1.4284	1979	342	0.983	1.74	0.067
26	Williams	Billy	1.4270	1974	2087	0.973	1.78	0.069
27	Williams	Cy	1.4235	1917	494	0.971	2.35	0.107
28	Moryn	Walt	1.4231	1960	563	0.976	1.92	0.082
29	Kelly	King	1.4198	1886	444	0.826	1.61	0.464
30	Brock	Lou	1.4157	1964	301	0.965	2.11	0.106

Rank	PITCHING		FV	Lyear	IP	FPCT	RF
1	Spalding	Al	1.1455	1877	540	0.948	2.42
2	Jackson	Larry	1.1230	1966	838	0.985	2.87
3	Maddux	Greg	1.1126	2006	2016	0.972	3.06
4	Clarkson	John	1.1083	1887	1731	0.904	2.79
5	Corcoran	Larry	1.0933	1885	2338	0.911	2.55
6	Tyler	Lefty	1.0923	1921	542	0.977	3.50
7	McCormick	Jim	1.0885	1886	563	0.944	2.70
8	Reuschel	Rick	1.0880	1984	2290	0.966	2.66
9	Alexander	Pete	1.0870	1926	1884	0.988	2.82
10	Warneke	Lon	1.0831	1945	1625	0.990	2.27

Franchise When and Where
Chicago Cubs (1903 to Present)
Chicago Orphans (1898-1902)
Chicago Colts (1890-1897)
Chicago White Stockings (1876-1889)

CINCINNATI REDS
Best Seasons and Careers of All-Time

The Big Red Machine is well represented on the Best Team of the Reds in Bench, Rose, Morgan, and Perez, even though some will be surprised that Joey Votto gets the nod at first base over Tony. That's just how good Joey Votto has been, even though it seems like some have been sleeping over his greatness. Don't be concerned, however, Tony is on the bench and he'll get plenty of playing time. As will George Foster and Dave Concepcion and Bid McPhee. Who's Bid McPhee? Just one of the best fielding second basemen in history. Don't let that fielding percentage fool you. Just try to catch anything with those gloves. Check out the Range Factor, it's awesome. So the bench is strong, just like the starting eight. The starting rotation is lesser known, from long past decades, although some, like Walters and Derringer had multiple seasons in the Top Ten best for the Reds.

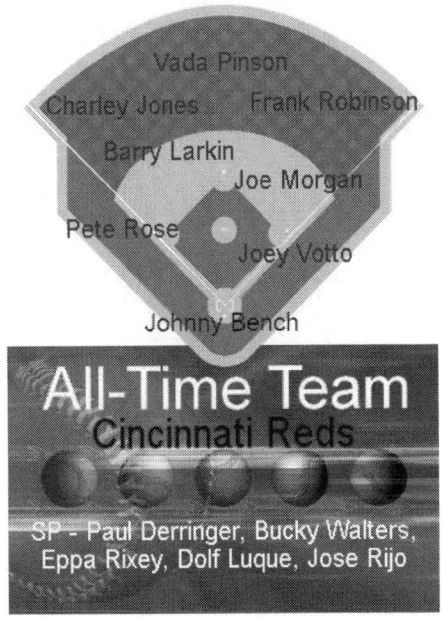

Reserves

Bench - George Foster (OF), Edd Roush (OF), John Reilly (1B/OF), Bid McPhee (2B), Tony Perez (1B), Dave Concepcion (SS), Ernie Lombardi (C).

Bullpen - Aroldis Chapman (CL), Rob Dibble (SU), Noodles Hahn, Pete Donohue, Mario Soto, Will White.

Cincinnati Reds - Best Position Player Years

Rank	Name	First	Year	Team	Lg	HR	RBI	AVG	Age	PEVA-B
1	Robinson	Frank	1962	CIN	NL	39	136	0.342	27	44.982
2	Bench	Johnny	1972	CIN	NL	40	125	0.270	25	42.271
3	Seymour	Cy	1905	CIN	NL	8	121	0.377	33	35.870
4	Foster	George	1977	CIN	NL	52	149	0.320	29	34.233
5	Votto	Joey	2010	CIN	NL	37	113	0.324	27	33.995
6	Bench	Johnny	1974	CIN	NL	33	129	0.280	27	33.034
7	Morgan	Joe	1976	CIN	NL	27	111	0.320	33	32.946
8	Jones	Charley	1878	CN1	NL	3	39	0.310	28	31.723
9	Votto	Joey	2017	CIN	NL	36	100	0.320	34	31.668
10	Morgan	Joe	1975	CIN	NL	17	94	0.327	32	30.407
11	Morgan	Joe	1972	CIN	NL	16	73	0.292	29	30.209
12	Perez	Tony	1970	CIN	NL	40	129	0.317	28	29.169
13	Jones	Charley	1884	CN2	AA	7	71	0.314	34	28.250
14	Kelly	King	1879	CN1	NL	2	47	0.348	22	28.236
15	Bench	Johnny	1970	CIN	NL	45	148	0.293	23	27.796
16	Robinson	Frank	1965	CIN	NL	33	113	0.296	30	27.669
17	Robinson	Frank	1964	CIN	NL	29	96	0.306	29	27.629
18	Morgan	Joe	1973	CIN	NL	26	82	0.290	30	27.309
19	Kluszewski	Ted	1954	CIN	NL	49	141	0.326	30	27.291
20	Rose	Pete	1973	CIN	NL	5	64	0.338	32	27.194

Cincinnati Reds - Best Pitcher Years

Rank	Name	First	Year	Team	Lg	W	L	SV	IP	ERA	Age	PEVA-P
1	Blackwell	Ewell	1947	CIN	NL	22	8	0	273.0	2.47	25	46.689
2	Luque	Dolf	1923	CIN	NL	27	8	2	322.0	1.93	33	42.654
3	Donohue	Pete	1925	CIN	NL	21	14	2	301.0	3.08	25	42.024
4	Walters	Bucky	1939	CIN	NL	27	11	0	319.0	2.29	30	41.246
5	Walters	Bucky	1940	CIN	NL	22	10	0	305.0	2.48	31	36.538
6	Luque	Dolf	1925	CIN	NL	16	18	0	291.0	2.63	35	35.862
7	Rixey	Eppa	1925	CIN	NL	21	11	1	287.3	2.88	34	34.428
8	Derringer	Paul	1939	CIN	NL	25	7	0	301.0	2.93	33	34.402
9	Derringer	Paul	1938	CIN	NL	21	14	3	307.0	2.93	32	34.132
10	Hahn	Noodles	1899	CIN	NL	23	8	0	309.0	2.68	20	33.291
11	Cueto	Johnny	2014	CIN	NL	20	9	0	243.7	2.25	28	33.132
12	Rijo	Jose	1993	CIN	NL	14	9	0	257.3	2.48	28	32.798
13	Derringer	Paul	1940	CIN	NL	20	12	0	296.7	3.06	34	31.160
14	Cueto	Johnny	2012	CIN	NL	19	9	0	217.0	2.78	26	30.769
15	Jackson	Danny	1988	CIN	NL	23	8	0	260.7	2.73	26	29.265
16	Rijo	Jose	1991	CIN	NL	15	6	0	204.3	2.51	26	27.931
17	White	Will	1879	CN1	NL	43	31	0	680.0	1.99	25	27.082
18	Soto	Mario	1982	CIN	NL	14	13	0	257.7	2.79	26	27.077
19	Arroyo	Bronson	2006	CIN	NL	14	11	0	240.7	3.29	29	27.027
20	Purkey	Bob	1962	CIN	NL	23	5	0	288.3	2.81	33	26.852

Cincinnati Reds (CN1, CN2, CIN) - Top Career Batters

RANK	NAME	FIRST	LYR	TEAM	LG	PEVA-B	YRS	PPYR	HR	RBI	H	AVE
1	Rose	Pete	1986	CIN	NL	294.862	19	15.519	152	1036	3358	0.307
2	Bench	Johnny	1983	CIN	NL	256.662	17	15.098	389	1376	2048	0.267

RANK	NAME	FIRST	LYR	TEAM	LG	PEVA-B	YRS	PPYR	HR	RBI	H	AVE
3	Robinson	Frank	1965	CIN	NL	237.493	10	23.749	324	1009	1673	0.303
4	Votto	Joey	2020	CIN	NL	223.308	14	15.951	295	966	1908	0.304
5	Perez	Tony	1986	CIN	NL	176.730	16	11.046	287	1192	1934	0.283
6	Morgan	Joe	1979	CIN	NL	176.447	8	22.056	152	612	1155	0.288
7	McPhee	Bid	1899	CIN	NL	166.066	18	9.226	53	1067	2250	0.271
8	Larkin	Barry	2004	CIN	NL	165.994	19	8.737	198	960	2340	0.295
9	Pinson	Vada	1968	CIN	NL	159.185	11	14.471	186	814	1881	0.297
10	Jones	Charley	1887	CN2	AA	152.726	9	16.970	39	407	835	0.301
11	Foster	George	1981	CIN	NL	151.263	11	13.751	244	861	1276	0.286
12	Roush	Edd	1931	CIN	NL	139.644	12	11.637	47	763	1784	0.331
13	Concepcion	Dave	1988	CIN	NL	130.003	19	6.842	101	950	2326	0.267
14	Reilly	John	1891	CIN	NL	128.015	10	12.802	69	740	1352	0.289
15	Kluszewski	Ted	1957	CIN	NL	126.670	11	11.515	251	886	1499	0.302
16	Groh	Heinie	1921	CIN	NL	122.139	9	13.571	17	408	1323	0.298
17	McCormick	Frank	1945	CIN	NL	101.295	10	10.130	110	800	1439	0.301
18	Bell	Gus	1961	CIN	NL	96.043	9	10.671	160	711	1343	0.288
19	Phillips	Brandon	2016	CIN	NL	92.705	11	8.428	191	851	1774	0.279
20	Griffey	Ken	1990	CIN	NL	91.377	12	7.615	71	466	1275	0.303
21	Holliday	Bug	1898	CIN	NL	90.136	10	9.014	65	617	1134	0.311
22	Davis	Eric	1996	CIN	NL	89.831	9	9.981	203	615	886	0.271
23	Bruce	Jay	2016	CIN	NL	88.794	9	9.866	233	718	1116	0.249
24	Dunn	Adam	2008	CIN	NL	86.913	8	10.864	270	646	920	0.247
25	Lombardi	Ernie	1941	CIN	NL	84.917	10	8.492	120	682	1238	0.311
26	Carpenter	Hick	1889	CN2	AA	81.800	9	9.089	16	492	1073	0.267
27	Seymour	Cy	1906	CIN	NL	78.800	5	15.760	26	326	738	0.332
28	Mitchell	Mike	1912	CIN	NL	77.302	6	12.884	19	420	892	0.283
29	Beckley	Jake	1903	CIN	NL	76.950	7	10.993	26	570	1125	0.325
30	Driessen	Dan	1984	CIN	NL	74.046	12	6.171	133	670	1277	0.271
31	Corcoran	Tommy	1906	CIN	NL	68.745	10	6.874	13	613	1205	0.249
32	Suarez	Eugenio	2020	CIN	NL	66.107	6	11.018	158	445	728	0.263
33	McMillan	Roy	1960	CIN	NL	64.399	10	6.440	42	395	1074	0.249
34	Casey	Sean	2005	CIN	NL	63.347	8	7.918	118	604	1223	0.305
35	Walker	Curt	1930	CIN	NL	62.948	7	8.993	43	482	1028	0.303
36	Goodman	Ival	1942	CIN	NL	61.883	8	7.735	91	464	995	0.279
37	Bescher	Bob	1913	CIN	NL	61.375	6	10.229	11	219	736	0.262
38	Cardenas	Leo	1968	CIN	NL	60.665	9	6.741	72	413	1058	0.261
39	May	Lee	1971	CIN	NL	60.077	7	8.582	147	449	779	0.274
40	Griffey	Ken	2008	CIN	NL	59.740	9	6.638	210	602	904	0.270
41	Fennelly	Frank	1888	CN2	AA	59.406	5	11.881	28	314	519	0.254
42	Post	Wally	1963	CIN	NL	58.942	12	4.912	172	525	805	0.266
43	Corkhill	Pop	1891	CIN	NL	58.132	7	8.305	18	437	760	0.267
44	Temple	Johnny	1964	CIN	NL	58.118	9	6.458	15	300	1058	0.291
45	Sanders	Reggie	1998	CIN	NL	57.122	8	7.140	125	431	781	0.271

RANK	NAME	FIRST	LYR	TEAM	LG	PEVA-B	YRS	PPYR	HR	RBI	H	AVE
46	Parker	Dave	1987	CIN	NL	56.450	4	14.112	107	432	694	0.281
47	Frey	Lonny	1946	CIN	NL	55.184	7	7.883	36	310	937	0.265
48	Hoblitzel	Dick	1914	CIN	NL	55.039	7	7.863	24	409	897	0.283
49	Tolan	Bobby	1973	CIN	NL	54.216	4	13.554	54	306	645	0.282
50	Sabo	Chris	1996	CIN	NL	53.790	7	7.684	104	373	812	0.270

Cincinnati Reds (CN1, CH2, CIN) - Top Career Pitchers

RANK	NAME	FIRST	LYEAR	TEAM	LG	PEVA	YRS	PPYR	W	L	SV	IP	ERA
1	Derringer	Paul	1942	CIN	NL	175.613	10	17.561	161	150	17	2615.3	3.36
2	Walters	Bucky	1948	CIN	NL	160.759	11	14.614	160	107	4	2355.7	2.93
3	Rixey	Eppa	1933	CIN	NL	157.828	13	12.141	179	148	8	2890.7	3.33
4	Luque	Dolf	1929	CIN	NL	145.848	12	12.154	154	152	10	2668.7	3.09
5	Rijo	Jose	2002	CIN	NL	129.993	10	12.999	97	61	0	1478.0	2.83
6	Hahn	Noodles	1905	CIN	NL	110.989	7	15.856	127	92	0	1987.3	2.52
7	Donohue	Pete	1930	CIN	NL	110.489	10	11.049	127	110	11	1996.3	3.73
8	Soto	Mario	1988	CIN	NL	109.458	12	9.121	100	92	4	1730.3	3.47
9	White	Will	1886	CN2	AA	108.243	8	13.530	227	163	0	3497.7	2.26
10	Cueto	Johnny	2015	CIN	NL	107.968	8	13.496	92	63	0	1339.0	3.21
11	Arroyo	Bronson	2017	CIN	NL	107.599	9	11.955	108	100	0	1761.3	4.18
12	Blackwell	Ewell	1952	CIN	NL	98.446	8	12.306	79	77	8	1281.3	3.32
13	Browning	Tom	1994	CIN	NL	89.064	11	8.097	123	88	0	1911.0	3.92
14	Vander Meer	Johnny	1949	CIN	NL	88.777	11	8.071	116	116	1	2028.0	3.41
15	Purkey	Bob	1964	CIN	NL	79.132	7	11.305	103	76	3	1588.0	3.49
16	Lucas	Red	1933	CIN	NL	77.958	8	9.745	109	99	6	1768.7	3.64
17	Nolan	Gary	1977	CIN	NL	74.062	10	7.406	110	67	0	1656.3	3.02
18	Seaver	Tom	1982	CIN	NL	73.586	6	12.264	75	46	0	1085.7	3.18
19	Raffensberger	Ken	1954	CIN	NL	73.018	8	9.127	89	99	7	1490.0	3.64
20	Maloney	Jim	1970	CIN	NL	72.308	11	6.573	134	81	4	1818.7	3.16
21	Harang	Aaron	2010	CIN	NL	71.915	8	8.989	75	80	0	1343.0	4.28
22	O'Toole	Jim	1966	CIN	NL	67.003	9	7.445	94	81	4	1561.0	3.59
23	Nuxhall	Joe	1966	CIN	NL	63.467	15	4.231	130	109	18	2169.3	3.80
24	Mullane	Tony	1893	CIN	NL	55.417	8	6.927	163	124	9	2599.0	3.15
25	Rhines	Billy	1897	CIN	NL	53.229	6	8.871	97	79	1	1557.0	3.27
26	Dwyer	Frank	1899	CIN	NL	52.587	8	6.573	132	101	5	1983.7	3.78
27	Chapman	Aroldis	2015	CIN	NL	50.812	6	8.469	19	20	146	319.0	2.17
28	Dibble	Rob	1993	CIN	NL	47.920	6	7.987	26	23	88	450.7	2.74
29	Ewing	Bob	1909	CIN	NL	47.689	8	5.961	108	103	4	2020.3	2.37
30	Franco	John	1989	CIN	NL	47.053	6	7.842	42	30	148	528.0	2.49
31	Carroll	Clay	1975	CIN	NL	44.534	8	5.567	71	43	119	856.0	2.73
32	Iglesias	Raisel	2020	CIN	NL	43.361	6	7.227	18	32	106	411.7	3.15
33	Gullett	Don	1976	CIN	NL	43.026	7	6.147	91	44	11	1187.0	3.03
34	Riddle	Elmer	1947	CIN	NL	42.967	8	5.371	52	34	6	757.7	3.20
35	Leake	Mike	2015	CIN	NL	42.832	6	7.139	62	47	0	1028.3	3.87

RANK	NAME	FIRST	LYEAR	TEAM	LG	PEVA	YRS	PPYR	W	L	SV	IP	ERA
36	Castillo	Luis	2020	CIN	NL	42.586	4	10.646	32	33	0	519.7	3.62
37	Bailey	Homer	2018	CIN	NL	41.073	12	3.423	67	77	0	1230.3	4.56
38	Toney	Fred	1918	CIN	NL	40.469	4	10.117	61	49	6	999.0	2.18
39	Smiley	John	1997	CIN	NL	40.081	5	8.016	48	48	0	775.3	4.16
40	Mays	Carl	1928	CIN	NL	38.467	5	7.693	49	34	4	703.3	3.26
41	Graves	Danny	2005	CIN	NL	38.365	9	4.263	39	43	182	733.0	3.94
42	Jay	Joey	1966	CIN	NL	37.168	6	6.195	75	63	4	1102.7	3.80
43	Benton	Rube	1925	CIN	NL	36.492	9	4.055	84	91	11	1504.7	3.28
44	Hume	Tom	1987	CIN	NL	36.236	10	3.624	52	66	88	921.0	3.83
45	Latos	Mat	2014	CIN	NL	35.512	3	11.837	33	16	0	522.3	3.31
46	Norman	Fred	1979	CIN	NL	35.198	7	5.028	85	64	1	1315.0	3.43
47	Breitenstein	Ted	1900	CIN	NL	34.138	4	8.535	66	45	0	1039.0	3.56
48	Harnisch	Pete	2001	CIN	NL	33.784	4	8.446	39	26	0	573.7	3.89
49	Beggs	Joe	1947	CIN	NL	33.467	7	4.781	42	30	27	569.0	2.56
50	Smith	Elmer	1898	CIN	NL	33.352	5	6.670	69	50	0	1072.3	3.31

Cincinnati Reds

Rank	FIRST BASE		FV	Lyear	G	FPCT	RF
1	McCormick	Frank	1.3536	1945	1206	0.995	10.44
2	Pipp	Wally	1.2520	1928	341	0.993	10.93
3	May	Lee	1.2134	1971	671	0.993	9.26
4	Comiskey	Charlie	1.2128	1894	265	0.980	10.56
5	Kluszewski	Ted	1.2040	1957	1255	0.993	9.19
6	Kelly	George	1.1840	1930	345	0.992	10.52
7	Benzinger	Todd	1.1730	1991	274	0.994	8.70
8	Driessen	Dan	1.1687	1984	1156	0.995	8.37
9	Perez	Tony	1.1460	1986	1092	0.993	8.29
10	Casey	Sean	1.1314	2005	1030	0.995	8.82

Rank	SECOND BASE		FV	Lyear	G	FPCT	RF
1	McPhee	Bid	1.4438	1899	2126	0.944	6.33
2	Rath	Morrie	1.4236	1920	264	0.975	5.70
3	Boone	Bret	1.4110	1998	677	0.990	4.69
4	Morgan	Joe	1.3792	1979	1116	0.986	5.10
5	Helms	Tommy	1.3705	1971	658	0.982	5.30
6	Frey	Lonny	1.3550	1946	889	0.974	5.65
7	Reese	Pokey	1.3400	2001	341	0.985	4.99
8	Egan	Dick	1.3277	1913	603	0.957	5.25
9	Huggins	Miller	1.3252	1909	757	0.950	5.45
10	Williams	Woody	1.3197	1945	300	0.971	5.59

Rank	SHORTSTOP		FV	Lyear	G	FPCT	RF
1	McMillan	Roy	1.6660	1960	1302	0.971	4.94
2	Miller	Eddie	1.6534	1947	697	0.972	5.39
3	Herzog	Buck	1.6508	1916	355	0.940	5.82
4	Smith	Germany	1.6265	1896	781	0.920	5.57
5	Beard	Ollie	1.5955	1890	254	0.896	5.18
6	Concepcion	Dave	1.5849	1988	2178	0.971	4.71
7	Cardenas	Leo	1.5787	1968	1138	0.969	4.54
8	Durocher	Leo	1.5713	1933	381	0.961	5.08
9	Corcoran	Tommy	1.5596	1906	1163	0.934	5.62
10	Cozart	Zak	1.5388	2017	721	0.980	4.11

Rank	THIRD BASE		FV	Lyear	G	FPCT	RF
1	Hoak	Don	1.6457	1958	261	0.968	3.21
2	Bell	Buddy	1.5906	1988	373	0.971	2.46
3	Groh	Heinie	1.5619	1921	883	0.965	3.24
4	Irwin	Charlie	1.5440	1900	603	0.928	3.47
5	Pinelli	Babe	1.5315	1927	579	0.949	3.41

			FV	Lyear	G	FPCT	RF	
6	Werber	Billy	1.5233	1941	397	0.950	3.21	
7	Sabo	Chris	1.4945	1996	792	0.963	2.40	
8	Mesner	Steve	1.4909	1945	398	0.956	3.19	
9	Rolen	Scott	1.4847	2012	319	0.972	2.43	
10	Perez	Tony	1.4736	1971	760	0.946	2.82	

Rank	CATCHER		FV	Lyear	G	FPCT	RF	CS%
1	Bench	Johnny	1.9703	1983	1742	0.990	5.80	0.432
2	Edwards	Johnny	1.9417	1967	731	0.991	7.10	0.396
3	Mueller	Ray	1.8982	1949	491	0.988	4.31	0.520
4	Hanigan	Ryan	1.8812	2013	460	0.995	6.93	0.404
5	Barnhart	Tucker	1.8766	2020	567	0.997	8.18	0.327
6	Oliver	Joe	1.8715	1997	738	0.990	6.50	0.328
7	Diaz	Bo	1.8543	1989	453	0.988	6.02	0.348
8	Peitz	Heinie	1.8510	1904	648	0.968	4.96	0.459
9	Lamanno	Ray	1.8387	1948	400	0.980	4.86	0.416
10	Keenan	Jim	1.8386	1891	320	0.940	6.22	0.375

Rank	OUTFIELD		FV	Lyear	G	FPCT	RF	ApG
1	Hamilton	Billy	1.6301	2018	664	0.994	2.42	0.078
2	Corkhill	Pop	1.6199	1891	644	0.941	2.19	0.225
3	Rose	Pete	1.5910	1978	1264	0.992	2.04	0.077
4	Pinson	Vada	1.5599	1968	1551	0.981	2.37	0.071
5	Craft	Harry	1.5459	1942	552	0.986	2.61	0.083
6	Jones	Charley	1.5447	1887	653	0.878	2.14	0.168
7	Bell	Gus	1.5349	1961	1186	0.987	2.36	0.073
8	Geronimo	Cesar	1.5283	1980	1141	0.989	2.32	0.065
9	Tolan	Bobby	1.5187	1973	569	0.978	2.50	0.054
10	Clay	Dain	1.5141	1946	403	0.987	2.72	0.065
11	Robinson	Frank	1.5137	1965	1278	0.986	2.05	0.070
12	Milner	Eddie	1.5106	1988	635	0.986	2.52	0.069
13	Seymour	Cy	1.5098	1905	554	0.937	2.51	0.143
14	Paskert	Dode	1.5094	1921	377	0.961	2.46	0.149
15	Stubbs	Drew	1.5040	2012	481	0.989	2.40	0.050
16	Allen	Ethan	1.5036	1930	388	0.985	2.73	0.077
17	Hatcher	Billy	1.4999	1992	275	0.988	2.18	0.051
18	Mitchell	Mike	1.4932	1912	842	0.960	1.95	0.160
19	Bescher	Bob	1.4911	1913	733	0.959	2.26	0.123
20	Roush	Edd	1.4865	1931	1360	0.971	2.63	0.111
21	O'Neill	Paul	1.4858	1992	711	0.988	2.04	0.073
22	Foster	George	1.4835	1981	1207	0.988	2.18	0.062
23	Hoy	Dummy	1.4779	1902	553	0.918	2.59	0.128
24	Harper	Tommy	1.4715	1967	616	0.990	1.86	0.045
25	Householder	Paul	1.4700	1984	286	0.992	1.81	0.080
26	Burns	George	1.4695	1924	400	0.968	2.31	0.110
27	Neale	Greasy	1.4683	1924	720	0.973	2.28	0.121
28	Baumholtz	Frank	1.4507	1949	280	0.980	2.08	0.107
29	Davis	Eric	1.4487	1996	934	0.986	2.37	0.046
30	Bates	Johnny	1.4478	1914	377	0.952	2.26	0.156

Rank	PITCHING		FV	Lyear	IP	FPCT	RF
1	Latos	Mat	1.1004	2014	522	0.991	1.86
2	Arroyo	Bronson	1.0931	2017	1761	0.980	2.05
3	Purkey	Bob	1.0871	1964	1588	0.966	2.74
4	Suggs	George	1.0795	1913	1029	0.967	3.09
5	Starr	Ray	1.0726	1943	528	0.978	2.23
6	Walters	Bucky	1.0705	1948	2356	0.971	2.42
7	Parrott	Tom	1.0700	1895	726	0.923	2.96
8	Mays	Carl	1.0664	1928	703	0.964	4.11
9	Breitenstein	Ted	1.0663	1900	1039	0.961	2.75
10	Rixey	Eppa	1.0646	1933	2891	0.983	2.48

Franchise When and Where
Cincinnati Reds (1876-1880, CN1); (1890-1953); (1960 to Present)
Cincinnati Redlegs (1954-1959)
Cincinnati Red Stockings (1882-1889, CN2)

CLEVELAND INDIANS
Best Seasons and Careers of All-Time

When you consider the history of the Cleveland Indians franchise, from the days when they were named after their best player, Nap Lajoie, i.e. the Cleveland Naps, to the years of the Indians in contention for playoff and World Series titles after the year 2000, you'll notice the domination of several players on the lists below. No, many current fans may not be as schooled on the exploits of Tris Speaker, but he had three of the five best batting seasons in team history. That's something you'd think a more current player like Jim Thome might have, though that takes away nothing from the fact that Thome is the best Indian first baseman ever. It just notes just how great Speaker was. The starters for your best ever team span those eras, and include some of the most stellar starting pitchers; yes, the two Bobs, Feller and Lemon, Early Wynn, and the more current Corey Kluber. And one current question. How long do we think it will take before Shane Bieber is on this roster, or maybe he should be here already?

Reserves

Bench - Albert Belle (OF), Manny Ramirez (OF), Joe Jackson (OF), Joe Sewell (SS/3B), Ken Keltner (3B), Hal Trosky (1B), Steve O'Neill (CATCHER).

Bullpen - Sam McDowell (CL), Doug Jones (SU), Addie Joss, Mike Garcia, C.C. Sabathia, Gaylord Perry.

Cleveland Indians - Best Position Player Years

Rank	Name	First	Year	Team	Lg	HR	RBI	AVG	Age	PEVA-B
1	Rosen	Al	1953	CLE	AL	43	145	0.336	29	48.401
2	Speaker	Tris	1916	CLE	AL	2	79	0.386	28	42.388
3	Jackson	Joe	1912	CLE	AL	3	90	0.395	23	37.904
4	Speaker	Tris	1923	CLE	AL	17	130	0.380	35	35.232
5	Speaker	Tris	1920	CLE	AL	8	107	0.388	32	35.002
6	Doby	Larry	1952	CLE	AL	32	104	0.276	29	34.855
7	Lajoie	Nap	1906	CLE	AL	0	91	0.355	32	34.293
8	Jackson	Joe	1911	CLE	AL	7	83	0.408	22	34.179
9	Lajoie	Nap	1904	CLE	AL	6	102	0.376	30	34.027
10	Rosen	Al	1952	CLE	AL	28	105	0.302	28	33.117
11	Belle	Albert	1995	CLE	AL	50	126	0.317	29	32.570
12	Lajoie	Nap	1910	CLE	AL	4	76	0.384	36	32.056
13	Boudreau	Lou	1948	CLE	AL	18	106	0.355	31	31.926
14	Brantley	Michael	2014	CLE	AL	20	97	0.327	27	31.045
15	Ramirez	Manny	1999	CLE	AL	44	165	0.333	27	30.231
16	Jackson	Joe	1913	CLE	AL	7	71	0.373	24	29.387
17	Bradley	Bill	1902	CLE	AL	11	77	0.340	24	29.269
18	Rosen	Al	1950	CLE	AL	37	116	0.287	26	29.097
19	Harrah	Toby	1982	CLE	AL	25	78	0.304	34	28.962
20	Averill	Earl	1936	CLE	AL	28	126	0.378	34	28.867

Cleveland Indians - Best Pitcher Years

Rank	Name	First	Year	Team	Lg	W	L	SV	IP	ERA	Age	PEVA-P
1	Kluber	Corey	2017	CLE	AL	18	4	0	203.7	2.25	31	48.424
2	Lee	Cliff	2008	CLE	AL	22	3	0	223.3	2.54	30	47.417
3	Feller	Bob	1940	CLE	AL	27	11	4	320.3	2.61	22	46.643
4	Bieber	Shane	2020	CLE	AL	8	1	0	77.3	1.63	25	40.664
5	Sabathia	C.C.	2007	CLE	AL	19	7	0	241.0	3.21	27	39.488
6	Feller	Bob	1946	CLE	AL	26	15	4	371.3	2.18	28	34.939
7	Perry	Gaylord	1972	CLE	AL	24	16	1	342.7	1.92	34	33.015
8	Perry	Gaylord	1974	CLE	AL	21	13	0	322.3	2.51	36	30.630
9	Feller	Bob	1947	CLE	AL	20	11	3	299.0	2.68	29	30.546
10	Kluber	Corey	2018	CLE	AL	20	7	0	215.0	2.89	32	25.421
11	Kluber	Corey	2016	CLE	AL	18	9	0	215.0	3.14	30	27.962
12	Bieber	Shane	2019	CLE	AL	15	8	0	214.3	3.28	24	27.744
13	Coveleski	Stan	1918	CLE	AL	22	13	1	311.0	1.82	29	27.680
14	Garcia	Mike	1954	CLE	AL	19	8	5	258.7	2.64	31	27.607
15	McDowell	Sam	1970	CLE	AL	20	12	0	305.0	2.92	28	27.561
16	Wynn	Early	1954	CLE	AL	23	11	2	270.7	2.73	34	27.349
17	Uhle	George	1926	CLE	AL	27	11	1	318.3	2.83	28	27.341
18	Blyleven	Bert	1984	CLE	AL	19	7	0	245.0	2.87	33	27.257
19	Carrasco	Carlos	2017	CLE	AL	18	6	0	200.0	3.29	30	27.201
20	Carmona	Fausto	2007	CLE	AL	19	8	0	215.0	3.06	24	26.017

Cleveland Indians - Top Career Batters

RANK	NAME	FIRST	LYR	TEAM	LG	PEVA-B	YRS	PPYR	HR	RBI	H	AVE
1	Speaker	Tris	1926	CLE	AL	268.546	11	24.413	73	884	1965	0.354
2	Lajoie	Nap	1914	CLE	AL	219.218	13	16.863	34	919	2046	0.339

RANK	NAME	FIRST	LYR	TEAM	LG	PEVA-B	YRS	PPYR	HR	RBI	H	AVE
3	Averill	Earl	1939	CLE	AL	183.365	11	16.670	226	1084	1903	0.322
4	Boudreau	Lou	1950	CLE	AL	166.252	13	12.789	63	740	1706	0.296
5	Doby	Larry	1958	CLE	AL	160.844	10	16.084	215	776	1234	0.286
6	Thome	Jim	2011	CLE	AL	159.758	13	12.289	337	937	1353	0.287
7	Rosen	Al	1956	CLE	AL	154.897	10	15.490	192	717	1063	0.285
8	Belle	Albert	1996	CLE	AL	134.867	8	16.858	242	751	1014	0.295
9	Sewell	Joe	1930	CLE	AL	131.698	11	11.973	30	869	1800	0.320
10	Keltner	Ken	1949	CLE	AL	129.826	12	10.819	163	850	1561	0.276
11	Ramirez	Manny	2000	CLE	AL	127.409	8	15.926	236	804	1086	0.313
12	Jackson	Joe	1915	CLE	AL	124.016	6	20.669	24	353	937	0.375
13	Trosky	Hal	1941	CLE	AL	118.782	9	13.198	216	911	1365	0.313
14	Santana	Carlos	2020	CLE	AL	114.385	10	11.438	216	710	1197	0.251
15	Flick	Elmer	1910	CLE	AL	113.194	9	12.577	19	376	1058	0.299
16	Bradley	Bill	1910	CLE	AL	112.334	10	11.233	26	473	1265	0.272
17	Lofton	Kenny	2007	CLE	AL	107.726	10	10.773	87	518	1512	0.300
18	Thornton	Andre	1987	CLE	AL	101.651	10	10.165	214	749	1095	0.254
19	Colavito	Rocky	1967	CLE	AL	101.466	8	12.683	190	574	851	0.267
20	Vizquel	Omar	2004	CLE	AL	96.572	11	8.779	60	584	1616	0.283
21	Hafner	Travis	2012	CLE	AL	93.142	10	9.314	200	688	1039	0.278
22	Heath	Jeff	1945	CLE	AL	90.393	10	9.039	122	619	1040	0.298
23	Jamieson	Charlie	1932	CLE	AL	90.119	14	6.437	18	492	1753	0.316
24	Brantley	Michael	2018	CLE	AL	87.534	10	8.753	87	528	1195	0.295
25	Chapman	Ray	1920	CLE	AL	85.317	9	9.480	17	364	1053	0.278
26	Sizemore	Grady	2011	CLE	AL	83.198	8	10.400	139	458	948	0.269
27	Harrah	Toby	1983	CLE	AL	80.074	5	16.015	70	324	725	0.281
28	Turner	Terry	1918	CLE	AL	79.022	15	5.268	8	521	1472	0.254
29	Jacoby	Brook	1992	CLE	AL	78.536	9	8.726	120	524	1178	0.273
30	Graney	Jack	1922	CLE	AL	77.490	14	5.535	18	420	1178	0.250
31	Ramirez	Jose	2020	CLE	AL	76.877	8	9.610	127	437	840	0.281
32	Lindor	Francisco	2020	CLE	AL	76.322	6	12.720	138	411	896	0.285
33	Avila	Bobby	1958	CLE	AL	76.135	10	7.613	74	442	1236	0.284
34	Martinez	Victor	2009	CLE	AL	75.639	8	9.455	103	518	900	0.297
35	O'Neill	Steve	1923	CLE	AL	75.483	13	5.806	11	458	1109	0.265
36	Franco	Julio	1997	CLE	AL	72.583	8	9.073	62	530	1272	0.297
37	Carter	Joe	1989	CLE	AL	72.528	6	12.088	151	530	876	0.269
38	Choo	Shin-Soo	2012	CLE	AL	69.824	7	9.975	83	372	736	0.292
39	Hegan	Jim	1957	CLE	AL	68.363	14	4.883	90	499	1026	0.230
40	Mitchell	Dale	1956	CLE	AL	67.759	11	6.160	41	402	1237	0.312
41	Baerga	Carlos	1999	CLE	AL	67.372	8	8.422	104	565	1097	0.299
42	Vosmik	Joe	1936	CLE	AL	64.154	7	9.165	44	556	1003	0.313
43	Francona	Tito	1964	CLE	AL	62.977	6	10.496	85	378	832	0.284
44	Kipnis	Jason	2019	CLE	AL	60.529	9	6.725	123	529	1120	0.261
45	Peralta	Jhonny	2010	CLE	AL	60.497	8	7.562	103	456	906	0.264

RANK	NAME	FIRST	LYR	TEAM	LG	PEVA-B	YRS	PPYR	HR	RBI	H	AVE
46	Hargrove	Mike	1985	CLE	AL	59.730	7	8.533	33	383	860	0.292
47	Hale	Odell	1940	CLE	AL	59.581	9	6.620	72	563	1046	0.293
48	Bell	Buddy	1978	CLE	AL	58.623	7	8.375	64	386	1016	0.274
49	Alvis	Max	1969	CLE	AL	56.533	8	7.067	108	361	874	0.249
50	Cabrera	Asdrubal	2014	CLE	AL	55.425	8	6.928	82	430	933	0.270

Cleveland Indians - Top Career Pitchers

RANK	NAME	FIRST	LYEAR	LTEAM	LG	PEVA	YRS	PPYR	W	L	SV	IP	ERA
1	Feller	Bob	1956	CLE	AL	246.330	18	13.685	266	162	21	3827.0	3.25
2	Lemon	Bob	1958	CLE	AL	165.840	13	12.757	207	128	22	2850.0	3.23
3	Kluber	Corey	2019	CLE	AL	150.613	9	16.735	98	58	0	1341.7	3.16
4	Coveleski	Stan	1924	CLE	AL	140.733	9	15.637	172	123	20	2502.3	2.80
5	Wynn	Early	1963	CLE	AL	136.070	10	13.607	164	102	10	2286.7	3.24
6	Garcia	Mike	1959	CLE	AL	123.307	12	10.276	142	96	21	2138.0	3.24
7	Joss	Addie	1910	CLE	AL	121.395	9	13.488	160	97	5	2327.0	1.89
8	Sabathia	C.C.	2008	CLE	AL	120.902	8	15.113	106	71	0	1528.7	3.83
9	Harder	Mel	1947	CLE	AL	116.071	20	5.804	223	186	23	3426.3	3.80
10	McDowell	Sam	1971	CLE	AL	104.898	11	9.536	122	109	11	2109.7	2.99
11	Lee	Cliff	2009	CLE	AL	94.650	8	11.831	83	48	0	1117.0	4.01
12	Nagy	Charles	2002	CLE	AL	92.023	13	7.079	129	103	0	1942.3	4.51
13	Carrasco	Carlos	2020	CLE	AL	89.892	11	8.172	88	73	2	1242.3	3.77
14	Perry	Gaylord	1975	CLE	AL	84.762	4	21.190	70	57	1	1130.7	2.71
15	Uhle	George	1936	CLE	AL	83.512	11	7.592	147	119	15	2200.3	3.92
16	Hudlin	Willis	1940	CLE	AL	81.421	15	5.428	157	151	31	2557.7	4.34
17	Bagby	Jim	1922	CLE	AL	72.142	7	10.306	122	85	26	1735.7	3.02
18	Bieber	Shane	2020	CLE	AL	71.857	3	23.952	34	14	0	406.3	3.32
19	Ferrell	Wes	1933	CLE	AL	71.005	7	10.144	102	62	12	1321.3	3.67
20	Bauer	Trevor	2019	CLE	AL	60.301	7	8.614	67	53	1	1044.3	3.89
21	Colon	Bartolo	2002	CLE	AL	58.031	6	9.672	75	45	0	1029.7	3.92
22	Candiotti	Tom	1999	CLE	AL	55.224	7	7.889	73	66	0	1201.7	3.62
23	Blyleven	Bert	1985	CLE	AL	54.199	5	10.840	48	37	0	760.7	3.23
24	Westbrook	Jake	2010	CLE	AL	50.284	9	5.587	69	69	0	1191.3	4.29
25	Carmona	Fausto	2012	CLE	AL	48.556	7	6.937	53	69	0	949.0	4.64
26	Jones	Doug	1998	CLE	AL	47.541	7	6.792	27	34	129	452.3	3.06
27	Gromek	Steve	1953	CLE	AL	47.303	13	3.639	78	67	16	1340.7	3.22
28	Swindell	Greg	1996	CLE	AL	47.254	7	6.751	61	56	0	1071.7	3.86
29	Tiant	Luis	1969	CLE	AL	46.562	6	7.760	75	64	12	1200.0	2.84
30	Gregg	Vean	1914	CLE	AL	45.689	4	11.422	72	36	5	898.3	2.31
31	Bell	Gary	1967	CLE	AL	44.613	10	4.461	96	92	45	1550.3	3.71
32	Perry	Jim	1975	CLE	AL	43.551	7	6.222	70	67	5	1131.7	3.76
33	Allen	Cody	2018	CLE	AL	42.426	7	6.061	24	29	149	440.7	2.98
34	Clevinger	Mike	2020	CLE	AL	42.264	5	8.453	42	22	0	523.3	3.20
35	Allen	Johnny	1940	CLE	AL	41.293	5	8.259	67	34	6	929.7	3.65

RANK	NAME	FIRST	LYEAR	LTEAM	LG	PEVA	YRS	PPYR	W	L	SV	IP	ERA
36	Siebert	Sonny	1969	CLE	AL	**40.437**	6	6.740	61	48	9	991.0	2.76
37	Score	Herb	1959	CLE	AL	**39.993**	5	7.999	49	34	3	714.3	3.17
38	Mesa	Jose	1998	CLE	AL	**39.444**	7	5.635	33	36	104	647.3	3.88
39	Masterson	Justin	2014	CLE	AL	**38.912**	6	6.485	48	61	0	950.7	4.23
40	Shaute	Joe	1930	CLE	AL	**37.606**	9	4.178	78	88	11	1447.0	4.11
41	Burba	Dave	2002	CLE	AL	**37.501**	5	7.500	57	35	0	799.7	4.65
42	Morton	Guy	1924	CLE	AL	**36.469**	11	3.315	98	88	6	1629.7	3.13
43	Moore	Earl	1907	CLE	AL	**34.713**	7	4.959	81	68	2	1337.7	2.58
44	Narleski	Ray	1958	CLE	AL	**33.588**	5	6.718	39	21	53	597.7	3.22
45	Bagby	Jim	1945	CLE	AL	**33.315**	5	6.663	55	54	5	982.7	3.45
46	Hargan	Steve	1972	CLE	AL	**32.771**	8	4.096	56	74	3	1053.3	3.78
47	Rhoads	Bob	1909	CLE	AL	**31.827**	7	4.547	88	66	1	1444.7	2.39
48	Hand	Brad	2020	CLE	AL	**31.660**	3	10.553	8	6	58	107.0	2.78
49	Bernhard	Bill	1907	CLE	AL	**31.250**	6	5.208	77	56	1	1175.0	2.45
50	Miller	Jake	1931	CLE	AL	**30.222**	8	3.778	55	52	3	964.0	3.92

Cleveland Indians – Top Fielders

Rank	FIRST BASE		FV	Lyear	G	FPCT	RF
1	Power	Vic	**1.3134**	1961	450	0.995	9.02
2	Vernon	Mickey	**1.2307**	1958	274	0.990	9.67
3	Fonseca	Lew	**1.2188**	1931	270	0.994	10.71
4	Chambliss	Chris	**1.2051**	1974	398	0.992	9.75
5	Stovall	George	**1.1762**	1911	802	0.985	11.29
6	Thornton	Andre	**1.1709**	1984	449	0.994	9.29
7	Rocco	Mickey	**1.1689**	1946	431	0.994	9.80
8	Hargrove	Mike	**1.1503**	1985	769	0.993	8.74
9	Fleming	Les	**1.1429**	1947	320	0.990	9.51
10	Morgan	Ed	**1.1156**	1933	456	0.985	10.37

Rank	SECOND BASE		FV	Lyear	G	FPCT	RF
1	Alomar	Roberto	**1.4219**	2001	468	0.988	4.61
2	Lajoie	Nap	**1.3823**	1914	1385	0.965	5.69
3	Hodapp	Johnny	**1.3403**	1932	354	0.971	5.93
4	Kuiper	Duane	**1.3194**	1981	774	0.984	5.00
5	Baerga	Carlos	**1.2956**	1999	735	0.974	5.22
6	Avila	Bobby	**1.2923**	1958	1098	0.979	5.15
7	Leon	Eddie	**1.2528**	1972	284	0.983	4.79
8	Bernazard	Tony	**1.2269**	1987	507	0.977	4.96
9	Gordon	Joe	**1.2261**	1950	549	0.975	5.11
10	Browne	Jerry	**1.2182**	1991	337	0.980	4.58

Rank	SHORTSTOP		FV	Lyear	G	FPCT	RF
1	Lary	Lyn	**1.6881**	1939	299	0.963	5.05
2	Vizquel	Omar	**1.6493**	2004	1472	0.985	4.40
3	Boudreau	Lou	**1.6473**	1950	1486	0.973	5.15
4	Sewell	Joe	**1.6089**	1928	1216	0.951	5.37
5	Duffy	Frank	**1.5968**	1977	797	0.979	4.47
6	Turner	Terry	**1.5710**	1918	722	0.953	5.18
7	Lindor	Francisco	**1.5568**	2020	763	0.981	3.79
8	Peralta	Jhonny	**1.5392**	2009	706	0.975	4.52
9	Veryzer	Tom	**1.5353**	1981	460	0.970	4.49
10	Fermin	Felix	**1.5334**	1993	624	0.971	4.38

Rank	THIRD BASE		FV	Lyear	G	FPCT	RF
1	Kamm	Willie	**1.6750**	1935	515	0.969	2.99
2	Nettles	Graig	**1.6610**	1972	462	0.966	3.28
3	Bell	Buddy	**1.5961**	1978	843	0.960	3.17
4	Keltner	Ken	**1.5778**	1949	1492	0.965	3.10
5	Hale	Odell	**1.5479**	1940	433	0.943	3.18

			FV	Lyear	G	FPCT	RF	
6	Bradley	Bill	1.5466	1910	1193	0.940	3.34	
7	Gardner	Larry	1.5375	1924	600	0.956	3.19	
8	Sewell	Joe	1.5279	1930	268	0.964	3.17	
9	Phillips	Bubba	1.5147	1962	373	0.964	2.88	
10	Jacoby	Brook	1.5059	1992	1109	0.957	2.45	

Rank	CATCHER		FV	Lyear	G	FPCT	RF	CS%
1	Azcue	Joe	1.9830	1969	561	0.994	7.20	0.471
2	Perez	Roberto	1.9757	2020	438	0.995	9.28	0.414
3	Hegan	Jim	1.9648	1957	1491	0.990	5.10	0.507
4	Hemsley	Rollie	1.9307	1941	377	0.986	5.44	0.445
5	Gomes	Yan	1.8819	2018	589	0.992	8.95	0.347
6	Fosse	Ray	1.8742	1977	577	0.986	6.65	0.381
7	Romano	Johnny	1.8634	1964	537	0.990	5.99	0.368
8	Diaz	Einar	1.8583	2002	453	0.990	7.42	0.338
9	O'Neill	Steve	1.8506	1923	1339	0.973	5.11	0.461
10	Pytlak	Frankie	1.8445	1940	598	0.991	4.76	0.441

Rank	OUTFIELD		FV	Lyear	G	FPCT	RF	ApG
1	Butler	Brett	1.6530	1987	601	0.993	2.92	0.075
2	Speaker	Tris	1.6138	1926	1475	0.976	2.75	0.151
3	Piersall	Jim	1.5699	1961	345	0.989	2.66	0.049
4	Manning	Rick	1.5614	1983	1051	0.986	2.81	0.059
5	Lofton	Kenny	1.5310	2007	1259	0.982	2.51	0.080
6	Sizemore	Grady	1.5245	2011	848	0.993	2.51	0.021
7	Cardenal	Jose	1.5244	1969	295	0.978	2.42	0.071
8	Hendrick	George	1.5207	1976	532	0.987	2.36	0.062
9	Davalillo	Vic	1.5178	1968	648	0.986	2.23	0.063
10	Snyder	Cory	1.5098	1990	599	0.983	2.22	0.109
11	Naquin	Tyler	1.5086	2020	313	0.997	1.84	0.077
12	Pinson	Vada	1.5000	1971	282	0.980	2.09	0.067
13	Minoso	Minnie	1.4956	1959	302	0.980	2.16	0.089
14	Uhlaender	Ted	1.4951	1971	265	0.992	1.82	0.042
15	Doby	Larry	1.4928	1958	1165	0.983	2.60	0.068
16	Averill	Earl	1.4899	1939	1483	0.970	2.62	0.073
17	Vosmik	Joe	1.4830	1936	808	0.981	2.31	0.078
18	Bourn	Michael	1.4742	2015	322	0.993	2.19	0.047
19	Birmingham	Joe	1.4720	1914	712	0.958	2.26	0.181
20	Bay	Harry	1.4719	1907	515	0.970	2.17	0.107
21	Brantley	Michael	1.4653	2018	1022	0.994	1.92	0.055
22	Kirkland	Willie	1.4637	1963	375	0.977	2.11	0.091
23	Vukovich	George	1.4478	1985	389	0.990	2.03	0.051
24	Colavito	Rocky	1.4459	1967	871	0.980	1.92	0.070
25	Jamieson	Charlie	1.4435	1932	1386	0.970	2.29	0.115
26	Chapman	Ben	1.4415	1940	286	0.968	2.40	0.077
27	Whiten	Mark	1.4206	2000	301	0.973	2.19	0.113
28	Belle	Albert	1.4199	1996	734	0.974	2.13	0.074
29	Norris	Jim	1.4146	1979	295	0.983	2.39	0.058
30	Carter	Joe	1.4140	1989	662	0.978	2.44	0.065

Rank	PITCHING		FV	Lyear	IP	FPCT	RF	
1	Perry	Gaylord	1.1121	1975	1131	0.977	2.03	
2	Lemon	Bob	1.1103	1958	2850	0.969	3.07	
3	Joss	Addie	1.1074	1910	2327	0.965	3.83	
4	Sutcliffe	Rick	1.1013	1984	554	0.985	2.10	
5	Coveleski	Stan	1.0959	1924	2502	0.976	3.05	
6	Ferrell	Wes	1.0928	1933	1321	0.978	2.47	
7	Candiotti	Tom	1.0848	1999	1202	0.976	2.39	
8	McLish	Cal	1.0770	1959	667	0.978	2.42	
9	Westbrook	Jake	1.0724	2010	1191	0.971	2.82	
10	Kluber	Corey	1.0673	2019	1342	0.986	1.46	

Franchise When and Where
Cleveland Indians (1915 to Present)
Cleveland Naps (1903-1914)
Cleveland Bronchos (1902); Cleveland Blues (1901)

COLORADO ROCKIES
Best Seasons and Careers of All-Time

It's another franchise with a shorter history and a ballpark with a Park Factor that skews the counting stats results, in a positive way for the batter, and a negative one for the pitcher, so in some ways it's difficult to choose a best ever team, and in other ways not. So for starters, there's not much doubt that decades from now when the Rockies have a longer history that several players on this list will still be at the franchise top. Larry Walker, Todd Helton, and Nolan Arenado will be making the All-Time Team for a long time. The pitchers, perhaps not so much. It's possible that not one will be there, outside German Marquez if he continues to impress.

Reserves

Bench - Carlos Gonzalez (OF), Brad Hawpe (OF/1B), Charlie Blackmon (OF), Vinny Castilla (3B), Andres Gallaraga (1B), Trevor Story (IF), Wilin Rosario (CATCHER).

Bullpen - Brian Fuentes (CL), Rafael Betancourt (SU), Jason Jennings, Pedro Astacio, Kyle Freeland, Jon Gray.

Colorado Rockies - Best Position Player Years

Rank	Name	First	Year	Team	Lg	HR	RBI	AVG	Age	PEVA-B
1	Walker	Larry	1997	COL	NL	49	130	0.366	31	28.501
2	Helton	Todd	2003	COL	NL	33	117	0.358	30	25.643
3	Blackmon	Charlie	2017	COL	NL	37	104	0.331	31	24.700
4	Holliday	Matt	2007	COL	NL	36	137	0.340	27	24.699
5	Arenado	Nolan	2016	COL	NL	41	133	0.294	25	22.940
6	Helton	Todd	2000	COL	NL	42	147	0.372	27	22.244
7	Arenado	Nolan	2017	COL	NL	37	130	0.309	26	22.085
8	Atkins	Garrett	2006	COL	NL	29	120	0.329	27	21.810
9	Helton	Todd	2001	COL	NL	49	146	0.336	28	20.540
10	Arenado	Nolan	2016	COL	NL	42	130	0.287	25	19.635
11	Gonzalez	Carlos	2010	COL	NL	34	117	0.336	25	19.250
12	Helton	Todd	2004	COL	NL	32	96	0.347	31	19.092
13	Holliday	Matt	2006	COL	NL	34	114	0.326	26	18.861
14	Arenado	Nolan	2018	COL	NL	38	110	0.297	27	18.782
15	Arenado	Nolan	2019	COL	NL	41	118	0.315	28	18.745
16	Tulowitzki	Troy	2009	COL	NL	32	92	0.297	25	17.461
17	Story	Trevor	2018	COL	NL	37	108	0.291	26	17.290
18	Castilla	Vinny	1998	COL	NL	46	144	0.319	31	17.100
19	Burks	Ellis	1996	COL	NL	40	128	0.344	32	16.456
20	Tulowitzki	Troy	2011	COL	NL	30	105	0.302	27	15.964

Colorado Rockies - Best Pitcher Years

Rank	Name	First	Year	Team	Lg	W	L	SV	IP	ERA	Age	PEVA-P
1	Jimenez	Ubaldo	2010	COL	NL	19	8	0	221.7	2.88	26	31.338
2	Jimenez	Ubaldo	2009	COL	NL	15	12	0	218.0	3.47	25	20.035
3	Freeland	Kyle	2018	COL	NL	17	7	0	202.3	2.85	25	20.020
4	Francis	Jeff	2007	COL	NL	17	9	0	215.3	4.22	26	15.645
5	Marquez	German	2018	COL	NL	14	11	0	196.0	3.77	23	14.901
6	Marquis	Jason	2009	COL	NL	15	13	0	216.0	4.04	31	14.173
7	Marquez	German	2020	COL	NL	4	6	0	81.7	3.75	25	14.127
8	Senzatela	Antonio	2020	COL	NL	5	3	0	73.3	3.44	25	13.920
9	Cook	Aaron	2008	COL	NL	16	9	0	211.3	3.96	29	13.582
10	Chacin	Jhoulys	2013	COL	NL	14	10	0	197.3	3.47	25	13.307
11	White	Gabe	2000	COL	NL	11	2	5	83.0	2.17	29	13.270
12	Francis	Jeff	2006	COL	NL	13	11	0	199.0	4.16	25	12.808
13	Astacio	Pedro	1999	COL	NL	17	11	0	232.0	5.04	30	12.605
14	Fuentes	Brian	2008	COL	NL	1	5	30	62.7	2.73	33	12.332
15	Marquez	German	2019	COL	NL	12	5	0	174.0	4.76	24	12.155
16	Jennings	Jason	2006	COL	NL	9	13	0	212.0	3.78	28	12.146
17	Jimenez	Ubaldo	2008	COL	NL	12	12	0	198.7	3.99	24	12.017
18	de la Rosa	Jorge	2013	COL	NL	16	6	0	167.7	3.49	32	11.515
19	de la Rosa	Jorge	2009	COL	NL	16	9	0	185.0	4.38	28	11.140
20	Ritz	Kevin	1996	COL	NL	17	11	0	213.0	5.28	31	10.928

Colorado Rockies - Top Career Batters

RANK	NAME	FIRST	LYR	TEAM	LG	PEVA-B	YRS	PPYR	HR	RBI	H	AVE
1	Helton	Todd	2013	COL	NL	195.680	17	11.511	369	1406	2519	0.316
2	Arenado	Nolan	2020	COL	NL	120.060	8	15.008	235	760	1206	0.293
3	Walker	Larry	2004	COL	NL	115.097	10	11.510	258	848	1361	0.334
4	Tulowitzki	Troy	2015	COL	NL	100.825	10	10.083	188	657	1165	0.299
5	Blackmon	Charlie	2020	COL	NL	97.190	10	9.719	178	553	1311	0.304
6	Gonzalez	Carlos	2018	COL	NL	83.913	10	8.391	227	749	1330	0.290
7	Bichette	Dante	1999	COL	NL	80.981	7	11.569	201	826	1278	0.316
8	Castilla	Vinny	2006	COL	NL	78.028	9	8.670	239	745	1206	0.294
9	Holliday	Matt	2018	COL	NL	69.103	6	11.517	130	486	863	0.319
10	Story	Trevor	2020	COL	NL	59.187	5	11.837	134	375	636	0.277
11	Galarraga	Andres	1997	COL	NL	55.236	5	11.047	172	579	843	0.316
12	Atkins	Garrett	2009	COL	NL	52.366	7	7.481	98	479	805	0.289
13	LeMahieu	DJ	2018	COL	NL	48.539	7	6.934	49	345	1011	0.299
14	Hawpe	Brad	2010	COL	NL	45.640	7	6.520	118	464	749	0.280
15	Burks	Ellis	1998	COL	NL	33.366	5	6.673	115	337	558	0.306
16	Perez	Neifi	2001	COL	NL	32.868	6	5.478	43	281	769	0.282
17	Fowler	Dexter	2013	COL	NL	29.279	6	4.880	40	210	606	0.270
18	Young	Eric	1997	COL	NL	27.044	5	5.409	30	227	626	0.295
19	Iannetta	Chris	2019	COL	NL	24.915	8	3.114	80	293	435	0.232
20	Weiss	Walt	1997	COL	NL	23.700	4	5.925	14	143	469	0.266
21	Barmes	Clint	2010	COL	NL	20.346	8	2.543	61	285	582	0.254
22	Cirillo	Jeff	2001	COL	NL	20.168	2	10.084	28	198	360	0.320
23	Rosario	Wilin	2015	COL	NL	19.588	5	3.918	71	241	413	0.273
24	Hayes	Charlie	1994	COL	NL	19.267	2	9.634	35	148	297	0.298
25	Wilson	Preston	2005	COL	NL	18.149	3	6.050	57	217	288	0.269
26	Smith	Seth	2011	COL	NL	17.318	5	3.464	51	181	354	0.275
27	Cuddyer	Michael	2014	COL	NL	16.738	3	5.579	46	173	318	0.307
28	Pierre	Juan	2002	COL	NL	14.945	3	4.982	3	110	434	0.308
29	Desmond	Ian	2019	COL	NL	14.314	3	4.771	49	193	337	0.252
30	Girardi	Joe	1995	COL	NL	13.862	3	4.621	15	120	302	0.274
31	Spilborghs	Ryan	2011	COL	NL	13.713	7	1.959	42	218	424	0.272
32	Payton	Jay	2010	COL	NL	13.588	3	4.529	36	118	250	0.311
33	Stewart	Ian	2011	COL	NL	13.328	5	2.666	54	187	293	0.236
34	Reynolds	Mark	2019	COL	NL	13.109	3	4.370	48	170	273	0.260
35	Dickerson	Corey	2015	COL	NL	13.061	3	4.354	39	124	255	0.299
36	Morneau	Justin	2015	COL	NL	11.542	2	5.771	20	97	212	0.316
37	Parra	Gerardo	2018	COL	NL	11.141	3	3.714	23	163	328	0.283
38	Reed	Jeff	1999	COL	NL	11.014	4	2.753	36	134	275	0.286
39	Kingery	Mike	1995	COL	NL	10.629	2	5.315	12	78	199	0.306
40	Uribe	Juan	2003	COL	NL	10.409	3	3.470	24	135	298	0.258
41	McMahon	Ryan	2020	COL	NL	10.155	4	2.539	38	129	202	0.237

Colorado Rockies - Top Career Pitchers

RANK	NAME	FIRST	LYEAR	LTEAM	LG	PEVA	YRS	PPYR	W	L	SV	IP	ERA
1	Jimenez	Ubaldo	2011	COL	NL	69.716	6	11.619	56	45	0	851.0	3.66
2	Marquez	German	2020	COL	NL	49.990	5	9.998	42	30	0	634.3	4.24
3	De La Rosa	Jorge	2016	COL	NL	49.125	9	5.458	86	61	0	1141.3	4.35
4	Cook	Aaron	2011	COL	NL	46.349	10	4.635	72	68	0	1312.3	4.53
5	Francis	Jeff	2013	COL	NL	43.790	8	5.474	64	62	0	1066.0	4.96
6	Fuentes	Brian	2008	COL	NL	41.071	7	5.867	16	26	115	410.3	3.38
7	Freeland	Kyle	2020	COL	NL	39.029	4	9.757	33	32	0	533.3	4.17
8	Jennings	Jason	2006	COL	NL	37.351	6	6.225	58	56	0	941.0	4.74
9	Astacio	Pedro	2001	COL	NL	34.466	5	6.893	53	48	0	827.3	5.43
10	Gray	Jon	2020	COL	NL	33.753	6	5.626	45	37	0	680.3	4.59
11	Chacin	Jhoulys	2014	COL	NL	31.724	6	5.287	38	48	0	672.0	3.78
12	Betancourt	Rafael	2015	COL	NL	27.984	6	4.664	15	15	58	275.7	3.53
13	Reed	Steve	2004	COL	NL	27.747	7	3.964	33	29	15	499.0	3.63
14	Belisle	Matt	2014	COL	NL	25.691	6	4.282	32	32	4	471.7	4.50
15	Senzatela	Antonio	2020	COL	NL	24.167	4	6.042	32	25	0	423.0	5.00
16	Ritz	Kevin	1998	COL	NL	23.826	5	4.765	39	38	2	576.3	5.20
17	Ottavino	Adam	2018	COL	NL	23.224	7	3.318	17	18	17	390.7	3.41
18	Jimenez	Jose	2003	COL	NL	20.928	4	5.232	15	23	102	300.7	4.13
19	Street	Huston	2011	COL	NL	20.371	3	6.790	9	9	84	167.3	3.50
20	Oberg	Scott	2019	COL	NL	19.901	5	3.980	18	8	7	257.3	3.85
21	Ruffin	Bruce	1997	COL	NL	18.840	5	3.768	17	18	60	321.0	3.84
22	Chatwood	Tyler	2017	COL	NL	18.466	5	3.693	34	35	2	505.7	4.18
23	Holmes	Darren	1997	COL	NL	17.893	5	3.579	23	13	46	328.0	4.42
24	Corpas	Manuel	2013	COL	NL	17.841	6	2.974	13	18	34	327.7	4.01
25	Wright	Jamey	2005	COL	NL	17.827	6	2.971	35	52	0	791.7	5.40
26	Reynoso	Armando	1996	COL	NL	17.434	4	4.358	30	31	0	503.0	4.65
27	Hammel	Jason	2011	COL	NL	16.547	3	5.516	27	30	1	524.7	4.63
28	Bettis	Chad	2019	COL	NL	16.252	7	2.322	31	31	1	600.7	5.12
29	Thomson	John	2002	COL	NL	15.909	5	3.182	27	43	0	611.0	5.01
30	Leskanic	Curt	1999	COL	NL	15.534	7	2.219	31	20	20	470.0	4.92
31	Bohanon	Brian	2001	COL	NL	14.973	3	4.991	29	30	0	471.3	5.82
32	Rusin	Chris	2019	COL	NL	14.868	5	2.974	16	19	2	356.7	4.52
33	Brothers	Rex	2015	COL	NL	14.831	5	2.966	16	11	20	242.3	3.42
34	Kile	Darryl	1999	COL	NL	14.476	2	7.238	21	30	0	421.0	5.84
35	White	Gabe	2001	COL	NL	14.415	2	7.208	12	9	5	150.7	4.00
36	Chacon	Shawn	2005	COL	NL	14.408	5	2.882	24	45	35	552.3	5.20
37	Marquis	Jason	2009	COL	NL	14.173	1	14.173	15	13	0	216.0	4.04
38	Freeman	Marvin	1996	COL	NL	13.811	3	4.604	20	18	0	337.0	4.91
39	Anderson	Tyler	2019	COL	NL	13.782	4	3.445	18	24	0	397.0	4.69
40	Fogg	Josh	2009	COL	NL	13.178	3	4.393	21	20	0	383.3	5.05
41	Hampton	Mike	2002	COL	NL	11.840	2	5.920	21	28	0	381.7	5.75

RANK	NAME	FIRST	LYEAR	LTEAM	LG	PEVA	YRS	PPYR	W	L	SV	IP	ERA
42	Buchholz	Taylor	2010	COL	NL	**11.701**	3	3.900	13	11	1	170.0	3.44
43	Dipoto	Jerry	2000	COL	NL	**11.333**	4	2.833	12	12	36	267.3	4.21
44	DeJean	Mike	2006	COL	NL	**10.057**	6	1.676	17	12	4	294.7	4.70

Colorado Rockies – Top Fielders

Rank	FIRST BASE		FV	Lyear	G	FPCT	RF
1	Helton	Todd	**1.3230**	2013	2178	0.996	9.46
2	Galarraga	Andres	**1.2741**	1997	677	0.991	10.01
3	Reynolds	Mark	**1.2412**	2019	285	0.994	8.87

Rank	SECOND BASE		FV	Lyear	G	FPCT	RF
1	LeMahieu	DJ	**1.4507**	2018	877	0.991	4.76
2	Young	Eric	**1.3378**	1997	413	0.977	5.37
3	Lansing	Mike	**1.3291**	2000	276	0.986	4.91
4	Barmes	Clint	**1.1485**	2010	306	0.982	4.40

Rank	SHORTSTOP		FV	Lyear	G	FPCT	RF
1	Tulowitzki	Troy	**1.6927**	2015	1033	0.985	4.72
2	Perez	Neifi	**1.6535**	2001	627	0.978	4.81
3	Story	Trevor	**1.6492**	2020	595	0.980	4.19
4	Weiss	Walt	**1.6074**	1997	520	0.971	4.45
5	Uribe	Juan	**1.5400**	2003	298	0.971	4.85
6	Barmes	Clint	**1.4108**	2010	333	0.969	4.48

Rank	THIRD BASE		FV	Lyear	G	FPCT	RF
1	Arenado	Nolan	**1.6700**	2020	1069	0.972	2.95
2	Cirillo	Jeff	**1.6681**	2001	292	0.973	2.68
3	Castilla	Vinny	**1.6114**	2006	931	0.964	2.73
4	Hayes	Charlie	**1.5833**	1994	264	0.950	2.66
5	Atkins	Garrett	**1.3998**	2009	642	0.954	2.36
6	Stewart	Ian	**1.3194**	2011	354	0.958	2.14

Rank	CATCHER		FV	Lyear	G	FPCT	RF	CS%
1	Girardi	Joe	**1.8134**	1995	299	0.989	6.42	0.299
2	Wolters	Tony	**1.7545**	2020	351	0.995	7.62	0.310
3	Iannetta	Chris	**1.7165**	2019	571	0.995	6.99	0.232
4	Torrealba	Yorvit	**1.6796**	2013	356	0.993	6.89	0.251
5	Manwaring	Kirt	**1.6524**	1999	252	0.989	5.43	0.253
6	Rosario	Wilin	**1.6315**	2015	323	0.987	6.94	0.280
7	Reed	Jeff	**1.6017**	1999	324	0.985	5.30	0.313

Rank	OUTFIELD		FV	Lyear	G	FPCT	RF	ApG
1	Walker	Larry	**1.4406**	2004	1108	0.987	1.87	0.086
2	Blackmon	Charlie	**1.4293**	2020	1078	0.988	2.00	0.038
3	Pierre	Juan	**1.4155**	2002	353	0.985	2.40	0.023
4	Bichette	Dante	**1.4126**	1999	997	0.973	1.81	0.073
5	Wilson	Preston	**1.3769**	2005	276	0.974	2.18	0.047
6	Gonzalez	Carlos	**1.3583**	2018	1227	0.987	1.71	0.059
7	Burks	Ellis	**1.3470**	1998	559	0.977	1.67	0.043
8	Fowler	Dexter	**1.3379**	2013	620	0.984	2.12	0.034
9	Holliday	Matt	**1.2982**	2018	700	0.978	1.81	0.049
10	Hawpe	Brad	**1.2362**	2010	747	0.978	1.70	0.064
11	Parra	Gerardo	**1.2302**	2018	313	0.978	1.57	0.086
12	Smith	Seth	**1.2098**	2011	354	0.983	1.59	0.040
13	Spilborghs	Ryan	**1.1496**	2011	495	0.981	1.37	0.040
14	Dahl	David	**1.1376**	2020	262	0.988	1.58	0.027

Rank	PITCHING		FV	Lyear	IP	FPCT	RF
1	Ritz	Kevin	**1.0679**	1998	576	1.000	2.65
2	Bettis	Chad	**1.0404**	2019	601	0.974	2.28
3	Astacio	Pedro	**1.0338**	2001	827	0.967	1.94
4	Cook	Aaron	**1.0270**	2011	1312	0.961	2.68
5	Francis	Jeff	**1.0266**	2013	1066	0.995	1.81
6	Jimenez	Ubaldo	**1.0195**	2011	851	0.943	2.09
7	Jennings	Jason	**1.0072**	2006	941	0.966	1.91
8	Chatwood	Tyler	**1.0069**	2017	506	0.950	2.35

| 9 | Hammel | Jason | **0.9931** | 2011 | 525 | 0.981 | 1.77 |
| 10 | Wright | Jamey | **0.9879** | 2005 | 792 | 0.954 | 2.36 |

Franchise When and Where
Colorado Rockies (1993 to Present)

DETROIT TIGERS
Best Seasons and Careers of All-Time

It's an All-Time team with a mix of eras, from Miguel Cabrera and Justin Verlander to the earlier stars of Ty Cobb, Sam Crawford, and Hal Newhouser. And those stars of the past ... well, sometimes I think we forget just how good Ty Cobb was. No, his reputation was not great, but his exploits on the field were dominant. He had nine of the Top 20 best seasons ever in Tiger history for a position player. Cobb got on base, and scored runs. Newhouser was not quite as dominant on the pitcher list of best seasons with only five of the Top 20, but his repertoire falls not far short. It adds up to second on the All-Time Best pitcher list for Detroit with recent star Justin Verlander taking the top. And there's some interesting players on the bench, like Norm Cash backing up Hank Greenberg at first base and Lou Whitaker waiting for his chance at playing time behind Charlie Gehringer.

Reserves

Bench - Harry Heilman (OF/1B), Bobby Veach (OF), Rudy York (1b/C), Norm Cash (1b), Lou Whitaker (SS), Donie Bush (SS), Lance Parrish (CATCHER).

Bullpen - John Hiller (CL), George Mullen (SU), Jim Bunning, Frank Lary, Denny McLain, Max Scherzer.

Detroit Tigers - Best Position Player Years

Rank	Name	First	Year	Team	Lg	HR	RBI	AVG	Age	PEVA-B
1	Cobb	Ty	1917	DET	AL	6	102	0.383	31	48.911
2	Cobb	Ty	1915	DET	AL	3	99	0.369	29	43.671
3	Cobb	Ty	1911	DET	AL	8	127	0.420	25	42.464
4	Cobb	Ty	1909	DET	AL	9	107	0.377	23	39.724
5	Cabrera	Miguel	2012	DET	AL	44	139	0.330	29	39.160
6	Cobb	Ty	1918	DET	AL	3	64	0.382	32	37.701
7	Cash	Norm	1961	DET	AL	41	132	0.361	27	36.206
8	Cobb	Ty	1912	DET	AL	7	83	0.409	26	36.188
9	Cabrera	Miguel	2010	DET	AL	38	126	0.328	27	36.079
10	Greenberg	Hank	1937	DET	AL	40	183	0.337	26	35.096
11	Cabrera	Miguel	2013	DET	AL	44	137	0.348	30	34.680
12	Cobb	Ty	1916	DET	AL	5	68	0.371	30	34.488
13	Cabrera	Miguel	2011	DET	AL	30	105	0.344	28	32.955
14	Cobb	Ty	1910	DET	AL	8	91	0.383	24	32.427
15	Greenberg	Hank	1935	DET	AL	36	170	0.328	24	32.405
16	Greenberg	Hank	1940	DET	AL	41	150	0.340	29	32.198
17	Cobb	Ty	1907	DET	AL	5	119	0.350	21	31.905
18	Ordonez	Magglio	2007	DET	AL	28	139	0.363	33	31.089
19	Greenberg	Hank	1938	DET	AL	58	146	0.315	27	30.495
20	Fielder	Cecil	1990	DET	AL	51	132	0.277	27	29.877

Detroit Tigers - Best Pitcher Years

Rank	Name	First	Year	Team	Lg	W	L	SV	IP	ERA	Age	PEVA-P
1	Newhouser	Hal	1945	DET	AL	25	9	2	313.3	1.81	24	48.483
2	Verlander	Justin	2011	DET	AL	24	5	0	251.0	2.40	28	43.997
3	Trout	Dizzy	1944	DET	AL	27	14	0	352.3	2.12	29	39.350
4	Newhouser	Hal	1946	DET	AL	26	9	1	292.7	1.94	25	38.936
5	Verlander	Justin	2012	DET	AL	17	8	0	238.3	2.64	29	36.365
6	Newhouser	Hal	1944	DET	AL	29	9	2	312.3	2.22	23	32.575
7	McLain	Denny	1968	DET	AL	31	6	0	336.0	1.96	24	32.509
8	Bunning	Jim	1957	DET	AL	20	8	1	267.3	2.69	26	32.324
9	McLain	Denny	1969	DET	AL	24	9	0	325.0	2.80	25	29.720
10	Scherzer	Max	2013	DET	AL	21	3	0	214.3	2.90	29	29.035
11	Verlander	Justin	2009	DET	AL	19	9	0	240.0	3.45	26	27.965
12	Verlander	Justin	2016	DET	AL	16	9	0	227.7	3.04	33	26.544
13	Newhouser	Hal	1947	DET	AL	17	17	2	285.0	2.87	26	26.043
14	Lary	Frank	1961	DET	AL	23	9	0	275.3	3.24	31	25.029
15	Bunning	Jim	1961	DET	AL	17	11	1	268.0	3.19	30	24.083
16	Fidrych	Mark	1976	DET	AL	19	9	0	250.3	2.34	22	23.725
17	Bunning	Jim	1960	DET	AL	11	14	0	252.0	2.79	29	23.650
18	Lolich	Mickey	1971	DET	AL	25	14	0	376.0	2.92	31	23.606
19	Newsom	Bobo	1940	DET	AL	21	5	0	264.0	2.83	33	23.291
20	Newhouser	Hal	1948	DET	AL	21	12	1	272.3	3.01	27	21.891

Detroit Tigers - Top Career Batters

RANK	NAME	FIRST	LYR	TEAM	LG	PEVA-B	YRS	PPYR	HR	RBI	H	AVE
1	Cobb	Ty	1926	DET	AL	553.520	22	25.160	111	1804	3900	0.368
2	Kaline	Al	1974	DET	AL	297.259	22	13.512	399	1583	3007	0.297

RANK	NAME	FIRST	LYR	TEAM	LG	PEVA-B	YRS	PPYR	HR	RBI	H	AVE
3	Cabrera	Miguel	2020	DET	AL	254.542	13	19.580	349	1206	2024	0.313
4	Crawford	Sam	1917	DET	AL	252.290	15	16.819	70	1264	2466	0.309
5	Heilmann	Harry	1929	DET	AL	235.849	15	15.723	164	1442	2499	0.342
6	Gehringer	Charlie	1942	DET	AL	233.202	19	12.274	184	1427	2839	0.320
7	Greenberg	Hank	1946	DET	AL	206.974	12	17.248	306	1202	1528	0.319
8	Trammell	Alan	1996	DET	AL	189.326	20	9.466	185	1003	2365	0.285
9	Veach	Bobby	1923	DET	AL	188.829	12	15.736	59	1042	1859	0.311
10	Cash	Norm	1974	DET	AL	173.654	15	11.577	373	1087	1793	0.272
11	Whitaker	Lou	1995	DET	AL	170.425	19	8.970	244	1084	2369	0.276
12	Bush	Donie	1921	DET	AL	149.331	14	10.667	9	427	1745	0.250
13	Freehan	Bill	1976	DET	AL	145.340	15	9.689	200	758	1591	0.262
14	York	Rudy	1945	DET	AL	124.435	10	12.444	239	936	1317	0.282
15	Parrish	Lance	1986	DET	AL	116.688	10	11.669	212	700	1123	0.263
16	Fielder	Cecil	1996	DET	AL	104.158	7	14.880	245	758	947	0.258
17	Horton	Willie	1977	DET	AL	102.064	15	6.804	262	886	1490	0.276
18	McAuliffe	Dick	1973	DET	AL	97.254	14	6.947	192	672	1471	0.249
19	Fryman	Travis	1997	DET	AL	92.871	8	11.609	149	679	1176	0.274
20	Gibson	Kirk	1995	DET	AL	92.140	12	7.678	195	668	1140	0.273
21	Lemon	Chet	1990	DET	AL	89.891	9	9.988	142	536	1071	0.263
22	Higginson	Bobby	2005	DET	AL	89.291	11	8.117	187	709	1336	0.272
23	Kuenn	Harvey	1959	DET	AL	87.661	8	10.958	53	423	1372	0.314
24	Kell	George	1952	DET	AL	81.711	7	11.673	25	414	1075	0.325
25	Northrup	Jim	1974	DET	AL	79.258	11	7.205	145	570	1184	0.267
26	Colavito	Rocky	1963	DET	AL	78.359	4	19.590	139	430	633	0.271
27	Rogell	Billy	1939	DET	AL	77.522	10	7.752	39	532	1210	0.274
28	Wertz	Vic	1963	DET	AL	71.279	9	7.920	109	531	798	0.286
29	Martinez	Victor	2018	DET	AL	69.271	7	9.896	115	540	1033	0.290
30	Ordonez	Magglio	2011	DET	AL	68.792	7	9.827	107	533	989	0.312
31	Phillips	Tony	1994	DET	AL	67.040	5	13.408	61	309	771	0.281
32	Barrett	Jimmy	1905	DET	AL	66.043	5	13.209	10	174	660	0.292
33	Kemp	Steve	1981	DET	AL	65.732	5	13.146	89	422	711	0.284
34	Tettleton	Mickey	1994	DET	AL	64.841	4	16.210	112	333	469	0.249
35	Stanley	Mickey	1978	DET	AL	64.185	15	4.279	117	500	1243	0.248
36	Inge	Brandon	2012	DET	AL	64.003	12	5.334	140	589	1083	0.234
37	Maxwell	Charlie	1962	DET	AL	63.983	8	7.998	133	455	723	0.268
38	Boone	Ray	1958	DET	AL	62.981	6	10.497	105	460	723	0.291
39	Fox	Pete	1940	DET	AL	60.724	8	7.591	59	493	1182	0.302
40	Evers	Hoot	1954	DET	AL	59.372	9	6.597	63	429	787	0.290
41	McIntyre	Matty	1910	DET	AL	59.065	7	8.438	3	211	783	0.261
42	Blue	Lu	1927	DET	AL	56.692	7	8.099	19	407	1002	0.295
43	Wert	Don	1970	DET	AL	56.509	8	7.064	77	364	927	0.244
44	Castellanos	Nicholas	2019	DET	AL	55.661	7	7.952	104	424	862	0.274
45	LeFlore	Ron	1979	DET	AL	55.056	6	9.176	51	265	970	0.297

RANK	NAME	FIRST	LYR	TEAM	LG	PEVA-B	YRS	PPYR	HR	RBI	H	AVE
46	Guillen	Carlos	2011	DET	AL	54.616	8	6.827	95	449	892	0.297
47	Higgins	Pinky	1946	DET	AL	54.140	7	7.734	60	472	878	0.280
48	Granderson	Curtis	2009	DET	AL	54.017	6	9.003	102	299	702	0.272
49	Evans	Darrell	1988	DET	AL	51.178	5	10.236	141	405	559	0.238
50	Rodriguez	Aurelio	1979	DET	AL	51.003	9	5.667	85	423	1040	0.239

Detroit Tigers - Top Career Pitchers

RANK	NAME	FIRST	LYEAR	LTEAM	LG	PEVA	YRS	PPYR	W	L	SV	IP	ERA
1	Verlander	Justin	2017	DET	AL	240.225	13	18.479	183	114	0	2511.0	3.49
2	Newhouser	Hal	1953	DET	AL	214.336	15	14.289	200	148	19	2944.0	3.07
3	Morris	Jack	1990	DET	AL	155.657	14	11.118	198	150	0	3042.7	3.73
4	Lolich	Mickey	1975	DET	AL	129.756	13	9.981	207	175	10	3361.7	3.45
5	Trout	Dizzy	1952	DET	AL	126.383	14	9.027	161	153	34	2591.7	3.20
6	Bunning	Jim	1963	DET	AL	124.530	9	13.837	118	87	12	1867.3	3.45
7	Bridges	Tommy	1946	DET	AL	117.328	16	7.333	194	138	10	2826.3	3.57
8	Lary	Frank	1964	DET	AL	116.661	11	10.606	123	110	7	2008.7	3.46
9	Mullin	George	1913	DET	AL	94.732	12	7.894	209	179	6	3394.0	2.76
10	McLain	Denny	1970	DET	AL	91.872	8	11.484	117	62	1	1593.0	3.13
11	Dauss	Hooks	1926	DET	AL	89.926	15	5.995	222	182	40	3390.7	3.30
12	Scherzer	Max	2014	DET	AL	77.820	5	15.564	82	35	0	1013.0	3.52
13	Petry	Dan	1991	DET	AL	73.495	11	6.681	119	93	0	1843.0	3.84
14	Trucks	Virgil	1956	DET	AL	69.230	12	5.769	114	96	13	1800.7	3.50
15	Whitehill	Earl	1932	DET	AL	67.701	10	6.770	133	119	7	2171.3	4.16
16	Hiller	John	1980	DET	AL	63.837	15	4.256	87	76	125	1242.0	2.83
17	Hutchinson	Fred	1953	DET	AL	59.270	10	5.927	95	71	7	1464.0	3.73
18	Rowe	Schoolboy	1942	DET	AL	54.275	10	5.427	105	62	8	1445.0	4.01
19	Tanana	Frank	1992	DET	AL	52.880	8	6.610	96	82	1	1551.3	4.08
20	Foytack	Paul	1963	DET	AL	49.068	10	4.907	81	81	7	1425.3	4.14
21	Coleman	Joe	1976	DET	AL	48.914	6	8.152	88	73	0	1407.7	3.82
22	Aguirre	Hank	1967	DET	AL	47.180	10	4.718	64	64	27	1179.0	3.29
23	Donovan	Bill	1918	DET	AL	46.856	11	4.260	141	96	3	2137.3	2.49
24	Wilcox	Milt	1985	DET	AL	45.783	9	5.087	97	75	0	1495.3	3.91
25	Porcello	Rick	2014	DET	AL	45.653	6	7.609	76	63	0	1073.3	4.30
26	Newsom	Bobo	1941	DET	AL	44.197	3	14.732	50	35	4	760.3	3.59
27	Henneman	Mike	1995	DET	AL	44.119	9	4.902	57	34	154	669.7	3.05
28	Mossi	Don	1963	DET	AL	43.850	5	8.770	59	44	4	929.7	3.49
29	Benton	Al	1948	DET	AL	42.970	9	4.774	71	64	45	1218.7	3.46
30	Bonderman	Jeremy	2013	DET	AL	42.148	9	4.683	68	78	0	1192.7	4.91
31	Hernandez	Willie	1989	DET	AL	41.936	6	6.989	36	31	120	483.7	2.98
32	Coveleski	Harry	1918	DET	AL	41.550	5	8.310	69	43	8	1023.3	2.34
33	Killian	Ed	1910	DET	AL	41.198	7	5.885	99	74	6	1536.7	2.38
34	Terrell	Walt	1992	DET	AL	40.914	7	5.845	79	76	0	1328.0	4.26
35	Sorrell	Vic	1937	DET	AL	39.637	10	3.964	92	101	10	1671.7	4.43

RANK	NAME	FIRST	LYEAR	LTEAM	LG	PEVA	YRS	PPYR	W	L	SV	IP	ERA
36	Hoeft	Billy	1959	DET	AL	38.379	8	4.797	74	78	11	1324.7	4.02
37	Robertson	Nate	2009	DET	AL	37.304	7	5.329	51	68	1	1042.7	4.87
38	Wilson	Earl	1970	DET	AL	37.219	5	7.444	64	45	0	962.3	3.18
39	Sanchez	Anibal	2017	DET	AL	36.295	6	6.049	46	49	0	798.3	4.43
40	Willett	Ed	1913	DET	AL	35.850	8	4.481	96	80	3	1545.7	2.89
41	Houtteman	Art	1953	DET	AL	35.448	8	4.431	53	69	16	1076.3	4.13
42	Lopez	Aurelio	1985	DET	AL	32.648	7	4.664	53	30	85	713.0	3.41
43	Moehler	Brian	2002	DET	AL	32.376	7	4.625	48	52	0	809.0	4.44
44	Jones	Todd	2008	DET	AL	31.898	8	3.987	23	32	235	479.3	4.07
45	Thompson	Justin	1999	DET	AL	31.875	4	7.969	36	43	0	647.0	3.98
46	Auker	Elden	1938	DET	AL	30.919	6	5.153	77	52	2	1083.7	4.26
47	Uhle	George	1933	DET	AL	30.071	5	6.014	44	41	10	828.3	3.91
48	Rozema	Dave	1984	DET	AL	29.768	8	3.721	57	46	10	1007.3	3.38
49	Gullickson	Bill	1994	DET	AL	29.401	4	7.350	51	36	0	722.7	4.68
50	Boyd	Matthew	2020	DET	AL	29.137	6	4.856	34	52	0	699.0	4.98

Detroit Tigers – Top Fielders

Rank	FIRST BASE		FV	Lyear	G	FPCT	RF
1	Thompson	Jason	1.2383	1980	602	0.993	10.23
2	Clark	Tony	1.1841	2001	681	0.992	9.43
3	Burns	George	1.1505	1917	469	0.985	11.65
4	Pena	Carlos	1.1396	2005	387	0.993	9.27
5	Greenberg	Hank	1.1248	1946	1019	0.991	10.04
6	Blue	Lu	1.1228	1927	894	0.988	10.84
7	Dropo	Walt	1.1218	1954	360	0.991	8.90
8	York	Rudy	1.1148	1945	945	0.989	9.91
9	Cash	Norm	1.1104	1974	1912	0.992	8.49
10	Fielder	Prince	1.1000	2013	310	0.994	8.42

Rank	SECOND BASE		FV	Lyear	G	FPCT	RF
1	Polanco	Placido	1.4189	2009	625	0.994	4.95
2	Priddy	Jerry	1.3781	1953	431	0.978	5.84
3	Easley	Damion	1.3567	2002	794	0.985	4.94
4	Kinsler	Ian	1.3511	2017	599	0.986	4.67
5	Gehringer	Charlie	1.3477	1942	2206	0.976	5.64
6	Whitaker	Lou	1.3093	1995	2308	0.984	4.95
7	Mayo	Eddie	1.2840	1948	544	0.978	5.33
8	Bolling	Frank	1.2812	1960	779	0.981	5.03
9	Bloodworth	Jimmy	1.2810	1946	334	0.973	5.53
10	Gleason	Kid	1.2647	1902	253	0.932	5.77

Rank	SHORTSTOP		FV	Lyear	G	FPCT	RF
1	Brinkman	Ed	1.6727	1974	628	0.978	4.67
2	Rogell	Billy	1.6125	1939	1148	0.957	5.18
3	Cruz	Deivi	1.6022	2001	702	0.979	4.40
4	Iglesias	Jose	1.5955	2018	549	0.985	4.01
5	Bush	Donie	1.5885	1921	1846	0.937	5.45
6	Kuenn	Harvey	1.5830	1957	747	0.964	4.63
7	Elberfeld	Kid	1.5758	1902	285	0.916	6.04
8	Trammell	Alan	1.5744	1996	2139	0.977	4.47
9	Peralta	Jhonny	1.5512	2013	446	0.989	4.06
10	Tavener	Jackie	1.5354	1928	537	0.952	5.05

Rank	THIRD BASE		FV	Lyear	G	FPCT	RF
1	Kell	George	1.6207	1952	826	0.971	3.14
2	Inge	Brandon	1.6119	2012	999	0.961	2.80
3	Rodriguez	Aurelio	1.5966	1979	1236	0.966	3.03
4	Boone	Ray	1.5762	1957	505	0.958	3.21
5	McManus	Marty	1.5686	1931	473	0.962	3.19

6	Fryman	Travis	**1.5619**	1997	767	0.966	2.72
7	Vitt	Ossie	**1.5471**	1918	565	0.955	3.51
8	Wert	Don	**1.5412**	1970	1036	0.968	2.79
9	Owen	Marv	**1.5317**	1937	717	0.954	2.93
10	Casey	Doc	**1.5002**	1902	259	0.896	3.63

Rank	CATCHER		FV	Lyear	G	FPCT	RF	CS%
1	Richards	Paul	**2.0601**	1946	327	0.988	5.65	0.581
2	Freehan	Bill	**1.9724**	1976	1581	0.993	6.74	0.368
3	Parrish	Lance	**1.9687**	1986	1039	0.991	5.65	0.439
4	Ausmus	Brad	**1.9632**	2000	350	0.994	6.47	0.388
5	Bassler	Johnny	**1.9070**	1927	730	0.982	4.35	0.467
6	Rodriguez	Ivan	**1.8896**	2008	578	0.993	6.50	0.398
7	McCann	James	**1.8736**	2018	434	0.997	7.55	0.368
8	Cochrane	Mickey	**1.8650**	1937	303	0.989	4.73	0.418
9	Avila	Alex	**1.8553**	2017	683	0.995	7.46	0.297
10	House	Frank	**1.8530**	1961	422	0.989	5.05	0.510

Rank	OUTFIELD		FV	Lyear	G	FPCT	RF	ApG
1	Barrett	Jimmy	**1.6374**	1905	587	0.958	2.38	0.172
2	Hunter	Brian	**1.6246**	1999	319	0.990	2.71	0.063
3	Granderson	Curtis	**1.5886**	2009	685	0.993	2.55	0.036
4	Tuttle	Bill	**1.5724**	1957	570	0.982	2.72	0.084
5	Bruton	Bill	**1.5669**	1964	519	0.987	2.52	0.042
6	Jackson	Austin	**1.5529**	2014	667	0.991	2.51	0.043
7	Colavito	Rocky	**1.5476**	1963	625	0.983	2.12	0.075
8	McIntyre	Matty	**1.5306**	1910	786	0.970	2.18	0.134
9	McCosky	Barney	**1.5235**	1946	586	0.983	2.63	0.048
10	Lemon	Chet	**1.5045**	1990	1170	0.986	2.48	0.051
11	Kaline	Al	**1.5011**	1973	2488	0.986	2.09	0.068
12	Castellanos	Nicholas	**1.5011**	2019	261	0.989	2.03	0.050
13	LeFlore	Ron	**1.4999**	1979	745	0.973	2.70	0.083
14	Evers	Hoot	**1.4987**	1951	708	0.983	2.65	0.079
15	Kuenn	Harvey	**1.4933**	1959	276	0.986	2.25	0.054
16	Veach	Bobby	**1.4815**	1923	1565	0.964	2.31	0.121
17	Cobb	Ty	**1.4793**	1926	2722	0.961	2.33	0.138
18	Stanley	Mickey	**1.4785**	1978	1290	0.991	2.23	0.047
19	Maxwell	Charlie	**1.4718**	1962	709	0.988	2.13	0.054
20	Cramer	Doc	**1.4611**	1948	655	0.985	2.39	0.075
21	Pettis	Gary	**1.4579**	1992	291	0.988	2.88	0.027
22	Curtis	Chad	**1.4500**	1996	272	0.981	2.26	0.040
23	Kemp	Steve	**1.4432**	1981	602	0.982	2.08	0.068
24	Delsing	Jim	**1.4266**	1955	377	0.991	2.26	0.040
25	Jones	JaCoby	**1.4307**	2020	292	0.991	2.35	0.031
26	Rice	Harry	**1.4222**	1930	291	0.960	2.70	0.096
27	Deer	Rob	**1.4196**	1993	324	0.979	2.32	0.065
28	Crawford	Sam	**1.4132**	1917	1906	0.972	1.63	0.103
29	Groth	Johnny	**1.4108**	1960	681	0.984	2.22	0.068
30	Higginson	Bobby	**1.4091**	2005	1311	0.977	2.07	0.095

Rank	PITCHING		FV	Lyear	IP	FPCT	RF
1	Garver	Ned	**1.1025**	1956	702	0.969	2.42
2	Coveleski	Harry	**1.1014**	1918	1023	0.944	3.72
3	Ehmke	Howard	**1.0947**	1922	1236	0.968	3.32
4	Mullin	George	**1.0885**	1913	3394	0.948	3.69
5	Moore	Mike	**1.0851**	1995	501	0.981	2.80
6	Petry	Dan	**1.0802**	1991	1843	0.977	2.54
7	Dauss	Hooks	**1.0782**	1926	3391	0.968	3.26
8	Terrell	Walt	**1.0688**	1992	1328	0.975	2.12
9	Dubuc	Jean	**1.0660**	1916	1145	0.958	3.91
10	Willett	Ed	**1.0640**	1913	1546	0.951	3.88

Franchise When and Where
Detroit Tigers (1901 to Present)

HOUSTON ASTROS
Best Seasons and Careers of All-Time

It starts with the killer B's in Craig Biggio, Jeff Bagwell, and Lance Berkman from a generation ago, with the addition of new star Alex Bregman, who might play shortstop with Doug Rader at third, to the list. Yes, some of the shine might be off the current team with trash can troubles in their recent World Series run, but that doesn't take too much away from the era of today when Bregman, Verlander, Altuve, Springer, and more are deserving members of their All-Time team, whether that be in the starting lineup or as a reserve. The starting staff has some great names in Nolan Ryan and Phil Niekro and the man at the top of the starting rotation, Roy Oswalt, just does not seem to get enough credit for how great he was as an Astro outside of Houston. And who'd like to go up against that bullpen? And who should get that last spot in the pen? Long timers like Dallas Keuchel, or perhaps Bob Knepper, or short time great pitchers like Clemens or Gerrit Cole.

Reserves

Bench - Cesar Cedeno (OF), Terry Puhl (OF), Bill Doran (IF), Bob Watson (1B/OF), Joe Morgan (2B), Jose Altuve (2B), Alan Ashby (CATCHER).

Bullpen - Billy Wagner (CL), Dave Smith (SU), Shane Reynolds, Justin Verlander, Larry Dierker, Dallas Keuchel.

Houston Astros - Best Position Player Years

Rank	Name	First	Year	Team	Lg	HR	RBI	AVG	Age	PEVA-B
1	Bagwell	Jeff	1994	HOU	NL	39	116	0.368	26	38.044
2	Bagwell	Jeff	1999	HOU	NL	42	126	0.304	31	35.960
3	Bagwell	Jeff	1996	HOU	NL	31	120	0.315	28	31.039
4	Bagwell	Jeff	1997	HOU	NL	43	135	0.286	29	29.539
5	Bregman	Alex	2019	HOU	AL	41	112	0.296	25	29.250
6	Cruz	Jose	1984	HOU	NL	12	95	0.312	37	27.975
7	Cedeno	Cesar	1972	HOU	NL	22	82	0.320	21	27.803
8	Wynn	Jimmy	1968	HOU	NL	26	67	0.269	26	27.640
9	Berkman	Lance	2006	HOU	NL	45	136	0.315	30	27.139
10	Wynn	Jimmy	1969	HOU	NL	33	87	0.269	27	27.134
11	Wynn	Jimmy	1972	HOU	NL	24	90	0.273	30	26.180
12	Altuve	Jose	2016	HOU	AL	24	96	0.338	26	26.036
13	Wynn	Jimmy	1965	HOU	NL	22	73	0.275	23	25.873
14	Altuve	Jose	2017	HOU	AL	24	81	0.346	27	25.494
15	Bagwell	Jeff	2000	HOU	NL	47	132	0.310	32	25.140
16	Berkman	Lance	2008	HOU	NL	29	106	0.312	32	24.959
17	Bregman	Alex	2018	HOU	AL	31	103	0.286	24	24.590
18	Biggio	Craig	1997	HOU	NL	22	81	0.309	32	23.961
19	Berkman	Lance	2004	HOU	NL	30	106	0.316	28	23.880
20	Cruz	Jose	1983	HOU	NL	14	92	0.318	36	22.088

Houston Astros - Best Pitcher Years

Rank	Name	First	Year	Team	Lg	W	L	SV	IP	ERA	Age	PEVA-P
1	Verlander	Justin	2019	HOU	AL	21	6	0	223.0	2.58	36	47.983
2	Scott	Mike	1986	HOU	NL	18	10	0	275.3	2.22	31	44.955
3	Cole	Gerrit	2019	HOU	AL	20	5	0	212.3	2.50	29	44.051
4	Richard	J.R.	1979	HOU	NL	18	13	0	292.3	2.71	29	35.177
5	Dierker	Larry	1969	HOU	NL	20	13	0	305.3	2.33	23	34.302
6	Verlander	Justin	2018	HOU	AL	16	9	0	214.0	2.52	35	30.623
7	Pettitte	Andy	2005	HOU	NL	17	9	0	222.3	2.39	33	29.658
8	Oswalt	Roy	2006	HOU	NL	15	8	0	220.7	2.98	29	29.269
9	Keutchel	Dallas	2015	HOU	NL	20	8	0	232.0	2.48	27	28.617
10	Niekro	Joe	1982	HOU	NL	17	12	0	270.0	2.47	38	28.453
11	Clemens	Roger	2005	HOU	NL	13	8	0	211.3	1.87	43	28.104
12	Scott	Mike	1987	HOU	NL	16	13	0	247.7	3.23	32	27.688
13	Oswalt	Roy	2005	HOU	NL	20	12	0	241.7	2.94	28	24.970
14	Kile	Darryl	1997	HOU	NL	19	7	0	255.7	2.57	29	24.432
15	Hampton	Mike	1999	HOU	NL	22	4	0	239.0	2.90	27	23.528
16	Sutton	Don	1981	HOU	NL	11	9	0	158.7	2.61	36	23.269
17	Oswalt	Roy	2004	HOU	NL	20	10	0	237.0	3.49	27	22.905
18	Oswalt	Roy	2002	HOU	NL	19	9	0	233.0	3.01	25	22.588
19	Clemens	Roger	2004	HOU	NL	18	4	0	214.3	2.98	42	22.379
20	Ryan	Nolan	1981	HOU	NL	11	5	0	149.0	1.69	34	21.204

Houston Astros - Top Career Batters

RANK	NAME	FIRST	LYR	TEAM	LG	PEVA-B	YRS	PPYR	HR	RBI	H	AVE
1	Bagwell	Jeff	2005	HOU	NL	293.606	15	19.574	449	1529	2314	0.297
2	Biggio	Craig	2007	HOU	NL	226.358	20	11.318	291	1175	3060	0.281

RANK	NAME	FIRST	LYR	TEAM	LG	PEVA-B	YRS	PPYR	HR	RBI	H	AVE
3	Berkman	Lance	2010	HOU	NL	178.988	12	14.916	326	1090	1648	0.296
4	Wynn	Jimmy	1973	HOU	NL	172.930	11	15.721	223	719	1291	0.255
5	Cruz	Jose	1987	HOU	NL	168.825	13	12.987	138	942	1937	0.292
6	Cedeno	Cesar	1981	HOU	NL	156.475	12	13.040	163	778	1659	0.289
7	Watson	Bob	1979	HOU	NL	121.311	14	8.665	139	782	1448	0.297
8	Altuve	Jose	2020	HOU	AL	118.010	10	11.801	133	556	1610	0.311
9	Springer	George	2020	HOU	AL	88.095	7	12.585	174	458	832	0.270
10	Puhl	Terry	1990	HOU	NL	84.066	14	6.005	62	432	1357	0.281
11	Morgan	Joe	1980	HOU	NL	80.052	10	8.005	72	327	972	0.261
12	Rader	Doug	1975	HOU	NL	79.441	9	8.827	128	600	1060	0.250
13	Bregman	Alex	2020	HOU	AL	74.115	5	14.823	105	342	582	0.283
14	Doran	Bill	1990	HOU	NL	69.842	9	7.760	69	404	1139	0.267
15	Davis	Glenn	1990	HOU	NL	67.815	7	9.688	166	518	795	0.262
16	Caminiti	Ken	2000	HOU	NL	67.204	10	6.720	103	546	1037	0.264
17	Bass	Kevin	1994	HOU	NL	61.995	10	6.200	87	468	990	0.278
18	Staub	Rusty	1968	HOU	NL	61.675	6	10.279	57	370	792	0.273
19	Hidalgo	Richard	2004	HOU	NL	57.353	8	7.169	134	465	787	0.278
20	Lee	Carlos	2012	HOU	NL	56.899	6	9.483	133	533	894	0.286
21	Cabell	Enos	1985	HOU	NL	55.861	8	6.983	45	405	1124	0.281
22	Pence	Hunter	2011	HOU	NL	54.923	5	10.985	103	377	768	0.290
23	Correa	Carlos	2020	HOU	AL	54.671	6	9.112	107	397	626	0.276
24	Aspromonte	Bob	1968	HOU	NL	52.820	7	7.546	51	385	925	0.258
25	Ausmus	Brad	2008	HOU	NL	51.180	10	5.118	41	386	970	0.246
26	Gonzalez	Luis	1997	HOU	NL	47.156	7	6.737	62	366	683	0.266
27	Bell	Derek	1999	HOU	NL	45.054	5	9.011	74	444	770	0.284
28	Metzger	Roger	1978	HOU	NL	43.808	8	5.476	5	206	844	0.229
29	Alou	Moises	2001	HOU	NL	43.503	3	14.501	95	346	513	0.331
30	Ensberg	Morgan	2007	HOU	NL	43.393	7	6.199	105	335	551	0.266
31	Menke	Denis	1974	HOU	NL	42.767	5	8.553	30	282	575	0.266
32	Ashby	Alan	1989	HOU	NL	42.059	11	3.824	69	388	736	0.252
33	May	Lee	1974	HOU	NL	38.478	3	12.826	81	288	464	0.274
34	Finley	Steve	1994	HOU	NL	37.868	4	9.467	32	186	595	0.281
35	Garner	Phil	1987	HOU	NL	37.068	7	5.295	49	320	659	0.260
36	Reynolds	Craig	1989	HOU	NL	33.925	11	3.084	32	300	860	0.252
37	Gurriel	Yuli	2020	HOU	AL	33.283	5	6.657	71	301	565	0287
38	Walling	Denny	1992	HOU	NL	32.724	13	2.517	47	345	726	0.277
39	Howe	Art	1982	HOU	NL	31.655	7	4.522	39	266	609	0.269
40	Bourn	Michael	2011	HOU	NL	31.044	4	7.761	11	134	552	0.271
41	Gonzalez	Marwin	2018	HOU	AL	30.165	7	4.309	76	292	650	0.264
42	Thon	Dickie	1987	HOU	NL	29.939	7	4.277	33	172	492	0.270
43	Gross	Greg	1989	HOU	NL	29.603	5	5.921	0	109	473	0.293
44	Edwards	Johnny	1974	HOU	NL	28.920	6	4.820	25	199	466	0.237
45	Gattis	Evan	2018	HOU	AL	28.699	4	7.175	96	293	422	0.245

RANK	NAME	FIRST	LYR	TEAM	LG	PEVA-B	YRS	PPYR	HR	RBI	H	AVE
46	Hatcher	Billy	1989	HOU	NL	27.408	4	6.852	27	195	507	0.266
47	Castro	Jason	2016	HOU	AL	27.297	6	4.549	62	212	469	0.232
48	Reddick	Josh	2020	HOU	AL	26.789	4	6.697	48	208	439	0.275
49	Tejada	Miguel	2009	HOU	NL	23.334	2	11.667	27	152	378	0.298
50	Johnson	Cliff	1977	HOU	NL	23.066	6	3.844	52	172	255	0.256

Houston Astros - Top Career Pitchers

RANK	NAME	FIRST	LYEAR	LTEAM	LG	PEVA	YRS	PPYR	W	L	SV	IP	ERA
1	Oswalt	Roy	2010	HOU	NL	179.194	10	17.919	143	82	0	1932.3	3.24
2	Scott	Mike	1991	HOU	NL	131.199	9	14.578	110	81	0	1704.0	3.30
3	Niekro	Joe	1985	HOU	NL	122.547	11	11.141	144	116	9	2270.0	3.22
4	Ryan	Nolan	1988	HOU	NL	110.250	9	12.250	106	94	0	1854.7	3.13
5	Richard	J.R.	1980	HOU	NL	99.479	10	9.948	107	71	0	1606.0	3.15
6	Reynolds	Shane	2002	HOU	NL	91.426	11	8.311	103	86	0	1622.3	3.95
7	Verlander	Justin	2020	HOU	AL	82.053	4	20.513	43	15	0	477.0	2.45
8	Dierker	Larry	1976	HOU	NL	81.453	13	6.266	137	117	1	2294.3	3.28
9	Knepper	Bob	1989	HOU	NL	80.903	9	8.989	93	100	1	1738.0	3.66
10	Wagner	Billy	2003	HOU	NL	74.263	9	8.251	26	29	225	504.3	2.53
11	Keuchel	Dallas	2018	HOU	AL	71.321	7	10.189	76	63	0	1189.3	3.66
12	Smith	Dave	1990	HOU	NL	68.474	11	6.225	53	47	199	762.0	2.53
13	Hampton	Mike	2009	HOU	NL	63.325	7	9.046	76	50	0	1138.0	3.59
14	Cole	Gerrit	2019	HOU	AL	63.051	2	31.525	35	10	0	412.7	2.68
15	Rodriguez	Wandy	2012	HOU	NL	61.851	8	7.731	80	84	0	1306.7	4.04
16	Clemens	Roger	2006	HOU	NL	61.294	3	20.431	38	18	0	539.0	2.40
17	Kile	Darryl	1997	HOU	NL	55.820	7	7.974	71	65	0	1200.0	3.79
18	Wilson	Don	1974	HOU	NL	53.550	9	5.950	104	92	2	1748.3	3.15
19	Forsch	Ken	1980	HOU	NL	49.929	11	4.539	78	81	50	1493.7	3.18
20	Pettitte	Andy	2006	HOU	NL	46.901	3	15.634	37	26	0	519.7	3.38
21	Lima	Jose	2001	HOU	NL	45.043	5	9.009	46	42	2	804.0	4.77
22	Harnisch	Pete	1994	HOU	NL	44.498	4	11.125	45	33	0	736.0	3.41
23	McHugh	Collin	2019	HOU	AL	43.065	6	7.177	58	35	0	753.3	3.63
24	Sambito	Joe	1984	HOU	NL	42.534	8	5.317	33	32	72	536.0	2.42
25	Deshaies	Jim	1991	HOU	NL	42.472	7	6.067	61	59	0	1102.0	3.67
26	Miller	Wade	2004	HOU	NL	40.081	6	6.680	58	39	0	768.0	3.87
27	Lidge	Brad	2007	HOU	NL	39.320	6	6.553	23	20	123	401.0	3.30
28	Drabek	Doug	1996	HOU	NL	38.106	4	9.526	38	42	0	762.7	4.00
29	Darwin	Danny	1996	HOU	NL	36.671	6	6.112	47	35	12	769.0	3.21
30	Portugal	Mark	1993	HOU	NL	36.305	5	7.261	52	30	1	782.3	3.34
31	Sutton	Don	1982	HOU	NL	35.618	2	17.809	24	17	0	353.7	2.82
32	Farrell	Turk	1967	HOU	NL	34.004	6	5.667	53	64	8	1015.0	3.42
33	Dotel	Octavio	2004	HOU	NL	31.961	5	6.392	22	24	42	449.0	3.25
34	Andersen	Larry	1990	HOU	NL	26.488	5	5.298	22	16	20	410.3	2.57
35	Cuellar	Mike	1968	HOU	NL	24.997	4	6.249	37	36	6	700.3	2.74

RANK	NAME	FIRST	LYEAR	LTEAM	LG	PEVA	YRS	PPYR	W	L	SV	IP	ERA
36	Myers	Brett	2012	HOU	NL	24.080	3	8.027	21	26	19	470.3	3.77
37	Bruce	Bob	1966	HOU	NL	23.983	5	4.797	42	58	0	907.0	3.78
38	McCullers, Jr.	Lance	2020	HOU	AL	22.717	5	4.543	32	25	0	508.7	3.70
39	Devenski	Chris	2020	HOU	AL	22.579	5	4.516	16	16	7	309.0	3.35
40	Osuna	Roberto	2020	HOU	AL	22.279	3	7.426	6	5	51	92.0	2.45
41	Jones	Doug	1993	HOU	NL	22.255	2	11.128	15	18	62	197.0	3.02
42	Johnson	Ken	1965	HOU	NL	22.098	4	5.524	32	51	1	690.7	3.41
43	Greinke	Zack	2020	HOU	AL	21.704	2	10.852	11	4	0	129.7	3.54
44	Morton	Charlie	2018	HOU	AL	21.543	2	10.771	29	10	0	313.7	3.36
45	Ruhle	Vern	1984	HOU	NL	21.229	7	3.033	39	46	7	749.7	3.35
46	Roberts	Dave	1975	HOU	NL	21.204	4	5.301	47	44	4	843.7	3.69
47	Qualls	Chad	2015	HOU	AL	21.178	6	3.530	27	22	29	384.7	3.51
48	Lopez	Wilton	2012	HOU	NL	20.773	4	5.193	13	13	11	223.7	3.14
49	Norris	Bud	2013	HOU	AL	20.585	5	4.117	34	46	0	689.7	4.33
50	Hernandez	Xavier	1996	HOU	NL	20.269	5	4.054	22	19	25	407.7	3.40

Houston Astros – Top Fielders

Rank	FIRST BASE		FV	Lyear	G	FPCT	RF
1	May	Lee	1.2805	1974	435	0.994	9.27
2	Bagwell	Jeff	1.2138	2005	2111	0.993	9.12
3	Davis	Glenn	1.1974	1990	810	0.992	9.26
4	Knight	Ray	1.1833	1984	263	0.993	9.76
5	Watson	Bob	1.1177	1979	790	0.992	8.83
6	Staub	Rusty	1.1106	1968	307	0.991	9.18
7	Berkman	Lance	1.0962	2010	709	0.995	8.95
8	Gurriel	Yuli	1.0897	2020	405	0.995	7.81
9	Cabell	Enos	1.0502	1985	263	0.993	7.13

Rank	SECOND BASE		FV	Lyear	G	FPCT	RF
1	Helms	Tommy	1.3329	1975	459	0.984	5.21
2	Biggio	Craig	1.3273	2007	1989	0.984	4.75
3	Kent	Jeff	1.3017	2004	267	0.986	4.80
4	Morgan	Joe	1.2879	1980	987	0.976	5.04
5	Doran	Bill	1.2694	1990	1138	0.983	4.73
6	Altuve	Jose	1.2289	2020	1252	0.985	4.04
7	Howe	Art	1.2018	1980	276	0.983	4.75

Rank	SHORTSTOP		FV	Lyear	G	FPCT	RF
1	Metzger	Roger	1.6300	1978	1007	0.977	4.69
2	Tejada	Miguel	1.6199	2009	315	0.976	4.18
3	Thon	Dickie	1.4958	1987	505	0.968	4.29
4	Everett	Adam	1.4901	2007	632	0.977	4.27
5	Jackson	Sonny	1.4898	1967	294	0.946	4.62
6	Reynolds	Craig	1.4801	1989	926	0.969	4.10
7	Correa	Carlos	1.4714	2020	601	0.981	3.78
8	Lillis	Bob	1.4050	1967	411	0.964	4.44
9	Menke	Denis	1.3780	1974	318	0.957	4.08
10	Bogar	Tim	1.3779	2000	320	0.979	3.86

Rank	THIRD BASE		FV	Lyear	G	FPCT	RF
1	Dominguez	Matt	1.5742	2014	333	0.969	2.64
2	Rader	Doug	1.5335	1975	1116	0.955	2.97
3	Aspromonte	Bob	1.4904	1968	931	0.962	2.71
4	Caminiti	Ken	1.4837	2000	1063	0.949	2.57
5	Cabell	Enos	1.4494	1980	744	0.951	2.61
6	Bregman	Alex	1.4358	2020	449	0.964	2.43
7	Blum	Geoff	1.4180	2010	378	0.976	2.30
8	Garner	Phil	1.3864	1987	497	0.942	2.51
9	Ensberg	Morgan	1.3709	2007	606	0.955	2.41

| 10 | Howe | | Art | **1.3625** | 1982 | 292 | 0.970 | 2.43 | |

Rank	CATCHER			FV	Lyear	G	FPCT	RF	CS%
1	Ausmus	Brad		**1.9978**	2008	1243	0.996	7.29	0.353
2	Edwards	Johnny		**1.9282**	1974	607	0.993	6.69	0.372
3	Biggio	Craig		**1.8409**	2007	428	0.989	6.21	0.222
4	Servais	Scott		**1.7768**	2001	284	0.993	6.31	0.229
5	Castro	Jason		**1.7700**	2016	572	0.995	7.52	0.261
6	Ashby	Alan		**1.7678**	1989	901	0.985	6.19	0.242
7	Quintero	Humberto		**1.7617**	2011	334	0.992	6.69	0.332
8	Eusebio	Tony		**1.7458**	2001	522	0.992	6.58	0.283
9	Bateman	John		**1.7344**	1968	526	0.982	6.72	0.332
10	Bailey	Mark		**1.7041**	1988	306	0.983	6.00	0.289

Rank	OUTFIELD			FV	Lyear	G	FPCT	RF	ApG
1	Bourn	Michael		**1.5703**	2011	525	0.990	2.49	0.059
2	Finley	Steve		**1.5691**	1994	545	0.988	2.43	0.077
3	Taveras	Willy		**1.5444**	2006	293	0.988	2.34	0.065
4	Cedeno	Cesar		**1.5364**	1981	1351	0.985	2.60	0.062
5	Pence	Hunter		**1.5131**	2011	677	0.985	2.29	0.083
6	Wynn	Jimmy		**1.5105**	1973	1379	0.980	2.20	0.076
7	Hidalgo	Richard		**1.5049**	2004	917	0.988	1.95	0.075
8	Warwick	Carl		**1.4971**	1963	269	0.987	1.94	0.071
9	Gonzalez	Luis		**1.4835**	1997	705	0.985	2.16	0.054
10	Everett	Carl		**1.4681**	1999	262	0.983	2.19	0.088
11	Young	Gerald		**1.4652**	1992	546	0.992	2.19	0.070
12	Hatcher	Billy		**1.4623**	1989	507	0.986	2.04	0.061
13	Puhl	Terry		**1.4493**	1990	1299	0.993	2.03	0.044
14	Gross	Greg		**1.4461**	1989	408	0.978	1.94	0.108
15	Springer	George		**1.4408**	2020	833	0.989	1.80	0.050
16	Mumphrey	Jerry		**1.4199**	1985	306	0.981	2.22	0.039
17	Scott	Tony		**1.4167**	1984	251	0.986	1.99	0.056
18	Marisnick	Jake		**1.4060**	2019	591	0.991	1.80	0.044
19	Cruz	Jose		**1.3988**	1987	1788	0.973	2.07	0.062
20	Bass	Kevin		**1.3977**	1994	943	0.983	1.93	0.060
21	Biggio	Craig		**1.3633**	2004	363	0.980	2.01	0.058
22	Bell	Derek		**1.3510**	1999	674	0.973	1.82	0.065
23	Staub	Rusty		**1.3462**	1968	506	0.959	1.93	0.087
24	Hunter	Brian		**1.3350**	2003	329	0.965	1.99	0.076
25	Mouton	James		**1.3271**	1997	365	0.986	1.53	0.047
26	Alou	Moises		**1.3126**	2001	411	0.981	1.60	0.063
27	Anthony	Eric		**1.3064**	1993	375	0.980	1.74	0.061
28	Berkman	Lance		**1.3058**	2007	963	0.978	1.59	0.048
29	Lee	Carlos		**1.3013**	2011	634	0.985	1.57	0.058
30	Watson	Bob		**1.3011**	1975	568	0.972	1.61	0.042

Rank	PITCHING			FV	Lyear	IP	FPCT	RF
1	Oswalt	Roy		**1.0700**	2010	1932	0.981	1.96
2	Keuchel	Dallas		**1.0538**	2018	1189	0.972	2.33
3	Giusti	Dave		**1.0529**	1968	913	0.970	2.25
4	Reynolds	Shane		**1.0499**	2002	1622	0.977	2.11
5	Niekro	Joe		**1.0430**	1985	2270	0.970	1.90
6	Clemens	Roger		**1.0257**	2006	539	0.980	1.65
7	Roberts	Dave		**1.0227**	1975	844	0.974	1.98
8	Pettitte	Andy		**1.0204**	2006	520	0.964	1.85
9	Scott	Mike		**1.0190**	1991	1704	0.960	1.80
10	Bruce	Bob		**1.0144**	1966	907	0.973	2.12

Franchise When and Where
Houston Astros (1965 to Present)
Houston Colt 45's (1962-1964)

KANSAS CITY ROYALS
Best Seasons and Careers of All-Time

Okay, we're going to start off here trying to pick out the batting order. Willie Wilson leading off, Amos Otis second, George Brett third, Hal McRae in the cleanup spot, followed by Mayberry, Frank White, Darrell Porter, and Alcides Escobar. What would your order be? In the more modern stat approach, most would probably slide Brett up to second. We like him batting third with the ability to knock in speedsters Wilson and Otis above him. And then there's the choice of Designated Hitters. We might add in Carlos Beltran and bat him sixth.

Reserves

Bench - Alex Gordon (OF), Danny Tartabull (OF), Carlos Beltran (OF), Billy Butler (1B), Mike Sweeney (1B/C), Kevin Seitzer (3B/1B), Salvador Perez (CATCHER).

Bullpen - Dan Quisenberry (CL), Jeff Montgomery (SU), Larry Gura, Paul Splittorff, Charlie Liebrandt, Greg Holland.

Kansas City Royals - Best Position Player Years

Rank	Name	First	Year	Team	Lg	HR	RBI	AVG	Age	PEVA-B
1	Brett	George	1985	KCA	AL	30	112	0.335	32	39.324
2	Porter	Darrell	1979	KCA	AL	20	112	0.291	27	31.378
3	Mayberry	John	1975	KCA	AL	34	106	0.291	26	28.634
4	Brett	George	1980	KCA	AL	24	118	0.390	27	27.571
5	McRae	Hal	1982	KCA	AL	27	133	0.308	37	27.210
6	Brett	George	1979	KCA	AL	23	107	0.329	26	25.426
7	Mayberry	John	1972	KCA	AL	25	100	0.298	23	22.654
8	Brett	George	1982	KCA	AL	21	82	0.301	29	22.248
9	Brett	George	1988	KCA	AL	24	103	0.306	35	21.193
10	Gordon	Alex	2011	KCA	AL	23	87	0.303	27	20.547
11	Tartabull	Danny	1987	KCA	AL	34	101	0.309	25	20.246
12	Brett	George	1976	KCA	AL	7	67	0.333	23	19.932
13	Gordon	Alex	2012	KCA	AL	14	72	0.294	28	19.558
14	Tartabull	Danny	1991	KCA	AL	31	100	0.316	29	19.129
15	Mayberry	John	1973	KCA	AL	26	100	0.278	24	18.772
16	Cowens	Al	1977	KCA	AL	23	112	0.312	26	18.749
17	Butler	Billy	2012	KCA	AL	29	107	0.313	26	18.708
18	Seitzer	Kevin	1987	KCA	AL	15	83	0.323	25	18.408
19	Solar	Jorge	2019	KCA	AL	48	117	0.265	27	18.044
20	Otis	Amos	1978	KCA	AL	22	96	0.298	31	18.024

Kansas City Royals - Best Pitcher Years

Rank	Name	First	Year	Team	Lg	W	L	SV	IP	ERA	Age	PEVA-P
1	Saberhagen	Bret	1989	KCA	AL	23	6	0	262.3	2.16	25	53.447
2	Greinke	Zack	2009	KCA	AL	16	8	0	229.3	2.16	26	42.305
3	Appier	Kevin	1993	KCA	AL	18	8	0	238.7	2.56	26	36.409
4	Leonard	Dennis	1977	KCA	AL	20	12	1	292.7	3.04	26	27.380
5	Saberhagen	Bret	1987	KCA	AL	18	10	0	257.0	3.36	23	26.693
6	Black	Bud	1984	KCA	AL	17	12	0	257.0	3.12	27	25.197
7	Quisenberry	Dan	1983	KCA	AL	5	3	45	139.0	1.94	30	24.535
8	Gubicza	Mark	1988	KCA	AL	20	8	0	269.7	2.70	26	23.085
9	Cone	David	1994	KCA	AL	16	5	0	171.7	2.94	31	22.648
10	Gura	Larry	1981	KCA	AL	11	8	0	172.3	2.72	34	20.054
11	Leonard	Dennis	1981	KCA	AL	13	11	0	201.7	2.99	30	19.981
12	Holland	Greg	2013	KCA	AL	1	2	47	67.0	1.21	28	19.447
13	Saberhagen	Bret	1985	KCA	AL	20	6	0	235.3	2.87	21	19.446
14	Appier	Kevin	1992	KCA	AL	15	8	0	208.3	2.46	25	19.157
15	Quisenberry	Dan	1984	KCA	AL	6	3	44	129.3	2.64	31	18.502
16	Montgomery	Jeff	1993	KCA	AL	7	5	45	87.3	2.27	31	18.356
17	Gubicza	Mark	1989	KCA	AL	15	11	0	255.0	3.04	27	18.146
18	Quisenberry	Dan	1982	KCA	AL	9	7	35	136.7	2.57	29	18.009
19	Gura	Larry	1980	KCA	AL	18	10	0	283.3	2.95	33	17.423
20	Byrd	Paul	2002	KCA	AL	17	11	0	228.3	3.90	32	17.059

Kansas City Royals - Top Career Batters

RANK	NAME	FIRST	LYR	TEAM	LG	PEVA-B	YRS	PPYR	HR	RBI	H	AVE
1	Brett	George	1993	KCA	AL	301.897	21	14.376	317	1595	3154	0.305
2	Otis	Amos	1983	KCA	AL	161.550	14	11.539	193	992	1977	0.280

RANK	NAME	FIRST	LYR	TEAM	LG	PEVA-B	YRS	PPYR	HR	RBI	H	AVE
3	McRae	Hal	1987	KCA	AL	125.000	15	8.333	169	1012	1924	0.293
4	Gordon	Alex	2020	KCA	AL	118.012	14	8.429	190	749	1643	0.257
5	Wilson	Willie	1990	KCA	AL	106.434	15	7.096	40	509	1968	0.289
6	Mayberry	John	1977	KCA	AL	94.598	6	15.766	143	552	816	0.261
7	White	Frank	1990	KCA	AL	93.076	18	5.171	160	886	2006	0.255
8	Butler	Billy	2014	KCA	AL	75.671	8	9.459	127	628	1273	0.295
9	Sweeney	Mike	2007	KCA	AL	68.382	13	5.260	197	837	1398	0.299
10	Perez	Salvador	2020	KCA	AL	68.267	9	7.585	152	535	992	0.269
11	Tartabull	Danny	1991	KCA	AL	67.175	5	13.435	124	425	674	0.290
12	Hosmer	Eric	2017	KCA	AL	65.702	7	9.386	127	566	1132	0.284
13	Beltran	Carlos	2004	KCA	AL	62.766	7	8.967	123	516	899	0.287
14	Porter	Darrell	1980	KCA	AL	60.035	4	15.009	61	301	514	0.271
15	Escobar	Alcides	2018	KCA	AL	59.595	8	7.449	36	390	1208	0.259
16	Seitzer	Kevin	1991	KCA	AL	59.378	6	9.896	33	265	809	0.294
17	Randa	Joe	2004	KCA	AL	55.767	8	6.971	86	533	1084	0.288
18	Patek	Freddie	1979	KCA	AL	55.332	9	6.148	28	382	1036	0.241
19	DeJesus	David	2010	KCA	AL	53.913	8	6.739	61	390	971	0.289
20	Moustakas	Mike	2018	KCA	AL	52.181	8	6.523	139	441	858	0.251
21	Damon	Johnny	2000	KCA	AL	49.516	6	8.253	65	352	894	0.292
22	Cowens	Al	1979	KCA	AL	45.245	6	7.541	45	374	784	0.282
23	Macfarlane	Mike	1998	KCA	AL	43.652	11	3.968	103	398	717	0.256
24	Merrifield	Whit	2020	KCA	AL	42.740	5	8.548	58	271	725	0.295
25	Piniella	Lou	1973	KCA	AL	41.461	5	8.292	45	348	734	0.286
26	Cain	Lorenzo	2017	KCA	AL	40.792	7	5.827	56	308	765	0.289
27	Dye	Jermaine	2001	KCA	AL	38.031	5	7.606	85	329	584	0.284
28	Aikens	Willie	1983	KCA	AL	37.346	4	9.337	77	297	499	0.282
29	McRae	Brian	1994	KCA	AL	36.012	5	7.202	30	248	627	0.262
30	Jackson	Bo	1990	KCA	AL	32.466	5	6.493	109	313	460	0.250
31	Schaal	Paul	1974	KCA	AL	32.410	6	5.402	32	198	525	0.263
32	Teahen	Mark	2009	KCA	AL	31.167	5	6.233	59	293	667	0.269
33	Rojas	Cookie	1977	KCA	AL	31.032	8	3.879	25	332	824	0.268
34	Kirkpatrick	Ed	1973	KCA	AL	30.892	5	6.178	56	245	471	0.248
35	Joyner	Wally	1995	KCA	AL	30.790	4	7.697	44	271	556	0.293
36	Balboni	Steve	1988	KCA	AL	30.019	5	6.004	119	318	459	0.230
37	Washington	U L	1984	KCA	AL	29.522	8	3.690	26	228	625	0.254
38	Berroa	Angel	2007	KCA	AL	26.877	7	3.840	45	235	606	0.263
39	Wathan	John	1985	KCA	AL	26.087	10	2.609	21	261	656	0.262
40	Soler	Jorge	2020	KCA	AL	23.310	4	5.827	67	175	263	0.249
41	Eisenreich	Jim	1992	KCA	AL	22.619	6	3.770	23	225	555	0.277
42	Stillwell	Kurt	1991	KCA	AL	22.532	4	5.633	26	209	464	0.256
43	Offerman	Jose	1998	KCA	AL	22.150	3	7.383	14	152	487	0.306
44	Gagne	Greg	1995	KCA	AL	20.796	3	6.932	23	157	358	0.266
45	Morales	Kendrys	2016	KCA	AL	20.764	2	10.382	52	199	312	0.277

RANK	NAME	FIRST	LYR	TEAM	LG	PEVA-B	YRS	PPYR	HR	RBI	H	AVE
46	Gaetti	Gary	1995	KCA	AL	20.403	3	6.801	61	199	300	0.267
47	Brown	Emil	2007	KCA	AL	19.992	3	6.664	38	229	401	0.279
48	Cabrera	Melky	2017	KCA	AL	19.659	2	9.830	22	116	261	0.296
49	Ibanez	Raul	2014	KCA	AL	19.273	4	4.818	57	252	418	0.286
50	Oliver	Bob	1972	KCA	AL	19.183	4	4.796	49	200	367	0.255

Kansas City Royals - Top Career Pitchers

RANK	NAME	FIRST	LYEAR	LTEAM	LG	PEVA	YRS	PPYR	W	L	SV	IP	ERA
1	Saberhagen	Bret	1991	KCA	AL	138.736	8	17.342	110	78	1	1660.3	3.21
2	Appier	Kevin	2004	KCA	AL	127.556	13	9.812	115	92	0	1843.7	3.49
3	Leonard	Dennis	1986	KCA	AL	104.156	12	8.680	144	106	1	2187.0	3.70
4	Quisenberry	Dan	1988	KCA	AL	100.751	10	10.075	51	44	238	920.3	2.55
5	Gubicza	Mark	1996	KCA	AL	96.379	13	7.414	132	135	2	2218.7	3.91
6	Greinke	Zack	2010	KCA	AL	78.499	7	11.214	60	67	1	1108.0	3.82
7	Gura	Larry	1985	KCA	AL	76.835	10	7.683	111	78	12	1701.3	3.72
8	Montgomery	Jeff	1999	KCA	AL	76.504	12	6.375	44	50	304	849.3	3.20
9	Splittorff	Paul	1984	KCA	AL	72.582	15	4.839	166	143	1	2554.7	3.81
10	Holland	Greg	2020	KCA	AL	61.340	7	8.763	21	12	151	348.0	2.38
11	Leibrandt	Charlie	1989	KCA	AL	55.642	6	9.274	76	61	0	1257.0	3.60
12	Soria	Joakim	2017	KCA	AL	55.005	7	7.858	22	26	162	438.0	2.82
13	Duffy	Danny	2020	KCA	AL	48.177	10	4.818	64	65	1	1111.3	4.02
14	Gordon	Tom	1995	KCA	AL	42.358	8	5.295	79	71	3	1149.7	4.02
15	Black	Bud	1988	KCA	AL	41.994	7	5.999	56	57	10	977.7	3.73
16	Busby	Steve	1980	KCA	AL	41.250	8	5.156	70	54	0	1060.7	3.72
17	Cone	David	1994	KCA	AL	38.388	3	12.796	27	19	0	448.3	3.29
18	Davis	Wade	2016	KCA	AL	35.201	4	8.800	27	15	47	318.0	2.94
19	Herrera	Kelvin	2018	KCA	AL	34.749	8	4.344	23	27	57	441.3	2.75
20	Belcher	Tim	1998	KCA	AL	32.914	3	10.971	42	37	0	686.0	4.38
21	Fitzmorris	Al	1976	KCA	AL	32.562	8	4.070	70	48	7	1098.0	3.46
22	Suppan	Jeff	2002	KCA	AL	32.457	5	6.491	39	51	0	864.7	4.73
23	Shields	James	2014	KCA	AL	32.002	2	16.001	27	17	0	455.7	3.18
24	Hochevar	Luke	2016	KCA	AL	30.611	9	3.401	46	65	3	929.3	4.98
25	Meche	Gil	2010	KCA	AL	28.720	4	7.180	29	39	0	617.0	4.27
26	Kennedy	Ian	2020	KCA	AL	27.847	5	5.569	22	37	30	546.7	4.48
27	Keller	Brad	2020	KCA	AL	27.183	3	9.061	21	23	0	360.3	3.50
28	Drago	Dick	1973	KCA	AL	27.004	5	5.401	61	70	1	1134.0	3.52
29	Rosado	Jose	2000	KCA	AL	25.895	5	5.179	37	45	1	720.3	4.27
30	Ventura	Yordano	2016	KCA	AL	25.642	4	6.410	38	31	0	547.7	3.89
31	Guthrie	Jeremy	2015	KCA	AL	25.530	4	6.382	41	34	0	653.7	4.38
32	Jackson	Danny	1987	KCA	AL	24.743	5	4.949	37	49	1	712.7	3.69
33	Bird	Doug	1978	KCA	AL	24.566	6	4.094	49	36	58	714.7	3.56
34	Vargas	Jason	2017	KCA	AL	24.216	4	6.054	34	23	0	421.7	3.88
35	Farr	Steve	1990	KCA	AL	23.505	6	3.917	34	24	49	511.0	3.05

RANK	NAME	FIRST	LYEAR	LTEAM	LG	PEVA	YRS	PPYR	W	L	SV	IP	ERA
36	Bannister	Brian	2010	KCA	AL	22.092	4	5.523	35	49	0	629.3	5.13
37	Chen	Bruce	2014	KCA	AL	22.069	6	3.678	47	43	1	718.7	4.53
38	Volquez	Edinson	2016	KCA	AL	20.120	2	10.060	23	20	0	389.7	4.43
39	May	Darrell	2004	KCA	AL	19.565	3	6.522	23	37	0	527.3	4.81
40	Mingori	Steve	1979	KCA	AL	18.585	7	2.655	16	25	27	439.0	3.05
41	Byrd	Paul	2002	KCA	AL	18.510	2	9.255	23	17	0	321.7	3.95
42	Pattin	Marty	1980	KCA	AL	18.409	7	2.630	43	39	21	825.7	3.48
43	Junis	Jakob	2020	KCA	AL	17.653	4	4.413	27	31	0	476.0	4.78
44	Nelson	Roger	1976	KCA	AL	15.820	5	3.164	18	22	3	418.3	3.08
45	Gale	Rich	1981	KCA	AL	15.631	4	3.908	42	33	1	666.3	4.38
46	Pichardo	Hipolito	1998	KCA	AL	14.879	7	2.126	42	39	19	669.7	4.48
47	Abernathy	Ted	1972	KCA	AL	14.804	3	4.935	16	13	40	195.0	2.31
48	Haney	Chris	1998	KCA	AL	14.625	7	2.089	33	40	0	625.7	5.24
49	Burgmeier	Tom	1973	KCA	AL	14.011	5	2.802	24	16	28	276.0	3.20
50	Davies	Kyle	2011	KCA	AL	13.034	5	2.607	29	44	0	531.0	5.34

Kansas City Royals – Top Fielders

Rank	FIRST BASE		FV	Lyear	G	FPCT	RF
1	Mayberry	John	1.2907	1977	837	0.993	9.85
2	King	Jeff	1.2740	1999	282	0.995	9.16
3	Balboni	Steve	1.2120	1988	490	0.989	9.90
4	Joyner	Wally	1.2035	1995	497	0.994	9.46
5	Brett	George	1.1277	1992	461	0.993	9.45
6	Hosmer	Eric	1.1250	2017	1028	0.995	8.66
7	Aikens	Willie	1.0354	1983	477	0.991	8.63
8	LaCock	Pete	1.0164	1980	329	0.995	6.47
9	Butler	Billy	1.0154	2014	394	0.992	8.29
10	Sweeney	Mike	1.0097	2007	553	0.990	9.18

Rank	SECOND BASE		FV	Lyear	G	FPCT	RF
1	White	Frank	1.3457	1990	2150	0.984	5.11
2	Rojas	Cookie	1.2656	1977	790	0.985	4.72
3	Grudzielanek	Mark	1.2315	2008	333	0.991	4.53
4	Merrifield	Whit	1.2015	2020	402	0.982	4.27
5	Offerman	Jose	1.2013	1998	291	0.978	4.53
6	Febles	Carlos	1.1020	2003	493	0.979	4.56
7	Getz	Chris	1.0956	2013	303	0.987	4.26
8	Shumpert	Terry	1.0954	1994	250	0.973	4.23
9	Infante	Omar	1.0571	2016	297	0.979	3.95

Rank	SHORTSTOP		FV	Lyear	G	FPCT	RF
1	Sanchez	Rey	1.7241	2001	377	0.989	4.92
2	Gagne	Greg	1.6784	1995	383	0.978	4.68
3	Escobar	Alcides	1.5833	2018	1209	0.978	4.11
4	Patek	Freddie	1.5484	1979	1241	0.963	4.79
5	Howard	David	1.4949	1997	332	0.977	4.31
6	Stillwell	Kurt	1.4392	1991	513	0.966	3.88
7	Washington	U L	1.4371	1984	676	0.957	4.30
8	Berroa	Angel	1.4360	2007	619	0.964	4.47
9	Concepcion	Onix	1.3779	1985	287	0.960	4.14

Rank	THIRD BASE		FV	Lyear	G	FPCT	RF
1	Randa	Joe	1.5343	2004	940	0.963	2.60
2	Brett	George	1.5220	1992	1692	0.951	2.98
3	Gaetti	Gary	1.5119	1995	280	0.968	2.56
4	Seitzer	Kevin	1.4959	1991	670	0.946	2.55
5	Moustakas	Mike	1.4864	2018	885	0.961	2.59
6	Gordon	Alex	1.3999	2010	329	0.949	2.48

			FV	Lyear	G	FPCT	RF	
7	Teahen	Mark	1.3857	2009	363	0.952	2.62	
8	Schaal	Paul	1.3241	1974	563	0.932	2.57	
9	Pryor	Greg	1.2365	1986	266	0.957	1.94	

Rank	CATCHER		FV	Lyear	G	FPCT	RF	CS%
1	Perez	Salvador	1.8669	2020	908	0.995	7.73	0.351
2	Porter	Darrell	1.8340	1980	492	0.983	4.98	0.423
3	Macfarlane	Mike	1.7686	1998	798	0.992	5.73	0.317
4	Mayne	Brent	1.7374	2003	620	0.993	5.70	0.298
5	Kirkpatrick	Ed	1.7202	1973	278	0.983	5.67	0.425
6	Healy	Fran	1.6743	1976	292	0.980	5.08	0.345
7	Quirk	Jamie	1.6719	1988	320	0.985	4.95	0.338
8	Buck	John	1.6697	2009	562	0.990	6.34	0.260
9	Martinez	Buck	1.6479	1977	334	0.981	4.95	0.329
10	Wathan	John	1.6204	1985	572	0.982	4.23	0.318

Rank	OUTFIELD		FV	Lyear	G	FPCT	RF	ApG
1	Otis	Amos	1.6048	1983	1845	0.991	2.67	0.063
2	DeJesus	David	1.5426	2010	911	0.992	2.30	0.053
3	Goodwin	Tom	1.5377	1997	383	0.989	2.21	0.042
4	Gordon	Alex	1.5328	2020	1392	0.994	2.05	0.073
5	McRae	Brian	1.5313	1994	606	0.990	2.65	0.028
6	Beltran	Carlos	1.5165	2004	756	0.982	2.78	0.082
7	Wilson	Willie	1.5151	1990	1732	0.988	2.59	0.041
8	Cain	Lorenzo	1.4969	2017	716	0.985	2.65	0.046
9	Damon	Johnny	1.4907	2000	806	0.987	2.26	0.042
10	Cowens	Al	1.4839	1979	783	0.985	2.07	0.073
11	Gathright	Joey	1.4700	2008	253	0.988	2.24	0.047
12	Teahen	Mark	1.4688	2009	298	0.986	2.18	0.081
13	Piniella	Lou	1.4463	1973	661	0.981	1.87	0.064
14	Maier	Mitch	1.4417	2012	347	0.990	2.03	0.049
15	Dye	Jermaine	1.4270	2001	532	0.980	2.22	0.085
16	Sheridan	Pat	1.4147	1985	306	0.986	2.11	0.056
17	Kirkpatrick	Ed	1.4115	1973	270	0.993	1.97	0.048
18	Tucker	Michael	1.3936	2003	349	0.990	1.92	0.069
19	Dyson	Jerrod	1.3923	2016	479	0.981	2.28	0.075
20	Francoeur	Jeff	1.3867	2013	355	0.986	1.98	0.107
21	Brown	Emil	1.3424	2007	380	0.973	2.00	0.071
22	Eisenreich	Jim	1.3330	1992	518	0.987	1.89	0.023
23	Wohlford	Jim	1.3216	1976	346	0.973	2.00	0.069
24	Jackson	Bo	1.3195	1990	464	0.960	2.05	0.088
25	Motley	Darryl	1.2936	1986	375	0.976	1.97	0.048
26	Poquette	Tom	1.2600	1982	310	0.974	1.91	0.042
27	Tartabull	Danny	1.2522	1991	526	0.970	1.64	0.051
28	Smith	Lonnie	1.2491	1987	269	0.957	1.89	0.063
29	McRae	Hal	1.2246	1982	329	0.967	1.95	0.073
30	Hurdle	Clint	1.1920	1981	291	0.966	1.87	0.055

Rank	PITCHING		FV	Lyear	IP	FPCT	RF
1	Gura	Larry	1.0680	1985	1701	0.983	2.10
2	Fitzmorris	Al	1.0561	1976	1098	0.979	2.65
3	Greinke	Zack	1.0542	2010	1108	0.982	1.78
4	Gubicza	Mark	1.0469	1996	2219	0.969	2.39
5	Leibrandt	Charlie	1.0434	1989	1257	0.958	2.27
6	Suppan	Jeff	1.0426	2002	865	0.964	1.94
7	Busby	Steve	1.0311	1980	1061	0.923	2.32
8	Belcher	Tim	1.0288	1998	686	0.970	1.72
9	Splittorff	Paul	1.0277	1984	2555	0.975	2.03
10	Saberhagen	Bret	1.0263	1991	1660	0.958	2.11

Franchise When and Where
Kansas City Royals (1969 to Present)

LOS ANGELES ANGELS OF ANAHEIM
Best Seasons and Careers of All-Time

It's a fact almost every Angels fan knows without thinking twice, Mike Trout is the best baseball player ever to put on an Anaheim uniform, ... in fact, he's twice as good a player as the second best. That's awesome, and accomplished in only ten years. There's almost no limit to the heights Trout might achieve on the All-Time baseball list, but Top Ten of All-Time certainly is not out of the question. The rest of the All-Time Angels team has its moments, in players like Second Baseman Bobby Grich and part-time Angel pitchers like Hall of Famer Nolan Ryan, but it's all about the Trout when you place the win, place, and show bets in franchise history. Just look at the Best Seasons Ever chart. Trout has the Top 7 best, and Number 12. For pitchers, it's less of a stellar collection, although the seasons of Dean Chance, in 1964, tops the list with a 20-9 record and 1.69 ERA, all at the age of 23.

Reserves

Bench - Vladimir Guerrero (OF), Darren Erstad (OF/1B), Chili Davis (OF), Wally Joyner (1B), Troy Glaus (3B), Erick Aybar (IF), Bob Boone (C).

Bullpen - Troy Percival (CL), Francisco Rodriguez (SU), Mike Witt, Mark Langston, Dean Chance, Clyde Wright, Kelvim Escobar.

Los Angeles Angels of Anaheim – Best Position Player Years

Rank	Name	First	Year	Team	Lg	HR	RBI	AVG	Age	PEVA-B
1	Trout	Mike	2014	LAA	AL	36	111	0.287	23	41.098
2	Trout	Mike	2016	LAA	AL	29	100	0.315	25	40.170
3	Trout	Mike	2013	LAA	AL	27	97	0.323	22	39.602
4	Trout	Mike	2018	LAA	AL	39	79	0.312	27	35.599
5	Trout	Mike	2015	LAA	AL	41	90	0.299	24	35.459
6	Trout	Mike	2012	LAA	AL	30	83	0.326	21	33.502
7	Trout	Mike	2019	LAA	AL	45	104	0.291	28	32.665
8	Salmon	Tim	1995	CAL	AL	34	105	0.330	27	29.547
9	DeCinces	Doug	1982	CAL	AL	30	97	0.301	32	27.834
10	Baylor	Don	1979	CAL	AL	36	139	0.296	30	25.905
11	Downing	Brian	1982	CAL	AL	28	84	0.281	32	25.802
12	Trout	Mike	2017	LAA	AL	33	72	0.306	26	24.502
13	Glaus	Troy	2000	ANA	AL	47	102	0.284	24	23.161
14	Downing	Brian	1979	CAL	AL	12	75	0.326	29	22.294
15	Jackson	Reggie	1982	CAL	AL	39	101	0.275	36	22.210
16	Trout	Mike	2020	LAA	AL	17	46	0.281	29	21.671
17	Guerrero	Vladimir	2004	ANA	AL	39	126	0.337	28	21.307
18	Erstad	Darin	2000	ANA	AL	25	100	0.355	26	21.163
19	Edmonds	Jim	1995	CAL	AL	33	107	0.290	25	20.927
20	Guerrero	Vladimir	2006	LAA	AL	33	116	0.329	30	20.282

Los Angeles Angels of Anaheim - Best Pitcher Years

Rank	Name	First	Year	Team	Lg	W	L	SV	IP	ERA	Age	PEVA-P
1	Chance	Dean	1964	LAA	AL	20	9	4	278.3	1.65	23	29.474
2	Tanana	Frank	1976	CAL	AL	19	10	0	288.3	2.43	23	28.912
3	Lackey	John	2007	LAA	AL	19	9	0	224.0	3.01	29	28.594
4	Weaver	Jered	2011	LAA	AL	18	8	0	235.7	2.41	29	27.853
5	Weaver	Jered	2012	LAA	AL	20	5	0	188.7	2.81	30	26.567
6	Langston	Mark	1993	CAL	AL	16	11	0	256.3	3.20	33	23.167
7	Langston	Mark	1991	CAL	AL	19	8	0	246.3	3.00	31	23.149
8	Wright	Clyde	1970	CAL	AL	22	12	0	260.7	2.83	29	22.880
9	Haren	Dan	2011	LAA	AL	16	10	0	238.3	3.17	29	22.878
10	Santana	Ervin	2008	LAA	AL	16	7	0	219.0	3.49	25	22.414
11	Ryan	Nolan	1974	CAL	AL	22	16	0	332.7	2.89	27	21.613
12	Witt	Mike	1986	CAL	AL	18	10	0	269.0	2.84	26	21.604
13	Weaver	Jered	2010	LAA	AL	13	12	0	224.3	3.01	28	21.203
14	Ryan	Nolan	1977	CAL	AL	19	16	0	299.0	2.77	30	20.766
15	Abbott	Jim	1991	CAL	AL	18	11	0	243.0	2.89	24	20.695
16	Blyleven	Bert	1989	CAL	AL	17	5	0	241.0	2.73	38	20.160
17	Tanana	Frank	1977	CAL	AL	15	9	0	241.3	2.54	24	19.687
18	Finley	Chuck	1993	CAL	AL	16	14	0	251.3	3.15	31	19.355
19	Escobar	Kelvim	2007	LAA	AL	18	7	0	195.7	3.40	31	18.934
20	Colon	Bartolo	2005	LAA	AL	21	8	0	222.7	3.48	32	18.290

Los Angeles Angels of Anaheim (ANA, CAL, LAA) - Top Career Batters

RANK	NAME	FIRST	LYR	TEAM	LG	PEVA-B	YRS	PPYR	HR	RBI	H	AVE
1	Trout	Mike	2020	LAA	AL	304.881	10	30.488	302	798	1380	0.304
2	Downing	Brian	1990	CAL	AL	157.437	13	12.111	222	846	1588	0.271

RANK	NAME	FIRST	LYR	TEAM	LG	PEVA-B	YRS	PPYR	HR	RBI	H	AVE
3	Salmon	Tim	2006	LAA	AL	150.732	14	10.767	299	1016	1674	0.282
4	Anderson	Garret	2008	LAA	AL	137.630	15	9.175	272	1292	2368	0.296
5	Fregosi	Jim	1971	CAL	AL	123.541	11	11.231	115	546	1408	0.268
6	Grich	Bobby	1986	CAL	AL	95.385	10	9.539	154	557	1103	0.269
7	Guerrero	Vladimir	2009	LAA	AL	92.851	6	15.475	173	616	1034	0.319
8	Pujols	Albert	2020	LAA	AL	83.216	9	9.246	217	771	1163	0.257
9	Erstad	Darin	2006	LAA	AL	77.974	11	7.089	114	625	1505	0.286
10	Davis	Chili	1996	CAL	AL	74.258	7	10.608	156	618	973	0.279
11	Joyner	Wally	2001	ANA	AL	72.753	7	10.393	117	532	961	0.286
12	Baylor	Don	1982	CAL	AL	71.347	6	11.891	141	523	813	0.262
13	DeCinces	Doug	1987	CAL	AL	71.314	6	11.886	130	481	765	0.265
14	Glaus	Troy	2004	ANA	AL	64.989	7	9.284	182	515	748	0.253
15	Calhoun	Kole	2019	LAA	AL	64.934	8	8.117	140	451	884	0.249
16	Hunter	Torii	2012	LAA	AL	64.628	5	12.926	105	432	768	0.286
17	Aybar	Erick	2015	LAA	AL	60.762	10	6.076	48	417	1223	0.276
18	Edmonds	Jim	1999	ANA	AL	60.298	7	8.614	121	408	768	0.290
19	Figgins	Chone	2009	LAA	AL	55.609	8	6.951	31	341	1045	0.291
20	Kendrick	Howie	2014	LAA	AL	52.194	9	5.799	78	501	1204	0.292
21	Carew	Rod	1985	CAL	AL	51.759	7	7.394	18	282	968	0.314
22	Lynn	Fred	1984	CAL	AL	51.617	4	12.904	71	270	456	0.271
23	Pearson	Albie	1966	CAL	AL	48.955	6	8.159	24	167	618	0.275
24	Jackson	Reggie	1986	CAL	AL	47.312	5	9.462	123	374	557	0.239
25	DiSarcina	Gary	2000	ANA	AL	42.152	12	3.513	28	355	966	0.258
26	Boone	Bob	1988	CAL	AL	40.915	7	5.845	39	318	742	0.245
27	Rodgers	Buck	1969	CAL	AL	39.958	9	4.440	31	288	704	0.232
28	Schofield	Dick	1996	CAL	AL	39.570	12	3.297	48	280	798	0.232
29	Reichardt	Rick	1970	CAL	AL	39.461	7	5.637	68	261	512	0.261
30	Wagner	Leon	1963	LAA	AL	37.692	3	12.564	91	276	451	0.279
31	Kennedy	Adam	2006	LAA	AL	36.917	7	5.274	51	353	935	0.280
32	White	Devon	1990	CAL	AL	36.813	6	6.136	59	241	551	0.247
33	Knoop	Bobby	1969	CAL	AL	33.140	6	5.523	44	236	629	0.240
34	Alomar	Sandy	1974	CAL	AL	32.889	6	5.481	8	162	758	0.248
35	Molina	Bengie	2005	LAA	AL	32.440	8	4.055	65	362	678	0.273
36	Trumbo	Mark	2013	LAA	AL	32.380	4	8.095	95	284	429	0.250
37	Simmons	Andrelton	2020	LAA	AL	32.441	5	6.448	36	238	592	0.281
38	Howell	Jack	1997	ANA	AL	31.642	9	3.516	100	313	581	0.241
39	Abreu	Bobby	2012	LAA	AL	31.626	4	7.907	43	246	443	0.267
40	Lansford	Carney	1980	CAL	AL	31.571	3	10.524	42	211	478	0.280
41	Eckstein	David	2004	ANA	AL	30.119	4	7.530	17	170	614	0.278
42	Robinson	Frank	1974	CAL	AL	28.964	2	14.482	50	160	249	0.259
43	Thomas	Lee	1964	LAA	AL	28.799	4	7.200	61	253	460	0.265
44	Chalk	Dave	1978	CAL	AL	28.737	6	4.789	12	205	631	0.255
45	Polonia	Luis	1993	CAL	AL	28.552	4	7.138	5	149	628	0.294

RANK	NAME	FIRST	LYR	TEAM	LG	PEVA-B	YRS	PPYR	HR	RBI	H	AVE
46	Cabrera	Orlando	2007	LAA	AL	27.885	3	9.295	25	215	502	0.281
47	Rivera	Juan	2010	LAA	AL	27.678	6	4.613	92	337	566	0.277
48	Napoli	Mike	2010	LAA	AL	26.714	5	5.343	92	249	389	0.251
49	Curtis	Chad	1994	CAL	AL	26.691	3	8.897	27	155	396	0.268
50	Pettis	Gary	1987	CAL	AL	25.911	6	4.319	13	143	451	0.242

Los Angeles Angels of Anaheim (ANA, CAL, LAA) - Top Career Pitchers

RANK	NAME	FIRST	LYEAR	LTEAM	LG	PEVA	YRS	PPYR	W	L	SV	IP	ERA
1	Weaver	Jered	2016	LAA	AL	149.719	11	13.611	150	93	0	2025.0	3.55
2	Finley	Chuck	1999	ANA	AL	138.133	14	9.867	165	140	0	2675.0	3.72
3	Ryan	Nolan	1979	CAL	AL	104.056	8	13.007	138	121	1	2181.3	3.07
4	Lackey	John	2009	LAA	AL	93.923	8	11.740	102	71	0	1501.0	3.81
5	Tanana	Frank	1980	CAL	AL	89.677	8	11.210	102	78	0	1615.3	3.08
6	Witt	Mike	1990	CAL	AL	84.436	10	8.444	109	107	6	1965.3	3.76
7	Langston	Mark	1997	ANA	AL	78.413	8	9.802	88	74	0	1445.3	3.97
8	Santana	Ervin	2012	LAA	AL	74.985	8	9.373	96	80	0	1475.7	4.33
9	Percival	Troy	2004	ANA	AL	66.072	10	6.607	29	38	316	586.7	2.99
10	Chance	Dean	1966	CAL	AL	62.961	6	10.493	74	66	16	1236.7	2.83
11	Rodriguez	Francisco	2008	LAA	AL	60.392	7	8.627	23	17	208	451.7	2.35
12	Wright	Clyde	1973	CAL	AL	48.718	8	6.090	87	85	3	1403.3	3.28
13	Washburn	Jarrod	2005	LAA	AL	47.648	8	5.956	75	57	0	1153.3	3.93
14	Abbott	Jim	1996	CAL	AL	46.499	6	7.750	54	74	0	1073.7	4.07
15	McCaskill	Kirk	1991	CAL	AL	44.068	7	6.295	78	74	0	1221.0	3.86
16	Escobar	Kelvim	2009	LAA	AL	44.054	5	8.811	43	36	1	658.0	3.60
17	Messersmith	Andy	1972	CAL	AL	42.182	5	8.436	59	47	13	972.3	2.78
18	Shields	Scot	2010	LAA	AL	38.771	10	3.877	46	44	21	697.0	3.18
19	Wilson	C.J.	2015	LAA	AL	36.292	4	9.073	51	35	0	722.3	3.87
20	Richards	Garrett	2018	LAA	AL	36.201	8	4.525	45	38	2	744.7	3.54
21	Harvey	Bryan	1992	CAL	AL	34.750	6	5.792	16	20	126	307.7	2.49
22	Haren	Danny	2012	LAA	AL	34.262	3	11.421	33	27	0	509.0	3.52
23	Zahn	Geoff	1985	CAL	AL	33.449	5	6.690	52	42	0	830.0	3.64
24	Saunders	Joe	2010	LAA	AL	33.444	6	5.574	54	32	0	692.0	4.29
25	Ortiz	Ramon	2004	ANA	AL	32.589	6	5.431	59	49	0	893.7	4.60
26	Colon	Bartolo	2007	LAA	AL	30.661	4	7.665	46	33	0	586.7	4.66
27	Brunet	George	1969	CAL	AL	30.158	6	5.026	54	69	3	1047.3	3.13
28	Forsch	Ken	1986	CAL	AL	26.464	5	5.293	36	32	1	633.7	3.81
29	Lee	Bob	1966	CAL	AL	26.158	3	8.719	20	16	58	370.0	1.99
30	Blyleven	Bert	1992	CAL	AL	25.035	3	8.345	33	24	0	508.0	3.92
31	McBride	Ken	1965	CAL	AL	24.077	5	4.815	40	48	2	780.3	3.81
32	May	Rudy	1974	CAL	AL	20.900	7	2.986	51	76	5	1138.7	3.67
33	Heaney	Andrew	2020	LAA	AL	20.564	5	3.427	24	26	0	475.3	4.35
34	Donnelly	Brendan	2006	LAA	AL	19.839	5	3.968	23	8	4	295.0	2.87
35	Newman	Fred	1967	CAL	AL	19.323	6	3.221	33	39	0	610.0	3.41

RANK	NAME	FIRST	LYEAR	LTEAM	LG	PEVA	YRS	PPYR	W	L	SV	IP	ERA
36	Shoemaker	Matt	2018	AA	AL	**19.069**	6	3.178	40	32	0	545.0	3.93
37	Singer	Bill	1975	AL	AL	**18.835**	3	6.278	34	33	1	603.3	3.70
38	Tatum	Ken	1970	CAL	AL	**17.888**	2	8.944	14	6	39	175.0	2.16
39	Murphy	Tom	1972	CAL	AL	**17.880**	5	3.576	37	52	0	795.3	3.85
40	McGlothlin	Jim	1969	CAL	AL	**17.261**	5	3.452	33	43	3	692.3	3.37
41	Aase	Don	1984	CAL	AL	**16.935**	6	2.822	39	39	27	695.3	3.91
42	Santiago	Hector	2016	LAA	AL	**16.906**	3	5.635	25	22	0	428.7	3.82
43	Moore	Donnie	1988	CAL	AL	**16.831**	4	4.208	19	17	61	235.3	2.75
44	LaRoche	Dave	1980	CAL	AL	**16.797**	6	2.800	35	32	65	512.3	3.65
45	Bedrosian	Cam	2020	LAA	AL	**16.773**	7	2.396	17	13	9	277.7	3.70
46	Hassler	Andy	1983	CAL	AL	**16.275**	9	1.808	21	46	24	659.3	3.78
47	Sutton	Don	1987	CAL	AL	**16.118**	3	5.373	28	24	0	430.3	4.16
48	Fowler	Art	1964	LAA	AL	**15.948**	4	3.987	14	16	27	262.3	3.16
49	Fraser	Willie	1990	CAL	AL	**15.834**	5	3.167	31	34	5	543.3	4.26
50	Eichhorn	Mark	1996	CAL	AL	**15.733**	4	3.933	8	14	16	253.3	2.81

Los Angeles Angels of Anaheim – Top Fielders

Rank	FIRST BASE		FV	Lyear	G	FPCT	RF
1	Joyner	Wally	**1.2681**	2001	879	0.994	9.48
2	Spencer	Jim	**1.2128**	1973	474	0.994	9.17
3	Kotchman	Casey	**1.1978**	2008	310	0.997	8.12
4	Snow	J.T.	**1.1698**	1996	487	0.995	8.65
5	Spiezio	Scott	**1.1511**	2003	391	0.997	7.55
6	Mincher	Don	**1.1281**	1968	255	0.993	8.91
7	Erstad	Darin	**1.1195**	2006	579	0.995	8.19
8	Carew	Rod	**1.1113**	1985	718	0.991	9.77
9	Trumbo	Mark	**1.1070**	2013	299	0.993	8.56
10	Adcock	Joe	**1.0989**	1966	273	0.995	8.98

Rank	SECOND BASE		FV	Lyear	G	FPCT	RF
1	Knoop	Bobby	**1.3727**	1969	801	0.979	5.20
2	Grich	Bobby	**1.3454**	1986	1097	0.984	5.24
3	Alomar Sr.	Sandy	**1.3233**	1974	703	0.979	5.05
4	Remy	Jerry	**1.3184**	1977	432	0.978	5.03
5	Moran	Billy	**1.3136**	1964	365	0.978	5.30
6	Velarde	Randy	**1.2741**	1999	260	0.984	4.64
7	Ray	Johnny	**1.2631**	1990	363	0.982	5.18
8	Kennedy	Adam	**1.2473**	2006	969	0.984	4.53
9	Kendrick	Howie	**1.1660**	2014	967	0.985	4.50
10	Wilfong	Rob	**1.0762**	1986	323	0.983	4.54

Rank	SHORTSTOP		FV	Lyear	G	FPCT	RF
1	Simmons	Andrelton	**1.6166**	2020	559	0.979	4.14
2	DiSarcina	Gary	**1.6003**	2000	1069	0.973	4.49
3	Schofield	Dick	**1.5952**	1996	1073	0.975	4.52
4	Fregosi	Jim	**1.5911**	1971	1367	0.963	4.73
5	Cabrera	Orlando	**1.5137**	2007	446	0.982	4.17
6	Aybar	Erick	**1.4883**	2015	1134	0.973	4.04
7	Eckstein	David	**1.4863**	2004	527	0.980	4.00
8	Chalk	Dave	**1.3296**	1978	324	0.954	4.32
9	Koppe	Joe	**1.3256**	1965	260	0.953	4.52

Rank	THIRD BASE		FV	Lyear	G	FPCT	RF
1	McMullen	Ken	**1.5875**	1972	417	0.965	2.95
2	DeCinces	Doug	**1.5351**	1987	748	0.959	2.83
3	Lansford	Carney	**1.4989**	1980	424	0.962	2.53
4	Chalk	Dave	**1.4627**	1978	399	0.963	2.77
5	Rodriguez	Aurelio	**1.4449**	1970	275	0.954	2.99
6	Glaus	Troy	**1.4392**	2004	778	0.944	2.52

			FV	Lyear	G	FPCT	RF	
7	Howell	Jack	1.4113	1997	600	0.955	2.43	
8	Schaal	Paul	1.4104	1974	490	0.956	2.69	
9	Callaspo	Alberto	1.4026	2013	398	0.960	2.52	
10	Torres	Felix	1.3925	1964	317	0.945	2.82	

Rank	CATCHER		FV	Lyear	G	FPCT	RF	CS%
1	Parrish	Lance	1.9965	1992	386	0.993	6.16	0.385
2	Boone	Bob	1.9163	1988	961	0.985	5.31	0.462
3	Molina	Bengie	1.8575	2005	685	0.994	6.37	0.360
4	Rodgers	Buck	1.8534	1969	895	0.988	5.83	0.433
5	Downing	Brian	1.8413	1981	310	0.990	5.48	0.302
6	Molina	Jose	1.8239	2007	348	0.990	6.53	0.413
7	Humphrey	Terry	1.7652	1979	255	0.984	5.86	0.346
8	Iannetta	Chris	1.7440	2015	380	0.996	7.25	0.244
9	Fabregas	Jorge	1.6299	2002	309	0.989	5.66	0.295
10	Mathis	Jeff	1.6260	2011	411	0.987	6.83	0.236

Rank	OUTFIELD		FV	Lyear	G	FPCT	RF	ApG
1	Curtis	Chad	1.5938	1994	400	0.982	2.62	0.095
2	Berry	Ken	1.5881	1973	346	0.995	2.42	0.066
3	Edmonds	Jim	1.5745	1999	654	0.990	2.67	0.076
4	Cardenal	Jose	1.5702	1967	376	0.981	2.30	0.085
5	Erstad	Darin	1.5648	2006	715	0.995	2.70	0.064
6	Trout	Mike	1.5590	2020	1235	0.993	2.37	0.031
7	Hunter	Torii	1.5457	2012	667	0.993	2.34	0.058
8	Miller	Rick	1.5380	1980	364	0.987	2.81	0.063
9	Pettis	Gary	1.5353	1987	569	0.985	2.82	0.072
10	White	Devon	1.5309	1990	595	0.979	2.73	0.076
11	Lynn	Fred	1.5127	1984	455	0.987	2.46	0.066
12	Bourjos	Peter	1.5107	2019	364	0.992	2.28	0.058
13	Anderson	Garret	1.4951	2008	1793	0.989	2.19	0.059
14	Downing	Brian	1.4904	1987	722	0.995	2.00	0.050
15	Calhoun	Cole	1.4503	2019	952	0.985	2.01	0.061
16	Pearson	Albie	1.4440	1966	589	0.980	2.15	0.053
17	Reichardt	Rick	1.4428	1970	541	0.981	1.89	0.076
18	Rivers	Mickey	1.4362	1975	426	0.978	2.45	0.063
19	Salmon	Tim	1.4296	2006	1267	0.978	2.20	0.078
20	Rudi	Joe	1.4236	1980	342	0.992	2.26	0.050
21	Johnstone	Jay	1.4195	1970	397	0.980	2.20	0.071
22	Repoz	Roger	1.4121	1971	432	0.988	1.85	0.051
23	Pinson	Vada	1.4091	1973	254	0.978	1.72	0.087
24	Polonia	Luis	1.3986	1993	468	0.981	1.92	0.068
25	Clark	Bobby	1.3634	1983	304	0.991	1.80	0.056
26	Wagner	Leon	1.3384	1963	413	0.967	1.78	0.063
27	Ford	Dan	1.3242	1981	283	0.967	2.16	0.057
28	Matthews	Gary	1.3143	2009	342	0.980	2.25	0.044
29	Davis	Chili	1.3116	1994	354	0.960	1.90	0.056
30	Jones	Ruppert	1.3098	1987	260	0.984	1.86	0.069

Rank	PITCHING		FV	Lyear	IP	FPCT	RF
1	McBride	Ken	1.0926	1965	780	0.969	2.92
2	Newman	Fred	1.0639	1967	610	0.963	3.11
3	Wright	Clyde	1.0538	1973	1403	0.960	2.33
4	Tanana	Frank	1.0504	1980	1615	0.980	1.67
5	Chance	Dean	1.0494	1966	1237	0.957	2.10
6	Blyleven	Bert	1.0359	1992	508	0.990	1.72
7	Abbott	Jim	1.0332	1996	1074	0.975	1.98
8	Witt	Mike	1.0120	1990	1965	0.950	1.90
9	Saunders	Joe	1.0112	2010	692	0.986	1.78
10	Langston	Mark	1.0063	1997	1445	0.948	2.02

Franchise When and Where
Los Angeles Angels of Anaheim (2005 to Present)
Anaheim Angels (1997-2004)
California Angels (1965-1996)
Los Angeles Angels (1961-1964)

LOS ANGELES DODGERS
Best Seasons and Careers of All-Time

It's hard not to lead with the amazing pitchers in that starting rotation. You can argue the order, but not the quality. Clayton Kershaw, Don Drysdale, Dazzy Vance, Sandy Koufax, and Don Sutton. Oh, my. There's power and guile, durability and the burst of amazing. Sandy Koufax had the best two seasons in Dodger history, no matter whether you were in Brooklyn or Chavez Ravine. His seasons in 1963 and 1965 were two of the best of All-Time, no matter the team. On the offensive side, two players, Jackie Robinson and Roy Campanella stand out for many reasons, and Duke Snider may have been the third best outfielder in New York City during his time, but he was the best of all Dodgers for position players. Zach Wheat is on the lesser known list, with his last year played in 1926, but when you have over 1,200 RBI, you should be known better. It will be interesting to see how a current player like Cody Bellinger moves up this list over time. Too short a career thus far to know, but ten years from now we might just be saying Bellinger is part of not only the team, but the starting lineup, too.

Reserves

Bench - Carl Furillo (OF), Dixie Walker (OF), Matt Kemp (OF), Steve Garvey (3B/1B), Jim Gilliam (2B/3B/OF), Maury Wills (SS), Mike Piazza (CATCHER).

Bullpen - Kenley Jansen (CL), Eric Gagne (SU), Orel Hershiser, Fernando Valenzuela, Don Newcombe, Whit Wyatt.

Los Angeles Dodgers - Best Position Player Years

Rank	Name	First	Year	Team	Lg	HR	RBI	AVG	Age	PEVA-B
1	Brouthers	Dan	1892	BRO	NL	5	124	0.335	34	42.196
2	Piazza	Mike	1997	LAN	NL	40	124	0.362	29	41.108
3	Snider	Duke	1953	BRO	NL	42	126	0.336	27	38.655
4	Campanella	Roy	1953	BRO	NL	41	142	0.312	32	38.348
5	Sheckard	Jimmy	1903	BRO	NL	9	75	0.332	25	36.040
6	Kemp	Matt	2011	LAN	NL	39	126	0.324	26	35.783
7	Snider	Duke	1955	BRO	NL	42	136	0.309	29	34.757
8	Bellinger	Cody	2019	LAN	NL	47	115	0.305	24	33.859
9	Snider	Duke	1954	BRO	NL	40	130	0.341	28	32.766
10	Galan	Augie	1944	BRO	NL	12	93	0.318	32	31.002
11	Campanella	Roy	1951	BRO	NL	33	108	0.325	30	30.592
12	Herman	Babe	1930	BRO	NL	35	130	0.393	27	30.341
13	Davis	Tommy	1962	LAN	NL	27	153	0.346	23	29.550
14	Piazza	Mike	1996	LAN	NL	36	105	0.336	28	29.100
15	Wynn	Jimmy	1974	LAN	NL	32	108	0.271	32	28.948
16	Walker	Dixie	1944	BRO	NL	13	91	0.357	34	28.465
17	Robinson	Jackie	1952	BRO	NL	19	75	0.308	33	25.988
18	Beltre	Adrian	2004	LAN	NL	48	121	0.334	25	25.807
19	Murray	Eddie	1990	LAN	NL	26	95	0.330	34	25.700
20	Robinson	Jackie	1951	BRO	NL	19	88	0.338	32	25.424

Los Angeles Dodgers - Best Pitcher Years

Rank	Name	First	Year	Team	Lg	W	L	SV	IP	ERA	Age	PEVA-P
1	Koufax	Sandy	1963	LAN	NL	25	5	0	311.0	1.88	28	50.345
2	Koufax	Sandy	1965	LAN	NL	26	8	2	335.7	2.04	30	46.321
3	Vance	Dazzy	1924	BRO	NL	28	6	0	308.3	2.16	33	44.534
4	Wyatt	Whit	1941	BRO	NL	22	10	1	288.3	2.34	34	42.854
5	Kershaw	Clayton	2013	LAN	NL	16	9	0	236.0	1.83	25	41.458
6	Greinke	Zach	2015	LAN	NL	19	3	0	222.7	1.66	32	41.195
7	Kershaw	Clayton	2014	LAN	NL	21	3	0	198.3	1.77	26	39.635
8	Kershaw	Clayton	2011	LAN	NL	21	5	0	233.3	2.28	23	39.502
9	Kershaw	Clayton	2015	LAN	NL	16	7	0	232.7	2.13	27	38.045
10	Koufax	Sandy	1966	LAN	NL	27	9	0	323.0	1.73	31	37.199
11	Vance	Dazzy	1928	BRO	NL	22	10	2	280.3	2.09	37	34.912
12	Singer	Bill	1969	LAN	NL	20	12	1	315.7	2.34	25	33.351
13	Drysdale	Don	1962	LAN	NL	25	9	1	314.3	2.83	26	33.051
14	Drysdale	Don	1964	LAN	NL	18	16	0	321.3	2.18	28	32.039
15	Kershaw	Clayton	2012	LAN	NL	14	9	0	227.7	2.53	24	31.904
16	Hershiser	Orel	1988	LAN	NL	23	8	1	267.0	2.26	30	31.540
17	Drysdale	Don	1960	LAN	NL	15	14	2	269.0	2.84	24	31.247
18	Vance	Dazzy	1925	BRO	NL	22	9	0	265.3	3.53	34	31.049
19	Newcombe	Don	1956	BRO	NL	27	7	0	268.0	3.06	30	30.309
20	Branca	Ralph	1947	BRO	NL	21	12	1	280.0	2.67	21	30.169

Los Angeles Dodgers (BR3, BRO, LAN) - Top Career Batters

RANK	NAME	FIRST	LYR	TEAM	LG	PEVA-B	YRS	PPYR	HR	RBI	H	AVE
1	Snider	Duke	1962	LAN	NL	246.786	16	15.424	389	1271	1995	0.300
2	Wheat	Zack	1926	BRO	NL	211.353	18	11.742	131	1210	2804	0.317

RANK	NAME	FIRST	LYR	TEAM	LG	PEVA-B	YRS	PPYR	HR	RBI	H	AVE
3	Hodges	Gil	1961	LAN	NL	168.075	16	10.505	361	1254	1884	0.274
4	Reese	Pee Wee	1958	LAN	NL	166.690	16	10.418	126	885	2170	0.269
5	Campanella	Roy	1957	BRO	NL	162.658	10	16.266	242	856	1161	0.276
6	Cey	Ron	1982	LAN	NL	151.942	12	12.662	228	842	1378	0.264
7	Garvey	Steve	1982	LAN	NL	147.511	14	10.537	211	992	1968	0.301
8	Robinson	Jackie	1956	BRO	NL	146.209	10	14.621	137	734	1518	0.311
9	Davis	Willie	1973	LAN	NL	144.813	14	10.344	154	849	2091	0.279
10	Piazza	Mike	1998	LAN	NL	140.487	7	20.070	177	563	896	0.331
11	Furillo	Carl	1960	LAN	NL	125.828	15	8.389	192	1058	1910	0.299
12	Walker	Dixie	1947	BRO	NL	124.757	9	13.862	67	725	1395	0.311
13	Guerrero	Pedro	1988	LAN	NL	122.716	11	11.156	171	585	1113	0.309
14	Kemp	Matt	2018	LAN	NL	122.154	10	12.215	203	733	1322	0.292
15	Griffin	Mike	1898	BRO	NL	118.042	8	14.755	29	477	1166	0.305
16	Gilliam	Jim	1966	LAN	NL	109.763	14	7.840	65	558	1889	0.265
17	Sheckard	Jimmy	1905	BRO	NL	102.943	8	12.868	36	420	966	0.295
18	Karros	Eric	2002	LAN	NL	100.842	12	8.404	270	976	1608	0.268
19	Ethier	Andre	2017	LAN	NL	98.504	12	8.209	162	687	1367	0.285
20	Wills	Maury	1972	LAN	NL	95.928	12	7.994	17	374	1732	0.281
21	Pinkney	George	1891	BRO	NL	90.886	7	12.984	20	436	1012	0.271
22	Baker	Dusty	1983	LAN	NL	89.486	8	11.186	144	586	1144	0.281
23	Herman	Babe	1945	BRO	NL	88.858	7	12.694	112	594	1093	0.339
24	Daubert	Jake	1918	BRO	NL	86.265	9	9.585	33	415	1387	0.305
25	Burns	Oyster	1895	BRO	NL	84.858	8	10.607	40	606	955	0.300
26	Russell	Bill	1986	LAN	NL	84.660	18	4.703	46	627	1926	0.263
27	Galan	Augie	1946	BRO	NL	82.123	6	13.687	33	316	640	0.301
28	Parker	Wes	1972	LAN	NL	81.514	9	9.057	64	470	1110	0.267
29	Green	Shawn	2004	LAN	NL	80.788	5	16.158	162	509	842	0.280
30	Roseboro	Johnny	1967	LAN	NL	80.055	11	7.278	92	471	1009	0.251
31	Camilli	Dolph	1943	BRO	NL	79.585	6	13.264	139	572	809	0.270
32	Mondesi	Raul	1999	LAN	NL	79.122	7	11.303	163	518	1004	0.288
33	Scioscia	Mike	1992	LAN	NL	78.273	13	6.021	68	446	1131	0.259
34	Lopes	Davey	1981	LAN	NL	72.592	10	7.259	99	384	1204	0.262
35	Fairly	Ron	1969	LAN	NL	72.505	12	6.042	90	541	1010	0.260
36	Daly	Tom	1901	BRO	NL	70.619	11	6.420	44	614	1181	0.294
37	Myers	Hy	1922	BRO	NL	70.435	11	6.403	29	496	1253	0.282
38	Sheffield	Gary	2001	LAN	NL	69.708	4	17.427	129	367	583	0.312
39	Beltre	Adrian	2004	LAN	NL	68.227	7	9.747	147	510	949	0.274
40	Davis	Tommy	1966	LAN	NL	67.330	8	8.416	86	465	912	0.304
41	Butler	Brett	1997	LAN	NL	67.170	7	9.596	14	191	837	0.298
42	Bellinger	Cody	2020	LAN	NL	66.876	4	16.719	123	318	494	0.273
43	Lumley	Harry	1910	BRO	NL	66.207	7	9.458	38	305	728	0.274
44	Fournier	Jack	1926	BRO	NL	61.439	4	15.360	82	396	629	0.337

RANK	NAME	FIRST	LYR	TEAM	LG	PEVA-B	YRS	PPYR	HR	RBI	H	AVE
45	Johnston	Jimmy	1925	BRO	NL	61.013	10	6.101	20	390	1440	0.297
46	Sax	Steve	1988	LAN	NL	60.277	8	7.535	30	333	1218	0.282
47	Seager	Corey	2020	LAN	NL	59.063	6	9.844	88	307	610	0.295
48	Gonzalez	Adrian	2017	LAN	NL	58.668	6	9.778	101	448	752	0.280
49	Keeler	Willie	1902	BRO	NL	58.313	5	11.663	8	219	833	0.352
50	Dahlen	Bill	1911	BRO	NL	55.834	7	7.976	12	365	645	0.266

Los Angeles Dodgers (BR3, BRO, LAN) - Top Career Pitchers

RANK	NAME	FIRST	LYEAR	LTEAM	LG	PEVA	YRS	PPYR	W	L	SV	IP	ERA
1	Kershaw	Clayton	2020	LAN	NL	322.730	13	24.825	175	76	0	2333.0	2.43
2	Drysdale	Don	1969	LAN	NL	228.992	14	16.357	209	166	6	3432.0	2.95
3	Vance	Dazzy	1935	BRO	NL	208.994	12	17.416	190	131	7	2757.7	3.17
4	Koufax	Sandy	1966	LAN	NL	206.787	12	17.232	165	87	9	2324.3	2.76
5	Sutton	Don	1988	LAN	NL	191.643	16	11.978	233	181	5	3816.3	3.09
6	Hershiser	Orel	2000	LAN	NL	158.331	13	12.179	135	107	5	2180.7	3.12
7	Valenzuela	Fernando	1990	LAN	NL	143.987	11	13.090	141	116	2	2348.7	3.31
8	Newcombe	Don	1958	LAN	NL	122.137	8	15.267	123	66	4	1662.7	3.51
9	Jansen	Kenley	2020	LAN	NL	117.627	11	10.693	33	22	312	636.0	2.39
10	Grimes	Burleigh	1926	BRO	NL	109.893	9	12.210	158	121	5	2426.0	3.46
11	Osteen	Claude	1973	LAN	NL	98.204	9	10.912	147	126	0	2396.7	3.09
12	Welch	Bob	1987	LAN	NL	96.199	10	9.620	115	86	8	1820.7	3.14
13	Hooton	Burt	1984	LAN	NL	93.717	10	9.372	112	84	6	1861.3	3.14
14	Wyatt	Whit	1944	BRO	NL	93.449	6	15.575	80	45	1	1072.3	2.86
15	Martinez	Ramon	1998	LAN	NL	92.094	11	8.372	123	77	0	1731.7	3.45
16	Reuss	Jerry	1987	LAN	NL	91.391	9	10.155	86	69	8	1407.7	3.11
17	Brown	Kevin	2003	LAN	NL	82.913	5	16.583	58	32	0	872.7	2.83
18	Clark	Watty	1937	BRO	NL	82.849	11	7.532	106	88	16	1659.0	3.55
19	Mungo	Van	1941	BRO	NL	81.720	11	7.429	102	99	14	1739.3	3.41
20	Podres	Johnny	1966	LAN	NL	80.285	13	6.176	136	104	6	2029.3	3.66
21	Roe	Preacher	1954	BRO	NL	77.500	7	11.071	93	37	4	1277.3	3.26
22	Kennedy	Brickyard	1901	BRO	NL	77.246	10	7.725	177	149	9	2857.0	3.98
23	Nomo	Hideo	2004	LAN	NL	74.737	7	10.677	81	66	0	1217.3	3.74
24	Park	Chan Ho	2008	LAN	NL	73.556	9	8.173	84	58	2	1279.0	3.77
25	Rucker	Nap	1916	BRO	NL	73.267	10	7.327	134	134	14	2375.3	2.42
26	Greinke	Zack	2015	LAN	NL	71.382	3	23.794	51	15	0	602.7	2.30
27	Lowe	Derek	2008	LAN	NL	70.244	4	17.561	54	48	0	850.3	3.59
28	Gagne	Eric	2006	LAN	NL	68.922	8	8.615	25	21	161	545.3	3.27
29	Pfeffer	Jeff	1921	BRO	NL	68.339	9	7.593	113	80	8	1748.3	2.31
30	Messersmith	Andy	1979	LAN	NL	63.483	4	15.871	55	34	1	926.0	2.67
31	Ryu	Hyun-Jin	2019	LAN	NL	61.083	6	10.180	54	33	1	740.3	2.98
32	Billingsley	Chad	2013	LAN	NL	60.805	8	7.601	81	61	0	1175.3	3.65
33	Singer	Bill	1972	LAN	NL	59.291	9	6.588	69	76	1	1274.3	3.03
34	Branca	Ralph	1956	BRO	NL	58.245	11	5.295	80	58	18	1324.0	3.70

RANK	NAME	FIRST	LYEAR	LTEAM	LG	PEVA	YRS	PPYR	W	L	SV	IP	ERA
35	Valdez	Ismael	2000	LAN	NL	56.747	7	8.107	61	57	1	1065.0	3.48
36	Hamlin	Luke	1941	BRO	NL	54.098	5	10.820	60	57	8	1011.0	3.61
37	Erskine	Carl	1959	LAN	NL	52.106	12	4.342	122	78	13	1718.7	4.00
38	John	Tommy	1978	LAN	NL	50.832	6	8.472	87	42	1	1198.0	2.97
39	Pena	Alejandro	1989	LAN	NL	50.832	9	5.648	38	38	32	769.3	2.92
40	Rau	Doug	1979	LAN	NL	50.488	8	6.311	80	58	3	1250.7	3.30
41	Brewer	Jim	1975	LAN	NL	49.255	12	4.105	61	51	125	822.3	2.62
42	Belcher	Tim	1991	LAN	NL	48.587	5	9.717	50	38	5	806.0	2.99
43	Labine	Clem	1960	LAN	NL	47.642	11	4.331	70	52	83	933.3	3.63
44	Casey	Hugh	1948	BRO	NL	46.065	7	6.581	70	41	50	867.7	3.34
45	Petty	Jesse	1928	BRO	NL	45.480	4	11.370	54	59	3	934.3	3.52
46	Candiotti	Tom	1997	LAN	NL	44.483	6	7.414	52	64	0	1048.0	3.57
47	Perranoski	Ron	1972	LAN	NL	44.431	8	5.554	54	41	101	766.7	2.56
48	Higbe	Kirby	1947	BRO	NL	42.742	5	8.548	70	38	4	931.0	3.29
49	Penny	Brad	2008	LAN	NL	41.933	5	8.387	46	33	0	678.7	4.07
50	Kuroda	Hiroki	2011	LAN	NL	40.156	4	10.039	41	46	0	699.0	3.45

Los Angeles Dodgers – Top Fielders

Rank	FIRST BASE		FV	Lyear	G	FPCT	RF
1	Garvey	Steve	1.3621	1982	1470	0.996	10.01
2	Parker	Wes	1.2788	1972	1108	0.996	9.33
3	Gonzalez	Adrian	1.2684	2017	704	0.995	8.78
4	LaChance	Candy	1.2495	1898	470	0.983	10.71
5	Murray	Eddie	1.2442	1991	458	0.995	9.17
6	Phillips	Bill	1.2371	1887	372	0.978	10.50
7	Karros	Eric	1.2241	2002	1579	0.993	9.19
8	Hodges	Gil	1.2240	1961	1851	0.993	8.76
9	Daubert	Jake	1.1894	1918	1207	0.991	10.13
10	Loney	James	1.1460	2012	860	0.994	8.35

Rank	SECOND BASE		FV	Lyear	G	FPCT	RF
1	Cutshaw	George	1.4201	1917	833	0.961	5.55
2	Robinson	Jackie	1.3349	1956	748	0.983	5.25
3	Stanky	Eddie	1.2951	1947	498	0.973	5.35
4	Cuccinello	Tony	1.2745	1935	439	0.975	5.68
5	Sax	Steve	1.2733	1988	1070	0.975	5.05
6	Lopes	Davey	1.2625	1981	1150	0.977	5.00
7	Sizemore	Ted	1.2489	1976	275	0.982	5.09
8	Hummel	John	1.2470	1914	547	0.963	5.04
9	Grudzielanek	Mark	1.2330	2002	428	0.983	4.50
10	Cora	Alex	1.2276	2004	335	0.981	4.18

Rank	SHORTSTOP		FV	Lyear	G	FPCT	RF
1	Dahlen	Bill	1.6135	1911	649	0.935	5.73
2	Corcoran	Tommy	1.6004	1896	654	0.918	5.73
3	Reese	Pee Wee	1.5879	1958	2014	0.962	4.93
4	Bancroft	Dave	1.5709	1929	251	0.951	5.45
5	Wills	Maury	1.5541	1972	1497	0.963	4.74
6	Smith	Germany	1.5338	1897	778	0.885	5.26
7	Izturis	Cesar	1.5227	2006	553	0.980	4.13
8	Russell	Bill	1.5173	1986	1746	0.960	4.63
9	Gagne	Greg	1.5129	1997	270	0.968	4.15
10	Durocher	Leo	1.5071	1943	325	0.961	4.76

Rank	THIRD BASE		FV	Lyear	G	FPCT	RF
1	Cey	Ron	1.5977	1982	1468	0.963	2.94
2	Casey	Doc	1.5458	1907	288	0.937	3.11
3	Smith	Red	1.5213	1914	394	0.933	3.27

Rank			FV	Lyear	G	FPCT	RF
4	Gilbert	Wally	1.4965	1931	476	0.950	2.90
5	Beltre	Adrian	1.4945	2004	957	0.951	2.65
6	Wallach	Tim	1.4923	1996	384	0.964	2.35
7	Shindle	Billy	1.4830	1898	617	0.904	3.35
8	Uribe	Juan	1.4753	2015	354	0.978	2.42
9	Stripp	Joe	1.4706	1937	589	0.961	2.83
10	Pinkney	George	1.4664	1891	865	0.895	3.16

Rank	CATCHER		FV	Lyear	G	FPCT	RF	CS%
1	Campanella	Roy	2.0572	1957	1183	0.988	5.98	0.574
2	Roseboro	Johnny	1.9971	1967	1218	0.990	6.95	0.449
3	Owen	Mickey	1.9734	1945	510	0.986	4.67	0.496
4	Grandal	Yasmany	1.9515	2018	474	0.995	8.97	0.294
5	Scioscia	Mike	1.9411	1992	1395	0.988	6.50	0.339
6	Ellis	A.J.	1.9385	2016	526	0.997	7.19	0.335
7	Martin	Russell	1.9116	2019	701	0.991	7.87	0.307
8	Piazza	Mike	1.8928	1998	700	0.989	7.40	0.254
9	Lo Duca	Paul	1.8809	2004	498	0.991	7.53	0.353
10	Lopez	Al	1.8704	1935	746	0.982	4.30	0.499

Rank	OUTFIELD		FV	Lyear	G	FPCT	RF	ApG
1	Griffin	Mike	1.6560	1898	981	0.967	2.69	0.156
2	Butler	Brett	1.5841	1997	750	0.996	2.27	0.048
3	Maloney	Billy	1.5591	1908	402	0.962	2.43	0.119
4	Wynn	Jimmy	1.5428	1975	268	0.988	2.47	0.060
5	Myers	Hy	1.5365	1922	1070	0.972	2.56	0.125
6	Rosen	Goody	1.5239	1946	388	0.991	2.70	0.101
7	Davis	Willie	1.5202	1973	1906	0.977	2.39	0.065
8	Cooney	Johnny	1.5196	1944	255	0.987	2.61	0.078
9	McTamany	Jim	1.5123	1887	280	0.906	2.14	0.211
10	Sheckard	Jimmy	1.4929	1905	838	0.949	2.34	0.153
11	Burch	Al	1.4702	1911	416	0.956	2.21	0.175
12	Snider	Duke	1.4636	1962	1769	0.985	2.28	0.066
13	Brown	Eddie	1.4574	1925	267	0.973	2.88	0.037
14	Medwick	Joe	1.4569	1946	434	0.984	2.11	0.058
15	Baker	Dusty	1.4544	1983	1092	0.987	1.87	0.057
16	Mondesi	Raul	1.4525	1999	913	0.977	2.07	0.076
17	Wheat	Zack	1.4508	1926	2275	0.966	2.25	0.098
18	Carey	Max	1.4472	1929	267	0.971	2.39	0.101
19	Frederick	Johnny	1.4464	1934	733	0.974	2.56	0.082
20	Keeler	Willie	1.4354	1902	543	0.966	1.67	0.140
21	Shelby	John	1.4315	1990	367	0.981	2.30	0.052
22	Moran	Herbie	1.4300	1913	258	0.956	2.10	0.151
23	Walker	Dixie	1.4263	1947	1176	0.974	2.13	0.099
24	Furillo	Carl	1.4236	1960	1739	0.979	2.00	0.087
25	Daniels	Kal	1.4216	1992	291	0.982	1.71	0.079
26	O'Brien	Darby	1.4211	1892	582	0.938	1.99	0.120
27	Reiser	Pete	1.4079	1948	510	0.979	2.34	0.080
28	Jones	Fielder	1.4067	1900	614	0.945	1.99	0.122
29	Smith	Reggie	1.4021	1980	470	0.977	2.00	0.081
30	Johnson	Lou	1.3999	1967	367	0.983	1.69	0.049

Rank	PITCHING		FV	Lyear	IP	FPCT	RF
1	Greinke	Zach	1.1101	2015	602	0.982	2.47
2	Osteen	Claude	1.0989	1973	2397	0.972	2.31
3	Morgan	Mike	1.0975	1991	600	0.974	2.87
4	Lowe	Derek	1.0962	2008	850	0.974	2.42
5	Caruthers	Bob	1.0809	1891	1434	0.921	2.64
6	Valenzuela	Fernando	1.0809	1990	2349	0.964	2.36
7	Kennedy	Brickyard	1.0768	1901	2857	0.940	2.67
8	Stricklett	Elmer	1.0756	1907	759	0.958	4.59
9	Stein	Ed	1.0743	1898	1394	0.945	2.54
10	Grimes	Burleigh	1.0692	1926	2426	0.950	3.32

Franchise When and Where

Los Angeles Dodgers (1958 to Present); Brooklyn Dodgers (1932-1957, 1911-1912, BRO); Brooklyn Robins (1914-1931, BRO); Brooklyn Superbas (1899-1910, 1913, BRO); Brooklyn Bridegrooms (1888-1889, BR3; 1890, 1896-1898, BRO); Brooklyn Grooms (1891-1895, BRO); Brooklyn Grays (1885-1887, BR3); Brooklyn Atlantics (1884, BR3)

MIAMI MARLINS
Best Seasons and Careers of All-Time

They've won more than you'd think they should, and as a Franchise, first known as Florida and now Miami, the players on this list, for the most part, are come and gone players due to the lack of consistent payroll to pay players as they reach toward free agency, but their All-Time team is interesting. Giancarlo Stanton in the middle of your order is outstanding. Miguel Cabrera batting either in front of or after makes them an interesting pair. Add in Gary Sheffield and the middle of the order would be hard to pitch to. Pitching would be where this team might struggle, not with individual seasons, some were great and helped the Marlins win World Series titles, but with duration. There's no ten year career pitcher on the list. But some of those years were outstanding; people tend to forget that Kevin Brown, in 1996, had one of the most underrated seasons of All-Time.

Reserves

Bench - Cliff Floyd (OF), Christian Yelich (OF), Marcell Ozuna (OF), Luis Castillo (2B), Derek Lee (1B), Alex Gonzalez (SS), Charles Johnson (CATCHER).

Bullpen - Robb Nen (CL), Steve Cishek (SU), A.J. Burnett, Anibel Sanchez, A.J. Ramos, Brad Penny.

Miami Marlins - Best Position Player Years

Rank	Name	First	Year	Team	Lg	HR	RBI	AVG	Age	PEVA-B
1	Stanton	Giancarlo	2017	MIA	NL	59	132	0.281	27	38.866
2	Sheffield	Gary	1996	FLO	NL	42	120	0.314	28	32.618
3	Cabrera	Miguel	2006	FLO	NL	26	114	0.339	23	32.126
4	Stanton	Giancarlo	2014	MIA	NL	37	105	0.288	24	27.604
5	Ozuna	Marcell	2017	MIA	NL	37	124	0.312	27	26.942
6	Cabrera	Miguel	2005	FLO	NL	33	116	0.323	22	23.720
7	Ramirez	Hanley	2009	FLO	NL	24	106	0.342	26	23.588
8	Cabrera	Miguel	2007	FLO	NL	34	119	0.320	24	22.708
9	Delgado	Carlos	2005	FLO	NL	33	115	0.301	33	21.013
10	Ramirez	Hanley	2008	FLO	NL	33	67	0.301	25	20.938
11	Ramirez	Hanley	2007	FLO	NL	29	81	0.332	24	19.908
12	Yelich	Christian	2017	MIA	NL	18	81	0.282	26	17.376
13	Uggla	Dan	2010	FLO	NL	33	105	0.287	30	16.698
14	Yelich	Christian	2016	MIA	NL	21	98	0.298	25	16.451
15	Floyd	Cliff	2001	FLO	NL	31	103	0.317	29	16.222
16	Stanton	Mike	2011	FLO	NL	34	87	0.262	21	15.379
17	Cabrera	Miguel	2004	FLO	NL	33	112	0.294	21	14.825
18	Rodriguez	Ivan	2003	FLO	NL	16	85	0.297	32	14.811
19	Alou	Moises	1997	FLO	NL	23	115	0.292	31	14.645
20	Lowell	Mike	2004	FLO	NL	27	85	0.293	30	14.639

Miami Marlins - Best Pitcher Years

Rank	Name	First	Year	Team	Lg	W	L	SV	IP	ERA	Age	PEVA-P
1	Brown	Kevin	1996	FLO	NL	17	11	0	233.0	1.89	31	40.004
2	Willis	Dontrelle	2005	FLO	NL	22	10	0	236.3	2.63	23	30.817
3	Brown	Kevin	1997	FLO	NL	16	8	0	237.3	2.69	32	22.694
4	Johnson	Josh	2009	FLO	NL	15	5	0	209.0	3.23	25	21.840
5	Johnson	Josh	2010	FLO	NL	11	8	0	183.7	2.30	26	21.819
6	Fernandez	Jose	2016	MIA	NL	16	8	0	182.3	2.86	24	20.464
7	Fernandez	Jose	2013	MIA	NL	12	6	0	172.7	2.19	21	19.799
8	Pavano	Carl	2004	FLO	NL	18	8	0	222.3	3.00	28	19.631
9	Nolasco	Ricky	2008	FLO	NL	15	8	0	212.3	3.52	26	19.070
10	Harvey	Bryan	1993	FLO	NL	1	5	45	69.0	1.70	30	16.133
11	Nen	Robb	1996	FLO	NL	5	1	35	83.0	1.95	27	15.924
12	Leiter	Al	1996	FLO	NL	16	12	0	215.3	2.93	31	15.083
13	Willis	Dontrelle	2006	FLO	NL	12	12	0	223.3	3.87	24	14.550
14	Fernandez	Alex	1997	FLO	NL	17	12	0	220.7	3.59	28	14.499
15	Jones	Todd	2005	FLO	NL	1	5	40	73.0	2.10	37	14.477
16	Dempster	Ryan	2000	FLO	NL	14	10	0	226.3	3.66	23	14.130
17	Benitez	Armando	2004	FLO	NL	2	2	47	69.7	1.29	32	13.658
18	Penny	Brad	2001	FLO	NL	10	10	0	205.0	3.69	23	12.356
19	Burnett	A.J.	2005	FLO	NL	12	12	0	209.0	3.44	28	12.274
20	Sanchez	Anibel	2010	FLO	NL	13	12	0	195.0	3.55	26	12.197

Florida/Miami Marlins (FLO, MIA) - Top Career Batters

RANK	NAME	FIRST	LYR	TEAM	LG	PEVA-B	YRS	PPYR	HR	RBI	H	AVE
1	Stanton	Giancarlo	2017	MIA	NL	120.215	8	15.027	267	672	960	0.268
2	Ramirez	Hanley	2012	MIA	NL	99.786	7	14.255	148	482	1103	0.300

RANK	NAME	FIRST	LYR	TEAM	LG	PEVA-B	YRS	PPYR	HR	RBI	H	AVE
3	Cabrera	Miguel	2007	FLO	NL	96.341	5	19.268	138	523	842	0.313
4	Sheffield	Gary	1998	FLO	NL	69.230	6	11.538	122	380	538	0.288
5	Lowell	Mike	2005	FLO	NL	68.068	7	9.724	143	578	965	0.272
6	Uggla	Dan	2010	FLO	NL	61.021	5	12.204	154	465	771	0.263
7	Conine	Jeff	2005	FLO	NL	58.808	8	7.351	120	553	1005	0.290
8	Yelich	Christian	2017	MIA	NL	56.224	5	11.245	59	293	719	0.290
9	Ozuna	Marcell	2017	MIA	NL	56.162	5	11.232	96	361	683	0.277
10	Castillo	Luis	2005	FLO	NL	54.996	10	5.500	20	271	1273	0.293
11	Lee	Derrek	2003	FLO	NL	46.603	6	7.767	129	417	746	0.264
12	Floyd	Cliff	2002	FLO	NL	45.583	6	7.597	110	409	661	0.294
13	Realmuto	J.T.	2018	MIA	NL	40.154	5	8.031	59	243	555	0.279
14	Wilson	Preston	2002	FLO	NL	37.729	5	7.546	104	329	549	0.262
15	Pierre	Juan	2013	MIA	NL	37.442	4	9.360	7	145	682	0.295
16	Gonzalez	Alex	2005	FLO	NL	36.315	8	4.539	81	375	788	0.245
17	Ross	Cody	2010	FLO	NL	32.001	5	6.400	80	297	502	0.265
18	Anderson	Brian	2020	MIA	NL	30.284	4	7.571	42	177	354	0.266
19	Johnson	Charles	2002	FLO	NL	29.358	7	4.194	75	277	467	0.241
20	Encarnacion	Juan	2005	FLO	NL	25.600	4	6.400	46	223	414	0.271
21	Millar	Kevin	2002	FLO	NL	23.757	5	4.751	59	251	443	0.296
22	Willingham	Josh	2008	FLO	NL	23.696	5	4.739	63	219	378	0.266
23	Hechavarria	Adeiny	2017	MIA	NL	22.796	5	4.559	13	168	541	0.255
24	Rojas	Miguel	2020	MIA	NL	22.731	6	3.788	23	176	465	0.273
25	Kotsay	Mark	2000	FLO	NL	22.547	4	5.637	31	179	463	0.280
26	Bour	Justin	2018	MIA	NL	22.383	5	4.477	83	272	396	0.262
27	Cantu	Jorge	2010	FLO	NL	22.133	3	7.378	55	249	441	0.278
28	Gordon	Dee	2017	MIA	NL	22.045	3	7.348	7	93	493	0.309
29	Dietrich	Derek	2018	MIA	NL	21.986	6	3.664	60	204	477	0.254
30	Delgado	Carlos	2005	FLO	NL	21.013	1	21.013	33	115	157	0.301
31	Renteria	Edgar	1998	FLO	NL	20.787	3	6.929	12	114	450	0.288
32	Prado	Martin	2019	MIA	NL	20.327	5	4.065	22	183	467	0.278
33	Hermida	Jeremy	2009	FLO	NL	20.182	5	4.036	57	210	452	0.265
34	Sanchez	Gaby	2012	MIA	NL	19.897	5	3.979	43	184	353	0.260
35	Castro	Starlin	2019	MIA	NL	16.788	2	8.394	34	140	337	0.274
36	Jacobs	Mike	2008	FLO	NL	16.413	3	5.471	69	224	354	0.258
37	Carr	Chuck	1995	FLO	NL	16.066	3	5.355	8	91	331	0.256
38	Colbrunn	Greg	1996	FLO	NL	14.888	3	4.963	45	189	339	0.284
39	Rodriguez	Ivan	2003	FLO	NL	14.811	1	14.811	16	85	152	0.297
40	Alou	Moises	1997	FLO	NL	14.645	1	14.645	23	115	157	0.292
41	Pendleton	Terry	1996	FLO	NL	14.190	2	7.095	21	136	251	0.273
42	Abbott	Kurt	1997	FLO	NL	13.919	4	3.480	40	156	343	0.257
43	Bonilla	Bobby	1998	FLO	NL	13.629	2	6.815	21	111	194	0.294
44	Coghlan	Chris	2013	MIA	NL	13.124	5	2.625	21	117	383	0.270
45	Redmond	Mike	2004	FLO	NL	12.855	7	1.836	11	132	380	0.284

RANK	NAME	FIRST	LYR	TEAM	LG	PEVA-B	YRS	PPYR	HR	RBI	H	AVE
46	Bonifacio	Emilio	2012	MIA	NL	12.841	4	3.210	7	84	393	0.271
47	Morrison	Logan	2013	MIA	NL	12.711	4	3.178	42	162	322	0.249
48	McGehee	Casey	2015	MIA	NL	12.511	2	6.256	4	85	197	0.271
49	Reyes	Jose	2012	MIA	NL	12.427	1	12.427	11	57	184	0.287
50	Santiago	Benito	1994	FLO	NL	12.229	2	6.114	24	91	200	0.248

Miami/Florida Marlins - Top Career Pitchers

RANK	NAME	FIRST	LYEAR	LTEAM	LG	PEVA	YRS	PPYR	W	L	SV	IP	ERA
1	Willis	Dontrelle	2007	FLO	NL	70.888	5	14.178	68	54	0	1022.7	3.78
2	Johnson	Josh	2012	MIA	NL	69.725	8	8.716	56	37	0	916.7	3.15
3	Brown	Kevin	1997	FLO	NL	62.698	2	31.349	33	19	0	470.3	2.30
4	Nolasco	Ricky	2013	MIA	NL	60.390	8	7.549	81	72	0	1225.7	4.44
5	Fernandez	Jose	2016	MIA	NL	46.784	4	11.696	38	17	0	471.3	2.58
6	Burnett	A.J.	2005	FLO	NL	36.538	7	5.220	49	50	0	853.7	3.73
7	Sanchez	Anibal	2012	MIA	NL	36.034	7	5.148	44	45	0	794.3	3.75
8	Penny	Brad	2014	MIA	NL	33.101	6	5.517	50	43	0	807.7	4.12
9	Nen	Robb	1997	FLO	NL	32.683	5	6.537	20	16	108	314.0	3.41
10	Dempster	Ryan	2002	FLO	NL	30.382	5	6.076	42	43	0	759.7	4.64
11	Cishek	Steve	2015	MIA	NL	28.526	6	4.754	17	20	94	289.7	2.86
12	Pavano	Carl	2004	FLO	NL	28.334	3	9.445	33	23	0	485.0	3.64
13	Ramos	AJ	2017	MIA	NL	27.121	6	4.520	15	16	92	327.3	2.78
14	Koehler	Tom	2017	MIA	NL	26.656	6	4.443	36	53	0	767.3	4.43
15	Beckett	Josh	2005	FLO	NL	26.235	5	5.247	41	34	0	609.0	3.46
16	Rapp	Pat	1997	FLO	NL	25.886	5	5.177	37	43	0	665.7	4.18
17	Olsen	Scott	2008	FLO	NL	24.917	4	6.229	31	37	0	579.3	4.63
18	Urena	Jose	2020	MIA	NL	21.858	6	3.643	32	46	4	597.0	4.60
19	Leiter	Al	2005	FLO	NL	21.615	3	7.205	30	28	0	446.7	4.07
20	Fernandez	Alex	2000	FLO	NL	21.268	3	7.089	28	24	0	414.0	3.59
21	Alfonseca	Antonio	2005	FLO	NL	19.039	6	3.173	19	25	102	333.0	3.86
22	Volstad	Chris	2011	FLO	NL	18.268	4	4.567	32	39	0	584.0	4.59
23	Burkett	John	1996	FLO	NL	17.392	2	8.696	20	24	0	342.3	4.31
24	Harvey	Bryan	1995	FLO	NL	16.533	3	5.511	1	5	51	79.3	2.50
25	Hammond	Chris	1998	FLO	NL	16.353	5	3.271	29	32	0	520.0	4.52
26	Looper	Braden	2003	FLO	NL	16.352	5	3.270	19	16	46	388.0	3.69
27	Alvarez	Henderson	2015	MIA	NL	15.759	3	5.253	17	17	0	312.0	3.23
28	Alcantara	Sandy	2020	MIA	NL	15.395	3	5.322	11	19	0	273.3	3.69
29	Lopez	Pablo	2020	MIA	NL	15.155	3	5.052	13	16	0	227.3	4.47
30	Hernandez	Livan	1999	FLO	NL	14.919	4	3.730	24	24	0	469.7	4.39
31	Jones	Todd	2005	FLO	NL	14.477	1	14.477	1	5	40	73.0	2.10
32	Benitez	Armando	2007	FLO	NL	14.432	2	7.216	4	7	47	102.7	2.72
33	Dunn	Mike	2016	MIA	NL	14.257	6	2.376	26	25	4	328.0	3.59
34	Straily	Dan	2018	MIA	NL	12.602	2	6.301	15	15	0	304.0	4.20
35	Gregg	Kevin	2014	MIA	NL	12.555	3	4.185	7	13	61	161.7	3.84

RANK	NAME	FIRST	LYEAR	LTEAM	LG	PEVA	YRS	PPYR	W	L	SV	IP	ERA
36	Nunez	Leo	2011	FLO	NL	**12.424**	3	4.141	9	13	92	198.0	3.86
37	Sanchez	Jesus	2001	FLO	NL	**12.093**	4	3.023	23	32	0	494.0	5.06
38	Buehrle	Mark	2012	MIA	NL	**12.067**	1	12.067	13	13	0	202.3	3.74
39	Nunez	Vladimir	2003	FLO	NL	**11.848**	5	2.370	14	27	20	343.3	4.77
40	Barraclough	Kyle	2018	MIA	NL	**11.661**	4	2.915	15	12	11	218.7	3.21
41	Phelps	David	2017	MIA	NL	**11.370**	3	3.790	13	18	4	245.7	3.52
42	Conley	Adam	2019	MIA	NL	**11.126**	5	2.225	25	30	5	414.3	4.82
43	Meadows	Brian	1999	FLO	NL	**10.835**	2	5.417	22	28	0	352.7	5.41
44	Hough	Charlie	1994	FLO	NL	**10.750**	2	5.375	14	25	0	318.0	4.58
45	Vazquez	Javier	2011	FLO	NL	**10.128**	1	10.128	13	11	0	192.7	3.69
46	Sanches	Brian	2011	FLO	NL	**10.011**	3	3.337	10	5	0	181.7	2.92

Miami Marlins – Top Fielders

Rank	FIRST BASE		FV	Lyear	G	FPCT	RF
1	Colbrunn	Greg	**1.2168**	1996	309	0.995	8.92
2	Sanchez	Gaby	**1.1876**	2012	360	0.994	8.51
3	Lee	Derrek	**1.1360**	2003	818	0.994	8.53
4	Bour	Justin	**1.0461**	2018	413	0.996	7.64
5	Conine	Jeff	**1.0057**	2005	398	0.992	6.64
6	Jacobs	Mike	**1.0000**	2008	351	0.991	7.73

Rank	SECOND BASE		FV	Lyear	G	FPCT	RF
1	Gordon	Dee	**1.3178**	2017	376	0.986	4.57
2	Castillo	Luis	**1.2612**	2005	1114	0.983	4.76
3	Uggla	Dan	**1.1811**	2010	769	0.980	4.64
4	Castro	Starlin	**1.1663**	2019	267	0.980	3.92

Rank	SHORTSTOP		FV	Lyear	G	FPCT	RF
1	Renteria	Edgar	**1.5886**	1998	388	0.973	4.46
2	Hechavarria	Adeiny	**1.5414**	2017	596	0.979	4.04
3	Rojas	Miguel	**1.4784**	2020	389	0.980	3.82
4	Gonzalez	Alex	**1.4546**	2005	880	0.968	4.31
5	Ramirez	Hanley	**1.4120**	2011	827	0.968	4.05
6	Abbott	Kurt	**1.3920**	1997	265	0.964	4.07

Rank	THIRD BASE		FV	Lyear	G	FPCT	RF
1	Lowell	Mike	**1.5768**	2005	939	0.976	2.59
2	Prado	Martin	**1.3944**	2019	378	0.973	2.20
3	Cabrera	Miguel	**1.3816**	2007	375	0.954	2.35

Rank	CATCHER		FV	Lyear	G	FPCT	RF	CS%
1	Johnson	Charles	**2.0097**	2002	582	0.995	7.16	0.438
2	Realmuto	J.T.	**1.7905**	2018	494	0.993	8.04	0.330
3	Redmond	Mike	**1.7726**	2004	447	0.994	6.26	0.332

Rank	OUTFIELD		FV	Lyear	G	FPCT	RF	ApG
1	Kotsay	Mark	**1.5691**	2000	444	0.986	2.17	0.126
2	Pierre	Juan	**1.5456**	2013	547	0.993	2.30	0.029
3	Carr	Chuck	**1.5392**	1995	346	0.984	2.68	0.055
4	Wilson	Preston	**1.4576**	2002	577	0.984	2.33	0.068
5	Encarnacion	Juan	**1.4519**	2005	422	0.991	1.91	0.043
6	Ross	Cody	**1.4457**	2010	601	0.989	1.94	0.047
7	Yelich	Christian	**1.4455**	2017	653	0.992	1.98	0.029
8	Ozuna	Marcell	**1.4418**	2017	645	0.988	2.25	0.064
9	Conine	Jeff	**1.3672**	2005	664	0.982	1.77	0.060
10	Sheffield	Gary	**1.3563**	1998	478	0.972	1.75	0.075
11	Stanton	Giancarlo	**1.3540**	2017	943	0.980	2.18	0.064
12	Coghlan	Chris	**1.3089**	2013	353	0.991	1.97	0.048
13	Willingham	Josh	**1.2988**	2008	371	0.984	1.64	0.057
14	Floyd	Cliff	**1.2520**	2002	579	0.968	1.86	0.066
15	Hermida	Jeremy	**1.2489**	2009	488	0.976	1.90	0.031

Rank							
16	Cabrera	Miguel	**1.2101**	2005	348	0.971	1.66	0.086

Rank	PITCHING		FV	Lyear	IP	FPCT	RF
1	Johnson	Josh	**1.0314**	2012	917	0.977	2.10
2	Dempster	Ryan	**1.0036**	2002	760	0.953	1.91
3	Volstad	Chris	**1.0021**	2011	584	0.983	1.79
4	Urena	Jose	**1.0012**	2020	597	0.975	1.73
5	Nolasco	Ricky	**0.9863**	2013	1226	0.953	1.50
6	Penny	Brad	**0.9841**	2014	808	0.975	1.77
7	Willis	Dontrelle	**0.9767**	2007	1023	0.917	1.86
8	Koehler	Tom	**0.9718**	2017	767	0.931	1.42
9	Sanchez	Anibal	**0.9554**	2012	794	0.912	1.88
10	Rapp	Pat	**0.9332**	1997	666	0.950	1.81

Franchise When and Where
Miami Marlins (2012 to present)
Florida Marlins (1993-2011)

MILWAUKEE BREWERS
Best Seasons and Careers of All-Time

It's a power collection of sluggers paving the way for Milwaukee with Prince Fielder, Ryan Braun, and Gorman Thomas vying to knock in the best players that the Brewers produced. Think Yount and Molitor heading the batting order. Okay, the starting rotation, like many of the more recent teams to enter the American or National leagues, might have some trouble against the Yankees, and are likely to be surpassed in the decades to come by more stellar names and accomplishments. We like the bullpen, even if Rollie Fingers is better known for his mustache because of seasons in other uniforms and Josh Hader is only four years into his career there.

Reserves

Bench - Geoff Jenkins (OF), Jeromy Burnitz (OF), Jeff Cirillo (3B), Cecil Cooper (1B), George Scott (1B), Jim Gantner (2B/3B), Jonathan Lucroy (CATCHER).

Bullpen - Rollie Fingers (CL), Dan Plesac (SU), Jim Slaton, Chris Bosio, Cal Eldred, Josh Hader.

Milwaukee Brewers - Best Position Player Years

Rank	Name	First	Year	Team	Lg	HR	RBI	AVG	Age	PEVA-B
1	Yount	Robin	1982	ML4	AL	29	114	0.331	27	45.717
2	Fielder	Prince	2009	MIL	NL	46	141	0.299	25	34.062
3	Braun	Ryan	2012	MIL	NL	41	112	0.319	29	28.403
4	Yount	Robin	1983	ML4	AL	17	80	0.308	28	28.042
5	Braun	Ryan	2011	MIL	NL	33	111	0.332	28	27.874
6	Fielder	Prince	2011	MIL	NL	38	120	0.299	27	27.347
7	Thomas	Gorman	1982	ML4	AL	39	112	0.245	32	26.667
8	Yelich	Christian	2019	MIL	NL	44	97	0.329	28	26.048
9	Yelich	Christian	2018	MIL	NL	36	110	0.326	27	26.040
10	Braun	Ryan	2009	MIL	NL	32	114	0.320	26	25.835
11	Yount	Robin	1989	ML4	AL	21	103	0.318	34	25.703
12	Molitor	Paul	1982	ML4	AL	19	71	0.302	26	25.602
13	Cooper	Cecil	1982	ML4	AL	32	121	0.313	33	24.686
14	Molitor	Paul	1991	ML4	AL	17	75	0.325	35	24.360
15	Cooper	Cecil	1983	ML4	AL	30	126	0.307	34	24.257
16	Oglivie	Ben	1980	ML4	AL	41	118	0.304	31	23.936
17	Cooper	Cecil	1980	ML4	AL	25	122	0.352	31	23.765
18	Yount	Robin	1984	ML4	AL	16	80	0.298	29	23.370
19	Lezcano	Sixto	1979	ML4	AL	28	101	0.321	26	22.688
20	Fielder	Prince	2007	MIL	NL	50	119	0.288	23	22.583

Milwaukee Brewers - Best Pitcher Years

Rank	Name	First	Year	Team	Lg	W	L	SV	IP	ERA	Age	PEVA-P
1	Sheets	Ben	2004	MIL	NL	12	14	0	237.0	2.70	26	27.681
2	Caldwell	Mike	1978	ML4	AL	22	9	1	293.3	2.36	29	24.297
3	Higuera	Teddy	1988	ML4	AL	16	9	0	227.3	2.45	30	22.403
4	Sabathia	C.C.	2008	MIL	NL	11	2	0	130.7	1.65	28	20.421
5	Higuera	Teddy	1987	ML4	AL	18	10	0	261.7	3.85	29	20.419
6	Fingers	Rollie	1981	ML4	AL	6	3	28	78.0	1.04	35	20.222
7	Higuera	Teddy	1986	ML4	AL	20	11	0	248.3	2.79	28	19.290
8	Sheets	Ben	2008	MIL	NL	13	9	0	198.3	3.09	30	18.905
9	Jones	Doug	1997	ML4	AL	6	6	36	80.3	2.02	40	18.476
10	Davies	Zach	2017	MIL	NL	17	9	0	191.3	3.90	24	16.851
11	Bosio	Chris	1989	ML4	AL	15	10	0	234.7	2.95	26	16.011
12	Chacin	Jhoulys	2018	MIL	NL	15	8	0	192.7	3.50	30	15.658
13	Hader	Josh	2019	MIL	NL	3	5	37	75.7	2.62	25	15.393
14	Navarro	Jaime	1992	ML4	AL	17	11	0	246.0	3.33	25	15.093
15	Gallardo	Yovani	2012	MIL	NL	16	9	0	204.0	3.66	26	15.080
16	Wegman	Bill	1992	ML4	AL	13	14	0	261.7	3.20	30	14.900
17	Capuano	Chris	2005	MIL	NL	18	12	0	219.0	3.99	27	14.873
18	Wegman	Bill	1991	ML4	AL	15	7	0	193.3	2.84	29	14.785
19	Sanders	Ken	1971	ML4	AL	7	12	31	136.3	1.91	30	14.657
20	Cordero	Francisco	2007	MIL	NL	0	4	44	63.3	2.98	32	14.631

Milwaukee Brewers (MIL, SE1) - Top Career Batters

RANK	NAME	FIRST	LYR	TEAM	LG	PEVA-B	YRS	PPYR	HR	RBI	H	AVE
1	Yount	Robin	1993	ML4	AL	291.976	20	14.599	251	1406	3142	0.285
2	Braun	Ryan	2020	MIL	NL	187.723	14	13.409	352	1154	1963	0.296

RANK	NAME	FIRST	LYR	TEAM	LG	PEVA-B	YRS	PPYR	HR	RBI	H	AVE
3	Molitor	Paul	1992	ML4	AL	177.049	15	11.803	160	790	2281	0.303
4	Cooper	Cecil	1987	ML4	AL	143.483	11	13.044	201	944	1815	0.302
5	Fielder	Prince	2011	MIL	NL	126.723	7	18.103	230	656	996	0.282
6	Thomas	Gorman	1986	ML4	AL	99.391	11	9.036	208	605	815	0.230
7	Oglivie	Ben	1986	ML4	AL	98.016	9	10.891	176	685	1144	0.277
8	Jenkins	Geoff	2007	MIL	NL	79.013	10	7.901	212	704	1221	0.277
9	Scott	George	1976	ML4	AL	72.764	5	14.553	115	463	851	0.283
10	Money	Don	1983	ML4	AL	69.513	11	6.319	134	529	1168	0.270
11	Gantner	Jim	1992	ML4	AL	66.603	17	3.918	47	568	1696	0.274
12	Cirillo	Jeff	2006	MIL	NL	65.226	8	8.153	73	418	1000	0.307
13	Burnitz	Jeromy	2001	MIL	NL	64.153	6	10.692	165	525	714	0.258
14	Hart	Corey	2012	MIL	NL	63.609	9	7.068	154	508	950	0.276
15	Lucroy	Jonathan	2016	MIL	NL	62.513	7	8.930	79	387	806	0.284
16	Yelich	Christian	2020	MIL	NL	61.628	3	20.543	92	229	389	0.308
17	Vaughn	Greg	1996	ML4	AL	61.395	8	7.674	169	566	799	0.246
18	Lezcano	Sixto	1980	ML4	AL	58.995	7	8.428	102	374	749	0.275
19	Surhoff	B.J.	1995	ML4	AL	57.810	9	6.423	57	524	1064	0.274
20	Weeks	Rickie	2014	MIL	NL	53.661	11	4.878	148	430	1009	0.249
21	Simmons	Ted	1985	ML4	AL	52.469	5	10.494	66	394	666	0.262
22	May	Dave	1978	ML4	AL	45.087	6	7.514	69	287	652	0.259
23	Sexson	Richie	2003	MIL	NL	44.362	4	11.091	133	398	549	0.276
24	Deer	Rob	1990	ML4	AL	43.296	5	8.659	137	385	535	0.229
25	Gomez	Carlos	2015	MIL	NL	42.958	6	7.160	87	288	622	0.267
26	Nilsson	Dave	1999	MIL	NL	42.185	8	5.273	105	470	789	0.284
27	Moore	Charlie	1986	ML4	AL	41.864	14	2.990	35	401	1029	0.262
28	Briggs	Johnny	1975	ML4	AL	40.066	5	8.013	80	259	492	0.258
29	Valentin	Jose	1999	MIL	NL	34.325	8	4.291	90	343	577	0.240
30	Harper	Tommy	1971	ML4	AL	34.110	3	11.370	54	175	456	0.264
31	Ramirez	Aramis	2015	MIL	NL	33.534	4	8.384	65	262	467	0.284
32	Seitzer	Kevin	1996	ML4	AL	32.437	5	6.487	34	281	598	0.300
33	Hall	Bill	2009	MIL	NL	32.316	8	4.039	102	367	677	0.253
34	Jaha	John	1998	MIL	NL	32.266	7	4.609	105	366	583	0.268
35	Hamilton	Darryl	1995	ML4	AL	31.766	7	4.538	23	253	637	0.290
36	Porter	Darrell	1976	ML4	AL	30.899	6	5.150	54	226	391	0.229
37	Bando	Sal	1981	ML4	AL	30.401	5	6.080	50	243	479	0.250
38	Hardy	J.J.	2009	MIL	NL	28.239	5	5.648	75	265	543	0.262
39	Loretta	Mark	2002	MIL	NL	26.180	8	3.272	29	272	751	0.289
40	McGehee	Casey	2011	MIL	NL	24.628	3	8.209	52	237	403	0.267
41	Clark	Brady	2006	MIL	NL	24.534	4	6.134	30	168	477	0.284
42	Shaw	Travis	2019	MIL	NL	24.505	3	8.168	70	203	303	0.239
43	Vina	Fernando	1999	MIL	NL	22.935	5	4.587	22	164	559	0.286
44	Hernandez	Jose	2002	MIL	NL	22.828	3	7.609	60	210	395	0.261

RANK	NAME	FIRST	LYR	TEAM	LG	PEVA-B	YRS	PPYR	HR	RBI	H	AVE
45	Lee	Carlos	2006	MIL	NL	22.632	2	11.316	60	195	275	0.273
46	Segura	Jean	2015	MIL	NL	21.466	4	5.366	23	144	482	0.266
47	Arcia	Orlando	2020	MIL	NL	21.456	5	4.291	42	179	421	0.244
48	Grissom	Marquis	2000	MIL	NL	21.420	3	7.140	44	205	453	0.260
49	Overbay	Lyle	2014	MIL	NL	20.970	3	6.990	39	194	382	0.278
50	Hisle	Larry	1982	ML4	AL	20.644	5	4.129	49	161	219	0.276

Milwaukee Brewers (MIL, ML4, SE1) - Top Career Pitchers

RANK	NAME	FIRST	LYEAR	LTEAM	LG	PEVA	YRS	PPYR	W	L	SV	IP	ERA
1	Sheets	Ben	2008	MIL	NL	90.234	8	11.279	86	83	0	1428.0	3.72
2	Higuera	Teddy	1994	ML4	AL	79.331	9	8.815	94	64	0	1380.0	3.61
3	Gallardo	Yovani	2014	MIL	NL	70.304	8	8.788	89	64	0	1289.3	3.69
4	Caldwell	Mike	1984	ML4	AL	64.597	8	8.075	102	80	2	1604.7	3.74
5	Wegman	Bill	1995	ML4	AL	55.455	11	5.041	81	90	2	1482.7	4.16
6	Slaton	Jim	1983	ML4	AL	50.213	12	4.184	117	121	11	2025.3	3.86
7	Bosio	Chris	1992	ML4	AL	49.803	7	7.115	67	62	8	1190.0	3.76
8	Eldred	Cal	1999	MIL	NL	44.631	9	4.959	64	65	0	1078.7	4.51
9	Haas	Moose	1985	ML4	AL	44.160	10	4.416	91	79	2	1542.0	4.03
10	Plesac	Dan	1992	ML4	AL	40.054	7	5.722	29	37	133	524.3	3.21
11	Navarro	Jaime	2000	MIL	NL	38.957	7	5.565	62	64	1	1061.7	4.44
12	Fingers	Rollie	1985	ML4	AL	38.411	4	9.603	13	17	97	259.0	2.54
13	Davis	Doug	2010	MIL	NL	35.970	5	7.194	38	40	0	724.0	4.11
14	Bush	David	2010	MIL	NL	34.815	5	6.963	46	53	0	870.0	4.80
15	Anderson	Chase	2019	MIL	NL	34.596	4	8.649	38	27	0	590.0	3.83
16	Bones	Ricky	1996	ML4	AL	34.402	5	6.880	47	56	0	883.0	4.64
17	Hader	Josh	2020	MIL	NL	33.784	4	8.446	12	11	62	223.7	2.54
18	Capuano	Chris	2016	MIL	NL	33.701	6	5.617	45	49	0	768.7	4.33
19	Karl	Scott	1999	MIL	NL	32.889	5	6.578	50	51	0	914.7	4.57
20	Davies	Zach	2019	MIL	NL	29.492	3	9.831	29	23	0	417.0	3.91
21	Nelson	Jimmy	2019	MIL	NL	28.492	6	4.749	33	46	0	633.3	4.22
22	Peralta	Wily	2017	MIL	NL	27.832	6	4.639	47	52	0	704.7	4.48
23	Woodruff	Brandon	2020	MIL	NL	27.830	4	6.957	19	11	1	280.7	3.66
24	Sanders	Ken	1972	ML4	AL	27.662	3	9.221	14	23	61	321.0	2.21
25	Sorensen	Lary	1980	ML4	AL	26.678	4	6.670	52	46	2	854.0	3.72
26	Travers	Bill	1980	ML4	AL	26.143	7	3.735	65	67	1	1068.3	3.99
27	Colborn	Jim	1976	ML4	AL	26.011	5	5.202	57	60	3	1118.0	3.65
28	Rodriguez	Francisco	2015	MIL	NL	25.897	5	5.179	13	16	95	250.7	2.91
29	Lohse	Kyle	2015	MIL	NL	25.340	3	8.447	29	32	2	549.3	4.11
30	Axford	John	2013	MIL	NL	24.986	5	4.997	21	19	106	263.3	3.35
31	Wolf	Randy	2012	MIL	NL	24.322	3	8.107	29	32	0	570.3	4.37
32	Jeffress	Jeremy	2019	MIL	NL	24.322	7	3.475	24	8	43	304.7	2.66
33	Vuckovich	Pete	1986	ML4	AL	23.663	5	4.733	40	26	0	533.0	3.88
34	Pattin	Marty	1971	ML4	AL	21.216	3	7.072	35	38	0	656.7	3.82

RANK	NAME	FIRST	LYEAR	LTEAM	LG	PEVA	YRS	PPYR	W	L	SV	IP	ERA
35	Fetters	Mike	1997	ML4	AL	21.141	6	3.523	13	19	79	334.3	2.99
36	Jones	Doug	1998	MIL	NL	21.080	4	5.270	14	10	49	168.7	3.42
37	Suppan	Jeff	2010	MIL	NL	20.456	4	5.114	29	36	0	577.0	5.08
38	Sabathia	C.C.	2008	MIL	NL	20.421	1	20.421	11	2	0	130.7	1.65
39	Wickman	Bob	2000	MIL	NL	19.823	5	3.965	21	25	79	315.0	3.20
40	Knebel	Corey	2020	MIL	NL	19.207	5	3.841	6	11	57	227.7	3.20
41	McClure	Bob	1986	ML4	AL	18.318	10	1.832	45	43	34	842.0	3.97
42	Burnes	Corbin	2020	MIL	NL	18.124	3	6.041	12	6	2	146.7	4.48
43	Greinke	Zack	2012	MIL	NL	17.594	2	8.797	25	9	0	294.7	3.67
44	Chacin	Jhoulys	2019	MIL	NL	17.554	2	8.777	18	18	0	281.3	4.22
45	Augustine	Jerry	1984	ML4	AL	17.528	10	1.753	55	59	11	944.0	4.23
46	Crim	Chuck	1991	ML4	AL	17.480	5	3.496	33	31	42	529.7	3.47
47	Castro	Bill	1980	ML4	AL	17.362	7	2.480	25	23	44	411.0	2.96
48	Cordero	Francisco	2007	MIL	NL	16.483	2	8.241	3	5	60	90.0	2.60
49	McDonald	Ben	1997	ML4	AL	16.461	2	8.231	20	17	0	354.3	3.96
50	Marcum	Shaun	2012	MIL	NL	16.257	2	8.129	20	11	0	324.7	3.60

Milwaukee Brewers – Top Fielders

Rank	FIRST BASE		FV	Lyear	G	FPCT	RF
1	Cooper	Cecil	1.2227	1986	1257	0.992	9.93
2	Scott	George	1.2160	1976	743	0.992	9.46
3	Sexson	Richie	1.1798	2003	531	0.994	9.15
4	Fielder	Prince	1.1299	2011	948	0.992	8.76
5	Hegan	Mike	1.1121	1977	263	0.994	8.08
6	Brock	Greg	1.0748	1991	495	0.994	8.50
7	Jaha	John	1.0650	1998	511	0.993	8.75
8	Overbay	Lyle	1.0572	2014	395	0.992	8.20

Rank	SECOND BASE		FV	Lyear	G	FPCT	RF
1	Vina	Fernando	1.3224	1999	508	0.984	5.10
2	Gantner	Jim	1.2993	1992	1449	0.985	5.17
3	Belliard	Ron	1.2708	2002	416	0.980	4.92
4	Garcia	Pedro	1.2682	1976	433	0.974	5.35
5	Molitor	Paul	1.2620	1990	400	0.979	5.50
6	Gennett	Scooter	1.0905	2016	413	0.980	4.18
7	Weeks	Rickie	1.0580	2014	1044	0.970	4.34

Rank	SHORTSTOP		FV	Lyear	G	FPCT	RF
1	Yount	Robin	1.5896	1984	1479	0.964	4.99
2	Segura	Jean	1.5539	2015	471	0.971	4.34
3	Arcia	Orlando	1.5349	2020	528	0.973	3.90
4	Hernandez	Jose	1.5141	2002	336	0.972	4.40
5	Valentin	Jose	1.4732	1999	716	0.957	4.40
6	Listach	Pat	1.4691	1996	302	0.968	4.38
7	Hardy	J.J.	1.4666	2009	557	0.979	3.94
8	Spiers	Bill	1.4533	1994	372	0.970	4.21
9	Riles	Ernest	1.4338	1988	287	0.961	4.00
10	Sveum	Dale	1.4053	1991	338	0.960	4.14

Rank	THIRD BASE		FV	Lyear	G	FPCT	RF
1	Cirillo	Jeff	1.5235	2006	848	0.962	2.52
2	Bando	Sal	1.4869	1981	450	0.962	2.86
3	Molitor	Paul	1.4829	1990	791	0.950	2.88
4	Money	Don	1.4729	1983	687	0.969	2.84
5	Shaw	Travis	1.4498	2019	321	0.970	2.25
6	Seitzer	Kevin	1.4412	1996	322	0.958	2.45
7	Harper	Tommy	1.4116	1971	257	0.943	3.02
8	Ramirez	Aramis	1.3655	2015	423	0.967	2.03

			FV	Lyear	G	FPCT	RF	
9	McGehee	Casey	1.3568	2011	371	0.942	2.20	
10	Gantner	Jim	1.2328	1992	360	0.956	2.18	

Rank	CATCHER		FV	Lyear	G	FPCT	RF	CS%
1	Kendall	Jason	1.9080	2009	282	0.993	7.31	0.324
2	Lucroy	Jonathan	1.8405	2016	725	0.992	7.92	0.275
3	Rodriguez	Ellie	1.8064	1973	303	0.987	5.11	0.500
4	Surhoff	B.J.	1.7974	1995	704	0.988	5.61	0.300
5	Simmons	Ted	1.7327	1985	297	0.985	4.96	0.329
6	Maldonado	Martin	1.6959	2016	304	0.987	7.51	0.353
7	Moore	Charlie	1.6835	1986	850	0.979	4.60	0.364
8	Porter	Darrell	1.6800	1976	482	0.977	4.91	0.379
9	Matheny	Mike	1.6465	1998	439	0.989	5.13	0.305
10	Schroeder	Bill	1.6295	1988	261	0.991	5.28	0.238

Rank	OUTFIELD		FV	Lyear	G	FPCT	RF	ApG
1	Podsednik	Scott	1.5780	2004	292	0.991	2.56	0.034
2	Coluccio	Bob	1.5731	1975	261	0.991	2.54	0.088
3	Yount	Robin	1.5595	1993	1218	0.990	2.67	0.044
4	Cameron	Mike	1.5400	2009	266	0.993	2.65	0.026
5	May	Dave	1.5384	1978	668	0.982	2.55	0.069
6	Grissom	Marquis	1.4964	2000	428	0.990	2.47	0.030
7	Hamilton	Darryl	1.4849	1995	620	0.994	2.26	0.050
8	Thomas	Gorman	1.4810	1983	1019	0.984	2.54	0.043
9	Cain	Lorenzo	1.4773	2020	326	0.987	2.27	0.058
10	Lezcano	Sixto	1.4599	1980	764	0.980	2.22	0.092
11	Aoki	Norichika	1.4526	2013	290	0.989	1.86	0.059
12	Gomez	Carlos	1.4410	2015	659	0.984	2.35	0.056
13	Deer	Rob	1.4365	1990	629	0.976	2.21	0.083
14	Clark	Brady	1.4325	2006	517	0.986	2.12	0.033
15	Oglivie	Ben	1.4313	1986	1000	0.979	2.27	0.070
16	Burnitz	Jeromy	1.4167	2001	777	0.978	1.97	0.075
17	Jenkins	Geoff	1.4015	2007	1188	0.984	1.96	0.077
18	Moore	Charlie	1.4009	1986	391	0.983	2.01	0.077
19	Yelich	Christian	1.3989	2020	367	0.988	1.53	0.033
20	Braun	Ryan	1.3901	2020	1531	0.989	1.78	0.051
21	Vaughn	Greg	1.3798	1996	672	0.983	2.13	0.046
22	Manning	Rick	1.3572	1987	457	0.984	2.07	0.020
23	Mieske	Matt	1.3507	1997	415	0.978	1.86	0.067
24	Briggs	Johnny	1.3501	1975	478	0.970	2.06	0.067
25	Hart	Corey	1.3413	2012	820	0.987	1.92	0.035
26	Braggs	Glenn	1.3165	1990	397	0.963	2.31	0.048
27	Felder	Mike	1.2995	1990	385	0.981	1.92	0.062
28	Lee	Carlos	1.2907	2006	260	0.979	1.78	0.046
29	Davis	Khris	1.2095	2015	276	0.981	1.72	0.014
30	Santana	Domingo	1.1620	2018	318	0.978	1.51	0.025

Rank	PITCHING		FV	Lyear	IP	FPCT	RF	
1	Caldwell	Mike	1.0663	1984	1605	0.977	2.13	
2	Sorensen	Lary	1.0539	1980	854	0.957	2.32	
3	Colborn	Jim	1.0392	1976	1118	0.969	1.99	
4	Lohse	Kyle	1.0355	2015	549	0.978	1.49	
5	Suppan	Jeff	1.0319	2010	577	0.977	1.98	
6	Pattin	Marty	1.0315	1971	657	0.971	1.85	
7	Gallardo	Yovani	1.0260	2014	1289	0.977	1.75	
8	Wegman	Bill	1.0139	1995	1483	0.954	2.27	
9	Parsons	Bill	1.0134	1973	518	0.990	1.68	
10	Davis	Doug	1.0127	2010	724	0.970	1.60	

Franchise When and Where
Milwaukee Brewers (1970 to Present)
Seattle Pilots (1969)

MINNESOTA TWINS
Best Seasons and Careers of All-Time

Plenty of old Washington Senators here, starting with standout pitcher Walter Johnson, and the best batting season by outfielder Ed Delahanty, but most of the players who most would place on the Twins All-Time team are actually Twins, particularly on the pitching side, after Johnson. One Twin we think should get more attention today is Rod Carew, one of the best bat control hitters in the history of baseball. Yes, we know that's not the most popular way to play the game now, but imagine attempting to employ the shift with Carew at the plate. With his ability to hit the ball almost wherever he wanted, they wouldn't even attempt it. Maybe he could have taught his teammates then, passing it down the baseball generations, and Minnesota would have avoided this brand of deploying fielders against them altogether.

Reserves

Bench - Goose Goslin (OF), Clyde Milan (OF), Bob Allison (OF/1B), Mickey Vernon (1B), Buddy Lewis (3B/OF), Joe Cronin (SS), Earl Battey (CATCHER).

Bullpen - Joe Nathan (CL), Firpo Marberry (SU), Frank Viola, Camilo Pasquel, Dutch Leonard, Jim Perry.

Minnesota Twins - Best Position Player Years

Rank	Name	First	Year	Team	Lg	HR	RBI	AVG	Age	PEVA-B
1	Delahanty	Ed	1902	WS1	AL	10	93	0.376	35	34.689
2	Killebrew	Harmon	1969	MIN	AL	49	140	0.276	33	33.634
3	Mauer	Joe	2009	MIN	AL	28	96	0.365	26	32.590
4	Carew	Rod	1977	MIN	AL	14	100	0.388	32	31.528
5	Spence	Stan	1944	WS1	AL	18	100	0.316	29	30.663
6	Puckett	Kirby	1988	MIN	AL	24	121	0.356	28	30.641
7	Killebrew	Harmon	1967	MIN	AL	44	113	0.269	31	29.312
8	Oliva	Tony	1964	MIN	AL	32	94	0.323	26	26.344
9	Puckett	Kirby	1986	MIN	AL	31	96	0.328	26	25.975
10	Travis	Cecil	1941	WS1	AL	7	101	0.359	28	25.776
11	Mauer	Joe	2006	MIN	AL	13	84	0.347	23	25.655
12	Killebrew	Harmon	1964	MIN	AL	49	111	0.270	28	25.257
13	Goslin	Goose	1926	WS1	AL	17	108	0.354	26	24.499
14	Vernon	Mickey	1953	WS1	AL	15	115	0.337	35	23.556
15	Killebrew	Harmon	1970	MIN	AL	41	113	0.271	34	23.140
16	Killebrew	Harmon	1966	MIN	AL	39	110	0.281	30	23.060
17	Allison	Bob	1963	MIN	AL	35	91	0.271	29	22.876
18	Allison	Bob	1964	MIN	AL	32	86	0.287	30	22.600
19	Mauer	Joe	2008	MIN	AL	9	85	0.328	25	22.034
20	Goslin	Goose	1924	WS1	AL	12	129	0.344	24	21.994

Minnesota Twins - Best Pitcher Years

Rank	Name	First	Year	Team	Lg	W	L	SV	IP	ERA	Age	PEVA-P
1	Johnson	Walter	1912	WS1	AL	33	12	2	369.0	1.39	25	52.347
2	Santana	Johan	2006	MIN	AL	19	6	0	233.7	2.77	27	46.748
3	Johnson	Walter	1910	WS1	AL	25	17	1	370.0	1.36	23	45.752
4	Johnson	Walter	1913	WS1	AL	36	7	2	346.0	1.14	26	43.737
5	Johnson	Walter	1918	WS1	AL	23	13	3	326.0	1.27	31	43.252
6	Santana	Johan	2004	MIN	AL	20	6	0	228.0	2.61	25	39.021
7	Johnson	Walter	1914	WS1	AL	28	18	1	371.7	1.72	27	36.936
8	Johnson	Walter	1915	WS1	AL	27	13	4	336.7	1.55	28	36.871
9	Marberry	Firpo	1929	WS1	AL	19	12	11	250.3	3.06	31	33.863
10	Johnson	Walter	1919	WS1	AL	20	14	2	290.3	1.49	32	32.304
11	Blyleven	Bert	1973	MIN	AL	20	17	0	325.0	2.52	22	32.194
12	Johnson	Walter	1916	WS1	AL	25	20	1	369.7	1.90	29	31.062
13	Viola	Frank	1987	MIN	AL	17	10	0	251.7	2.90	27	30.300
14	Perry	Jim	1970	MIN	AL	24	12	0	278.7	3.04	35	30.121
15	Santana	Johan	2005	MIN	AL	16	7	0	231.7	2.87	26	29.297
16	Johnson	Walter	1911	WS1	AL	25	13	1	322.3	1.90	24	27.861
17	Viola	Frank	1988	MIN	AL	24	7	0	255.3	2.64	28	26.964
18	Johnson	Walter	1924	WS1	AL	23	7	0	277.7	2.72	37	25.968
19	Viola	Frank	1984	MIN	AL	18	12	0	257.7	3.21	24	25.678
20	Wolff	Roger	1945	WS1	AL	20	10	2	250.0	2.12	34	25.554

Minnesota Twins (WS1, MIN) - Top Career Batters

RANK	NAME	FIRST	LYR	TEAM	LG	PEVA-B	YRS	PPYR	HR	RBI	H	AVE
1	Killebrew	Harmon	1974	MIN	AL	268.631	21	12.792	559	1540	2024	0.258
2	Puckett	Kirby	1995	MIN	AL	204.074	12	17.006	207	1085	2304	0.318

RANK	NAME	FIRST	LYR	TEAM	LG	PEVA-B	YRS	PPYR	HR	RBI	H	AVE
3	Mauer	Joe	2018	MIN	AL	188.930	15	12.595	143	923	2123	0.306
4	Rice	Sam	1933	WS1	AL	180.318	19	9.490	33	1045	2889	0.323
5	Carew	Rod	1978	MIN	AL	156.323	12	13.027	74	733	2085	0.334
6	Oliva	Tony	1976	MIN	AL	155.848	15	10.390	220	947	1917	0.304
7	Yost	Eddie	1958	WS1	AL	148.898	14	10.636	101	550	1521	0.253
8	Vernon	Mickey	1955	WS1	AL	141.926	14	10.138	121	1026	1993	0.288
9	Goslin	Goose	1938	WS1	AL	139.781	12	11.648	127	931	1659	0.323
10	Milan	Clyde	1922	WS1	AL	139.763	16	8.735	17	617	2100	0.285
11	Allison	Bob	1970	MIN	AL	135.670	13	10.436	256	796	1281	0.255
12	Hrbek	Kent	1994	MIN	AL	134.078	14	9.577	293	1086	1749	0.282
13	Judge	Joe	1932	WS1	AL	121.719	18	6.762	71	1001	2291	0.299
14	Myer	Buddy	1941	WS1	AL	107.428	16	6.714	35	759	1828	0.303
15	Lewis	Buddy	1949	WS1	AL	107.224	11	9.748	71	607	1563	0.297
16	Gaetti	Gary	1990	MIN	AL	102.866	10	10.287	201	758	1276	0.256
17	Spence	Stan	1947	WS1	AL	99.298	5	19.860	66	427	852	0.296
18	Travis	Cecil	1947	WS1	AL	97.425	12	8.119	27	657	1544	0.314
19	Cronin	Joe	1934	WS1	AL	94.086	7	13.441	51	673	1090	0.304
20	Morneau	Justin	2013	MIN	AL	93.956	11	8.541	221	860	1318	0.278
21	Bluege	Ossie	1939	WS1	AL	87.540	18	4.863	43	848	1751	0.272
22	Hunter	Torii	2015	MIN	AL	87.417	12	7.285	214	792	1343	0.268
23	Knoblauch	Chuck	1997	MIN	AL	87.235	7	12.462	43	391	1197	0.304
24	Sievers	Roy	1959	WS1	AL	81.073	6	13.512	180	574	823	0.267
25	Battey	Earl	1967	MIN	AL	79.725	8	9.966	91	410	894	0.277
26	Kuhel	Joe	1946	WS1	AL	76.472	11	6.952	56	667	1338	0.288
27	Dozier	Brian	2018	MIN	AL	76.142	7	10.877	167	491	927	0.248
28	Case	George	1947	WS1	AL	72.800	10	7.280	20	355	1306	0.288
29	Brunansky	Tom	1988	MIN	AL	70.600	7	10.086	163	469	829	0.250
30	Manush	Heinie	1935	WS1	AL	70.250	6	11.708	47	491	1078	0.328
31	Tovar	Cesar	1972	MIN	AL	70.105	8	8.763	38	319	1164	0.281
32	Foster	Eddie	1919	WS1	AL	69.225	8	8.653	6	355	1177	0.266
33	Smalley	Roy	1987	MIN	AL	69.056	10	6.906	110	485	1046	0.262
34	McBride	George	1920	WS1	AL	68.249	13	5.250	5	393	1068	0.221
35	Versalles	Zoilo	1967	MIN	AL	67.563	9	7.507	87	406	1061	0.250
36	Cuddyer	Michael	2011	MIN	AL	65.308	11	5.937	141	580	1106	0.272
37	Lemon	Jim	1963	MIN	AL	64.406	10	6.441	159	509	855	0.265
38	Harris	Bucky	1928	WS1	AL	63.959	10	6.396	9	506	1295	0.275
39	Shanks	Howie	1922	WS1	AL	63.546	11	5.777	21	520	1232	0.252
40	Ruel	Muddy	1930	WS1	AL	58.224	8	7.278	2	371	834	0.290
41	Hisle	Larry	1977	MIN	AL	55.187	5	11.037	87	409	697	0.286
42	Mack	Shane	1994	MIN	AL	53.186	5	10.637	67	315	668	0.309
43	West	Sam	1941	WS1	AL	52.902	10	5.290	30	485	984	0.297
44	Koskie	Corey	2004	MIN	AL	51.038	7	7.291	101	437	781	0.280
45	Wynegar	Butch	1982	MIN	AL	50.991	7	7.284	37	325	697	0.254

RANK	NAME	FIRST	LYR	TEAM	LG	PEVA-B	YRS	PPYR	HR	RBI	H	AVE
46	Runnels	Pete	1957	WS1	AL	50.062	7	7.152	18	355	921	0.274
47	Jones	Jacque	2005	MIN	AL	50.037	7	7.148	132	476	974	0.279
48	Rollins	Rich	1968	MIN	AL	49.237	8	6.155	71	369	830	0.272
49	Hall	Jimmie	1966	MIN	AL	47.792	4	11.948	98	288	507	0.269
50	Rosario	Eddie	2020	MIN	AL	47.330	6	7.888	119	388	738	0.277

Minnesota Twins (WS1, MIN) - Top Career Pitchers

RANK	NAME	FIRST	LYEAR	LTEAM	LG	PEVA	YRS	PPYR	W	L	SV	IP	ERA
1	Johnson	Walter	1927	WS1	AL	479.881	21	22.851	417	279	34	5914.7	2.17
2	Santana	Johan	2007	MIN	AL	153.720	8	19.215	93	44	1	1308.7	3.22
3	Blyleven	Bert	1988	MIN	AL	144.556	11	13.141	149	138	0	2566.7	3.28
4	Radke	Brad	2006	MIN	AL	130.309	12	10.859	148	139	0	2451.0	4.22
5	Kaat	Jim	1973	MIN	AL	128.252	15	8.550	190	159	6	3014.3	3.34
6	Viola	Frank	1989	MIN	AL	115.982	8	14.498	112	93	0	1772.7	3.86
7	Pascual	Camilo	1966	MIN	AL	110.796	13	8.523	145	141	10	2465.0	3.66
8	Marberry	Firpo	1936	WS1	AL	99.087	11	9.008	117	71	96	1654.0	3.59
9	Nathan	Joe	2011	MIN	AL	95.196	7	13.599	24	13	260	463.3	2.16
10	Leonard	Dutch	1946	WS1	AL	93.004	9	10.334	118	101	2	1899.3	3.27
11	Perry	Jim	1972	MIN	AL	80.186	10	8.019	128	90	5	1883.3	3.15
12	Tapani	Kevin	1995	MIN	AL	64.625	7	9.232	75	63	0	1171.3	4.06
13	Crowder	Alvin	1934	WS1	AL	59.546	7	8.507	98	69	12	1331.0	3.98
14	Aguilera	Rick	1999	MIN	AL	58.838	11	5.349	40	47	254	694.0	3.50
15	Goltz	Dave	1979	MIN	AL	54.265	8	6.783	96	79	3	1638.0	3.48
16	Ramos	Pedro	1961	MIN	AL	49.523	7	7.075	78	112	12	1544.3	4.19
17	Hadley	Bump	1935	WS1	AL	48.246	7	6.892	68	71	10	1299.0	3.98
18	Berrios	Jose	2020	MIN	AL	47.859	5	9.572	48	38	0	659.7	4.19
19	Erickson	Scott	1995	MIN	AL	47.705	6	7.951	61	60	0	979.3	4.22
20	Gibson	Kyle	2019	MIN	AL	46.476	7	6.639	67	68	0	1087.0	4.52
21	Zachary	Tom	1928	WS1	AL	44.702	9	4.967	96	103	8	1589.0	3.78
22	Perkins	Glen	2017	MIN	AL	42.492	12	3.541	35	25	120	624.3	3.88
23	Shaw	Jim	1921	WS1	AL	41.703	9	4.634	84	98	17	1600.3	3.07
24	Porterfield	Bob	1955	WS1	AL	41.695	5	8.339	67	64	0	1041.7	3.38
25	Braxton	Garland	1930	WS1	AL	41.326	4	10.332	38	32	28	583.0	3.40
26	Wynn	Early	1948	WS1	AL	41.166	8	5.146	72	87	2	1266.7	3.94
27	Chance	Dean	1969	MIN	AL	41.159	3	13.720	41	34	2	664.0	2.67
28	Milton	Eric	2003	MIN	AL	40.396	6	6.733	57	51	0	987.3	4.76
29	Hudson	Sid	1952	WS1	AL	40.111	10	4.011	88	130	6	1819.3	4.38
30	Hawkins	LaTroy	2003	MIN	AL	39.774	9	4.419	44	57	44	818.0	5.05
31	Baker	Scott	2011	MIN	AL	38.740	7	5.534	63	48	0	958.0	4.15
32	Mogridge	George	1925	WS1	AL	38.655	5	7.731	68	55	1	1016.7	3.35
33	Silva	Carlos	2007	MIN	AL	38.005	4	9.501	47	45	0	773.7	4.42
34	Guardado	Eddie	2008	MIN	AL	37.307	12	3.109	37	48	116	704.7	4.55
35	Mays	Joe	2005	MIN	AL	37.052	6	6.175	48	65	0	946.3	4.85

RANK	NAME	FIRST	LYEAR	LTEAM	LG	PEVA	YRS	PPYR	W	L	SV	IP	ERA
36	Masterson	Walt	1953	WS1	AL	35.992	11	3.272	62	88	13	1347.0	3.98
37	Groom	Bob	1913	WS1	AL	35.655	5	7.131	72	89	3	1353.3	3.04
38	Haefner	Mickey Francis	1949	WS1	AL	35.645	7	5.092	73	77	12	1291.7	3.29
39	Liriano	co	2012	MIN	AL	35.453	7	5.065	50	52	1	783.3	4.33
40	Newsom	Bobo	1952	WS1	AL	35.022	8	4.378	61	66	7	1079.7	4.28
41	Coveleski	Stan	1927	WS1	AL	34.486	3	11.495	36	17	1	500.7	2.98
42	Patten	Case	1908	WS1	AL	33.516	8	4.190	105	127	5	2059.3	3.34
43	Stobbs	Chuck	1961	MIN	AL	33.417	9	3.713	66	92	16	1238.3	4.27
44	Whitehill	Earl	1936	WS1	AL	33.396	4	8.349	64	43	1	996.7	4.21
45	Santana	Ervin	2018	MIN	AL	33.354	4	8.339	30	25	0	525.3	3.68
46	Smithson	Mike	1987	MIN	AL	32.057	4	8.014	47	48	0	816.0	4.46
47	Rogers	Taylor	2020	MIN	AL	31.850	5	6.370	15	14	41	274.3	3.12
48	Anderson	Allan	1991	MIN	AL	31.668	6	5.278	49	54	0	818.7	4.11
49	Wolff	Roger	1946	WS1	AL	30.999	3	10.333	29	33	4	527.0	3.07
50	Lohse	Kyle	2006	MIN	AL	30.461	6	5.077	51	57	0	908.3	4.88

Minnesota Twins – Top Fielders

Rank	FIRST BASE		FV	Lyear	G	FPCT	RF
1	Carew	Rod	1.2198	1978	466	0.990	10.06
2	Mientkiewicz	Doug	1.1781	2004	628	0.996	8.52
3	Hrbek	Kent	1.1768	1994	1609	0.994	9.18
4	Jackson	Ron	1.1761	1981	312	0.992	9.54
5	Vernon	Mickey	1.1539	1955	1775	0.990	9.49
6	Morneau	Justin	1.1448	2013	1124	0.996	9.14
7	Gandil	Chick	1.1274	1915	541	0.989	10.08
8	Mauer	Joe	1.1243	2018	603	0.996	8.70
9	Power	Vic	1.1168	1964	278	0.992	8.61
10	Kuhel	Joe	1.1104	1946	1176	0.992	9.88

Rank	SECOND BASE		FV	Lyear	G	FPCT	RF
1	Bloodworth	Jimmy	1.3690	1941	315	0.972	5.92
2	Dozier	Brian	1.3676	2018	865	0.988	4.63
3	Knoblauch	Chuck	1.3578	1997	1000	0.986	4.65
4	Priddy	Jerry	1.3006	1947	418	0.971	5.67
5	Harris	Bucky	1.2962	1928	1246	0.965	5.80
6	Myer	Buddy	1.2669	1941	1339	0.974	5.64
7	Teufel	Tim	1.2609	1985	312	0.983	4.78
8	Castillo	Luis	1.2517	2007	227	0.991	4.49
9	Randall	Bob	1.2258	1980	442	0.979	4.85
10	Wilfong	Rob	1.2163	1982	514	0.982	4.70

Rank	SHORTSTOP		FV	Lyear	G	FPCT	RF
1	Cardenas	Leo	1.6940	1971	473	0.975	4.99
2	McBride	George	1.6751	1920	1445	0.949	5.46
3	Cronin	Joe	1.6137	1934	935	0.951	5.38
4	Cassidy	Joe	1.6087	1905	250	0.935	5.91
5	Smalley	Roy	1.5804	1987	809	0.968	4.90
6	Peckinpaugh	Roger	1.5702	1926	626	0.954	5.00
7	Versalles	Zoilo	1.5291	1967	1106	0.956	4.56
8	Gagne	Greg	1.5243	1992	1112	0.971	4.12
9	Meares	Pat	1.5126	1998	737	0.965	4.36
10	Guzman	Cristian	1.4976	2004	833	0.972	4.23

Rank	THIRD BASE		FV	Lyear	G	FPCT	RF
1	Gaetti	Gary	1.6207	1990	1311	0.965	2.87
2	Castino	John	1.5841	1984	416	0.967	3.01
3	Coughlin	Bill	1.5819	1903	386	0.934	3.57
4	Yost	Eddie	1.5436	1958	1625	0.958	3.07

			FV	Lyear	G	FPCT	RF	
5	Bluege	Ossie	1.5154	1939	1487	0.957	3.09	
6	Koskie	Corey	1.5024	2004	762	0.966	2.51	
7	Soderholm	Eric	1.4528	1975	375	0.954	3.02	
8	Valencia	Danny	1.4460	2012	262	0.958	2.46	
9	Lewis	Buddy	1.4409	1941	671	0.927	3.12	
10	Shanks	Howie	1.4349	1922	354	0.946	3.43	

Rank	CATCHER		FV	Lyear	G	FPCT	RF	CS%
1	Ruel	Muddy	2.0262	1930	874	0.985	4.76	0.481
2	Street	Gabby	1.9710	1911	422	0.977	6.40	0.453
3	Battey	Earl	1.9584	1967	967	0.990	6.33	0.416
4	Wynegar	Butch	1.9284	1982	759	0.988	5.17	0.419
5	Henry	John	1.9146	1917	591	0.979	6.30	0.468
6	Spencer	Roy	1.8810	1932	377	0.983	4.39	0.500
7	Ferrell	Rick	1.8588	1947	634	0.983	4.66	0.444
8	Mauer	Joe	1.8570	2018	921	0.995	6.68	0.332
9	Mitterwald	George	1.8558	1973	496	0.989	6.07	0.405
10	Borgmann	Glenn	1.8444	1979	439	0.988	5.33	0.369

Rank	OUTFIELD		FV	Lyear	G	FPCT	RF	ApG
1	Busby	Jim	1.6316	1955	480	0.990	3.25	0.054
2	Puckett	Kirby	1.6107	1995	1696	0.989	2.67	0.084
3	Spence	Stan	1.6022	1947	739	0.982	2.87	0.101
4	Becker	Rich	1.5924	1997	417	0.988	2.67	0.091
5	Ward	Gary	1.5757	1983	399	0.982	2.43	0.113
6	West	Sam	1.5556	1941	852	0.983	2.76	0.103
7	Brunansky	Tom	1.5425	1988	884	0.984	2.26	0.080
8	Hunter	Torii	1.5384	2015	1326	0.990	2.55	0.059
9	Buxton	Byron	1.5286	2019	386	0.990	2.72	0.041
10	Bostock	Lyman	1.5250	1977	365	0.988	2.41	0.063
11	Kepler	Max	1.5233	2020	627	0.991	1.95	0.046
12	Uhlaender	Ted	1.5120	1969	501	0.991	2.20	0.044
13	Tovar	Cesar	1.5109	1972	735	0.983	2.24	0.076
14	Schulte	Fred	1.5081	1935	332	0.982	2.70	0.051
15	Cordova	Marty	1.5069	1999	529	0.985	2.31	0.072
16	Jones	Charlie	1.4995	1907	381	0.967	2.35	0.131
17	Hall	Jimmie	1.4980	1966	524	0.981	2.15	0.074
18	Span	Denard	1.4955	2012	646	0.989	2.40	0.037
19	Mack	Shane	1.4787	1994	607	0.985	2.34	0.054
20	Milan	Clyde	1.4744	1922	1903	0.953	2.31	0.154
21	Gladden	Dan	1.4673	1991	627	0.983	2.17	0.072
22	Green	Lenny	1.4665	1964	593	0.987	2.04	0.034
23	Rice	Sam	1.4655	1933	2192	0.965	2.24	0.126
24	Ganley	Bob	1.4621	1909	321	0.953	1.90	0.112
25	Oliva	Tony	1.4573	1972	1178	0.975	2.04	0.060
26	Hisle	Larry	1.4524	1977	626	0.978	2.28	0.070
27	Jones	Jacque	1.4524	2005	917	0.986	2.22	0.059
28	Manush	Heinie	1.4345	1935	767	0.983	2.13	0.051
29	Goslin	Goose	1.4322	1938	1310	0.961	2.36	0.110
30	Brye	Steve	1.4222	1976	493	0.989	2.09	0.071

Rank	PITCHING		FV	Lyear	IP	FPCT	RF	
1	Radke	Brad	1.0776	2006	2451	0.987	1.94	
2	Kralick	Jack	1.0762	1963	674	0.988	2.20	
3	Coveleski	Stan	1.0744	1927	501	0.962	2.71	
4	Pavano	Carl	1.0721	2012	580	0.984	1.96	
5	Grant	Mudcat	1.0652	1967	781	0.968	2.09	
6	Tapani	Kevin	1.0584	1995	1171	0.980	1.91	
7	Orth	Al	1.0530	1903	677	0.928	3.40	
8	Lee	Watty	1.0513	1903	527	0.962	3.42	
9	Ramos	Pedro	1.0506	1961	1544	0.988	1.84	
10	Porterfield	Bob	1.0504	1955	1042	0.977	2.09	

Franchise When and Where
Minnesota Twins (1961 to Present)
Washington Senators (1901-1960)

NEW YORK YANKEES
Best Seasons and Careers of All-Time

Whether this is the team you root for or one you root against, I think most people would admit that the batting order that a New York Yankees All-Time Team could bring to the box is by far the best that any franchise could muster. Ruth, DiMaggio, and Mantle in the outfield, relegating Dave Winfield to the bench and perhaps not even allowing Reggie Jackson, Mr. October, to make the team, or Roger Maris, Mr. 61 to make the team, or Rickey Henderson, Mr. Stolen Base, to make the team. I'm sure some would choose them instead of others, but that's just the start of the difficult selection process. Don Mattingly backing up Lou Gehrig. Bill Dickey backing up Yogi Berra. Boy, there's such a great bench, you could pick out the designated hitter by fan ballot. No, the pitching staff may not equal the Dodgers, but it's still good, and it only pales in comparison to the lineup of the men from the Bronx. And with a reliever, Mariano Rivera, being their best pitcher, they'd sure have the ability to close a game.

Reserves

Bench - Bernie Williams (OF), Dave Winfield (OF), Charlie Keller (OF), Don Mattingly (1B), Robinson Cano (2B), Jorge Posada (C), Bill Dickey (CATCHER).

Bullpen - Mariano Rivera (CL), Hoyt Waite (SU), Mike Mussina, CC Sabathia, Mel Stottlemyre, Spud Chandler.

New York Yankees - Best Position Player Years

Rank	Name	First	Year	Team	Lg	HR	RBI	AVG	Age	PEVA-B
1	Ruth	Babe	1923	NYA	AL	41	131	0.393	28	58.931
2	Ruth	Babe	1920	NYA	AL	54	137	0.376	25	55.754
3	Ruth	Babe	1921	NYA	AL	59	171	0.378	26	54.876
4	Ruth	Babe	1927	NYA	AL	60	164	0.356	32	51.850
5	Ruth	Babe	1926	NYA	AL	47	146	0.372	31	51.603
6	Ruth	Babe	1924	NYA	AL	46	121	0.378	29	51.324
7	Gehrig	Lou	1927	NYA	AL	47	175	0.373	24	50.953
8	Gehrig	Lou	1934	NYA	AL	49	165	0.363	31	50.136
9	Mantle	Mickey	1956	NYA	AL	52	130	0.353	25	47.236
10	Gehrig	Lou	1936	NYA	AL	49	152	0.354	33	45.995
11	Mantle	Mickey	1961	NYA	AL	54	128	0.317	30	42.398
12	Mantle	Mickey	1960	NYA	AL	40	94	0.275	29	42.394
13	Ruth	Babe	1931	NYA	AL	46	163	0.373	36	41.968
14	Rodriguez	Alex	2007	NYA	AL	54	156	0.314	32	40.717
15	Mantle	Mickey	1957	NYA	AL	34	94	0.365	26	40.637
16	Gehrig	Lou	1931	NYA	AL	46	184	0.341	28	40.131
17	Ruth	Babe	1928	NYA	AL	54	142	0.323	33	40.061
18	Gehrig	Lou	1930	NYA	AL	41	174	0.379	27	39.839
19	Ruth	Babe	1930	NYA	AL	49	153	0.359	35	39.019
20	DiMaggio	Joe	1941	NYA	AL	30	125	0.357	27	37.809

New York Yankees - Best Pitcher Years

Rank	Name	First	Year	Team	Lg	W	L	SV	IP	ERA	Age	PEVA-P
1	Chandler	Spud	1943	NYA	AL	20	4	0	253.0	1.64	36	42.384
2	Chesbro	Jack	1904	NYA	AL	41	12	0	454.7	1.82	30	41.233
3	Guidry	Ron	1978	NYA	AL	25	3	0	273.7	1.74	28	39.576
4	Gomez	Lefty	1937	NYA	AL	21	11	0	278.3	2.33	29	35.814
5	Hunter	Catfish	1975	NYA	AL	23	14	0	328.0	2.58	29	34.002
6	Mussina	Mike	2001	NYA	AL	17	11	0	228.7	3.15	33	31.025
7	Mays	Carl	1921	NYA	AL	27	9	7	336.7	3.05	30	28.720
8	Peterson	Fritz	1969	NYA	AL	17	16	0	272.0	2.55	27	27.915
9	Ford	Whitey	1958	NYA	AL	14	7	1	219.3	2.01	30	26.457
10	Gomez	Lefty	1934	NYA	AL	26	5	1	281.7	2.33	26	26.325
11	Ford	Russ	1910	NYA	AL	26	6	1	299.7	1.65	27	25.360
12	Mussina	Mike	2008	NYA	AL	20	9	0	200.3	3.37	40	25.277
13	Terry	Ralph	1962	NYA	AL	23	12	2	298.7	3.19	26	25.227
14	Key	Jimmy	1993	NYA	AL	18	6	0	236.7	3.00	32	25.024
15	Sabathia	C.C.	2010	NYA	AL	21	7	0	237.7	3.18	30	24.796
16	Pettitte	Andy	1997	NYA	AL	18	7	0	240.3	2.88	25	24.405
17	Severino	Luis	2017	NYA	AL	14	6	0	193.3	2.98	23	24.367
18	Bonham	Tiny	1942	NYA	AL	21	5	0	226.0	2.27	29	24.208
19	Sabathia	C.C.	2009	NYA	AL	19	8	0	230.0	3.37	29	23.949
20	Ford	Whitey	1961	NYA	AL	25	4	0	283.0	3.21	33	23.895

New York Yankees (NYA, BLA) - Top Career Batters

RANK	NAME	FIRST	LYR	TEAM	LG	PEVA-B	YRS	PPYR	HR	RBI	H	AVE
1	Ruth	Babe	1934	NYA	AL	566.741	15	37.783	659	1975	2518	0.349
2	Gehrig	Lou	1939	NYA	AL	479.522	17	28.207	493	1995	2721	0.340
3	Mantle	Mickey	1968	NYA	AL	455.611	18	25.312	536	1509	2415	0.298

RANK	NAME	FIRST	LYR	TEAM	LG	PEVA-B	YRS	PPYR	HR	RBI	H	AVE
4	DiMaggio	Joe	1951	NYA	AL	297.630	13	22.895	361	1537	2214	0.325
5	Jeter	Derek	2014	NYA	AL	259.537	20	12.977	260	1311	3465	0.310
6	Berra	Yogi	1963	NYA	AL	251.424	18	13.968	358	1430	2148	0.285
7	Dickey	Bill	1946	NYA	AL	202.680	17	11.922	202	1209	1969	0.313
8	Williams	Bernie	2006	NYA	AL	201.884	16	12.618	287	1257	2336	0.297
9	Mattingly	Don	1995	NYA	AL	193.054	14	13.790	222	1099	2153	0.307
10	Rodriguez	Alex	2016	NYA	AL	186.731	12	15.561	351	1096	1580	0.283
11	White	Roy	1979	NYA	AL	164.619	15	10.975	160	758	1803	0.271
12	Posada	Jorge	2011	NYA	AL	159.103	17	9.359	275	1065	1664	0.273
13	Winfield	Dave	1990	NYA	AL	157.533	9	17.504	205	818	1300	0.290
14	Keller	Charlie	1952	NYA	AL	143.887	11	13.081	184	723	1053	0.286
15	Munson	Thurman	1979	NYA	AL	134.322	11	12.211	113	701	1558	0.292
16	Combs	Earle	1935	NYA	AL	131.405	12	10.950	58	632	1866	0.325
17	Murcer	Bobby	1983	NYA	AL	130.882	13	10.068	175	687	1231	0.278
18	Cano	Robinson	2013	NYA	AL	129.190	9	14.354	204	822	1649	0.309
19	Nettles	Graig	1983	NYA	AL	127.229	11	11.566	250	834	1396	0.253
20	Lazzeri	Tony	1937	NYA	AL	124.158	12	10.346	169	1154	1784	0.293
21	O'Neill	Paul	2001	NYA	AL	121.196	9	13.466	185	858	1426	0.303
22	Henrich	Tommy	1950	NYA	AL	113.881	11	10.353	183	795	1297	0.282
23	Rizzuto	Phil	1956	NYA	AL	111.989	13	8.615	38	563	1588	0.273
24	Howard	Elston	1967	NYA	AL	111.621	13	8.586	161	733	1405	0.279
25	Randolph	Willie	1988	NYA	AL	110.299	13	8.485	48	549	1731	0.275
26	Pipp	Wally	1925	NYA	AL	102.933	11	9.358	80	827	1577	0.282
27	Maris	Roger	1966	NYA	AL	101.427	7	14.490	203	548	797	0.265
28	Rolfe	Red	1942	NYA	AL	98.122	10	9.812	69	497	1394	0.289
29	Meusel	Bob	1929	NYA	AL	96.448	10	9.645	146	1006	1565	0.311
30	Bauer	Hank	1959	NYA	AL	95.306	12	7.942	158	654	1326	0.277
31	Gardner	Brett	2020	NYA	AL	93.792	13	7.215	129	539	1384	0.259
32	Crosetti	Frankie	1948	NYA	AL	93.230	17	5.484	98	649	1541	0.245
33	Tresh	Tom	1969	NYA	AL	91.420	9	10.158	140	493	967	0.247
34	Giambi	Jason	2008	NYA	AL	90.653	7	12.950	209	604	764	0.260
35	Gordon	Joe	1946	NYA	AL	88.660	7	12.666	153	617	1000	0.271
36	McDougald	Gil	1960	NYA	AL	86.538	10	8.654	112	576	1291	0.276
37	Peckinpaugh	Roger	1921	NYA	AL	86.139	9	9.571	36	428	1170	0.257
38	Chapman	Ben	1936	NYA	AL	84.807	7	12.115	60	589	1079	0.305
39	Teixeira	Mark	2016	NYA	AL	75.868	8	9.484	206	622	873	0.248
40	Henderson	Rickey	1989	NYA	AL	75.723	5	15.145	78	255	663	0.288
41	Jackson	Reggie	1981	NYA	AL	74.364	5	14.873	144	461	661	0.281
42	Skowron	Bill	1962	NYA	AL	71.989	9	7.999	165	672	1103	0.294
43	Matsui	Hideki	2009	NYA	AL	71.059	7	10.151	140	597	977	0.292
44	Williams	Jimmy	1907	NYA	AL	70.643	7	10.092	31	537	978	0.277
45	Martinez	Tino	2005	NYA	AL	69.580	7	9.940	192	739	1039	0.276
46	Selkirk	George	1942	NYA	AL	69.096	9	7.677	108	576	810	0.290

RANK	NAME	FIRST	LYR	TEAM	LG	PEVA-B	YRS	PPYR	HR	RBI	H	AVE
47	Stirnweiss	Snuffy	1950	NYA	AL	65.122	8	8.140	27	253	899	0.274
48	Baker	Frank	1922	NYA	AL	60.418	6	10.070	48	375	735	0.288
49	Richardson	Bobby	1966	NYA	AL	60.389	12	5.032	34	390	1432	0.266
50	Clarke	Horace	1974	NYA	AL	58.469	10	5.847	27	300	1213	0.257

New York Yankees - Top Career Pitchers

RANK	NAME	FIRST	LYEAR	LTEAM	LG	PEVA	YRS	PPYR	W	L	SV	IP	ERA
1	Rivera	Mariano	2013	NYA	AL	245.654	19	12.929	82	60	652	1283.7	2.21
2	Ford	Whitey	1967	NYA	AL	200.553	16	12.535	236	106	10	3170.3	2.75
3	Pettitte	Andy	2013	NYA	AL	163.109	15	10.874	219	127	0	2796.3	3.94
4	Guidry	Ron	1988	NYA	AL	144.658	14	10.333	170	91	4	2392.0	3.29
5	Ruffing	Red	1946	NYA	AL	137.320	15	9.155	231	124	8	3168.7	3.47
6	Gomez	Lefty	1942	NYA	AL	135.369	13	10.413	189	101	9	2498.3	3.34
7	Sabathia	CC	2019	NYA	AL	127.926	11	11.630	134	88	0	1918.0	3.81
8	Mussina	Mike	2008	NYA	AL	124.700	8	15.587	123	72	0	1553.0	3.88
9	Stottlemyre	Mel	1974	NYA	AL	105.938	11	9.631	164	139	1	2661.3	2.97
10	Hoyt	Waite	1930	NYA	AL	102.845	10	10.284	157	98	28	2272.3	3.48
11	Chandler	Spud	1947	NYA	AL	99.944	11	9.086	109	43	6	1485.0	2.84
12	Pennock	Herb	1933	NYA	AL	96.556	11	8.778	162	90	20	2203.3	3.54
13	Shawkey	Bob	1927	NYA	AL	88.534	13	6.810	168	131	26	2488.7	3.12
14	Chesbro	Jack	1909	NYA	AL	84.045	7	12.006	128	93	2	1952.0	2.58
15	Peterson	Fritz	1974	NYA	AL	83.654	9	9.295	109	106	1	1857.3	3.10
16	Reynolds	Allie	1954	NYA	AL	82.812	8	10.352	131	60	41	1700.0	3.30
17	Raschi	Vic	1953	NYA	AL	76.467	8	9.558	120	50	3	1537.0	3.47
18	Righetti	Dave	1990	NYA	AL	72.977	11	6.634	74	61	224	1136.7	3.11
19	Lopat	Ed	1955	NYA	AL	72.869	8	9.109	113	59	2	1497.3	3.19
20	Tanaka	Masahiro	2020	NYA	AL	69.401	7	9.914	78	46	0	1054.3	3.74
21	John	Tommy	1989	NYA	AL	67.807	8	8.476	91	60	0	1367.0	3.59
22	Gossage	Rich	1989	NYA	AL	65.037	7	9.291	42	28	151	533.0	2.14
23	Bonham	Tiny	1946	NYA	AL	62.625	7	8.946	79	50	6	1176.7	2.73
24	Lyle	Sparky	1978	NYA	AL	60.206	7	8.601	57	40	141	745.7	2.41
25	Clemens	Roger	2007	NYA	AL	58.308	6	9.718	83	42	0	1103.0	4.01
26	Ford	Russ	1913	NYA	AL	58.124	5	11.625	73	56	3	1112.7	2.54
27	Mays	Carl	1923	NYA	AL	56.963	5	11.393	79	39	11	1090.0	3.25
28	Terry	Ralph	1964	NYA	AL	55.122	8	6.890	78	59	8	1198.0	3.44
29	Cone	David	2000	NYA	AL	53.308	6	8.885	64	40	0	922.0	3.91
30	Wells	David	2003	NYA	AL	51.842	4	12.961	68	28	0	851.7	3.90
31	Hunter	Catfish	1979	NYA	AL	51.639	5	10.328	63	53	0	993.0	3.58
32	Turley	Bob	1962	NYA	AL	50.610	8	6.326	82	52	12	1269.0	3.62
33	Key	Jimmy	1996	NYA	AL	50.586	4	12.647	48	23	0	604.3	3.68
34	Pipgras	George	1933	NYA	AL	48.244	9	5.360	93	64	11	1351.7	4.04
35	Murphy	Johnny	1946	NYA	AL	46.664	12	3.889	93	53	104	990.3	3.54

RANK	NAME	FIRST	LYEAR	LTEAM	LG	PEVA	YRS	PPYR	W	L	SV	IP	ERA
36	Severino	Luis	2019	NYA	AL	44.963	5	8.993	42	26	0	530.0	3.46
37	Wang	Chien-Ming	2009	NYA	AL	44.370	5	8.874	55	26	1	670.7	4.16
38	Kuroda	Hiroki	2014	NYA	AL	41.166	3	13.722	38	33	0	620.0	3.44
39	Robertson	David	2018	NYA	AL	40.839	9	4.538	38	22	53	498.0	2.75
40	Page	Joe	1950	NYA	AL	40.779	7	5.826	57	49	76	780.3	3.44
41	Chapman	Aroldis	2020	NYA	AL	39.275	5	7.855	14	6	114	201.7	2.54
42	Downing	Al	1969	NYA	AL	36.764	9	4.085	72	57	2	1235.3	3.23
43	Betances	Dellin	2019	NYA	AL	36.609	8	4.576	21	22	36	381.7	2.36
44	Hernandez	Orlando	2004	NYA	AL	36.570	6	6.095	61	40	1	876.3	3.96
45	Bouton	Jim	1968	NYA	AL	36.058	7	5.151	55	51	4	1013.7	3.36
46	Bush	Joe	1924	NYA	AL	36.054	3	12.018	62	38	4	783.0	3.44
47	Borowy	Hank	1945	NYA	AL	34.470	4	8.618	56	30	3	780.7	2.74
48	Figueroa	Ed	1980	NYA	AL	34.443	5	6.889	62	39	1	911.7	3.53
49	Orth	Al	1909	NYA	AL	34.255	6	5.709	72	73	0	1172.7	2.72
50	May	Rudy	1983	NYA	AL	33.984	7	4.855	54	46	7	841.7	3.12

New York Yankees – Top Fielders

Rank	FIRST BASE		FV	Lyear	G	FPCT	RF
1	Mattingly	Don	1.2701	1995	1634	0.996	9.33
2	Pipp	Wally	1.2479	1925	1468	0.992	10.98
3	Pepitone	Joe	1.2394	1969	698	0.993	9.40
4	Martinez	Tino	1.2382	2005	1026	0.994	8.51
5	Chambliss	Chris	1.2371	1979	854	0.993	9.56
6	Mantle	Mickey	1.1700	1968	262	0.991	9.35
7	Teixeira	Mark	1.1685	2016	916	0.997	8.60
8	Skowron	Bill	1.1628	1962	986	0.992	8.82
9	Gehrig	Lou	1.1330	1939	2137	0.991	9.64
10	Dahlgren	Babe	1.0699	1940	305	0.991	9.71

Rank	SECOND BASE		FV	Lyear	G	FPCT	RF
1	Clarke	Horace	1.4176	1974	1081	0.983	5.34
2	Pratt	Del	1.4173	1920	420	0.970	5.72
3	Sax	Steve	1.3796	1991	461	0.988	4.85
4	Stirnweiss	Snuffy	1.3477	1950	700	0.980	5.38
5	Randolph	Willie	1.3326	1988	1688	0.980	5.32
6	Cano	Robinson	1.3188	2013	1350	0.986	4.78
7	Williams	Jimmy	1.3117	1907	919	0.954	5.41
8	Gordon	Joe	1.3095	1946	970	0.967	5.67
9	Ward	Aaron	1.3039	1926	669	0.972	5.50
10	Richardson	Bobby	1.2723	1966	1339	0.979	4.91

Rank	SHORTSTOP		FV	Lyear	G	FPCT	RF
1	Scott	Everett	1.6625	1925	477	0.965	4.95
2	Espinoza	Alvaro	1.6195	1991	444	0.972	4.70
3	Dent	Bucky	1.6164	1982	694	0.976	4.64
4	Rizzuto	Phil	1.5868	1956	1647	0.968	4.79
5	McDougald	Gil	1.5707	1959	284	0.973	4.86
6	Peckinpaugh	Roger	1.5702	1921	1214	0.947	5.34
7	Kubek	Tony	1.5474	1965	882	0.967	4.85
8	Michael	Gene	1.5372	1974	709	0.965	4.91
9	Gregorius	Didi	1.4870	2019	655	0.980	3.69
10	Tresh	Tom	1.4864	1969	274	0.963	4.85
11	Jeter	Derek	1.4814	2014	2674	0.976	3.90

Rank	THIRD BASE		FV	Lyear	G	FPCT	RF
1	Boyer	Clete	1.6393	1966	909	0.965	3.43
2	Nettles	Graig	1.6160	1983	1509	0.962	3.06
3	Boggs	Wade	1.5514	1997	543	0.973	2.48

			FV	Lyear	G	FPCT	RF	
4	Baker	Frank	1.5414	1922	652	0.956	3.40	
5	Sewell	Joe	1.5383	1933	375	0.963	2.79	
6	Rolfe	Red	1.5376	1942	1084	0.956	3.09	
7	Kenney	Jerry	1.5105	1972	328	0.962	3.01	
8	Brosius	Scott	1.4959	2001	536	0.953	2.57	
9	Carey	Andy	1.4891	1960	656	0.957	3.02	
10	Dugan	Joe	1.4725	1928	774	0.961	2.88	

Rank	CATCHER		FV	Lyear	G	FPCT	RF	CS%
1	Dickey	Bill	1.9752	1946	1708	0.988	5.22	0.466
2	Berra	Yogi	1.9696	1963	1697	0.989	5.61	0.487
3	McCann	Brian	1.9531	2016	326	0.995	8.52	0.327
4	Howard	Elston	1.9256	1967	1029	0.992	6.08	0.465
5	Cerone	Rick	1.9142	1990	567	0.992	5.68	0.387
6	Wynegar	Butch	1.8830	1986	434	0.991	6.14	0.359
7	Munson	Thurman	1.8822	1979	1278	0.982	5.47	0.441
8	Girardi	Joe	1.8613	1999	374	0.993	7.48	0.285
9	Stanley	Mike	1.8234	1995	356	0.992	5.90	0.317
10	Posada	Jorge	1.8035	2011	1574	0.992	6.81	0.278

Rank	OUTFIELD		FV	Lyear	G	FPCT	RF	ApG
1	Granderson	Curtis	1.5760	2013	498	0.996	2.30	0.040
2	Murcer	Bobby	1.5506	1980	1012	0.983	2.27	0.080
3	DiMaggio	Joe	1.5447	1951	1721	0.978	2.71	0.089
4	Rivers	Mickey	1.5368	1979	479	0.982	2.81	0.061
5	Barfield	Jesse	1.5096	1992	391	0.978	2.25	0.115
6	Witt	Whitey	1.5093	1925	437	0.977	2.48	0.080
7	Cabrera	Melky	1.5026	2009	609	0.990	2.07	0.062
8	Williams	Bernie	1.5005	2006	1926	0.990	2.48	0.034
9	White	Roy	1.4921	1979	1625	0.988	2.12	0.053
10	Kelly	Roberto	1.4903	2000	625	0.985	2.55	0.050
11	Mumphrey	Jerry	1.4848	1983	285	0.979	2.80	0.060
12	Chapman	Ben	1.4762	1936	757	0.964	2.41	0.120
13	Ellsbury	Jacoby	1.4713	2017	496	0.994	2.20	0.028
14	Winfield	Dave	1.4651	1990	1123	0.985	2.05	0.051
15	Gardner	Brett	1.4648	2020	1557	0.992	1.89	0.049
16	Abreu	Bobby	1.4647	2008	365	0.989	1.97	0.060
17	Mantle	Mickey	1.4620	1966	2019	0.982	2.26	0.058
18	Henderson	Rickey	1.4580	1989	557	0.980	2.77	0.043
19	Suzuki	Ichiro	1.4547	2014	364	0.993	1.52	0.030
20	O'Neill	Paul	1.4538	2001	1221	0.988	1.95	0.048
21	Tresh	Tom	1.4391	1968	716	0.979	1.97	0.068
22	Woodling	Gene	1.4340	1954	658	0.991	2.10	0.074
23	Maris	Roger	1.4233	1966	806	0.985	1.85	0.043
24	Combs	Earle	1.4168	1935	1387	0.974	2.54	0.050
25	High	Hugh	1.4042	1918	331	0.972	2.13	0.124
26	Bodie	Ping	1.4008	1921	378	0.964	2.15	0.116
27	Noren	Irv	1.3981	1956	408	0.984	2.01	0.081
28	Henrich	Tommy	1.3891	1949	1017	0.981	2.07	0.094
29	Lindell	Johnny	1.3857	1949	654	0.980	2.51	0.072
30	Judge	Aaron	1.3802	2020	376	0.988	1.91	0.064

Rank	PITCHING		FV	Lyear	IP	FPCT	RF	
1	Bush	Joe	1.1226	1924	783	0.984	2.87	
2	Mays	Carl	1.1033	1923	1090	0.973	3.52	
3	Stottlemyre	Mel	1.1015	1974	2661	0.969	2.75	
4	Wang	Chien-Ming	1.0858	2009	671	0.989	2.33	
5	Borowy	Hank	1.0745	1945	781	0.986	2.35	
6	Kuroda	Hiroki	1.0742	2014	620	0.991	1.64	
7	Chandler	Spud	1.0710	1947	1485	0.980	2.98	
8	Chesbro	Jack	1.0565	1909	1952	0.951	3.32	
9	Shocker	Urban	1.0557	1928	932	0.982	2.57	
10	Peterson	Fritz	1.0511	1974	1857	0.962	2.23	

Franchise When and Where
New York Yankees (1913 to Present)
New York Highlanders (1903-1912)
Baltimore Orioles (1901-1902, BLA)

NEW YORK METS
Best Seasons and Careers of All-Time

For the New York Mets, it's all about the pitching. For most of the seasons of the franchise after the opening years of futility, the Mets won games, and World Series, because of their pitching. Whether that be Jacob deGrom today, or Tom Seaver, Dwight Gooden, and others in the past. Yes, there were the great seasons of Darryl Strawberry or Pete Alonso in 2019, but compared to the pitching side of the equation, they were few and far between. Just look at the best seasons on both sides; seven pitchers over 30.000 PEVA in one season, none for the hitters. There's some nice players, Keith Hernandez and David Wright and Hall of Famer Mike Piazza, just to name three, but it's still pitching, pitching, pitching, that would lead this All-Time team, taking nothing away from the great position players.

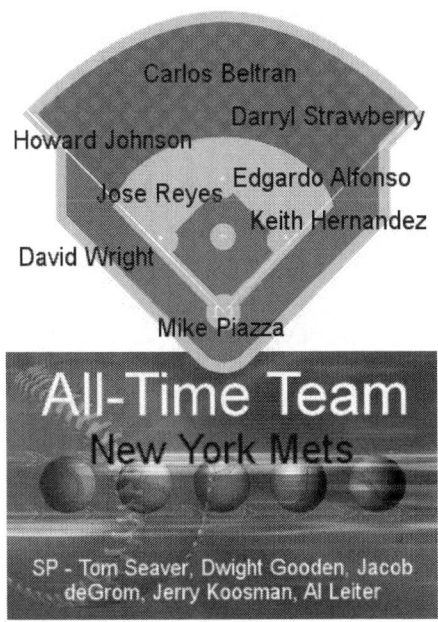

Reserves

Bench - Cleon Jones (OF), Kevin McReynolds (OF), Lee Mazzilli (OF), Rusty Staub (1B/OF), Bud Harrelson (SS), Robin Ventura (3B), Todd Hundley (CATCHER).

Bullpen - John Franco (CL), Jesse Orosco (SU), Sid Fernandez, David Cone, Jon Matlack, Noah Syndergaard.

New York Mets - Best Position Player Years

Rank	Name	First	Year	Team	Lg	HR	RBI	AVG	Age	PEVA-B
1	Beltran	Carlos	2006	NYN	NL	41	116	0.275	29	29.035
2	Wright	David	2007	NYN	NL	30	107	0.325	25	28.574
3	Wright	David	2012	NYN	NL	21	93	0.306	30	27.139
4	Strawberry	Darryl	1987	NYN	NL	39	104	0.284	25	26.929
5	Alonso	Pete	2019	NYN	NL	53	120	0.260	25	25.470
6	Johnson	Howard	1989	NYN	NL	36	101	0.287	29	25.048
7	Piazza	Mike	2000	NYN	NL	38	113	0.324	32	25.007
8	Wright	David	2008	NYN	NL	33	124	0.302	26	24.501
9	Strawberry	Darryl	1988	NYN	NL	39	101	0.269	26	23.327
10	Carter	Gary	1985	NYN	NL	32	100	0.281	31	23.097
11	Gilkey	Bernard	1996	NYN	NL	30	117	0.317	30	22.529
12	Hernandez	Keith	1984	NYN	NL	15	94	0.311	31	22.367
13	Beltran	Carlos	2008	NYN	NL	27	112	0.284	31	21.453
14	Staub	Rusty	1975	NYN	NL	19	105	0.282	31	21.008
15	Johnson	Howard	1991	NYN	NL	38	117	0.259	31	20.769
16	Wright	David	2006	NYN	NL	26	116	0.311	24	20.464
17	Strawberry	Darryl	1990	NYN	NL	37	108	0.277	28	20.252
18	Wright	David	2010	NYN	NL	29	103	0.283	28	20.236
19	Ventura	Robin	1999	NYN	NL	32	120	0.301	32	19.984
20	Wright	David	2005	NYN	NL	27	102	0.306	23	19.979

New York Mets - Best Pitcher Years

Rank	Name	First	Year	Team	Lg	W	L	SV	IP	ERA	Age	PEVA-P
1	Gooden	Dwight	1985	NYN	NL	24	4	0	276.7	1.53	21	45.645
2	Gooden	Dwight	1984	NYN	NL	17	9	0	218.0	2.60	20	37.956
3	Dickey	R.A.	2012	NYN	NL	20	6	0	233.7	2.73	38	35.214
4	deGrom	Jacob	2018	NYN	NL	10	9	0	217.0	1.70	30	32.813
5	Seaver	Tom	1969	NYN	NL	25	7	0	273.3	2.21	25	31.954
6	Seaver	Tom	1971	NYN	NL	20	10	0	286.3	1.76	27	31.022
7	Seaver	Tom	1973	NYN	NL	19	10	0	290.0	2.08	29	30.181
8	Seaver	Tom	1975	NYN	NL	22	9	0	280.3	2.38	31	29.900
9	Seaver	Tom	1970	NYN	NL	18	12	0	290.7	2.82	26	29.421
10	Santana	Johan	2008	NYN	NL	16	7	0	234.3	2.53	29	28.994
11	Saberhagen	Bret	1994	NYN	NL	14	4	0	177.3	2.74	30	28.916
12	deGrom	Jacob	2019	NYN	NL	11	8	0	204.0	2.43	31	28.752
13	Viola	Frank	1990	NYN	NL	20	12	0	249.7	2.67	30	25.299
14	Martinez	Pedro	2005	NYN	NL	15	8	0	217.0	2.82	34	24.921
15	Syndergaard	Noah	2016	NYN	NL	14	9	0	183.7	2.60	24	22.931
16	Koosman	Jerry	1969	NYN	NL	17	9	0	241.0	2.28	27	21.934
17	Leiter	Al	1998	NYN	NL	17	6	0	193.0	2.47	33	20.800
18	Harvey	Matt	2013	NYN	NL	9	5	0	178.3	2.27	24	20.754
19	Cone	David	1988	NYN	NL	20	3	0	231.3	2.22	25	20.404
20	Matlack	Jon	1974	NYN	NL	13	15	0	265.3	2.41	24	19.734

New York Mets - Top Career Batters

RANK	NAME	FIRST	LYR	TEAM	LG	PEVA-B	YRS	PPYR	HR	RBI	H	AVE
1	Wright	David	2018	NYN	NL	183.995	14	13.142	242	970	1777	0.296
2	Strawberry	Darryl	1990	NYN	NL	131.391	8	16.424	252	733	1025	0.263

RANK	NAME	FIRST	LYR	TEAM	LG	PEVA-B	YRS	PPYR	HR	RBI	H	AVE
3	Piazza	Mike	2005	NYN	NL	**105.622**	8	13.203	220	655	1028	0.296
4	Beltran	Carlos	2011	NYN	NL	**96.735**	7	13.819	149	559	878	0.280
5	Johnson	Howard	1993	NYN	NL	**94.784**	9	10.532	192	629	997	0.251
6	Reyes	Jose	2018	NYN	NL	**84.558**	12	7.047	108	521	1534	0.282
7	Hernandez	Keith	1989	NYN	NL	**81.195**	7	11.599	80	468	939	0.297
8	Alfonzo	Edgardo	2002	NYN	NL	**80.065**	8	10.008	120	538	1136	0.292
9	Jones	Cleon	1975	NYN	NL	**75.788**	12	6.316	93	521	1188	0.281
10	Conforto	Michael	2020	NYN	NL	**67.666**	6	11.278	118	341	556	0.259
11	McReynolds	Kevin	1994	NYN	NL	**66.957**	6	11.159	122	456	791	0.272
12	Mazzilli	Lee	1989	NYN	NL	**61.912**	10	6.191	68	353	796	0.264
13	Staub	Rusty	1985	NYN	NL	**58.491**	9	6.499	75	399	709	0.276
14	Wilson	Mookie	1989	NYN	NL	**58.240**	10	5.824	60	342	1112	0.276
15	Hundley	Todd	1998	NYN	NL	**54.779**	9	6.087	124	397	612	0.240
16	Carter	Gary	1989	NYN	NL	**54.024**	5	10.805	89	349	542	0.249
17	Olerud	John	1999	NYN	NL	**53.907**	3	17.969	63	291	524	0.315
18	Kranepool	Ed	1979	NYN	NL	**52.975**	18	2.943	118	614	1418	0.261
19	Grote	Jerry	1977	NYN	NL	**52.327**	12	4.361	35	357	994	0.256
20	Harrelson	Bud	1977	NYN	NL	**50.685**	13	3.899	6	242	1029	0.234
21	Stearns	John	1984	NYN	NL	**47.579**	10	4.758	46	312	695	0.259
22	Granderson	Curtis	2017	NYN	NL	**43.492**	4	10.873	95	247	484	0.239
23	Agee	Tommie	1972	NYN	NL	**43.201**	5	8.640	82	265	632	0.262
24	Duda	Lucas	2017	NYN	NL	**42.938**	8	5.367	125	378	614	0.246
25	Kingman	Dave	1983	NYN	NL	**40.985**	6	6.831	154	389	509	0.219
26	Bonilla	Bobby	1999	NYN	NL	**40.412**	5	8.082	95	295	481	0.270
27	Garrett	Wayne	1976	NYN	NL	**38.813**	8	4.852	55	295	667	0.237
28	Murphy	Daniel	2014	NYN	NL	**38.304**	6	6.384	48	329	827	0.290
29	Delgado	Carlos	2009	NYN	NL	**38.157**	4	9.539	104	339	468	0.267
30	Foster	George	1986	NYN	NL	**38.032**	5	7.606	99	361	602	0.252
31	Ventura	Robin	2001	NYN	NL	**36.035**	3	12.012	77	265	394	0.260
32	Milner	John	1977	NYN	NL	**35.625**	7	5.089	94	338	586	0.245
33	Gilkey	Bernard	1998	NYN	NL	**34.845**	3	11.615	52	223	370	0.273
34	Alonso	Pete	2020	NYN	NL	**34.143**	2	17.071	69	155	203	0.252
35	Magadan	Dave	1992	NYN	NL	**33.292**	7	4.756	21	254	610	0.292
36	Nimmo	Brandon	2020	NYN	NL	**32.025**	5	6.405	39	121	276	0.258
37	Henderson	Steve	1980	NYN	NL	**31.879**	4	7.970	35	227	516	0.287
38	Brooks	Hubie	1991	NYN	NL	**31.634**	6	5.272	44	269	640	0.267
39	Swoboda	Ron	1970	NYN	NL	**30.402**	6	5.067	69	304	536	0.242
40	Millan	Felix	1977	NYN	NL	**29.809**	5	5.962	8	182	743	0.278
41	Ordonez	Rey	2002	NYN	NL	**28.109**	7	4.016	8	260	720	0.245
42	Dykstra	Lenny	1989	NYN	NL	**27.940**	5	5.588	30	153	469	0.278
43	Youngblood	Joel	1982	NYN	NL	**27.534**	6	4.589	38	216	519	0.274
44	Floyd	Cliff	2006	NYN	NL	**27.497**	4	6.874	81	273	440	0.268
45	Kent	Jeff	1996	NYN	NL	**25.478**	5	5.096	67	267	510	0.279

RANK	NAME	FIRST	LYR	TEAM	LG	PEVA-B	YRS	PPYR	HR	RBI	H	AVE
46	Cespedes	Yoenis	2020	NYN	NL	25.325	5	5.065	76	205	327	0.279
47	Backman	Wally	1988	NYN	NL	23.985	9	2.665	7	165	670	0.283
48	Jefferies	Gregg	1991	NYN	NL	23.957	5	4.791	42	205	472	0.276
49	Christopher	Joe	1965	NYN	NL	23.935	4	5.984	28	156	371	0.265
50	McNeil	Jeff	2020	NYN	NL	23.692	3	7.897	30	117	293	0.319

New York Mets - Top Career Pitchers

RANK	NAME	FIRST	LYEAR	LTEAM	LG	PEVA	YRS	PPYR	W	L	SV	IP	ERA
1	Seaver	Tom	1983	NYN	NL	235.428	12	19.619	198	124	1	3045.3	2.57
2	Gooden	Dwight	1994	NYN	NL	176.442	11	16.040	157	85	1	2169.7	3.10
3	deGrom	Jacob	2020	NYN	NL	128.750	7	18.393	70	51	0	1169.7	2.61
4	Koosman	Jerry	1978	NYN	NL	102.649	12	8.554	140	137	5	2544.7	3.09
5	Leiter	Al	2004	NYN	NL	85.459	7	12.208	95	67	0	1360.0	3.42
6	Fernandez	Sid	1993	NYN	NL	84.206	10	8.421	98	78	1	1584.7	3.14
7	Cone	David	2003	NYN	NL	74.974	7	10.711	81	51	1	1209.3	3.13
8	Darling	Ron	1991	NYN	NL	67.663	9	7.518	99	70	0	1620.0	3.50
9	Matlack	Jon	1977	NYN	NL	62.324	7	8.903	82	81	0	1448.0	3.03
10	Franco	John	2004	NYN	NL	59.854	14	4.275	48	56	276	702.7	3.10
11	Dickey	R.A.	2012	NYN	NL	55.579	3	18.526	39	28	0	616.7	2.95
12	Glavine	Tom	2007	NYN	NL	55.345	5	11.069	61	56	0	1005.3	3.97
13	Syndergaard	Noah	2019	NYN	NL	54.924	5	10.985	47	30	0	716.0	3.31
14	Jones	Bobby	2000	NYN	NL	54.087	8	6.761	74	56	0	1215.7	4.13
15	Santana	Johan	2012	NYN	NL	53.475	4	13.369	46	34	0	717.0	3.18
16	Reed	Rick	2001	NYN	NL	53.269	5	10.654	59	36	0	888.7	3.66
17	Trachsel	Steve	2006	NYN	NL	44.517	6	7.420	66	59	0	956.3	4.09
18	Ojeda	Bob	1990	NYN	NL	43.710	5	8.742	51	40	0	764.0	3.12
19	Saberhagen	Bret	1995	NYN	NL	42.807	4	10.702	29	21	0	524.3	3.16
20	Harvey	Matt	2018	NYN	NL	42.164	6	7.027	34	37	0	639.3	3.66
21	Orosco	Jesse	1987	NYN	NL	41.499	8	5.187	47	47	107	595.7	2.73
22	Niese	Jon	2016	NYN	NL	40.456	9	4.495	61	62	0	1079.3	3.99
23	Benitez	Armando	2003	NYN	NL	39.664	5	7.933	18	14	160	347.0	2.70
24	Viola	Frank	1991	NYN	NL	38.753	3	12.918	38	32	0	566.3	3.31
25	Pelfrey	Mike	2012	NYN	NL	37.719	7	5.388	50	54	1	896.3	4.36
26	Familia	Jeurys	2020	NYN	NL	36.448	9	4.050	19	19	123	408.0	3.18
27	Swan	Craig	1984	NYN	NL	35.859	12	2.988	59	71	2	1230.7	3.72
28	Wheeler	Zack	2019	NYN	NL	35.796	5	7.159	44	38	0	749.3	3.77
29	McGraw	Tug	1974	NYN	NL	35.605	9	3.956	47	55	86	792.7	3.17
30	Martinez	Pedro	2008	NYN	NL	33.456	4	8.364	32	23	0	486.7	3.88
31	Wagner	Billy	2009	NYN	NL	32.567	4	8.142	5	5	101	189.7	2.37
32	Colon	Bartolo	2016	NYN	NL	30.585	3	10.195	44	34	0	588.7	3.90
33	Lockwood	Skip	1979	NYN	NL	26.393	5	5.279	24	36	65	379.7	2.80
34	McDowell	Roger	1989	NYN	NL	24.942	5	4.988	33	29	84	468.3	3.13
35	Matz	Steven	2020	NYN	NL	24.448	6	4.075	31	41	0	579.7	4.35

RANK	NAME	FIRST	LYEAR	LTEAM	LG	PEVA	YRS	PPYR	W	L	SV	IP	ERA
36	Lugo	Seth	2020	NYN	NL	22.532	5	4.506	25	19	12	383.3	3.45
37	Maine	John	2010	NYN	NL	22.261	5	4.452	39	32	0	542.0	4.17
38	Perez	Oliver	2010	NYN	NL	21.861	5	4.372	29	29	0	520.0	4.71
39	Feliciano	Pedro	2013	NYN	NL	21.711	9	2.412	22	21	4	383.7	3.33
40	Gee	Dillon	2015	NYN	NL	21.547	6	3.591	40	37	0	679.3	4.03
41	Myers	Randy	1989	NYN	NL	21.178	5	4.236	17	13	56	240.0	2.74
42	Heilman	Aaron	2008	NYN	NL	20.323	6	3.387	22	33	9	450.3	4.24
43	Parnell	Bobby	2015	NYN	NL	19.769	8	2.471	20	28	37	331.3	3.78
44	Gentry	Gary	1972	NYN	NL	19.217	4	4.804	41	42	1	789.3	3.56
45	Fisher	Jack	1967	NYN	NL	19.178	4	4.794	38	73	1	931.7	4.12
46	Jackson	Al	1969	NYN	NL	18.756	6	3.126	43	80	6	980.7	4.26
47	Clark	Mark	1997	NYN	NL	18.737	2	9.368	22	18	0	354.3	3.76
48	Reed	Addison	2017	NYN	NL	18.037	3	6.012	6	5	21	142.0	2.09
49	Sisk	Doug	1987	NYN	NL	17.955	6	2.993	17	16	33	412.3	3.10
50	Mlicki	Dave	1998	NYN	NL	17.431	4	4.358	24	30	1	501.3	4.15

New York Mets – Top Fielders

Rank	FIRST BASE		FV	Lyear	G	FPCT	RF
1	Olerud	John	1.3591	1999	463	0.995	9.15
2	Hernandez	Keith	1.2748	1989	854	0.995	9.11
3	Montanez	Willie	1.1569	1979	266	0.992	9.15
4	Murray	Eddie	1.1300	1993	308	0.989	9.12
5	Kranepool	Ed	1.1005	1979	1304	0.994	8.64
6	Duda	Lucas	1.0918	2017	472	0.995	8.16
7	Magadan	Dave	1.0865	1992	417	0.994	7.87
8	Milner	John	1.0807	1977	366	0.993	8.51
9	Delgado	Carlos	1.0627	2009	458	0.994	8.78
10	Zeile	Todd	1.0534	2004	367	0.992	8.18

Rank	SECOND BASE		FV	Lyear	G	FPCT	RF
1	Flynn	Doug	1.3297	1981	533	0.987	4.84
2	Baerga	Carlos	1.2809	1998	276	0.982	4.53
3	Millan	Felix	1.2578	1977	674	0.979	4.92
4	Alfonzo	Edgardo	1.2567	2001	524	0.987	4.37
5	Alomar	Roberto	1.2310	2003	219	0.982	4.25
6	Hunt	Ron	1.2225	1966	420	0.972	5.33
7	Kent	Jeff	1.2005	1995	390	0.976	4.77
8	Backman	Wally	1.1093	1988	680	0.979	4.17
9	Boswell	Ken	1.1035	1974	506	0.978	4.38
10	Castillo	Luis	1.0785	2010	342	0.986	4.23

Rank	SHORTSTOP		FV	Lyear	G	FPCT	RF
1	McMillan	Roy	1.5810	1966	335	0.970	4.81
2	Santana	Rafael	1.5538	1987	478	0.970	4.34
3	Ordonez	Rey	1.5530	2002	907	0.976	4.26
4	Harrelson	Bud	1.5304	1977	1281	0.970	4.65
5	Elster	Kevin	1.4844	1992	524	0.971	3.98
6	Taveras	Frank	1.4816	1981	372	0.956	4.34
7	Reyes	Jose	1.4239	2018	1117	0.974	3.99
8	Tejada	Ruben	1.4023	2019	433	0.976	3.99
9	Rosario	Amed	1.3576	2020	387	0.969	3.34
10	Johnson	Howard	1.1979	1991	263	0.952	3.19

Rank	THIRD BASE		FV	Lyear	G	FPCT	RF
1	Ventura	Robin	1.6067	2001	436	0.965	2.64
2	Alfonzo	Edgardo	1.5271	2002	515	0.969	2.54
3	Wright	David	1.4598	2018	1572	0.955	2.57
4	Brooks	Hubie	1.3971	1984	516	0.936	2.57
5	Garrett	Wayne	1.3652	1976	709	0.953	2.62

| 6 | Johnson | Howard | 1.2907 | 1993 | 835 | 0.931 | 2.12 | |

Rank	CATCHER		FV	Lyear	G	FPCT	RF	CS%
1	Carter	Gary	1.9817	1989	566	0.990	7.15	0.269
2	Grote	Jerry	1.9226	1977	1176	0.992	6.67	0.388
3	Stearns	John	1.8450	1984	698	0.985	5.96	0.369
4	Dyer	Duffy	1.8090	1974	326	0.991	6.42	0.398
5	Piazza	Mike	1.8001	2005	826	0.990	7.00	0.218
6	Hundley	Todd	1.7650	1998	745	0.990	5.90	0.254
7	d'Arnaud	Travis	1.7392	2019	378	0.994	8.49	0.215
8	Sasser	Mackey	1.6249	1992	261	0.983	5.42	0.262
9	Hodges	Ron	1.6166	1984	445	0.978	5.18	0.297

Rank	OUTFIELD		FV	Lyear	G	FPCT	RF	ApG
1	Beltran	Carlos	1.5728	2011	814	0.992	2.57	0.053
2	Gilkey	Bernard	1.5559	1998	369	0.986	1.97	0.119
3	Mazzilli	Lee	1.5050	1989	684	0.987	2.42	0.061
4	McReynolds	Kevin	1.5010	1994	774	0.985	1.96	0.078
5	Staub	Rusty	1.4902	1985	550	0.980	1.89	0.107
6	Thompson	Ryan	1.4879	1995	277	0.987	2.84	0.054
7	Dykstra	Lenny	1.4722	1989	494	0.991	2.23	0.045
8	Youngblood	Joel	1.4528	1982	444	0.982	2.11	0.131
9	Granderson	Curtis	1.4414	2017	551	0.992	1.92	0.051
10	Wilson	Mookie	1.4402	1989	1037	0.980	2.49	0.043
11	Lagares	Juan	1.4305	2020	676	0.986	2.01	0.052
12	Agee	Tommie	1.4303	1972	639	0.974	2.33	0.047
13	McRae	Brian	1.4295	1999	282	0.985	1.87	0.035
14	Payton	Jay	1.4284	2002	348	0.985	2.12	0.057
15	Henderson	Steve	1.4124	1980	482	0.978	2.16	0.073
16	Foster	George	1.4067	1986	617	0.977	1.97	0.066
17	Conforto	Michael	1.4035	2020	622	0.989	1.78	0.055
18	Strawberry	Darryl	1.3968	1990	1085	0.979	1.95	0.053
19	Pagan	Angel	1.3941	2011	386	0.981	2.36	0.052
20	Thomas	Frank	1.3876	1964	253	0.976	1.80	0.095
21	Perez	Timo	1.3803	2003	354	0.986	1.77	0.062
22	Johnson	Lance	1.3759	1997	223	0.972	2.49	0.058
23	Nimmo	Brandon	1.3679	2020	377	0.990	1.65	0.024
24	Jones	Cleon	1.3676	1975	1103	0.978	1.87	0.058
25	Shamsky	Art	1.3571	1971	256	0.993	1.65	0.063
26	Cedeno	Roger	1.3514	2003	421	0.981	1.73	0.038
27	Floyd	Cliff	1.3385	2006	443	0.986	1.77	0.070
28	Swoboda	Ron	1.3367	1970	639	0.971	1.67	0.072
29	Christopher	Joe	1.3295	1965	396	0.979	1.62	0.048
30	Bonilla	Bobby	1.3285	1999	262	0.982	1.90	0.080

Rank	PITCHING		FV	Lyear	IP	FPCT	RF
1	Dickey	R.A.	1.0838	2012	617	0.968	2.66
2	Fisher	Jack	1.0768	1967	932	0.970	2.48
3	Seaver	Tom	1.0698	1983	3045	0.961	1.98
4	deGrom	Jacob	1.0595	2020	1169	0.980	1.85
5	Glavine	Tom	1.0568	2007	1005	0.969	2.22
6	Jackson	Al	1.0407	1969	981	0.960	2.62
7	Saberhagen	Bret	1.0360	1995	524	0.975	2.68
8	Ojeda	Bob	1.0334	1990	764	0.970	2.32
9	Reed	Rick	1.0253	2001	889	0.971	2.02
10	Pelfrey	Mike	1.0234	2012	896	0.969	1.90

Franchise When and Where
New York Mets (1962 to Present)

OAKLAND ATHLETICS
Best Seasons and Careers of All-Time

They started out in Philadelphia, headed to Kansas City, and ended up in Oakland, and the Athletics team reflects best players from all those eras, but predominantly from the early days in Philadelphia and the decades on the West Coast. Whether that be in players like Frank Baker and Jimmie Foxx and Lefty Grove (early days) or the championship teams of Reggie Jackson, Bert Campaneris, Rickey Henderson, Catfish Hunter, and Vida (I don't want to be called True) Blue (Oakland years). And you have a spectacular choice of Designated Hitters, albeit some of the substance variety. The strength of the team might even be in the bullpen where Rollie Fingers and Dennis Eckersley head a great group. We've chosen Eckersley to close, but actually think we'd probably use both in that role.

Rickey Henderson
Bob Johnson   Reggie Jackson
Bert Campaneris
Eddie Collins
Frank Baker
Jimmie Foxx

Mickey Cochrane

All-Time Team
Oakland Athletics

SP - Lefty Grove, Eddie Plank, Vida
Blue, Catfish Hunter, Eddie Rommel

Reserves

Bench - Al Simmons (OF), Jose Canseco (OF), Jason Giambi (1B/OF), Mark McGwire (1B), Sal Bando (3B), Eddie Joost (IF), Terry Steinbach (CATCHER).

Bullpen - Dennis Eckersley (CL), Rollie Fingers (SU), Barry Zito, Chief Bender, Rube Waddell, Tim Hudson.

Oakland Athletics - Best Position Player Years

Rank	Name	First	Year	Team	Lg	HR	RBI	AVG	Age	PEVA-B
1	Foxx	Jimmie	1933	PHA	AL	48	163	0.356	26	42.539
2	Foxx	Jimmie	1932	PHA	AL	58	169	0.364	25	41.252
3	Lajoie	Nap	1901	PHA	AL	14	125	0.426	27	38.604
4	Baker	Frank	1912	PHA	AL	10	130	0.347	26	36.589
5	Canseco	Jose	1988	OAK	AL	42	124	0.307	24	36.135
6	Giambi	Jason	2000	OAK	AL	43	137	0.333	29	34.676
7	Foxx	Jimmie	1934	PHA	AL	44	130	0.334	27	33.948
8	Jackson	Reggie	1969	OAK	AL	47	118	0.275	23	33.898
9	Collins	Eddie	1914	PHA	AL	2	85	0.344	27	32.932
10	Baker	Frank	1913	PHA	AL	12	117	0.337	27	31.860
11	Henderson	Rickey	1990	OAK	AL	28	61	0.325	32	30.896
12	Foxx	Jimmie	1935	PHA	AL	36	115	0.346	28	29.569
13	Giambi	Jason	2001	OAK	AL	38	120	0.342	30	29.030
14	Collins	Eddie	1909	PHA	AL	3	56	0.347	22	28.689
15	Bando	Sal	1969	OAK	AL	31	113	0.281	25	27.934
16	Johnson	Bob	1939	PHA	AL	23	114	0.338	34	27.839
17	Collins	Eddie	1913	PHA	AL	3	73	0.345	26	27.774
18	McGwire	Mark	1996	OAK	AL	52	113	0.312	33	27.171
19	McGwire	Mark	1987	OAK	AL	49	118	0.289	24	26.438
20	Canseco	Jose	1991	OAK	AL	44	122	0.266	27	26.059

Oakland Athletics - Best Pitcher Years

Rank	Name	First	Year	Team	Lg	W	L	SV	IP	ERA	Age	PEVA-P
1	Grove	Lefty	1930	PHA	AL	28	5	9	291.0	2.54	30	52.344
2	Grove	Lefty	1931	PHA	AL	31	4	5	288.7	2.06	31	46.335
3	Grove	Lefty	1929	PHA	AL	20	6	4	275.3	2.81	29	38.544
4	Hunter	Catfish	1974	OAK	AL	25	12	0	318.3	2.49	28	35.949
5	Blue	Vida	1971	OAK	AL	24	8	0	312.0	1.82	22	34.160
6	Coombs	Jack	1910	PHA	AL	31	9	1	353.0	1.30	28	32.981
7	Blue	Vida	1976	OAK	AL	18	13	0	298.3	2.35	27	29.573
8	Grove	Lefty	1928	PHA	AL	24	8	4	261.7	2.58	28	28.141
9	Zito	Barry	2002	OAK	AL	23	5	0	229.3	2.75	24	27.825
10	Rommel	Eddie	1922	PHA	AL	27	13	2	294.0	3.28	25	27.744
11	Shantz	Bobby	1952	PHA	AL	24	7	0	279.7	2.48	27	26.992
12	Grove	Lefty	1932	PHA	AL	25	10	7	291.7	2.84	32	26.783
13	Norris	Mike	1980	OAK	AL	22	9	0	284.3	2.53	25	26.018
14	Stewart	Dave	1990	OAK	AL	22	11	0	267.0	2.56	33	24.907
15	Mulder	Mark	2001	OAK	AL	21	8	0	229.3	3.45	24	24.581
16	McCatty	Steve	1981	OAK	AL	14	7	0	185.7	2.33	27	24.432
17	Hudson	Tim	2003	OAK	AL	16	7	0	240.0	2.70	28	24.250
18	Earnshaw	George	1929	PHA	AL	24	8	1	254.7	3.29	29	23.280
19	Waddell	Rube	1905	PHA	AL	27	10	0	328.7	1.48	29	23.151
20	Perry	Scott	1918	PHA	AL	20	19	2	332.3	1.98	27	22.807

Oakland Athletics (PHA, KC1, OAK) - Top Career Batters

RANK	NAME	FIRST	LYR	TEAM	LG	PEVA-B	YRS	PPYR	HR	RBI	H	AVE
1	Foxx	Jimmie	1935	PHA	AL	215.477	11	19.589	302	1075	1492	0.339
2	Henderson	Rickey	1998	OAK	AL	214.434	14	15.317	167	648	1768	0.288

RANK	NAME	FIRST	LYR	TEAM	LG	PEVA-B	YRS	PPYR	HR	RBI	H	AVE
3	Johnson	Bob	1942	PHA	AL	181.433	10	18.143	252	1040	1617	0.298
4	McGwire	Mark	1997	OAK	AL	169.899	12	14.158	363	941	1157	0.260
5	Jackson	Reggie	1987	OAK	AL	164.741	10	16.474	269	776	1228	0.262
6	Simmons	Al	1944	PHA	AL	163.521	12	13.627	209	1178	1827	0.356
7	Collins	Eddie	1930	PHA	AL	161.283	13	12.406	16	496	1308	0.337
8	Bando	Sal	1976	OAK	AL	158.997	11	14.454	192	796	1311	0.255
9	Baker	Frank	1914	PHA	AL	144.082	7	20.583	48	612	1103	0.321
10	Cochrane	Mickey	1933	PHA	AL	138.530	9	15.392	108	680	1317	0.321
11	Canseco	Jose	1997	OAK	AL	130.460	9	14.496	254	793	1048	0.264
12	Giambi	Jason	2009	OAK	AL	117.960	8	14.745	198	715	1100	0.300
13	Davis	Harry	1917	PHA	AL	113.195	16	7.075	69	761	1500	0.279
14	Campaneris	Bert	1976	OAK	AL	111.655	13	8.589	70	529	1882	0.262
15	Murphy	Dwayne	1987	OAK	AL	108.184	10	10.818	153	563	999	0.247
16	Chapman	Sam	1951	PHA	AL	99.023	11	9.002	174	737	1273	0.268
17	Murphy	Danny	1913	PHA	AL	98.297	12	8.191	40	664	1489	0.290
18	Chavez	Eric	2010	OAK	AL	97.252	13	7.481	230	787	1276	0.267
19	Joost	Eddie	1954	PHA	AL	92.011	8	11.501	116	435	840	0.249
20	Hartsel	Topsy	1911	PHA	AL	89.716	10	8.972	21	266	1087	0.266
21	Lansford	Carney	1992	OAK	AL	88.626	10	8.863	94	548	1317	0.288
22	Seybold	Socks	1908	PHA	AL	86.437	8	10.805	51	548	1066	0.296
23	Valo	Elmer	1956	KC1	AL	82.062	15	5.471	47	491	1229	0.285
24	Strunk	Amos	1924	PHA	AL	80.227	13	6.171	11	352	977	0.283
25	Moses	Wally	1951	PHA	AL	78.441	10	7.844	64	409	1316	0.307
26	Dykes	Jimmie	1932	PHA	AL	77.676	15	5.178	86	764	1705	0.283
27	Steinbach	Terry	1996	OAK	AL	76.283	11	6.935	132	595	1144	0.275
28	Tejada	Miguel	2003	OAK	AL	76.167	7	10.881	156	604	968	0.270
29	McInnis	Stuffy	1917	PHA	AL	74.176	9	8.242	13	532	1192	0.313
30	Rudi	Joe	1982	OAK	AL	73.113	11	6.647	116	540	1087	0.272
31	Hayes	Frankie	1945	PHA	AL	72.548	11	6.595	101	503	906	0.270
32	Miller	Bing	1934	PHA	AL	72.365	12	6.030	94	762	1480	0.311
33	Tenace	Gene	1976	OAK	AL	71.230	8	8.904	121	389	603	0.245
34	Semien	Marcus	2020	OAK	AL	66.662	6	11.110	107	345	758	0.256
35	Fain	Ferris	1952	PHA	AL	66.107	6	11.018	35	436	887	0.297
36	Zernial	Gus	1957	KC1	AL	65.332	7	9.333	191	592	806	0.259
37	Bishop	Max	1933	PHA	AL	62.896	10	6.290	39	343	1122	0.272
38	Cross	Lave	1905	PHA	AL	61.594	5	12.319	5	419	825	0.302
39	Henderson	Dave	1993	OAK	AL	61.030	6	10.172	104	377	672	0.263
40	Walker	Tilly	1923	PHA	AL	60.947	6	10.158	100	410	771	0.287
41	Oldring	Rube	1918	PHA	AL	60.630	12	5.052	25	453	1222	0.271
42	Siebern	Norm	1963	KC1	AL	57.592	4	14.398	78	367	647	0.289
43	Davis	Khris	2020	OAK	AL	53.816	5	10.763	158	418	542	0.240
44	Higgins	Pinky	1936	PHA	AL	50.329	5	10.066	64	363	677	0.307
45	Barry	Jack	1915	PHA	AL	48.617	8	6.077	8	351	768	0.250

RANK	NAME	FIRST	LYR	TEAM	LG	PEVA-B	YRS	PPYR	HR	RBI	H	AVE
46	Lajoie	Nap	1916	PHA	AL	48.401	4	12.100	17	222	475	0.324
47	Perkins	Cy	1930	PHA	AL	48.399	15	3.227	30	402	921	0.259
48	Armas	Tony	1982	OAK	AL	48.360	6	8.060	111	374	622	0.250
49	Charles	Ed	1967	KC1	AL	47.783	6	7.964	65	319	703	0.268
50	Siebert	Dick	1945	PHA	AL	47.315	8	5.914	32	480	1094	0.283

Oakland Athletics (PHA, KC1, OAK) - Top Career Pitchers

RANK	NAME	FIRST	LYEAR	LTEAM	LG	PEVA	YRS	PPYR	W	L	SV	IP	ERA
1	Grove	Lefty	1933	PHA	AL	251.486	9	27.943	195	79	51	2401.0	2.88
2	Plank	Eddie	1914	PHA	AL	148.985	14	10.642	284	162	16	3860.7	2.39
3	Blue	Vida	1977	OAK	AL	120.100	9	13.344	124	86	2	1945.7	2.95
4	Hunter	Catfish	1974	OAK	AL	119.807	10	11.981	161	113	1	2456.3	3.13
5	Rommel	Eddie	1932	PHA	AL	107.495	13	8.269	171	119	29	2556.3	3.54
6	Zito	Barry	2006	OAK	AL	106.442	7	15.206	102	63	0	1430.3	3.55
7	Bender	Chief	1914	PHA	AL	99.665	12	8.305	193	102	28	2602.0	2.32
8	Stewart	Dave	1995	OAK	AL	97.757	8	12.220	119	78	0	1717.3	3.73
9	Waddell	Rube	1907	PHA	AL	95.353	6	15.892	131	82	0	1869.3	1.97
10	Hudson	Tim	2004	OAK	AL	93.684	6	15.614	92	39	0	1240.7	3.30
11	Eckersley	Dennis	1995	OAK	AL	92.686	9	10.298	41	31	320	637.0	2.74
12	Walberg	Rube	1933	PHA	AL	78.745	11	7.159	134	114	27	2186.7	4.11
13	Mulder	Mark	2004	OAK	AL	67.653	5	13.531	81	42	0	1003.0	3.92
14	Earnshaw	George	1933	PHA	AL	66.290	6	11.048	98	58	10	1353.7	4.18
15	Coombs	Jack	1914	PHA	AL	61.912	9	6.879	115	67	8	1629.7	2.60
16	Fingers	Rollie	1976	OAK	AL	61.804	9	6.867	67	61	136	1016.0	2.91
17	Welch	Bob	1994	OAK	AL	61.494	7	8.785	96	60	0	1271.3	3.94
18	Moore	Mike	1992	OAK	AL	53.509	4	13.377	66	46	0	874.0	3.54
19	Holtzman	Ken	1975	OAK	AL	52.037	4	13.009	77	55	0	1084.3	2.92
20	Haren	Danny	2007	OAK	AL	49.646	3	16.549	43	34	0	662.7	3.64
21	Langford	Rick	1986	OAK	AL	47.848	10	4.785	73	105	0	1468.0	3.97
22	Shantz	Bobby	1956	KC1	AL	45.865	8	5.733	69	65	11	1166.7	3.80
23	Norris	Mike	1990	OAK	AL	44.166	10	4.417	58	59	0	1124.3	3.89
24	Hendriks	Liam	2020	OAK	AL	42.187	5	8.437	11	12	40	263.0	3.08
25	Gray	Sonny	2017	OAK	AL	41.617	5	8.323	44	36	0	705.0	3.42
26	McCatty	Steve	1985	OAK	AL	41.417	9	4.602	63	63	5	1188.3	3.99
27	Blanton	Joe	2008	OAK	AL	40.987	5	8.197	47	46	0	760.7	4.25
28	Marchildon	Phil	1949	PHA	AL	40.760	8	5.095	68	75	2	1213.0	3.92
29	Kellner	Alex	1958	KC1	AL	39.860	11	3.624	92	108	5	1730.3	4.54
30	Cahill	Trevor	2018	OAK	AL	39.132	4	9.783	47	39	0	693.0	3.88
31	Quinn	Jack	1930	PHA	AL	36.286	6	6.048	69	47	11	926.7	3.51
32	Morgan	Cy	1912	PHA	AL	35.182	4	8.796	52	38	1	862.7	2.15
33	Fowler	Dick	1952	PHA	AL	35.120	10	3.512	66	79	4	1303.0	4.11
34	Street	Huston	2008	OAK	AL	35.070	4	8.768	21	12	94	269.0	2.88
35	Duchscherer	Justin	2010	OAK	AL	34.584	7	4.941	32	24	14	440.0	2.82

RANK	NAME	FIRST	LYEAR	LTEAM	LG	PEVA	YRS	PPYR	W	L	SV	IP	ERA
36	Harriss	Slim	1926	PHA	AL	34.495	7	4.928	67	93	14	1291.3	4.21
37	Anderson	Brett Blue	2019	OAK	AL	33.680	7	4.811	43	43	3	707.0	3.91
38	Odom	Moon	1975	OAK	AL	33.082	12	2.757	80	76	1	1414.7	3.53
39	Manaea	Sean	2020	OAK	AL	32.282	5	6.456	39	31	0	547.7	3.85
40	Harden	Rich	2011	OAK	AL	31.816	7	4.545	40	23	0	624.3	3.65
41	Gonzalez	Gio	2011	OAK	AL	31.289	4	7.822	38	32	0	535.3	3.93
42	Perry	Scott	1921	PHA	AL	30.856	4	7.714	38	67	5	849.7	3.01
43	Keough	Matt	1983	OAK	AL	30.725	7	4.389	50	75	0	1060.3	4.13
44	Dobson	Chuck	1973	OAK	AL	30.469	7	4.353	72	64	0	1200.3	3.66
45	Bailey	Andrew	2011	OAK	AL	26.681	3	8.894	7	10	75	174.0	2.07
46	Fiers	Mike	2020	OAK	AL	26.205	3	8.735	26	9	0	296.7	4.00
47	Doolittle	Sean	2017	OAK	AL	26.057	6	4.343	13	13	36	253.0	3.09
48	Christopher	Russ	1947	PHA	AL	25.948	6	4.325	51	62	18	940.7	3.40
49	Flores	Jesse	1947	PHA	AL	25.648	5	5.130	41	55	2	914.7	3.15
50	Segui	Diego	1972	OAK	AL	25.529	9	2.837	59	71	15	1147.7	3.65

Oakland Athletics Top Fielders

Rank	FIRST BASE		FV	Lyear	IP	FPCT	RF
1	Power	Vic	1.2540	1958	404	0.994	9.55
2	Olson	Matt	1.2426	2020	392	0.995	8.73
3	McInnis	Stuffy	1.2326	1917	956	0.990	10.60
4	Siebern	Norm	1.1865	1963	471	0.991	9.50
5	McGwire	Mark	1.1808	1997	1251	0.994	8.84
6	Giambi	Jason	1.1732	2009	728	0.993	9.10
7	Hauser	Joe	1.1279	1928	539	0.990	10.53
8	Hatteberg	Scott	1.1276	2005	420	0.992	9.35
9	Fain	Ferris	1.1223	1952	830	0.986	9.51
10	Davis	Harry	1.0912	1915	1391	0.981	10.24

Rank	SECOND BASE		FV	Lyear	G	FPCT	RF
1	Collins	Eddie	1.3933	1928	996	0.965	5.18
2	Lajoie	Nap	1.3865	1916	334	0.965	5.80
3	Hall	Irv	1.3693	1946	289	0.977	5.81
4	Lumpe	Jerry	1.3571	1963	653	0.984	5.22
5	Ellis	Mark	1.3402	2011	1021	0.990	4.95
6	Spiezio	Scott	1.2921	1999	300	0.984	4.64
7	Garner	Phil	1.2784	1976	322	0.971	5.05
8	Green	Dick	1.2541	1974	1158	0.983	4.82
9	Gates	Brent	1.2451	1996	397	0.979	4.93
10	Lowrie	Jed	1.2387	2018	378	0.989	4.02

Rank	SHORTSTOP		FV	Lyear	G	FPCT	RF
1	Bordick	Mike	1.6187	1996	715	0.978	4.41
2	Joost	Eddie	1.6171	1954	907	0.965	5.19
3	DeMaestri	Joe	1.5761	1959	890	0.968	4.63
4	Tejada	Miguel	1.5738	2003	935	0.970	4.61
5	Griffin	Alfredo	1.5651	1987	461	0.963	4.45
6	Semien	Marcus	1.5650	2020	769	0.968	4.14
7	Campaneris	Bert	1.5520	1976	1702	0.965	4.67
8	Causey	Wayne	1.5060	1966	400	0.970	4.71
9	Cross	Monte	1.4954	1907	712	0.937	5.21
10	Pennington	Cliff	1.4867	2012	466	0.967	4.34

Rank	THIRD BASE		FV	Lyear	G	FPCT	RF
1	Chapman	Matt	1.6216	2020	421	0.965	3.04
2	Kell	George	1.6141	1946	313	0.963	3.46
3	Majeski	Hank	1.5796	1952	583	0.974	3.17
4	Baker	Frank	1.5776	1914	896	0.934	3.45
5	Chavez	Eric	1.5724	2009	1233	0.969	2.76

6	Bando	Sal	1.5441	1976	1446	0.958	2.82	
7	Donaldson	Josh	1.5235	2014	376	0.954	2.82	
8	Charles	Ed	1.5203	1967	695	0.960	2.93	
9	Werber	Billy	1.5145	1938	259	0.946	3.19	
10	Lansford	Carney	1.5053	1992	1096	0.969	2.33	

Rank	CATCHER		FV	Lyear	G	FPCT	RF	CS%
1	Rosar	Buddy	2.0062	1949	425	0.995	4.63	0.613
2	Cochrane	Mickey	1.9765	1933	1148	0.984	5.07	0.390
3	Thomas	Ira	1.9458	1915	318	0.976	6.40	0.498
4	Schreckengost	Ossee	1.9421	1908	670	0.975	7.48	0.441
5	Perkins	Cy	1.8686	1930	1095	0.978	4.38	0.484
6	Kendall	Jason	1.8420	2007	368	0.994	6.89	0.227
7	Steinbach	Terry	1.8287	1996	1050	0.988	5.84	0.373
8	Suzuki	Kurt	1.8178	2013	684	0.994	7.11	0.286
9	Hernandez	Ramon	1.7910	2003	591	0.988	6.50	0.313
10	Astroth	Joe	1.7817	1956	511	0.987	4.48	0.496

Rank	OUTFIELD		FV	Lyear	G	FPCT	RF	ApG
1	Tuttle	Bill	1.5783	1961	439	0.985	2.48	0.103
2	Murphy	Dwayne	1.5755	1987	1177	0.987	2.94	0.066
4	North	Billy	1.5702	1978	627	0.982	2.98	0.069
4	Philley	Dave	1.5487	1953	426	0.985	2.54	0.107
5	Chapman	Sam	1.5322	1950	1225	0.971	2.91	0.092
6	Henderson	Dave	1.5253	1993	636	0.986	2.68	0.050
7	Simmons	Al	1.5073	1944	1256	0.980	2.41	0.084
8	Sweeney	Ryan	1.5053	2011	467	0.996	1.90	0.051
9	Armas	Tony	1.5021	1982	679	0.982	2.53	0.078
10	Haas	Mule	1.4926	1938	603	0.982	2.68	0.071
11	Kotsay	Mark	1.4919	2007	465	0.987	2.36	0.062
12	Cramer	Doc	1.4836	1935	616	0.976	2.69	0.071
13	Hershberger	Mike	1.4804	1969	542	0.982	1.77	0.092
14	Strunk	Amos	1.4759	1924	927	0.980	2.27	0.129
15	Johnson	Bob	1.4644	1942	1399	0.964	2.42	0.114
16	Del Greco	Bobby	1.4560	1963	307	0.983	2.09	0.072
17	Henderson	Rickey	1.4506	1998	1606	0.980	2.43	0.055
18	Piscotty	Stephen	1.4455	2020	285	0.994	1.84	0.032
19	Estalella	Bobby	1.4389	1949	355	0.985	2.52	0.079
20	Monday	Rick	1.4369	1971	611	0.975	2.26	0.062
21	Javier	Stan	1.4316	1995	589	0.990	2.26	0.034
22	Pickering	Ollie	1.4313	1904	256	0.956	2.03	0.117
23	Walker	Tilly	1.4277	1923	689	0.950	2.35	0.155
24	Young	Ernie	1.4262	1997	265	0.986	2.12	0.053
25	Crisp	Coco	1.4488	2015	577	0.993	2.32	0.019
26	Rudi	Joe	1.4196	1982	852	0.990	1.86	0.050
27	Cimoli	Geno	1.4158	1964	287	0.977	1.79	0.077
28	McCosky	Barney	1.4136	1950	404	0.985	2.32	0.050
29	Gosger	Jim	1.4063	1968	254	0.990	1.86	0.055
30	Grieve	Ben	1.4043	2000	458	0.990	1.73	0.046

Rank	PITCHING		FV	Lyear	IP	FPCT	RF
1	Morgan	Cy	1.0973	1912	863	0.955	3.31
2	Myers	Elmer	1.0676	1918	621	0.952	3.43
3	Langford	Rick	1.0676	1986	1468	0.983	2.15
4	Holtzman	Ken	1.0674	1975	1084	0.966	1.89
5	Rommel	Eddie	1.0671	1932	2556	0.968	3.41
6	Hudson	Tim	1.0635	2004	1241	0.959	2.23
7	Shantz	Bobby	1.0623	1956	1167	0.973	2.73
8	Moore	Mike	1.0587	1992	874	0.964	2.18
9	Christopher	Russ	1.0580	1947	941	0.978	3.75
10	Cahill	Trevor	1.0507	2018	693	0.976	2.08

Franchise When and Where
Oakland Athletics (1968 to Present)
Kansas City Athletics (1955-1967, KC1)
Philadelphia Athletics (1901-1954, PHA)

PHILADELPHIA PHILLIES
Best Seasons and Careers of All-Time

Richie Ashburn, Robin Roberts, and Del Ennis. Mike Schmidt and Steve Carlton. Chase Utley, Ryan Howard, Jimmy Rollins, and Cole Hamels. Just a short list of the great players from the three Championship eras of Phillies baseball, with the latter two bringing a World Series parade. And yes, they're all on the list somewhere, all but Ennis as the best at their position. Ed Delahanty, often forgotten when some in Philadelphia discuss the best of All-Time, deserves more than a passing mention. He's the second best hitting Phillie, batting 0.348 with 1,286 Runs Batted In. And, yes, Bobby Abreu almost made the starting outfield, I'm sure to the chagrin of some fans, though that may not be fair. But don't worry, Sherry Magee got the nod. You can see that historically the Phillies had more trouble pitching, beyond the first few, than they did pitching. We've chosen current ace Aaron Nola for the last spot in the bullpen. Some will say that should go to Cliff Lee. That would be a good choice, too.

Reserves

Bench - Bobby Abreu (OF), Sam Thompson (OF), Chuck Klein (OF), Larry Bowa (SS), Dick Allen (3B/1B/OF), Mike Lieberthal (CATCHER).

Bullpen - Ron Reed (CL), Tug McGraw (SU), Jim Bunning, Roy Halladay, Chris Short, Aaron Nola.

Philadelphia Phillies - Best Position Player Years

Rank	Name	First	Year	Team	Lg	HR	RBI	AVG	Age	PEVA-B
1	Delahanty	Ed	1899	PHI	NL	9	137	0.410	32	42.557
2	Schmidt	Mike	1981	PHI	NL	31	91	0.316	32	40.963
3	Delahanty	Ed	1896	PHI	NL	13	126	0.397	29	40.317
4	Flick	Elmer	1900	PHI	NL	11	110	0.367	24	37.675
5	Delahanty	Ed	1893	PHI	NL	19	146	0.368	26	36.872
6	Magee	Sherry	1910	PHI	NL	6	123	0.331	26	36.256
7	Howard	Ryan	2006	PHI	NL	58	149	0.313	27	35.507
8	Delahanty	Ed	1897	PHI	NL	5	96	0.377	30	35.320
9	Hamilton	Billy	1894	PHI	NL	4	87	0.404	28	34.987
10	Schmidt	Mike	1974	PHI	NL	36	116	0.282	25	34.027
11	Klein	Chuck	1930	PHI	NL	40	170	0.386	26	33.052
12	O'Doul	Lefty	1929	PHI	NL	32	122	0.398	32	31.823
13	Delahanty	Ed	1895	PHI	NL	11	106	0.404	28	31.733
14	Delahanty	Ed	1898	PHI	NL	4	92	0.334	31	30.919
15	Allen	Dick	1964	PHI	NL	29	91	0.318	22	30.770
16	Schmidt	Mike	1983	PHI	NL	40	109	0.255	34	30.565
17	Schmidt	Mike	1982	PHI	NL	35	87	0.280	33	30.250
18	Allen	Dick	1966	PHI	NL	40	110	0.317	24	29.910
19	Thompson	Sam	1895	PHI	NL	18	165	0.392	35	29.754
20	Schmidt	Mike	1984	PHI	NL	36	106	0.277	35	29.652

Philadelphia Phillies - Best Pitcher Years

Rank	Name	First	Year	Team	Lg	W	L	SV	IP	ERA	Age	PEVA-P
1	Alexander	Pete	1915	PHI	NL	31	10	3	376.3	1.22	28	52.205
2	Carlton	Steve	1980	PHI	NL	24	9	0	304.0	2.34	36	48.494
3	Alexander	Pete	1916	PHI	NL	33	12	3	389.0	1.55	29	47.561
4	Halladay	Roy	2010	PHI	NL	21	10	0	250.7	2.44	33	43.316
5	Halladay	Roy	2011	PHI	NL	19	6	0	233.7	2.35	34	42.710
6	Alexander	Pete	1917	PHI	NL	30	13	0	388.0	1.83	30	39.958
7	Carlton	Steve	1972	PHI	NL	27	10	0	346.3	1.97	28	39.105
8	Roberts	Robin	1951	PHI	NL	21	15	2	315.0	3.03	25	38.640
9	Roberts	Robin	1952	PHI	NL	28	7	2	330.0	2.59	26	38.501
10	Roberts	Robin	1953	PHI	NL	23	16	2	346.7	2.75	27	38.372
11	Roberts	Robin	1954	PHI	NL	23	15	4	336.7	2.97	28	35.774
12	Carlton	Steve	1982	PHI	NL	23	11	0	295.7	3.10	38	35.010
13	Lee	Cliff	2011	PHI	NL	17	8	0	232.7	2.40	33	33.297
14	Roberts	Robin	1950	PHI	NL	20	11	1	304.3	3.02	24	30.767
15	Nola	Aaron	2018	PHI	NL	17	6	0	212.3	2.37	25	30.543
16	Schilling	Curt	1997	PHI	NL	17	11	0	254.3	2.97	31	30.295
17	Roberts	Robin	1955	PHI	NL	23	14	3	305.0	3.28	29	28.350
18	Bunning	Jim	1967	PHI	NL	17	15	0	302.3	2.29	36	28.202
19	Schilling	Curt	1998	PHI	NL	15	14	0	268.7	3.25	32	28.183
20	Denny	John	1983	PHI	NL	19	6	0	242.7	2.37	31	28.177

Philadelphia Phillies - Top Career Batters

RANK	NAME	FIRST	LYR	TEAM	LG	PEVA-B	YRS	PPYR	HR	RBI	H	AVE
1	Schmidt	Mike	1989	PHI	NL	383.574	18	21.310	548	1595	2234	0.267
2	Delahanty	Ed	1901	PHI	NL	305.971	13	23.536	87	1286	2213	0.348
3	Magee	Sherry	1914	PHI	NL	196.074	11	17.825	75	886	1647	0.299

RANK	NAME	FIRST	LYR	TEAM	LG	PEVA-B	YRS	PPYR	HR	RBI	H	AVE
4	Ashburn	Richie	1959	PHI	NL	177.326	12	14.777	22	499	2217	0.311
5	Abreu	Bobby	2006	PHI	NL	156.932	9	17.437	195	814	1474	0.303
6	Thompson	Sam	1898	PHI	NL	156.862	10	15.686	95	957	1469	0.333
7	Thomas	Roy	1911	PHI	NL	155.658	12	12.972	6	264	1364	0.295
8	Ennis	Del	1956	PHI	NL	152.246	11	13.841	259	1124	1812	0.286
9	Rollins	Jimmy	2014	PHI	NL	150.061	15	10.004	216	887	2306	0.267
10	Klein	Chuck	1944	PHI	NL	149.923	15	9.995	243	983	1705	0.326
11	Allen	Dick	1976	PHI	NL	148.577	9	16.509	204	655	1143	0.290
12	Howard	Ryan	2016	PHI	NL	143.152	13	11.012	382	1194	1475	0.258
13	Callison	Johnny	1969	PHI	NL	137.833	10	13.783	185	666	1438	0.271
14	Hamilton	Billy	1895	PHI	NL	133.809	6	22.302	23	367	1079	0.361
15	Cravath	Gavvy	1920	PHI	NL	129.501	9	14.389	117	676	1054	0.291
16	Luzinski	Greg	1980	PHI	NL	122.236	11	11.112	223	811	1299	0.281
17	Utley	Chase	2015	PHI	NL	119.147	13	9.165	233	916	1623	0.282
18	Titus	John	1912	PHI	NL	115.622	10	11.562	31	475	1209	0.278
19	Jones	Willie	1959	PHI	NL	110.196	13	8.477	180	753	1400	0.258
20	Williams	Cy	1930	PHI	NL	109.600	13	8.431	217	795	1553	0.306
21	Flick	Elmer	1901	PHI	NL	93.454	4	23.363	29	377	683	0.338
22	Burrell	Pat	2008	PHI	NL	90.901	9	10.100	251	827	1166	0.257
23	Bowa	Larry	1981	PHI	NL	88.897	12	7.408	13	421	1798	0.264
24	Hayes	Von	1991	PHI	NL	88.131	9	9.792	124	568	1173	0.272
25	Daulton	Darren	1997	PHI	NL	86.715	14	6.194	134	567	858	0.245
26	Luderus	Fred	1920	PHI	NL	83.327	11	7.575	83	630	1322	0.278
27	Gonzalez	Tony	1968	PHI	NL	83.001	9	9.222	77	438	1110	0.295
28	Hamner	Granny	1959	PHI	NL	80.920	16	5.058	103	705	1518	0.263
29	Rolen	Scott	2002	PHI	NL	80.855	7	11.551	150	559	880	0.282
30	Clements	Jack	1897	PHI	NL	72.050	14	5.146	70	636	1074	0.289
31	Whitney	Pinky	1939	PHI	NL	70.340	10	7.034	69	734	1329	0.307
32	Lajoie	Nap	1900	PHI	NL	70.316	5	14.063	32	458	721	0.345
33	Paskert	Dode	1917	PHI	NL	69.604	7	9.943	28	291	933	0.272
34	Taylor	Tony	1976	PHI	NL	69.057	15	4.604	51	461	1511	0.261
35	Lieberthal	Mike	2006	PHI	NL	68.861	13	5.297	150	609	1137	0.275
36	Maddox	Garry	1986	PHI	NL	68.036	12	5.670	85	566	1333	0.284
37	Dykstra	Lenny	1996	PHI	NL	67.668	8	8.459	51	251	829	0.289
38	Ruiz	Carlos	2016	PHI	NL	63.351	11	5.759	68	401	898	0.266
39	Victorino	Shane	2012	PHI	NL	63.081	8	7.885	88	390	998	0.279
40	Doolan	Mickey	1913	PHI	NL	62.182	9	6.909	11	445	1077	0.236
41	Kruk	John	1994	PHI	NL	61.255	6	10.209	62	390	790	0.309
42	Seminick	Andy	1957	PHI	NL	60.377	12	5.031	123	411	716	0.244
43	Samuel	Juan	1989	PHI	NL	59.966	7	8.567	100	413	921	0.263
44	Boone	Bob	1981	PHI	NL	56.448	10	5.645	65	456	957	0.259
45	Lopata	Stan	1958	PHI	NL	56.130	11	5.103	116	393	655	0.257
46	Hallman	Bill	1903	PHI	NL	54.050	11	4.914	12	571	1179	0.278

RANK	NAME	FIRST	LYR	TEAM	LG	PEVA-B	YRS	PPYR	HR	RBI	H	AVE
47	Rose	Pete	1983	PHI	NL	51.470	5	10.294	8	255	826	0.291
48	Werth	Jayson	2010	PHI	NL	51.123	4	12.781	95	300	507	0.282
49	Hurst	Don	1934	PHI	NL	50.914	7	7.273	112	598	946	0.303
50	Northey	Ron	1957	PHI	NL	48.699	6	8.117	60	273	556	0.269

Philadelphia Phillies - Top Career Pitchers

RANK	NAME	FIRST	LYEAR	LTEAM	LG	PEVA	YRS	PPYR	W	L	SV	IP	ERA
1	Carlton	Steve	1986	PHI	NL	278.981	15	18.599	241	161	0	3697.3	3.09
2	Roberts	Robin	1961	PHI	NL	275.929	14	19.709	234	199	24	3739.3	3.46
3	Alexander	Pete	1930	PHI	NL	207.112	8	25.889	190	91	15	2513.7	2.18
4	Hamels	Cole	2015	PHI	NL	147.094	10	14.709	114	90	0	1930.0	3.30
5	Schilling	Curt	2000	PHI	NL	126.818	9	14.091	101	78	2	1659.3	3.35
6	Bunning	Jim	1971	PHI	NL	100.697	6	16.783	89	73	4	1520.7	2.93
7	Halladay	Roy	2013	PHI	NL	90.648	4	22.662	55	29	0	702.7	3.25
8	Short	Chris	1972	PHI	NL	80.283	14	5.734	132	127	16	2253.0	3.38
9	Lee	Cliff	2014	PHI	NL	79.119	5	15.824	48	34	0	827.3	2.94
10	Nola	Aaron	2020	PHI	NL	74.751	6	12.459	58	40	0	842.7	3.47
11	Simmons	Curt	1960	PHI	NL	73.304	13	5.639	115	110	4	1939.7	3.66
12	Myers	Brett	2009	PHI	NL	50.608	8	6.326	73	63	21	1183.7	4.40
13	Reed	Ron	1983	PHI	NL	48.807	8	6.101	57	38	90	809.3	3.06
14	Orth	Al	1901	PHI	NL	48.441	7	6.920	100	72	4	1504.7	3.49
15	Mulholland	Terry	1996	PHI	NL	48.326	6	8.054	62	57	0	1070.3	3.81
16	Denny	John	1985	PHI	NL	46.283	4	11.571	37	29	0	650.0	2.96
17	Ferguson	Charlie	1887	PHI	NL	45.301	4	11.325	99	64	4	1514.7	2.67
18	Wolf	Randy	2006	PHI	NL	44.760	8	5.595	69	60	0	1175.0	4.21
19	McGraw	Tug	1984	PHI	NL	44.635	10	4.464	49	37	94	722.0	3.10
20	Rixey	Eppa	1920	PHI	NL	44.172	8	5.521	87	103	6	1604.0	2.83
21	Madson	Ryan	2011	PHI	NL	42.427	9	4.714	47	30	52	630.0	3.59
22	Christenson	Larry	1983	PHI	NL	42.223	11	3.838	83	71	4	1402.7	3.79
23	Sparks	Tully	1910	PHI	NL	41.974	9	4.664	95	95	7	1698.0	2.48
24	Kendrick	Kyle	2014	PHI	NL	39.964	8	4.996	74	68	0	1138.7	4.42
25	Ring	Jimmy	1928	PHI	NL	39.573	6	6.595	68	98	3	1458.0	4.46
26	Taylor	Jack	1897	PHI	NL	38.786	6	6.464	96	77	6	1505.3	4.34
27	Ruthven	Dick	1983	PHI	NL	38.616	9	4.291	78	65	1	1262.7	4.00
28	Moore	Earl	1913	PHI	NL	38.258	6	6.376	67	64	2	1151.3	2.63
29	Papelbon	Jonathan	2015	PHI	NL	37.848	4	9.462	14	11	123	237.7	2.31
30	Leonard	Dutch	1948	PHI	NL	37.447	2	18.724	29	29	0	460.7	2.60
31	Buffinton	Charlie	1889	PHI	NL	36.063	3	12.021	77	50	0	1112.7	2.89
32	Farrell	Turk	1969	PHI	NL	35.952	9	3.995	47	41	65	601.0	3.25
33	Lonborg	Jim	1979	PHI	NL	35.727	7	5.104	75	60	1	1142.3	3.98
34	Gross	Kevin	1988	PHI	NL	34.716	6	5.786	60	66	1	1104.7	3.87
35	Konstanty	Jim	1954	PHI	NL	34.538	7	4.934	51	39	54	675.3	3.64
36	McQuillan	George	1916	PHI	NL	34.019	6	5.670	54	49	7	926.3	1.79

RANK	NAME	FIRST	LYEAR	LTEAM	LG	PEVA	YRS	PPYR	W	L	SV	IP	ERA
37	Moyer	Jamie	2010	PHI	NL	**32.622**	5	6.524	56	40	0	720.7	4.55
38	Wise	Rick	1971	PHI	NL	**32.172**	7	4.596	75	76	0	1244.3	3.60
39	Davis	Curt	1936	PHI	NL	**31.969**	3	10.656	37	35	7	565.7	3.42
40	Padilla	Vicente	2005	PHI	NL	**31.716**	6	5.286	49	49	2	741.3	3.98
41	Donahue	Red	1901	PHI	NL	**31.432**	4	7.858	72	48	1	1098.7	3.26
42	Benge	Ray	1936	PHI	NL	**31.387**	6	5.231	58	82	15	1141.3	4.69
43	Johnson	Syl	1940	PHI	NL	**31.271**	7	4.467	36	51	23	792.0	4.05
44	Carlson	Hal	1927	PHI	NL	**31.112**	4	7.778	42	48	3	768.7	4.13
45	Duggleby	Bill	1907	PHI	NL	**30.852**	8	3.857	90	99	6	1683.7	3.20
46	Passeau	Claude	1939	PHI	NL	**30.433**	4	7.608	38	55	6	802.0	4.15
47	Carman	Don	1990	PHI	NL	**30.283**	8	3.785	53	52	10	883.3	4.06
48	Rowe	Schoolboy	1949	PHI	NL	**30.192**	5	6.038	52	39	4	744.0	3.54
49	Garber	Gene	1978	PHI	NL	**29.909**	5	5.982	33	22	51	392.7	2.68
50	Gleason	Kid	1891	PHI	NL	**29.709**	4	7.427	78	70	4	1328.7	3.39

Philadelphia Phillies Top Fielders

Rank	FIRST BASE		FV	Lyear	G	FPCT	RF
1	Rose	Pete	**1.2591**	1983	702	0.995	9.25
2	Brogna	Rico	**1.2467**	2000	487	0.995	8.58
3	Lee	Travis	**1.2350**	2002	351	0.996	8.88
4	White	Bill	**1.2224**	1968	364	0.994	9.39
5	Waitkus	Eddie	**1.1961**	1955	588	0.992	9.26
6	Thome	Jim	**1.1887**	2012	346	0.996	8.97
7	Farrar	Sid	**1.1827**	1889	816	0.974	10.55
8	Johnson	Deron	**1.1798**	1973	380	0.992	8.63
9	Holke	Walter	**1.1700**	1925	317	0.992	10.33
10	Luderus	Fred	**1.1585**	1920	1298	0.986	10.55

Rank	SECOND BASE		FV	Lyear	G	FPCT	RF
1	Trillo	Manny	**1.4572**	1982	501	0.988	5.55
2	Cash	Dave	**1.4567**	1976	482	0.982	5.45
3	Lajoie	Nap	**1.4221**	1900	315	0.952	6.13
4	Sizemore	Ted	**1.3785**	1978	259	0.983	5.05
5	Herr	Tom	**1.3235**	1990	258	0.990	4.75
6	Verban	Emil	**1.3089**	1948	347	0.973	5.38
7	Samuel	Juan	**1.3012**	1988	792	0.972	5.10
8	Thompson	Fresco	**1.2953**	1930	565	0.963	6.03
9	Rojas	Cookie	**1.2874**	1969	617	0.983	4.90
10	Morandini	Mickey	**1.2740**	2000	926	0.988	4.54

Rank	SHORTSTOP		FV	Lyear	G	FPCT	RF
1	Bartell	Dick	**1.7227**	1934	585	0.954	5.71
2	Allen	Bob	**1.6965**	1894	567	0.915	5.92
3	Bowa	Larry	**1.6646**	1981	1730	0.981	4.61
4	Galvis	Freddie	**1.6471**	2017	498	0.984	4.06
5	Bancroft	Dave	**1.6198**	1920	670	0.937	5.99
6	Doolan	Mickey	**1.6100**	1913	1297	0.938	5.44
7	Irwin	Arthur	**1.6029**	1894	341	0.893	4.65
8	Cross	Monte	**1.6002**	1901	573	0.916	5.92
9	Rollins	Jimmy	**1.5748**	2014	2058	0.983	4.12
10	Fernandez	Chico	**1.5702**	1959	337	0.967	4.42

Rank	THIRD BASE		FV	Lyear	G	FPCT	RF
1	Polanco	Placido	**1.6230**	2012	416	0.983	2.81
2	Rolen	Scott	**1.6191**	2002	842	0.965	2.80
3	Jones	Willie	**1.6076**	1959	1495	0.963	3.12
4	Feliz	Pedro	**1.5978**	2009	284	0.969	2.53
5	May	Pinky	**1.5815**	1943	646	0.962	3.29
6	Schmidt	Mike	**1.5777**	1989	2212	0.955	3.00
7	Money	Don	**1.5609**	1972	338	0.967	2.97

			FV	Lyear	G	FPCT	RF	
8	Whitney	Pinky	1.5583	1939	1078	0.960	3.00	
9	Cross	Lave	1.5570	1897	428	0.927	3.94	
10	Hayes	Charlie	1.5421	1995	507	0.951	2.68	

Rank	CATCHER		FV	Lyear	G	FPCT	RF	CS%
1	Killefer	Bill	1.9858	1917	614	0.980	6.33	0.477
2	Diaz	Bo	1.9228	1985	325	0.987	6.74	0.325
3	McFarland	Ed	1.8977	1901	419	0.964	4.69	0.446
4	Dalrymple	Clay	1.8921	1968	944	0.987	6.15	0.481
5	Boone	Bob	1.8906	1981	1095	0.986	5.71	0.349
6	Ruiz	Carlos	1.8565	2016	1029	0.994	7.65	0.273
7	Lieberthal	Mike	1.8470	2006	1139	0.992	7.17	0.297
8	Ryan	Mike	1.8255	1973	390	0.992	5.85	0.479
9	Daulton	Darren	1.8235	1995	965	0.989	6.07	0.292
10	Clements	Jack	1.8093	1897	953	0.936	5.54	0.331

Rank	OUTFIELD		FV	Lyear	G	FPCT	RF	ApG
1	Ashburn	Richie	1.6389	1959	1785	0.984	3.14	0.086
2	Allen	Ethan	1.6314	1936	331	0.977	2.65	0.139
3	Fogarty	Jim	1.6298	1889	594	0.936	2.53	0.259
4	Thomas	Roy	1.6072	1911	1257	0.971	2.42	0.137
5	Callison	Johnny	1.5892	1969	1379	0.985	2.06	0.111
6	Victorino	Shane	1.5785	2012	929	0.996	2.22	0.058
7	Glanville	Doug	1.5684	2004	792	0.991	2.43	0.067
8	Delahanty	Ed	1.5629	1901	1175	0.949	2.41	0.188
9	Paskert	Dode	1.5579	1917	918	0.974	2.45	0.131
10	Cooley	Duff	1.5397	1899	358	0.943	2.45	0.103
11	Rowand	Aaron	1.5272	2007	268	0.990	2.46	0.063
12	Litwhiler	Danny	1.5253	1943	369	0.981	2.40	0.081
13	Maddox	Garry	1.5212	1986	1282	0.985	2.73	0.060
14	Williams	Cy	1.5203	1930	1324	0.974	2.45	0.131
15	Dykstra	Lenny	1.5154	1996	727	0.985	2.84	0.050
16	Arnovich	Morrie	1.5136	1940	422	0.979	2.53	0.100
17	Montanez	Willie	1.5092	1974	350	0.979	2.26	0.094
18	Hamilton	Billy	1.5057	1895	729	0.922	2.49	0.137
19	Manning	Jack	1.5005	1885	309	0.864	1.66	0.272
20	Leach	Freddy	1.4988	1928	481	0.975	2.65	0.114
21	Unser	Del	1.4973	1982	338	0.986	2.27	0.080
22	Herrera	Odubel	1.4971	2019	609	0.987	2.36	0.039
23	McBride	Bake	1.4748	1981	528	0.990	2.10	0.064
24	Gonzalez	Tony	1.4698	1968	1054	0.988	1.98	0.058
25	Sothern	Denny	1.4664	1930	304	0.966	2.80	0.145
26	Magee	Sherry	1.4580	1914	1415	0.967	2.10	0.096
27	Thompson	Sam	1.4549	1898	1030	0.943	1.72	0.196
28	Wilson	Glenn	1.4530	1987	575	0.974	2.08	0.104
29	Andrews	Ed	1.4517	1889	435	0.904	2.01	0.177
30	Werth	Jayson	1.4516	2010	561	0.987	1.89	0.066

Rank	PITCHING		FV	Lyear	IP	FPCT	RF
1	Walters	Bucky	1.1266	1938	745	0.981	3.20
2	Buffinton	Charlie	1.1076	1889	1113	0.930	2.90
3	Alexander	Pete	1.1072	1930	2514	0.982	2.86
4	Coleman	John	1.0811	1884	693	0.901	2.48
5	Ferguson	Charlie	1.0781	1887	1515	0.919	2.43
6	Jackson	Larry	1.0761	1968	752	0.953	2.68
7	Davis	Curt	1.0745	1936	566	0.944	3.23
8	Mulcahy	Hugh	1.0732	1946	1155	0.960	2.77
9	Taylor	Jack	1.0727	1897	1505	0.903	2.83
10	Passeau	Claude	1.0679	1939	802	0.969	2.44

Franchise When and Where
Philadelphia Phillies (1890 to Present); unofficially known as Blue Jays 1943-4
Philadelphia Quakers (1883-1889)

PITTSBURGH PIRATES
Best Seasons and Careers of All-Time

For most of a certain age, they harken back to the days of Roberto Clemente or Willie Stargell. Others recall the footage of Bill Mazeroski and that walk off home run. However, three of the best players of the Pirates played much longer ago, ... Honus Wagner, Pie Traynor, and Paul Waner. Wagner had the Pirates best season (seven of the Top Twenty) and best career. Waner batted 0.340 over fifteen seasons, ending in 1940. Traynor batted in over 1,200 runs. For some, they'd be surprised that Andrew McCutchen had enough seasons in Pittsburgh to grab the Center Field job, but he played nine there, and had the second best batting season for the franchise in 2012, going 31, 96, 0.327. No, the pitching staff will not make you forget the Giants or the Dodgers. It's doubtful many would be able to name more than one in the Starting Five. And outside the Top Two relievers, not sure If most who work for the Pirates would know most of the names of the pitching reserves. But with that power in the offense, the Pirates All-Time team might just be able to hold their own against most franchises in history.

Andrew McCutchen

Paul Waner　　　Roberto Clemente

Honus Wagner　Bill Mazeroski

　　　　　　Willie Stargell

Pie Traynor

Jason Kendall

All-Time Team
Pittsburgh Pirates

SP - Bob Friend, Wilbur Cooper, Babe Adams, John Candelaria, Vern Law

Reserves

Bench - Ralph Kiner (OF), Max Carey (OF), Bobby Leach (3B/OF), Barry Bonds (OF), Jay Bell (IF), Manny Sanguillen (CATCHER).

Bullpen - Roy Face (CL), Kent Tekulvie (SU), Ray Kremer, Doug Drabek, Jesse Tannehill, Sam Leever.

Pittsburgh Pirates - Best Position Player Years

Rank	Name	First	Year	Team	Lg	HR	RBI	AVG	Age	PEVA-B
1	Wagner	Honus	1908	PIT	NL	10	109	0.354	34	48.837
2	McCutchen	Andrew	2012	PIT	NL	31	96	0.327	26	38.647
3	Kiner	Ralph	1951	PIT	NL	42	109	0.309	29	37.003
4	Bonds	Barry	1990	PIT	NL	33	114	0.301	26	36.095
5	Wagner	Honus	1907	PIT	NL	6	82	0.350	33	35.816
6	Wagner	Honus	1905	PIT	NL	6	101	0.363	31	35.473
7	Bonds	Barry	1992	PIT	NL	34	103	0.311	28	35.418
8	Stargell	Willie	1973	PIT	NL	44	119	0.299	33	33.533
9	Wagner	Honus	1900	PIT	NL	4	100	0.381	26	33.466
10	Wagner	Honus	1903	PIT	NL	5	101	0.355	29	32.062
11	Wagner	Honus	1906	PIT	NL	2	71	0.339	32	31.968
12	Wagner	Honus	1909	PIT	NL	5	100	0.339	35	31.677
13	Clemente	Roberto	1967	PIT	NL	23	110	0.357	33	31.045
14	Stargell	Willie	1971	PIT	NL	48	125	0.295	31	30.420
15	Kiner	Ralph	1947	PIT	NL	51	127	0.313	25	30.272
16	Williams	Jimmy	1899	PIT	NL	9	116	0.355	23	28.883
17	McCutheon	Andrew	2014	PIT	NL	25	83	0.314	28	28.419
18	Kiner	Ralph	1949	PIT	NL	54	127	0.310	27	28.368
19	Bonds	Barry	1991	PIT	NL	25	116	0.292	27	28.310
20	Vaughan	Arky	1935	PIT	NL	19	99	0.385	23	26.511

Pittsburgh Pirates - Best Pitcher Years

Rank	Name	First	Year	Team	Lg	W	L	SV	IP	ERA	Age	PEVA-P
1	Friend	Bob	1960	PIT	NL	18	12	1	275.7	3.00	30	38.546
2	Morris	Ed	1886	PT1	AA	41	20	1	555.3	2.45	24	33.289
3	Blanton	Cy	1935	PIT	NL	18	13	1	254.3	2.58	27	32.884
4	Hawley	Pink	1895	PIT	NL	31	22	1	444.3	3.18	23	31.890
5	Killen	Frank	1893	PIT	NL	36	14	0	415.0	3.64	23	30.320
6	Cooper	Wilbur	1920	PIT	NL	24	15	2	327.0	2.39	28	29.361
7	Law	Vern	1960	PIT	NL	20	9	0	271.7	3.08	30	28.689
8	Grimes	Burleigh	1928	PIT	NL	25	14	3	330.7	2.99	35	28.344
9	Adams	Babe	1911	PIT	NL	22	12	0	293.3	2.33	29	28.103
10	Adams	Babe	1919	PIT	NL	17	10	1	263.3	1.98	37	26.879
11	Candelaria	John	1977	PIT	NL	20	5	0	230.7	2.34	24	24.674
12	Cole	Gerrit	2015	PIT	NL	19	8	0	208.0	2.60	25	24.066
13	Adams	Babe	1920	PIT	NL	17	13	2	263.0	2.16	38	23.725
14	Killen	Frank	1896	PIT	NL	30	18	0	432.3	3.41	26	23.686
15	Drabek	Doug	1992	PIT	NL	15	11	0	256.7	2.77	30	23.331
16	Morris	Ed	1885	PT1	AA	39	24	0	581.0	2.35	23	23.155
17	Drabek	Doug	1990	PIT	NL	22	6	0	231.3	2.76	28	22.627
18	Friend	Bob	1963	PIT	NL	17	16	0	268.7	2.34	33	22.183
19	Kremer	Ray	1927	PIT	NL	19	8	2	226.0	2.47	34	21.882
20	Rhoden	Rick	1984	PIT	NL	14	9	0	238.3	2.72	31	21.773

Pittsburgh Pirates (PIT, PT1) - Top Career Batters

RANK	NAME	FIRST	LYR	TEAM	LG	PEVA-B	YRS	PPYR	HR	RBI	H	AVE
1	Wagner	Honus	1917	PIT	NL	418.765	18	23.265	82	1475	2967	0.328
2	Clemente	Roberto	1972	PIT	NL	264.635	18	14.702	240	1305	3000	0.317
3	Stargell	Willie	1982	PIT	NL	241.847	21	11.517	475	1540	2232	0.282

RANK	NAME	FIRST	LYR	TEAM	LG	PEVA-B	YRS	PPYR	HR	RBI	H	AVE
4	Waner	Paul	1940	PIT	NL	228.401	15	15.227	109	1177	2868	0.340
5	Carey	Max	1926	PIT	NL	183.198	17	10.776	67	719	2416	0.287
6	McCutchen	Andrew	2017	PIT	NL	178.703	9	19.856	203	725	1463	0.291
7	Kiner	Ralph	1953	PIT	NL	175.644	8	21.955	301	801	1097	0.280
8	Vaughan	Arky	1941	PIT	NL	162.788	10	16.279	84	764	1709	0.324
9	Clarke	Fred	1915	PIT	NL	159.569	15	10.638	33	622	1638	0.299
10	Bonds	Barry	1992	PIT	NL	148.339	7	21.191	176	556	984	0.275
11	Traynor	Pie	1937	PIT	NL	141.423	17	8.319	58	1273	2416	0.320
12	Leach	Tommy	1918	PIT	NL	125.144	14	8.939	43	626	1603	0.271
13	Parker	Dave	1983	PIT	NL	118.404	11	10.764	166	758	1479	0.305
14	Oliver	Al	1977	PIT	NL	106.312	10	10.631	135	717	1490	0.296
15	Waner	Lloyd	1945	PIT	NL	104.120	17	6.125	27	577	2317	0.319
16	Kendall	Jason	2004	PIT	NL	103.018	9	11.446	67	471	1409	0.306
17	Van Slyke	Andy	1994	PIT	NL	102.157	8	12.770	117	564	1108	0.283
18	Beaumont	Ginger	1906	PIT	NL	100.065	8	12.508	31	421	1292	0.321
19	Smith	Elmer	1901	PIT	NL	99.667	7	14.238	30	467	958	0.324
20	Mazeroski	Bill	1972	PIT	NL	98.836	17	5.814	138	853	2016	0.260
21	Giles	Brian	2003	PIT	NL	98.218	5	19.644	165	506	782	0.308
22	Bonilla	Bobby	1991	PIT	NL	94.109	6	15.685	114	500	868	0.284
23	Elliott	Bob	1946	PIT	NL	89.446	8	11.181	50	633	1142	0.292
24	Sanguillen	Manny	1980	PIT	NL	86.402	12	7.200	59	527	1343	0.299
25	Beckley	Jake	1896	PIT	NL	84.726	8	10.591	43	661	1137	0.300
26	Bell	Jay	1996	PIT	NL	83.505	8	10.438	78	423	1124	0.269
27	Hebner	Richie	1983	PIT	NL	79.997	11	7.272	128	520	1079	0.277
28	Fletcher	Elbie	1947	PIT	NL	78.226	7	11.175	60	464	875	0.279
29	Groat	Dick	1962	PIT	NL	77.194	9	8.577	30	454	1435	0.290
30	Virdon	Bill	1968	PIT	NL	75.938	11	6.903	72	425	1431	0.266
31	Suhr	Gus	1939	PIT	NL	74.482	10	7.448	79	789	1379	0.278
32	Bay	Jason	2008	PIT	NL	74.050	6	12.342	139	452	729	0.281
33	Skinner	Bob	1963	PIT	NL	72.878	9	8.098	90	462	1050	0.280
34	Thomas	Frank	1958	PIT	NL	72.869	8	9.109	163	562	950	0.275
35	Clendenon	Donn	1968	PIT	NL	71.764	8	8.970	106	488	986	0.280
36	Wilson	Chief	1913	PIT	NL	69.314	6	11.552	44	427	915	0.274
37	Donovan	Patsy	1899	PIT	NL	65.560	8	8.195	13	424	1283	0.307
38	Stenzel	Jake	1896	PIT	NL	65.222	5	13.044	26	337	631	0.361
39	Marte	Starling	2019	PIT	NL	63.636	8	7.955	108	420	1047	0.287
40	Ritchey	Claude	1906	PIT	NL	62.123	7	8.875	5	420	965	0.277
41	Alou	Matty	1970	PIT	NL	61.942	5	12.388	6	202	986	0.327
42	Russell	Jim	1947	PIT	NL	60.539	6	10.090	40	288	729	0.277
43	Madlock	Bill	1985	PIT	NL	59.083	7	8.440	68	390	870	0.297
44	Zisk	Richie	1976	PIT	NL	58.684	6	9.781	69	324	600	0.299
45	Bigbee	Carson	1926	PIT	NL	58.483	11	5.317	17	324	1205	0.287
46	Grantham	George	1931	PIT	NL	57.003	7	8.143	74	508	992	0.315

RANK	NAME	FIRST	LYR	TEAM	LG	PEVA-B	YRS	PPYR	HR	RBI	H	AVE
47	Pena	Tony	1986	PIT	NL	56.712	7	8.102	63	340	821	0.286
48	Moreno	Omar	1982	PIT	NL	54.889	8	6.861	25	263	915	0.255
49	Cuyler	Kiki	1927	PIT	NL	53.878	7	7.697	38	312	680	0.336
50	Miller	Doggie	1893	PIT	NL	53.770	10	5.377	19	374	985	0.254

Pittsburgh Pirates (PIT, PT1) - Top Career Pitchers

RANK	NAME	FIRST	LYEAR	LTEAM	LG	PEVA	YRS	PPYR	W	L	SV	IP	ERA
1	Friend	Bob	1965	PIT	NL	175.551	15	11.703	191	218	10	3480.3	3.55
2	Cooper	Wilbur	1924	PIT	NL	158.666	13	12.205	202	159	14	3199.0	2.74
3	Adams	Babe	1926	PIT	NL	158.236	18	8.791	194	139	15	2991.3	2.74
4	Candelaria	John	1993	PIT	NL	107.249	12	8.937	124	87	16	1873.0	3.17
5	Law	Vern	1967	PIT	NL	103.746	16	6.484	162	147	13	2672.0	3.77
6	Kremer	Ray	1933	PIT	NL	101.477	10	10.148	143	85	10	1954.7	3.76
7	Drabek	Doug	1992	PIT	NL	99.151	6	16.525	92	62	0	1362.7	3.02
8	Leever	Sam	1910	PIT	NL	96.852	13	7.450	194	100	13	2660.7	2.47
9	Phillippe	Deacon	1911	PIT	NL	96.644	12	8.054	168	92	11	2286.0	2.50
10	Face	Roy	1968	PIT	NL	88.354	15	5.890	100	93	188	1314.7	3.46
11	Tannehill	Jesse	1902	PIT	NL	80.132	6	13.355	116	58	5	1499.0	2.73
12	Sewell	Rip	1949	PIT	NL	77.735	12	6.478	143	97	15	2108.7	3.43
13	Veale	Bob	1972	PIT	NL	76.671	11	6.970	116	91	6	1868.7	3.06
14	Tekulve	Kent	1985	PIT	NL	76.544	12	6.379	70	61	158	1017.0	2.68
15	Killen	Frank	1898	PIT	NL	72.982	6	12.164	112	82	0	1661.3	3.97
16	Rhoden	Rick	1986	PIT	NL	72.112	8	9.014	79	73	1	1448.0	3.51
17	Morris	Ed	1889	PIT	NL	72.078	5	14.416	129	102	1	2104.0	2.81
18	French	Larry	1934	PIT	NL	68.367	6	11.395	87	83	9	1502.7	3.50
19	Blanton	Cy	1939	PIT	NL	66.710	6	11.118	58	51	4	955.3	3.28
20	Swift	Bill	1939	PIT	NL	61.922	8	7.740	91	79	18	1555.0	3.57
21	Meadows	Lee	1929	PIT	NL	60.877	7	8.697	88	52	1	1248.3	3.50
22	Camnitz	Howie	1913	PIT	NL	58.023	9	6.447	116	84	13	1754.3	2.63
23	Melancon	Mark	2016	PIT	NL	57.281	4	14.320	10	10	130	260.3	1.80
24	Hawley	Pink	1897	PIT	NL	54.194	3	18.065	71	61	1	1133.7	3.76
25	Morrison	Johnny	1927	PIT	NL	51.720	8	6.465	89	71	14	1363.7	3.52
26	Willis	Vic	1909	PIT	NL	49.194	4	12.299	89	46	3	1209.0	2.08
27	Cole	Gerrit	2017	PIT	NL	49.190	5	9.838	59	42	0	782.3	3.50
28	Grimes	Burleigh	1934	PIT	NL	47.338	5	9.468	48	42	5	830.3	3.26
29	Leifield	Lefty	1912	PIT	NL	46.475	8	5.809	109	84	7	1578.0	2.38
30	Smith	Zane	1996	PIT	NL	46.053	6	7.676	47	41	0	768.3	3.35
31	Smiley	John	1991	PIT	NL	45.988	6	7.665	60	42	4	854.0	3.57
32	Ellis	Dock	1979	PIT	NL	44.064	9	4.896	96	80	0	1430.0	3.16
33	Walk	Bob	1993	PIT	NL	41.973	10	4.197	82	61	5	1303.0	3.83
34	Reuschel	Rick	1987	PIT	NL	41.483	3	13.828	31	30	1	586.7	3.04
35	Rooker	Jim	1980	PIT	NL	41.252	8	5.157	82	65	6	1317.7	3.29
36	Blass	Steve	1974	PIT	NL	40.634	10	4.063	103	76	2	1597.3	3.63

RANK	NAME	FIRST	LYEAR	LTEAM	LG	PEVA	YRS	PPYR	W	L	SV	IP	ERA
37	Dickson	Murry	1953	PIT	NL	39.837	5	7.967	66	85	11	1216.3	3.83
38	Maholm	Paul	2011	PIT	NL	39.474	7	5.639	53	73	0	1143.7	4.36
39	McBean	Al	1970	PIT	NL	39.426	9	4.381	65	43	59	1016.0	3.08
40	Galvin	Pud	1892	PIT	NL	39.070	7	5.581	125	110	0	2084.7	3.10
41	Vazquez	Felipe	2019	PIT	NL	38.849	4	9.712	15	9	86	232.7	2.17
42	Kline	Ron	1969	PIT	NL	38.643	8	4.830	66	91	14	1251.3	3.77
43	Hill	Carmen	1929	PIT	NL	37.975	8	4.747	47	31	8	735.3	3.26
44	Giusti	Dave	1976	PIT	NL	37.390	7	5.341	47	28	133	618.0	2.94
45	Chesbro	Jack	1902	PIT	NL	36.451	4	9.113	70	38	3	938.7	2.89
46	Watson	Tony	2017	PIT	NL	36.196	7	5.171	31	16	30	433.0	2.68
47	Neagle	Denny	1996	PIT	NL	35.633	5	7.127	43	35	3	697.0	4.02
48	Duke	Zach	2010	PIT	NL	35.344	6	5.891	45	70	0	964.3	4.54
49	Liriano	Francisco	2019	PIT	NL	34.315	5	6.863	46	39	0	693.7	3.65
50	Robinson	Don	1987	PIT	NL	34.054	10	3.405	65	69	43	1203.0	3.85

Pittsburgh Pirates Top Fielders

Rank	FIRST BASE		FV	Lyear	G	FPCT	RF
1	Fletcher	Elbie	1.2989	1947	894	0.993	10.29
2	Clendenon	Donn	1.2888	1968	910	0.988	10.38
3	Beckley	Jake	1.2403	1896	924	0.980	10.60
4	Young	Kevin	1.2276	2003	1022	0.992	8.80
5	Grimm	Charlie	1.2260	1924	768	0.994	10.47
6	Dahlgren	Babe	1.2144	1945	302	0.992	10.05
7	LaRoche	Adam	1.2065	2009	367	0.996	9.33
8	Long	Dale	1.1863	1957	265	0.985	9.18
9	Bream	Sid	1.1743	1990	615	0.991	9.01
10	Thompson	Jason	1.1615	1985	650	0.992	9.20

Rank	SECOND BASE		FV	Lyear	G	FPCT	RF
1	Lind	Jose	1.4309	1992	774	0.987	5.23
2	Mazeroski	Bill	1.4054	1972	2094	0.983	5.57
3	Ritchey	Claude	1.3543	1906	973	0.958	5.22
4	Bierbauer	Lou	1.3523	1896	707	0.947	6.00
5	Ray	Johnny	1.3337	1987	914	0.982	5.07
6	Walker	Neil	1.3226	2015	802	0.989	4.69
7	Womack	Tony	1.3226	1998	311	0.974	4.95
8	Stennett	Rennie	1.3121	1979	919	0.978	5.48
9	Cutshaw	George	1.2959	1921	478	0.967	5.51
10	Cash	Dave	1.2704	1973	366	0.985	5.57

Rank	SHORTSTOP		FV	Lyear	G	FPCT	RF
1	Maranville	Rabbit	1.7047	1923	432	0.963	5.79
2	Bell	Jay	1.6713	1996	1103	0.976	4.69
3	Groat	Dick	1.6218	1962	1242	0.962	5.12
4	Wilson	Jack	1.6186	2009	1128	0.978	4.68
5	Foli	Tim	1.6127	1985	351	0.976	4.87
6	Wagner	Honus	1.5922	1917	1887	0.940	5.63
7	Smith	Pop	1.5843	1889	264	0.901	4.91
8	Ely	Bones	1.5798	1900	735	0.929	5.59
9	Alley	Gene	1.5728	1973	977	0.970	4.92
10	Vaughan	Arky	1.5724	1941	1381	0.950	5.27

Rank	THIRD BASE		FV	Lyear	G	FPCT	RF
1	Hoak	Don	1.5484	1962	569	0.957	2.92
2	Lyons	Denny	1.5220	1897	320	0.906	3.65
3	Traynor	Pie	1.5164	1937	1863	0.947	3.12
4	Gustine	Frankie	1.5033	1948	321	0.938	3.30
5	Williams	Jimmy	1.4954	1900	255	0.896	3.97
6	Byrne	Bobby	1.4817	1913	586	0.940	2.96
7	Wills	Maury	1.4801	1968	285	0.952	2.88

8	King	Jeff	**1.4780**	1996	582	0.953	2.61	
9	Leach	Tommy	**1.4404**	1911	850	0.911	3.57	
10	Elliott	Bob	**1.4301**	1946	557	0.939	3.15	

Rank	CATCHER		FV	Lyear	G	FPCT	RF	SB
1	Pena	Tony	**1.9783**	1986	787	0.987	6.61	0.388
2	Gibson	George	**1.9030**	1916	1155	0.977	5.59	0.463
3	Schmidt	Walter	**1.8878**	1924	703	0.981	4.75	0.500
4	Mack	Connie	**1.8834**	1896	287	0.943	5.47	0.402
5	Todd	Al	**1.8828**	1938	330	0.978	5.23	0.412
6	Lopez	Al	**1.8710**	1946	650	0.988	3.80	0.530
7	Sanguillen	Manny	**1.8512**	1979	1037	0.986	5.93	0.381
8	LaValliere	Mike	**1.8463**	1993	584	0.992	5.52	0.344
9	Kendall	Jason	**1.8255**	2004	1205	0.988	6.84	0.310
10	Ott	Ed	**1.8141**	1980	430	0.984	5.62	0.347

Rank	OUTFIELD		FV	Lyear	G	FPCT	RF	ApG
1	Carey	Max	**1.6009**	1926	2154	0.966	2.82	0.145
2	Moreno	Omar	**1.5773**	1982	926	0.982	2.81	0.069
3	Waner	Lloyd	**1.5532**	1945	1680	0.984	2.82	0.084
4	Van Slyke	Andy	**1.5516**	1994	1024	0.989	2.54	0.065
5	Sunday	Billy	**1.5504**	1890	287	0.924	2.45	0.233
6	Virdon	Bill	**1.5503**	1968	1376	0.983	2.53	0.066
7	DiMaggio	Vince	**1.5466**	1944	654	0.980	2.68	0.104
8	Bonds	Barry	**1.5355**	1992	986	0.985	2.34	0.075
9	Southworth	Billy	**1.5214**	1920	327	0.981	2.35	0.125
10	Leach	Tommy	**1.5148**	1918	653	0.975	2.54	0.126
11	Wilson	Chief	**1.5144**	1913	897	0.965	2.03	0.129
12	Waner	Paul	**1.5030**	1940	2019	0.976	2.29	0.109
13	McCarthy	Jack	**1.5000**	1899	275	0.948	2.23	0.135
14	McCutchen	Andrew	**1.4933**	2017	1327	0.988	2.27	0.048
15	Thomas	Frank	**1.4901**	1958	575	0.985	2.45	0.108
16	Clarke	Fred	**1.4897**	1915	1431	0.971	2.23	0.101
17	Cuyler	Kiki	**1.4881**	1927	509	0.964	2.56	0.130
18	Alou	Matty	**1.4865**	1970	729	0.979	2.04	0.073
19	Clemente	Roberto	**1.4832**	1972	2370	0.973	2.09	0.112
20	Wynne	Marvell	**1.4620**	1985	355	0.987	2.37	0.051
21	Russell	Jim	**1.4592**	1947	679	0.979	2.45	0.085
22	McLouth	Nate	**1.4571**	2012	437	0.991	1.99	0.030
23	Zisk	Richie	**1.4518**	1976	535	0.983	2.01	0.075
24	Westlake	Wally	**1.4508**	1950	511	0.985	2.37	0.067
25	Oliver	Al	**1.4462**	1977	970	0.982	2.44	0.037
26	Bigbee	Carson	**1.4408**	1926	1031	0.966	2.37	0.138
27	Stenzel	Jake	**1.4321**	1896	421	0.919	2.29	0.152
28	Smith	Elmer	**1.4201**	1897	745	0.915	2.24	0.137
29	Beaumont	Ginger	**1.4191**	1906	970	0.952	2.11	0.103
30	Elliot	Bob	**1.4162**	1946	470	0.980	2.18	0.081

Rank	PITCHING		FV	Lyear	IP	FPCT	RF	
1	Galvin	Pud	**1.0902**	1892	2085	0.915	2.60	
2	Reuschel	Rick	**1.0895**	1987	587	0.978	2.76	
3	Rhoden	Rick	**1.0878**	1986	1448	0.991	2.16	
4	Dickson	Murry	**1.0801**	1953	1216	0.961	2.75	
5	Willis	Vic	**1.0800**	1909	1209	0.963	3.29	
6	Friend	Bob	**1.0707**	1965	3480	0.972	2.14	
7	Drabek	Doug	**1.0689**	1992	1363	0.948	2.31	
8	Duke	Zach	**1.0670**	2010	964	0.979	2.22	
9	Hendrix	Claude	**1.0626**	1913	648	0.966	3.17	
10	Hawley	Pink	**1.0604**	1897	1134	0.924	2.59	

Franchise When and Where

Pittsburgh Pirates (1891 to Present)
Pittsburgh Alleghenys (1882-1886, PT1; 1887-1890, PIT);
also known as Innocents 1890.

SAN DIEGO PADRES
Best Seasons and Careers of All-Time

We get the feeling that with the young talent on the current roster of the Padres, that much is going to change on this All-Time team list over the next five years. Players like Fernando Tatis, Jr. and Manny Machado are likely to replace some of the names below, or at least push them to the bench. Machado already has the Number 5 Best Season for a Padre hitter, with Tatis, Jr. the Number 8 Best Season, both in the odd short season of 2020. For now, the team is led by Tony Gwynn, Dave Winfield, and a great bullpen, that led by Hall of Fame closer Trevor Hoffman. There's some nice bats off the bench, and you could not do better for a defensive replacement than having Ozzie Smith ready to somersault onto the field. Yes, we realize that more than a few would start him.

Reserves

Bench - Nate Colbert (OF/1B), Gene Richards (OF/1B), Ryan Klesko (1B/OF), Ozzie Smith (SS), Ken Caminiti (3B), Phil Nevin (3B), Gene Tenace (CATCHER).

Bullpen - Trevor Hoffman (CL), Heath Bell (SU), Eric Show, Bruce Hurst, Rollie Fingers, Joey Hamilton.

San Diego Padres - Best Position Player Years

Rank	Name	First	Year	Team	Lg	HR	RBI	AVG	Age	PEVA-B
1	Headley	Chase	2012	SDN	NL	31	115	0.286	28	33.091
2	Winfield	Dave	1979	SDN	NL	34	118	0.308	28	32.688
3	Gonzalez	Adrian	2009	SDN	NL	40	99	0.277	27	27.865
4	Gwynn	Tony	1987	SDN	NL	7	54	0.370	27	27.822
5	Machado	Manny	2020	SDN	NL	16	47	0.304	28	27.131
6	Caminiti	Ken	1996	SDN	NL	40	130	0.326	33	26.999
7	Gonzalez	Adrian	2010	SDN	NL	31	101	0.298	28	26.068
8	Tatis, Jr.	Fernando	2020	SDN	NL	17	45	0.277	21	25.006
9	Gwynn	Tony	1984	SDN	NL	5	71	0.351	24	24.767
10	Sheffield	Gary	1992	SDN	NL	33	100	0.330	24	23.846
11	Giles	Brian	2005	SDN	NL	15	83	0.301	34	23.632
12	Gwynn	Tony	1997	SDN	NL	17	119	0.372	37	22.316
13	Winfield	Dave	1978	SDN	NL	24	97	0.308	27	21.529
14	Colbert	Nate	1972	SDN	NL	38	111	0.250	26	21.351
15	Gwynn	Tony	1986	SDN	NL	14	59	0.329	26	21.280
16	Gwynn	Tony	1994	SDN	NL	12	64	0.394	34	21.228
17	Lezcano	Sixto	1982	SDN	NL	16	84	0.289	29	21.143
18	Gonzalez	Adrian	2008	SDN	NL	36	119	0.279	26	20.657
19	Vaughn	Greg	1998	SDN	NL	50	119	0.272	33	20.269
20	McGriff	Fred	1992	SDN	NL	35	104	0.286	29	20.225

San Diego Padres - Best Pitcher Years

Rank	Name	First	Year	Team	Lg	W	L	SV	IP	ERA	Age	PEVA-P
1	Brown	Kevin	1998	SDN	NL	18	7	0	257.0	2.38	33	42.712
2	Peavy	Jake	2007	SDN	NL	19	6	0	223.3	2.54	26	41.135
3	Jones	Randy	1976	SDN	NL	22	14	0	315.3	2.74	26	31.744
4	Jones	Randy	1975	SDN	NL	20	12	0	285.0	2.24	25	27.108
5	Yates	Kirby	2019	SDN	NL	0	5	41	60.7	1.19	32	20.633
6	Whitson	Ed	1989	SDN	NL	16	11	0	227.0	2.66	34	19.683
7	Benes	Andy	1991	SDN	NL	15	11	0	223.0	3.03	24	19.087
8	Whitson	Ed	1990	SDN	NL	14	9	0	228.7	2.60	35	18.998
9	Lamet	Dinelson	2020	SDN	NL	3	1	0	69.0	2.09	28	18.787
10	Davies	Zach	2020	SDN	NL	7	4	0	69.3	2.73	27	18.525
11	Hoffman	Trevor	1998	SDN	NL	4	2	53	73.0	1.48	31	18.234
12	Hurst	Bruce	1989	SDN	NL	15	11	0	244.7	2.69	31	18.221
13	Perry	Gaylord	1978	SDN	NL	21	6	0	260.7	2.73	40	16.718
14	Peavy	Jake	2005	SDN	NL	13	7	0	203.0	2.88	24	16.518
15	Hoffman	Trevor	1996	SDN	NL	9	5	42	88.0	2.25	29	16.509
16	Hoffman	Trevor	1999	SDN	NL	2	3	40	67.3	2.14	32	15.899
17	Peavy	Jake	2004	SDN	NL	15	6	0	166.3	2.27	23	15.750
18	Latos	Matt	2010	SDN	NL	14	10	0	184.7	2.92	23	15.614
19	Ashby	Andy	1998	SDN	NL	17	9	0	226.7	3.34	31	15.490
20	Roberts	Dave	1971	SDN	NL	14	17	0	269.7	2.10	27	14.958

San Diego Padres - Top Career Batters

RANK	NAME	FIRST	LYR	TEAM	LG	PEVA-B	YRS	PPYR	HR	RBI	H	AVE
1	Gwynn	Tony	2001	SDN	NL	238.944	20	11.947	135	1138	3141	0.338
2	Winfield	Dave	1980	SDN	NL	123.090	8	15.386	154	626	1134	0.284

RANK	NAME	FIRST	LYR	TEAM	LG	PEVA-B	YRS	PPYR	HR	RBI	H	AVE
3	Gonzalez	Adrian	2010	SDN	NL	100.592	5	20.118	161	501	856	0.288
4	Headley	Chase	2018	SDN	NL	75.366	9	8.374	87	405	879	0.263
5	Giles	Brian	2009	SDN	NL	74.100	7	10.586	83	415	872	0.279
6	Colbert	Nate	1974	SDN	NL	71.102	6	11.850	163	481	780	0.253
7	Caminiti	Ken	1998	SDN	NL	68.417	4	17.104	121	396	592	0.295
8	Kennedy	Terry	1986	SDN	NL	65.188	6	10.865	76	424	817	0.274
9	Richards	Gene	1983	SDN	NL	61.836	7	8.834	26	251	994	0.291
10	Klesko	Ryan	2006	SDN	NL	61.417	7	8.774	133	493	786	0.279
11	Nevin	Phil	2005	SDN	NL	60.293	7	8.613	156	573	842	0.288
12	Finley	Steve	1998	SDN	NL	50.714	4	12.679	82	298	662	0.276
13	Tenace	Gene	1980	SDN	NL	49.386	4	12.347	68	239	384	0.237
14	Templeton	Garry	1991	SDN	NL	47.904	10	4.790	43	427	1135	0.252
15	Santiago	Benito	1992	SDN	NL	47.661	7	6.809	85	375	758	0.264
16	Myers	Wil	2020	SDN	NL	47.045	6	7.841	110	329	590	0.253
17	McGriff	Fred	1993	SDN	NL	46.102	3	15.367	84	256	382	0.281
18	McReynolds	Kevin	1986	SDN	NL	40.028	4	10.007	65	260	470	0.263
19	Gaston	Cito	1974	SDN	NL	39.616	6	6.603	77	316	672	0.257
20	Venable	Will	2015	SDN	NL	37.626	8	4.703	81	304	694	0.252
21	Machado	Manny	2020	SDN	NL	37.331	2	18.666	48	132	218	0.269
22	Martinez	Carmelo	1989	SDN	NL	34.515	6	5.753	82	337	577	0.248
23	Smith	Ozzie	1981	SDN	NL	33.585	4	8.396	1	129	516	0.231
24	Garvey	Steve	1987	SDN	NL	33.059	5	6.612	61	316	631	0.275
25	Tatis, Jr.	Fernando	2020	SDN	NL	31.967	2	15.984	39	98	168	0.301
26	Grubb	Johnny	1976	SDN	NL	31.616	5	6.323	25	145	513	0.286
27	Loretta	Mark	2005	SDN	NL	31.607	3	10.536	32	186	506	0.314
28	Greene	Khalil	2008	SDN	NL	30.959	6	5.160	84	328	594	0.248
29	Roberts	Bip	1995	SDN	NL	30.152	7	4.307	20	169	673	0.298
30	Brown	Ollie	1972	SDN	NL	30.142	4	7.535	52	208	450	0.272
31	Vaughn	Greg	1998	SDN	NL	28.468	3	9.489	78	198	263	0.245
32	Sheffield	Gary	1993	SDN	NL	27.851	2	13.925	43	136	260	0.319
33	Clark	Jack	1990	SDN	NL	27.507	2	13.753	51	156	199	0.252
34	Kouzmanoff	Kevin	2009	SDN	NL	26.450	3	8.817	59	246	430	0.263
35	Kotsay	Mark	2013	SDN	NL	26.240	5	5.248	37	183	482	0.273
36	Alomar	Roberto	1990	SDN	NL	25.724	3	8.575	22	157	497	0.283
37	Jones	Ruppert	1983	SDN	NL	25.321	3	8.440	28	149	297	0.257
38	Salazar	Luis	1989	SDN	NL	25.041	7	3.577	40	226	598	0.267
39	Joyner	Wally	1999	SDN	NL	24.902	4	6.225	38	271	480	0.291
40	Lezcano	Sixto	1983	SDN	NL	24.659	2	12.329	24	133	210	0.267
41	Denorfia	Chris	2014	SDN	NL	24.133	5	4.827	33	154	456	0.275
42	Kendall	Fred	1980	SDN	NL	24.079	10	2.408	28	201	516	0.233
43	Kruk	John	1989	SDN	NL	23.333	4	5.833	36	179	331	0.281
44	Hoser	Eric	2020	SDN	NL	22.801	3	7.600	49	204	360	0.262
45	Cameron	Mike	2007	SDN	NL	22.248	2	11.124	43	161	286	0.255

RANK	NAME	FIRST	LYR	TEAM	LG	PEVA-B	YRS	PPYR	HR	RBI	H	AVE
46	Veras	Quilvio	1999	SDN	NL	22.169	3	7.390	15	131	414	0.270
47	Hendrick	George	1978	SDN	NL	21.376	2	10.688	26	89	195	0.299
48	Kemp	Matt	2016	SDN	NL	21.337	2	10.668	46	169	265	0.264
49	Solarte	Yangervis	2017	SDN	NL	20.612	4	5.153	51	215	435	0.270
50	Gomez	Chris	2001	SDN	NL	19.551	6	3.258	13	147	430	0.253

San Diego Padres - Top Career Pitchers

RANK	NAME	FIRST	LYEAR	LTEAM	LG	PEVA	YRS	PPYR	W	L	SV	IP	ERA
1	Hoffman	Trevor	2008	SDN	NL	151.267	16	9.454	54	64	552	952.3	2.76
2	Peavy	Jake	2009	SDN	NL	107.744	8	13.468	92	68	0	1342.7	3.29
3	Jones	Randy	1980	SDN	NL	88.355	8	11.044	92	105	2	1766.0	3.30
4	Benes	Andy	1995	SDN	NL	68.733	7	9.819	69	75	0	1235.0	3.57
5	Whitson	Ed	1991	SDN	NL	66.290	8	8.286	77	72	1	1354.3	3.69
6	Ashby	Andy	2004	SDN	NL	65.177	8	8.147	70	62	0	1212.0	3.59
7	Show	Eric	1990	SDN	NL	62.499	10	6.250	100	87	7	1603.3	3.59
8	Hurst	Bruce	1993	SDN	NL	55.228	5	11.046	55	38	0	911.7	3.27
9	Bell	Heath	2011	SDN	NL	46.978	5	9.396	27	19	134	374.0	2.53
10	Hamilton	Joey	1998	SDN	NL	43.336	5	8.667	55	44	0	934.7	3.83
11	Brown	Kevin	1998	SDN	NL	42.712	1	42.712	18	7	0	257.0	2.38
12	Richard	Clayton	2018	SDN	NL	38.746	8	4.843	58	68	0	1046.3	4.37
13	Lawrence	Brian	2005	SDN	NL	37.932	5	7.586	49	61	0	934.0	4.10
14	Dravecky	Dave	1987	SDN	NL	34.872	6	5.812	53	50	10	900.3	3.12
15	Lefferts	Craig	1992	SDN	NL	34.087	7	4.870	42	40	64	659.0	3.24
16	Williams	Woody	2006	SDN	NL	33.849	5	6.770	51	45	0	826.3	4.32
17	Hawkins	Andy	1988	SDN	NL	33.432	7	4.776	60	58	0	1102.7	3.84
18	Young	Chris	2010	SDN	NL	31.955	5	6.391	33	25	0	550.7	3.60
19	Ross	Tyson	2018	SDN	NL	31.098	5	6.220	32	44	0	645.3	3.40
20	Yates	Kirby	2020	SDN	NL	31.084	4	7.771	9	14	56	183.7	2.55
21	Harris	Greg	1993	SDN	NL	30.337	6	5.056	41	39	15	673.3	2.95
22	Fingers	Rollie	1980	SDN	NL	30.243	4	7.561	34	40	108	426.3	3.12
23	Perry	Gaylord	1979	SDN	NL	27.401	2	13.700	33	17	0	493.3	2.88
24	Davis	Mark	1994	SDN	NL	27.326	5	5.465	14	20	78	308.0	2.75
25	Gossage	Rich	1987	SDN	NL	25.608	4	6.402	25	20	83	298.0	2.99
26	Kirby	Clay	1973	SDN	NL	24.761	5	4.952	52	81	0	1128.0	3.73
27	Latos	Mat	2011	SDN	NL	24.715	3	8.238	27	29	0	429.7	3.37
28	Gregerson	Luke	2013	SDN	NL	24.633	5	4.927	17	22	16	347.0	2.88
29	Adams	Mike	2011	SDN	NL	24.463	4	6.116	9	5	1	217.0	1.66
30	Lamet	Dinelson	2020	SDN	NL	23.568	3	7.856	13	14	0	256.3	3.76
31	Linebrink	Scott	2007	SDN	NL	23.120	5	4.624	27	12	4	339.0	2.73
32	Eaton	Adam	2005	SDN	NL	22.479	6	3.747	47	41	0	796.0	4.34
33	Lollar	Tim	1984	SDN	NL	22.477	4	5.619	36	42	1	680.7	4.07
34	Hand	Brad	2018	SDN	NL	21.287	3	7.096	9	12	46	213.0	2.66
35	Lucas	Gary	1983	SDN	NL	20.950	4	5.237	18	33	49	428.3	2.90

RANK	NAME	FIRST	LYEAR	LTEAM	LG	PEVA	YRS	PPYR	W	L	SV	IP	ERA
36	Street	Huston	2014	SDN	NL	20.895	3	6.965	5	6	80	128.7	2.03
37	Rasmussen	Dennis	1991	SDN	NL	20.886	5	4.177	41	42	0	680.0	3.80
38	Stammen	Craig	2020	SDN	NL	20.845	4	5.211	22	15	4	265.3	3.29
39	Hitchcock	Sterling	2004	SDN	NL	20.667	6	3.445	34	42	1	649.0	4.47
40	Cashner	Andrew	2016	SDN	NL	19.955	5	3.991	28	43	0	608.7	3.67
41	Stauffer	Tim	2014	SDN	NL	19.621	9	2.180	32	34	0	575.0	3.87
42	DeLeon	Luis	1985	SDN	NL	19.283	4	4.821	17	16	31	294.3	3.06
43	Maddux	Greg	2008	SDN	NL	18.921	2	9.460	20	20	0	351.3	4.07
44	Davies	Zach	2020	SDN	NL	18.525	1	18.525	7	4	0	69.3	2.73
45	Roberts	Dave	1971	SDN	NL	18.413	3	6.138	22	34	2	500.0	2.99
46	Stults	Eric	2014	SDN	NL	18.007	3	6.002	27	33	0	472.0	3.87
47	Paddack	Chris	2020	SDN	NL	17.958	2	8.979	13	12	0	199.7	3.74
48	McCullers	Lance	1988	SDN	NL	17.955	4	4.489	21	28	36	392.0	2.96
49	Kennedy	Ian	2015	SDN	NL	17.358	3	5.786	26	30	0	426.7	3.97
50	Thurmond	Mark	1986	SDN	NL	16.907	4	4.227	31	29	2	503.0	3.67

San Diego Padres – Top Fielders

Rank	FIRST BASE		FV	Lyear	G	FPCT	RF
1	Garvey	Steve	1.2680	1987	589	0.997	8.75
2	Colbert	Nate	1.2496	1974	813	0.992	9.38
3	Myers	Wil	1.2397	2020	336	0.996	8.69
4	Hosmer	Eric	1.2001	2020	346	0.993	8.11
5	Gonzalez	Adrian	1.1591	2010	792	0.995	9.11
6	Joyner	Wally	1.1545	1999	482	0.996	8.56
7	McGriff	Fred	1.1120	1993	387	0.989	8.97
8	Alonso	Yonder	1.0664	2015	420	0.995	8.73
9	Ivie	Mike	1.0474	1977	329	0.993	7.92
10	Perkins	Broderick	1.0231	1982	285	0.993	8.49

Rank	SECOND BASE		FV	Lyear	G	FPCT	RF
1	Reed	Jody	1.4425	1996	275	0.990	4.91
2	Veras	Quilvio	1.3568	1999	391	0.984	4.99
3	Loretta	Mark	1.3363	2005	409	0.988	4.61
4	Fuentes	Tito	1.3275	1976	269	0.970	5.81
5	Alomar	Roberto	1.3225	1990	437	0.974	5.25
6	Bonilla	Juan	1.2659	1983	291	0.980	5.16
7	Campbell	Dave	1.2282	1973	250	0.973	5.19
8	Gyorko	Jedd	1.1112	2015	319	0.987	4.11
9	Thomas	Derrel	1.1100	1978	274	0.972	4.90
10	Flannery	Tim	1.0909	1989	544	0.982	4.29

Rank	SHORTSTOP		FV	Lyear	G	FPCT	RF
1	Smith	Ozzie	1.7310	1981	582	0.974	5.45
2	Fernandez	Tony	1.6406	1992	299	0.977	4.45
3	Templeton	Garry	1.5356	1991	1224	0.965	4.51
4	Gomez	Chris	1.5096	2001	510	0.970	4.06
5	Hernandez	Enzo	1.4699	1977	681	0.964	4.62
6	Greene	Khalil	1.3759	2008	648	0.976	4.12
7	Cabrera	Everth	1.3421	2014	461	0.967	4.18

Rank	THIRD BASE		FV	Lyear	G	FPCT	RF
1	Headley	Chase	1.5172	2018	691	0.965	2.37
2	Caminiti	Ken	1.4932	1998	547	0.941	2.70
3	Kouzmanoff	Kevin	1.4822	2009	429	0.966	2.36
4	Nettles	Graig	1.4300	1986	363	0.946	2.48
5	Salazar	Luis	1.3975	1989	551	0.951	2.66
6	Burroughs	Sean	1.3813	2005	388	0.959	2.47
7	Nevin	Phil	1.3700	2002	425	0.937	2.46
8	Spiezio	Ed	1.3676	1972	287	0.950	2.67

9	Roberts	Dave	**1.3301**	1977	330	0.941	2.70

Rank	CATCHER		FV	Lyear	G	FPCT	RF	CS%
1	Santiago	Benito	**1.8769**	1992	778	0.980	6.05	0.367
2	Ausmus	Brad	**1.8729**	1996	294	0.987	7.11	0.355
3	Kennedy	Terry	**1.8259**	1986	792	0.984	5.50	0.310
4	Tenace	Gene	**1.7760**	1980	368	0.986	4.96	0.386
5	Kendall	Fred	**1.7757**	1980	688	0.987	5.09	0.319
6	Hedges	Austin	**1.7439**	2020	375	0.989	8.78	0.325
7	Cannizzaro	Chris	**1.6911**	1974	287	0.984	5.48	0.362
8	Hundley	Nick	**1.6780**	**2014**	467	0.990	7.52	0.277

Rank	OUTFIELD		FV	Lyear	G	FPCT	RF	ApG
1	McReynolds	Kevin	**1.5443**	1986	485	0.988	2.69	0.072
2	Finley	Steve	**1.5207**	1998	595	0.982	2.35	0.062
3	Jackson	Darrin	**1.5049**	1992	314	0.990	2.63	0.073
4	Jones	Ruppert	**1.5029**	1983	329	0.986	2.65	0.046
5	Kotsay	Mark	**1.4934**	2013	438	0.989	2.37	0.071
6	Cameron	Mike	**1.4897**	2007	291	0.985	2.56	0.045
7	Plantier	Phil	**1.4862**	1997	267	0.985	1.95	0.090
8	Owens	Eric	**1.4784**	2000	310	0.996	1.69	0.032
9	Gwynn	Tony	**1.4768**	2001	2326	0.987	2.01	0.069
10	Winfield	Dave	**1.4718**	1980	1065	0.976	2.20	0.086
11	Margot	Manuel	**1.4699**	2019	404	0.991	2.10	0.025
12	Brown	Ollie	**1.4507**	1972	436	0.975	1.97	0.083
13	Grubb	Johnny	**1.4466**	1976	467	0.983	2.37	0.054
14	Maybin	Cameron	**1.4330**	2014	381	0.989	2.29	0.018
15	Gaston	Cito	**1.4166**	1974	664	0.971	2.05	0.090
16	Clark	Jerald	**1.4113**	1992	261	0.988	1.97	0.069
17	Richards	Gene	**1.3704**	1983	780	0.973	2.02	0.094
18	Kemp	Matt	**1.3703**	2016	246	0.978	1.84	0.073
19	Martinez	Carmelo	**1.3652**	1989	559	0.979	1.98	0.089
20	Rivera	Ruben	**1.3545**	2000	384	0.979	1.96	0.055
21	Denorfia	Chris	**1.3511**	2014	654	0.987	1.36	0.050
22	Giles	Brian	**1.3342**	2009	832	0.981	1.98	0.041
23	Venable	Will	**1.3306**	2015	908	0.988	1.71	0.020
24	Renfroe	Hunter	**1.3241**	2019	394	0.969	1.68	0.074
25	Wynne	Marvell	**1.3028**	1989	405	0.982	1.72	0.042
26	Henderson	Rickey	**1.2393**	2001	325	0.972	1.71	0.037
27	Hairston	Scott	**1.2286**	2010	277	0.985	1.68	0.036
28	Murrell	Ivan	**1.2134**	1973	283	0.968	1.90	0.053
29	Turner	Jerry	**1.1793**	1983	372	0.960	1.67	0.083

Rank	PITCHING		FV	Lyear	IP	FPCT	RF
1	Jones	Randy	**1.0756**	1980	1766	0.968	2.65
2	Hurst	Bruce	**1.0492**	1993	912	0.978	1.72
3	Ashby	Andy	**1.0488**	2004	1212	0.974	1.98
4	Lawrence	Brian	**1.0478**	2005	934	0.962	2.21
5	Roberts	Dave	**1.0461**	1971	500	0.981	1.89
6	Thurmond	Mark	**1.0365**	1986	503	0.992	2.31
7	Cashner	Andrew	**1.0327**	2016	608	0.980	2.13
8	Benes	Andy	**1.0239**	1995	1235	0.981	1.50
9	Stauffer	Tim	**1.0230**	2014	575	0.993	2.10
10	Shirley	Bob	**1.0106**	1980	722	0.971	2.12

Franchise When and Where
San Diego Padres (1969 to Present)

SEATTLE MARINERS
Best Seasons and Careers of All-Time

Okay, we're starting Edgar Martinez at Third Base, but realize he'd probably take the spot at Designated Hitter while Kyle Seager manned the bag. There's a lot of good choices at Third with Adrian Beltre also making the team. We just like Edgar better. One thing we know for certain, we'd bat Ichiro first; followed somewhere in the order by Ken Griffey, Jr. and Alex Rodriguez. Sabermetrics would likely dictate one of those bat second. The starting pitching is surprising strong for a more recent franchise. When you can trot out Felix Hernandez and Randy Johnson as your Top Two, that's pretty great. There's a good mix of relievers, too, with Sasaki and Putz. For now, Marco Gonzales takes a role in the pen. That's not likely to last long; he's probably bound for the starting five All-Time, as long as he remains a Mariner for a few more seasons.

Reserves

Bench - Raul Ibanez (OF), Nelson Cruz (OF), Adrian Beltre (3B), John Olerud (1B), Kyle Seager (3B), Bret Boone (2B), Dave Valle (CATCHER).

Bullpen - Kazahiro Sasaki (CL), J.J. Putz (SU), Hisashi Iwakuma, Erik Hanson, Edwin Diaz, Marco Gonzales.

Seattle Mariners - Best Position Player Years

Rank	Name	First	Year	Team	Lg	HR	RBI	AVG	Age	PEVA-B
1	Martinez	Edgar	1995	SEA	AL	29	113	0.356	32	34.622
2	Rodriguez	Alex	2000	SEA	AL	41	132	0.316	25	34.588
3	Griffey, Jr.	Ken	1997	SEA	AL	56	147	0.304	28	30.208
4	Rodriguez	Alex	1996	SEA	AL	36	123	0.358	21	29.207
5	Griffey, Jr.	Ken	1993	SEA	AL	45	109	0.309	24	28.976
6	Davis	Alvin	1984	SEA	AL	27	116	0.284	24	26.893
7	Martinez	Edgar	2000	SEA	AL	37	145	0.324	37	26.156
8	Griffey, Jr.	Ken	1994	SEA	AL	40	90	0.323	25	24.873
9	Griffey, Jr.	Ken	1991	SEA	AL	22	100	0.327	22	24.792
10	Martinez	Edgar	1997	SEA	AL	28	108	0.330	34	23.979
11	Griffey, Jr.	Ken	1996	SEA	AL	49	140	0.303	27	23.477
12	Martinez	Edgar	1996	SEA	AL	26	103	0.327	33	22.840
13	Griffey, Jr.	Ken	1998	SEA	AL	56	146	0.284	29	22.701
14	Cano	Robinson	2016	SEA	AL	39	103	0.298	34	22.255
15	Cano	Robinson	2014	SEA	AL	14	82	0.314	32	20.710
16	Rodriguez	Alex	1998	SEA	AL	42	124	0.310	23	20.656
17	Seager	Kyle	2016	SEA	AL	30	99	0.278	29	20.517
18	Cruz	Nelson	2016	SEA	AL	43	105	0.287	36	20.393
19	Griffey, Jr.	Ken	1999	SEA	AL	48	134	0.285	30	20.133
20	Cruz	Nelson	2015	SEA	AL	43	93	0.302	35	20.099

Seattle Mariners - Best Pitcher Years

Rank	Name	First	Year	Team	Lg	W	L	SV	IP	ERA	Age	PEVA-P
1	Johnson	Randy	1995	SEA	AL	18	2	0	214.3	2.48	32	34.064
2	Hernandez	Felix	2009	SEA	AL	19	5	0	238.7	2.49	23	33.947
3	Hernandez	Felix	2014	SEA	AL	15	6	0	236.0	2.14	28	30.118
4	Hernandez	Felix	2010	SEA	AL	13	12	0	249.7	2.27	24	28.650
5	Johnson	Randy	1993	SEA	AL	19	8	1	255.3	3.24	30	26.278
6	Johnson	Randy	1997	SEA	AL	20	4	0	213.0	2.28	34	25.435
7	Garcia	Freddy	2001	SEA	AL	18	6	0	238.7	3.05	26	25.267
8	Moyer	Jamie	2001	SEA	AL	20	6	0	209.7	3.43	39	20.937
9	Diaz	Edwin	2018	SEA	AL	0	4	57	73.3	1.96	24	20.848
10	Iwakuma	Hisashi	2013	SEA	AL	14	6	0	219.7	2.66	32	20.843
11	Gonzales	Marco	2020	SEA	AL	7	2	0	69.7	3.10	28	20.509
12	Putz	J.J.	2006	SEA	AL	4	1	36	78.3	2.30	29	19.452
13	Hernandez	Felix	2012	SEA	AL	13	9	0	232.0	3.06	26	19.376
14	Moyer	Jamie	2003	SEA	AL	21	7	0	215.0	3.27	41	18.423
15	Hanson	Erik	1990	SEA	AL	18	9	0	236.0	3.24	25	18.227
16	Putz	J.J.	2007	SEA	AL	6	1	40	71.7	1.38	30	17.859
17	Langston	Mark	1987	SEA	AL	19	13	0	272.0	3.84	27	17.850
18	Gonzales	Marco	2019	SEA	AL	16	13	0	203.0	3.99	27	17.699
19	Moyer	Jamie	1998	SEA	AL	15	9	0	234.3	3.53	36	17.212
20	Fassero	Jeff	1997	SEA	AL	16	9	0	234.3	3.61	34	16.405

Seattle Mariners - Top Career Batters

RANK	NAME	FIRST	LYR	TEAM	LG	PEVA-B	YRS	PPYR	HR	RBI	H	AVE
1	Martinez	Edgar	2004	SEA	AL	225.436	18	12.524	309	1261	2247	0.312
2	Griffey	Ken	2010	SEA	AL	224.565	13	17.274	417	1216	1843	0.292

RANK	NAME	FIRST	LYR	TEAM	LG	PEVA-B	YRS	PPYR	HR	RBI	H	AVE
3	Suzuki	Ichiro	2019	SEA	AL	164.602	14	11.757	99	633	2542	0.321
4	Seager	Kyle	2020	SEA	AL	122.852	10	12.285	207	706	1267	0.256
5	Buhner	Jay	2001	SEA	AL	116.173	14	8.298	307	951	1255	0.255
6	Rodriguez	Alex	2000	SEA	AL	109.585	7	15.655	189	595	966	0.309
7	Davis	Alvin	1991	SEA	AL	104.099	8	13.012	160	667	1163	0.281
8	Cruz	Nelson	2018	SEA	AL	72.838	4	18.210	163	414	640	0.284
9	Ibanez	Raul	2013	SEA	AL	71.329	11	6.484	156	612	1077	0.279
10	Cano	Robinson	2018	SEA	AL	69.250	5	13.850	107	411	821	0.296
11	Boone	Bret	2005	SEA	AL	60.059	7	8.580	143	535	863	0.277
12	Wilson	Dan	2005	SEA	AL	54.699	12	4.558	88	508	1071	0.262
13	Bradley	Phil	1987	SEA	AL	53.524	5	10.705	52	234	649	0.301
14	Olerud	John	2004	SEA	AL	53.523	5	10.705	72	405	709	0.285
15	Reynolds	Harold	1992	SEA	AL	51.115	10	5.111	17	295	1063	0.260
16	Presley	Jim	1989	SEA	AL	49.017	6	8.170	115	418	736	0.250
17	Beltre	Adrian	2009	SEA	AL	48.640	5	9.728	103	396	751	0.266
18	Cameron	Mike	2003	SEA	AL	46.313	4	11.578	87	344	554	0.256
19	Bochte	Bruce	1982	SEA	AL	45.799	5	9.160	58	329	697	0.290
20	Lopez	Jose	2010	SEA	AL	39.252	7	5.607	80	431	897	0.266
21	Sexson	Richie	2008	SEA	AL	34.758	4	8.690	105	321	447	0.244
22	Winn	Randy	2005	SEA	AL	34.029	3	11.343	31	193	462	0.287
23	Valle	Dave	1993	SEA	AL	33.708	10	3.371	72	318	588	0.235
24	Jones	Ruppert	1979	SEA	AL	32.630	3	10.877	51	200	434	0.257
25	Phelps	Ken	1988	SEA	AL	32.115	6	5.352	105	255	349	0.249
26	Henderson	Dave	1986	SEA	AL	30.239	6	5.040	79	271	545	0.257
27	Martinez	Tino	1995	SEA	AL	29.911	6	4.985	88	312	502	0.265
28	Cruz	Julio	1983	SEA	AL	29.661	7	4.237	17	162	649	0.243
29	Cowens	Al	1986	SEA	AL	28.819	5	5.764	56	266	504	0.255
30	Paciorek	Tom	1981	SEA	AL	27.526	4	6.882	39	197	410	0.296
31	Meyer	Dan	1981	SEA	AL	27.347	5	5.469	64	313	618	0.265
32	Zunino	Mike	2018	SEA	AL	27.322	6	4.554	95	241	391	0.207
33	Haniger	Mitch	2019	SEA	AL	25.857	3	8.619	57	172	328	0.271
34	Roberts	Leon	1980	SEA	AL	24.521	3	8.174	47	179	358	0.276
35	Cora	Joey	1998	SEA	AL	23.956	4	5.989	26	164	600	0.293
36	Gutierrez	Franklin	2013	SEA	AL	23.749	5	4.750	45	194	446	0.255
37	Betancourt	Yuniesky	2009	SEA	AL	23.443	5	4.689	27	202	582	0.279
38	Ackley	Dustin	2015	SEA	AL	22.809	5	4.562	42	201	488	0.243
39	Johjima	Kenji	2009	SEA	AL	22.539	4	5.635	48	198	431	0.268
40	Saunders	Michael	2014	SEA	AL	21.617	6	3.603	51	182	396	0.231
41	Vizquel	Omar	1993	SEA	AL	21.511	5	4.302	6	131	531	0.252
42	Blowers	Mike	1999	SEA	AL	19.730	6	3.288	55	231	366	0.270
43	Bell	David	2001	SEA	AL	18.898	4	4.725	47	197	420	0.262
44	McLemore	Mark	2003	SEA	AL	18.124	4	4.531	17	181	398	0.259
45	Owen	Spike	1986	SEA	AL	18.108	4	4.527	11	136	380	0.239

RANK	NAME	FIRST	LYR	TEAM	LG	PEVA-B	YRS	PPYR	HR	RBI	H	AVE
46	Guillen	Carlos	2003	SEA	AL	18.078	6	3.013	29	211	439	0.264
47	Zisk	Richie	1983	SEA	AL	16.817	3	5.606	49	141	327	0.286
48	Segura	Jean	2018	SEA	AL	16.705	2	8.353	21	108	335	0.302
49	Davis	Russ	1999	SEA	AL	16.166	4	4.041	66	222	389	0.256
50	Cotto	Henry	1993	SEA	AL	15.098	6	2.516	34	156	420	0.261

Seattle Mariners - Top Career Pitchers

RANK	NAME	FIRST	LYEAR	LTEAM	LG	PEVA	YRS	PPYR	W	L	SV	IP	ERA
1	Hernandez	Felix	2019	SEA	AL	197.663	15	13.178	169	136	0	2729.7	3.42
2	Johnson	Randy	1998	SEA	AL	145.762	10	14.576	130	74	2	1838.3	3.42
3	Moyer	Jamie	2006	SEA	AL	125.477	11	11.407	145	87	0	2093.0	3.97
4	Garcia	Freddy	2004	SEA	AL	63.854	6	10.642	76	50	0	1096.3	3.89
5	Langston	Mark	1989	SEA	AL	59.270	6	9.878	74	67	0	1197.7	4.01
6	Iwakuma	Hisashi	2017	SEA	AL	50.931	6	8.489	63	39	2	883.7	3.42
7	Gonzales	Marco	2020	SEA	AL	46.777	4	11.694	37	25	0	476.0	3.97
8	Hanson	Erik	1993	SEA	AL	42.617	6	7.103	56	54	0	967.3	3.69
9	Putz	J.J.	2008	SEA	AL	42.423	6	7.071	22	15	101	323.0	3.07
10	Moore	Mike	1988	SEA	AL	40.810	7	5.830	66	96	2	1457.0	4.38
11	Pineiro	Joel	2006	SEA	AL	38.578	7	5.511	58	55	1	996.0	4.48
12	Diaz	Edwin	2018	SEA	AL	33.266	3	11.089	4	14	109	191.0	2.64
13	Rhodes	Arthur	2008	SEA	AL	30.835	5	6.167	28	16	9	283.0	3.05
14	Paxton	James	2018	SEA	AL	30.290	6	5.048	41	26	0	582.3	3.42
15	Fassero	Jeff	1999	SEA	AL	29.545	3	9.848	33	35	0	598.0	4.62
16	Sasaki	Kazuhiro	2003	SEA	AL	28.187	4	7.047	7	16	129	223.3	3.14
17	Sele	Aaron	2005	SEA	AL	28.057	3	9.352	38	27	0	542.7	4.39
18	Young	Matt	1990	SEA	AL	27.166	5	5.433	45	66	14	864.3	4.13
19	Bannister	Floyd	1982	SEA	AL	26.981	4	6.745	40	50	0	768.3	3.75
20	Swift	Bill	1998	SEA	AL	26.796	7	3.828	41	49	24	903.7	4.33
21	Beattie	Jim	1986	SEA	AL	26.725	7	3.818	43	72	1	944.7	4.14
22	Vargas	Jason	2012	SEA	AL	26.548	4	6.637	36	42	0	702.7	4.09
23	Franklin	Ryan	2005	SEA	AL	25.105	6	4.184	35	50	0	811.3	4.34
24	Meche	Gil	2006	SEA	AL	24.657	6	4.110	55	44	0	815.3	4.65
25	Washburn	Jarrod	2009	SEA	AL	23.589	4	5.897	31	49	1	667.3	4.17
26	Fleming	Dave	1995	SEA	AL	22.878	5	4.576	38	31	0	578.3	4.73
27	Nelson	Jeff	2005	SEA	AL	22.820	8	2.853	24	23	23	447.3	3.26
28	Schooler	Mike	1992	SEA	AL	21.193	5	4.239	12	29	98	267.3	3.30
29	Wilhelmsen	Tom	2016	SEA	AL	21.082	6	3.514	11	11	68	337.3	3.01
30	Bankhead	Scott	1991	SEA	AL	20.392	5	4.078	33	31	0	568.3	4.16
31	Jackson	Mike	1996	SEA	AL	18.312	5	3.662	23	26	34	436.7	3.38
32	Fister	Doug	2011	SEA	AL	18.004	3	6.001	12	30	0	378.0	3.81
33	Bosio	Chris	1996	SEA	AL	17.970	4	4.493	27	31	1	520.0	4.43
34	Abbott	Glenn	1983	SEA	AL	17.889	6	2.981	44	62	0	904.0	4.54
35	Leake	Mike	2019	SEA	AL	17.681	3	5.894	22	19	0	354.7	4.16

RANK	NAME	FIRST	LYEAR	LTEAM	LG	PEVA	YRS	PPYR	W	L	SV	IP	ERA
36	Charlton	Norm	2001	SEA	AL	**17.350**	5	3.470	14	21	67	275.0	4.03
37	Abbott	Paul	2002	SEA	AL	**17.007**	5	3.401	36	17	0	465.7	4.48
38	Holman	Brian	1991	SEA	AL	**17.001**	3	5.667	32	35	0	544.7	3.73
39	League	Brandon	2012	SEA	AL	**16.014**	3	5.338	10	17	52	185.0	3.26
40	Walker	Tijuan	2020	SEA	AL	**15.822**	5	3.164	24	24	0	384.0	4.17
41	Halama	John	2002	SEA	AL	**15.695**	4	3.924	41	31	0	557.0	4.46
42	Ayala	Bobby	1998	SEA	AL	**15.488**	5	3.098	27	26	56	367.0	4.88
43	Caudill	Bill	1983	SEA	AL	**15.466**	2	7.733	14	17	52	168.3	3.37
44	Batista	Miguel	2009	SEA	AL	**14.592**	3	4.864	27	29	2	379.3	4.84
45	Hasegawa	Shigetoshi	2005	SEA	AL	**13.966**	4	3.491	15	16	17	278.0	3.46
46	Elias	Roenis	2019	SEA	AL	**13.491**	4	3.373	22	23	14	377.0	3.75
47	Vande Berg	Ed	1985	SEA	AL	**13.306**	4	3.326	21	21	20	338.3	3.75
48	Aardsma	David	2010	SEA	AL	**13.267**	2	6.633	3	12	69	121.0	2.90
49	Soriano	Rafael	2006	SEA	AL	**12.807**	5	2.561	4	8	4	171.0	2.89
50	Mateo	Julio	2007	SEA	AL	**12.206**	6	2.034	18	12	2	318.3	3.68

Seattle Mariners – Top Fielders

Rank	FIRST BASE		FV	Lyear	G	FPCT	RF
1	Olerud	John	**1.2391**	2004	697	0.996	8.36
2	Bochte	Bruce	**1.1974**	1982	397	0.994	9.91
3	Davis	Alvin	**1.1915**	1991	865	0.992	9.45
4	Meyer	Dan	**1.1602**	1981	302	0.991	9.34
5	Sexson	Richie	**1.1429**	2008	490	0.997	8.77
6	Martinez	Tino	**1.1192**	1995	454	0.995	8.95
7	O'Brien	Pete	**1.1190**	1993	319	0.996	8.84
8	Sorrento	Paul	**1.0602**	1997	277	0.993	7.41
9	Smoak	Justin	**1.0535**	2014	468	0.995	8.69

Rank	SECOND BASE		FV	Lyear	G	FPCT	RF
1	Cruz	Julio	**1.3711**	1983	720	0.984	5.38
2	Cano	Robinson	**1.3430**	2018	675	0.990	4.40
3	Reynolds	Harold	**1.3088**	1992	1133	0.978	5.06
4	Perconte	Jack	**1.2864**	1985	275	0.983	4.97
5	Boone	Bret	**1.2577**	2005	795	0.985	4.36
6	Lopez	Jose	**1.2218**	2009	627	0.981	4.78
7	Ackley	Dustin	**1.1541**	2015	282	0.990	4.39
8	Cora	Joey	**1.1473**	1998	524	0.968	4.15

Rank	SHORTSTOP		FV	Lyear	G	FPCT	RF
1	Vizquel	Omar	**1.6189**	1993	653	0.980	4.49
2	Owen	Spike	**1.6102**	1986	460	0.974	4.78
3	Rodriguez	Alex	**1.5632**	2000	786	0.973	4.40
4	Reynolds	Craig	**1.5321**	1978	280	0.958	4.64
5	Ryan	Brendan	**1.5120**	2013	345	0.977	4.30
6	Betancourt	Yuniesky	**1.4562**	2009	577	0.969	4.28
7	Mendoza	Mario	**1.4491**	1980	262	0.964	3.96
8	Quinones	Rey	**1.4426**	1989	313	0.958	4.36
9	Segura	Jean	**1.3313**	2018	268	0.966	3.59
10	Guillen	Carlos	**1.2563**	2003	369	0.969	3.72

Rank	THIRD BASE		FV	Lyear	G	FPCT	RF
1	Seager	Kyle	**1.5985**	2020	1278	0.966	2.73
2	Beltre	Adrian	**1.5756**	2009	707	0.963	2.80
3	Presley	Jim	**1.5084**	1989	762	0.952	2.59
4	Martinez	Edgar	**1.4255**	2004	563	0.946	2.42
5	Stein	Bill	**1.4057**	1980	359	0.953	2.75
6	Blowers	Mike	**1.3722**	1999	334	0.949	2.22
7	Davis	Russ	**1.3329**	1999	429	0.933	2.24

Rank	CATCHER		FV	Lyear	G	FPCT	RF	CS%
1	Kearney	Bob	1.9231	1987	344	0.990	5.91	0.422
2	Wilson	Dan	1.9126	2005	1237	0.995	6.77	0.347
3	Valle	Dave	1.9084	1993	798	0.992	6.00	0.369
4	Johjima	Kenji	1.9052	2009	447	0.994	6.52	0.400
5	Zunino	Mike	1.8290	2018	575	0.995	8.03	0.283
6	Bradley	Scott	1.6820	1992	425	0.991	5.68	0.241
7	Olivo	Miguel	1.6526	2012	303	0.990	6.75	0.303
8	Stinson	Bob	1.6414	1980	358	0.983	4.52	0.265

Rank	OUTFIELD		FV	Lyear	G	FPCT	RF	ApG
1	Jones	Ruppert	1.6350	1979	444	0.985	3.03	0.077
2	Winn	Randy	1.6128	2005	429	0.993	2.41	0.026
3	Cameron	Mike	1.5692	2003	608	0.988	2.85	0.039
4	Gutierrez	Franklin	1.5614	2013	467	0.993	2.76	0.034
5	Suzuki	Ichiro	1.5548	2019	1818	0.992	2.29	0.054
6	Griffey	Ken	1.5487	2009	1499	0.986	2.51	0.072
7	Henderson	Dave	1.5023	1986	607	0.985	2.43	0.099
8	Bradley	Phil	1.4867	1987	595	0.988	1.96	0.064
9	Buhner	Jay	1.4439	2001	1368	0.988	1.87	0.072
10	Reed	Jeremy	1.4393	2008	300	0.989	2.45	0.040
11	Roberts	Leon	1.4172	1980	368	0.980	2.29	0.060
12	Saunders	Michael	1.4100	2014	545	0.991	2.10	0.039
13	Heredia	Felix	1.4073	2018	299	0.995	1.90	0.040
14	Cowens	Al	1.4067	1986	474	0.982	1.90	0.086
15	Brantley	Mickey	1.3904	1989	277	0.984	2.19	0.043
16	Paciorek	Tom	1.3690	1981	292	0.985	2.08	0.062
17	Cotto	Henry	1.3637	1993	510	0.991	1.87	0.045
18	Haniger	Mitch	1.3559	2019	350	0.979	2.10	0.051
19	Ibanez	Raul	1.3402	2013	879	0.984	1.79	0.063
20	Simpson	Joe	1.3401	1982	409	0.977	1.94	0.078
21	Moses	John	1.3357	1992	349	0.986	1.83	0.074
22	Amaral	Rich	1.3298	1998	296	0.995	1.48	0.041
23	Briley	Greg	1.2416	1992	390	0.974	1.61	0.038
24	Gamel	Ben	1.1865	2018	254	0.981	1.61	0.043

Rank	PITCHING		FV	Lyear	IP	FPCT	RF	
1	Moyer	Jamie	1.0797	2006	2093	0.981	2.03	
2	Moore	Mike	1.0495	1988	1457	0.941	2.19	
3	Garcia	Freddy	1.0389	2004	1096	0.961	2.02	
4	Iwakuma	Hisashi	1.0382	2017	884	0.981	1.60	
5	Fassero	Jeff	1.0340	1999	598	0.976	1.84	
6	Hernandez	Felix	1.0267	2019	2730	0.964	1.68	
7	Beattie	Jim	1.0160	1986	945	0.977	2.07	
8	Pineiro	Joel	1.0033	2006	996	0.976	1.83	
9	Fleming	Dave	1.0000	1995	578	0.983	1.81	
10	Langston	Mark	0.9991	1989	1198	0.935	1.74	

Franchise When and Where
Seattle Mariners (1977 to Present)

SAN FRANCISCO GIANTS
Best Seasons and Careers of All-Time

Willie Mays and Barry Bonds. It's hard to go wrong when you start with those two. Carl Hubbell and Christy Mathewson. It's hard to go wrong when you start with those two, either. Add in Mel Ott as your number three, and Willlie McCovery as your four, and probably cleanup at the plate, with Juan Marichal as your number three in the rotation, and you might just have the start of something big. While others may disagree with this, we just might think that the All-Time team for the Giants, New York and San Francisco style, might be the second best All-Time team behind the Yankees. There's pop off the bench. Clutch at the back end of the starting rotation. Can we say not mentioned enough Amos Rusie and World Series hero Madison Bumgarner? There's even some interesting names in the bullpen.

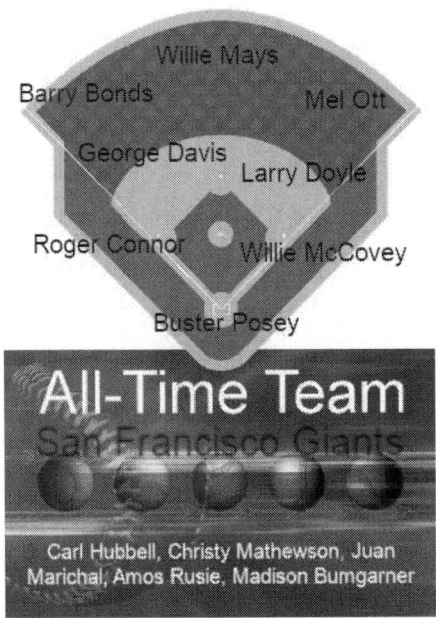

Reserves

Bench - Mike Tiernan (OF), George Burns (OF), Travis Jackson (SS/3B), Bill Terry (1B), Will Clark (1B), Orlando Cepeda (1B), Buck Ewing (CATCHER).

Bullpen - Robb Nen (CL), Joe McGinnity (SU), Matt Cain, Gaylord Perry, Tim Lincecum, Larry Jansen.

San Francisco Giants - Best Position Player Years

Rank	Name	First	Year	Team	Lg	HR	RBI	AVG	Age	PEVA-B
1	Bonds	Barry	2001	SFN	NL	73	137	0.328	37	55.207
2	Bonds	Barry	2002	SFN	NL	46	110	0.370	38	54.848
3	Bonds	Barry	2004	SFN	NL	45	101	0.362	40	48.632
4	Bonds	Barry	1993	SFN	NL	46	123	0.336	29	43.404
5	Mays	Willie	1965	SFN	NL	52	112	0.317	34	43.109
6	Mays	Willie	1962	SFN	NL	49	141	0.304	31	40.947
7	Posey	Buster	2012	SFN	NL	24	103	0.336	25	39.507
8	Mays	Willie	1955	NY1	NL	51	127	0.319	24	39.404
9	Mays	Willie	1960	SFN	NL	29	103	0.319	29	38.898
10	McCovey	Willie	1969	SFN	NL	45	126	0.320	31	36.924
11	Mays	Willie	1958	SFN	NL	29	96	0.347	27	36.606
12	Ott	Mel	1929	NY1	NL	42	151	0.328	20	36.437
13	Mays	Willie	1964	SFN	NL	47	111	0.296	33	36.258
14	Mays	Willie	1963	SFN	NL	38	103	0.314	32	34.477
15	Mays	Willie	1954	NY1	NL	41	110	0.345	23	33.994
16	Bonds	Barry	1996	SFN	NL	42	129	0.308	32	33.905
17	Connor	Roger	1885	NY1	NL	1	65	0.371	28	33.375
18	Mitchell	Kevin	1989	SFN	NL	47	125	0.291	27	33.233
19	McCovey	Willie	1970	SFN	NL	39	126	0.289	32	32.785
20	Bonds	Barry	2000	SFN	NL	49	106	0.306	36	32.041

San Francisco Giants - Best Pitcher Years

Rank	Name	First	Year	Team	Lg	W	L	SV	IP	ERA	Age	PEVA-P
1	Rusie	Amos	1894	NY1	NL	36	13	1	444.0	2.78	23	55.357
2	Hubbell	Carl	1933	NY1	NL	23	12	5	308.7	1.66	30	52.001
3	Hubbell	Carl	1936	NY1	NL	26	6	3	304.0	2.31	33	48.808
4	Hubbell	Carl	1934	NY1	NL	21	12	8	313.0	2.30	31	43.860
5	Marichal	Juan	1969	SFN	NL	21	11	0	299.7	2.10	32	42.465
6	Rusie	Amos	1893	NY1	NL	33	21	1	482.0	3.23	22	37.905
7	Lincecum	Tim	2009	SFN	NL	15	7	0	225.3	2.48	25	37.546
8	Maglie	Sal	1951	NY1	NL	23	6	4	298.0	2.93	34	35.603
9	Lincecum	Tim	2008	SFN	NL	18	5	0	227.0	2.62	24	34.883
10	Mathewson	Christy	1909	NY1	NL	25	6	2	275.3	1.14	29	34.761
11	McGinnity	Joe	1904	NY1	NL	35	8	5	408.0	1.61	33	33.860
12	Marichal	Juan	1966	SFN	NL	25	6	0	307.3	2.23	29	33.441
13	Melton	Cliff	1937	NY1	NL	20	9	7	248.0	2.61	25	32.906
14	Mathewson	Christy	1905	NY1	NL	31	9	2	338.7	1.28	25	32.837
15	Marichal	Juan	1965	SFN	NL	22	13	1	295.3	2.13	28	32.690
16	Meekin	Jouett	1894	NY1	NL	33	9	2	409.0	3.70	27	32.597
17	Mathewson	Christy	1911	NY1	NL	26	13	3	307.0	1.99	31	32.300
18	Mathewson	Christy	1908	NY1	NL	37	11	5	390.7	1.43	28	32.234
19	Jansen	Larry	1951	NY1	NL	23	11	0	278.7	3.04	31	32.060
20	Rusie	Amos	1897	NY1	NL	28	10	0	322.3	2.54	26	31.574

San Francisco Giants (NY1, SFN) - Top Career Batters

RANK	NAME	FIRST	LYR	TEAM	LG	PEVA-B	YRS	PPYR	HR	RBI	H	AVE
1	Mays	Willie	1972	SFN	NL	516.157	21	24.579	646	1859	3187	0.304
2	Bonds	Barry	2007	SFN	NL	458.361	15	30.557	586	1440	1951	0.312
3	Ott	Mel	1947	NY1	NL	369.518	22	16.796	511	1860	2876	0.304

RANK	NAME	FIRST	LYR	TEAM	LG	PEVA-B	YRS	PPYR	HR	RBI	H	AVE
4	McCovey	Willie	1980	SFN	NL	241.730	19	12.723	469	1388	1974	0.274
5	Connor	Roger	1894	NY1	NL	204.857	10	20.486	76	786	1388	0.319
6	Tiernan	Mike	1899	NY1	NL	180.026	13	13.848	106	851	1834	0.311
7	Terry	Bill	1936	NY1	NL	157.226	14	11.230	154	1078	2193	0.341
8	Posey	Buster	2019	SFN	NL	149.896	11	13.627	140	673	1380	0.302
9	Burns	George	1921	NY1	NL	143.471	11	13.043	34	458	1541	0.290
10	Davis	George	1903	NY1	NL	136.080	10	13.608	53	816	1427	0.332
11	Clark	Will	1993	SFN	NL	135.831	8	16.979	176	709	1278	0.299
12	Van Haltren	George	1903	NY1	NL	132.330	10	13.233	29	604	1575	0.321
13	Cepeda	Orlando	1966	SFN	NL	128.383	9	14.265	226	767	1286	0.308
14	Bonds	Bobby	1974	SFN	NL	123.893	7	17.699	186	552	1106	0.273
15	Doyle	Larry	1920	NY1	NL	123.810	13	9.524	67	725	1751	0.292
16	Youngs	Ross	1926	NY1	NL	110.998	10	11.100	42	592	1491	0.322
17	Clark	Jack	1984	SFN	NL	105.185	10	10.518	163	595	1034	0.277
18	Williams	Matt	1996	SFN	NL	104.459	10	10.446	247	732	1092	0.264
19	Thomson	Bobby	1957	NY1	NL	102.946	9	11.438	189	704	1171	0.277
20	Jackson	Travis	1936	NY1	NL	98.655	15	6.577	135	929	1768	0.291
21	Ewing	Buck	1892	NY1	NL	98.270	9	10.919	47	459	905	0.306
22	Devlin	Art	1911	NY1	NL	96.646	8	12.081	10	439	1011	0.268
23	Kent	Jeff	2002	SFN	NL	96.260	6	16.043	175	689	1021	0.297
24	Fletcher	Art	1920	NY1	NL	90.940	12	7.578	21	584	1311	0.275
25	Hart	Jim Ray	1973	SFN	NL	85.908	11	7.810	157	526	965	0.282
26	Bresnahan	Roger	1908	NY1	NL	85.385	7	12.198	15	291	731	0.293
27	Evans	Darrell	1983	SFN	NL	84.293	8	10.537	142	525	952	0.255
28	Lockman	Whitey	1958	SFN	NL	80.590	13	6.199	113	543	1571	0.281
29	Dark	Alvin	1956	NY1	NL	80.563	7	11.509	98	429	1106	0.292
30	Mize	Johnny	1949	NY1	NL	79.250	5	15.850	157	505	733	0.299
31	Lindstrom	Freddie	1932	NY1	NL	78.503	9	8.723	91	603	1347	0.318
32	Kelly	George	1926	NY1	NL	76.811	11	6.983	123	762	1270	0.301
33	Ward	John	1894	NY1	NL	76.733	9	8.526	17	546	1245	0.279
34	Crawford	Brandon	2020	SFN	NL	75.666	10	7.567	106	564	1099	0.250
35	O'Rourke	Jim	1904	NY1	NL	75.021	8	9.378	21	446	966	0.299
36	Sandoval	Pablo	2020	SFN	NL	73.697	11	6.700	135	569	1130	0.285
37	Belt	Brandon	2020	SFN	NL	73.216	10	7.322	138	502	1003	0.263
38	Mitchell	Kevin	1991	SFN	NL	73.149	5	14.630	143	411	614	0.278
39	Moore	Jo-Jo	1941	NY1	NL	72.692	12	6.058	79	513	1615	0.298
40	Meyers	Chief	1915	NY1	NL	67.629	7	9.661	14	335	722	0.301
41	Frisch	Frankie	1926	NY1	NL	67.281	8	8.410	54	524	1303	0.321
42	Davis	Chili	1987	SFN	NL	64.973	7	9.282	101	418	840	0.267
43	Snow	J.T.	2008	SFN	NL	63.470	10	6.347	124	615	1043	0.273
44	Thompson	Robby	1996	SFN	NL	62.919	11	5.720	119	458	1187	0.257
45	Aurilia	Rich	2009	SFN	NL	62.425	12	5.202	143	574	1226	0.275
46	Thompson	Hank	1956	NY1	NL	62.421	8	7.803	129	477	781	0.267

RANK	NAME	FIRST	LYR	TEAM	LG	PEVA-B	YRS	PPYR	HR	RBI	H	AVE
47	Speier	Chris	1989	SFN	NL	61.331	10	6.133	70	409	924	0.248
48	Donlin	Mike	1914	NY1	NL	59.398	6	9.900	18	218	498	0.333
49	Merkle	Fred	1916	NY1	NL	59.370	10	5.937	49	508	1042	0.272
50	Kauff	Benny	1920	NY1	NL	58.686	5	11.737	29	274	582	0.287

San Francisco Giants (NY1, SFN) - Top Career Pitchers

RANK	NAME	FIRST	LYEAR	LTEAM	LG	PEVA	YRS	PPYR	W	L	SV	IP	ERA
1	Hubbell	Carl	1943	NY1	NL	301.955	16	18.872	253	154	33	3590.3	2.98
2	Mathewson	Christy	1916	NY1	NL	290.825	17	17.107	372	188	28	4771.7	2.12
3	Marichal	Juan	1973	SFN	NL	230.597	14	16.471	238	140	2	3444.0	2.84
4	Rusie	Amos	1898	NY1	NL	207.458	8	25.932	233	163	5	3522.7	2.89
5	Bumgarner	Madison	2019	SFN	NL	138.047	11	12.550	119	92	0	1846.0	3.13
6	Lincecum	Tim	2015	SFN	NL	128.900	9	14.322	108	83	1	1643.7	3.61
7	Cain	Matt	2017	SFN	NL	128.865	13	9.913	104	118	0	2085.7	3.68
8	Perry	Gaylord	1971	SFN	NL	120.599	10	12.060	134	109	10	2294.7	2.96
9	Jansen	Larry	1954	NY1	NL	118.311	8	14.789	120	86	9	1731.0	3.55
10	Schumacher	Hal	1946	NY1	NL	113.603	13	8.739	158	121	7	2482.3	3.36
11	Fitzsimmons	Freddie	1937	NY1	NL	105.185	13	8.091	170	114	9	2514.3	3.54
12	Antonelli	Johnny	1960	SFN	NL	104.345	7	14.906	108	84	19	1600.7	3.13
13	Keefe	Tim	1891	NY1	NL	101.563	6	16.927	174	82	1	2265.0	2.53
14	McGinnity	Joe	1908	NY1	NL	97.683	7	13.955	151	88	21	2151.3	2.38
15	Welch	Mickey	1892	NY1	NL	89.061	10	8.906	238	146	4	3579.0	2.69
16	Schmidt	Jason	2006	SFN	NL	86.771	6	14.462	78	37	0	1069.7	3.36
17	Maglie	Sal	1955	NY1	NL	78.428	7	11.204	95	42	8	1297.7	3.13
18	McCormick	Mike	1970	SFN	NL	72.810	11	6.619	107	96	11	1822.7	3.68
19	Rueter	Kirk	2005	SFN	NL	71.357	10	7.136	105	80	0	1614.0	4.32
20	Melton	Cliff	1944	NY1	NL	69.463	8	8.683	86	80	16	1453.7	3.42
21	Nen	Robb	2002	SFN	NL	64.914	5	12.983	24	25	206	378.3	2.43
22	Meekin	Jouett	1899	NY1	NL	64.830	6	10.805	116	74	2	1741.0	4.01
23	Tesreau	Jeff	1918	NY1	NL	59.461	7	8.494	115	72	9	1679.0	2.43
24	Lavelle	Gary	1984	SFN	NL	58.997	11	5.363	73	67	127	980.3	2.82
25	Barr	Jim	1983	SFN	NL	58.938	10	5.894	90	96	11	1800.3	3.41
26	Barnes	Jesse	1923	NY1	NL	56.784	6	9.464	82	43	8	1150.3	2.92
27	Sanford	Jack	1965	SFN	NL	53.654	7	7.665	89	67	4	1405.7	3.61
28	Beck	Rod	1997	SFN	NL	53.336	7	7.619	21	28	199	463.0	2.97
29	Nehf	Art	1926	NY1	NL	53.238	8	6.655	107	60	7	1436.0	3.45
30	Burkett	John	1994	SFN	NL	52.534	6	8.756	67	42	1	997.3	3.83
31	Marquard	Rube	1915	NY1	NL	51.567	8	6.446	103	76	12	1546.0	2.85
32	Romo	Sergio	2016	SFN	NL	51.440	9	5.716	32	26	84	439.7	2.58
33	Ortiz	Russ	2007	SFN	NL	51.220	6	8.537	69	47	0	973.7	4.09
34	Wiltse	Hooks	1914	NY1	NL	47.792	11	4.345	136	85	29	2053.0	2.48
35	Garrelts	Scott	1991	SFN	NL	46.894	10	4.689	69	53	48	959.3	3.29
36	Blue	Vida	1986	SFN	NL	44.760	6	7.460	72	58	0	1131.3	3.52

RANK	NAME	FIRST	LYEAR	LTEAM	LG	PEVA	YRS	PPYR	W	L	SV	IP	ERA
37	Koslo	Dave	1953	NY1	NL	**44.592**	10	4.459	91	104	21	1559.7	3.69
38	Swift	Bill	1994	SFN	NL	**44.543**	3	14.848	39	19	1	506.7	2.70
39	Zito	Barry	2013	SFN	NL	**44.438**	7	6.348	63	80	0	1139.3	4.62
40	Montefusco	John	1980	SFN	NL	**44.327**	7	6.332	59	62	0	1182.7	3.47
41	Minton	Greg	1987	SFN	NL	**43.529**	13	3.348	45	52	125	870.3	3.23
42	Hearn	Jim	1956	NY1	NL	**42.521**	7	6.074	78	66	3	1242.7	3.74
43	Gomez	Ruben	1958	SFN	NL	**42.220**	6	7.037	71	72	2	1253.3	3.90
44	Estes	Shawn	2001	SFN	NL	**41.712**	7	5.959	64	50	0	990.0	4.25
45	Walker	Bill	1932	NY1	NL	**41.492**	6	6.915	58	49	6	905.7	3.45
46	Cueto	Johnny	2020	SFN	NL	**41.105**	5	8.221	32	20	0	499.3	3.75
47	Taylor	Dummy	1908	NY1	NL	**40.845**	9	4.538	115	103	3	1882.3	2.77
48	Krukow	Mike	1989	SFN	NL	**40.718**	7	5.817	66	56	1	1154.0	3.84
49	Ames	Red	1913	NY1	NL	**39.565**	11	3.597	108	77	12	1802.7	2.45
50	Grissom	Marv	1958	SFN	NL	**38.845**	7	5.549	31	25	58	543.3	2.88

San Francisco Giants – Top Fielders

Rank	FIRST BASE		FV	Lyear	G	FPCT	RF
1	Terry	Bill	**1.3118**	1936	1579	0.992	10.82
2	Mize	Johnny	**1.2811**	1949	646	0.993	9.93
3	Kelly	George	**1.2771**	1926	919	0.992	11.25
4	Clark	Will	**1.2489**	1993	1124	0.992	9.81
5	Tenney	Fred	**1.2395**	1909	254	0.988	11.26
6	McGann	Dan	**1.2340**	1907	681	0.991	10.64
7	Connor	Roger	**1.2239**	1894	1002	0.977	10.60
8	McCarthy	Johnny	**1.1813**	1948	271	0.990	10.80
9	Snow	J.T.	**1.1794**	2008	1139	0.996	8.36
10	Lockman	Whitey	**1.1667**	1958	722	0.990	9.67

Rank	SECOND BASE		FV	Lyear	G	FPCT	RF
1	Whitehead	Burgess	**1.4021**	1941	557	0.972	6.09
2	Critz	Hughie	**1.3634**	1935	658	0.976	6.02
3	Kent	Jeff	**1.3208**	2002	854	0.981	4.80
4	Richardson	Danny	**1.3159**	1891	483	0.939	5.99
5	Stanky	Eddie	**1.3148**	1951	291	0.977	5.47
6	Frisch	Frankie	**1.3066**	1926	622	0.971	5.93
7	Gleason	Kid	**1.3028**	1900	660	0.937	5.73
8	Witek	Mickey	**1.2922**	1947	437	0.969	5.62
9	Thompson	Robby	**1.2883**	1996	1279	0.983	4.94
10	Fuentes	Tito	**1.2610**	1974	842	0.976	5.07

Rank	SHORTSTOP		FV	Lyear	G	FPCT	RF
1	Bancroft	Dave	**1.6770**	1930	521	0.947	6.30
2	Davis	George	**1.6759**	1903	635	0.936	6.23
3	Lanier	Hal	**1.6303**	1971	620	0.971	4.91
4	Bartell	Dick	**1.6236**	1943	621	0.956	5.69
5	Jackson	Travis	**1.6075**	1936	1326	0.952	5.67
6	Kerr	Buddy	**1.6007**	1949	820	0.967	5.22
7	Speier	Chris	**1.5930**	1989	910	0.969	4.80
8	Clayton	Royce	**1.5839**	1995	499	0.968	4.53
9	Vizquel	Omar	**1.5821**	2008	529	0.990	4.13
10	Fletcher	Art	**1.5798**	1920	1240	0.937	5.48

Rank	THIRD BASE		FV	Lyear	G	FPCT	RF
1	Williams	Matt	**1.5688**	1996	1011	0.959	2.75
2	Groh	Heinie	**1.5293**	1926	404	0.973	2.78
3	Devlin	Art	**1.5227**	1911	1097	0.935	3.26
4	Mueller	Bill	**1.4966**	2002	560	0.961	2.49
5	Evans	Darrell	**1.4962**	1983	697	0.948	2.98
6	Lindstrom	Freddie	**1.4773**	1932	776	0.959	2.97

			FV	Lyear	G	FPCT	RF	
7	Davis	George	1.4744	1901	426	0.899	3.61	
8	Zimmerman	Heinie	1.4725	1919	412	0.946	3.25	
9	Feliz	Pedro	1.4687	2007	615	0.961	2.38	
10	Herzog	Buck	1.4375	1916	324	0.941	3.18	

Rank	CATCHER		FV	Lyear	G	FPCT	RF	CS%
1	Warner	John	2.0003	1904	606	0.966	5.88	0.479
2	Bresnahan	Roger	1.9856	1908	430	0.976	6.22	0.498
3	Ewing	Buck	1.9624	1892	475	0.933	7.03	0.353
4	Molina	Bengie	1.9411	2010	446	0.994	7.57	0.279
5	Meyers	Chief	1.9326	1915	769	0.973	6.08	0.461
6	Danning	Harry	1.9003	1942	801	0.985	4.63	0.469
7	Bowerman	Frank	1.8943	1907	554	0.968	6.09	0.493
8	Haller	Tom	1.8723	1967	719	0.992	6.38	0.338
9	Posey	Buster	1.8608	2019	987	0.995	8.09	0.331
10	Snyder	Frank	1.8563	1926	686	0.985	3.99	0.498

Rank	OUTFIELD		FV	Lyear	G	FPCT	RF	ApG
1	Lewis	Darren	1.5541	1995	479	0.998	2.55	0.033
2	Mays	Willie	1.5498	1972	2748	0.981	2.57	0.069
3	Winn	Randy	1.5494	2009	724	0.994	2.07	0.036
4	Butler	Brett	1.5466	1990	466	0.986	2.66	0.039
5	Selbach	Kip	1.5249	1901	266	0.948	2.17	0.135
6	Van Haltren	George	1.5168	1903	1212	0.932	2.20	0.185
7	Rowand	Aaron	1.5025	2011	480	0.993	2.25	0.038
8	Burns	George	1.5018	1921	1356	0.969	2.21	0.106
9	Snodgrass	Fred	1.4936	1915	690	0.962	2.25	0.165
10	Thomson	Bobby	1.4931	1953	851	0.979	2.71	0.081
11	Bonds	Bobby	1.4858	1974	1005	0.976	2.22	0.070
12	Roush	Edd	1.4782	1929	299	0.974	2.47	0.154
13	Marshall	Willard	1.4627	1949	667	0.976	2.16	0.112
14	Ott	Mel	1.4610	1946	2313	0.980	2.06	0.111
15	Seymour	Cy	1.4449	1910	556	0.953	2.14	0.131
16	Kauff	Benny	1.4381	1920	559	0.961	2.37	0.131
17	Davis	Chili	1.4359	1987	824	0.974	2.38	0.069
18	Maddox	Garry	1.4357	1975	405	0.979	2.59	0.042
19	Demaree	Frank	1.4336	1941	279	0.984	2.15	0.065
20	Clark	Jack	1.4286	1984	995	0.978	2.04	0.094
21	Mertes	Sam	1.4240	1906	505	0.964	1.82	0.121
22	North	Billy	1.4212	1981	282	0.982	2.52	0.053
23	Grissom	Marquis	1.4209	2005	326	0.986	2.33	0.018
24	Gladden	Dan	1.4162	1986	316	0.984	2.54	0.057
25	Murray	Red	1.4155	1917	812	0.959	1.78	0.145
26	Torres	Andres	1.4084	2013	438	0.989	1.78	0.037
27	Hamilton	Darryl	1.4067	1998	215	0.989	2.07	0.023
28	Burke	Eddie	1.4053	1895	340	0.920	2.09	0.153
29	Gillespie	Pete	1.4037	1887	474	0.911	1.63	0.108
30	Bernard	Marvin	1.4005	2003	797	0.986	1.81	0.045

Rank	PITCHING		FV	Lyear	IP	FPCT	RF
1	Hernandez	Livan	1.1217	2002	746	0.986	2.52
2	Mathewson	Christy	1.1059	1916	4772	0.972	3.36
3	Gumbert	Harry	1.1036	1941	1113	0.980	3.51
4	Barnes	Jesse	1.0973	1923	1150	0.973	3.34
5	Jansen	Larry	1.0933	1954	1731	0.977	2.42
6	Fitzsimmons	Freddie	1.0926	1937	2514	0.974	3.28
7	Perry	Gaylord	1.0876	1971	2295	0.972	2.34
8	Nehf	Art	1.0852	1926	1436	0.977	2.95
9	Ortiz	Russ	1.0742	2007	974	0.987	2.15
10	Schumacher	Hal	1.0731	1946	2482	0.971	2.90

Franchise When and Where
San Francisco Giants (1958 to Present)
New York Giants (1885-1957); New York Gothams (1883-1884)

ST. LOUIS CARDINALS
Best Seasons and Careers of All-Time

Kinda ashamed they lost Albert Pujols west in free agency, although that did not matter to his inclusion, here. He's flanked by Hall of Famers Rogers Hornsby, Ozzie Smith, Ted Simmons, Stan Musial, Enos Slaughter, and Lou Brock in a rather impressive lineup. And anytime your starting pitcher for your most important game is Bob Gibson, you've got a chance to win. For some outside of St. Louis, they might be surprised that Adam Wainwright would be listed as the second best pitcher In franchise history, ahead of Dizzy Dean, but he pitched twice as many seasons for the Cardinals, although that shouldn't take away from any of his accomplishments. Durability and consistency are great qualities, too. We've added Silver King to the back of the bullpen, even though he pitched for only three seasons as a Cardinal. But boy, that 1888 season was so great, we thought he should be included.

Reserves

Bench - Joe Medwick (OF), Jim Edmonds (OF), Ray Lankford (OF), Jim Bottomley (1B), Red Schoendienst (2B), Joe Torre (C/1B/3B), Yadier Molina (CATCHER).

Bullpen - Jason Isringhausen (CL), Joaquin Andujar (SU), Jesse Haines, Harry Breechen, Bob Forsch, Silver King.

St. Louis Cardinals - Best Position Player Years

Rank	Name	First	Year	Team	Lg	HR	RBI	AVG	Age	PEVA-B
1	Hornsby	Rogers	1922	SLN	NL	42	152	0.401	26	45.149
2	Pujols	Albert	2009	SLN	NL	47	135	0.327	29	43.955
3	Musial	Stan	1943	SLN	NL	13	81	0.357	23	41.278
4	McGwire	Mark	1998	SLN	NL	70	147	0.299	35	40.809
5	Musial	Stan	1953	SLN	NL	30	113	0.337	33	40.502
6	Pujols	Albert	2010	SLN	NL	42	118	0.312	30	39.067
7	Musial	Stan	1944	SLN	NL	12	94	0.347	24	38.717
8	Musial	Stan	1952	SLN	NL	21	91	0.336	32	37.889
9	Hornsby	Rogers	1925	SLN	NL	39	143	0.403	29	37.655
10	Musial	Stan	1951	SLN	NL	32	108	0.355	31	37.339
11	Pujols	Albert	2006	SLN	NL	49	137	0.331	26	36.422
12	Musial	Stan	1948	SLN	NL	39	131	0.376	28	35.811
13	Torre	Joe	1971	SLN	NL	24	137	0.363	31	34.530
14	Hornsby	Rogers	1924	SLN	NL	25	94	0.424	28	34.349
15	Pujols	Albert	2003	SLN	NL	43	124	0.359	23	33.510
16	Pujols	Albert	2008	SLN	NL	37	116	0.357	28	33.388
17	Musial	Stan	1954	SLN	NL	35	126	0.330	34	33.159
18	Burkett	Jesse	1901	SLN	NL	10	75	0.376	33	32.782
19	Pujols	Albert	2005	SLN	NL	41	117	0.330	25	32.329
20	O'Neill	Tip	1887	SL4	AA	14	123	0.435	29	31.789

St. Louis Cardinals - Best Pitcher Years

Rank	Name	First	Year	Team	Lg	W	L	SV	IP	ERA	Age	PEVA-P
1	King	Silver	1888	SL4	AA	45	21	0	585.7	1.64	20	56.728
2	Cooper	Mort	1942	SLN	NL	22	7	0	278.7	1.78	29	47.763
3	Young	Cy	1899	SLN	NL	26	16	1	369.3	2.58	32	40.907
4	Tudor	John	1985	SLN	NL	21	8	0	275.0	1.93	31	38.832
5	Brecheen	Harry	1948	SLN	NL	20	7	1	233.3	2.24	34	37.896
6	Gibson	Bob	1968	SLN	NL	22	9	0	304.7	1.12	33	36.485
7	Wainwright	Adam	2010	SLN	NL	20	11	0	230.3	2.42	29	35.716
8	Dean	Dizzy	1934	SLN	NL	30	7	7	311.7	2.66	24	35.666
9	Carpenter	Chris	2009	SLN	NL	17	4	0	192.7	2.24	34	35.125
10	Andujar	Joaquin	1982	SLN	NL	15	10	0	265.7	2.47	30	34.352
11	Tewksbury	Bob	1992	SLN	NL	16	5	0	233.0	2.16	32	32.658
12	Haines	Jesse	1927	SLN	NL	24	10	1	300.7	2.72	34	32.652
13	Gibson	Bob	1969	SLN	NL	20	13	0	314.0	2.18	34	32.616
14	Dean	Dizzy	1935	SLN	NL	28	12	5	325.3	3.04	25	32.595
15	Carpenter	Chris	2005	SLN	NL	21	5	0	241.7	2.83	30	32.538
16	Wainwright	Adam	2013	SLN	NL	19	9	0	241.7	2.94	32	30.443
17	Dean	Dizzy	1936	SLN	NL	24	13	11	315.0	3.17	26	30.183
18	Carpenter	Chris	2006	SLN	NL	15	8	0	221.7	3.09	31	29.268
19	Cooper	Mort	1943	SLN	NL	21	8	3	274.0	2.30	30	28.795
20	Wainwright	Adam	2014	SLN	NL	20	9	0	227.0	2.38	33	28.068

St. Louis Cardinals (SL4, SLN) - Top Career Batters

RANK	NAME	FIRST	LYR	TEAM	LG	PEVA-B	YRS	PPYR	HR	RBI	H	AVE
1	Musial	Stan	1963	SLN	NL	481.184	22	21.872	475	1951	3630	0.331
2	Pujols	Albert	2011	SLN	NL	330.820	11	30.075	445	1329	2073	0.328

RANK	NAME	FIRST	LYR	TEAM	LG	PEVA-B	YRS	PPYR	HR	RBI	H	AVE
3	Hornsby	Rogers	1933	SLN	NL	258.875	13	19.913	193	1072	2110	0.359
4	Simmons	Ted	1980	SLN	NL	184.755	13	14.212	172	929	1704	0.298
5	Boyer	Ken	1965	SLN	NL	164.783	11	14.980	255	1001	1855	0.293
6	Slaughter	Enos	1953	SLN	NL	164.390	13	12.645	146	1148	2064	0.305
7	Brock	Lou	1979	SLN	NL	162.510	16	10.157	129	814	2713	0.297
8	Molina	Yadier	2020	SLN	NL	139.280	17	8.193	160	932	2001	0.281
9	Medwick	Joe	1948	SLN	NL	130.327	11	11.848	152	923	1590	0.335
10	Smith	Ozzie	1996	SLN	NL	128.467	15	8.564	27	664	1944	0.272
11	Edmonds	Jim	2007	SLN	NL	124.000	8	15.500	241	713	1033	0.285
12	Lankford	Ray	2004	SLN	NL	123.023	13	9.463	228	829	1479	0.273
13	Bottomley	Jim	1932	SLN	NL	122.406	11	11.128	181	1105	1727	0.325
14	Flood	Curt	1969	SLN	NL	120.736	12	10.061	84	633	1853	0.293
15	O'Neill	Tip	1891	SL4	AA	118.748	7	16.964	47	625	1092	0.343
16	Hernandez	Keith	1983	SLN	NL	118.120	10	11.812	81	595	1217	0.299
17	Schoendienst	Red	1963	SLN	NL	110.289	15	7.353	65	651	1980	0.289
18	Holliday	Matt	2016	SLN	NL	109.416	8	13.677	156	616	1048	0.293
19	Carpenter	Matt	2019	SLN	NL	101.956	9	11.328	148	531	1092	0.269
20	Mize	Johnny	1941	SLN	NL	101.247	6	16.874	158	653	1048	0.336
21	Torre	Joe	1974	SLN	NL	101.068	6	16.845	98	558	1062	0.308
22	Konetchy	Ed	1913	SLN	NL	95.329	7	13.618	36	476	1013	0.283
23	McGwire	Mark	2001	SLN	NL	91.288	5	18.258	220	473	469	0.270
24	McGee	Willie	1999	SLN	NL	88.801	13	6.831	63	678	1683	0.294
25	Kurowski	Whitey	1949	SLN	NL	86.394	9	9.599	106	529	925	0.286
26	White	Bill	1969	SLN	NL	84.655	8	10.582	140	631	1241	0.298
27	Burkett	Jesse	1901	SLN	NL	80.170	3	26.723	24	214	650	0.378
28	Comiskey	Charlie	1891	SL4	AA	77.386	9	8.598	26	694	1198	0.273
29	Hendrick	George	1984	SLN	NL	75.574	7	10.796	122	582	978	0.294
30	Marion	Marty	1950	SLN	NL	74.923	11	6.811	34	605	1402	0.264
31	Frisch	Frankie	1937	SLN	NL	74.514	11	6.774	51	720	1577	0.312
32	Latham	Arlie	1896	SLN	NL	71.383	8	8.923	11	250	982	0.266
33	McCarver	Tim	1974	SLN	NL	70.330	12	5.861	66	453	1029	0.272
34	Rolen	Scott	2007	SLN	NL	67.858	6	11.310	111	453	678	0.286
35	Hafey	Chick	1931	SLN	NL	66.082	8	8.260	127	618	963	0.326
36	Moore	Terry	1948	SLN	NL	64.835	11	5.894	80	513	1318	0.280
37	Renteria	Edgar	2004	SLN	NL	59.144	6	9.857	71	451	973	0.290
38	Herr	Tom	1988	SLN	NL	58.866	10	5.887	19	435	1021	0.274
39	Douthit	Taylor	1931	SLN	NL	58.506	9	6.501	29	342	1006	0.300
40	Huggins	Miller	1916	SLN	NL	57.712	7	8.245	5	164	740	0.270
41	Gleason	Bill	1887	SL4	AA	57.581	6	9.597	7	232	781	0.275
42	Martin	Pepper	1944	SLN	NL	56.421	13	4.340	59	501	1227	0.298
43	Javier	Julian	1971	SLN	NL	55.037	12	4.586	76	494	1450	0.258
44	Collins	Ripper	1936	SLN	NL	54.151	6	9.025	106	516	852	0.307
45	Pendleton	Terry	1990	SLN	NL	53.441	7	7.634	44	442	888	0.259

RANK	NAME	FIRST	LYR	TEAM	LG	PEVA-B	YRS	PPYR	HR	RBI	H	AVE
46	McCarthy	Tommy	1891	SL4	AA	52.755	4	13.189	17	295	687	0.307
47	Hemus	Solly	1959	SLN	NL	52.245	9	5.805	38	198	567	0.275
48	Zeile	Todd	1995	SLN	NL	51.770	7	7.396	75	394	719	0.267
49	Smoot	Homer	1906	SLN	NL	51.030	5	10.206	14	252	706	0.292
50	Smith	Jack	1926	SLN	NL	50.271	12	4.189	36	299	1067	0.284

St. Louis Cardinals (SL4, SLN) - Top Career Pitchers

RANK	NAME	FIRST	LYEAR	LTEAM	LG	PEVA	YRS	PPYR	W	L	SV	IP	ERA
1	Gibson	Bob	1975	SLN	NL	225.768	17	13.280	251	174	6	3884.3	2.91
2	Wainwright	Adam	2020	SLN	NL	198.362	15	13.224	167	98	3	2169.3	3.38
3	Dean	Dizzy	1937	SLN	NL	152.623	7	21.803	134	75	30	1737.3	2.99
4	Carpenter	Chris	2012	SLN	NL	141.904	9	15.767	95	44	0	1348.7	3.07
5	Cooper	Mort	1945	SLN	NL	118.364	8	14.795	105	50	12	1480.3	2.77
6	Haines	Jesse	1937	SLN	NL	116.240	18	6.458	210	158	10	3203.7	3.64
7	Brecheen	Harry	1952	SLN	NL	107.820	11	9.802	128	79	17	1790.3	2.91
8	Forsch	Bob	1988	SLN	NL	93.912	15	6.261	163	127	3	2658.7	3.67
9	Morris	Matt	2005	SLN	NL	84.692	8	10.586	101	62	4	1377.3	3.61
10	King	Silver	1889	SL4	AA	84.369	3	28.123	111	50	2	1433.7	2.71
11	Andujar	Joaquin	1985	SLN	NL	81.975	5	16.395	68	53	1	1077.0	3.33
12	Jackson	Larry	1962	SLN	NL	80.627	8	10.078	101	86	20	1672.3	3.67
13	Lanier	Max	1951	SLN	NL	79.002	12	6.583	101	69	12	1454.7	2.84
14	Pollet	Howie	1951	SLN	NL	78.541	9	8.727	97	65	11	1401.7	3.06
15	Sherdel	Bill	1932	SLN	NL	75.363	14	5.383	153	131	25	2450.7	3.64
16	Tudor	John	1990	SLN	NL	72.894	5	14.579	62	26	0	881.7	2.52
17	Doak	Bill	1929	SLN	NL	72.526	13	5.579	144	136	13	2387.0	2.93
18	Tewksbury	Bob	1994	SLN	NL	72.388	6	12.065	67	46	1	968.7	3.48
19	Lynn	Lance	2017	SLN	NL	66.168	6	11.028	72	47	1	977.7	3.38
20	Breitenstein	Ted	1901	SLN	NL	62.958	7	8.994	94	125	3	1925.3	4.30
21	Young	Cy	1900	SLN	NL	62.390	2	31.195	45	35	1	690.7	2.78
22	Martinez	Carlos	2020	SLN	NL	57.089	8	7.136	58	43	31	884.7	3.51
23	Brazle	Al	1954	SLN	NL	56.660	10	5.666	97	64	60	1376.7	3.31
24	Caruthers	Bob	1892	SLN	NL	54.385	5	10.877	108	48	1	1395.0	2.75
25	Isringhausen	Jason	2008	SLN	NL	53.288	7	7.613	17	20	217	408.0	2.98
26	Lohse	Kyle	2012	SLN	NL	51.398	5	10.280	55	35	0	809.0	3.90
27	Warneke	Lon	1942	SLN	NL	51.117	6	8.519	83	49	2	1157.7	3.67
28	Broglio	Ernie	1964	SLN	NL	51.099	6	8.516	70	55	0	1124.0	3.43
29	Sallee	Slim	1916	SLN	NL	49.678	9	5.520	106	107	26	1905.3	2.67
30	McDaniel	Lindy	1962	SLN	NL	49.142	8	6.143	66	54	64	884.7	3.88
31	Alexander	Pete	1929	SLN	NL	48.273	4	12.068	55	34	7	792.0	3.08
32	Staley	Gerry	1954	SLN	NL	46.543	8	5.818	89	76	18	1274.7	4.03
33	Simmons	Curt	1966	SLN	NL	46.532	7	6.647	69	58	0	1214.7	3.25
34	Hallahan	Bill	1936	SLN	NL	46.367	10	4.637	93	68	8	1453.3	3.82
35	Magrane	Joe	1993	SLN	NL	45.418	6	7.570	51	54	0	921.0	3.34

RANK	NAME	FIRST	LYEAR	LTEAM	LG	PEVA	YRS	PPYR	W	L	SV	IP	ERA
36	Carlton	Steve	1971	SLN	NL	45.129	7	6.447	77	62	1	1265.0	3.10
37	Foutz	Dave	1887	SL4	AA	44.691	4	11.173	114	48	1	1457.7	2.67
38	DeLeon	Jose	1992	SLN	NL	44.329	5	8.866	43	57	0	917.7	3.59
39	Garcia	Jaime	2016	SLN	NL	42.863	8	5.358	62	45	0	896.0	3.57
40	Sutter	Bruce	1984	SLN	NL	40.992	4	10.248	26	30	127	396.7	2.72
41	Wilks	Ted	1951	SLN	NL	39.925	8	4.991	51	20	29	742.7	3.25
42	Mizell	Vinegar Bend	1960	SLN	NL	39.468	7	5.638	69	70	0	1218.7	3.72
43	Haddix	Harvey	1956	SLN	NL	39.340	5	7.868	53	40	6	786.3	3.65
44	Kile	Darryl	2002	SLN	NL	39.253	3	13.084	41	24	0	544.3	3.54
45	Stivetts	Jack	1891	SL4	AA	39.214	3	13.071	72	50	2	1051.0	3.01
46	Dickson	Murry	1957	SLN	NL	38.883	9	4.320	72	54	7	1180.3	3.38
47	Cox	Danny	1988	SLN	NL	38.685	6	6.448	56	56	0	985.7	3.40
48	Worrell	Todd	1992	SLN	NL	37.778	6	6.296	33	33	129	425.7	2.56
49	Dean	Paul	1939	SLN	NL	37.111	6	6.185	46	30	8	669.0	3.70
50	Wacha	Michael	2019	SLN	NL	37.091	7	5.299	59	39	0	867.7	3.91

St. Louis Cardinals – Top Fielders

Rank	FIRST BASE		FV	Lyear	G	FPCT	RF
1	Pujols	Albert	1.3126	2011	1337	0.994	9.81
2	Konetchy	Ed	1.3039	1913	981	0.988	10.94
3	Hernandez	Keith	1.3013	1983	1118	0.994	10.24
4	Martinez	Tino	1.2594	2003	275	0.997	8.79
5	White	Bill	1.2239	1969	972	0.992	9.15
6	Cepeda	Orlando	1.2235	1968	425	0.990	9.45
7	Comiskey	Charlie	1.1739	1891	1010	0.971	10.50
8	Musial	Stan	1.1692	1960	1016	0.992	9.25
9	Torre	Joe	1.1438	1974	425	0.993	8.88
10	McGwire	Mark	1.1353	2001	512	0.993	8.66

Rank	SECOND BASE		FV	Lyear	G	FPCT	RF
1	Schoendienst	Red	1.3835	1962	1429	0.983	5.47
2	Blasingame	Don	1.3730	1959	542	0.978	5.50
3	Herr	Tom	1.3547	1988	987	0.988	5.08
4	Oquendo	Jose	1.3253	1995	649	0.992	4.70
5	Huggins	Miller	1.3248	1916	773	0.961	5.17
6	Frisch	Frankie	1.3032	1937	1140	0.975	5.86
7	Farrell	John	1.2940	1905	373	0.935	5.83
8	Vina	Fernando	1.2900	2003	483	0.984	4.72
9	Wong	Kolten	1.2664	2020	785	0.981	4.37
10	Verban	Emil	1.2624	1945	301	0.973	4.99

Rank	SHORTSTOP		FV	Lyear	G	FPCT	RF
1	Smith	Ozzie	1.6745	1996	1929	0.980	4.90
2	Ryan	Brendan	1.6551	2010	312	0.979	4.34
3	Wallace	Bobby	1.6345	1918	374	0.927	6.21
4	Marion	Marty	1.6261	1950	1484	0.968	5.10
5	Clayton	Royce	1.6081	1998	355	0.972	4.57
6	Peralta	Jhonny	1.5996	2016	307	0.984	3.96
7	Durocher	Leo	1.5891	1937	681	0.962	5.00
8	Eckstein	David	1.5710	2007	390	0.977	4.55
9	Templeton	Garry	1.5703	1981	700	0.955	5.36
10	Cross	Monte	1.5691	1897	256	0.907	5.98

Rank	THIRD BASE		FV	Lyear	G	FPCT	RF
1	Pendleton	Terry	1.6390	1990	908	0.959	3.14
2	Rolen	Scott	1.5847	2007	659	0.968	2.88
3	Byrne	Bobby	1.5796	1909	375	0.922	3.75
4	Reitz	Ken	1.5496	1980	1081	0.971	2.60
5	Mowrey	Mike	1.5419	1913	516	0.939	3.28

			FV	Lyear	G	FPCT	RF	
6	Boyer	Ken	1.5392	1965	1539	0.953	2.94	
7	Gaetti	Gary	1.5261	1998	348	0.977	2.30	
8	Latham	Arlie	1.5115	1896	839	0.866	3.52	
9	Zeile	Todd	1.5042	1994	567	0.942	2.58	
10	Oberkfell	Ken	1.4902	1984	447	0.964	2.68	

Rank	CATCHER		FV	Lyear	G	FPCT	RF	CS%
1	Pena	Tony	1.9780	1989	388	0.993	5.82	0.319
2	Matheny	Mike	1.9587	2004	611	0.996	6.49	0.396
3	Wilson	Jimmie	1.9571	1933	630	0.982	4.76	0.538
4	Molina	Yadier	1.9501	2020	1990	0.995	7.40	0.403
5	O'Dea	Ken	1.9411	1946	287	0.990	4.87	0.526
6	Sarni	Bill	1.9079	1956	296	0.991	4.83	0.477
7	Boyle	Jack	1.8864	1891	327	0.928	5.99	0.354
8	Owen	Mickey	1.8853	1940	433	0.979	4.17	0.552
9	Simmons	Ted	1.8797	1980	1439	0.987	5.71	0.343
10	Mancuso	Gus	1.8759	1942	318	0.978	5.37	0.519

Rank	OUTFIELD		FV	Lyear	G	FPCT	RF	ApG
1	Welch	Curt	1.6847	1887	373	0.946	2.53	0.196
2	Nicol	Hugh	1.5935	1886	339	0.897	2.06	0.363
3	Flood	Curt	1.5859	1969	1687	0.987	2.44	0.068
4	Moore	Terry	1.5343	1948	1189	0.985	2.71	0.086
5	Douthit	Taylor	1.5292	1931	835	0.970	3.10	0.066
6	Heidrick	Emmet	1.5262	1901	346	0.943	2.18	0.202
7	Magee	Lee	1.5200	1914	295	0.970	2.41	0.180
8	McBride	Bake	1.5198	1977	367	0.988	2.71	0.057
9	Wilson	Chief	1.5194	1916	372	0.977	2.13	0.175
10	Oakes	Rebel	1.5098	1913	559	0.955	2.40	0.123
11	Edmonds	Jim	1.4995	2007	1048	0.987	2.40	0.069
12	Scott	Tony	1.4898	1981	495	0.988	2.48	0.065
13	Jay	Jon	1.4858	2015	718	0.995	2.00	0.026
14	Shannon	Spike	1.4841	1905	353	0.979	2.11	0.096
15	Burkett	Jesse	1.4835	1901	423	0.932	2.35	0.128
16	Jose	Felix	1.4817	1992	303	0.985	2.01	0.086
17	Hendrick	George	1.4755	1984	790	0.990	2.04	0.073
18	McCarthy	Tommy	1.4748	1891	486	0.905	1.89	0.257
19	Medwick	Joe	1.4635	1948	1161	0.976	2.26	0.076
20	Smoot	Homer	1.4540	1905	619	0.954	2.14	0.115
21	Brunansky	Tom	1.4476	1990	315	0.984	1.95	0.063
22	Gilkey	Bernard	1.4443	1995	557	0.980	1.95	0.099
23	Ludwick	Ryan	1.4421	2010	471	0.994	1.75	0.051
24	Ellis	Rube	1.4395	1912	510	0.943	2.26	0.165
25	Slaughter	Enos	1.4369	1953	1751	0.980	2.06	0.081
26	Rothrock	Jack	1.4358	1935	281	0.977	2.28	0.053
27	Jordan	Brian	1.4298	1998	632	0.987	2.10	0.062
28	Lankford	Ray	1.4252	2004	1492	0.984	2.30	0.045
29	Coleman	Vince	1.4220	1990	861	0.973	2.02	0.087
30	Mumphrey	Jerry	1.4187	1979	461	0.984	2.05	0.059

Rank	PITCHING		FV	Lyear	IP	FPCT	RF	
1	Hart	Bill	1.1266	1897	631	0.935	3.31	
2	Breitenstein	Ted	1.1160	1901	1925	0.933	2.88	
3	Gleason	Kid	1.1089	1894	838	0.919	3.03	
4	Foutz	Dave	1.1060	1887	1458	0.923	2.59	
5	Wise	Rick	1.1004	1973	528	0.983	1.98	
6	Wainwright	Adam	1.0822	2020	2169	0.983	1.95	
7	Carpenter	Chris	1.0815	2012	1349	0.980	2.01	
8	Lohse	Kyle	1.0799	2012	809	0.990	2.25	
9	Staley	Gerry	1.0733	1954	1275	0.976	2.90	
10	Young	Cy	1.0709	1900	691	0.917	2.88	

Franchise When and Where
St. Louis Cardinals (1900 to Present)
St. Louis Perfectos (1899)
St. Louis Browns (1883-1898, SL4)
St. Louis Brown Stockings (1882, SL4)

TAMPA BAY RAYS
Best Seasons and Careers of All-Time

Another one of those younger franchises that's gonna have a lot of changes in their All-Time team soon, particularly with the emergence of their young pitching staff. Yes, Blake Snell is already one of their best five starting pitchers of All-Time. Others will soon be rising up the list. You can say the same for position players such as Brandon Lowe. For now, franchise best players include those that started their careers in Tampa Bay, but left for other pastures, whether Evan Longoria, as a Third Baseman, or David Price, on the mound. Here's hoping that some of these younger players on their way up the lists will see the ability for the Rays to keep them in Tampa Bay a bit longer than those of the past.

B.J. Upton
Carl Crawford
Aubrey Huff
Julio Lugo
Ben Zobrist
Evan Longoria
Carlos Pena
Toby Hall

All-Time Team
Tampa Bay Rays

SP - James Shields, David Price, Scott Kazmir, Chris Archer, Blake Snell

Reserves

Bench - Matthew Joyce (OF), Desmond Jennings (OF), Kevin Kiermaier (OF), Fred McGriff (1B), Jason Bartlett (SS), Logan Forsythe (IF), Dionar Navarro (CATCHER).

Bullpen - Fernando Rodney (CL), Jake McGee (SU), Matt Garza, Alex Colome, Jake Odorizzi, Alex Cobb.

Tampa Bay Rays - Best Position Player Years

Rank	Name	First	Year	Team	Lg	HR	RBI	AVG	Age	PEVA-B
1	Longoria	Evan	2010	TBA	AL	22	104	0.294	25	23.815
2	Pena	Carlos	2007	TBA	AL	46	121	0.282	29	23.368
3	Longoria	Evan	2009	TBA	AL	33	113	0.281	24	19.499
4	Crawford	Carl	2010	TBA	AL	19	90	0.307	29	19.483
5	Longoria	Evan	2013	TBA	AL	32	88	0.269	28	18.924
6	Longoria	Evan	2016	TBA	AL	36	98	0.273	31	17.143
7	Longoria	Evan	2011	TBA	AL	31	99	0.244	26	16.843
8	Zobrist	Ben	2012	TBA	AL	20	74	0.270	31	16.786
9	Zobrist	Ben	2009	TBA	AL	27	91	0.297	28	16.721
10	Zobrist	Ben	2011	TBA	AL	20	91	0.269	30	16.197
11	Longoria	Evan	2014	TBA	AL	22	91	0.253	29	14.639
12	Huff	Aubrey	2003	TBA	AL	34	107	0.311	27	14.625
13	Meadows	Austin	2019	TBA	AL	33	89	0.291	24	13.821
14	Lowe	Brandon	2020	TBA	AL	14	37	0.269	26	12.984
15	Upton	B.J.	2011	TBA	AL	23	81	0.243	27	12.936
16	Crawford	Carl	2005	TBA	AL	15	81	0.301	24	12.677
17	McGriff	Fred	1999	TBA	AL	32	104	0.310	36	12.146
18	Pham	Tommy	2019	TBA	AL	21	68	0.273	31	12.025
19	Huff	Aubrey	2004	TBA	AL	29	104	0.297	28	11.992
20	Baldelli	Rocco	2003	TBA	AL	11	78	0.289	22	11.878

Tampa Bay Rays - Best Pitcher Years

Rank	Name	First	Year	Team	Lg	W	L	SV	IP	ERA	Age	PEVA-P
1	Snell	Blake	2018	TBA	AL	21	5	0	180.7	1.89	26	31.010
2	Price	David	2012	TBA	AL	20	5	0	211.0	2.56	27	27.912
3	Morton	Charlie	2019	TBA	AL	16	6	0	194.7	3.05	36	27.783
4	Shields	James	2011	TBA	AL	16	12	0	249.3	2.82	30	22.433
5	Rodney	Fernando	2012	TBA	AL	2	2	48	74.7	0.60	35	20.284
6	Price	David	2010	TBA	AL	19	8	0	208.7	2.72	25	19.161
7	Shields	James	2008	TBA	AL	14	8	0	215.0	3.56	27	18.346
8	Shields	James	2007	TBA	AL	12	8	0	215.0	3.85	26	16.713
9	Kazmir	Scott	2007	TBA	AL	13	9	0	206.7	3.48	23	16.131
10	Shields	James	2012	TBA	AL	15	10	0	227.7	3.52	31	15.147
11	Soriano	Rafael	2010	TBA	AL	3	2	45	62.3	1.73	31	14.501
12	Archer	Chris	2015	TBA	AL	12	13	0	212.0	3.23	27	14.284
13	Pagan	Emilio	2019	TBA	AL	4	2	20	70.0	2.31	28	12.553
14	Price	David	2011	TBA	AL	12	13	0	224.3	3.49	26	12.484
15	Arrojo	Rolando	1998	TBA	AL	14	12	0	202.0	3.56	30	12.370
16	McGee	Jake	2014	TBA	AL	5	2	19	71.3	1.89	28	12.069
17	Archer	Chris	2017	TBA	AL	10	12	0	201.0	4.07	29	11.977
18	Price	David	2014	TBA	AL	11	8	0	170.7	3.11	29	11.908
19	Hellickson	Jeremy	2012	TBA	AL	10	11	0	177.0	3.10	25	11.322
20	Colome	Alex	2016	TBA	AL	2	4	37	56.7	1.91	28	11.278

Tampa Bay Rays - Top Career Batters

RANK	NAME	FIRST	LYR	TEAM	LG	PEVA-B	YRS	PPYR	HR	RBI	H	AVE
1	Longoria	Evan	2017	TBA	AL	148.496	10	14.850	261	892	1471	0.270
2	Crawford	Carl	2010	TBA	AL	88.864	9	9.874	104	592	1480	0.296

RANK	NAME	FIRST	LYR	TEAM	LG	PEVA-B	YRS	PPYR	HR	RBI	H	AVE
3	Zobrist	Ben	2014	TBA	AL	83.688	9	9.299	114	511	1016	0.264
4	Upton	B.J.	2012	TBA	AL	65.737	8	8.217	118	447	910	0.255
5	Pena	Carlos	2012	TBA	AL	59.035	5	11.807	163	468	559	0.230
6	Huff	Aubrey	2006	TBA	AL	46.522	7	6.646	128	449	870	0.287
7	McGriff	Fred	2004	TBA	AL	36.431	5	7.286	99	359	603	0.291
8	Joyce	Matthew	2014	TBA	AL	34.467	6	5.744	76	280	485	0.250
9	Kiermaier	Kevin	2020	TBA	AL	32.800	8	4.100	71	257	619	0.248
10	Lugo	Julio	2006	TBA	AL	29.375	4	7.344	40	212	550	0.287
11	Jennings	Desmond	2016	TBA	AL	27.454	7	3.922	55	191	508	0.245
12	Baldelli	Rocco	2010	TBA	AL	26.041	6	4.340	53	239	493	0.280
13	Winn	Randy	2002	TBA	AL	21.673	5	4.335	24	182	513	0.279
14	Bartlett	Jason	2010	TBA	AL	20.969	3	6.990	19	150	409	0.288
15	Hall	Toby	2006	TBA	AL	20.404	7	2.915	44	251	538	0.262
16	Souza	Steven	2017	TBA	AL	19.169	3	6.390	63	167	315	0.238
17	Loney	James	2015	TBA	AL	18.812	3	6.271	26	176	439	0.291
18	Dickerson	Corey	2017	TBA	AL	18.530	2	9.265	51	132	291	0.265
19	Lowe	Brandon	2020	TBA	AL	17.654	3	5.885	37	113	162	0.262
20	Forsythe	Logan	2016	TBA	AL	16.915	3	5.638	43	146	354	0.262
21	Adames	Willy	2020	TBA	AL	16.700	3	5.567	38	109	263	0.262
22	Grieve	Ben	2003	TBA	AL	15.880	3	5.293	34	153	302	0.254
23	Meadows	Austin	2020	TBA	AL	15.840	3	5.280	38	106	187	0.273
24	Iwamura	Akinori	2009	TBA	AL	15.525	3	5.175	14	104	379	0.281
25	Navarro	Dioner	2010	TBA	AL	15.525	5	3.105	29	157	367	0.243
26	Pham	Tommy	2019	TBA	AL	15.247	2	7.624	28	90	204	0.287
27	Flaherty	John	2002	TBA	AL	14.726	5	2.945	35	196	422	0.252
28	Vaughn	Greg	2002	TBA	AL	14.717	3	4.906	60	185	271	0.226
29	Cantu	Jorge	2007	TBA	AL	14.386	4	3.597	44	200	338	0.272
30	Gomes	Jonny	2008	TBA	AL	14.364	6	2.394	66	184	297	0.235
31	Morrison	Logan	2017	TBA	AL	14.203	2	7.102	52	128	210	0.243
32	Lee	Travis	2006	TBA	AL	13.198	3	4.399	42	150	336	0.261
33	Escobar	Yunel	2014	TBA	AL	12.772	2	6.386	16	95	253	0.257
34	Wendle	Joey	2020	TBA	AL	12.482	3	4.161	14	97	249	0.279
35	Miller	Brad	2018	TBA	AL	12.331	3	4.110	44	142	241	0.231
36	Rodriguez	Sean	2014	TBA	AL	11.891	5	2.378	40	172	331	0.228
37	Cox	Steve	2002	TBA	AL	11.806	4	2.951	39	158	324	0.262
38	Jaso	John	2015	TBA	AL	11.147	4	2.787	15	93	199	0.255
39	Cairo	Miguel	2000	TBA	AL	10.965	3	3.655	9	116	373	0.275
40	Williams	Gerald	2001	TBA	AL	10.749	2	5.374	25	106	221	0.256
41	Guyer	Brandon	2016	TBA	AL	10.677	5	2.135	21	76	217	0.255
42	Martinez	Dave	2000	TBA	AL	10.566	3	3.522	10	98	252	0.272

Tampa Bay Rays - Top Career Pitchers

RANK	NAME	FIRST	LYEAR	LTEAM	LG	PEVA	YRS	PPYR	W	L	SV	IP	ERA
1	Shields	James	2012	TBA	AL	93.591	7	13.370	87	73	0	1454.7	3.89
2	Price	David	2014	TBA	AL	85.328	7	12.190	82	47	0	1143.7	3.18
3	Archer	Chris	2018	TBA	AL	53.680	7	7.669	54	68	0	1063.0	3.69
4	Snell	Blake	2020	TBA	AL	50.098	5	10.020	42	30	0	556.0	3.24
5	Kazmir	Scott	2009	TBA	AL	46.339	6	7.723	55	44	0	834.0	3.92
6	Odorizzi	Jake	2017	TBA	AL	31.487	5	6.297	40	37	1	698.0	3.82
7	Cobb	Alex	2017	TBA	AL	31.391	6	5.232	48	35	0	700.0	3.50
8	Hellickson	Jeremy	2014	TBA	AL	31.167	5	6.233	40	36	0	640.0	3.78
9	Morton	Charlie	2020	TBA	AL	30.338	2	15.169	18	8	0	232.7	3.33
10	Garza	Matt	2010	TBA	AL	29.795	3	9.932	34	31	1	592.3	3.86
11	McGee	Jake	2015	TBA	AL	28.801	6	4.800	21	11	26	259.7	2.77
12	Rodney	Fernando	2013	TBA	AL	25.663	2	12.831	7	6	85	141.3	1.91
13	Moore	Matt	2016	TBA	AL	25.458	6	4.243	39	28	0	540.0	3.88
14	Colome	Alex	2018	TBA	AL	24.678	6	4.113	17	18	95	294.3	3.21
15	Niemann	Jeff	2012	TBA	AL	20.441	5	4.088	40	26	0	544.3	4.08
16	Yarbrough	Ryan	2020	TBA	AL	18.482	3	6.161	28	16	0	344.7	3.94
17	Hernandez	Roberto	2000	TBA	AL	18.374	3	6.125	8	16	101	218.0	3.43
18	Davis	Wade	2012	TBA	AL	18.174	4	4.544	28	22	0	458.7	3.94
19	Howell	J.P.	2012	TBA	AL	17.929	6	2.988	18	18	21	330.3	4.03
20	Balfour	Grant	2015	TBA	AL	17.161	6	2.860	16	13	20	269.7	3.74
21	Lopez	Albie	2001	TBA	AL	16.280	4	4.070	26	31	4	453.7	4.27
22	Zambrano	Victor	2004	TBA	AL	15.939	4	3.985	35	27	3	481.7	4.47
23	Glasnow	Tyler	2020	TBA	AL	15.771	3	5.257	12	7	0	173.7	3.32
24	Wheeler	Dan	2010	TBA	AL	15.090	7	2.156	13	25	18	268.7	4.32
25	Arrojo	Rolando	1999	TBA	AL	14.832	2	7.416	21	24	0	342.7	4.23
26	Soriano	Rafael	2010	TBA	AL	14.501	1	14.501	3	2	45	62.3	1.73
27	Castillo	Diego	2020	TBA	AL	14.332	3	4.777	12	10	12	147.0	3.06
28	Hendrickson	Mark	2006	TBA	AL	13.932	3	4.644	25	31	0	451.3	5.05
29	Sonnanstine	Andy	2011	TBA	AL	13.871	5	2.774	28	31	1	540.3	5.26
30	Jackson	Edwin	2008	TBA	AL	13.059	3	4.353	19	26	0	380.7	5.08
31	Boxberger	Brad	2017	TBA	AL	12.926	4	3.232	17	19	43	181.3	3.33
32	Anderson	Nick	2020	TBA	AL	12.624	2	6.312	5	1	6	37.7	1.43
33	Pagan	Emilio	2019	TBA	AL	12.553	1	12.553	4	2	20	70.0	2.31
34	Peralta	Joel	2014	TBA	AL	12.245	4	3.061	11	22	10	269.3	3.58
35	Yan	Esteban	2002	TBA	AL	12.145	5	2.429	26	30	42	418.7	5.01
36	Sturtze	Tanyon	2002	TBA	AL	11.929	3	3.976	19	30	1	472.0	4.58
37	Baez	Danys	2005	TBA	AL	11.405	2	5.703	9	8	71	140.3	3.21
38	Ramirez	Erasmo	2017	TBA	AL	11.191	3	3.730	22	20	3	323.3	3.98
39	Farnsworth	Kyle	2013	TBA	AL	10.254	3	3.418	8	7	25	114.3	3.54

Tampa Bay Rays – Top Fielders

Rank	FIRST BASE		FV	Lyear	G	FPCT	RF
1	Lee	Travis	1.1737	2006	378	0.997	8.40
2	McGriff	Fred	1.1547	2004	484	0.991	9.11
3	Pena	Carlos	1.0797	2012	704	0.994	8.30
4	Loney	James	1.0755	2014	306	0.994	8.07

Rank	SECOND BASE		FV	Lyear	G	FPCT	RF
1	Cairo	Miguel	1.2979	2000	373	0.982	4.97
2	Zobrist	Ben	1.1338	2014	547	0.987	3.89

Rank	SHORTSTOP		FV	Lyear	G	FPCT	RF
1	Lugo	Julio	1.4578	2006	489	0.966	4.61
2	Escobar	Yunel	1.4137	2014	289	0.978	3.59
3	Bartlett	Jason	1.3493	2010	390	0.969	3.80
4	Adames	Willy	1.3356	2020	280	0.961	3.44

Rank	THIRD BASE		FV	Lyear	G	FPCT	RF
1	Longoria	Evan	1.5526	2017	1345	0.968	2.57
2	Huff	Aubrey	1.2021	2006	283	0.940	2.29

Rank	CATCHER		FV	Lyear	G	FPCT	RF	CS%
1	Navarro	Dioner	1.8244	2010	442	0.989	7.26	0.329
2	Flaherty	John	1.7701	2002	467	0.991	6.49	0.325
3	Hall	Toby	1.7056	2006	578	0.989	6.09	0.366

Rank	OUTFIELD		FV	Lyear	G	FPCT	RF	ApG
1	Baldelli	Rocco	1.5596	2010	400	0.983	2.79	0.088
2	Upton	B.J.	1.5571	2012	813	0.989	2.56	0.064
3	Crawford	Carl	1.4911	2010	1219	0.991	2.24	0.042
4	Kiermaier	Kevin	1.4642	2020	569	0.987	2.36	0.060
5	Winn	Randy	1.4614	2002	487	0.988	2.35	0.082
6	Jennings	Desmond	1.4299	2016	554	0.995	2.10	0.031
7	Zobrist	Ben	1.4241	2014	431	0.997	1.62	0.058
8	Joyce	Matthew	1.2844	2014	549	0.987	1.62	0.038
9	Smith	Mallex	1.1332	2018	240	0.978	1.68	0.021

Rank	PITCHING		FV	Lyear	IP	FPCT	RF
1	Shields	James	1.0276	2012	1455	0.947	1.76
2	Price	David	0.9844	2014	1144	0.951	1.36
3	Sonnanstine	Andy	0.9792	2011	540	0.957	1.85
4	Hellickson	Jeremy	0.9582	2014	640	0.972	1.49
5	Niemann	Jeff	0.9495	2012	544	0.988	1.37
6	Cobb	Alex	0.9494	2017	700	0.936	2.06
7	Odorizzi	Jake	0.9460	2017	529	0.944	1.14
8	Archer	Chris	0.9296	2018	851	0.905	1.11
9	Garza	Matt	0.9220	2010	592	0.945	1.05
10	Kazmir	Scott	0.8791	2009	834	0.907	1.06

Franchise When and Where
Tampa Bay Rays (2008 to Present)
Tampa Bay Devil Rays (1998-2007)

TEXAS RANGERS
Best Seasons and Careers of All-Time

Well, you know the catching's going to be good. Ivan Rodriguez behind the plate. Adrian Beltre, another very good fielder, at third. Not sure you want Juan Gonzalez playing center field every day, but with the designated hitter, he might move there at times in a platoon. There's a good amount of home run power in the lineup surrounding Gonzalez with Rafael Palmeiro, Ruben Sierra, and Frank Howard in the batter's box. Charlie Hough is the top starting pitcher; challenge for Ivan with that nasty knuckleball, but he's up for it. The remainder of the starting rotation may have its moments, particularly with Ferguson Jenkins and Kevin Brown, but might not be the caliber of other staffs. The reserves are an interesting bunch. Any time you can call on Nolan Ryan for a trip to the mound is a good day. And Jim Sundberg is one fine defensive replacement when Rodriguez needs a day off.

Reserves

Bench - Rusty Greer (OF), Josh Hamilton (OF), Jeff Burroughs (3B), Mark Teixeira (1B), Buddy Bell (3B), Elvis Andrus (SS), Jim Sundberg (CATCHER).

Bullpen - John Wetteland (CL), Jeff Russell (SU), Bobby Witt, Nolan Ryan, Colby Lewis, Yu Darvish.

Texas Rangers - Best Position Player Years

Rank	Name	First	Year	Team	Lg	HR	RBI	AVG	Age	PEVA-B
1	Howard	Frank	1969	WS2	AL	48	111	0.296	33	30.491
2	Howard	Frank	1970	WS2	AL	44	126	0.283	34	29.338
3	Howard	Frank	1968	WS2	AL	44	106	0.274	32	28.584
4	Rodriguez	Alex	2001	TEX	AL	52	135	0.318	26	27.632
5	Rodriguez	Alex	2002	TEX	AL	57	142	0.300	27	25.524
6	Palmeiro	Rafael	1991	TEX	AL	26	88	0.322	27	25.081
7	Burroughs	Jeff	1974	TEX	AL	25	118	0.301	23	24.708
8	Hamilton	Josh	2010	TEX	AL	32	100	0.359	29	23.840
9	Rodriguez	Alex	2003	TEX	AL	47	118	0.298	28	23.712
10	Sierra	Ruben	1991	TEX	AL	25	116	0.307	26	23.040
11	Teixeira	Mark	2005	TEX	AL	43	144	0.301	25	22.742
12	Palmeiro	Rafael	1999	TEX	AL	47	148	0.324	35	22.557
13	Beltre	Adrian	2014	TEX	AL	19	77	0.324	35	21.712
14	Sierra	Ruben	1989	TEX	AL	29	119	0.306	24	21.583
15	Bell	Buddy	1984	TEX	AL	11	83	0.315	33	20.732
16	Palmeiro	Rafael	1993	TEX	AL	37	105	0.295	29	20.393
17	Gonzalez	Juan	1993	TEX	AL	46	118	0.310	24	19.823
18	Hamilton	Josh	2008	TEX	AL	32	130	0.304	27	19.261
19	Rodriguez	Ivan	1999	TEX	AL	35	113	0.332	28	19.153
20	Harrah	Toby	1975	TEX	AL	20	93	0.293	27	18.954

Texas Rangers - Best Pitcher Years

Rank	Name	First	Year	Team	Lg	W	L	SV	IP	ERA	Age	PEVA-P
1	Jenkins	Fergie	1974	TEX	AL	25	12	0	328.3	2.82	32	34.395
2	Lynn	Lance	2019	TEX	AL	16	11	0	208.3	3.67	32	24.601
3	Wilson	C.J.	2011	TEX	AL	16	7	0	223.3	2.94	31	22.523
4	Lynn	Lance	2020	TEX	AL	6	3	0	84.0	3.32	33	21.090
5	Hough	Charlie	1987	TEX	AL	18	13	0	285.3	3.79	39	19.948
6	Harrison	Matt	2012	TEX	AL	18	11	0	213.3	3.29	27	19.939
7	Brown	Kevin	1992	TEX	AL	21	11	0	265.7	3.32	27	19.711
8	Minor	Mike	2019	TEX	AL	14	10	0	208.3	3.59	32	19.475
9	Darvish	Yu	2013	TEX	AL	13	9	0	209.7	2.83	27	18.259
10	Kern	Jim	1979	TEX	AL	13	5	29	143.0	1.57	30	18.109
11	Matlack	Jon	1978	TEX	AL	15	13	1	270.0	2.27	28	17.730
12	Rogers	Kenny	1995	TEX	AL	17	7	0	208.0	3.38	31	17.288
13	Ryan	Nolan	1989	TEX	AL	16	10	0	239.3	3.20	42	16.581
14	Nathan	Joe	2013	TEX	AL	6	2	43	64.7	1.39	39	16.240
15	Blyleven	Bert	1977	TEX	AL	14	12	0	234.7	2.72	26	16.187
16	Tanana	Frank	1984	TEX	AL	15	15	0	246.3	3.25	31	15.957
17	Hill	Ken	1996	TEX	AL	16	10	0	250.7	3.63	31	15.910
18	Wilson	C.J.	2010	TEX	AL	15	8	0	204.0	3.35	30	15.167
19	Hamels	Cole	2016	TEX	AL	15	5	0	200.7	3.32	33	14.974
20	Russell	Jeff	1989	TEX	AL	6	4	38	72.7	1.98	28	14.931

Texas Rangers - Top Career Batters

RANK	NAME	FIRST	LYR	TEAM	LG	PEVA-B	YRS	PPYR	HR	RBI	H	AVE
1	Palmeiro	Rafael	2003	TEX	AL	157.511	10	15.751	321	1039	1692	0.290
2	Howard	Frank	1972	TEX	AL	146.881	8	18.360	246	701	1141	0.277

RANK	NAME	FIRST	LYR	TEAM	LG	PEVA-B	YRS	PPYR	HR	RBI	H	AVE
3	Young	Michael	2012	TEX	AL	134.504	13	10.346	177	984	2230	0.301
4	Gonzalez	Juan	2003	TEX	AL	134.135	13	10.318	372	1180	1595	0.293
5	Rodriguez	Ivan	2009	TEX	AL	127.258	13	9.789	217	842	1747	0.304
6	Beltre	Adrian	2018	TEX	AL	107.307	8	13.413	199	699	1277	0.304
7	Sierra	Ruben	2003	TEX	AL	100.532	10	10.053	180	742	1281	0.280
8	Bell	Buddy	1989	TEX	AL	99.017	8	12.377	87	499	1060	0.293
9	Andrus	Elvis	2020	TEX	AL	98.565	12	8.214	76	636	1743	0.274
10	Sundberg	Jim	1989	TEX	AL	90.856	12	7.571	60	480	1180	0.252
11	Harrah	Toby	1986	TEX	AL	89.156	11	8.105	124	568	1174	0.257
12	Greer	Rusty	2002	TEX	AL	77.166	9	8.574	119	614	1166	0.305
13	Rodriguez	Alex	2003	TEX	AL	76.868	3	25.623	156	395	569	0.305
14	Hamilton	Josh	2015	TEX	AL	73.044	6	12.174	150	531	814	0.302
15	Burroughs	Jeff	1976	TEX	AL	65.070	7	9.296	108	412	645	0.255
16	Kinsler	Ian	2013	TEX	AL	64.523	8	8.065	156	539	1145	0.273
17	Teixeira	Mark	2007	TEX	AL	63.627	5	12.725	153	499	746	0.283
18	O'Brien	Pete	1988	TEX	AL	60.585	7	8.655	114	487	914	0.273
19	McMullen	Ken	1970	WS2	AL	57.483	6	9.580	86	327	709	0.251
20	Franco	Julio	1993	TEX	AL	55.682	5	11.136	55	331	725	0.307
21	Parrish	Larry	1988	TEX	AL	54.765	7	7.824	149	522	852	0.264
22	Hargrove	Mike	1978	TEX	AL	51.842	5	10.368	47	295	730	0.293
23	Blalock	Hank	2009	TEX	AL	51.220	8	6.402	152	535	943	0.269
24	Palmer	Dean	1997	TEX	AL	51.196	8	6.400	154	451	677	0.247
25	Oliver	Al	1981	TEX	AL	49.584	4	12.396	49	337	668	0.319
26	Clark	Will	1998	TEX	AL	46.371	5	9.274	77	397	686	0.308
27	Cruz	Nelson	2013	TEX	AL	45.768	8	5.721	157	489	773	0.268
28	Choo	Shin-Soo	2020	TEX	AL	44.170	7	6.310	114	355	771	0.260
29	Lock	Don	1966	WS2	AL	44.089	5	8.818	99	286	498	0.240
30	Wills	Bump	1981	TEX	AL	43.832	5	8.766	30	264	693	0.265
31	Brinkman	Ed	1975	TEX	AL	43.009	11	3.910	31	273	868	0.226
32	Incaviglia	Pete	1990	TEX	AL	42.566	5	8.513	124	388	607	0.248
33	Odor	Rougned	2020	TEX	AL	39.429	7	5.633	146	458	749	0.237
34	Buechele	Steve	1995	TEX	AL	38.265	8	4.783	94	338	654	0.240
35	Hinton	Chuck	1964	WS2	AL	36.475	4	9.119	49	217	549	0.280
36	Murphy	David	2013	TEX	AL	35.886	7	5.127	85	362	733	0.275
37	King	Jim	1967	WS2	AL	33.836	7	4.834	89	290	511	0.239
38	Unser	Del	1971	WS2	AL	32.592	4	8.148	22	158	543	0.256
39	Fletcher	Scott	1989	TEX	AL	32.376	4	8.094	8	182	545	0.280
40	Epstein	Mike	1973	TEX	AL	32.243	6	5.374	74	218	414	0.248
41	Gallo	Joey	2010	TEX	AL	30.021	6	5.004	120	262	316	0.208
42	Rivers	Mickey	1984	TEX	AL	29.776	6	4.963	22	168	596	0.303
43	Ward	Gary	1986	TEX	AL	29.557	3	9.852	41	200	461	0.293
44	McLemore	Mark	1999	TEX	AL	28.920	5	5.784	22	210	632	0.268
45	Sample	Bill	1984	TEX	AL	28.452	7	4.065	39	201	587	0.270

RANK	NAME	FIRST	LYR	TEAM	LG	PEVA-B	YRS	PPYR	HR	RBI	H	AVE
46	McDowell	Oddibe	1994	TEX	AL	27.926	5	5.585	57	195	503	0.251
47	Mazara	Nomar	2019	TEX	AL	26.686	4	6.671	79	308	518	0.261
48	Wright	George	1986	TEX	AL	26.355	5	5.271	42	203	507	0.248
49	Casanova	Paul	1971	WS2	AL	25.237	7	3.605	41	216	527	0.228
50	Moreland	Mitch	2016	TEX	AL	24.643	7	3.520	110	354	633	0.254

Texas Rangers (WS2, TEX) - Top Career Pitchers

RANK	NAME	FIRST	LYEAR	LTEAM	LG	PEVA	YRS	PPYR	W	L	SV	IP	ERA
1	Hough	Charlie	1990	TEX	AL	104.223	11	9.475	139	123	1	2308.0	3.68
2	Rogers	Kenny	2005	TEX	AL	96.190	12	8.016	133	96	28	1909.0	4.16
3	Jenkins	Fergie	1981	TEX	AL	71.298	6	11.883	93	72	0	1410.3	3.56
4	Brown	Kevin	1994	TEX	AL	59.377	8	7.422	78	64	0	1278.7	3.81
5	Wilson	C.J.	2011	TEX	AL	51.917	7	7.417	43	35	52	708.0	3.60
6	Lewis	Colby	2016	TEX	AL	50.546	9	5.616	77	70	0	1174.3	4.65
7	Witt	Bobby	1998	TEX	AL	50.054	11	4.550	104	104	0	1680.7	4.85
8	Darvish	Yu	2017	TEX	AL	48.659	5	9.732	52	39	0	782.7	3.42
9	Ryan	Nolan	1993	TEX	AL	48.016	5	9.603	51	39	0	840.0	3.43
10	Helling	Rick	2001	TEX	AL	47.706	8	5.963	68	51	0	1008.0	4.86
11	Lynn	Lance	2020	TEX	AL	45.692	2	22.846	22	14	0	292.3	3.57
12	Oliver	Darren	2011	TEX	AL	40.120	10	4.012	60	54	5	955.3	4.94
13	Bosman	Dick	1973	TEX	AL	39.545	8	4.943	59	64	2	1103.3	3.35
14	Holland	Derek	2016	TEX	AL	39.520	8	4.940	62	50	0	985.0	4.35
15	Russell	Jeff	1996	TEX	AL	39.226	10	3.923	42	40	134	752.7	3.73
16	Perry	Gaylord	1980	TEX	AL	38.047	4	9.512	48	43	0	827.3	3.26
17	Millwood	Kevin	2009	TEX	AL	36.162	4	9.040	48	46	0	755.0	4.57
18	Wetteland	John	2000	TEX	AL	35.347	4	8.837	20	12	150	253.0	2.95
19	Harrison	Matt	2015	TEX	AL	35.182	8	4.398	50	35	2	668.3	4.21
20	Guzman	Jose	1992	TEX	AL	34.705	6	5.784	66	62	0	1013.7	3.90
21	Cordero	Francisco	2006	TEX	AL	34.114	7	4.873	21	20	117	397.0	3.45
22	Hamels	Cole	2018	TEX	AL	32.804	4	8.201	38	21	0	546.7	3.90
23	Minor	Mike	2020	TEX	AL	31.015	3	10.338	26	23	0	400.7	4.00
24	Matlack	Jon	1983	TEX	AL	30.682	6	5.114	43	45	3	915.0	3.41
25	Feliz	Neftali	2015	TEX	AL	30.420	7	4.346	13	10	93	261.3	2.69
26	Nathan	Joe	2013	TEX	AL	28.647	2	14.323	9	7	80	129.0	2.09
27	Darwin	Danny	1995	TEX	AL	28.432	8	3.554	55	52	15	872.0	3.72
28	Kline	Ron	1966	WS2	AL	26.053	4	6.513	26	25	83	364.7	2.54
29	Tanana	Frank	1985	TEX	AL	25.483	4	6.371	31	49	0	677.7	3.81
30	Pavlik	Roger	1998	TEX	AL	25.480	7	3.640	47	39	1	743.0	4.58
31	Perez	Martin	2018	TEX	AL	25.355	7	3.622	43	49	0	761.3	4.63
32	Ogando	Alexi	2014	TEX	AL	25.294	5	5.059	28	16	4	406.0	3.35
33	Knowles	Darold	1977	TEX	AL	25.089	6	4.181	25	29	64	424.0	2.46
34	Feldman	Scott	2012	TEX	AL	24.306	8	3.038	39	44	0	727.7	4.81
35	Sele	Aaron	1999	TEX	AL	23.896	2	11.948	37	20	0	417.7	4.50

RANK	NAME	FIRST	LYEAR	LTEAM	LG	PEVA	YRS	PPYR	W	L	SV	IP	ERA
36	Padilla	Vicente	2009	TEX	AL	23.467	4	5.867	43	34	0	599.3	4.90
37	Blyleven	Bert	1977	TEX	AL	22.022	2	11.011	23	23	0	437.0	2.74
38	Honeycutt	Rick	1994	TEX	AL	21.229	4	5.307	31	33	1	491.3	3.85
39	Medich	Doc	1982	TEX	AL	21.199	5	4.240	50	43	2	790.3	3.95
40	Zimmerman	Jeff	2001	TEX	AL	21.032	3	7.011	17	12	32	228.7	3.27
41	Kern	Jim	1981	TEX	AL	20.550	3	6.850	17	18	37	236.3	2.59
42	Comer	Steve	1982	TEX	AL	19.917	5	3.983	39	29	13	575.7	3.80
43	Hill	Ken	1997	TEX	AL	19.610	2	9.805	21	18	0	361.7	4.11
44	Coleman	Joe	1970	WS2	AL	19.587	6	3.265	43	50	1	850.3	3.51
45	Osteen	Claude	1964	WS2	AL	18.064	4	4.516	33	41	1	638.0	3.46
46	Burkett	John	1999	TEX	AL	17.987	4	4.497	32	35	0	600.3	5.13
47	Otsuka	Akinori	2007	TEX	AL	17.793	2	8.896	4	5	36	92.0	2.25
48	Richert	Pete	1967	WS2	AL	17.739	3	5.913	31	32	0	494.0	3.21
49	Ortega	Phil	1968	WS2	AL	16.771	4	4.193	39	49	0	712.3	4.12
50	Leclerc	Jose	2020	TEX	AL	16.501	5	3.300	6	10	29	189.0	3.19

Texas Rangers – Top Fielders

Rank	FIRST BASE		FV	Lyear	G	FPCT	RF
1	O'Brien	Pete	1.2441	1988	904	0.993	9.32
2	Teixeira	Mark	1.2200	2007	646	0.996	9.32
3	Stevens	Lee	1.1809	1999	250	0.994	8.66
4	Clark	Will	1.1643	1998	580	0.993	9.19
5	Spencer	Jim	1.1597	1975	258	0.997	8.48
6	Palmeiro	Rafael	1.1422	2003	1167	0.994	8.89
7	Hargrove	Mike	1.1182	1978	572	0.988	9.15
8	Moreland	Mitch	1.0803	2016	661	0.996	8.00
9	Epstein	Mike	1.0662	1973	479	0.989	9.42
10	Putnam	Pat	1.0244	1982	377	0.993	8.35

Rank	SECOND BASE		FV	Lyear	G	FPCT	RF
1	Wills	Bump	1.4558	1981	697	0.981	5.60
2	Young	Michael	1.3523	2012	446	0.986	4.72
3	McLemore	Mark	1.2993	1999	559	0.983	4.93
4	Franco	Julio	1.2395	1992	447	0.977	4.68
5	Soriano	Alfonso	1.2284	2005	295	0.971	4.94
6	Odor	Roughned	1.2192	2020	834	0.975	4.46
7	Kinsler	Ian	1.2096	2013	1029	0.978	4.90
8	Nelson	Dave	1.1979	1975	317	0.977	4.99
9	Blasingame	Don	1.1792	1966	367	0.983	4.54
10	Cottier	Chuck	1.1787	1964	372	0.977	5.14

Rank	SHORTSTOP		FV	Lyear	G	FPCT	RF
1	Rodriguez	Alex	1.6950	2003	481	0.984	4.48
2	Andrus	Elvis	1.5822	2020	1628	0.973	4.31
3	Brinkman	Ed	1.5763	1970	1104	0.967	4.77
4	Young	Michael	1.5658	2012	792	0.977	4.29
5	Gil	Benji	1.5512	1997	263	0.967	4.71
6	Fletcher	Scott	1.5488	1989	511	0.972	4.22
7	Clayton	Royce	1.4783	2000	333	0.969	4.58
8	Harrah	Toby	1.4665	1985	773	0.960	4.72
9	Huson	Jeff	1.3171	1993	329	0.961	3.48
10	Wilkerson	Curtis	1.2530	1988	348	0.953	3.39

Rank	THIRD BASE		FV	Lyear	G	FPCT	RF
1	Bell	Buddy	1.6725	1989	901	0.967	3.32
2	McMullen	Ken	1.6031	1970	742	0.963	3.29
3	Buechele	Steve	1.5350	1995	835	0.970	2.54
4	Beltre	Adrian	1.5100	2018	941	0.966	2.59
5	Palmer	Dean	1.4120	1997	728	0.938	2.34

			FV	Lyear	G	FPCT	RF	
6	Blalock	Hank	1.3851	2009	697	0.960	2.45	
7	Young	Michael	1.3650	2012	358	0.958	2.22	
8	Harrah	Toby	1.3563	1978	345	0.960	2.42	
9	Howell	Roy	1.2533	1977	258	0.928	2.60	

Rank	CATCHER		FV	Lyear	G	FPCT	RF	CS%
1	Sundberg	Jim	2.0138	1989	1495	0.992	5.63	0.418
2	Rodriguez	Ivan	1.9683	2009	1451	0.990	6.55	0.501
3	Casanova	Paul	1.7594	1971	657	0.986	5.73	0.417
4	Slaught	Don	1.7464	1987	278	0.990	5.84	0.263
5	Petralli	Geno	1.6801	1993	556	0.987	5.20	0.319
6	Chirinos	Robinson	1.6477	2020	432	0.993	6.76	0.264
7	Barajas	Rod	1.6344	2006	318	0.987	6.40	0.340
8	Laird	Gerald	1.6259	2008	356	0.984	6.08	0.376
9	Stanley	Mike	1.5631	1991	275	0.984	4.68	0.165

Rank	OUTFIELD		FV	Lyear	G	FPCT	RF	ApG
1	Martin	Leonys	1.5763	2015	424	0.987	2.44	0.092
2	Beniquez	Juan	1.5621	1978	390	0.982	2.73	0.092
3	Unser	Del	1.5564	1971	559	0.981	2.40	0.086
4	Wright	George	1.5254	1986	534	0.984	2.51	0.062
5	Rivers	Mickey	1.5238	1984	348	0.985	2.46	0.112
6	Lock	Don	1.5156	1966	627	0.978	2.39	0.078
7	McDowell	Oddibe	1.4857	1994	542	0.990	2.36	0.057
8	Ward	Gary	1.4805	1986	405	0.983	2.34	0.074
9	Goodwin	Tom	1.4733	1999	311	0.990	2.50	0.039
10	Pettis	Gary	1.4712	1991	254	0.986	2.15	0.055
11	Matthews	Gary	1.4463	2006	368	0.983	2.38	0.063
12	Byrd	Marlon	1.4420	2009	394	0.986	2.18	0.056
13	Kapler	Gabe	1.4411	2002	329	0.983	2.40	0.061
14	Hinton	Chuck	1.4273	1964	484	0.983	2.00	0.058
15	Maddox	Elliott	1.4228	1973	286	0.988	1.96	0.073
16	Mazara	Nomar	1.4213	2019	505	0.989	1.91	0.051
17	Valentine	Fred	1.4202	1968	369	0.985	1.92	0.046
18	Gonzalez	Juan	1.4183	2003	1097	0.983	2.08	0.069
19	Sample	Bill	1.4147	1984	600	0.987	2.08	0.050
20	Oliver	Al	1.4022	1980	383	0.977	2.14	0.068
21	Gallo	Joey	1.3948	2020	280	0.987	1.90	0.079
22	Mench	Kevin	1.3866	2006	514	0.990	1.77	0.051
23	King	Jim	1.3811	1967	640	0.981	1.79	0.078
24	Espy	Cecil	1.3799	1990	278	0.984	2.01	0.061
25	Burroughs	Jeff	1.3785	1976	673	0.974	1.84	0.074
26	Sierra	Ruben	1.3758	2003	1070	0.971	1.93	0.072
27	Greer	Rusty	1.3633	2002	989	0.979	2.00	0.040
28	DeShields	Delino	1.3552	2019	506	0.980	2.22	0.047
29	Stroud	Ed	1.3425	1970	366	0.986	1.77	0.033
30	Hamilton	Josh	1.3387	2015	704	0.984	1.96	0.045

Rank	PITCHING		FV	Lyear	IP	FPCT	RF
1	Hough	Charlie	1.0811	1990	2308	0.976	2.05
2	Jenkins	Fergie	1.0645	1981	1410	0.959	2.24
3	Tanana	Frank	1.0498	1985	678	0.975	2.03
4	Rogers	Kenny	1.0413	2005	1909	0.956	2.54
5	Brown	Kevin	1.0293	1994	1279	0.940	2.42
6	Perry	Gaylord	1.0291	1980	827	0.973	1.57
7	Bosman	Dick	1.0186	1973	1103	0.980	1.98
8	Coleman	Joe	1.0121	1970	850	0.969	1.96
9	Osteen	Claude	1.0100	1964	638	0.979	1.95
10	Guzman	Jose	1.0055	1992	1014	0.968	1.87

Franchise When and Where
Texas Rangers (1972 to Present)
Washington Senators (1961-1971,WS2)

TORONTO BLUE JAYS
Best Seasons and Careers of All-Time

Two World Series victories in the relatively short span of Toronto Blue Jay baseball surprisingly does not populate the starting lineup or starting staff of the All-Time franchise team as much as you'd think. There's no Joe Carter, although you could argue that he should be, and might be considered better for the Outfield than DH candidates George Bell or Jose Bautista. Roberto Alomar is there, his double play mate Tony Fernandez, too. Jimmy Key, Pat Hentgen, and Dave Stieb, too, in a variety or roles. Jose Bautista and Carlos Delgado head the list of best players overall, and Roy Halladay is the best pitcher in Blue Jay history. For some, adding Roger Clemens to the staff seems most appropriate for his two great seasons; for others it wasn't enough time to be included.

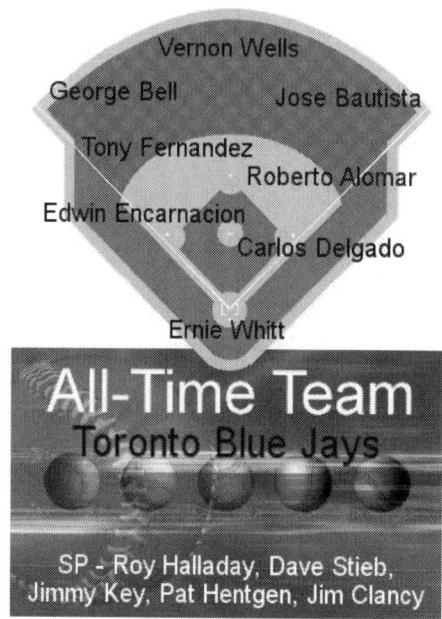

Vernon Wells

George Bell   Jose Bautista

Tony Fernandez
Roberto Alomar

Edwin Encarnacion
Carlos Delgado

Ernie Whitt

All-Time Team
Toronto Blue Jays

SP - Roy Halladay, Dave Stieb,
Jimmy Key, Pat Hentgen, Jim Clancy

Reserves

Bench - Lloyd Moseby (OF), Jesse Barfield (OF), Joe Carter (OF), Fred McGriff (1B), John Olerud (1B), Josh Donaldson (3B), Aaron Hill (IF), Pat Borders (CATCHER).

Bullpen - Tom Henke (CL), Duane Ward (SU), Juan Guzman, David Wells, Ricky Romero, Marcus Stroman.

Toronto Blue Jays - Best Position Player Years

Rank	Name	First	Year	Team	Lg	HR	RBI	AVG	Age	PEVA-B
1	Delgado	Carlos	2000	TOR	AL	41	137	0.344	28	34.143
2	Bautista	Jose	2014	TOR	AL	35	103	0.286	34	31.646
3	Bautista	Jose	2011	TOR	AL	43	103	0.302	31	30.892
4	Bautista	Jose	2010	TOR	AL	54	124	0.260	30	30.577
5	Olerud	John	1993	TOR	AL	24	107	0.363	25	28.968
6	Donaldson	Josh	2015	TOR	AL	41	123	0.297	30	28.923
7	Barfield	Jesse	1986	TOR	AL	40	108	0.289	27	28.916
8	Donaldson	Josh	2016	TOR	AL	37	99	0.284	31	26.376
9	McGriff	Fred	1989	TOR	AL	36	92	0.269	26	25.384
10	Delgado	Carlos	2003	TOR	AL	42	145	0.302	31	24.444
11	Bell	George	1987	TOR	AL	47	134	0.308	28	24.361
12	Encarnacion	Edwin	2012	TOR	AL	42	110	0.280	29	22.161
13	Moseby	Lloyd	1984	TOR	AL	18	92	0.280	25	22.132
14	Green	Shawn	1999	TOR	AL	42	123	0.309	27	21.898
15	McGriff	Fred	1990	TOR	AL	35	88	0.300	27	21.863
16	McGriff	Fred	1988	TOR	AL	34	82	0.282	25	21.613
17	Bautista	Jose	2015	TOR	AL	40	114	0.250	35	21.082
18	Bell	George	1986	TOR	AL	31	108	0.309	27	21.052
19	Molitor	Paul	1993	TOR	AL	22	111	0.332	37	19.716
20	Gruber	Kelly	1990	TOR	AL	31	118	0.274	28	19.660

Toronto Blue Jays - Best Pitcher Years

Rank	Name	First	Year	Team	Lg	W	L	SV	IP	ERA	Age	PEVA-P
1	Clemens	Roger	1997	TOR	AL	21	7	0	264.0	2.05	35	47.079
2	Halladay	Roy	2008	TOR	AL	20	11	0	246.0	2.78	31	46.107
3	Halladay	Roy	2003	TOR	AL	22	7	0	266.0	3.25	26	36.858
4	Key	Jimmy	1987	TOR	AL	17	8	0	261.0	2.76	26	36.007
5	Clemens	Roger	1998	TOR	AL	20	6	0	234.7	2.65	36	33.173
6	Halladay	Roy	2009	TOR	AL	17	10	0	239.0	2.79	32	31.554
7	Halladay	Roy	2006	TOR	AL	16	5	0	220.0	3.19	29	30.499
8	Stieb	Dave	1984	TOR	AL	16	8	0	267.0	2.83	27	29.332
9	Alexander	Doyle	1984	TOR	AL	17	6	0	261.7	3.13	34	26.207
10	Halladay	Roy	2002	TOR	AL	19	7	0	239.3	2.93	25	23.939
11	Stieb	Dave	1982	TOR	AL	17	14	0	288.3	3.25	25	22.711
12	Stieb	Dave	1983	TOR	AL	17	12	0	278.0	3.04	26	22.592
13	Hentgen	Pat	1996	TOR	AL	20	10	0	265.7	3.22	28	22.520
14	Wells	David	2000	TOR	AL	20	8	0	229.7	4.11	37	21.659
15	Stroman	Marcus	2017	TOR	AL	13	9	0	201.0	3.09	26	19.518
16	Happ	J.A.	2016	TOR	AL	20	4	0	195.0	3.18	34	19.155
17	Romero	Ricky	2011	TOR	AL	15	11	0	225.0	2.92	26	18.736
18	Key	Jimmy	1991	TOR	AL	16	12	0	209.3	3.05	30	18.636
19	Stieb	Dave	1981	TOR	AL	11	10	0	183.7	3.19	24	18.245
20	Eichorn	Mark	1986	TOR	AL	14	6	10	157.0	1.72	26	18.200

Toronto Blue Jays - Top Career Batters

RANK	NAME	FIRST	LYR	TEAM	LG	PEVA-B	YRS	PPYR	HR	RBI	H	AVE
1	Bautista	Jose	2017	TOR	AL	151.500	10	15.150	288	766	1103	0.253
2	Delgado	Carlos	2004	TOR	AL	143.926	12	11.994	336	1058	1413	0.282

RANK	NAME	FIRST	LYR	TEAM	LG	PEVA-B	YRS	PPYR	HR	RBI	H	AVE
3	Bell	George	1990	TOR	AL	108.429	9	12.048	202	740	1294	0.286
4	Wells	Vernon	2010	TOR	AL	107.719	12	8.977	223	813	1529	0.280
5	Moseby	Lloyd	1989	TOR	AL	105.798	10	10.580	149	651	1319	0.257
6	Encarnacion	Edwin	2016	TOR	AL	100.983	8	12.623	239	679	977	0.268
7	Fernandez	Tony	2001	TOR	AL	95.931	12	7.994	60	613	1583	0.297
8	Barfield	Jesse	1989	TOR	AL	88.455	9	9.828	179	527	919	0.265
9	Carter	Joe	1997	TOR	AL	84.649	7	12.093	203	736	1051	0.257
10	McGriff	Fred	1990	TOR	AL	73.370	5	14.674	125	305	540	0.278
11	Olerud	John	1996	TOR	AL	69.764	8	8.721	109	471	910	0.293
12	Donaldson	Josh	2018	TOR	AL	66.705	4	16.676	116	316	492	0.281
13	Whitt	Ernie	1989	TOR	AL	65.164	12	5.430	131	518	888	0.253
14	Alomar	Roberto	1995	TOR	AL	59.926	5	11.985	55	342	832	0.307
15	Upshaw	Willie	1987	TOR	AL	59.524	9	6.614	112	478	982	0.265
16	Gruber	Kelly	1992	TOR	AL	58.353	9	6.484	114	434	800	0.259
17	Stewart	Shannon	2008	TOR	AL	52.918	10	5.292	74	370	1082	0.298
18	Green	Shawn	1999	TOR	AL	51.706	7	7.387	119	376	718	0.286
19	Lind	Adam	2014	TOR	AL	51.249	9	5.694	146	519	931	0.273
20	White	Devon	1995	TOR	AL	50.795	5	10.159	72	274	733	0.270
21	Rios	Alexis	2009	TOR	AL	47.865	6	7.977	81	395	875	0.285
22	Sprague	Ed	1998	TOR	AL	44.458	8	5.557	113	418	773	0.245
23	Mulliniks	Rance	1992	TOR	AL	44.028	11	4.003	68	389	843	0.280
24	Hill	Aaron	2011	TOR	AL	43.559	7	6.223	96	409	881	0.265
25	Molitor	Paul	1995	TOR	AL	41.129	3	13.710	51	246	508	0.315
26	Gonzalez	Alex	2001	TOR	AL	39.673	8	4.959	83	350	798	0.245
27	Overbay	Lyle	2010	TOR	AL	38.873	5	7.775	83	336	672	0.268
28	Cruz	Jose	2002	TOR	AL	37.228	6	6.205	122	355	640	0.250
29	Garcia	Damaso	1986	TOR	AL	35.365	7	5.052	32	296	1028	0.288
30	Griffin	Alfredo	1993	TOR	AL	35.175	8	4.397	13	231	844	0.249
31	Smoak	Justin	2019	TOR	AL	33.147	5	6.629	117	321	491	0.237
32	Pillar	Kevin	2019	TOR	AL	32.449	7	4.636	55	231	641	0.260
33	Hinske	Eric	2006	TOR	AL	32.064	5	6.413	78	313	584	0.259
34	Borders	Pat	1999	TOR	AL	29.373	8	3.672	54	272	590	0.256
35	Mayberry	John	1982	TOR	AL	28.360	5	5.672	92	272	461	0.256
36	Grichuk	Randal	2020	TOR	AL	27.097	3	9.032	68	176	299	0.244
37	Johnson	Reed	2007	TOR	AL	26.643	5	5.329	42	234	585	0.281
38	Martin	Russell	2018	TOR	AL	26.378	4	6.595	66	211	335	0.225
39	Batista	Tony	2001	TOR	AL	25.183	3	8.394	80	238	326	0.258
40	Howell	Roy	1980	TOR	AL	25.069	4	6.267	43	234	532	0.272
41	Velez	Otto	1982	TOR	AL	23.499	6	3.916	72	243	394	0.257
42	Fletcher	Darrin	2002	TOR	AL	23.094	5	4.619	61	268	490	0.276
43	Rasmus	Colby	2014	TOR	AL	21.742	4	5.436	66	194	342	0.234
44	Zaun	Gregg	2008	TOR	AL	21.264	5	4.253	45	219	417	0.255
45	Scutaro	Marco	2009	TOR	AL	20.841	2	10.420	19	120	300	0.275

RANK	NAME	FIRST	LYR	TEAM	LG	PEVA-B	YRS	PPYR	HR	RBI	H	AVE
46	Johnson	Cliff	1986	TOR	AL	20.795	4	5.199	54	202	321	0.273
47	Catalanotto	Frank	2006	TOR	AL	20.084	4	5.021	29	200	476	0.299
48	Glaus	Troy	2007	TOR	AL	19.903	2	9.951	58	166	237	0.256
49	Bonnell	Barry	1983	TOR	AL	19.588	4	4.897	33	187	422	0.281
50	Hudson	Orlando	2005	TOR	AL	19.233	4	4.808	35	201	437	0.270

Toronto Blue Jays - Top Career Pitchers

RANK	NAME	FIRST	LYEAR	LTEAM	LG	PEVA	YRS	PPYR	W	L	SV	IP	ERA
1	Halladay	Roy	2009	TOR	AL	214.098	12	17.841	148	76	1	2046.7	3.43
2	Stieb	Dave	1998	TOR	AL	173.801	15	11.587	175	134	3	2873.0	3.42
3	Key	Jimmy	1992	TOR	AL	105.710	9	11.746	116	81	10	1695.7	3.42
4	Hentgen	Pat	2004	TOR	AL	88.578	10	8.858	107	85	0	1636.0	4.28
5	Clancy	Jim	1988	TOR	AL	84.708	12	7.059	128	140	1	2204.7	4.10
6	Clemens	Roger	1998	TOR	AL	80.252	2	40.126	41	13	0	498.7	2.33
7	Henke	Tom	1992	TOR	AL	74.479	8	9.310	29	29	217	563.0	2.48
8	Guzman	Juan	1998	TOR	AL	65.588	8	8.199	76	62	0	1215.7	4.07
9	Wells	David	2000	TOR	AL	61.483	8	7.685	84	55	13	1148.7	4.06
10	Ward	Duane	1995	TOR	AL	52.059	9	5.784	32	36	121	650.7	3.18
11	Stroman	Marcus	2019	TOR	AL	46.913	6	7.819	47	45	1	789.7	3.76
12	Romero	Ricky	2013	TOR	AL	44.108	5	8.822	51	45	0	801.3	4.16
13	Alexander	Doyle	1986	TOR	AL	43.563	4	10.891	46	26	0	750.0	3.56
14	Happ	J.A.	2018	TOR	AL	41.908	6	6.985	59	41	0	745.3	3.88
15	Osuna	Roberto	2018	TOR	AL	39.219	4	9.805	8	13	104	223.0	2.87
16	Dickey	R.A.	2016	TOR	AL	38.987	4	9.747	49	52	0	824.3	4.05
17	Janssen	Casey	2014	TOR	AL	37.703	8	4.713	29	24	90	493.0	3.52
18	Estrada	Marco	2018	TOR	AL	34.816	4	8.704	39	40	0	686.7	4.25
19	Stottlemyre	Todd	1994	TOR	AL	34.472	7	4.925	69	70	1	1139.0	4.39
20	Eichhorn	Mark	1993	TOR	AL	31.812	6	5.302	29	19	15	493.0	3.03
21	Buehrle	Mark	2015	TOR	AL	31.787	3	10.596	40	28	0	604.3	3.78
22	Escobar	Kelvim	2003	TOR	AL	30.725	7	4.389	58	55	58	849.0	4.58
23	Leal	Luis	1985	TOR	AL	30.387	6	5.064	51	58	1	946.0	4.14
24	Sanchez	Aaron	2019	TOR	AL	28.837	6	4.806	32	33	3	571.0	3.96
25	Marcum	Shaun	2010	TOR	AL	28.722	5	5.744	37	25	1	592.0	3.85
26	Burnett	A.J.	2008	TOR	AL	28.502	3	9.501	38	26	0	522.7	3.94
27	Quantrill	Paul	2001	TOR	AL	26.825	6	4.471	30	34	15	517.7	3.67
28	Downs	Scott	2010	TOR	AL	26.267	6	4.378	20	18	16	407.7	3.13
29	Carpenter	Chris	2002	TOR	AL	25.937	6	4.323	49	50	0	870.7	4.83
30	Cecil	Brett	2016	TOR	AL	25.425	8	3.178	41	42	11	656.0	4.20
31	Lilly	Ted	2006	TOR	AL	24.752	3	8.251	37	34	0	505.3	4.52
32	Ryan	B.J.	2009	TOR	AL	22.485	4	5.621	5	9	75	155.3	2.95
33	Frasor	Jason	2012	TOR	AL	21.782	9	2.420	25	29	36	504.7	3.73
34	Morrow	Brandon	2014	TOR	AL	19.707	5	3.941	34	31	0	538.0	4.40
35	Cerutti	John	1990	TOR	AL	19.656	6	3.276	46	37	2	772.3	3.87

RANK	NAME	FIRST	LYEAR	LTEAM	LG	PEVA	YRS	PPYR	W	L	SV	IP	ERA
36	Timlin	Mike	1997	TOR	AL	19.576	7	2.797	23	22	52	393.3	3.62
37	Williams	Woody	1998	TOR	AL	18.901	6	3.150	28	34	0	613.3	4.30
38	Loup	Aaron	2018	TOR	AL	18.599	7	2.657	12	20	6	318.7	3.47
39	Towers	Josh	2007	TOR	AL	18.406	5	3.681	37	42	1	558.3	4.93
40	Koch	Billy	2001	TOR	AL	17.258	3	5.753	11	13	100	211.7	3.57
41	McGowan	Dustin	2014	TOR	AL	15.737	7	2.248	25	27	1	482.3	4.57
42	Morris	Jack	1993	TOR	AL	15.714	2	7.857	28	18	0	393.3	4.87
43	Leiter	Al	1995	TOR	AL	15.674	7	2.239	26	24	2	415.3	4.20
44	Ryu	Hyun Jin	2020	TOR	AL	15.147	1	15.147	5	2	0	67.0	2.69
45	Litsch	Jesse	2011	TOR	AL	15.079	5	3.016	27	27	1	417.7	4.16
46	Chacin	Gustavo	2007	TOR	AL	14.795	4	3.699	25	15	0	331.7	4.18
47	Cone	David	1995	TOR	AL	14.617	2	7.308	13	9	0	183.3	3.14
48	Garvin	Jerry	1982	TOR	AL	14.516	6	2.419	20	41	8	606.0	4.43
49	Jackson	Roy Lee	1984	TOR	AL	13.280	4	3.320	24	21	30	337.0	3.50
50	Hutchison	Drew	2016	TOR	AL	13.264	4	3.316	30	21	0	406.3	4.92

Toronto Blue Jays – Top Fielders

Rank	FIRST BASE		FV	Lyear	G	FPCT	RF
1	McGriff	Fred	1.3085	1990	474	0.993	9.50
2	Overbay	Lyle	1.2604	2010	703	0.996	9.42
3	Delgado	Carlos	1.1933	2004	1168	0.992	9.38
4	Smoak	Justin	1.1814	2019	595	0.997	7.75
5	Upshaw	Willie	1.1667	1987	950	0.990	8.92
6	Olerud	John	1.1366	1996	766	0.995	8.71
7	Mayberry	John	1.1321	1982	494	0.994	9.12
8	Lind	Adam	1.0662	2014	304	0.993	8.84
9	Encarnacion	Edwin	1.0053	2016	386	0.992	8.69

Rank	SECOND BASE		FV	Lyear	G	FPCT	RF
1	Hudson	Orlando	1.4560	2005	454	0.986	5.36
2	Alomar	Roberto	1.3399	1995	694	0.987	4.65
3	Bush	Homer	1.2797	2002	284	0.987	5.22
4	Hill	Aaron	1.2597	2011	746	0.987	4.76
5	Garcia	Damaso	1.2525	1986	869	0.980	4.99
6	Lee	Manuel	1.1987	1990	344	0.987	4.39
7	Johnson	Kelly	1.1647	2012	169	0.981	4.57
8	Liriano	Nelson	1.1309	1990	288	0.978	4.55
9	Travis	Devon	1.0323	2018	312	0.978	4.25
10	Iorg	Garth	1.0302	1987	338	0.976	4.06

Rank	SHORTSTOP		FV	Lyear	G	FPCT	RF
1	Fernandez	Tony	1.6727	1993	1104	0.981	4.69
2	Gonzalez	Alex	1.5965	2001	874	0.976	4.58
3	Griffin	Alfredo	1.5146	1993	907	0.959	4.62
4	Lee	Manuel	1.4639	1992	365	0.974	3.75
5	Escobar	Yunel	1.4638	2012	335	0.977	4.40
6	McDonald	John	1.3245	2011	361	0.973	3.76
7	Reyes	Jose	1.2962	2015	303	0.965	3.72
8	Woodward	Chris	1.2634	2011	283	0.967	4.28

Rank	THIRD BASE		FV	Lyear	G	FPCT	RF
1	Gruber	Kelly	1.5136	1992	829	0.955	2.67
2	Howell	Roy	1.4879	1980	489	0.953	2.91
3	Lawrie	Brett	1.4783	2014	332	0.962	2.70
4	Sprague	Ed	1.4536	1998	814	0.945	2.37
5	Donaldson	Josh	1.4385	2018	417	0.958	2.63
6	Hinske	Eric	1.3617	2006	435	0.953	2.32
7	Mulliniks	Rance	1.3211	1991	725	0.961	1.92
8	Iorg	Garth	1.2526	1987	556	0.955	1.77

Rank	CATCHER		FV	Lyear	G	FPCT	RF	CS%
1	Whitt	Ernie	1.8540	1989	1159	0.991	5.30	0.334
2	Borders	Pat	1.8390	1999	691	0.988	5.92	0.349
3	Cerone	Rick	1.8222	1979	251	0.986	5.02	0.410
4	Fletcher	Darrin	1.7874	2002	516	0.994	6.16	0.253
5	Martin	Russell	1.7841	2018	398	0.995	8.11	0.255
6	Arencibia	J.P.	1.7668	2013	355	0.992	7.22	0.263
7	Martinez	Buck	1.7141	1986	441	0.991	4.22	0.363
8	Myers	Greg	1.6523	2005	316	0.986	5.13	0.279
9	Zaun	Gregg	1.6248	2008	483	0.989	6.31	0.225

Rank	OUTFIELD		FV	Lyear	G	FPCT	RF	ApG
1	White	Devon	1.5846	1995	650	0.989	2.83	0.049
2	Bosetti	Rick	1.5814	1981	367	0.981	2.96	0.106
3	Pillar	Kevin	1.5523	2019	685	0.991	2.36	0.050
4	Wells	Vernon	1.5489	2010	1367	0.993	2.34	0.045
5	Barfield	Jesse	1.5171	1989	996	0.982	2.24	0.117
6	Moseby	Lloyd	1.5141	1989	1349	0.985	2.53	0.047
7	Grichuk	Randal	1.4955	2020	331	0.993	1.84	0.039
8	Bailor	Bob	1.4857	1980	404	0.980	2.30	0.141
9	Green	Shawn	1.4795	1999	657	0.986	2.05	0.070
10	Cruz Jr.	Jose	1.4645	2002	752	0.988	2.25	0.056
11	Nixon	Otis	1.4629	1997	227	0.993	1.96	0.026
12	Rios	Alexis	1.4448	2009	819	0.988	1.96	0.067
13	Rasmus	Colby	1.4307	2014	381	0.985	2.46	0.029
14	Bonnell	Barry	1.3825	1983	430	0.978	2.08	0.070
15	Johnson	Reed	1.3822	2007	659	0.990	1.51	0.053
16	Bautista	Jose	1.3652	2017	998	0.984	1.91	0.086
17	Carter	Joe	1.3621	1997	835	0.974	1.95	0.061
18	Stewart	Shannon	1.3586	2008	849	0.983	1.94	0.037
19	Bell	George	1.3235	1990	1066	0.964	1.96	0.070
20	Catalanotto	Frank	1.3169	2006	358	0.993	1.50	0.050
21	Davis	Rajai	1.3035	2013	343	0.980	1.73	0.041
22	Woods	Al	1.2841	1982	531	0.974	2.08	0.055
23	Mondesi	Raul	1.2817	2002	307	0.973	1.99	0.088
24	Hernandez	Toscar	1.2377	2020	321	0.976	1.91	0.087
25	Carrera	Ezequiel	1.1227	2017	329	0.982	1.16	0.043

Rank	PITCHING		FV	Lyear	IP	FPCT	RF
1	Halladay	Roy	1.0930	2009	2047	0.980	2.12
2	Stieb	Dave	1.0788	1998	2873	0.973	2.39
3	Dickey	R.A.	1.0619	2016	825	0.970	1.76
4	Buehrle	Mark	1.0601	2015	604	0.955	1.91
5	Key	Jimmy	1.0562	1992	1696	0.970	2.23
6	Garvin	Jerry	1.0542	1982	606	0.982	2.50
7	Alexander	Doyle	1.0453	1986	750	0.963	1.87
8	Romero	Rickey	1.0445	2013	801	0.959	2.10
9	Stroman	Marcus	1.0437	2019	763	0.958	2.15
10	Marcum	Shaun	1.0309	2010	592	1.000	2.05

Franchise When and Where
Toronto Blue Jays (1977 to Present)

WASHINGTON NATIONALS
Best Seasons and Careers of All-Time

It took two cities, two countries, and until 2019 before the franchise once known as the Montreal Expos could claim a World Series championship. The players who man the All-Time list reflect both those cities, and countries, from the speed at the top of the lineup represented by Tim Raines of those Montreal days to the professional hitter of Anthony Rendon, of Nationals lore. In fact, there's five tool ability in Andre Dawson and Vladimir Guerrero starting in the outfield and Bryce Harper coming off the bench. And the starting pitching has some great entrants; Max Scherzer, Steve Rogers, Stephen Strasburg, Padro Martinez, and, not his brother, Dennis.

Reserves

Bench - Rusty Staub (1B/OF), Bryce Harper (OF), Larry Walker (OF), Bob Bailey (3B/1B/OF), Larry Parrish (3B/OF), Jose Vidro (IF), Brian Schneider (CATCHER).

Bullpen - Tim Burke (CL), Jeff Riordan (SU), Livan Hernandez, Gio Gonzalez, Jordan Zimmermann, Jeff Fassero.

Washington Nationals - Best Position Player Years

Rank	Name	First	Year	Team	Lg	HR	RBI	AVG	Age	PEVA-B
1	Harper	Bryce	2015	WAS	NL	42	99	0.330	23	33.903
2	Carter	Gary	1982	MON	NL	29	97	0.293	28	33.521
3	Carter	Gary	1984	MON	NL	27	106	0.294	30	31.258
4	Singleton	Ken	1973	MON	NL	23	103	0.302	26	28.768
5	Raines	Tim	1984	MON	NL	8	60	0.309	25	26.337
6	Rendon	Anthony	2019	WAS	NL	34	126	0.319	29	26.321
7	Oliver	Al	1982	MON	NL	22	109	0.331	36	25.696
8	Dawson	Andre	1983	MON	NL	32	113	0.299	29	25.631
9	Staub	Rusty	1969	MON	NL	29	79	0.302	25	24.146
10	Staub	Rusty	1971	MON	NL	19	97	0.311	27	23.695
11	Staub	Rusty	1970	MON	NL	30	94	0.274	26	22.827
12	Soto	Juan	2020	WAS	NL	13	37	0.351	22	22.177
13	Guerrero	Vladimir	2000	MON	NL	44	123	0.345	24	22.091
14	Dawson	Andre	1981	MON	NL	24	64	0.302	27	22.054
15	Raines	Tim	1983	MON	NL	11	71	0.298	24	21.966
16	Guerrero	Vladimir	2002	MON	NL	39	111	0.336	26	21.831
17	Raines	Tim	1987	MON	NL	18	68	0.330	28	21.635
18	Zimmerman	Ryan	2009	WAS	NL	33	106	0.292	25	21.206
19	Turner	Trea	2020	WAS	NL	12	41	0.335	27	20.691
20	Soto	Juan	2019	WAS	NL	34	110	0.282	21	20.629

Washington Nationals - Best Pitcher Years

Rank	Name	First	Year	Team	Lg	W	L	SV	IP	ERA	Age	PEVA-P
1	Martinez	Pedro	1997	MON	NL	17	8	0	241.3	1.90	26	38.574
2	Rogers	Steve	1982	MON	NL	19	8	0	277.0	2.40	33	36.926
3	Scherzer	Max	2017	WAS	NL	16	6	0	200.7	2.51	33	36.052
4	Scherzer	Max	2018	WAS	NL	18	7	0	220.7	2.53	34	35.063
5	Scherzer	Max	2016	WAS	NL	20	7	0	228.3	2.96	32	33.220
6	Gonzalez	Gio	2012	WAS	NL	21	8	0	199.3	2.89	27	30.161
7	Strasburg	Stephen	2019	WAS	NL	18	6	0	209.0	3.32	31	29.823
8	Strasburg	Stephen	2017	WAS	NL	15	4	0	175.3	2.52	29	28.878
9	Scherzer	Max	2015	WAS	NL	14	12	0	228.7	2.79	31	25.289
10	Martinez	Dennis	1992	MON	NL	16	11	0	226.3	2.47	37	24.770
11	Vazquez	Javier	2001	MON	NL	16	11	0	223.7	3.42	25	24.621
12	Martinez	Dennis	1991	MON	NL	14	11	0	222.0	2.39	36	23.324
13	Scherzer	Max	2019	WAS	NL	11	7	0	172.3	2.92	35	22.974
14	Rogers	Steve	1977	MON	NL	17	16	0	301.7	3.10	28	21.900
15	Vazquez	Javier	2003	MON	NL	13	12	0	230.7	3.24	27	21.294
16	Gonzalez	Gio	2017	WAS	NL	15	9	0	201.0	2.96	32	20.878
17	Corbin	Patrick	2019	WAS	NL	14	7	0	202.0	3.25	30	20.792
18	Wetteland	John	1993	MON	NL	9	3	43	85.3	1.37	27	20.171
19	Hernandez	Livan	2003	MON	NL	15	10	0	233.3	3.20	28	19.856
20	Zimmermann	Jordan	2014	WAS	NL	14	5	0	199.7	2.66	28	19.823

Washington Nationals (WAS, MON) - Top Career Batters

RANK	NAME	FIRST	LYR	TEAM	LG	PEVA-B	YRS	PPYR	HR	RBI	H	AVE
1	Carter	Gary	1992	MON	NL	174.379	12	14.532	220	823	1427	0.269
2	Raines	Tim	2001	MON	NL	160.252	13	12.327	96	556	1622	0.301
3	Dawson	Andre	1986	MON	NL	143.855	11	13.078	225	838	1575	0.280

RANK	NAME	FIRST	LYR	TEAM	LG	PEVA-B	YRS	PPYR	HR	RBI	H	AVE
4	Zimmerman	Ryan	2019	WAS	NL	130.665	15	8.711	270	1015	1784	0.279
5	Wallach	Tim	1992	MON	NL	128.113	13	9.855	204	905	1694	0.259
6	Guerrero	Vladimir	2003	MON	NL	103.212	8	12.902	234	702	1215	0.323
7	Harper	Bryce	2018	WAS	NL	102.532	7	14.647	184	521	922	0.279
8	Rendon	Anthony	2019	WAS	NL	94.904	7	13.558	136	546	994	0.290
9	Staub	Rusty	1979	MON	NL	71.327	4	17.832	81	284	531	0.295
10	Bailey	Bob	1975	MON	NL	66.559	7	9.508	118	466	791	0.264
11	Werth	Jayson	2017	WAS	NL	57.302	7	8.186	109	393	781	0.263
12	Walker	Larry	1994	MON	NL	56.370	6	9.395	99	384	666	0.281
13	Parrish	Larry	1981	MON	NL	56.177	8	7.022	100	444	896	0.263
14	Cromartie	Warren	1983	MON	NL	56.137	9	6.237	60	371	1063	0.280
15	Desmond	Ian	2015	WAS	NL	56.065	7	8.009	110	432	917	0.264
16	Vidro	Jose	2006	WAS	NL	55.678	10	5.568	115	550	1280	0.301
17	Soto	Juan	2020	WAS	NL	53.488	3	17.829	69	217	328	0.295
18	Galarraga	Andres	2002	MON	NL	52.354	8	6.544	115	473	906	0.269
19	Turner	Trea	2020	WAS	NL	52.124	6	8.687	75	257	644	0.296
20	Grissom	Marquis	1994	MON	NL	49.187	6	8.198	54	276	747	0.279
21	Singleton	Ken	1974	MON	NL	49.019	3	16.340	46	227	449	0.285
22	Alou	Moises	1996	MON	NL	43.808	6	7.301	84	373	626	0.292
23	Cabrera	Orlando	2004	MON	NL	43.448	8	5.431	66	381	877	0.267
24	Fairly	Ron	1974	MON	NL	41.908	6	6.985	86	331	615	0.276
25	White	Rondell	2000	MON	NL	40.860	8	5.107	101	384	808	0.293
26	Brooks	Hubie	1989	MON	NL	39.992	5	7.998	75	390	689	0.279
27	Wilkerson	Brad	2005	WAS	NL	38.909	5	7.782	83	265	580	0.256
28	Johnson	Nick	2009	WAS	NL	38.619	5	7.724	56	248	467	0.280
29	Valentine	Ellis	1981	MON	NL	38.259	7	5.466	95	358	676	0.288
30	Ramos	Wilson	2016	WAS	NL	36.813	7	5.259	83	320	566	0.268
31	Dunn	Adam	2010	WAS	NL	35.534	2	17.767	76	208	291	0.264
32	Oliver	Al	1983	MON	NL	34.600	2	17.300	30	193	388	0.315
33	Speier	Chris	1984	MON	NL	33.360	8	4.170	29	255	710	0.245
34	LaRoche	Adam	2014	WAS	NL	33.123	4	8.281	82	269	430	0.249
35	Lansing	Mike	1997	MON	NL	33.036	5	6.607	49	265	709	0.276
36	Espinosa	Danny	2016	WAS	NL	30.284	7	4.326	92	285	598	0.226
37	Jorgensen	Mike	1977	MON	NL	29.172	6	4.862	57	243	477	0.254
38	Webster	Mitch	1988	MON	NL	28.822	4	7.205	36	155	456	0.279
39	DeShields	Delino	1993	MON	NL	28.650	4	7.162	23	181	575	0.277
40	Cordero	Wil	2005	WAS	NL	28.240	7	4.034	59	280	591	0.274
41	Schneider	Brian	2007	WAS	NL	28.006	8	3.501	47	294	586	0.252
42	Hunt	Ron	1974	MON	NL	27.326	4	6.831	5	100	489	0.277
43	Fletcher	Darrin	1997	MON	NL	27.252	6	4.542	61	300	520	0.266
44	Foli	Tim	1977	MON	NL	27.086	6	4.514	11	196	642	0.246
45	Span	Denard	2015	WAS	NL	24.334	3	8.111	14	106	428	0.292

RANK	NAME	FIRST	LYR	TEAM	LG	PEVA-B	YRS	PPYR	HR	RBI	H	AVE
46	Owen	Spike	1992	MON	NL	23.889	4	5.972	21	142	420	0.247
47	Morse	Mike	2012	WAS	NL	23.294	4	5.824	67	208	366	0.294
48	Grudzielanek	Mark	1998	MON	NL	22.939	4	5.735	19	161	553	0.281
49	Perez	Tony	1979	MON	NL	22.434	3	7.478	46	242	448	0.281
50	Guzman	Cristian	2010	WAS	NL	20.992	5	4.198	23	177	581	0.282

Washington Nationals (WAS, MON) - Top Career Pitchers

RANK	NAME	FIRST	LYEAR	LTEAM	LG	PEVA	YRS	PPYR	W	L	SV	IP	ERA
1	Scherzer	Max	2020	WAS	NL	164.053	6	27.342	84	43	0	1118.0	2.80
2	Rogers	Steve	1985	MON	NL	159.201	13	12.246	158	152	2	2837.7	3.17
3	Strasburg	Stephen	2019	WAS	NL	127.798	11	11.618	112	59	0	1443.7	3.19
4	Martinez	Dennis	1993	MON	NL	118.829	8	14.854	100	72	1	1609.0	3.06
5	Gonzalez	Gio	2018	WAS	NL	91.521	7	13.074	86	65	0	1253.3	3.62
6	Martinez	Pedro	1997	MON	NL	80.240	4	20.060	55	33	1	797.3	3.06
7	Zimmerman n	Jordan	2015	WAS	NL	78.589	7	11.227	70	50	0	1094.0	3.32
8	Vazquez	Javier	2003	MON	NL	75.095	6	12.516	64	68	0	1229.3	4.16
9	Hernandez	Livan	2011	WAS	NL	72.016	7	10.288	70	72	0	1317.0	3.98
10	Smith	Bryn	1989	MON	NL	68.521	9	7.613	81	71	6	1400.3	3.28
11	Fassero	Jeff	1996	MON	NL	63.444	6	10.574	58	48	10	850.0	3.20
12	Roark	Tanner	2018	WAS	NL	58.651	6	9.775	64	54	1	935.0	3.59
13	Gullickson	Bill	1985	MON	NL	56.505	7	8.072	72	61	0	1186.3	3.44
14	Burke	Tim	1991	MON	NL	42.498	7	6.071	43	26	101	600.3	2.61
15	Hill	Ken	1994	MON	NL	41.059	3	13.686	41	21	0	556.3	3.04
16	Rojas	Mel	1999	MON	NL	39.056	8	4.882	29	23	109	512.3	3.11
17	Sanderson	Scott	1983	MON	NL	39.053	6	6.509	56	47	2	883.0	3.33
18	Reardon	Jeff	1986	MON	NL	38.090	6	6.348	32	37	152	506.3	2.84
19	Lea	Charlie	1987	MON	NL	38.025	6	6.337	55	41	0	793.3	3.32
20	Clippard	Tyler	2014	WAS	NL	37.440	7	5.349	34	24	34	464.0	2.68
21	Hermanson	Dustin	2000	MON	NL	36.488	4	9.122	43	47	4	759.7	3.98
22	Wetteland	John	1994	MON	NL	35.557	3	11.852	17	13	105	232.3	2.32
23	Cordero	Chad	2008	WAS	NL	35.248	6	5.875	20	14	128	320.7	2.78
24	Storen	Drew	2015	WAS	NL	33.594	6	5.599	21	13	95	334.0	3.02
25	Lannan	John	2012	WAS	NL	32.377	6	5.396	42	52	0	783.7	4.01
26	Urbina	Ugueth	2001	MON	NL	30.955	7	4.422	31	26	125	406.7	3.52
27	Fryman	Woodie	1983	MON	NL	30.931	8	3.866	51	52	52	721.7	3.24
28	Perez	Pascual	1989	MON	NL	30.691	3	10.230	28	21	0	456.7	2.80
29	Renko	Steve	1976	MON	NL	30.041	8	3.755	68	82	3	1359.3	3.90
30	Armas	Tony	2006	WAS	NL	27.513	8	3.439	48	60	0	820.3	4.45
31	Marshall	Mike	1973	MON	NL	27.000	4	6.750	36	34	75	471.0	2.94
32	Ohka	Tomokazu	2005	WAS	NL	25.876	5	5.175	31	34	0	585.0	3.71
33	Stoneman	Bill	1973	MON	NL	25.578	5	5.116	51	72	1	1085.3	3.98
34	Corbin	Patrick	2020	WAS	NL	25.553	2	12.777	16	14	0	267.7	3.60
35	Perez	Carlos	1998	MON	NL	25.205	3	8.402	29	31	0	511.3	3.78

RANK	NAME	FIRST	LYEAR	LTEAM	LG	PEVA	YRS	PPYR	W	L	SV	IP	ERA
36	Doolittle	Sean	2019	WAS	NL	23.917	3	7.972	10	8	75	135.0	2.87
37	McGaffigan	Andy	1989	MON	NL	22.678	5	4.536	27	16	21	475.3	2.92
38	Schatzeder	Dan	1986	MON	NL	22.321	8	2.790	37	31	5	749.7	3.09
39	Ayala	Luis	2008	WAS	NL	21.428	5	4.286	27	32	9	332.3	3.33
40	Nabholz	Chris	1993	MON	NL	19.398	4	4.850	34	29	0	535.3	3.51
41	Morton	Carl	1972	MON	NL	19.288	4	4.822	35	45	1	699.7	4.09
42	Hesketh	Joe	1990	MON	NL	18.228	7	2.604	29	19	14	435.7	3.35
43	Palmer	David	1985	MON	NL	17.785	6	2.964	38	26	2	576.7	3.26
44	Rauch	Jon	2008	WAS	NL	17.077	5	3.415	21	15	23	280.3	3.24
45	Lee	Bill	1982	MON	NL	16.894	4	4.223	25	22	6	441.0	3.57
46	Stammen	Craig	2015	WAS	NL	16.321	7	2.332	26	24	1	490.7	3.91
47	Grimsley	Ross	1980	MON	NL	16.230	3	5.410	32	24	0	455.7	4.11
48	Murray	Dale	1980	MON	NL	15.774	5	3.155	21	21	33	337.0	3.26
49	Fister	Doug	2015	WAS	NL	14.718	2	7.359	21	13	1	267.0	3.10
50	Gardner	Mark	1992	MON	NL	14.571	4	3.643	28	33	0	527.0	3.96

Washington Nationals – Top Fielders

Rank	FIRST BASE		FV	Lyear	G	FPCT	RF
1	Galarraga	Andres	1.1903	2002	922	0.991	9.20
2	Segui	David	1.1612	1997	335	0.995	9.16
3	Jorgensen	Mike	1.1568	1977	509	0.995	8.77
4	Oliver	Al	1.1292	1983	312	0.988	8.66
5	LaRoche	Adam	1.1184	2014	481	0.994	8.74
6	Cartwright	Ed	1.1100	1897	420	0.977	9.87
7	Perez	Tony	1.1001	1979	422	0.992	9.16
8	Fairly	Ron	1.0744	1974	445	0.992	8.73
9	Stevens	Lee	1.0719	2002	333	0.989	9.29
10	Johnson	Nick	1.0470	2009	480	0.993	8.84

Rank	SECOND BASE		FV	Lyear	G	FPCT	RF
1	Cash	Dave	1.4035	1979	359	0.984	4.86
2	Lansing	Mike	1.3748	1997	537	0.986	4.71
3	Scott	Rodney	1.2910	1982	353	0.981	5.09
4	Espinosa	Danny	1.2514	2015	522	0.989	4.60
5	DeShields	Delino	1.2133	1993	533	0.975	4.75
6	Hunt	Ron	1.1963	1974	388	0.980	4.91
7	Law	Vance	1.1887	1987	326	0.986	4.70
8	Vidro	Jose	1.1817	2006	1036	0.985	4.38
9	Sutherland	Gary	1.1399	1971	292	0.971	4.67
10	Flynn	Doug	1.1308	1985	259	0.983	4.49

Rank	SHORTSTOP		FV	Lyear	G	FPCT	RF
1	Foli	Tim	1.6369	1977	701	0.970	5.12
2	Owen	Spike	1.5824	1992	539	0.984	4.14
3	Speier	Chris	1.5738	1984	863	0.971	4.63
4	Wine	Bobby	1.5736	1972	400	0.969	4.73
5	Cabrera	Orlando	1.5660	2004	862	0.977	4.44
6	Grudzielanek	Mark	1.4960	1998	448	0.958	4.25
7	Turner	Trea	1.4621	2020	443	0.974	3.64
8	Desmond	Ian	1.4296	2015	913	0.962	4.12
9	Brooks	Hubie	1.4072	1987	344	0.956	4.02
10	Guzman	Cristian	1.3971	2010	459	0.968	4.10

Rank	THIRD BASE		FV	Lyear	G	FPCT	RF
1	Wallach	Tim	1.6033	1992	1624	0.959	2.86
2	Zimmerman	Ryan	1.5141	2014	1133	0.957	2.68
3	Rendon	Anthony	1.5052	2019	759	0.971	2.34
4	Andrews	Shane	1.4552	1999	421	0.950	2.52
5	Parrish	Larry	1.4233	1981	946	0.941	2.74

			FV	Lyear	G	FPCT	RF	
6	Bailey	Bob	1.3682	1975	520	0.952	2.35	
7	Berry	Sean	1.3312	1995	299	0.938	2.26	
8	Laboy	Coco	1.3178	1973	397	0.944	2.28	

Rank	CATCHER		FV	Lyear	G	FPCT	RF	CS%
1	Carter	Gary	1.9993	1992	1342	0.991	6.10	0.394
2	Ramos	Wilson	1.8853	2016	564	0.994	8.18	0.341
3	Schneider	Brian	1.8706	2007	711	0.993	6.34	0.386
4	Foote	Barry	1.8483	1977	346	0.986	5.73	0.380
5	Bateman	John	1.7915	1972	347	0.984	6.21	0.344
6	Fletcher	Darrin	1.7715	1997	570	0.993	6.30	0.224
7	Barrett	Michael	1.7247	2003	399	0.991	6.78	0.236
8	Widger	Chris	1.6947	2000	411	0.985	6.39	0.226
9	Santovenia	Nelson	1.6941	1991	257	0.981	6.06	0.283
10	Boccabella	John	1.6911	1973	283	0.983	4.97	0.421

Rank	OUTFIELD		FV	Lyear	G	FPCT	RF	ApG
1	Span	Denard	1.6350	2014	300	0.995	2.56	0.040
2	Dawson	Andre	1.5418	1986	1412	0.983	2.59	0.073
3	Grissom	Marquis	1.5237	1994	671	0.983	2.58	0.064
4	Staub	Rusty	1.4994	1979	479	0.965	1.91	0.104
5	Chavez	Endy	1.4989	2005	303	0.987	2.28	0.083
6	Walker	Larry	1.4946	1994	580	0.986	2.12	0.093
7	Raines	Tim	1.4802	2001	1338	0.987	2.10	0.065
8	Kearns	Austin	1.4703	2009	370	0.987	2.21	0.054
9	Cromartie	Warren	1.4663	1983	774	0.977	2.17	0.096
10	Webster	Mitch	1.4425	1988	434	0.984	2.08	0.058
11	White	Rondell	1.4417	2000	752	0.986	2.17	0.047
12	Church	Ryan	1.4365	2007	311	0.993	2.16	0.035
13	Alou	Moises	1.4105	1996	602	0.984	1.78	0.058
14	Bergeron	Peter	1.4093	2004	308	0.984	2.18	0.078
15	Soto	Juan	1.4069	2020	306	0.993	1.79	0.016
16	Singleton	Ken	1.4001	1974	441	0.971	1.76	0.082
17	Martinez	Dave	1.3853	1991	398	0.982	2.04	0.063
18	Day	Boots	1.3822	1974	339	0.984	2.02	0.059
19	Valentine	Ellis	1.3816	1981	619	0.973	1.99	0.103
20	Bernadina	Roger	1.3665	2013	436	0.991	1.44	0.055
21	Santangelo	F.P.	1.3578	1998	352	0.987	1.73	0.040
22	Harper	Bryce	1.3448	2018	969	0.983	1.80	0.055
23	Nixon	Otis	1.3437	1990	268	0.992	1.84	0.034
24	Wilkerson	Brad	1.3395	2005	562	0.980	1.88	0.071
25	Werth	Jayson	1.3264	2017	795	0.984	1.84	0.049

Rank	PITCHING		FV	Lyear	IP	FPCT	RF
1	Hernandez	Livan	1.1006	2011	1317	0.980	2.30
2	Morton	Carl	1.0927	1972	700	0.975	2.51
3	Torrez	Mike	1.0790	1974	641	0.974	2.61
4	Martinez	Dennis	1.0745	1993	1609	0.955	2.38
5	Rogers	Steve	1.0604	1985	2838	0.958	2.22
6	Vazquez	Javier	1.0601	2003	1229	0.982	1.96
7	Roark	Tanner	1.0470	2018	935	0.973	1.70
8	Hill	Ken	1.0315	1994	556	0.960	2.70
9	Stoneman	Bill	1.0289	1973	1085	0.972	1.74
10	Ziimmermann	Jordan	1.0235	2015	1094	0.957	1.81

Franchise When and Where
Washington Nationals (2005 to Present)
Montreal Expos (1969-2004, MON)

Note1: For players with more than one team during the year, actual stats reflect stint with team only. Note2: Franchises with less than 5 players above 10.000 PEVA are listed with the five highest players. For Team careers lists, Top 50 players are listed above 10.000 PEVA. Note3: Age = Player age at end of year.

Fielding Note: For each current franchise, listed are the Top Ten Fielders at each position who played a minimum of 250 games for that that team or 500 innings pitched. At times, listed are players with less than that for recently added teams, and several players outside the Top Ten for interesting players, just for context.

ALTOONA MOUNTAIN CITY
Best Seasons and Careers of All-Time

Altoona Mountain City - Best Position Player Years

Rank	Name	First	Year	Team	Lg	HR	RBI	AVG	Age	PEVA-B
1	Smith	Germany	1884	ALT	UA	0	NA	0.315	21	5.227
2	Shafer	Taylor	1884	ALT	UA	0	NA	0.284	18	1.717
3	Moore	Jerrie	1884	ALT	UA	1	NA	0.313	29	0.940
4	Brown	Jim	1884	ALT	UA	1	NA	0.250	24	0.724
5	Cross	Clarence	1884	ALT	UA	0	NA	0.571	28	0.642

Altoona Mountain City - Best Pitcher Years

Rank	Name	First	Year	Team	Lg	W	L	SV	IP	ERA	Age	PEVA-P
1	Murphy	John	1884	ALT	UA	5	6	0	111.7	3.87	NA	1.076
2	Brown	Jim	1884	ALT	UA	1	9	0	74.0	5.35	24	0.944
3	Leary	Jack	1884	ALT	UA	0	3	0	24.0	5.25	27	0.680
4	Smith	Germany	1884	ALT	UA	0	0	0	1.0	9.00	21	0.200
5	Connors	Joe	1884	ALT	UA	0	1	0	9.0	7.00	NA	0.200

Altoona Mountain City - Best Career Batters

Rank	Name	First	LYear	LTeam	Lg	PEVA-B	YRS	PER	HR	RBI	H	AVE.
1	Smith	Germany	1884	ALT	UA	1.415	1	1.415	0	0	34	0.315
2	Moore	Jerrie	1884	ALT	UA	0.684	1	0.684	1	0	25	0.313
3	Brown	Jim	1884	ALT	UA	0.596	1	0.596	1	0	22	0.250
4	Dougherty	Charlie	1884	ALT	UA	0.587	1	0.587	0	0	22	0.259
5	Harris	Frank	1884	ALT	UA	0.559	1	0.559	0	0	25	0.263

Altoona Mountain City - Top Career Pitchers

Rank	Name	First	LYear	LTeam	Lg	PEVA-P	YRS	PER	W	L	SV	IP	ERA
1	Murphy	John	1884	ALT	UA	0.752	1	0.752	5	6	0	111.7	3.87
2	Brown	Jim	1884	ALT	UA	0.587	1	0.587	1	9	0	74.0	5.35
3	Leary	Jack	1884	ALT	UA	0.480	1	0.480	0	3	0	24.0	5.25
4	Smith	Germany	1884	ALT	UA	0.200	1	0.200	0	0	0	1.0	9.00
5	Connors	Joe	1884	ALT	UA	0.086	1	0.086	0	1	0	9.0	7.00

Note: Altoona Mountain City franchise folded after 25 games of their only season.

BUFFALO BISONS
Best Seasons and Careers of All-Time

Buffalo Bisons - Best Position Player Years

Rank	Name	First	Year	Team	Lg	HR	RBI	AVG	Age	PEVA-B
1	Brouthers	Dan	1883	BFN	NL	3	97	0.374	25	39.597
2	Brouthers	Dan	1882	BFN	NL	6	63	0.368	24	34.359
3	O'Rourke	Jim	1884	BFN	NL	5	63	0.347	34	25.770
4	Brouthers	Dan	1884	BFN	NL	14	79	0.327	26	21.208
5	White	Deacon	1884	BFN	NL	5	74	0.325	37	20.391
6	Brouthers	Dan	1885	BFN	NL	7	59	0.359	27	20.230
7	O'Rourke	Jim	1883	BFN	NL	1	38	0.328	33	17.804
8	Rowe	Jack	1884	BFN	NL	4	61	0.315	28	16.672
9	Richardson	Hardy	1881	BFN	NL	2	53	0.291	26	15.906
10	Richardson	Hardy	1883	BFN	NL	1	56	0.311	28	15.819
11	Foley	Curry	1882	BFN	NL	3	49	0.305	26	13.418
12	O'Rourke	Jim	1881	BFN	NL	0	30	0.302	31	12.725
13	Richardson	Hardy	1884	BFN	NL	6	60	0.301	29	12.683
14	Purcell	Blondie	1882	BFN	NL	2	40	0.276	28	12.622
15	Richardson	Hardy	1882	BFN	NL	2	57	0.271	27	12.574
16	Shaffer	Orator	1883	BFN	NL	0	41	0.292	32	12.566
17	Richardson	Hardy	1885	BFN	NL	6	44	0.319	30	12.478
18	Richardson	Hardy	1879	BFN	NL	0	37	0.283	24	11.797
19	O'Rourke	Jim	1882	BFN	NL	2	37	0.281	32	11.548
20	Brouthers	Dan	1881	BFN	NL	8	45	0.319	23	11.243

Buffalo Bisons - Best Pitcher Years

Rank	Name	First	Year	Team	Lg	W	L	SV	IP	ERA	Age	PEVA-P
1	Galvin	Pud	1884	BFN	NL	46	22	0	636.3	1.99	28	25.160
2	Galvin	Pud	1883	BFN	NL	46	29	0	656.3	2.72	27	23.316
3	Galvin	Pud	1879	BFN	NL	37	27	0	593.0	2.28	23	23.153
4	Galvin	Pud	1881	BFN	NL	28	24	0	474.0	2.37	25	18.358
5	Galvin	Pud	1882	BFN	NL	28	23	0	445.3	3.17	26	6.267

Buffalo Bisons - Top Career Batters

Rank	Name	First	LYear	LTeam	Lg	PEVA-B	YRS	PER	HR	RBI	H	AVE.
1	Brouthers	Dan	1885	BFN	NL	126.636	5	25.327	38	343	650	0.351
2	Richardson	Hardy	1885	BFN	NL	90.063	7	12.866	17	324	772	0.292
3	O'Rourke	Jim	1884	BFN	NL	67.848	4	16.962	8	168	514	0.317
4	White	Deacon	1885	BFN	NL	56.284	5	11.257	6	264	573	0.301
5	Rowe	Jack	1885	BFN	NL	53.651	7	7.664	10	279	610	0.289
6	Force	Davy	1885	BFN	NL	24.398	7	3.485	1	154	454	0.207
7	Foley	Curry	1883	BFN	NL	20.207	3	6.736	4	80	230	0.278
8	Crowley	Bill	1885	BFN	NL	18.240	3	6.080	1	86	253	0.264
9	Hornung	Joe	1880	BFN	NL	16.862	2	8.431	1	80	176	0.266
10	Lillie	Jim	1885	BFN	NL	15.588	3	5.196	6	112	259	0.235
11	Purcell	Blondie	1882	BFN	NL	13.142	2	6.571	2	57	138	0.280
12	Shaffer	Orator	1883	BFN	NL	12.566	1	12.566	0	41	117	0.292

Buffalo Bisons - Top Career Pitchers

Rank	Name	First	LYear	LTeam	Lg	PEVA-P	YRS	PER	W	L	SV	IP	ERA
1	Galvin	Pud	1885	BFN	NL	**102.507**	7	14.644	218	179	1	3547.7	2.63
2	Serad	Billy	1885	BFN	NL	**3.688**	2	1.844	23	41	0	549.3	4.19
3	McGunnigle	Bill	1880	BFN	NL	**2.218**	2	1.109	11	8	0	157.0	2.81
4	Daily	Hugh	1882	BFN	NL	**1.979**	1	1.979	15	14	0	255.7	2.99
5	Purcell	Blondie	1882	BFN	NL	**1.359**	2	0.680	6	2	0	92.7	3.50

BUFFALO BISONS (PACIFIC COAST LEAGUE)
Best Seasons and Careers of All-Time

Buffalo Bisons (Pacific Coast League) - Best Position Player Years

Rank	Name	First	Year	Team	Lg	HR	RBI	AVG	Age	PEVA-B
1	Hoy	Dummy	1890	BFP	PL	1	53	0.298	28	15.291
2	Wise	Sam	1890	BFP	PL	6	102	0.293	33	12.640
3	Mack	Connie	1890	BFP	PL	0	53	0.266	28	10.921
4	Beecher	Ed	1890	BFP	PL	3	90	0.297	30	9.205
5	Rowe	Jack	1890	BFP	PL	2	76	0.250	34	8.439

Buffalo Bisons (Pacific Coast League) - Best Pitcher Years

Rank	Name	First	Year	Team	Lg	W	L	SV	IP	ERA	Age	PEVA-P
1	Cunningham	Bert	1890	BFP	PL	9	15	0	211.0	5.84	25	2.308
2	Haddock	George	1890	BFP	PL	9	26	0	290.7	5.76	24	1.851
3	Keefe	George	1890	BFP	PL	6	16	0	196.0	6.52	23	0.966
4	Twitchell	Larry	1890	BFP	PL	5	7	0	104.3	4.57	26	0.600
5	Stafford	General	1890	BFP	PL	3	9	0	98.0	5.14	22	0.578

Buffalo Bisons (Pacific Coast League) - Top Career Batters

Rank	Name	First	LYear	LTeam	Lg	PEVA-B	YRS	PER	HR	RBI	H	AVE.
1	Hoy	Dummy	1890	BFP	PL	15.291	1	15.291	1	53	147	0.298
2	Wise	Sam	1890	BFP	PL	12.640	1	12.640	6	102	148	0.293
3	Mack	Connie	1890	BFP	PL	10.921	1	10.921	0	53	134	0.266
4	Beecher	Ed	1890	BFP	PL	9.205	1	9.205	3	90	159	0.297
5	Rowe	Jack	1890	BFP	PL	8.439	1	8.439	2	76	126	0.250

Buffalo Bisons (Pacific Coast League) - Top Career Pitchers

Rank	Name	First	LYear	LTeam	Lg	PEVA-P	YRS	PER	W	L	SV	IP	ERA
1	Haddock	George	1890	BFP	PL	1.851	1	1.851	9	26	0	290.7	5.76
2	Cunningham	Bert	1890	BFP	PL	1.524	1	1.524	9	15	0	211.0	5.84
3	Keefe	George	1890	BFP	PL	0.966	1	0.966	6	16	0	196.0	6.52
4	Twitchell	Larry	1890	BFP	PL	0.600	1	0.600	5	7	0	104.3	4.57
5	Stafford	General	1890	BFP	PL	0.578	1	0.578	3	9	0	98.0	5.14

BALTIMORE CANARIES
Best Seasons and Careers of All-Time

Baltimore Canaries - Best Position Player Years

Rank	Name	First	Year	Team	Lg	HR	RBI	AVG	Age	PEVA-B
1	Pike	Lip	1872	BL1	NA	6	60	0.292	27	17.098
2	Hall	George	1872	BL1	NA	1	37	0.336	23	15.242
3	Radcliff	John	1872	BL1	NA	1	44	0.290	26	14.113
4	Higham	Dick	1872	BL1	NA	2	38	0.343	21	12.788
5	York	Tom	1872	BL1	NA	1	41	0.266	22	11.840
6	Pike	Lip	1873	BL1	NA	4	50	0.315	28	11.676
7	York	Tom	1873	BL1	NA	2	49	0.303	23	11.520
8	Mills	Everett	1873	BL1	NA	0	57	0.331	28	10.791
9	Force	Davy	1873	BL1	NA	0	31	0.368	24	10.477
10	Carey	Tom	1873	BL1	NA	1	55	0.334	24	10.238

Baltimore Canaries - Best Pitcher Years

Rank	Name	First	Year	Team	Lg	W	L	SV	IP	ERA	Age	PEVA-P
1	Cummings	Candy	1873	BL1	NA	28	14	0	382.0	2.66	25	11.758
2	Mathews	Bobby	1872	BL1	NA	25	18	0	405.3	3.15	21	11.404
3	Fisher	Cherokee	1872	BL1	NA	10	1	1	110.3	2.53	27	5.924
4	Brainard	Asa	1874	BL1	NA	5	22	0	239.0	4.93	33	0.944
5	Brainard	Asa	1873	BL1	NA	5	7	0	108.7	4.14	32	0.909

Baltimore Canaries - Top Career Batters

Rank	Name	First	LYear	LTeam	Lg	PEVA-B	YRS	PER	HR	RBI	H	AVE.
1	Pike	Lip	1873	BL1	NA	28.774	2	14.387	10	110	174	0.303
2	York	Tom	1873	BL1	NA	23.360	2	11.680	3	90	150	0.286
3	Hall	George	1873	BL1	NA	18.938	2	9.469	1	67	142	0.340
4	Mills	Everett	1873	BL1	NA	18.843	2	9.422	0	91	166	0.314
5	Force	Davy	1873	BL1	NA	18.415	2	9.207	0	44	127	0.386
6	Radcliff	John	1873	BL1	NA	18.184	2	9.092	1	77	156	0.288
7	Carey	Tom	1873	BL1	NA	13.845	2	6.923	3	82	154	0.316
8	Higham	Dick	1872	BL1	NA	12.788	1	12.788	2	38	84	0.343

Baltimore Canaries - Top Career Pitchers

Rank	Name	First	LYear	LTeam	Lg	PEVA-P	YRS	PER	W	L	SV	IP	ERA
1	Cummings	Candy	1873	BL1	NA	11.758	1	11.758	28	14	0	382.0	2.66
2	Mathews	Bobby	1872	BL1	NA	11.290	1	11.290	25	18	0	405.3	3.15
3	Fisher	Cherokee	1872	BL1	NA	5.672	1	5.672	10	1	1	110.3	2.53
4	Brainard	Asa	1874	BL1	NA	1.853	2	0.927	10	29	0	347.7	4.69
5	Manning	Jack	1874	BL1	NA	0.784	1	0.784	4	16	0	179.7	3.41

BALTIMORE ORIOLES
(AMERICAN ASSOCIATION/NATIONAL LEAGUE)
Best Seasons and Careers of All-Time

Baltimore Orioles (American Assoc./National League) - Best Position Player Years

Rank	Name	First	Year	Team	Lg	HR	RBI	AVG	Age	PEVA-B
1	Kelley	Joe	1896	BLN	NL	8	100	0.364	25	36.936
2	Keeler	Willie	1897	BLN	NL	0	74	0.424	25	34.488
3	Jennings	Hughie	1896	BLN	NL	0	121	0.401	27	34.143
4	Kelley	Joe	1894	BLN	NL	6	111	0.393	23	28.190
5	Kelley	Joe	1895	BLN	NL	10	134	0.365	24	28.125
6	Jennings	Hughie	1895	BLN	NL	4	125	0.386	26	28.104
7	Kelley	Joe	1897	BLN	NL	5	118	0.362	26	27.788
8	Jennings	Hughie	1897	BLN	NL	2	79	0.355	28	26.148
9	Jennings	Hughie	1898	BLN	NL	1	87	0.328	29	25.255
10	Keeler	Willie	1896	BLN	NL	4	82	0.386	24	24.026
11	Tucker	Tommy	1889	BL2	AA	5	99	0.372	26	23.829
12	Burns	Oyster	1887	BL2	AA	9	99	0.341	23	21.296
13	Van Haltren	George	1891	BL3	AA	9	83	0.318	25	21.128
14	Stenzel	Jake	1897	BLN	NL	4	116	0.353	30	20.222
15	Keeler	Willie	1895	BLN	NL	4	78	0.377	23	20.191
16	McGraw	John	1898	BLN	NL	0	53	0.342	25	20.148
17	McGraw	John	1899	BLN	NL	1	33	0.391	26	17.875
18	Burns	Oyster	1888	BL2	AA	4	42	0.298	24	17.554
19	Van Haltren	George	1892	BLN	NL	7	57	0.302	26	16.603
20	Kelley	Joe	1893	BLN	NL	9	76	0.305	22	15.463

Baltimore Orioles (American Association/National League) - Best Pitcher Years

Rank	Name	First	Year	Team	Lg	W	L	SV	IP	ERA	Age	PEVA-P
1	McGinnity	Joe	1899	BLN	NL	28	16	2	366.3	2.68	28	34.184
2	Kilroy	Matt	1887	BL2	AA	46	19	0	589.3	3.07	21	29.854
3	McJames	Doc	1898	BLN	NL	27	15	0	374.0	2.36	24	23.828
4	Kitson	Frank	1899	BLN	NL	22	16	0	327.7	2.77	30	23.707
5	McMahon	Sadie	1891	BL3	AA	35	24	1	503.0	2.81	24	22.650
6	Corbett	Joe	1897	BLN	NL	24	8	0	313.0	3.11	22	20.492
7	Kilroy	Matt	1889	BL2	AA	29	25	0	480.7	2.85	23	19.075
8	Hoffer	Bill	1895	BLN	NL	31	6	0	314.0	3.21	25	17.949
9	Hoffer	Bill	1896	BLN	NL	25	7	0	309.0	3.38	26	16.948
10	Maul	Al	1898	BLN	NL	20	7	0	239.7	2.10	33	13.619
11	Kilroy	Matt	1886	BL2	AA	29	34	0	583.0	3.37	20	13.318
12	Foreman	Frank	1889	BL2	AA	23	21	0	414.0	3.52	26	11.443
13	McMahon	Sadie	1894	BLN	NL	25	8	0	275.7	4.21	27	10.426
14	Nops	Jerry	1897	BLN	NL	20	6	0	220.7	2.81	22	10.388

Baltimore Orioles (American Assoc./National League) - Top Career Batters

Rank	Name	First	LYear	LTeam	Lg	PEVA-B	YRS	PER	HR	RBI	H	AVE.
1	Kelley	Joe	1898	BLN	NL	151.911	7	21.702	40	653	1069	0.351
2	Jennings	Hughie	1899	BLN	NL	127.498	7	18.214	12	529	929	0.359
3	Keeler	Willie	1898	BLN	NL	108.922	5	21.784	14	372	1097	0.388
4	McGraw	John	1899	BLN	NL	86.517	9	9.613	10	392	1063	0.336

5	Brodie	Steve	1899	BLN	NL	**51.992**	6	8.665	10	459	776	0.331
6	Tucker	Tommy	1889	BL2	AA	**44.242**	3	14.747	17	244	489	0.311
7	Griffin	Mike	1889	BL2	AA	**44.007**	3	14.669	7	188	447	0.279
8	Shindle	Billy	1893	BLN	NL	**40.560**	4	10.140	8	242	577	0.260
9	Burns	Oyster	1888	BL2	AA	**37.883**	4	9.471	24	201	398	0.300
10	Van Haltren	George	1892	BLN	NL	**36.236**	2	18.118	16	140	348	0.310
11	Sommer	Joe	1890	BL3	AA	**36.221**	7	5.174	7	255	670	0.241
12	Robinson	Wilbert	1899	BLN	NL	**34.867**	10	3.487	10	456	836	0.295
13	Reitz	Heinie	1897	BLN	NL	**31.908**	5	6.382	9	400	618	0.291
14	Stenzel	Jake	1898	BLN	NL	**22.731**	2	11.365	4	138	224	0.332
15	Doyle	Jack	1897	BLN	NL	**21.305**	2	10.653	3	188	328	0.346
16	Clinton	Jim	1886	BL2	AA	**18.925**	3	6.308	4	6	258	0.281
17	Welch	Curt	1892	BLN	NL	**17.721**	3	5.907	4	82	203	0.248
18	Purcell	Blondie	1888	BL2	AA	**15.896**	3	5.299	6	143	257	0.243
19	DeMontreville	Gene	1899	BLN	NL	**15.641**	2	7.820	1	122	253	0.314
20	Holmes	Ducky	1899	BLN	NL	**15.606**	2	7.803	5	130	303	0.305

Baltimore Orioles (American Association/National League) - Top Career Pitchers

Rank	Name	First	LYear	LTeam	Lg	PEVA-P	YRS	PER	W	L	SV	IP	ERA
1	Kilroy	Matt	1889	BL2	AA	**65.201**	4	16.300	121	99	0	1974.0	3.26
2	McMahon	Sadie	1896	BLN	NL	**58.921**	7	8.417	130	91	3	1919.0	3.46
3	Hoffer	Bill	1898	BLN	NL	**42.819**	4	10.705	78	28	0	960.7	3.76
4	McGinnity	Joe	1899	BLN	NL	**34.184**	1	34.184	28	16	2	366.3	2.68
5	Kitson	Frank	1899	BLN	NL	**25.482**	2	12.741	30	21	0	447.0	2.90
6	Corbett	Joe	1897	BLN	NL	**25.055**	2	12.528	27	8	1	354.0	3.00
7	McJames	Doc	1898	BLN	NL	**23.828**	1	23.828	27	15	0	374.0	2.36
8	Nops	Jerry	1899	BLN	NL	**21.214**	4	5.304	55	27	0	736.7	3.58
9	Henderson	Hardie	1886	BL2	AA	**18.246**	4	4.562	65	105	0	1508.3	3.38
10	Pond	Arlie	1898	BLN	NL	**15.089**	4	3.772	35	19	2	496.0	3.45
11	Maul	Al	1898	BLN	NL	**13.778**	2	6.889	20	7	0	247.3	2.26
12	Foreman	Frank	1892	BLN	NL	**12.249**	3	4.083	25	25	0	466.0	3.84
13	Smith	Phenomenal	1888	BL2	AA	**12.058**	2	6.029	39	49	0	783.3	3.72
14	Emslie	Bob	1885	BL2	AA	**10.236**	3	3.412	44	40	0	763.7	3.08
15	Hemming	George	1896	BLN	NL	**10.126**	3	3.375	39	19	0	509.7	4.06

Note: Previous Names of Franchise: Baltimore Orioles (BL2) 1882-1889; (BL3) 1890-1891; (BLN) 1892-1899.

BALTIMORE MARYLANDS
Best Seasons and Careers of All-Time

Baltimore Marylands - Best Position Player Years

Rank	Name	First	Year	Team	Lg	HR	RBI	AVG	Age	PEVA-B
1	Woodhead	Red	1873	BL4	NA	0	0	0.000	22	0.200
2	Johns	Tommy	1873	BL4	NA	0	0	0.000	22	0.200
3	Smith	Bill	1873	BL4	NA	0	1	0.174	NA	0.200
4	Goldsmith	Wally	1873	BL4	NA	0	0	0.000	24	0.200
5	Stratton	Ed	1873	BL4	NA	0	0	0.125	NA	0.200

Baltimore Marylands - Best Pitcher Years

Rank	Name	First	Year	Team	Lg	W	L	SV	IP	ERA	Age	PEVA-P
1	Stratton	Ed	1873	BL4	NA	0	3	0	27.0	8.33	NA	0.377
2	Selman	Frank	1873	BL4	NA	0	1	0	9.0	8.00	21	0.200
3	French	Bill	1873	BL4	NA	0	1	0	9.0	12.00	NA	0.200
4	McDoolan	NA	1873	BL4	NA	0	1	0	9.0	3.00	NA	0.200

Baltimore Marylands - Top Career Batters

Rank	Name	First	LYear	LTeam	Lg	PEVA-B	YRS	PER	HR	RBI	H	AVE.
1	French	Bill	1873	BL4	NA	0.200	1	0.200	0	1	4	0.222
2	Hooper	Mike	1873	BL4	NA	0.200	1	0.200	0	2	3	0.214
3	Lennon	Bill	1873	BL4	NA	0.200	1	0.200	0	2	4	0.211
4	Say	Lou	1873	BL4	NA	0.200	1	0.200	0	2	2	0.167
5	Smith	Bill	1873	BL4	NA	0.200	1	0.200	0	1	4	0.174

Baltimore Marylands - Top Career Pitchers

Rank	Name	First	LYear	LTeam	Lg	PEVA-P	YRS	PER	W	L	SV	IP	ERA
1	Stratton	Ed	1873	BL4	NA	0.377	1	0.377	0	3	0	27.0	8.33
2	French	Bill	1873	BL4	NA	0.200	1	0.200	0	1	0	9.0	12.00
3	Selman	Frank	1873	BL4	NA	0.200	1	0.200	0	1	0	9.0	8.00
4	McDoolan	NA	1873	BL4	NA	0.200	1	0.200	0	1	0	9.0	3.00

BALTIMORE TERRAPINS
Best Seasons and Careers of All-Time

Baltimore Terrapins - Best Position Player Years

Rank	Name	First	Year	Team	Lg	HR	RBI	AVG	Age	PEVA-B
1	Duncan	Vern	1914	BLF	FL	2	53	0.287	24	12.622
2	Meyer	Benny	1914	BLF	FL	5	40	0.304	29	10.742
3	Swacina	Harry	1914	BLF	FL	0	90	0.280	33	10.267
4	Jacklitsch	Fred	1914	BLF	FL	2	48	0.276	38	9.357
5	Walsh	Jimmy	1914	BLF	FL	10	65	0.308	28	8.307

Baltimore Terrapins - Best Pitcher Years

Rank	Name	First	Year	Team	Lg	W	L	SV	IP	ERA	Age	PEVA-P
1	Quinn	Jack	1914	BLF	FL	26	14	1	342.7	2.60	31	18.114
2	Suggs	George	1914	BLF	FL	24	14	4	319.3	2.90	32	10.789
3	Quinn	Jack	1915	BLF	FL	9	22	1	273.7	3.45	32	3.286
4	Wilhelm	Kaiser	1914	BLF	FL	12	17	5	243.7	4.03	40	3.270
5	Suggs	George	1915	BLF	FL	11	17	3	232.7	4.14	33	2.635

Baltimore Terrapins - Top Career Batters

Rank	Name	First	LYear	LTeam	Lg	PEVA-B	YRS	PER	HR	RBI	H	AVE.
1	Duncan	Vern	1915	BLF	FL	20.247	2	10.124	4	96	302	0.278
2	Walsh	Jimmy	1915	BLF	FL	14.932	2	7.466	19	125	253	0.305
3	Doolan	Mickey	1915	BLF	FL	12.543	2	6.271	3	74	194	0.218
4	Meyer	Benny	1915	BLF	FL	12.041	2	6.021	5	45	181	0.292
5	Swacina	Harry	1915	BLF	FL	11.880	2	5.940	1	128	247	0.269
6	Jacklitsch	Fred	1915	BLF	FL	11.714	2	5.857	4	61	125	0.265

Baltimore Terrapins - Top Career Pitchers

Rank	Name	First	LYear	LTeam	Lg	PEVA-P	YRS	PER	W	L	SV	IP	ERA
1	Quinn	Jack	1915	BLF	FL	21.400	2	10.700	35	36	2	616.3	2.98
2	Suggs	George	1915	BLF	FL	13.424	2	6.712	35	31	7	552.0	3.42
3	Wilhelm	Kaiser	1915	BLF	FL	3.470	2	1.735	12	17	5	244.7	4.01
4	Bailey	Bill	1915	BLF	FL	3.366	2	1.683	13	28	0	319.0	4.01
5	Smith	Frank	1915	BLF	FL	2.807	2	1.404	14	12	2	263.3	3.55

BALTIMORE MONUMENTALS
Best Seasons and Careers of All-Time

Baltimore Monumentals - Best Position Player Years

Rank	Name	First	Year	Team	Lg	HR	RBI	AVG	Age	PEVA-B
1	Seery	Emmett	1884	BLU	UA	2	NA	0.311	23	12.602
2	Robinson	Yank	1884	BLU	UA	2	NA	0.267	25	7.959
3	Say	Lou	1884	BLU	UA	2	NA	0.239	30	4.524
4	Fusselback	Eddie	1884	BLU	UA	1	NA	0.284	28	3.994
5	Phelan	Dick	1884	BLU	UA	3	NA	0.246	30	3.499

Baltimore Monumentals - Best Pitcher Years

Rank	Name	First	Year	Team	Lg	W	L	SV	IP	ERA	Age	PEVA-P
1	Sweeney	Bill	1884	BLU	UA	40	21	0	538.0	2.59	NA	12.261
2	Atkinson	Al	1884	BLU	UA	3	5	0	69.7	2.33	23	4.069
3	Lee	Tom	1884	BLU	UA	5	8	0	122.0	3.39	22	1.034
4	Robinson	Yank	1884	BLU	UA	3	3	0	75.0	3.48	25	0.874
5	Ryan	John	1884	BLU	UA	3	2	0	51.0	3.35	NA	0.713

Baltimore Monumentals - Top Career Batters

Rank	Name	First	LYear	LTeam	Lg	PEVA-B	YRS	PER	HR	RBI	H	AVE.
1	Seery	Emmett	1884	BLU	UA	12.494	1	12.494	2	0	144	0.311
2	Robinson	Yank	1884	BLU	UA	7.959	1	7.959	2	0	111	0.267
3	Fusselback	Eddie	1884	BLU	UA	3.994	1	3.994	1	0	86	0.284
4	Say	Lou	1884	BLU	UA	3.749	1	3.749	2	0	81	0.239
5	Phelan	Dick	1884	BLU	UA	3.499	1	3.499	3	0	99	0.246

Baltimore Monumentals - Top Career Pitchers

Rank	Name	First	LYear	LTeam	Lg	PEVA-P	YRS	PER	W	L	SV	IP	ERA
1	Sweeney	Bill	1884	BLU	UA	12.261	1	12.261	40	21	0	538.0	2.59
2	Robinson	Yank	1884	BLU	UA	0.874	1	0.874	3	3	0	75.0	3.48
3	Lee	Tom	1884	BLU	UA	0.754	1	0.754	5	8	0	122.0	3.39
4	Atkinson	Al	1884	BLU	UA	0.720	1	0.720	3	5	0	69.7	2.33
5	Ryan	John	1884	BLU	UA	0.713	1	0.713	3	2	0	51.0	3.35

BROOKLYN ECKFORDS
Best Seasons and Careers of All-Time

Brooklyn Eckfords - Best Position Player Years

Rank	Name	First	Year	Team	Lg	HR	RBI	AVG	Age	PEVA-B
1	Allison	Doug	1872	BR1	NA	0	5	0.342	26	7.853
2	Wood	Jimmy	1872	BR1	NA	0	0	0.200	30	6.086
3	Martin	Phonney	1872	BR1	NA	0	9	0.154	27	3.387
4	Gedney	Count	1872	BR1	NA	0	7	0.183	23	2.157
5	Holdsworth	Jim	1872	BR1	NA	0	0	0.286	22	1.597

Brooklyn Eckfords - Best Pitcher Years

Rank	Name	First	Year	Team	Lg	W	L	SV	IP	ERA	Age	PEVA-P
1	Zettlein	George	1872	BR1	NA	1	8	0	75.3	2.99	28	6.833
2	Martin	Phonney	1872	BR1	NA	2	7	0	85.0	4.45	27	0.686
3	McDermott	Joe	1872	BR1	NA	0	7	0	63.0	8.29	NA	0.444
4	Malone	Martin	1872	BR1	NA	0	3	0	27.0	11.33	NA	0.377
5	O'Rourke	NA	1872	BR1	NA	0	1	0	9.0	6.00	NA	0.200

Brooklyn Eckfords - Top Career Batters

Rank	Name	First	LYear	LTeam	Lg	PEVA-B	YRS	PER	HR	RBI	H	AVE.
1	Allison	Doug	1872	BR1	NA	3.198	1	3.198	0	5	27	0.342
2	Martin	Phonney	1872	BR1	NA	1.355	1	1.355	0	9	12	0.154
3	Gedney	Count	1872	BR1	NA	1.298	1	1.298	0	7	13	0.183
4	Wood	Jimmy	1872	BR1	NA	1.277	1	1.277	0	0	6	0.200
5	Snyder	Jim	1872	BR1	NA	1.135	1	1.135	0	11	28	0.262

Brooklyn Eckfords - Top Career Pitchers

Rank	Name	First	LYear	LTeam	Lg	PEVA-P	YRS	PER	W	L	SV	IP	ERA
1	Zettlein	George	1872	BR1	NA	1.957	1	1.957	1	8	0	75.3	2.99
2	Martin	Phonney	1872	BR1	NA	0.477	1	0.477	2	7	0	85.0	4.45
3	McDermott	Joe	1872	BR1	NA	0.444	1	0.444	0	7	0	63.0	8.29
4	Malone	Martin	1872	BR1	NA	0.377	1	0.377	0	3	0	27.0	11.33
5	O'Rourke	0.000	1872	BR1	NA	0.200	1	0.200	0	1	0	9.0	6.00

BROOKLYN ATLANTICS
Best Seasons and Careers of All-Time

Brooklyn Atlantics - Best Position Player Years

Rank	Name	First	Year	Team	Lg	HR	RBI	AVG	Age	PEVA-B
1	Pabor	Charlie	1873	BR2	NA	0	42	0.360	27	9.654
2	Pearce	Dickey	1874	BR2	NA	0	25	0.294	38	7.157
3	Pearce	Dickey	1873	BR2	NA	1	26	0.275	37	5.297
4	Barlow	Tom	1873	BR2	NA	1	14	0.273	21	5.275
5	Burdock	Jack	1873	BR2	NA	2	36	0.253	21	4.967

Brooklyn Atlantics - Best Pitcher Years

Rank	Name	First	Year	Team	Lg	W	L	SV	IP	ERA	Age	PEVA-P
1	Britt	Jim	1873	BR2	NA	17	36	0	480.7	3.89	17	7.291
2	Bond	Tommy	1874	BR2	NA	22	32	0	497.0	3.19	18	4.309
3	Britt	Jim	1872	BR2	NA	9	28	0	336.0	5.06	16	2.874
4	Cassidy	John	1875	BR2	NA	1	20	0	214.7	3.98	18	1.076
5	Clinton	Jim	1875	BR2	NA	1	14	0	123.0	3.22	25	1.039

Brooklyn Atlantics - Top Career Batters

Rank	Name	First	LYear	LTeam	Lg	PEVA-B	YRS	PER	HR	RBI	H	AVE.
1	Pearce	Dickey	1874	BR2	NA	12.454	2	6.227	1	51	147	0.284
2	Pabor	Charlie	1875	BR2	NA	11.655	2	5.828	0	53	118	0.310
3	Ferguson	Bob	1874	BR2	NA	10.748	3	3.583	0	62	169	0.265
4	Barlow	Tom	1875	BR2	NA	8.599	3	2.866	1	24	127	0.285
5	Dehlman	Herman	1874	BR2	NA	8.068	3	2.689	0	49	137	0.227

Brooklyn Atlantics - Top Career Pitchers

Rank	Name	First	LYear	LTeam	Lg	PEVA-P	YRS	PER	W	L	SV	IP	ERA
1	Britt	Jim	1873	BR2	NA	10.101	2	5.050	26	64	0	816.7	4.38
2	Bond	Tommy	1874	BR2	NA	4.309	1	4.309	22	32	0	497.0	3.19
3	Cassidy	John	1875	BR2	NA	1.076	1	1.076	1	20	0	214.7	3.98
4	Clinton	Jim	1875	BR2	NA	1.039	1	1.039	1	14	0	123.0	3.22
5	Ferguson	Bob	1874	BR2	NA	0.400	2	0.200	0	2	0	28.3	5.40

BROOKLYN GLADIATORS
Best Seasons and Careers of All-Time

Brooklyn Gladiators - Best Position Player Years

Rank	Name	First	Year	Team	Lg	HR	RBI	AVG	Age	PEVA-B
1	Simon	Hank	1890	BR4	AA	0	38	0.257	28	9.569
2	Daily	Ed	1890	BR4	AA	1	39	0.239	28	5.020
3	Peltz	John	1890	BR4	AA	1	33	0.227	29	4.916
4	Gerhardt	Joe	1890	BR4	AA	2	40	0.203	35	4.772
5	O'Brien	Billy	1890	BR4	AA	4	67	0.278	30	3.832

Brooklyn Gladiators - Best Pitcher Years

Rank	Name	First	Year	Team	Lg	W	L	SV	IP	ERA	Age	PEVA-P
1	Daily	Ed	1890	BR4	AA	10	15	0	235.7	4.05	28	5.199
2	McCullough	Charlie	1890	BR4	AA	4	21	0	215.7	4.59	24	1.280
3	Mattimore	Mike	1890	BR4	AA	6	13	0	178.3	4.54	32	0.955
4	Toole	Steve	1890	BR4	AA	2	4	0	53.3	4.05	31	0.831
5	Murphy	Bob	1890	BR4	AA	3	9	0	96.0	5.72	24	0.639

Brooklyn Gladiators - Top Career Batters

Rank	Name	First	LYear	LTeam	Lg	PEVA-B	YRS	PER	HR	RBI	H	AVE.
1	Simon	Hank	1890	BR4	AA	6.747	1	6.747	0	38	96	0.257
2	Daily	Ed	1890	BR4	AA	4.045	1	4.045	1	39	94	0.239
3	Peltz	John	1890	BR4	AA	3.983	1	3.983	1	33	87	0.227
4	O'Brien	Billy	1890	BR4	AA	3.832	1	3.832	4	67	108	0.278
5	Gerhardt	Joe	1890	BR4	AA	3.565	1	3.565	2	40	75	0.203

Brooklyn Gladiators - Top Career Pitchers

Rank	Name	First	LYear	LTeam	Lg	PEVA-P	YRS	PER	W	L	SV	IP	ERA
1	Daily	Ed	1890	BR4	AA	3.555	1	3.555	10	15	0	235.7	4.05
2	McCullough	Charlie	1890	BR4	AA	1.142	1	1.142	4	21	0	215.7	4.59
3	Mattimore	Mike	1890	BR4	AA	0.955	1	0.955	6	13	0	178.3	4.54
4	Toole	Steve	1890	BR4	AA	0.831	1	0.831	2	4	0	53.3	4.05
5	Murphy	Bob	1890	BR4	AA	0.538	1	0.538	3	9	0	96.0	5.72

BROOKLYN TIP TOPS
Best Seasons and Careers of All-Time

Brooklyn Tip Tops - Best Position Player Years

Rank	Name	First	Year	Team	Lg	HR	RBI	AVG	Age	PEVA-B
1	Kauff	Benny	1915	BRF	FL	12	83	0.342	25	32.472
2	Evans	Steve	1914	BRF	FL	12	96	0.348	29	28.788
3	Evans	Steve	1915	BRF	FL	3	30	0.296	30	16.293
4	Cooper	Claude	1915	BRF	FL	2	63	0.294	23	15.763
5	Shaw	Al	1914	BRF	FL	5	49	0.324	33	11.926
6	Hofman	Solly	1914	BRF	FL	5	83	0.287	32	11.721

Brooklyn Tip-Tops - Best Pitcher Years

Rank	Name	First	Year	Team	Lg	W	L	SV	IP	ERA	Age	PEVA-P
1	Seaton	Tom	1914	BRF	FL	25	14	2	302.7	3.03	27	9.669
2	Lafitte	Ed	1914	BRF	FL	18	15	2	290.7	2.63	28	7.529
3	Seaton	Tom	1915	BRF	FL	12	11	3	189.3	4.56	28	4.319
4	Wiltse	Hooks	1915	BRF	FL	3	5	5	59.3	2.28	36	3.540
5	Falkenberg	Cy	1915	BRF	FL	3	3	0	48.0	1.50	35	3.257

Brooklyn Tip-Tops - Top Career Batters

Rank	Name	First	LYear	LTeam	Lg	PEVA-B	YRS	PER	HR	RBI	H	AVE.
1	Evans	Steve	1915	BRF	FL	35.118	2	17.559	15	126	243	0.333
2	Kauff	Benny	1915	BRF	FL	32.472	1	32.472	12	83	165	0.342
3	Cooper	Claude	1915	BRF	FL	19.456	2	9.728	4	88	251	0.271
4	Anderson	George	1915	BRF	FL	13.206	2	6.603	5	63	250	0.286
5	Shaw	Al	1914	BRF	FL	11.926	1	11.926	5	49	122	0.324
6	Hofman	Solly	1914	BRF	FL	11.721	1	11.721	5	83	148	0.287
7	Wisterzil	Tex	1915	BRF	FL	11.303	2	5.652	0	87	170	0.266

Brooklyn Tip-Tops - Top Career Pitchers

Rank	Name	First	LYear	LTeam	Lg	PEVA-P	YRS	PER	W	L	SV	IP	ERA
1	Seaton	Tom	1915	BRF	FL	12.763	2	6.381	37	25	5	492.0	3.62
2	Lafitte	Ed	1915	BRF	FL	8.538	2	4.269	24	24	2	408.3	3.02
3	Finneran	Happy	1915	BRF	FL	4.789	2	2.395	22	23	3	390.7	2.97
4	Wiltse	Hooks	1915	BRF	FL	3.540	1	3.540	3	5	5	59.3	2.28
5	Marion	Dan	1915	BRF	FL	3.292	2	1.646	15	11	0	297.7	3.42

BROOKLYN WARD'S WONDERS
Best Seasons and Careers of All-Time

Brooklyn Ward's Wonders - Best Position Player Years

Rank	Name	First	Year	Team	Lg	HR	RBI	AVG	Age	PEVA-B
1	Ward	John	1890	BRP	PL	4	60	0.335	30	15.619
2	Orr	Dave	1890	BRP	PL	6	124	0.371	31	15.509
3	Bierbauer	Lou	1890	BRP	PL	7	99	0.306	25	14.454
4	Joyce	Bill	1890	BRP	PL	1	78	0.252	25	13.176
5	Van Haltren	George	1890	BRP	PL	5	54	0.335	24	6.382

Brooklyn Ward's Wonders - Best Pitcher Years

Rank	Name	First	Year	Team	Lg	W	L	SV	IP	ERA	Age	PEVA-P
1	Weyhing	Gus	1890	BRP	PL	30	16	0	390.0	3.60	24	7.634
2	Sowders	John	1890	BRP	PL	19	16	0	309.0	3.82	24	4.114
3	Van Haltren	George	1890	BRP	PL	15	10	2	223.0	4.28	24	1.564
4	Murphy	Con	1890	BRP	PL	4	10	2	139.0	4.79	27	0.907
5	Hemming	George	1890	BRP	PL	8	4	3	123.0	3.80	22	0.891

Brooklyn Ward's Wonders - Top Career Batters

Rank	Name	First	LYear	LTeam	Lg	PEVA-B	YRS	PER	HR	RBI	H	AVE.
1	Ward	John	1890	BRP	PL	15.619	1	15.619	4	60	188	0.335
2	Orr	Dave	1890	BRP	PL	15.509	1	15.509	6	124	172	0.371
3	Bierbauer	Lou	1890	BRP	PL	14.454	1	14.454	7	99	180	0.306
4	Joyce	Bill	1890	BRP	PL	13.176	1	13.176	1	78	123	0.252
5	Van Haltren	George	1890	BRP	PL	6.382	1	6.382	5	54	126	0.335

Brooklyn Ward's Wonders - Top Career Pitchers

Rank	Name	First	LYear	LTeam	Lg	PEVA-P	YRS	PER	W	L	SV	IP	ERA
1	Weyhing	Gus	1890	BRP	PL	7.634	1	7.634	30	16	0	390.0	3.60
2	Van Haltren	George	1890	BRP	PL	1.564	1	1.564	15	10	2	223.0	4.28
3	Sowders	John	1890	BRP	PL	4.114	1	4.114	19	16	0	309.0	3.82
4	Murphy	Con	1890	BRP	PL	0.907	1	0.907	4	10	2	139.0	4.79
5	Hemming	George	1890	BRP	PL	0.761	1	0.761	8	4	3	123.0	3.80

BOSTON RED STOCKINGS
Best Seasons and Careers of All-Time

Boston Red Stockings - Best Position Player Years

Rank	Name	First	Year	Team	Lg	HR	RBI	AVG	Age	PEVA-B
1	Barnes	Ross	1873	BS1	NA	2	62	0.425	23	42.762
2	McVey	Cal	1875	BS1	NA	3	87	0.355	26	35.627
3	White	Deacon	1875	BS1	NA	1	60	0.367	28	35.065
4	Barnes	Ross	1871	BS1	NA	0	34	0.401	21	32.973
5	Barnes	Ross	1872	BS1	NA	1	44	0.432	22	32.428
6	Barnes	Ross	1875	BS1	NA	1	58	0.364	25	32.311
7	Wright	George	1873	BS1	NA	3	50	0.388	26	30.121
8	McVey	Cal	1874	BS1	NA	3	71	0.359	25	28.884
9	Wright	George	1875	BS1	NA	2	61	0.333	28	28.148
10	McVey	Cal	1871	BS1	NA	0	43	0.431	22	26.529
11	White	Deacon	1873	BS1	NA	0	66	0.390	26	24.754
12	Leonard	Andy	1875	BS1	NA	1	74	0.321	29	20.750
13	Wright	George	1874	BS1	NA	2	44	0.329	27	19.712
14	Wright	George	1872	BS1	NA	2	32	0.337	25	19.266
15	O'Rourke	Jim	1875	BS1	NA	6	72	0.296	25	18.580
16	O'Rourke	Jim	1874	BS1	NA	5	61	0.314	24	17.832
17	White	Deacon	1874	BS1	NA	3	52	0.300	27	15.492
18	Spalding	Al	1874	BS1	NA	0	54	0.329	24	14.447
19	Leonard	Andy	1874	BS1	NA	0	51	0.319	28	13.215
20	Spalding	Al	1872	BS1	NA	0	47	0.354	22	12.841

Boston Red Stockings - Best Pitcher Years

Rank	Name	First	Year	Team	Lg	W	L	SV	IP	ERA	Age	PEVA-P
1	Spalding	Al	1872	BS1	NA	38	8	0	404.7	1.98	22	31.314
2	Spalding	Al	1874	BS1	NA	52	16	0	616.3	2.35	24	30.873
3	Spalding	Al	1871	BS1	NA	19	10	0	257.3	3.36	21	28.490
4	Spalding	Al	1875	BS1	NA	55	5	8	575.0	1.52	25	27.761
5	Spalding	Al	1873	BS1	NA	41	14	2	497.7	2.46	23	26.662

Boston Red Stockings - Top Career Batters

Rank	Name	First	LYear	LTeam	Lg	PEVA-B	YRS	PER	HR	RBI	H	AVE.
1	Barnes	Ross	1875	BS1	NA	151.486	5	30.297	4	239	530	0.390
2	McVey	Cal	1875	BS1	NA	101.404	4	25.351	6	242	403	0.359
3	Wright	George	1875	BS1	NA	101.045	5	20.209	9	198	484	0.350
4	White	Deacon	1875	BS1	NA	75.311	3	25.104	4	178	363	0.351
5	Spalding	Al	1875	BS1	NA	55.859	5	11.172	2	248	455	0.323
6	Leonard	Andy	1875	BS1	NA	54.782	4	13.695	3	229	414	0.324
7	O'Rourke	Jim	1875	BS1	NA	47.885	3	15.962	12	181	308	0.318
8	Schafer	Harry	1875	BS1	NA	38.416	5	7.683	4	173	337	0.277
9	Wright	Harry	1875	BS1	NA	23.237	5	4.647	4	111	222	0.274
10	Gould	Charlie	1872	BS1	NA	11.796	2	5.898	2	65	97	0.268

Boston Red Stockings - Top Career Pitchers

Rank	Name	First	LYear	LTeam	Lg	PEVA-P	YRS	PER	W	L	SV	IP	ERA
1	Spalding	Al	1875	BS1	NA	**144.902**	5	28.980	205	53	10	2351.0	2.22
2	Manning	Jack	1875	BS1	NA	**4.323**	1	4.323	15	2	7	139.7	2.19
3	Wright	Harry	1874	BS1	NA	**4.142**	4	1.036	4	4	8	99.3	3.81
4	McVey	Cal	1875	BS1	NA	**0.200**	1	0.200	1	0	1	11.0	3.27
5	Wright	George	1875	BS1	NA	**0.200**	1	0.200	0	1	0	4.0	2.25

BOSTON REDS
(PACIFIC COAST LEAGUE/AMERICAN ASSOCIATION)
Best Seasons and Careers of All-Time

Boston Reds (Pacific Coast League/American Assoc.) - Best Position Player Years

Rank	Name	First	Year	Team	Lg	HR	RBI	AVG	Age	PEVA-B
1	Brouthers	Dan	1891	BS2	AA	5	109	0.350	33	34.762
2	Brown	Tom	1891	BS2	AA	5	72	0.321	31	27.645
3	Duffy	Hugh	1891	BS2	AA	9	110	0.336	25	23.866
4	Richardson	Hardy	1890	BSP	PL	13	146	0.326	35	20.434
5	Farrell	Duke	1891	BS2	AA	12	110	0.302	25	20.311
6	Brouthers	Dan	1890	BSP	PL	1	97	0.330	32	19.035
7	Stovey	Harry	1890	BSP	PL	12	84	0.299	34	16.612
8	Brown	Tom	1890	BSP	PL	4	61	0.274	30	13.226
9	Radford	Paul	1891	BS2	AA	0	65	0.259	30	12.663
10	Nash	Billy	1890	BSP	PL	5	90	0.266	25	11.930

Boston Reds (Pacific Coast League/American Association) - Best Pitcher Years

Rank	Name	First	Year	Team	Lg	W	L	SV	IP	ERA	Age	PEVA-P
1	Haddock	George	1891	BS2	AA	34	11	1	379.7	2.49	25	17.269
2	Buffinton	Charlie	1891	BS2	AA	29	9	1	363.7	2.55	30	16.050
3	Radbourn	Charley	1890	BSP	PL	27	12	0	343.0	3.31	36	7.308
4	Gumbert	Ad	1890	BSP	PL	23	12	0	277.3	3.96	22	3.317
5	Daley	Bill	1890	BSP	PL	18	7	2	235.0	3.60	22	2.526

Boston Reds (Pacific Coast League/American Assoc.) (BS2, BSP) - Top Career Batters

Rank	Name	First	Year	Team	Lg	PEVA-B	YRS	PER	HR	RBI	H	AVE.
1	Brouthers	Dan	1891	BS2	AA	53.797	2	26.899	6	206	322	0.340
2	Brown	Tom	1891	BS2	AA	40.871	2	20.435	9	133	338	0.299
3	Duffy	Hugh	1891	BS2	AA	23.866	1	23.866	9	110	180	0.336
4	Richardson	Hardy	1891	BS2	AA	23.522	2	11.761	20	198	252	0.303
5	Farrell	Duke	1891	BS2	AA	20.311	1	20.311	12	110	143	0.302
6	Stovey	Harry	1890	BSP	PL	16.612	1	16.612	12	84	144	0.299
7	Radford	Paul	1891	BS2	AA	12.663	1	12.663	0	65	118	0.259
8	Nash	Billy	1890	BSP	PL	11.930	1	11.930	5	90	130	0.266

Boston Reds (Pacific Coast League/American Assoc.) (BS2, BSP) - Top Career Pitchers

Rank	Name	First	LYear	LTeam	Lg	PEVA-P	YRS	PER	W	L	SV	IP	ERA
1	Haddock	George	1891	BS2	AA	17.269	1	17.269	34	11	1	379.7	2.49
2	Buffinton	Charlie	1891	BS2	AA	16.050	1	16.050	29	9	1	363.7	2.55
3	Radbourn	Charley	1890	BSP	PL	7.308	1	7.308	27	12	0	343.0	3.31
4	Daley	Bill	1891	BS2	AA	4.200	2	2.100	26	13	4	361.7	3.38
5	Gumbert	Ad	1890	BSP	PL	3.317	1	3.317	23	12	0	277.3	3.96

BOSTON REDS (UA)
Best Seasons and Careers of All-Time

Boston Reds (UA) - Best Position Player Years

Rank	Name	First	Year	Team	Lg	HR	RBI	AVG	Age	PEVA-B
1	Crane	Ed	1884	BSU	UA	12	NA	0.285	22	10.742
2	O'Brien	Tom	1884	BSU	UA	4	NA	0.263	24	6.013
3	Irwin	John	1884	BSU	UA	1	NA	0.234	23	5.791
4	Hackett	Walter	1884	BSU	UA	1	NA	0.243	27	5.602
5	Slattery	Mike	1884	BSU	UA	0	NA	0.208	18	4.100

Boston Reds (UA) - Best Pitcher Years

Rank	Name	First	Year	Team	Lg	W	L	SV	IP	ERA	Age	PEVA-P
1	Shaw	Dupee	1884	BSU	UA	21	15	0	315.7	1.77	25	12.916
2	Burke	James	1884	BSU	UA	19	15	0	322.0	2.85	NA	3.920
3	Tenney	Fred	1884	BSU	UA	3	1	0	35.0	2.31	25	2.110
4	Bond	Tommy	1884	BSU	UA	13	9	0	189.0	3.00	28	1.831
5	McCarthy	Tommy	1884	BSU	UA	0	7	0	56.0	4.82	21	0.557

Boston Reds (UA) - Top Career Batters

Rank	Name	First	LYear	LTeam	Lg	PEVA-B	YRS	PER	HR	RBI	H	AVE.
1	Crane	Ed	1884	BSU	UA	10.742	1	10.742	12	0	122	0.285
2	O'Brien	Tom	1884	BSU	UA	6.013	1	6.013	4	0	118	0.263
3	Irwin	John	1884	BSU	UA	5.791	1	5.791	1	0	101	0.234
4	Hackett	Walter	1884	BSU	UA	5.602	1	5.602	1	0	101	0.243
5	Slattery	Mike	1884	BSU	UA	4.100	1	4.100	0	0	86	0.208

Boston Reds - Top Career Pitchers

Rank	Name	First	LYear	LTeam	Lg	PEVA-P	YRS	PER	W	L	SV	IP	ERA
1	Shaw	Dupee	1884	BSU	UA	7.504	1	7.504	21	15	0	315.7	1.77
2	Burke	James	1884	BSU	UA	3.920	1	3.920	19	15	0	322.0	2.85
3	Tenney	Fred	1884	BSU	UA	1.718	1	1.718	3	1	0	35.0	2.31
4	Bond	Tommy	1884	BSU	UA	1.492	1	1.492	13	9	0	189.0	3.00
5	McCarthy	Tommy	1884	BSU	UA	0.557	1	0.557	0	7	0	56.0	4.82

BUFFALO BUFFEDS AND BLUES
Best Seasons and Careers of All-Time

Buffalo Buffeds & Blues - Best Position Player Years

Rank	Name	First	Year	Team	Lg	HR	RBI	AVG	Age	PEVA-B
1	Hanford	Charlie	1914	BUF	FL	12	90	0.291	32	17.564
2	Chase	Hal	1915	BUF	FL	17	89	0.291	32	13.941
3	Louden	Baldy	1914	BUF	FL	6	63	0.313	31	11.388
4	Louden	Baldy	1915	BUF	FL	4	48	0.281	32	8.621
5	Dalton	Jack	1915	BUF	FL	2	46	0.293	30	7.691

Buffalo Buffeds & Blues - Best Pitcher Years

Rank	Name	First	Year	Team	Lg	W	L	SV	IP	ERA	Age	PEVA-P
1	Ford	Russ	1914	BUF	FL	21	6	6	247.3	1.82	31	13.668
2	Bedient	Hugh	1915	BUF	FL	16	18	10	269.3	3.17	26	8.280
3	Schulz	Al	1915	BUF	FL	21	14	0	309.7	3.08	26	7.604
4	Anderson	Fred	1915	BUF	FL	19	13	0	240.0	2.51	30	6.632
5	Krapp	Gene	1914	BUF	FL	16	14	0	252.7	2.49	27	5.677

Buffalo Buffeds & Blues - Top Career Batters

Rank	Name	First	LYear	LTeam	Lg	PEVA-B	YRS	PER	HR	RBI	H	AVE.
1	Louden	Baldy	1915	BUF	FL	20.009	2	10.005	10	111	267	0.297
2	Chase	Hal	1915	BUF	FL	19.588	2	9.794	20	137	266	0.310
3	Hanford	Charlie	1914	BUF	FL	17.564	1	17.564	12	90	174	0.291
4	McDonald	Tex	1915	BUF	FL	8.299	2	4.150	9	71	142	0.283
5	Blair	Walter	1915	BUF	FL	7.696	2	3.848	2	53	157	0.235

Buffalo Buffeds & Blues - Top Career Pitchers

Rank	Name	First	LYear	LTeam	Lg	PEVA-P	YRS	PER	W	L	SV	IP	ERA
1	Ford	Russ	1915	BUF	FL	14.482	2	7.241	26	15	6	374.7	2.74
2	Anderson	Fred	1915	BUF	FL	10.664	2	5.332	32	28	0	500.3	2.81
3	Schulz	Al	1915	BUF	FL	9.554	2	4.777	30	26	2	480.7	3.18
4	Krapp	Gene	1915	BUF	FL	8.421	2	4.210	25	33	0	483.7	2.98
5	Bedient	Hugh	1915	BUF	FL	8.280	1	8.280	16	18	10	269.3	3.17

CHICAGO WHITE STOCKINGS
Best Seasons and Careers of All-Time

Chicago White Stockings (National Association) - Best Position Player Years

Rank	Name	First	Year	Team	Lg	HR	RBI	AVG	Age	PEVA-B
1	Wood	Jimmy	1871	CH1	NA	1	29	0.378	29	14.911
2	Meyerle	Levi	1874	CH2	NA	1	47	0.394	29	14.600
3	Hines	Paul	1875	CH2	NA	0	36	0.328	20	11.256
4	Treacey	Fred	1871	CH1	NA	4	33	0.339	24	8.368
5	Force	Davy	1874	CH2	NA	0	26	0.313	25	7.817

Chicago White Stockings (American Association) - Best Pitcher Years

Rank	Name	First	Year	Team	Lg	W	L	SV	IP	ERA	Age	PEVA-P
1	Zettlein	George	1871	CH1	NA	18	9	0	240.7	2.73	27	32.500
2	Zettlein	George	1875	CH2	NA	17	14	0	282.0	1.82	31	11.035
3	Zettlein	George	1874	CH2	NA	27	30	0	515.7	3.07	30	6.230
4	Golden	Mike	1875	CH2	NA	6	7	0	119.0	2.87	24	1.716
5	Devlin	Jim	1875	CH2	NA	7	16	0	224.0	2.89	26	1.544

Chicago White Stockings (National Association) (CH1, CH2) - Top Career Batters

Rank	Name	First	LYear	LTeam	Lg	PEVA-B	YRS	PER	HR	RBI	H	AVE.
1	Hines	Paul	1875	CH2	NA	17.390	2	8.695	0	70	181	0.313
2	Wood	Jimmy	1871	CH1	NA	14.911	1	14.911	1	29	51	0.378
3	Meyerle	Levi	1874	CH2	NA	14.600	1	14.600	1	47	100	0.394
4	Peters	John	1875	CH2	NA	11.009	2	5.505	1	59	154	0.287
5	Devlin	Jim	1875	CH2	NA	9.465	2	4.733	0	67	150	0.288

Chicago White Stockings (National Association) (CH1, CH2) - Top Career Pitchers

Rank	Name	First	LYear	LTeam	Lg	PEVA-P	YRS	PER	W	L	SV	IP	ERA
1	Zettlein	George	1875	CH2	NA	45.460	3	15.153	62	53	0	1038.3	2.65
2	Devlin	Jim	1875	CH2	NA	1.544	1	1.544	7	16	0	224.0	2.89
3	Golden	Mike	1875	CH2	NA	0.884	1	0.884	6	7	0	119.0	2.87
4	Force	Davy	1874	CH2	NA	0.200	1	0.200	0	0	0	7.0	24.43
5	Pinkham	Ed	1871	CH1	NA	0.200	1	0.200	1	0	1	10.3	3.48

CHICAGO CHI-FEDS
Best Seasons and Careers of All-Time

Chicago Chi-Feds - Best Position Player Years

Rank	Name	First	Year	Team	Lg	HR	RBI	AVG	Age	PEVA-B
1	Wilson	Art	1914	CHF	FL	10	64	0.291	29	25.707
2	Zwilling	Dutch	1914	CHF	FL	16	95	0.313	26	25.300
3	Zwilling	Dutch	1915	CHF	FL	13	94	0.286	27	22.595
4	Wickland	Al	1914	CHF	FL	6	68	0.276	26	17.925
5	Flack	Max	1915	CHF	FL	3	45	0.314	25	15.520
6	Mann	Les	1915	CHF	FL	4	58	0.306	23	14.224
7	Wilson	Art	1915	CHF	FL	7	31	0.305	30	12.652
8	Wickland	Al	1915	CHF	FL	1	5	0.244	27	11.088
9	Beck	Fred	1914	CHF	FL	11	77	0.279	28	10.316
10	Fischer	William	1915	CHF	FL	4	50	0.329	24	10.030

Chicago Chi-Feds - Best Pitcher Years

Rank	Name	First	Year	Team	Lg	W	L	SV	IP	ERA	Age	PEVA-P
1	Hendrix	Claude	1914	CHF	FL	29	10	5	362.0	1.69	25	27.456
2	McConnell	George	1915	CHF	FL	25	10	1	303.0	2.20	38	11.452
3	Brown	Mordecai	1915	CHF	FL	17	8	4	236.3	2.09	39	7.083
4	Prendergast	Mike	1915	CHF	FL	14	12	0	253.7	2.48	27	5.064
5	Hendrix	Claude	1915	CHF	FL	16	15	4	285.0	3.00	26	4.944

Chicago Chi-Feds - Top Career Batters

Rank	Name	First	LYear	LTeam	Lg	PEVA-B	YRS	PER	HR	RBI	H	AVE.
1	Zwilling	Dutch	1915	CHF	FL	47.895	2	23.947	29	189	342	0.300
2	Wilson	Art	1915	CHF	FL	38.359	2	19.180	17	95	210	0.296
3	Flack	Max	1915	CHF	FL	22.698	2	11.349	5	84	288	0.281
4	Wickland	Al	1915	CHF	FL	19.932	2	9.966	7	73	169	0.272
5	Mann	Les	1915	CHF	FL	14.224	1	14.224	4	58	144	0.306
6	Beck	Fred	1915	CHF	FL	13.168	2	6.584	16	115	238	0.256
7	Zeider	Rollie	1915	CHF	FL	11.358	2	5.679	1	70	236	0.249
8	Fischer	William	1915	CHF	FL	10.030	1	10.030	4	50	96	0.329

Chicago Chi-Feds - Top Career Pitchers

Rank	Name	First	LYear	LTeam	Lg	PEVA-P	YRS	PER	W	L	SV	IP	ERA
1	Hendrix	Claude	1915	CHF	FL	32.400	2	16.200	45	25	9	647.0	2.27
2	McConnell	George	1915	CHF	FL	11.452	1	11.452	25	10	1	303.0	2.20
3	Brown	Mordecai	1915	CHF	FL	7.083	1	7.083	17	8	4	236.3	2.09
4	Prendergast	Mike	1915	CHF	FL	6.604	2	3.302	19	21	0	389.7	2.45
5	Watson	Doc	1914	CHF	FL	3.592	1	3.592	9	8	1	172.0	2.04

CHICAGO PIRATES
Best Seasons and Careers of All-Time

Chicago Pirates - Best Position Player Years

Rank	Name	First	Year	Team	Lg	HR	RBI	AVG	Age	PEVA-B
1	Duffy	Hugh	1890	CHP	PL	7	82	0.320	24	23.069
2	Ryan	Jimmy	1890	CHP	PL	6	89	0.340	27	16.850
3	O'Neill	Tip	1890	CHP	PL	3	75	0.302	32	12.577
4	Farrell	Duke	1890	CHP	PL	2	84	0.290	24	9.023
5	Pfeffer	Fred	1890	CHP	PL	5	80	0.257	30	7.185

Chicago Pirates - Best Pitcher Years

Rank	Name	First	Year	Team	Lg	W	L	SV	IP	ERA	Age	PEVA-P
1	King	Silver	1890	CHP	PL	30	22	0	461.0	2.69	22	18.015
2	Baldwin	Mark	1890	CHP	PL	34	24	0	501.0	3.31	27	13.556
3	Bartson	Charlie	1890	CHP	PL	8	10	1	188.0	4.26	25	1.003
4	Dwyer	Frank	1890	CHP	PL	3	6	1	69.3	6.23	22	0.543

Chicago Pirates - Top Career Batters

Rank	Name	First	LYear	LTeam	Lg	PEVA-B	YRS	PER	HR	RBI	H	AVE
1	Duffy	Hugh	1890	CHP	PL	23.069	1	23.069	7	82	191	0.320
2	Ryan	Jimmy	1890	CHP	PL	16.850	1	16.850	6	89	165	0.340
3	O'Neill	Tip	1890	CHP	PL	12.577	1	12.577	3	75	174	0.302
4	Farrell	Duke	1890	CHP	PL	9.023	1	9.023	2	84	131	0.290
5	Pfeffer	Fred	1890	CHP	PL	7.185	1	7.185	5	80	128	0.257

Chicago Pirates - Top Career Pitchers

Rank	Name	First	LYear	LTeam	Lg	PEVA-P	YRS	PER	W	L	SV	IP	ERA
1	King	Silver	1890	CHP	PL	18.015	1	18.015	30	22	0	461.0	2.69
2	Baldwin	Mark	1890	CHP	PL	13.556	1	13.556	34	24	0	501.0	3.31
3	Bartson	Charlie	1890	CHP	PL	1.003	1	1.003	8	10	1	188.0	4.26
4	Dwyer	Frank	1890	CHP	PL	0.543	1	0.543	3	6	1	69.3	6.23

CHICAGO/PITTSBURGH (UNION LEAGUE)
Best Seasons and Careers of All-Time

Chicago/Pittsburgh (Union League) - Best Position Player Years

Rank	Name	First	Year	Team	Lg	HR	RBI	AVG	Age	PEVA-B
1	Schoeneck	Jumbo	1884	CHU	UA	2	NA	0.317	22	6.118
2	Ellick	Joe	1884	CHU	UA	0	NA	0.236	30	4.672
3	Gross	Emil	1884	CHU	UA	4	NA	0.358	26	3.217
4	Krieg	Bill	1884	CHU	UA	0	NA	0.247	25	3.184
5	Householder	Charlie	1884	CHU	UA	1	NA	0.239	28	2.194

Chicago/Pittsburgh (Union League) - Best Pitcher Years

Rank	Name	First	Year	Team	Lg	W	L	SV	IP	ERA	Age	PEVA-P
1	Daily	Hugh	1884	CHU	UA	27	27	0	484.7	2.43	27	10.851
2	Atkinson	Al	1884	CHU	UA	6	10	0	140.0	2.76	23	4.069
3	Horan	John	1884	CHU	UA	3	6	0	98.0	3.49	21	0.984
4	Cady	Charlie	1884	CHU	UA	3	1	0	35.0	2.83	19	0.933
5	Foreman	Frank	1884	CHU	UA	1	2	0	18.0	4.00	21	0.743

Chicago/Pittsburgh (Union League) - Top Career Batters

Rank	Name	First	LYear	LTeam	Lg	PEVA-B	YRS	PER	HR	RBI	H	AVE.
1	Schoeneck	Jumbo	1884	CHU	UA	5.256	1	5.256	2	0	116	0.317
2	Ellick	Joe	1884	CHU	UA	4.290	1	4.290	0	0	93	0.236
3	Gross	Emil	1884	CHU	UA	3.217	1	3.217	4	0	34	0.358
4	Krieg	Bill	1884	CHU	UA	3.184	1	3.184	0	0	69	0.247
5	Householder	Charlie	1884	CHU	UA	2.194	1	2.194	1	0	74	0.239

Chicago/Pittsburgh (Union League) - Top Career Pitchers

Rank	Name	First	LYear	LTeam	Lg	PEVA-P	YRS	PER	W	L	SV	IP	ERA
1	Daily	Hugh	1884	CHU	UA	10.504	1	10.504	27	27	0	484.7	2.43
2	Atkinson	Al	1884	CHU	UA	1.447	1	1.447	6	10	0	140.0	2.76
3	Horan	John	1884	CHU	UA	0.984	1	0.984	3	6	0	98.0	3.49
4	Cady	Charlie	1884	CHU	UA	0.933	1	0.933	3	1	0	35.0	2.83
5	Foreman	Frank	1884	CHU	UA	0.514	1	0.514	1	2	0	18.0	4.00

CLEVELAND FOREST CITYS
Best Seasons and Careers of All-Time

Cleveland Forest Citys - Best Position Player Years

Rank	Name	First	Year	Team	Lg	HR	RBI	AVG	Age	PEVA-B
1	White	Deacon	1871	CL1	NA	1	21	0.322	24	12.018
2	Sutton	Ezra	1871	CL1	NA	3	23	0.352	21	11.624
3	Hastings	Scott	1872	CL1	NA	0	16	0.391	25	7.720
4	Allison	Art	1871	CL1	NA	0	19	0.292	22	4.591
5	Pratt	Al	1871	CL1	NA	0	20	0.262	23	3.548

Cleveland Forest Citys - Best Pitcher Years

Rank	Name	First	Year	Team	Lg	W	L	SV	IP	ERA	Age	PEVA-P
1	Pratt	Al	1871	CL1	NA	10	17	0	224.7	3.77	23	6.902
2	Pratt	Al	1872	CL1	NA	2	9	0	104.7	4.39	24	0.570
3	Wolters	Rynie	1872	CL1	NA	3	6	0	76.3	5.19	30	0.506
4	Pabor	Charlie	1871	CL1	NA	0	2	0	29.3	6.75	25	0.377
5	Pabor	Charlie	1872	CL1	NA	1	1	0	18.0	3.00	26	0.200

Cleveland Forest Citys - Top Career Batters

Rank	Name	First	LYear	LTeam	Lg	PEVA-B	YRS	PER	HR	RBI	H	AVE.
1	White	Deacon	1872	CL1	NA	14.827	2	7.413	1	43	84	0.329
2	Sutton	Ezra	1872	CL1	NA	12.885	2	6.443	3	33	75	0.319
3	Allison	Art	1872	CL1	NA	5.186	2	2.593	0	27	63	0.281
4	Hastings	Scott	1872	CL1	NA	5.016	1	5.016	0	16	45	0.391
5	Pratt	Al	1872	CL1	NA	4.000	2	2.000	0	32	52	0.267

Cleveland Forest Citys - Top Career Pitchers

Rank	Name	First	LYear	LTeam	Lg	PEVA-P	YRS	PER	W	L	SV	IP	ERA
1	Pratt	Al	1872	CL1	NA	7.439	2	3.720	12	26	0	329.3	3.96
2	Pabor	Charlie	1872	CL1	NA	0.577	2	0.289	1	3	0	47.3	5.32
3	Wolters	Rynie	1872	CL1	NA	0.486	1	0.486	3	6	0	76.3	5.19

CLEVELAND BLUES
Best Seasons and Careers of All-Time

Cleveland Blues - Best Position Player Years

Rank	Name	First	Year	Team	Lg	HR	RBI	AVG	Age	PEVA-B
1	Glasscock	Jack	1882	CL2	NL	4	46	0.291	25	21.812
2	Glasscock	Jack	1884	CL2	NL	1	22	0.249	27	17.209
3	Dunlap	Fred	1883	CL2	NL	4	37	0.326	24	17.162
4	Dunlap	Fred	1880	CL2	NL	4	30	0.276	21	15.702
5	Shaffer	Orator	1880	CL2	NL	0	21	0.266	29	14.687
6	Dunlap	Fred	1881	CL2	NL	3	24	0.325	22	14.446
7	Dunlap	Fred	1882	CL2	NL	0	28	0.280	23	13.374
8	York	Tom	1883	CL2	NL	2	46	0.260	33	11.469
9	Glasscock	Jack	1883	CL2	NL	0	46	0.287	26	11.330
10	Muldoon	Mike	1882	CL2	NL	6	45	0.246	24	10.186

Cleveland Blues - Best Pitcher Years

Rank	Name	First	Year	Team	Lg	W	L	SV	IP	ERA	Age	PEVA-P
1	McCormick	Jim	1880	CL2	NL	45	28	0	657.7	1.85	24	21.965
2	McCormick	Jim	1882	CL2	NL	36	30	0	595.7	2.37	26	18.813
3	McCormick	Jim	1881	CL2	NL	26	30	0	526.0	2.45	25	17.833
4	McCormick	Jim	1884	CL2	NL	19	22	0	359.0	2.86	28	15.537
5	McCormick	Jim	1883	CL2	NL	28	12	1	342.0	1.84	27	10.611

Cleveland Blues - Top Career Batters

Rank	Name	First	LYear	LTeam	Lg	PEVA-B	YRS	PER	HR	RBI	H	AVE.
1	Glasscock	Jack	1884	CL2	NL	61.663	6	10.277	5	203	510	0.258
2	Dunlap	Fred	1883	CL2	NL	60.683	4	15.171	11	119	448	0.302
3	Phillips	Bill	1884	CL2	NL	44.308	6	7.385	11	242	590	0.264
4	Shaffer	Orator	1882	CL2	NL	29.336	3	9.779	4	83	245	0.246
5	Hotaling	Pete	1884	CL2	NL	23.115	3	7.705	3	98	285	0.248
6	Muldoon	Mike	1884	CL2	NL	21.802	3	7.267	8	112	271	0.238
7	McCormick	Jim	1884	CL2	NL	12.089	6	2.015	2	123	356	0.239
8	York	Tom	1883	CL2	NL	11.469	1	11.469	2	46	99	0.260

Cleveland Blues - Top Career Pitchers

Rank	Name	First	LYear	LTeam	Lg	PEVA-P	YRS	PER	W	L	SV	IP	ERA
1	McCormick	Jim	1884	CL2	NL	85.338	6	14.223	174	162	1	3026.7	2.28
2	Daily	Hugh	1883	CL2	NL	6.392	1	6.392	23	19	1	378.7	2.42
3	Harkins	John	1884	CL2	NL	2.934	1	2.934	12	32	0	391.0	3.68
4	Hankinson	Frank	1880	CL2	NL	2.879	1	2.879	1	1	1	25.0	1.08
5	Sawyer	Will	1883	CL2	NL	2.182	1	2.182	4	10	0	141.0	2.36

CLEVELAND BLUES AND SPIDERS
Best Seasons and Careers of All-Time

Cleveland Blues & Spiders - Best Position Player Years

Rank	Name	First	Year	Team	Lg	HR	RBI	AVG	Age	PEVA-B
1	Burkett	Jesse	1896	CL4	NL	6	72	0.410	28	28.983
2	Burkett	Jesse	1895	CL4	NL	5	83	0.409	27	23.591
3	Burkett	Jesse	1897	CL4	NL	2	60	0.383	29	22.708
4	Childs	Cupid	1896	CL4	NL	1	106	0.355	29	21.580
5	Childs	Cupid	1892	CL4	NL	3	53	0.317	25	20.676
6	Burkett	Jesse	1893	CL4	NL	6	82	0.348	25	18.979
7	McKean	Ed	1888	CL3	AA	6	68	0.299	24	18.637
8	Wallace	Bobby	1897	CL4	NL	4	112	0.335	24	18.517
9	Burkett	Jesse	1898	CL4	NL	0	42	0.341	30	17.717
10	McKean	Ed	1890	CL4	NL	7	61	0.296	26	17.400
11	McKean	Ed	1895	CL4	NL	8	119	0.342	31	15.760
12	McKean	Ed	1896	CL4	NL	7	112	0.338	32	14.719
13	Davis	George	1891	CL4	NL	3	89	0.289	21	14.708
14	Virtue	Jake	1892	CL4	NL	2	89	0.282	27	14.526
15	Childs	Cupid	1891	CL4	NL	2	83	0.281	24	14.432
16	Wallace	Bobby	1898	CL4	NL	3	99	0.270	25	14.090
17	McKean	Ed	1893	CL4	NL	4	133	0.310	29	13.841
18	Burkett	Jesse	1894	CL4	NL	8	94	0.358	26	13.431
19	McKean	Ed	1889	CL4	NL	4	75	0.318	25	13.389
20	Childs	Cupid	1893	CL4	NL	3	65	0.326	26	13.360

Cleveland Blues & Spiders - Best Pitcher Years

Rank	Name	First	Year	Team	Lg	W	L	SV	IP	ERA	Age	PEVA-P
1	Young	Cy	1893	CL4	NL	34	16	1	422.7	3.36	26	43.542
2	Young	Cy	1896	CL4	NL	28	15	3	414.3	3.24	29	38.520
3	Young	Cy	1895	CL4	NL	35	10	0	369.7	3.26	28	32.941
4	Young	Cy	1892	CL4	NL	36	12	0	453.0	1.93	25	31.345
5	Young	Cy	1898	CL4	NL	25	13	0	377.7	2.53	31	26.356
6	Young	Cy	1894	CL4	NL	26	21	1	408.7	3.94	27	26.323
7	Cuppy	Nig	1896	CL4	NL	25	14	1	358.0	3.12	27	22.116
8	Young	Cy	1897	CL4	NL	21	19	0	333.7	3.80	30	18.713
9	Cuppy	Nig	1895	CL4	NL	26	14	2	353.0	3.54	26	16.908
10	Young	Cy	1891	CL4	NL	27	22	2	423.7	2.85	24	14.082
11	Powell	Jack	1898	CL4	NL	23	15	0	342.0	3.00	24	12.785
12	Cuppy	Nig	1892	CL4	NL	28	13	1	376.0	2.51	23	11.417
13	Clarkson	John	1892	CL4	NL	17	10	1	243.3	2.55	31	10.721

Cleveland Blues & Spiders (CL3, CL4) - Top Career Batters

Rank	Name	First	LYear	LTeam	Lg	PEVA-B	YRS	PER	HR	RBI	H	AVE.
1	McKean	Ed	1898	CL4	NL	155.581	12	12.965	63	1084	2011	0.304
2	Burkett	Jesse	1898	CL4	NL	138.866	8	17.358	33	512	1453	0.356
3	Childs	Cupid	1898	CL4	NL	103.775	8	12.972	17	541	1238	0.318
4	Zimmer	Chief	1899	CL4	NL	51.049	13	3.927	23	503	945	0.272
5	McAleer	Jimmy	1898	CL4	NL	44.872	9	4.986	11	427	913	0.252
6	Tebeau	Patsy	1898	CL4	NL	42.527	9	4.725	21	625	1076	0.282

7	Davis	George	1892	CL4	NL	**35.366**	3	11.789	14	244	448	0.265
8	Wallace	Bobby	1898	CL4	NL	**33.255**	5	6.651	8	239	391	0.286
9	Virtue	Jake	1894	CL4	NL	**29.040**	5	5.808	7	256	483	0.274
10	O'Connor	Jack	1898	CL4	NL	**26.275**	7	3.754	11	410	765	0.277
11	Stricker	Cub	1889	CL4	NL	**22.024**	3	7.341	4	133	398	0.250
12	McGarr	Chippy	1896	CL4	NL	**17.091**	4	4.273	5	214	454	0.276
13	Hotaling	Pete	1888	CL3	AA	**16.755**	2	8.378	3	149	252	0.278
14	Blake	Harry	1898	CL4	NL	**14.672**	5	2.934	6	212	403	0.254
15	Ewing	Buck	1894	CL4	NL	**12.875**	2	6.438	8	161	225	0.316
16	Gilks	Bob	1890	CL4	NL	**10.530**	4	2.633	1	135	303	0.229

Cleveland Blues & Spiders (CL3, CL4) - Top Career Pitchers

Rank	Name	First	LYear	LTeam	Lg	PEVA-P	YRS	PER	W	L	SV	IP	ERA
1	Young	Cy	1898	CL4	NL	**234.004**	9	26.000	241	135	7	3351.0	3.10
2	Cuppy	Nig	1898	CL4	NL	**68.450**	7	9.779	139	80	4	1914.0	3.50
3	Powell	Jack	1898	CL4	NL	**22.120**	2	11.060	38	25	0	567.0	3.06
4	Clarkson	John	1894	CL4	NL	**15.430**	3	5.143	41	37	1	689.0	3.78
5	Wilson	Zeke	1898	CL4	NL	**14.760**	4	3.690	49	39	1	803.0	3.95
6	Bakely	Jersey	1889	CL4	NL	**14.743**	2	7.371	37	55	0	837.0	2.97
7	Beatin	Ed	1891	CL4	NL	**11.523**	3	3.841	42	48	0	821.0	3.78

COLUMBUS BUCKEYES
Best Seasons and Careers of All-Time

Columbus Buckeyes - Best Position Player Years

Rank	Name	First	Year	Team	Lg	HR	RBI	AVG	Age	PEVA-B
1	Brown	Tom	1884	CL5	AA	5	32	0.273	24	13.429
2	Mann	Fred	1884	CL5	AA	7	0	0.276	26	12.439
3	Brown	Tom	1883	CL5	AA	5	32	0.274	23	11.146
4	Smith	Pop	1883	CL5	AA	4	0	0.262	27	9.359
5	Richmond	John	1883	CL5	AA	0	0	0.283	29	8.609

Columbus Buckeyes - Best Pitcher Years

Rank	Name	First	Year	Team	Lg	W	L	SV	IP	ERA	Age	PEVA-P
1	Morris	Ed	1884	CL5	AA	34	13	0	429.7	2.18	22	15.285
2	Mountain	Frank	1883	CL5	AA	26	33	0	503.0	3.60	23	5.599
3	Mountain	Frank	1884	CL5	AA	23	17	1	360.7	2.45	24	5.549
4	Valentine	John	1883	CL5	AA	2	10	0	102.0	3.53	28	0.859
5	Dundon	Ed	1883	CL5	AA	3	16	0	166.7	4.48	24	0.777

Columbus Buckeyes - Top Career Batters

Rank	Name	First	LYear	LTeam	Lg	PEVA-B	YRS	PER	HR	RBI	H	AVE.
1	Brown	Tom	1884	CL5	AA	24.575	2	12.287	10	64	238	0.273
2	Mann	Fred	1884	CL5	AA	18.400	2	9.200	8	0	199	0.262
3	Smith	Pop	1884	CL5	AA	17.836	2	8.918	10	0	212	0.249
4	Richmond	John	1884	CL5	AA	17.102	2	8.551	3	0	209	0.267
5	Kuehne	Bill	1884	CL5	AA	9.440	2	4.720	6	0	183	0.232

Columbus Buckeyes - Top Career Pitchers

Rank	Name	First	LYear	LTeam	Lg	PEVA-P	YRS	PER	W	L	SV	IP	ERA
1	Morris	Ed	1884	CL5	AA	15.285	1	15.285	34	13	0	429.7	2.18
2	Mountain	Frank	1884	CL5	AA	11.148	2	5.574	49	50	1	863.7	3.12
3	Dundon	Ed	1884	CL5	AA	1.446	2	0.723	9	20	0	247.7	4.25
4	Valentine	John	1883	CL5	AA	0.859	1	0.859	2	10	0	102.0	3.53
5	Sullivan	Tom	1884	CL5	AA	0.481	1	0.481	2	2	0	31.0	4.06

COLUMBUS SOLONS
Best Seasons and Careers of All-Time

Columbus Solons - Best Position Player Years

Rank	Name	First	Year	Team	Lg	HR	RBI	AVG	Age	PEVA-B
1	Johnson	Spud	1890	CL6	AA	1	113	0.346	30	23.376
2	Marr	Lefty	1889	CL6	AA	1	75	0.306	27	16.611
3	Duffee	Charlie	1891	CL6	AA	10	90	0.301	25	16.545
4	O'Connor	Jack	1890	CL6	AA	2	66	0.324	21	15.537
5	McTamany	Jim	1889	CL6	AA	4	52	0.276	26	15.356
6	McTamany	Jim	1890	CL6	AA	1	48	0.258	27	14.589
7	McTamany	Jim	1891	CL6	AA	3	35	0.250	28	13.031
8	Crooks	Jack	1891	CL6	AA	0	46	0.245	26	12.304
9	Orr	Dave	1889	CL6	AA	4	87	0.327	30	10.793
10	Reilly	Charlie	1890	CL6	AA	4	77	0.266	23	10.281

Columbus Solons - Best Pitcher Years

Rank	Name	First	Year	Team	Lg	W	L	SV	IP	ERA	Age	PEVA-P
1	Knell	Phil	1891	CL6	AA	28	27	0	462.0	2.92	26	14.684
2	Gastright	Hank	1890	CL6	AA	30	14	0	401.3	2.94	25	13.178
3	Baldwin	Mark	1889	CL6	AA	27	34	1	513.7	3.61	26	10.311
4	Knauss	Frank	1890	CL6	AA	17	12	2	275.7	2.81	22	8.110
5	Chamberlain	Elton	1890	CL6	AA	12	6	0	175.0	2.21	23	4.450

Columbus Salons - Top Career Batters

Rank	Name	First	LYear	LTeam	Lg	PEVA-B	YRS	PER	HR	RBI	H	AVE.
1	McTamany	Jim	1891	CL6	AA	37.534	3	12.511	8	135	342	0.263
2	Johnson	Spud	1890	CL6	AA	30.007	2	15.003	3	192	316	0.317
3	O'Connor	Jack	1891	CL6	AA	23.383	3	7.794	6	163	316	0.292
4	Crooks	Jack	1891	CL6	AA	21.499	3	7.166	1	115	248	0.237
5	Sneed	John	1891	CL6	AA	17.891	2	8.946	3	126	235	0.276
6	Marr	Lefty	1889	CL6	AA	16.611	1	16.611	1	75	167	0.306
7	Duffee	Charlie	1891	CL6	AA	16.545	1	16.545	10	90	166	0.301
8	Orr	Dave	1889	CL6	AA	10.793	1	10.793	4	87	183	0.327
9	Reilly	Charlie	1890	CL6	AA	10.481	2	5.240	7	83	152	0.275

Columbus Salons - Top Career Pitchers

Rank	Name	First	LYear	LTeam	Lg	PEVA-P	YRS	PER	W	L	SV	IP	ERA
1	Gastright	Hank	1891	CL6	AA	16.582	3	5.527	52	49	0	907.7	3.60
2	Knell	Phil	1891	CL6	AA	14.684	1	14.684	28	27	0	462.0	2.92
3	Baldwin	Mark	1889	CL6	AA	10.311	1	10.311	27	34	1	513.7	3.61
4	Knauss	Frank	1890	CL6	AA	8.110	1	8.110	17	12	2	275.7	2.81
5	Easton	Jack	1891	CL6	AA	4.289	4	1.072	21	26	2	424.0	3.84

CLEVELAND INFANTS
Best Seasons and Careers of All-Time

Cleveland Infants - Best Position Player Years

Rank	Name	First	Year	Team	Lg	HR	RBI	AVG	Age	PEVA-B
1	Browning	Pete	1890	CLP	PL	5	93	0.373	29	29.964
2	Larkin	Henry	1890	CLP	PL	5	112	0.330	30	23.049
3	Radford	Paul	1890	CLP	PL	2	62	0.292	29	13.819
4	Tebeau	Patsy	1890	CLP	PL	5	74	0.298	26	10.414
5	Delahanty	Ed	1890	CLP	PL	3	64	0.296	23	9.191

Cleveland Infants - Best Pitcher Years

Rank	Name	First	Year	Team	Lg	W	L	SV	IP	ERA	Age	PEVA-P
1	Gruber	Henry	1890	CLP	PL	22	23	0	383.3	4.27	27	4.143
2	Bakely	Jersey	1890	CLP	PL	12	25	0	326.3	4.47	26	2.445
3	O'Brien	Darby	1890	CLP	PL	8	16	0	206.3	3.40	23	1.719
4	McGill	Willie	1890	CLP	PL	11	9	0	183.7	4.12	17	1.069
5	Hemming	George	1890	CLP	PL	0	1	0	21.0	6.86	22	0.891

Cleveland Infants - Top Career Batters

Rank	Name	First	LYear	LTeam	Lg	PEVA-B	YRS	PER	HR	RBI	H	AVE.
1	Browning	Pete	1890	CLP	PL	29.964	1	29.964	5	93	184	0.373
2	Larkin	Henry	1890	CLP	PL	23.049	1	23.049	5	112	167	0.330
3	Radford	Paul	1890	CLP	PL	13.819	1	13.819	2	62	136	0.292
4	Tebeau	Patsy	1890	CLP	PL	10.414	1	10.414	5	74	134	0.298
5	Delahanty	Ed	1890	CLP	PL	9.191	1	9.191	3	64	153	0.296

Cleveland Infants - Top Career Pitchers

Rank	Name	First	LYear	LTeam	Lg	PEVA-P	YRS	PER	W	L	SV	IP	ERA
1	Gruber	Henry	1890	CLP	PL	4.143	1	4.143	22	23	0	383.3	4.27
2	Bakely	Jersey	1890	CLP	PL	2.445	1	2.445	12	25	0	326.3	4.47
3	O'Brien	Darby	1890	CLP	PL	1.719	1	1.719	8	16	0	206.3	3.40
4	McGill	Willie	1890	CLP	PL	1.069	1	1.069	11	9	0	183.7	4.12
5	Gleason	Bill	1890	CLP	PL	0.200	1	0.200	0	1	0	4.0	27.00

CINCINNATI KELLY'S KILLERS
Best Seasons and Careers of All-Time

Cincinnati Kelly's Killers - Best Position Player Years

Rank	Name	First	Year	Team	Lg	HR	RBI	AVG	Age	PEVA-B
1	Canavan	Jim	1891	CN3	AA	7	66	0.228	25	9.146
2	Seery	Emmett	1891	CN3	AA	4	36	0.285	30	7.099
3	Kelly	King	1891	CN3	AA	1	53	0.297	34	5.852
4	Carney	John	1891	CN3	AA	3	43	0.278	25	5.535
5	Johnston	Dick	1891	CN3	AA	6	51	0.221	28	3.338

Cincinnati Kelly's Killers - Best Pitcher Years

Rank	Name	First	Year	Team	Lg	W	L	SV	IP	ERA	Age	PEVA-P
1	Crane	Ed	1891	CN3	AA	14	14	0	250.0	2.45	29	7.790
2	McGill	Willie	1891	CN3	AA	2	5	0	65.0	4.98	18	5.515
3	Dwyer	Frank	1891	CN3	AA	13	19	0	289.0	4.52	23	4.025
4	Mains	Willard	1891	CN3	AA	12	12	0	204.0	2.69	23	3.145
5	Kilroy	Matt	1891	CN3	AA	1	4	0	45.3	2.98	25	0.973

Cincinnati Kelly's Killers - Top Career Batters

Rank	Name	First	LYear	LTeam	Lg	PEVA-B	YRS	PER	HR	RBI	H	AVE.
1	Seery	Emmett	1891	CN3	AA	7.099	1	7.099	4	36	106	0.285
2	Canavan	Jim	1891	CN3	AA	6.859	1	6.859	7	66	97	0.228
3	Kelly	King	1891	CN3	AA	4.732	1	4.732	1	53	84	0.297
4	Carney	John	1891	CN3	AA	4.259	1	4.259	3	43	102	0.278
5	Johnston	Dick	1891	CN3	AA	3.338	1	3.338	6	51	83	0.221

Cincinnati Kelly's Killers - Top Career Pitchers

Rank	Name	First	LYear	LTeam	Lg	PEVA-P	YRS	PER	W	L	SV	IP	ERA
1	Crane	Ed	1891	CN3	AA	5.311	1	5.311	14	14	0	250.0	2.45
2	Dwyer	Frank	1891	CN3	AA	3.102	1	3.102	13	19	0	289.0	4.52
3	Mains	Willard	1891	CN3	AA	2.998	1	2.998	12	12	0	204.0	2.69
4	McGill	Willie	1891	CN3	AA	1.142	1	1.142	2	5	0	65.0	4.98
5	Kilroy	Matt	1891	CN3	AA	0.973	1	0.973	1	4	0	45.3	2.98

CINCINNATI OUTLAW REDS
Best Seasons and Careers of All-Time

Cincinnati Outlaw Reds - Best Position Player Years

Rank	Name	First	Year	Team	Lg	HR	RBI	AVG	Age	PEVA-B
1	Burns	Dick	1884	CNU	UA	4	NA	0.306	21	5.365
2	Harbidge	Bill	1884	CNU	UA	2	NA	0.279	29	5.304
3	Sylvester	Lou	1884	CNU	UA	2	NA	0.267	29	4.341
4	Hawes	Bill	1884	CNU	UA	4	NA	0.278	31	3.537
5	Crane	Sam	1884	CNU	UA	1	NA	0.233	30	2.184

Cincinnati Outlaw Reds - Best Pitcher Years

Rank	Name	First	Year	Team	Lg	W	L	SV	IP	ERA	Age	PEVA-P
1	McCormick	Jim	1884	CNU	UA	21	3	0	210.0	1.54	28	15.537
2	Bradley	George	1884	CNU	UA	25	15	0	342.0	2.71	32	6.254
3	Burns	Dick	1884	CNU	UA	23	15	0	329.7	2.46	21	5.938
4	Sylvester	Lou	1884	CNU	UA	0	1	1	32.7	3.58	29	0.904

Cincinnati Outlaw Reds - Top Career Batters

Rank	Name	First	LYear	LTeam	Lg	PEVA-B	YRS	PER	HR	RBI	H	AVE.
1	Glasscock	Jack	1884	CNU	UA	6.534	1	6.534	2	0	72	0.419
2	Burns	Dick	1884	CNU	UA	5.365	1	5.365	4	0	107	0.306
3	Harbidge	Bill	1884	CNU	UA	5.304	1	5.304	2	0	95	0.279
4	Sylvester	Lou	1884	CNU	UA	4.341	1	4.341	2	0	89	0.267
5	Hawes	Bill	1884	CNU	UA	3.537	1	3.537	4	0	97	0.278

Cincinnati Outlaw Reds - Top Career Pitchers

Rank	Name	First	LYear	LTeam	Lg	PEVA-P	YRS	PER	W	L	SV	IP	ERA
1	Bradley	George	1884	CNU	UA	6.254	1	6.254	25	15	0	342.0	2.71
2	Burns	Dick	1884	CNU	UA	5.938	1	5.938	23	15	0	329.7	2.46
3	McCormick	Jim	1884	CNU	UA	5.734	1	5.734	21	3	0	210.0	1.54
4	Sylvester	Lou	1884	CNU	UA	0.904	1	0.904	0	1	1	32.7	3.58

DETROIT WOLVERINES
Best Seasons and Careers of All-Time

Detroit Wolverines - Best Position Player Years

Rank	Name	First	Year	Team	Lg	HR	RBI	AVG	Age	PEVA-B
1	Brouthers	Dan	1888	DTN	NL	9	66	0.307	30	28.646
2	Brouthers	Dan	1886	DTN	NL	11	72	0.370	28	26.852
3	Thompson	Sam	1887	DTN	NL	11	166	0.372	27	23.822
4	Wood	George	1883	DTN	NL	5	47	0.302	25	22.913
5	Bennett	Charlie	1882	DTN	NL	5	51	0.301	28	22.544
6	Bennett	Charlie	1883	DTN	NL	5	55	0.305	29	20.547
7	Brouthers	Dan	1887	DTN	NL	12	101	0.338	29	20.013
8	Richardson	Hardy	1886	DTN	NL	11	61	0.351	31	19.201
9	Bennett	Charlie	1881	DTN	NL	7	64	0.301	27	18.960
10	Hanlon	Ned	1884	DTN	NL	5	39	0.264	27	16.317
11	Hanlon	Ned	1885	DTN	NL	1	29	0.302	28	15.291
12	Thompson	Sam	1886	DTN	NL	8	89	0.310	26	14.910
13	Wood	George	1882	DTN	NL	7	29	0.269	24	14.263
14	Bennett	Charlie	1885	DTN	NL	5	60	0.269	31	14.160
15	Wood	George	1884	DTN	NL	8	29	0.252	26	13.984
16	Rowe	Jack	1887	DTN	NL	6	96	0.318	31	12.622
17	Hanlon	Ned	1882	DTN	NL	5	38	0.231	25	12.267
18	White	Deacon	1888	DTN	NL	4	71	0.298	41	12.053
19	Knight	Lon	1881	DTN	NL	1	52	0.271	28	11.598
20	Richardson	Hardy	1887	DTN	NL	8	94	0.328	32	11.298

Detroit Wolverines - Best Pitcher Years

Rank	Name	First	Year	Team	Lg	W	L	SV	IP	ERA	Age	PEVA-P
1	Baldwin	Lady	1886	DTN	NL	42	13	0	487.0	2.24	27	30.125
2	Derby	George	1881	DTN	NL	29	26	0	494.7	2.20	24	22.265
3	Shaw	Dupee	1884	DTN	NL	9	18	0	227.7	3.04	25	12.916
4	Conway	Pete	1888	DTN	NL	30	14	0	391.0	2.26	22	12.719
5	Getzein	Charlie	1887	DTN	NL	29	13	0	366.7	3.73	23	7.624

Detroit Wolverines - Top Career Batters

Rank	Name	First	LYear	LTeam	Lg	PEVA-B	YRS	PER	HR	RBI	H	AVE.
1	Bennett	Charlie	1888	DTN	NL	98.664	8	12.333	37	353	654	0.278
2	Hanlon	Ned	1888	DTN	NL	82.480	8	10.310	27	342	879	0.261
3	Brouthers	Dan	1888	DTN	NL	75.511	3	25.170	32	239	510	0.338
4	Wood	George	1885	DTN	NL	68.560	5	13.712	27	165	558	0.281
5	Thompson	Sam	1888	DTN	NL	49.145	4	12.286	32	339	503	0.327
6	Richardson	Hardy	1888	DTN	NL	33.801	3	11.267	25	187	444	0.330

Detroit Wolverines - Top Career Pitchers

Rank	Name	First	LYear	LTeam	Lg	PEVA-P	YRS	PER	W	L	SV	IP	ERA
1	Baldwin	Lady	1888	DTN	NL	39.645	4	9.911	69	35	1	930.3	2.71
2	Getzein	Charlie	1888	DTN	NL	25.902	5	5.180	95	86	0	1634.7	3.09
3	Derby	George	1882	DTN	NL	25.471	2	12.736	46	46	0	856.7	2.65
4	Wiedman	Stump	1887	DTN	NL	19.243	6	3.207	84	101	2	1654.0	3.34
5	Conway	Pete	1888	DTN	NL	17.549	3	5.850	44	28	0	628.0	2.57

ELIZABETH RESOLUTES
Best Seasons and Careers of All-Time

Elizabeth Resolutes - Best Position Player Years

Rank	Name	First	Year	Team	Lg	HR	RBI	AVG	Age	PEVA-B
1	Booth	Eddie	1873	ELI	NA	0	4	0.292	NA	1.074
2	Allison	Doug	1873	ELI	NA	0	8	0.289	27	1.005
3	Allison	Art	1873	ELI	NA	0	11	0.323	24	0.869
4	Austin	Henry	1873	ELI	NA	0	11	0.248	29	0.441
5	Fleet	Frank	1873	ELI	NA	0	10	0.256	25	0.350

Elizabeth Resolutes - Best Pitcher Years

Rank	Name	First	Year	Team	Lg	W	L	SV	IP	ERA	Age	PEVA-P
1	Campbell	Hugh	1873	ELI	NA	2	16	0	165.0	2.84	27	1.710
2	Fleet	Frank	1873	ELI	NA	0	3	0	24.0	5.62	25	0.200
3	Wolters	Rynie	1873	ELI	NA	0	1	0	9.0	0.00	31	0.200
4	Lovett	Len	1873	ELI	NA	0	1	0	9.0	7.00	21	0.200

Elizabeth Resolutes - Top Career Batters

Rank	Name	First	LYear	LTeam	Lg	PEVA-B	YRS	PER	HR	RBI	H	AVE.
1	Allison	Art	1873	ELI	NA	0.869	1	0.869	0	11	32	0.323
2	Allison	Doug	1873	ELI	NA	0.637	1	0.637	0	8	24	0.289
3	Booth	Eddie	1873	ELI	NA	0.548	1	0.548	0	4	21	0.292
4	Austin	Henry	1873	ELI	NA	0.441	1	0.441	0	11	25	0.248
5	Fleet	Frank	1873	ELI	NA	0.350	1	0.350	0	10	23	0.256

Elizabeth Resolutes - Top Career Pitchers

Rank	Name	First	LYear	LTeam	Lg	PEVA-P	YRS	PER	W	L	SV	IP	ERA
1	Campbell	Hugh	1873	ELI	NA	1.710	1	1.710	2	16	0	165.0	2.84
2	Fleet	Frank	1873	ELI	NA	0.200	1	0.200	0	3	0	24.0	5.63
3	Lovett	Len	1873	ELI	NA	0.200	1	0.200	0	1	0	9.0	7.00
4	Wolters	Rynie	1873	ELI	NA	0.200	1	0.200	0	1	0	9.0	0.00

FORT WAYNE KEKIONGAS
Best Seasons and Careers of All-Time

Fort Wayne Kekiongas - Best Position Player Years

Rank	Name	First	Year	Team	Lg	HR	RBI	AVG	Age	PEVA-B
1	Foran	Jim	1871	FW1	NA	1	18	0.348	23	**1.456**
2	Mathews	Bobby	1871	FW1	NA	0	10	0.270	20	**0.589**
3	Goldsmith	Wally	1871	FW1	NA	0	12	0.205	22	**0.578**
4	Carey	Tom	1871	FW1	NA	0	10	0.230	22	**0.573**
5	Kelly	Bill	1871	FW1	NA	0	7	0.224	NA	**0.484**

Fort Wayne Kekiogas - Best Pitcher Years

Rank	Name	First	Year	Team	Lg	W	L	SV	IP	ERA	Age	PEVA-P
1	Mathews	Bobby	1871	FW1	NA	6	11	0	169.0	5.17	20	**1.663**

Fort Wayne Kekiongas - Top Career Batters

Rank	Name	First	LYear	LTeam	Lg	PEVA-B	YRS	PER	HR	RBI	H	AVE.
1	Foran	Jim	1871	FW1	NA	**1.456**	1	1.456	1	18	31	0.348
2	Mathews	Bobby	1871	FW1	NA	**0.589**	1	0.589	0	10	24	0.270
3	Goldsmith	Wally	1871	FW1	NA	**0.578**	1	0.578	0	12	18	0.205
4	Carey	Tom	1871	FW1	NA	**0.573**	1	0.573	0	10	20	0.230
5	Kelly	Bill	1871	FW1	NA	**0.484**	1	0.484	0	7	15	0.224

Fort Wayne Kekiongas - Top Career Pitchers

Rank	Name	First	LYear	LTeam	Lg	PEVA-P	YRS	PER	W	L	SV	IP	ERA
1	Mathews	Bobby	1871	FW1	NA	**1.663**	1	1.663	6	11	0	169.0	5.17

HARTFORD DARK BLUES (NATIONAL LEAGUE)
Best Seasons and Careers of All-Time

Hartford Dark Blues (National League) - Best Position Player Years

Rank	Name	First	Year	Team	Lg	HR	RBI	AVG	Age	PEVA-B
1	Cassidy	John	1877	HAR	NL	0	27	0.378	20	22.778
2	Start	Joe	1877	HAR	NL	1	21	0.332	35	19.559
3	York	Tom	1877	HAR	NL	1	37	0.283	27	13.799
4	Higham	Dick	1876	HAR	NL	0	35	0.327	25	11.623
5	Ferguson	Bob	1877	HAR	NL	0	35	0.256	32	11.164

Hartford Dark Blues (National League) - Best Pitcher Years

Rank	Name	First	Year	Team	Lg	W	L	SV	IP	ERA	Age	PEVA-P
1	Bond	Tommy	1876	HAR	NL	31	13	0	408.0	1.68	20	19.434
2	Larkin	Terry	1877	HAR	NL	29	25	0	501.0	2.14	NA	18.656
3	Cummings	Candy	1876	HAR	NL	16	8	0	216.0	1.67	28	4.764
4	Ferguson	Bob	1877	HAR	NL	1	1	0	25.0	3.96	32	0.629
5	Cassidy	John	1877	HAR	NL	1	1	0	18.0	5.00	20	0.200

Hartford Dark Blues (National League) - Top Career Batters

Rank	Name	First	LYear	LTeam	Lg	PEVA-B	YRS	PER	HR	RBI	H	AVE.
1	Cassidy	John	1877	HAR	NL	22.978	2	11.489	0	35	108	0.362
2	York	Tom	1877	HAR	NL	21.181	2	10.591	2	76	135	0.270
3	Start	Joe	1877	HAR	NL	19.559	1	19.559	1	21	90	0.332
4	Ferguson	Bob	1877	HAR	NL	18.223	2	9.111	0	67	147	0.261
5	Carey	Tom	1877	HAR	NL	13.346	2	6.673	1	46	148	0.263
6	Burdock	Jack	1877	HAR	NL	12.431	2	6.215	0	32	152	0.259
7	Higham	Dick	1876	HAR	NL	11.623	1	11.623	0	35	102	0.327

Hartford Dark Blues (National League) - Top Career Pitchers

Rank	Name	First	LYear	LTeam	Lg	PEVA-P	YRS	PER	W	L	SV	IP	ERA
1	Bond	Tommy	1876	HAR	NL	19.434	1	19.434	31	13	0	408.0	1.68
2	Larkin	Terry	1877	HAR	NL	18.656	1	18.656	29	25	0	501.0	2.14
3	Cummings	Candy	1876	HAR	NL	4.764	1	4.764	16	8	0	216.0	1.67
4	Ferguson	Bob	1877	HAR	NL	0.629	1	0.629	1	1	0	25.0	3.96
5	Cassidy	John	1877	HAR	NL	0.200	1	0.200	1	1	0	18.0	5.00

HARTFORD DARK BLUES (NATIONAL ASSOCIATION)
Best Seasons and Careers of All-Time

Hartford Dark Blues (National Association) - Best Position Player Years

Rank	Name	First	Year	Team	Lg	HR	RBI	AVG	Age	PEVA-B
1	York	Tom	1875	HR1	NA	0	37	0.296	25	14.808
2	Pike	Lip	1874	HR1	NA	1	51	0.355	29	13.501
3	Remsen	Jack	1875	HR1	NA	0	34	0.268	25	11.122
4	Ferguson	Bob	1875	HR1	NA	0	43	0.240	30	10.643
5	Burdock	Jack	1875	HR1	NA	0	35	0.294	23	9.859

Hartford Dark Blues (National Association) - Best Pitcher Years

Rank	Name	First	Year	Team	Lg	W	L	SV	IP	ERA	Age	PEVA-P
1	Cummings	Candy	1875	HR1	NA	35	12	0	417.0	1.60	27	19.393
2	Bond	Tommy	1875	HR1	NA	19	16	0	352.0	1.56	19	13.404
3	Fisher	Cherokee	1874	HR1	NA	14	23	0	317.0	3.04	29	2.732
4	Stearns	Bill	1874	HR1	NA	2	14	1	164.0	4.50	21	0.877
5	Ferguson	Bob	1875	HR1	NA	0	0	0	2.0	18.00	30	0.200

Hartford Dark Blues (National Association) - Top Career Batters

Rank	Name	First	LYear	LTeam	Lg	PEVA-B	YRS	PER	HR	RBI	H	AVE.
1	York	Tom	1875	HR1	NA	14.808	1	14.808	0	37	111	0.296
2	Pike	Lip	1874	HR1	NA	13.501	1	13.501	1	51	83	0.355
3	Remsen	Jack	1875	HR1	NA	11.122	1	11.122	0	34	96	0.268
4	Ferguson	Bob	1875	HR1	NA	10.643	1	10.643	0	43	88	0.240
5	Burdock	Jack	1875	HR1	NA	9.859	1	9.859	0	35	103	0.294

Hartford Dark Blues (National Association) - Top Career Pitchers

Rank	Name	First	LYear	LTeam	Lg	PEVA-P	YRS	PER	W	L	SV	IP	ERA
1	Cummings	Candy	1875	HR1	NA	19.393	1	19.393	35	12	0	417.0	1.60
2	Bond	Tommy	1875	HR1	NA	13.404	1	13.404	19	16	0	352.0	1.56
3	Fisher	Cherokee	1874	HR1	NA	2.732	1	2.732	14	23	0	317.0	3.04
4	Stearns	Bill	1874	HR1	NA	0.877	1	0.877	2	14	1	164.0	4.50
5	Ferguson	Bob	1875	HR1	NA	0.200	1	0.200	0	0	0	2.0	18.00

INDIANAPOLIS BLUES
Best Seasons and Careers of All-Time

Indianapolis Blues - Best Position Player Years

Rank	Name	First	Year	Team	Lg	HR	RBI	AVG	Age	PEVA-B
1	Shaffer	Orator	1878	IN1	NL	0	30	0.338	27	50.240
2	Clapp	John	1878	IN1	NL	0	29	0.304	27	20.427
3	McKelvy	Russ	1878	IN1	NL	2	36	0.225	24	10.612
4	Quest	Joe	1878	IN1	NL	0	13	0.205	26	6.698
5	Williamson	Ned	1878	IN1	NL	1	19	0.232	21	5.895

Indianapolis Blues - Best Pitcher Years

Rank	Name	First	Year	Team	Lg	W	L	SV	IP	ERA	Age	PEVA-P
1	Nolan	The Only	1878	IN1	NL	13	22	0	347.0	2.57	21	3.014
2	McCormick	Jim	1878	IN1	NL	5	8	0	117.0	1.69	22	2.216
3	Healey	Tom	1878	IN1	NL	6	4	1	89.0	2.22	25	0.596
4	McKelvy	Russ	1878	IN1	NL	0	2	0	25.0	2.16	24	0.456

Indianapolis Blues - Top Career Batters

Rank	Name	First	LYear	LTeam	Lg	PEVA-B	YRS	PER	HR	RBI	H	AVE.
1	Shaffer	Orator	1878	IN1	NL	50.240	1	50.240	0	30	90	0.338
2	Clapp	John	1878	IN1	NL	20.427	1	20.427	0	29	80	0.304
3	McKelvy	Russ	1878	IN1	NL	10.612	1	10.612	2	36	57	0.225
4	Quest	Joe	1878	IN1	NL	6.698	1	6.698	0	13	57	0.205
5	Williamson	Ned	1878	IN1	NL	5.895	1	5.895	1	19	58	0.232

Indianapolis Blues - Top Career Pitchers

Rank	Name	First	LYear	LTeam	Lg	PEVA-P	YRS	PER	W	L	SV	IP	ERA
1	Nolan	The Only	1878	IN1	NL	3.014	1	3.014	13	22	0	347.0	2.57
2	McCormick	Jim	1878	IN1	NL	2.216	1	2.216	5	8	0	117.0	1.69
3	Healey	Tom	1878	IN1	NL	0.470	1	0.470	6	4	1	89.0	2.22
4	McKelvy	Russ	1878	IN1	NL	0.456	1	0.456	0	2	0	25.0	2.16

INDIANAPOLIS HOOSIERS (AMERICAN ASSOCIATION)
Best Seasons and Careers of All-Time

Indianapolis Hoosiers (American Association) - Best Position Player Years

Rank	Name	First	Year	Team	Lg	HR	RBI	AVG	Age	PEVA-B
1	Keenan	Jim	1884	IN2	AA	3	0	0.293	26	6.327
2	Phillips	Marr	1884	IN2	AA	0	0	0.269	27	5.336
3	Peltz	John	1884	IN2	AA	3	0	0.219	23	4.633
4	Kerins	John	1884	IN2	AA	6	0	0.214	26	3.299
5	Weihe	Podge	1884	IN2	AA	4	0	0.254	22	2.474

Indianapolis Hoosiers (American Association) - Best Pitcher Years

Rank	Name	First	Year	Team	Lg	W	L	SV	IP	ERA	Age	PEVA-P
1	McKeon	Larry	1884	IN2	AA	18	41	0	512.0	3.50	18	5.217
2	Barr	Bob	1884	IN2	AA	3	11	0	132.0	4.98	28	3.228
3	Bond	Tommy	1884	IN2	AA	0	5	0	43.0	5.65	28	1.831
4	Aydelott	Jake	1884	IN2	AA	5	7	0	106.0	4.92	23	1.005
5	McCauley	Al	1884	IN2	AA	2	7	0	76.0	5.09	21	0.613

Indianapolis Hoosiers (American Association) - Top Career Batters

Rank	Name	First	LYear	LTeam	Lg	PEVA-B	YRS	PER	HR	RBI	H	AVE.
1	Keenan	Jim	1884	IN2	AA	6.327	1	6.327	3	0	73	0.293
2	Phillips	Marr	1884	IN2	AA	5.336	1	5.336	0	0	111	0.269
3	Peltz	John	1884	IN2	AA	4.633	1	4.633	3	0	86	0.219
4	Kerins	John	1884	IN2	AA	3.299	1	3.299	6	0	78	0.214
5	Weihe	Podge	1884	IN2	AA	2.474	1	2.474	4	0	65	0.254

Indianapolis Hoosiers (American Association) - Top Career Pitchers

Rank	Name	First	LYear	LTeam	Lg	PEVA-P	YRS	PER	W	L	SV	IP	ERA
1	McKeon	Larry	1884	IN2	AA	5.217	1	5.217	18	41	0	512.0	3.50
2	Barr	Bob	1884	IN2	AA	1.032	1	1.032	3	11	0	132.0	4.98
3	Aydelott	Jake	1884	IN2	AA	1.005	1	1.005	5	7	0	106.0	4.92
4	McCauley	Al	1884	IN2	AA	0.613	1	0.613	2	7	0	76.0	5.09
5	MacArthur	Mac	1884	IN2	AA	0.599	1	0.599	1	5	0	52.0	5.02

INDIANAPOLIS HOOSIERS (NATIONAL LEAGUE)
Best Seasons and Careers of All-Time

Indianapolis Hoosiers (National League) - Best Position Player Years

Rank	Name	First	Year	Team	Lg	HR	RBI	AVG	Age	PEVA-B
1	Glasscock	Jack	1889	IN3	NL	7	85	0.352	32	24.296
2	Seery	Emmett	1889	IN3	NL	8	59	0.314	28	16.268
3	Denny	Jerry	1889	IN3	NL	18	112	0.282	30	14.488
4	Denny	Jerry	1887	IN3	NL	11	97	0.324	28	12.665
5	Hines	Paul	1888	IN3	NL	4	58	0.281	33	12.664
6	Denny	Jerry	1888	IN3	NL	12	63	0.261	29	11.619
7	Seery	Emmett	1888	IN3	NL	5	50	0.220	27	10.417

Indianapolis Hoosiers (National League) - Best Pitcher Years

Rank	Name	First	Year	Team	Lg	W	L	SV	IP	ERA	Age	PEVA-P
1	Boyle	Henry	1887	IN3	NL	13	24	0	328.0	3.65	27	5.295
2	Boyle	Henry	1889	IN3	NL	21	23	0	378.7	3.92	29	4.998
3	Getzein	Charlie	1889	IN3	NL	18	22	1	349.0	4.54	25	3.074
4	Healy	John	1887	IN3	NL	12	29	0	341.0	5.17	21	2.641
5	Boyle	Henry	1888	IN3	NL	15	22	0	323.0	3.26	28	2.508

Indianapolis Hoosiers (National League) - Top Career Batters

Rank	Name	First	LYear	LTeam	Lg	PEVA-B	YRS	PER	HR	RBI	H	AVE.
1	Glasscock	Jack	1889	IN3	NL	39.030	3	13.010	8	170	466	0.309
2	Denny	Jerry	1889	IN3	NL	38.772	3	12.924	41	272	465	0.288
3	Seery	Emmett	1889	IN3	NL	32.706	3	10.902	17	137	379	0.254
4	Hines	Paul	1889	IN3	NL	19.750	2	9.875	10	130	292	0.292
5	Bassett	Charley	1889	IN3	NL	13.730	3	4.577	7	175	337	0.239
6	McGeachy	Jack	1889	IN3	NL	13.203	3	4.401	3	149	350	0.252

Indianapolis Hoosiers (National League) - Top Career Pitchers

Rank	Name	First	LYear	LTeam	Lg	PEVA-P	YRS	PER	W	L	SV	IP	ERA
1	Boyle	Henry	1889	IN3	NL	12.800	3	4.267	49	69	0	1029.7	3.63
2	Healy	John	1888	IN3	NL	4.937	2	2.468	24	53	0	662.3	4.55
3	Getzein	Charlie	1889	IN3	NL	3.074	1	3.074	18	22	1	349.0	4.54
4	Shreve	Lev	1889	IN3	NL	2.869	3	0.956	16	36	0	435.3	4.98
5	Burdick	Bill	1889	IN3	NL	1.880	2	0.940	12	14	1	221.7	3.17

INDIANAPOLIS HOOSIERS AND NEWARK PEPPERS
(FEDERAL LEAGUE)
Best Seasons and Careers of All-Time

Indianapolis Hoosiers & Newark Peppers (Federal League) - Best Position Player Years

Rank	Name	First	Year	Team	Lg	HR	RBI	AVG	Age	PEVA-B
1	Kauff	Benny	1914	IND	FL	8	95	0.370	24	35.356
2	Roush	Edd	1915	NEW	FL	3	60	0.298	22	14.470
3	Scheer	Al	1915	NEW	FL	2	60	0.267	27	13.949
4	Rariden	Bill	1915	NEW	FL	0	40	0.270	27	13.550
5	McKechnie	Bill	1914	IND	FL	2	38	0.304	28	12.768
6	Esmond	Jimmy	1915	NEW	FL	5	62	0.258	26	12.217
7	LaPorte	Frank	1914	IND	FL	4	107	0.311	34	11.995

Indianapolis Hoosiers & Newark Peppers (Federal League) - Best Pitcher Years

Rank	Name	First	Year	Team	Lg	W	L	SV	IP	ERA	Age	PEVA-P
1	Falkenberg	Cy	1914	IND	FL	25	16	3	377.3	2.22	34	23.241
2	Moseley	Earl	1915	NEW	FL	15	15	1	268.0	1.91	31	8.189
3	Reulbach	Ed	1915	NEW	FL	21	10	1	270.0	2.23	33	8.067
4	Moseley	Earl	1914	IND	FL	19	18	1	316.7	3.47	30	7.377
5	Kaiserling	George	1915	NEW	FL	15	15	2	261.3	2.24	22	6.622

Indianapolis Hoosiers & Newark Peppers (Federal League) (IND, NEW) - Top Career Batters

Rank	Name	First	LYear	LTeam	Lg	PEVA-B	YRS	PER	HR	RBI	H	AVE.
1	Kauff	Benny	1914	IND	FL	35.356	1	35.356	8	95	211	0.370
2	Esmond	Jimmy	1915	NEW	FL	22.057	2	11.029	7	111	307	0.276
3	Rariden	Bill	1915	NEW	FL	20.840	2	10.420	0	87	213	0.254
4	Scheer	Al	1915	NEW	FL	20.832	2	10.416	5	105	257	0.283
5	LaPorte	Frank	1915	NEW	FL	19.779	2	9.889	6	163	296	0.281
6	Campbell	Vin	1915	NEW	FL	19.521	2	9.760	8	88	336	0.314
7	McKechnie	Bill	1915	NEW	FL	19.064	2	9.532	3	81	286	0.280
8	Roush	Edd	1915	NEW	FL	16.881	2	8.440	4	90	218	0.304

Indianapolis Hoosiers & Newark Peppers (Federal League) - Top Career Pitchers

Rank	Name	First	LYear	LTeam	Lg	PEVA-P	YRS	PER	W	L	SV	IP	ERA
1	Falkenberg	Cy	1915	NEW	FL	25.787	2	12.894	34	27	4	549.3	2.54
2	Moseley	Earl	1915	NEW	FL	15.566	2	7.783	34	33	2	584.7	2.76
3	Kaiserling	George	1915	NEW	FL	12.402	2	6.201	32	25	2	536.7	2.68
4	Reulbach	Ed	1915	NEW	FL	8.067	1	8.067	21	10	1	270.0	2.23
5	Mullin	George	1915	NEW	FL	3.735	2	1.867	16	12	2	235.3	3.14

Note: Previous Names of Franchise: Indianapolis Hoosiers (IND) 1914; Newark Peppers (NEW) 1915.

KANSAS CITY COWBOYS
(AMERICAN ASSOCIATION)
Best Seasons and Careers of All-Time

Kansas City Cowboys (American Association) - Best Position Player Years

Rank	Name	First	Year	Team	Lg	HR	RBI	AVG	Age	PEVA-B
1	Hamilton	Billy	1889	KC2	AA	3	77	0.301	23	15.432
2	Long	Herman	1889	KC2	AA	3	60	0.275	23	13.249
3	McTamany	Jim	1888	KC2	AA	4	41	0.246	25	11.901
4	Burns	Jim	1889	KC2	AA	5	97	0.304	NA	11.228
5	Stearns	Ecky	1889	KC2	AA	3	87	0.286	28	8.475

Kansas City Cowboys (American Association) - Best Pitcher Years

Rank	Name	First	Year	Team	Lg	W	L	SV	IP	ERA	Age	PEVA-P
1	Conway	Jim	1889	KC2	AA	19	19	0	335.0	3.25	31	7.431
2	Porter	Henry	1888	KC2	AA	18	37	0	474.0	4.16	30	5.473
3	Swartzel	Park	1889	KC2	AA	19	27	1	410.3	4.32	24	4.020
4	Sullivan	Tom	1888	KC2	AA	8	16	0	214.7	3.40	28	1.319
5	Hoffman	Frank	1888	KC2	AA	3	9	0	104.0	2.77	NA	1.120

Kansas City Cowboys (American Association) - Top Career Batters

Rank	Name	First	LYear	LTeam	Lg	PEVA-B	YRS	PER	HR	RBI	H	AVE.
1	Hamilton	Billy	1889	KC2	AA	16.213	2	8.107	3	88	195	0.294
2	Long	Herman	1889	KC2	AA	13.249	1	13.249	3	60	158	0.275
3	McTamany	Jim	1888	KC2	AA	11.901	1	11.901	4	41	127	0.246
4	Burns	Jim	1889	KC2	AA	11.650	2	5.825	5	101	196	0.304
5	Stearns	Ecky	1889	KC2	AA	8.475	1	8.475	3	87	160	0.286

Kansas City Cowboys (American Association) - Top Career Pitchers

Rank	Name	First	LYear	LTeam	Lg	PEVA-P	YRS	PER	W	L	SV	IP	ERA
1	Conway	Jim	1889	KC2	AA	7.431	1	7.431	19	19	0	335.0	3.25
2	Porter	Henry	1889	KC2	AA	5.673	2	2.837	18	40	0	497.0	4.55
3	Swartzel	Park	1889	KC2	AA	4.020	1	4.020	19	27	1	410.3	4.32
4	Sullivan	Tom	1889	KC2	AA	1.998	2	0.999	10	24	0	302.0	4.05
5	Hoffman	Frank	1888	KC2	AA	1.120	1	1.120	3	9	0	104.0	2.77

KANSAS CITY PACKERS
Best Seasons and Careers of All-Time

Kansas City Packers - Best Position Player Years

Rank	Name	First	Year	Team	Lg	HR	RBI	AVG	Age	PEVA-B
1	Kenworthy	Bill	1914	KCF	FL	15	91	0.317	28	**23.988**
2	Easterly	Ted	1914	KCF	FL	1	67	0.335	29	**17.642**
3	Chadbourne	Chet	1914	KCF	FL	1	37	0.277	30	**12.792**
4	Perring	George	1914	KCF	FL	2	69	0.278	30	**10.555**
5	Perring	George	1915	KCF	FL	7	67	0.259	31	**9.935**

Kansas City Packers - Best Pitcher Years

Rank	Name	First	Year	Team	Lg	W	L	SV	IP	ERA	Age	PEVA-P
1	Cullop	Nick	1915	KCF	FL	22	11	2	302.3	2.44	28	**9.555**
2	Cullop	Nick	1914	KCF	FL	14	19	1	295.7	2.34	27	**8.157**
3	Packard	Gene	1914	KCF	FL	20	14	5	302.0	2.89	27	**7.764**
4	Packard	Gene	1915	KCF	FL	20	12	2	281.7	2.68	28	**6.620**
5	Johnson	Chief	1915	KCF	FL	17	17	2	281.3	2.75	29	**6.210**

Kansas City Packers - Top Career Batters

Rank	Name	First	LYear	LTeam	Lg	PEVA-B	YRS	PER	HR	RBI	H	AVE.
1	Kenworthy	Bill	1915	KCF	FL	**31.636**	2	15.818	18	143	291	0.309
2	Easterly	Ted	1915	KCF	FL	**22.776**	2	11.388	4	99	230	0.309
3	Chadbourne	Chet	1915	KCF	FL	**21.925**	2	10.963	2	72	294	0.252
4	Perring	George	1915	KCF	FL	**20.490**	2	10.245	9	136	281	0.268
5	Gilmore	Grover	1915	KCF	FL	**18.288**	2	9.144	2	79	269	0.286

Kansas City Packers - Top Career Pitchers

Rank	Name	First	LYear	LTeam	Lg	PEVA-P	YRS	PER YR	W	L	SV	IP	ERA
1	Cullop	Nick	1915	KCF	FL	**17.620**	2	8.810	36	30	3	598.0	2.39
2	Packard	Gene	1915	KCF	FL	**14.384**	2	7.192	40	26	7	583.7	2.79
3	Johnson	Chief	1915	KCF	FL	**7.673**	2	3.837	26	27	2	415.3	2.88
4	Main	Alex	1915	KCF	FL	**4.588**	1	4.588	13	14	3	230.0	2.54
5	Henning	Pete	1915	KCF	FL	**2.873**	2	1.436	14	25	4	345.0	3.83

KANSAS CITY COWBOYS
(NATIONAL LEAGUE)
Best Seasons and Careers of All-Time

Kansas City Cowboys (National League) - Best Position Player Years

Rank	Name	First	Year	Team	Lg	HR	RBI	AVG	Age	PEVA-B
1	Myers	Al	1886	KCN	NL	4	51	0.277	23	5.041
2	Radford	Paul	1886	KCN	NL	0	20	0.229	25	4.964
3	McQuery	Mox	1886	KCN	NL	4	38	0.247	25	4.197
4	Bassett	Charley	1886	KCN	NL	2	32	0.260	23	3.605
5	Rowe	Dave	1886	KCN	NL	3	57	0.240	32	3.549

Kansas City Cowboys (National League) - Best Pitcher Years

Rank	Name	First	Year	Team	Lg	W	L	SV	IP	ERA	Age	PEVA-P
1	Wiedman	Stump	1886	KCN	NL	12	36	0	427.7	4.50	25	3.572
2	Whitney	Jim	1886	KCN	NL	12	32	0	393.0	4.49	29	3.297
3	Conway	Pete	1886	KCN	NL	5	15	0	180.0	5.75	20	1.622
4	McKeon	Larry	1886	KCN	NL	0	2	0	21.0	10.71	20	0.933
5	King	Silver	1886	KCN	NL	1	3	0	39.0	4.85	18	0.763

Kansas City Cowboys (National League) - Top Career Batters

Rank	Name	First	LYear	LTeam	Lg	PEVA-B	YRS	PER	HR	RBI	H	AVE.
1	Myers	Al	1886	KCN	NL	5.041	1	5.041	4	51	131	0.277
2	Radford	Paul	1886	KCN	NL	4.964	1	4.964	0	20	113	0.229
3	McQuery	Mox	1886	KCN	NL	4.197	1	4.197	4	38	111	0.247
4	Bassett	Charley	1886	KCN	NL	3.605	1	3.605	2	32	89	0.260
5	Rowe	Dave	1886	KCN	NL	3.549	1	3.549	3	57	103	0.240

Kansas City Cowboys (National League) - Top Career Pitchers

Rank	Name	First	LYear	LTeam	Lg	PEVA-P	YRS	PER	W	L	SV	IP	ERA
1	Wiedman	Stump	1886	KCN	NL	3.572	1	3.572	12	36	0	427.7	4.50
2	Whitney	Jim	1886	KCN	NL	3.297	1	3.297	12	32	0	393.0	4.49
3	Conway	Pete	1886	KCN	NL	1.078	1	1.078	5	15	0	180.0	5.75
4	King	Silver	1886	KCN	NL	0.763	1	0.763	1	3	0	39.0	4.85
5	Lillie	Jim	1886	KCN	NL	0.200	1	0.200	0	0	0	6.0	4.50
6	McKeon	Larry	1886	KCN	NL	0.111	1	0.111	0	2	0	21.0	10.71

KANSAS CITY COWBOYS
(UNION LEAGUE)
Best Seasons and Careers of All-Time

Kansas City Cowboys (Union League) - Best Position Player Years

Rank	Name	First	Year	Team	Lg	HR	RBI	AVG	Age	PEVA-B
1	Seery	Emmett	1884	KCU	UA	0	NA	0.500	23	12.602
2	Ellick	Joe	1884	KCU	UA	0	NA	0.000	30	4.672
3	Say	Lou	1884	KCU	UA	1	NA	0.200	30	4.524
4	Whitehead	Milt	1884	KCU	UA	0	NA	0.136	22	3.837
5	Wheeler	Harry	1884	KCU	UA	0	NA	0.258	26	2.302

Kansas City Cowboys (Union League) - Best Pitcher Years

Rank	Name	First	Year	Team	Lg	W	L	SV	IP	ERA	Age	PEVA-P
1	Bakely	Jersey	1884	KCU	UA	2	3	0	33.0	2.45	20	3.870
2	Veach	Peek-A-Boo	1884	KCU	UA	3	9	0	104.0	2.42	22	2.327
3	Voss	Alex	1884	KCU	UA	0	6	0	53.0	4.25	26	1.420
4	Crothers	Doug	1884	KCU	UA	1	2	0	25.0	1.80	25	1.348
5	Black	Bob	1884	KCU	UA	4	9	0	123.0	3.22	22	1.201

Kansas City Cowboys (Union League) - Top Career Batters

Rank	Name	First	LYear	LTeam	Lg	PEVA-B	YRS	PER	HR	RBI	H	AVE.
1	Black	Bob	1884	KCU	UA	1.493	1	1.493	1	0	36	0.247
2	Shafer	Taylor	1884	KCU	UA	1.122	1	1.122	0	0	28	0.171
3	McLaughlin	Barney	1884	KCU	UA	0.992	1	0.992	0	0	37	0.228
4	McLaughlin	Frank	1884	KCU	UA	0.906	1	0.906	1	0	28	0.228
5	Say	Lou	1884	KCU	UA	0.774	1	0.774	1	0	14	0.200

Kansas City Cowboys (Union League) - Top Career Pitchers

Rank	Name	First	LYear	LTeam	Lg	PEVA-P	YRS	PER	W	L	SV	IP	ERA
1	Veach	Peek-A-Boo	1884	KCU	UA	2.327	1	2.327	3	9	0	104.0	2.42
2	Crothers	Doug	1884	KCU	UA	1.348	1	1.348	1	2	0	25.0	1.80
3	Black	Bob	1884	KCU	UA	1.201	1	1.201	4	9	0	123.0	3.22
4	Hickman	Ernie	1884	KCU	UA	0.793	1	0.793	4	13	0	137.3	4.52
5	Blaisdell	Dick	1884	KCU	UA	0.668	1	0.668	0	3	0	26.0	8.65

Note: All players on 2nd stint of year (partial year with club).

KEOKUK WESTERNS
Best Seasons and Careers of All-Time

Keokuk Westerns - Best Position Player Years

Rank	Name	First	Year	Team	Lg	HR	RBI	AVG	Age	PEVA-B
1	Hallinan	Jimmy	1875	KEO	NA	0	3	0.275	26	4.411
2	Golden	Mike	1875	KEO	NA	0	1	0.130	24	1.613
3	Quinn	Paddy	1875	KEO	NA	0	5	0.326	26	0.941
4	Jones	Charley	1875	KEO	NA	0	10	0.277	25	0.729
5	Simmons	Joe	1875	KEO	NA	0	4	0.170	30	0.200

Keokuk Westerns - Best Pitcher Years

Rank	Name	First	Year	Team	Lg	W	L	SV	IP	ERA	Age	PEVA-P
1	Golden	Mike	1875	KEO	NA	1	12	0	112.0	2.81	24	1.716

Keokuk Westerns - Top Career Batters

Rank	Name	First	LYear	LTeam	Lg	PEVA-B	YRS	PER	HR	RBI	H	AVE.
1	Hallinan	Jimmy	1875	KEO	NA	0.886	1	0.886	0	3	14	0.275
2	Jones	Charley	1875	KEO	NA	0.672	1	0.672	0	10	13	0.277
3	Golden	Mike	1875	KEO	NA	0.369	1	0.369	0	1	6	0.130
4	Quinn	Paddy	1875	KEO	NA	0.346	1	0.346	0	5	14	0.326
5	Goldsmith	Wally	1875	KEO	NA	0.200	1	0.200	0	1	6	0.118

Keokuk Westerns - Top Career Pitchers

Rank	Name	First	LYear	LTeam	Lg	PEVA-P	YRS	PER	W	L	SV	IP	ERA
1	Golden	Mike	1875	KEO	NA	0.832	1	0.832	1	12	0	112.0	2.81

LOUISVILLE GRAYS
Best Seasons and Careers of All-Time

Louisville Grays - Best Position Player Years

Rank	Name	First	Year	Team	Lg	HR	RBI	AVG	Age	PEVA-B
1	Hall	George	1877	LS1	NL	0	26	0.323	28	14.527
2	Shaffer	Orator	1877	LS1	NL	3	34	0.285	26	10.281
3	Gerhardt	Joe	1877	LS1	NL	1	35	0.304	22	8.914
4	Snyder	Pop	1877	LS1	NL	2	28	0.258	23	6.368
5	Latham	Juice	1877	LS1	NL	0	22	0.291	25	6.334

Louisville Grays - Best Pitcher Years

Rank	Name	First	Year	Team	Lg	W	L	SV	IP	ERA	Age	PEVA-P
1	Devlin	Jim	1877	LS1	NL	35	25	0	559.0	2.25	28	41.423
2	Devlin	Jim	1876	LS1	NL	30	35	0	622.0	1.56	27	31.066
3	Pearce	Frank	1876	LS1	NL	0	0	0	4.0	4.50	16	0.200
4	Ryan	Johnny	1876	LS1	NL	0	0	0	8.0	5.62	23	0.200
5	Clinton	Jim	1876	LS1	NL	0	1	0	9.0	6.00	26	0.200

Louisville Grays - Top Career Batters

Rank	Name	First	LYear	LTeam	Lg	PEVA-B	YRS	PER	HR	RBI	H	AVE.
1	Hall	George	1877	LS1	NL	14.527	1	14.527	0	26	87	0.323
2	Gerhardt	Joe	1877	LS1	NL	12.420	2	6.210	3	53	152	0.280
3	Shaffer	Orator	1877	LS1	NL	10.281	1	10.281	3	34	74	0.285
4	Devlin	Jim	1877	LS1	NL	9.716	2	4.858	1	55	166	0.293
5	Hague	Bill	1877	LS1	NL	9.284	2	4.642	2	46	148	0.266

Louisville Grays - Top Career Pitchers

Rank	Name	First	LYear	LTeam	Lg	PEVA-P	YRS	PER	W	L	SV	IP	ERA
1	Devlin	Jim	1877	LS1	NL	72.489	2	36.245	65	60	0	1181.0	1.89
2	Clinton	Jim	1876	LS1	NL	0.200	1	0.200	0	1	0	9.0	6.00
3	Pearce	Frank	1876	LS1	NL	0.200	1	0.200	0	0	0	4.0	4.50
4	Ryan	Johnny	1876	LS1	NL	0.200	1	0.200	0	0	0	8.0	5.63

LOUISVILLE ECLIPSE AND COLONELS
Best Seasons and Careers of All-Time

Louisville Eclipse & Colonels - Best Position Player Years

Rank	Name	First	Year	Team	Lg	HR	RBI	AVG	Age	PEVA-B
1	Browning	Pete	1885	LS2	AA	9	73	0.362	24	35.668
2	Clarke	Fred	1897	LS3	NL	6	67	0.390	25	31.409
3	Browning	Pete	1887	LS2	AA	4	118	0.402	26	27.217
4	Wolf	Jimmy	1890	LS2	AA	4	98	0.363	28	22.630
5	Collins	Hub	1888	LS2	AA	2	50	0.307	24	22.619
6	Browning	Pete	1884	LS2	AA	4	47	0.336	23	18.743
7	Clarke	Fred	1899	LS3	NL	5	70	0.342	27	17.629
8	Hoy	Dummy	1898	LS3	NL	6	66	0.304	36	17.456
9	Wolf	Jimmy	1884	LS2	AA	3	73	0.300	22	17.063
10	Wagner	Honus	1899	LS3	NL	7	113	0.336	25	16.590
11	Clarke	Fred	1898	LS3	NL	3	47	0.307	26	16.279
12	Browning	Pete	1882	LS2	AA	5	NA	0.378	21	15.646
13	Clarke	Fred	1896	LS3	NL	9	79	0.325	24	15.479
14	McCreery	Tom	1896	LS3	NL	7	65	0.351	22	14.077
15	Wolf	Jimmy	1885	LS2	AA	1	52	0.292	23	13.649
16	Browning	Pete	1883	LS2	AA	4	0	0.338	22	13.647
17	Wagner	Honus	1898	LS3	NL	10	105	0.299	24	13.502
18	Cline	Monk	1884	LS2	AA	2	39	0.290	26	12.997
19	Clarke	Fred	1895	LS3	NL	4	82	0.347	23	12.740
20	Browning	Pete	1888	LS2	AA	3	72	0.313	27	12.258

Louisville Eclipse & Colonels - Best Pitcher Years

Rank	Name	First	Year	Team	Lg	W	L	SV	IP	ERA	Age	PEVA-P
1	Hecker	Guy	1884	LS2	AA	52	20	0	670.7	1.80	28	39.319
2	Ramsey	Toad	1886	LS2	AA	38	27	0	588.7	2.45	22	32.963
3	Stratton	Scott	1890	LS2	AA	34	14	0	431.0	2.36	21	32.787
4	Ramsey	Toad	1887	LS2	AA	37	27	0	561.0	3.43	23	26.103
5	Phillippe	Deacon	1899	LS3	NL	21	17	1	321.0	3.17	27	17.432
6	Cunningham	Bert	1898	LS3	NL	28	15	0	362.0	3.16	33	15.085
7	Hecker	Guy	1885	LS2	AA	30	23	0	480.0	2.18	29	14.512
8	Ehret	Red	1890	LS2	AA	25	14	2	359.0	2.53	22	14.253
9	Mullane	Tony	1882	LS2	AA	30	24	0	460.3	1.88	23	13.305

Louisville Eclipse & Colonels - Top Career Batters

Rank	Name	First	LYear	LTeam	Lg	PEVA-B	YRS	PER	HR	RBI	H	AVE.
1	Browning	Pete	1893	LS3	NL	139.219	10	13.922	34	451	1233	0.343
2	Wolf	Jimmy	1891	LS2	AA	112.272	10	11.227	18	592	1438	0.290
3	Clarke	Fred	1899	LS3	NL	95.443	6	15.907	34	393	1034	0.334
4	Weaver	Farmer	1894	LS3	NL	39.297	7	5.614	9	320	816	0.275
5	Wagner	Honus	1899	LS3	NL	32.707	3	10.902	19	257	448	0.321
6	Collins	Hub	1888	LS2	AA	29.769	3	9.923	3	126	340	0.297
7	Hoy	Dummy	1899	LS3	NL	29.444	2	14.722	11	115	371	0.305
8	Brown	Tom	1894	LS3	NL	29.240	3	9.747	16	156	413	0.239
9	Hecker	Guy	1889	LS2	AA	28.731	8	3.591	19	240	735	0.290

10	Kerins	John	1889	LS2	AA	**27.046**	5	5.409	14	202	460	0.263
11	Mack	Reddy	1888	LS2	AA	**23.014**	4	5.754	5	164	372	0.257
12	Clingman	Billy	1899	LS3	NL	**20.972**	4	5.243	6	178	423	0.246
13	McCreery	Tom	1897	LS3	NL	**20.362**	3	6.787	11	115	286	0.322
14	Taylor	Harry	1892	LS3	NL	**20.356**	3	6.785	2	124	402	0.287
15	White	Bill	1888	LS2	AA	**20.293**	3	6.764	4	175	327	0.258
16	Werrick	Joe	1888	LS2	AA	**20.183**	3	6.728	10	212	381	0.253
17	Maskrey	Leech	1886	LS2	AA	**19.765**	5	3.953	2	84	341	0.227
18	Pfeffer	Fred	1895	LS3	NL	**18.135**	4	4.534	10	215	389	0.272
19	Dexter	Charlie	1899	LS3	NL	**14.563**	4	3.641	7	182	392	0.285
20	Cline	Monk	1891	LS2	AA	**14.336**	3	4.779	2	53	140	0.291

Louisville Eclipse & Colonels - Top Career Pitchers

Rank	Name	First	LYear	LTeam	Lg	PEVA-P	YRS	PER	W	L	SV	IP	ERA
1	Hecker	Guy	1889	LS2	AA	**78.200**	8	9.775	171	137	1	2786.3	2.83
2	Ramsey	Toad	1889	LS2	AA	**65.347**	5	13.069	87	106	0	1711.0	3.20
3	Stratton	Scott	1894	LS3	NL	**49.144**	7	7.021	87	104	1	1715.7	3.63
4	Cunningham	Bert	1899	LS3	NL	**31.479**	5	6.296	77	75	1	1340.7	4.04
5	Ehret	Red	1898	LS3	NL	**20.056**	4	5.014	51	63	2	1032.7	3.81
6	Phillippe	Deacon	1899	LS3	NL	**17.432**	1	17.432	21	17	1	321.0	3.17
7	Fraser	Chick	1898	LS3	NL	**13.381**	3	4.460	34	63	1	838.7	4.71
8	Mullane	Tony	1882	LS2	AA	**13.305**	1	13.305	30	24	0	460.3	1.88
9	Dowling	Pete	1899	LS3	NL	**12.291**	3	4.097	27	39	0	601.3	3.73
10	Hemming	George	1897	LS3	NL	**11.691**	4	2.923	36	42	2	728.3	4.78
11	Chamberlain	Elton	1888	LS2	AA	**10.544**	3	3.515	32	28	0	536.3	3.49

MIDDLETOWN MANSFIELDS
Best Seasons and Careers of All-Time

Middletown Mansfields - Best Position Player Years

Rank	Name	First	Year	Team	Lg	HR	RBI	AVG	Age	PEVA-B
1	Booth	Eddie	1872	MID	NA	0	12	0.325	NA	3.992
2	Murnane	Tim	1872	MID	NA	0	13	0.359	20	2.056
3	Clapp	John	1872	MID	NA	1	10	0.289	21	1.747
4	O'Rourke	Jim	1872	MID	NA	0	12	0.307	22	1.704
5	McCarton	Frank	1872	MID	NA	0	10	0.329	18	1.395

Middletown Mansfields - Best Pitcher Years

Rank	Name	First	Year	Team	Lg	W	L	SV	IP	ERA	Age	PEVA-P
1	Bentley	Cy	1872	MID	NA	2	15	0	154.0	6.14	22	0.737
2	Brainard	Asa	1872	MID	NA	0	2	0	8.0	7.88	31	0.696
3	Buttery	Frank	1872	MID	NA	3	2	0	49.0	5.14	21	0.630

Middletown Mansfields - Top Career Batters

Rank	Name	First	LYear	LTeam	Lg	PEVA-B	YRS	PER	HR	RBI	H	AVE
1	Booth	Eddie	1872	MID	NA	2.609	1	2.609	0	12	38	0.325
2	Murnane	Tim	1872	MID	NA	2.056	1	2.056	0	13	42	0.359
3	Clapp	John	1872	MID	NA	1.747	1	1.747	1	10	28	0.289
4	O'Rourke	Jim	1872	MID	NA	1.704	1	1.704	0	12	31	0.307
5	McCarton	Frank	1872	MID	NA	1.395	1	1.395	0	10	28	0.329

Middletown Mansfields - Top Career Pitchers

Rank	Name	First	LYear	LTeam	Lg	PEVA-P	YRS	PER	W	L	SV	IP	ERA
1	Bentley	Cy	1872	MID	NA	0.693	1	0.693	2	15	0	154.0	6.14
2	Buttery	Frank	1872	MID	NA	0.630	1	0.630	3	2	0	49.0	5.14
3	Brainard	Asa	1872	MID	NA	0.045	1	0.045	0	2	0	8.0	7.88

MILWAUKEE GRAYS
Best Seasons and Careers of All-Time

Milwaukee Grays - Best Position Player Years

Rank	Name	First	Year	Team	Lg	HR	RBI	AVG	Age	PEVA-B
1	Dalrymple	Abner	1878	ML2	NL	0	15	0.354	21	21.930
2	Peters	John	1878	ML2	NL	0	22	0.309	28	4.881
3	Foley	Will	1878	ML2	NL	0	22	0.271	23	3.871
4	Goodman	Jake	1878	ML2	NL	1	27	0.246	25	3.847
5	Golden	Mike	1878	ML2	NL	0	20	0.206	27	1.479

Milwaukee Grays - Best Pitcher Years

Rank	Name	First	Year	Team	Lg	W	L	SV	IP	ERA	Age	PEVA-P
1	Weaver	Sam	1878	ML2	NL	12	31	0	383.0	1.95	23	12.351
2	Golden	Mike	1878	ML2	NL	3	13	0	161.0	4.14	27	0.822
3	Ellick	Joe	1878	ML2	NL	0	1	0	3.0	3.00	24	0.200

Milwaukee Grays - Top Career Batters

Rank	Name	First	LYear	LTeam	Lg	PEVA-B	YRS	PER	HR	RBI	H	AVE.
1	Dalrymple	Abner	1878	ML2	NL	21.930	1	21.930	0	15	96	0.354
2	Peters	John	1878	ML2	NL	4.881	1	4.881	0	22	76	0.309
3	Foley	Will	1878	ML2	NL	3.871	1	3.871	0	22	62	0.271
4	Goodman	Jake	1878	ML2	NL	3.847	1	3.847	1	27	62	0.246
5	Golden	Mike	1878	ML2	NL	1.479	1	1.479	0	20	44	0.206

Milwaukee Grays - Top Career Pitchers

Rank	Name	First	LYear	LTeam	Lg	PEVA-P	YRS	PER	W	L	SV	IP	ERA
1	Weaver	Sam	1878	ML2	NL	12.351	1	12.351	12	31	0	383.0	1.95
2	Golden	Mike	1878	ML2	NL	0.822	1	0.822	3	13	0	161.0	4.14
3	Ellick	Joe	1878	ML2	NL	0.200	1	0.200	0	1	0	3.0	3.00

MILWAUKEE BREWERS
(AMERICAN ASSOCIATION)
Best Seasons and Careers of All-Time

Milwaukee Brewers (American Association) - Best Position Player Years

Rank	Name	First	Year	Team	Lg	HR	RBI	AVG	Age	PEVA-B
1	Canavan	Jim	1891	ML3	AA	3	21	0.268	25	**9.146**
2	Carney	John	1891	ML3	AA	3	23	0.300	25	**5.535**
3	Vaughn	Farmer	1891	ML3	AA	0	9	0.333	27	**1.755**
4	Shoch	George	1891	ML3	AA	1	16	0.315	32	**1.361**
5	Dalrymple	Abner	1891	ML3	AA	1	22	0.311	34	**0.887**

Milwaukee Brewers (American Association) - Best Pitcher Years

Rank	Name	First	Year	Team	Lg	W	L	SV	IP	ERA	Age	PEVA-P
1	Davies	George	1891	ML3	AA	7	5	0	102.0	2.65	23	**4.217**
2	Dwyer	Frank	1891	ML3	AA	6	4	0	86.0	2.20	23	**4.025**
3	Killen	Frank	1891	ML3	AA	7	4	0	96.7	1.68	21	**3.860**
4	Mains	Willard	1891	ML3	AA	0	2	0	10.0	10.80	23	**3.145**
5	Hughey	Jim	1891	ML3	AA	1	0	0	15.0	3.00	22	**0.200**

Milwaukee Brewers (American Association) - Top Career Batters

Rank	Name	First	LYear	LTeam	Lg	PEVA-B	YRS	PER	HR	RBI	H	AVE.
1	Canavan	Jim	1891	ML3	AA	**2.286**	1	2.286	3	21	38	0.268
2	Shoch	George	1891	ML3	AA	**1.361**	1	1.361	1	16	40	0.315
3	Carney	John	1891	ML3	AA	**1.277**	1	1.277	3	23	33	0.300
4	Dalrymple	Abner	1891	ML3	AA	**0.887**	1	0.887	1	22	42	0.311
5	Vaughn	Farmer	1891	ML3	AA	**0.634**	1	0.634	0	9	33	0.333

Milwaukee Brewers (American Association) - Top Career Pitchers

Rank	Name	First	LYear	LTeam	Lg	PEVA-P	YRS	PER	W	L	SV	IP	ERA
1	Davies	George	1891	ML3	AA	**4.217**	1	4.217	7	5	0	102.0	2.65
2	Killen	Frank	1891	ML3	AA	**3.860**	1	3.860	7	4	0	96.7	1.68
3	Dwyer	Frank	1891	ML3	AA	**0.923**	1	0.923	6	4	0	86.0	2.20
4	Hughey	Jim	1891	ML3	AA	**0.200**	1	0.200	1	0	0	15.0	3.00
5	Mains	Willard	1891	ML3	AA	**0.147**	1	0.147	0	2	0	10.0	10.80

MILWAUKEE BREWERS
(UNION LEAGUE)
Best Seasons and Careers of All-Time

Milwaukee Brewers (Union League) - Best Position Player Years

Rank	Name	First	Year	Team	Lg	HR	RBI	AVG	Age	PEVA-B
1	Sexton	Tom	1884	MLU	UA	0	NA	0.234	19	0.804
2	Cushman	Ed	1884	MLU	UA	0	NA	0.091	32	0.200
3	Morrissey	Tom	1884	MLU	UA	0	NA	0.170	24	0.200
4	Bignell	George	1884	MLU	UA	0	NA	0.222	26	0.200
5	Myers	Al	1884	MLU	UA	0	NA	0.326	21	0.200

Milwaukee Brewers (Union League) - Best Pitcher Years

Rank	Name	First	Year	Team	Lg	W	L	SV	IP	ERA	Age	PEVA-P
1	Cushman	Ed	1884	MLU	UA	4	0	0	36.0	1.00	32	5.306
2	Porter	Henry	1884	MLU	UA	3	3	0	51.0	3.00	26	1.144
3	Baldwin	Lady	1884	MLU	UA	1	1	0	17.0	2.65	25	0.200

Milwaukee Brewers (Union League) - Top Career Batters

Rank	Name	First	LYear	LTeam	Lg	PEVA-B	YRS	PER	HR	RBI	H	AVE.
1	Sexton	Tom	1884	MLU	UA	0.804	1	0.804	0	0	11	0.234
2	Baldwin	Lady	1884	MLU	UA	0.200	1	0.200	0	0	6	0.222
3	Behel	Steve	1884	MLU	UA	0.200	1	0.200	0	0	8	0.242
4	Broughton	Cal	1884	MLU	UA	0.200	1	0.200	0	0	12	0.308
5	Cushman	Ed	1884	MLU	UA	0.200	1	0.200	0	0	1	0.091

Milwaukee Brewers (Union League) - Top Career Pitchers

Rank	Name	First	LYear	LTeam	Lg	PEVA-P	YRS	PER	W	L	SV	IP	ERA
1	Cushman	Ed	1884	MLU	UA	5.306	1	5.306	4	0	0	36.0	1.00
2	Porter	Henry	1884	MLU	UA	1.144	1	1.144	3	3	0	51.0	3.00
3	Baldwin	Lady	1884	MLU	UA	0.200	1	0.200	1	1	0	17.0	2.65

NEW HAVEN ELM CITYS
Best Seasons and Careers of All-Time

New Haven Elm Citys - Best Position Player Years

Rank	Name	First	Year	Team	Lg	HR	RBI	AVG	Age	PEVA-B
1	McGinley	Tim	1875	NH1	NA	0	10	0.275	NA	2.581
2	Luff	Henry	1875	NH1	NA	2	18	0.271	19	2.444
3	Pabor	Charlie	1875	NH1	NA	0	2	0.348	29	2.302
4	Somerville	Ed	1875	NH1	NA	0	7	0.213	22	1.558
5	McKelvey	John	1875	NH1	NA	0	10	0.229	28	1.415

New Haven Elm Citys - Best Pitcher Years

Rank	Name	First	Year	Team	Lg	W	L	SV	IP	ERA	Age	PEVA-P
1	Nichols	Tricky	1875	NH1	NA	4	29	0	288.0	3.03	25	1.569
2	Luff	Henry	1875	NH1	NA	1	6	0	69.7	4.78	19	0.789
3	Ryan	Johnny	1875	NH1	NA	1	5	0	59.3	3.34	22	0.535
4	Knight	George	1875	NH1	NA	1	0	0	9.0	2.00	20	0.200

New Haven Elm Citys - Top Career Batters

Rank	Name	First	LYear	LTeam	Lg	PEVA-B	YRS	PER	HR	RBI	H	AVE.
1	Luff	Henry	1875	NH1	NA	2.444	1	2.444	2	18	45	0.271
2	McGinley	Tim	1875	NH1	NA	1.847	1	1.847	0	10	36	0.275
3	McKelvey	John	1875	NH1	NA	1.415	1	1.415	0	10	43	0.229
4	Geer	Billy	1875	NH1	NA	1.325	1	1.325	0	9	40	0.244
5	Gould	Charlie	1875	NH1	NA	1.133	1	1.133	0	8	29	0.266

New Haven Elm Citys - Top Career Pitchers

Rank	Name	First	LYear	LTeam	Lg	PEVA-P	YRS	PER	W	L	SV	IP	ERA
1	Nichols	Tricky	1875	NH1	NA	1.569	1	1.569	4	29	0	288.0	3.03
2	Luff	Henry	1875	NH1	NA	0.789	1	0.789	1	6	0	69.7	4.78
3	Ryan	Johnny	1875	NH1	NA	0.535	1	0.535	1	5	0	59.3	3.34
4	Knight	George	1875	NH1	NA	0.200	1	0.200	1	0	0	9.0	2.00

Note: McGinley, Pabor, Somerville 2nd stint players (partial year).

NEW YORK MUTUALS
(NATIONAL ASSOCIATION)
Best Seasons and Careers of All-Time

New York Mutuals (National Association) - Best Position Player Years

Rank	Name	First	Year	Team	Lg	HR	RBI	AVG	Age	PEVA-B
1	Eggler	Dave	1872	NY2	NA	0	20	0.338	23	25.075
2	Wolters	Rynie	1871	NY2	NA	0	44	0.370	29	21.178
3	Hatfield	John	1872	NY2	NA	1	45	0.319	25	18.990
4	Hicks	Nat	1872	NY2	NA	0	33	0.306	27	16.985
5	Start	Joe	1872	NY2	NA	0	50	0.270	30	12.845
6	Start	Joe	1871	NY2	NA	1	34	0.360	29	12.116
7	Eggler	Dave	1873	NY2	NA	0	34	0.336	24	11.226
8	Bechtel	George	1872	NY2	NA	0	41	0.298	24	11.150
9	Start	Joe	1874	NY2	NA	2	45	0.314	32	11.139
10	Eggler	Dave	1871	NY2	NA	0	18	0.320	22	10.199

New York Mutuals (National Association) - Best Pitcher Years

Rank	Name	First	Year	Team	Lg	W	L	SV	IP	ERA	Age	PEVA-P
1	Mathews	Bobby	1874	NY2	NA	42	22	0	578.0	2.30	23	29.885
2	Cummings	Candy	1872	NY2	NA	33	20	0	497.0	2.52	24	26.548
3	Wolters	Rynie	1871	NY2	NA	16	16	0	283.0	3.43	29	21.840
4	Mathews	Bobby	1873	NY2	NA	29	23	0	443.0	2.56	22	20.558
5	Mathews	Bobby	1875	NY2	NA	29	38	0	626.7	2.41	24	12.808

New York Mutuals (National Association) - Top Career Batters

Rank	Name	First	LYear	LTeam	Lg	PEVA-B	YRS	PER	HR	RBI	H	AVE.
1	Start	Joe	1875	NY2	NA	46.839	5	9.368	8	187	387	0.295
2	Eggler	Dave	1873	NY2	NA	46.499	3	15.500	0	72	235	0.333
3	Hatfield	John	1875	NY2	NA	39.408	5	7.882	3	143	281	0.279
4	Hicks	Nat	1875	NY2	NA	22.618	3	7.539	1	69	178	0.271
5	Wolters	Rynie	1871	NY2	NA	21.178	1	21.178	0	44	51	0.370
6	Higham	Dick	1875	NY2	NA	16.542	4	4.135	1	90	223	0.303
7	Holdsworth	Jim	1875	NY2	NA	11.953	2	5.976	0	51	167	0.300
8	Bechtel	George	1872	NY2	NA	11.150	1	11.150	0	41	74	0.298
9	Pearce	Dickey	1872	NY2	NA	10.719	2	5.360	1	43	84	0.228

New York Mutuals (National Association) - Top Career Pitchers

Rank	Name	First	LYear	LTeam	Lg	PEVA-P	YRS	PER	W	L	SV	IP	ERA
1	Mathews	Bobby	1875	NY2	NA	63.252	3	21.084	100	83	0	1647.7	2.41
2	Cummings	Candy	1872	NY2	NA	26.548	1	26.548	33	20	0	497.0	2.52
3	Wolters	Rynie	1871	NY2	NA	21.840	1	21.840	16	16	0	283.0	3.43
4	Martin	Phonney	1873	NY2	NA	0.652	1	0.652	0	1	0	34.0	3.44
5	Hatfield	John	1874	NY2	NA	0.200	1	0.200	0	1	0	8.0	2.25

NEW YORK MUTUALS
(NATIONAL LEAGUE)
Best Seasons and Careers of All-Time

New York Mutuals (National League) - Best Position Player Years

Rank	Name	First	Year	Team	Lg	HR	RBI	AVG	Age	PEVA-B
1	Force	Davy	1876	NY3	NL	0	0	0.000	27	5.219
2	Hallinan	Jimmy	1876	NY3	NL	2	36	0.279	27	4.913
3	Treacey	Fred	1876	NY3	NL	0	18	0.211	29	4.126
4	Start	Joe	1876	NY3	NL	0	21	0.277	34	3.497
5	Holdsworth	Jim	1876	NY3	NL	0	19	0.266	26	3.157

New York Mutuals (National League) - Best Pitcher Years

Rank	Name	First	Year	Team	Lg	W	L	SV	IP	ERA	Age	PEVA-P
1	Mathews	Bobby	1876	NY3	NL	21	34	0	516.0	2.86	25	5.545
2	Booth	Eddie	1876	NY3	NL	0	0	0	5.0	10.80	NA	0.200
3	Larkin	Terry	1876	NY3	NL	0	1	0	9.0	3.00	NA	0.200

New York Mutuals (National League) - Top Career Batters

Rank	Name	First	LYear	LTeam	Lg	PEVA-B	YRS	PER	HR	RBI	H	AVE.
1	Hallinan	Jimmy	1876	NY3	NL	4.913	1	4.913	2	36	67	0.279
2	Treacey	Fred	1876	NY3	NL	4.126	1	4.126	0	18	54	0.211
3	Start	Joe	1876	NY3	NL	3.497	1	3.497	0	21	73	0.277
4	Holdsworth	Jim	1876	NY3	NL	3.157	1	3.157	0	19	64	0.266
5	Craver	Bill	1876	NY3	NL	2.237	1	2.237	0	22	55	0.224

New York Mutuals (National League) - Top Career Pitchers

Rank	Name	First	LYear	LTeam	Lg	PEVA-P	YRS	PER	W	L	SV	IP	ERA
1	Mathews	Bobby	1876	NY3	NL	5.545	1	5.545	21	34	0	516.0	2.86
2	Larkin	Terry	1876	NY3	NL	0.200	1	0.200	0	1	0	9.0	3.00
3	Booth	Eddie	1876	NY3	NL	0.200	1	0.200	0	0	0	5.0	10.80

NEW YORK METROPOLITANS
Best Seasons and Careers of All-Time

New York Metropolitans - Best Position Player Years

Rank	Name	First	Year	Team	Lg	HR	RBI	AVG	Age	PEVA-B
1	Orr	Dave	1884	NY4	AA	9	112	0.354	25	28.656
2	Orr	Dave	1885	NY4	AA	6	77	0.342	26	25.379
3	Orr	Dave	1886	NY4	AA	7	91	0.338	27	21.791
4	Esterbrook	Dude	1884	NY4	AA	1	0	0.314	27	18.169
5	Nelson	Candy	1884	NY4	AA	1	0	0.255	35	16.469
6	Nelson	Candy	1885	NY4	AA	1	30	0.255	36	15.627
7	Roseman	Chief	1884	NY4	AA	4	0	0.298	28	13.761
8	Brady	Steve	1885	NY4	AA	3	58	0.295	34	13.032
9	Roseman	Chief	1885	NY4	AA	4	46	0.278	29	12.838
10	Nelson	Candy	1883	NY4	AA	0	0	0.305	34	10.308

New York Metropolitans - Best Pitcher Years

Rank	Name	First	Year	Team	Lg	W	L	SV	IP	ERA	Age	PEVA-P
1	Keefe	Tim	1883	NY4	AA	41	27	0	619.0	2.41	26	28.675
2	Keefe	Tim	1884	NY4	AA	37	17	0	483.0	2.25	27	13.989
3	Lynch	Jack	1884	NY4	AA	37	15	0	496.0	2.67	27	12.508
4	Lynch	Jack	1886	NY4	AA	20	30	0	432.7	3.95	29	4.657
5	Mays	Al	1887	NY4	AA	17	34	0	441.3	4.73	22	4.609

New York Metropolitans - Top Career Batters

Rank	Name	First	LYear	LTeam	Lg	PEVA-B	YRS	PER	HR	RBI	H	AVE.
1	Orr	Dave	1887	NY4	AA	81.804	6	13.634	26	357	650	0.348
2	Nelson	Candy	1887	NY4	AA	48.971	5	9.794	2	77	500	0.258
3	Roseman	Chief	1887	NY4	AA	39.418	5	7.884	14	126	526	0.257
4	Brady	Steve	1886	NY4	AA	30.906	4	7.727	4	97	479	0.264
5	Esterbrook	Dude	1887	NY4	AA	22.793	3	7.598	1	7	270	0.274
6	Hankinson	Frank	1887	NY4	AA	21.168	3	7.056	5	178	344	0.246
7	Kennedy	Ed	1885	NY4	AA	10.343	3	3.448	5	21	221	0.204

New York Metropolitans - Top Career Pitchers

Rank	Name	First	LYear	LTeam	Lg	PEVA-P	YRS	PER	W	L	SV	IP	ERA
1	Keefe	Tim	1884	NY4	AA	42.664	2	21.332	78	44	0	1102.0	2.34
2	Lynch	Jack	1887	NY4	AA	23.697	5	4.739	100	95	0	1749.7	3.66
3	Cushman	Ed	1887	NY4	AA	7.498	3	2.499	35	49	0	736.7	3.89
4	Mays	Al	1887	NY4	AA	7.452	2	3.726	28	62	0	791.3	4.14
5	Shaffer	John	1887	NY4	AA	4.122	2	2.061	7	14	0	181.0	4.57

NEW YORK GIANTS
(PACIFIC LEAGUE)
Best Seasons and Careers of All-Time

New York Giants (Pacific League) - Best Position Player Years

Rank	Name	First	Year	Team	Lg	HR	RBI	AVG	Age	PEVA-B
1	Connor	Roger	1890	NYP	PL	14	103	0.349	33	25.866
2	O'Rourke	Jim	1890	NYP	PL	9	115	0.360	40	16.853
3	Ewing	Buck	1890	NYP	PL	8	72	0.338	31	12.724
4	Gore	George	1890	NYP	PL	10	55	0.318	33	10.430
5	Richardson	Danny	1890	NYP	PL	4	80	0.256	27	7.003

New York Giants (Pacific League) - Best Pitcher Years

Rank	Name	First	Year	Team	Lg	W	L	SV	IP	ERA	Age	PEVA-P
1	Keefe	Tim	1890	NYP	PL	17	11	0	229.0	3.38	33	3.709
2	O'Day	Hank	1890	NYP	PL	22	13	3	329.0	4.21	28	3.441
3	Crane	Ed	1890	NYP	PL	16	19	0	330.3	4.63	28	2.641
4	Ewing	John	1890	NYP	PL	18	12	2	267.3	4.24	27	2.579
5	Hatfield	Gil	1890	NYP	PL	1	1	1	7.7	3.52	35	0.200

New York Giants (Pacific League) - Top Career Batters

Rank	Name	First	LYear	LTeam	Lg	PEVA-B	YRS	PER	HR	RBI	H	AVE.
1	Connor	Roger	1890	NYP	PL	25.866	1	25.866	14	103	169	0.349
2	O'Rourke	Jim	1890	NYP	PL	16.853	1	16.853	9	115	172	0.360
3	Ewing	Buck	1890	NYP	PL	12.724	1	12.724	8	72	119	0.338
4	Gore	George	1890	NYP	PL	10.430	1	10.430	10	55	127	0.318
5	Richardson	Danny	1890	NYP	PL	7.003	1	7.003	4	80	135	0.256

New York Giants (Pacific League) - Top Career Pitchers

Rank	Name	First	LYear	LTeam	Lg	PEVA-P	YRS	PER	W	L	SV	IP	ERA
1	Keefe	Tim	1890	NYP	PL	3.709	1	3.709	17	11	0	229.0	3.38
2	O'Day	Hank	1890	NYP	PL	3.441	1	3.441	22	13	3	329.0	4.21
3	Crane	Ed	1890	NYP	PL	2.641	1	2.641	16	19	0	330.3	4.63
4	Ewing	John	1890	NYP	PL	2.579	1	2.579	18	12	2	267.3	4.24
5	Hatfield	Gil	1890	NYP	PL	0.200	1	0.200	1	1	1	7.7	3.52

PHILADELPHIA ATHLETICS
(NATIONAL ASSOCIATION)
Best Seasons and Careers of All-Time

Philadelphia Athletics (National Association) - Best Position Player Years

Rank	Name	First	Year	Team	Lg	HR	RBI	AVG	Age	PEVA-B
1	Anson	Cap	1872	PH1	NA	0	50	0.415	20	27.329
2	Meyerle	Levi	1871	PH1	NA	4	40	0.492	26	24.682
3	Force	Davy	1875	PH1	NA	0	49	0.311	26	17.860
4	Sutton	Ezra	1875	PH1	NA	1	59	0.324	25	16.597
5	Hall	George	1875	PH1	NA	4	62	0.299	26	16.453
6	Cuthbert	Ned	1872	PH1	NA	1	47	0.338	27	16.386
7	McGeary	Mike	1872	PH1	NA	0	35	0.360	21	15.043
8	Malone	Fergy	1871	PH1	NA	1	33	0.343	29	13.373
9	Craver	Bill	1875	PH1	NA	2	40	0.319	31	13.098
10	Fisler	Wes	1872	PH1	NA	0	48	0.350	31	12.846
11	Anson	Cap	1875	PH1	NA	0	58	0.325	23	12.033
12	Mack	Denny	1872	PH1	NA	0	34	0.288	21	10.386

Philadelphia Athletics (National Association) - Best Pitcher Years

Rank	Name	First	Year	Team	Lg	W	L	SV	IP	ERA	Age	PEVA-P
1	McBride	Dick	1874	PH1	NA	33	22	0	487.0	2.55	29	17.928
2	McBride	Dick	1875	PH1	NA	44	14	0	538.0	1.97	30	16.714
3	McBride	Dick	1872	PH1	NA	30	14	0	419.0	3.01	27	16.138
4	McBride	Dick	1873	PH1	NA	24	19	0	382.7	3.32	28	9.485
5	McBride	Dick	1871	PH1	NA	18	5	0	222.0	4.58	26	7.556

Philadelphia Athletics (National Association) - Top Career Batters

Rank	Name	First	LYear	LTeam	Lg	PEVA-B	YRS	PER	HR	RBI	H	AVE.
1	Anson	Cap	1875	PH1	NA	53.497	4	13.374	0	181	384	0.364
2	Meyerle	Levi	1872	PH1	NA	28.933	2	14.466	5	71	112	0.406
3	McGeary	Mike	1874	PH1	NA	27.884	3	9.295	0	88	251	0.326
4	Fisler	Wes	1875	PH1	NA	27.606	5	5.521	1	159	334	0.316
5	Sutton	Ezra	1875	PH1	NA	27.018	3	9.006	1	120	268	0.318
6	Cuthbert	Ned	1872	PH1	NA	26.003	2	13.001	4	77	125	0.305
7	Malone	Fergy	1872	PH1	NA	20.018	2	10.009	1	72	106	0.305
8	McBride	Dick	1875	PH1	NA	18.444	5	3.689	0	174	306	0.260
9	Force	Davy	1875	PH1	NA	17.860	1	17.860	0	49	120	0.311
10	Hall	George	1875	PH1	NA	16.453	1	16.453	4	62	107	0.299
11	Clapp	John	1875	PH1	NA	15.941	3	5.314	4	87	187	0.283
12	McMullin	John	1874	PH1	NA	14.411	2	7.206	2	61	152	0.312
13	Reach	Al	1875	PH1	NA	11.160	5	2.232	0	57	97	0.247
14	Craver	Bill	1875	PH1	NA	10.479	1	10.479	2	40	83	0.319
15	Mack	Denny	1872	PH1	NA	10.386	1	10.386	0	34	59	0.288

Philadelphia Athletics (National Association) - Top Career Pitchers

Rank	Name	First	LYear	LTeam	Lg	PEVA-P	YRS	PER	W	L	SV	IP	ERA
1	McBride	Dick	1875	PH1	NA	67.696	5	13.539	149	74	0	2048.7	2.86
2	Fisher	Cherokee	1873	PH1	NA	4.479	1	4.479	3	4	1	84.3	1.81
3	Knight	Lon	1875	PH1	NA	1.367	1	1.367	6	5	0	107.0	2.44

| 4 | Bechtel | George | 1875 | PH1 | NA | **0.975** | 2 | 0.488 | 4 | 3 | 0 | 62.0 | 4.65 |
| 5 | Sutton | Ezra | 1875 | PH1 | NA | **0.200** | 1 | 0.200 | 0 | 0 | 0 | 6.0 | 7.50 |

PHILADELPHIA ATHLETICS
(AMERICAN ASSOCIATION)
Best Seasons and Careers of All-Time

Philadelphia Athletics (American Association) - Best Position Player Years

Rank	Name	First	Year	Team	Lg	HR	RBI	AVG	Age	PEVA-B
1	Stovey	Harry	1889	PH4	AA	19	119	0.308	33	34.320
2	Larkin	Henry	1885	PH4	AA	8	88	0.329	25	29.794
3	Stovey	Harry	1885	PH4	AA	13	75	0.315	29	27.677
4	Stovey	Harry	1884	PH4	AA	10	83	0.326	28	26.587
5	Stovey	Harry	1888	PH4	AA	9	65	0.287	32	26.048
6	Lyons	Denny	1889	PH4	AA	9	82	0.329	23	25.426
7	Lyons	Denny	1887	PH4	AA	6	102	0.367	21	23.589
8	Larkin	Henry	1886	PH4	AA	2	74	0.319	26	23.297
9	Stovey	Harry	1883	PH4	AA	14	66	0.304	27	21.352
10	Milligan	Jocko	1891	PH4	AA	11	106	0.303	30	21.264
11	Welch	Curt	1888	PH4	AA	1	61	0.282	26	20.921
12	Larkin	Henry	1888	PH4	AA	7	101	0.269	28	17.228
13	Lyons	Denny	1890	PH4	AA	7	73	0.354	24	16.142
14	Moynahan	Mike	1883	PH4	AA	1	67	0.310	27	16.073
15	Larkin	Henry	1889	PH4	AA	3	74	0.318	29	15.376
16	Lyons	Denny	1888	PH4	AA	6	83	0.296	22	15.309
17	Wood	George	1891	PH4	AA	3	61	0.309	33	15.229
18	Larkin	Henry	1891	PH4	AA	10	93	0.279	31	14.140
19	McTamany	Jim	1891	PH4	AA	3	21	0.225	28	13.031
20	Stovey	Harry	1886	PH4	AA	7	59	0.294	30	12.617

Philadelphia Athletics (American Association) - Best Pitcher Years

Rank	Name	First	Year	Team	Lg	W	L	SV	IP	ERA	Age	PEVA-P
1	Seward	Ed	1888	PH4	AA	35	19	0	518.7	2.01	21	23.438
2	McMahon	Sadie	1890	PH4	AA	29	18	1	410.0	3.34	23	17.442
3	Taylor	Billy	1884	PH4	AA	18	12	0	260.0	2.53	29	16.180
4	Mathews	Bobby	1885	PH4	AA	30	17	0	422.3	2.43	34	15.060
5	Weyhing	Gus	1891	PH4	AA	31	20	0	450.0	3.18	25	13.895
6	Weyhing	Gus	1888	PH4	AA	28	18	0	404.0	2.25	22	11.171
7	Weyhing	Gus	1889	PH4	AA	30	21	0	449.0	2.95	23	11.167
8	Mathews	Bobby	1883	PH4	AA	30	13	0	381.0	2.46	32	10.018

Philadelphia Athletics (American Association) - Top Career Batters

Rank	Name	First	LYear	LTeam	Lg	PEVA-B	YRS	PER	HR	RBI	H	AVE.
1	Stovey	Harry	1889	PH4	AA	157.628	7	22.518	76	544	1036	0.302
2	Larkin	Henry	1891	PH4	AA	116.041	7	16.577	36	555	1031	0.301
3	Lyons	Denny	1890	PH4	AA	80.785	5	16.157	28	351	658	0.329
4	Welch	Curt	1890	PH4	AA	40.991	3	13.664	3	140	401	0.274
5	Milligan	Jocko	1891	PH4	AA	36.912	5	7.382	23	240	476	0.286
6	O'Brien	Jack	1890	PH4	AA	35.196	6	5.866	10	273	505	0.273
7	Bierbauer	Lou	1889	PH4	AA	31.800	4	7.950	10	314	572	0.268
8	Knight	Lon	1885	PH4	AA	21.689	3	7.230	2	67	264	0.256
9	Purcell	Blondie	1890	PH4	AA	20.622	4	5.155	2	172	389	0.290
10	Houck	Sadie	1885	PH4	AA	19.045	2	9.523	0	54	239	0.278

11	Coleman	John	1889	PH4	AA	**18.954**	4	4.739	5	136	263	0.259
12	Birchall	Jud	1884	PH4	AA	**17.291**	3	5.764	1	51	254	0.252
13	Corey	Fred	1885	PH4	AA	**16.690**	3	5.563	7	78	292	0.260
14	Stricker	Cub	1885	PH4	AA	**16.474**	4	4.118	3	99	334	0.239
15	Moynahan	Mike	1884	PH4	AA	**16.146**	2	8.073	1	67	124	0.307
16	Wood	George	1891	PH4	AA	**15.229**	1	15.229	3	61	163	0.309
17	Poorman	Tom	1888	PH4	AA	**14.528**	2	7.264	6	105	242	0.250
18	Hallman	Bill	1891	PH4	AA	**10.783**	1	10.783	6	69	166	0.283
19	Robinson	Wilbert	1890	PH4	AA	**10.004**	5	2.001	7	155	330	0.227

Philadelphia Athletics (American Association) - Top Career Pitchers

Rank	Name	First	LYear	LTeam	Lg	PEVA-P	YRS	PER	W	L	SV	IP	ERA
1	Weyhing	Gus	1891	PH4	AA	**43.174**	4	10.793	115	87	0	1769.3	3.19
2	Seward	Ed	1890	PH4	AA	**36.855**	4	9.214	87	71	0	1463.3	3.41
3	Mathews	Bobby	1887	PH4	AA	**32.970**	5	6.594	106	61	0	1489.7	3.06
4	McMahon	Sadie	1890	PH4	AA	**17.088**	2	8.544	43	30	1	652.0	3.41
5	Taylor	Billy	1887	PH4	AA	**9.066**	3	3.022	20	17	0	321.3	2.66

PHILADELPHIA WHITES
Best Seasons and Careers of All-Time

Philadelphia Whites - Best Position Player Years

Rank	Name	First	Year	Team	Lg	HR	RBI	AVG	Age	PEVA-B
1	Craver	Bill	1874	PH2	NA	0	56	0.343	30	15.032
2	Eggler	Dave	1874	PH2	NA	0	31	0.318	25	12.715
3	Malone	Fergy	1873	PH2	NA	0	43	0.290	31	9.974
4	Meyerle	Levi	1875	PH2	NA	1	54	0.316	30	9.652
5	Meyerle	Levi	1873	PH2	NA	3	58	0.349	28	9.621

Philadelphia Whites - Best Pitcher Years

Rank	Name	First	Year	Team	Lg	W	L	SV	IP	ERA	Age	PEVA-P
1	Zettlein	George	1873	PH2	NA	36	15	0	460.0	2.70	29	17.432
2	Zettlein	George	1875	PH2	NA	12	8	0	180.3	2.40	31	11.035
3	Fisher	Cherokee	1875	PH2	NA	22	19	0	356.7	1.92	30	8.534
4	Cummings	Candy	1874	PH2	NA	28	26	0	482.0	2.88	26	6.770
5	Borden	Joe	1875	PH2	NA	2	4	0	66.0	1.64	21	3.528

Philadelphia Whites - Top Career Batters

Rank	Name	First	LYear	LTeam	Lg	PEVA-B	YRS	PER	HR	RBI	H	AVE.
1	Meyerle	Levi	1875	PH2	NA	19.272	2	9.636	4	112	178	0.330
2	Craver	Bill	1874	PH2	NA	15.032	1	15.032	0	56	91	0.343
3	Fulmer	Chick	1875	PH2	NA	14.106	3	4.702	1	99	203	0.257
4	Eggler	Dave	1874	PH2	NA	12.715	1	12.715	0	31	95	0.318
5	Malone	Fergy	1875	PH2	NA	10.427	2	5.213	0	53	103	0.270

Philadelphia Whites - Top Career Pitchers

Rank	Name	First	LYear	LTeam	Lg	PEVA-P	YRS	PER	W	L	SV	IP	ERA
1	Zettlein	George	1875	PH2	NA	21.736	2	10.868	48	23	0	640.3	2.61
2	Fisher	Cherokee	1875	PH2	NA	8.534	1	8.534	22	19	0	356.7	1.92
3	Cummings	Candy	1874	PH2	NA	6.770	1	6.770	28	26	0	482.0	2.88
4	Borden	Joe	1875	PH2	NA	3.528	1	3.528	2	4	0	66.0	1.64
5	Bechtel	George	1874	PH2	NA	0.832	2	0.416	1	5	0	58.0	4.03

PHILADELPHIA CENTENNIALS
Best Seasons and Careers of All-Time

Philadelphia Centennials - Best Position Player Years

Rank	Name	First	Year	Team	Lg	HR	RBI	AVG	Age	PEVA-B
1	Craver	Bill	1875	PH3	NA	0	5	0.277	31	13.098
2	Bechtel	George	1875	PH3	NA	0	7	0.279	27	3.286
3	Treacey	Fred	1875	PH3	NA	0	2	0.261	28	2.806
4	McGinley	Tim	1875	PH3	NA	0	5	0.231	NA	2.581
5	Somerville	Ed	1875	PH3	NA	0	6	0.228	22	1.558

Philadelphia Centennials - Best Pitcher Years

Rank	Name	First	Year	Team	Lg	W	L	SV	IP	ERA	Age	PEVA-P
1	Bechtel	George	1875	PH3	NA	2	12	0	126.0	3.93	27	1.542

Philadelphia Centennials - Top Career Batters

Rank	Name	First	LYear	LTeam	Lg	PEVA-B	YRS	PER	HR	RBI	H	AVE.
1	Craver	Bill	1875	PH3	NA	2.620	1	2.620	0	5	18	0.277
2	Bechtel	George	1875	PH3	NA	0.891	1	0.891	0	7	17	0.279
3	McGinley	Tim	1875	PH3	NA	0.733	1	0.733	0	5	12	0.231
4	Warner	Fred	1875	PH3	NA	0.706	1	0.706	0	2	14	0.246
5	Treacey	Fred	1875	PH3	NA	0.574	1	0.574	0	2	12	0.261

Philadelphia Centennials - Top Career Pitchers

Rank	Name	First	LYear	LTeam	Lg	PEVA-P	YRS	PER	W	L	SV	IP	ERA
1	Bechtel	George	1875	PH3	NA	1.200	1	1.200	2	12	0	126.0	3.93

PHILADELPHIA ATHLETICS
(NATIONAL LEAGUE)
Best Seasons and Careers of All-Time

Philadelphia Athletics (National League) - Best Position Player Years

Rank	Name	First	Year	Team	Lg	HR	RBI	AVG	Age	PEVA-B
1	Hall	George	1876	PHN	NL	5	45	0.366	27	19.290
2	Meyerle	Levi	1876	PHN	NL	0	34	0.340	31	8.147
3	Force	Davy	1876	PHN	NL	0	17	0.232	27	5.219
4	Fisler	Wes	1876	PHN	NL	1	30	0.288	35	4.809
5	Sutton	Ezra	1876	PHN	NL	1	31	0.297	26	4.636

Philadelphia Athletics (National League) - Best Pitcher Years

Rank	Name	First	Year	Team	Lg	W	L	SV	IP	ERA	Age	PEVA-P
1	Knight	Lon	1876	PHN	NL	10	22	0	282.0	2.62	23	1.878
2	Zettlein	George	1876	PHN	NL	4	20	2	234.0	3.88	32	1.477
3	Coon	William	1876	PHN	NL	0	0	0	7.0	5.14	21	0.200
4	Lafferty	Flip	1876	PHN	NL	0	1	0	9.0	0.00	22	0.200
5	Meyerle	Levi	1876	PHN	NL	0	2	0	18.0	5.00	31	0.200

Philadelphia Athletics (National League) - Top Career Batters

Rank	Name	First	LYear	LTeam	Lg	PEVA-B	YRS	PER	HR	RBI	H	AVE.
1	Hall	George	1876	PHN	NL	19.290	1	19.290	5	45	98	0.366
2	Meyerle	Levi	1876	PHN	NL	8.147	1	8.147	0	34	87	0.340
3	Force	Davy	1876	PHN	NL	5.165	1	5.165	0	17	66	0.232
4	Fisler	Wes	1876	PHN	NL	4.809	1	4.809	1	30	80	0.288
5	Sutton	Ezra	1876	PHN	NL	4.636	1	4.636	1	31	70	0.297

Philadelphia Athletics (National League) - Top Career Pitchers

Rank	Name	First	LYear	LTeam	Lg	PEVA-P	YRS	PER	W	L	SV	IP	ERA
1	Knight	Lon	1876	PHN	NL	1.878	1	1.878	10	22	0	282.0	2.62
2	Zettlein	George	1876	PHN	NL	1.477	1	1.477	4	20	2	234.0	3.88
3	Coon	William	1876	PHN	NL	0.200	1	0.200	0	0	0	7.0	5.14
4	Meyerle	Levi	1876	PHN	NL	0.200	1	0.200	0	2	0	18.0	5.00
5	Lafferty	Flip	1876	PHN	NL	0.200	1	0.200	0	1	0	9.0	0.00

PHILADELPHIA ATHLETICS
(PACIFIC LEAGUE)
Best Seasons and Careers of All-Time

Philadelphia Athletics (Pacific League) - Best Position Player Years

Rank	Name	First	Year	Team	Lg	HR	RBI	AVG	Age	PEVA-B
1	Shindle	Billy	1890	PHP	PL	10	90	0.324	30	19.068
2	Wood	George	1890	PHP	PL	9	102	0.289	32	15.312
3	Griffin	Mike	1890	PHP	PL	6	54	0.286	25	12.624
4	Mulvey	Joe	1890	PHP	PL	6	87	0.287	32	9.179
5	Farrar	Sid	1890	PHP	PL	1	69	0.256	31	5.644

Philadelphia Athletics (Pacific League) - Best Pitcher Years

Rank	Name	First	Year	Team	Lg	W	L	SV	IP	ERA	Age	PEVA-P
1	Sanders	Ben	1890	PHP	PL	19	18	1	346.7	3.76	25	4.233
2	Knell	Phil	1890	PHP	PL	22	11	0	286.7	3.83	25	3.221
3	Buffinton	Charlie	1890	PHP	PL	19	15	1	283.3	3.81	29	2.990
4	Cunningham	Bert	1890	PHP	PL	3	9	0	108.7	5.22	25	2.308
5	Husted	Bill	1890	PHP	PL	5	10	0	129.0	4.88	24	0.841

Philadelphia Athletics (Pacific League) - Top Career Batters

Rank	Name	First	LYear	LTeam	Lg	PEVA-B	YRS	PER	HR	RBI	H	AVE.
1	Shindle	Billy	1890	PHP	PL	19.068	1	19.068	10	90	189	0.324
2	Wood	George	1890	PHP	PL	15.312	1	15.312	9	102	156	0.289
3	Griffin	Mike	1890	PHP	PL	12.624	1	12.624	6	54	140	0.286
4	Mulvey	Joe	1890	PHP	PL	9.179	1	9.179	6	87	149	0.287
5	Farrar	Sid	1890	PHP	PL	5.644	1	5.644	1	69	123	0.256

Philadelphia Athletics (Pacific League) - Top Career Pitchers

Rank	Name	First	LYear	LTeam	Lg	PEVA-P	YRS	PER	W	L	SV	IP	ERA
1	Sanders	Ben	1890	PHP	PL	4.233	1	4.233	19	18	1	346.7	3.76
2	Knell	Phil	1890	PHP	PL	3.221	1	3.221	22	11	0	286.7	3.83
3	Buffinton	Charlie	1890	PHP	PL	2.990	1	2.990	19	15	1	283.3	3.81
4	Husted	Bill	1890	PHP	PL	0.841	1	0.841	5	10	0	129.0	4.88
5	Cunningham	Bert	1890	PHP	PL	0.785	1	0.785	3	9	0	108.7	5.22

PHILADELPHIA KEYSTONES
(NATIONAL ASSOCIATION)
Best Seasons and Careers of All-Time

Philadelphia Keystones - Best Position Player Years

Rank	Name	First	Year	Team	Lg	HR	RBI	AVG	Age	PEVA-B
1	Hoover	Buster	1884	PHU	UA	0	NA	0.364	21	9.374
2	Geer	Billy	1884	PHU	UA	0	NA	0.250	25	7.793
3	McCormick	Jerry	1884	PHU	UA	0	NA	0.285	NA	5.672
4	Kienzle	Bill	1884	PHU	UA	0	NA	0.254	NA	4.253
5	Clements	Jack	1884	PHU	UA	3	NA	0.282	20	3.395

Philadelphia Keystones - Best Pitcher Years

Rank	Name	First	Year	Team	Lg	W	L	SV	IP	ERA	Age	PEVA-P
1	Bakely	Jersey	1884	PHU	UA	14	25	0	344.7	4.47	20	3.870
2	Fisher	J.	1884	PHU	UA	1	7	0	70.7	3.57	NA	0.919
3	Weaver	Sam	1884	PHU	UA	5	10	0	136.0	5.76	29	0.903
4	Gallagher	Bill	1884	PHU	UA	1	2	0	25.0	3.24	NA	0.462
5	McCormick	Jerry	1884	PHU	UA	0	0	0	2.0	9.00	NA	0.200

Philadelphia Keystones - Top Career Batters

Rank	Name	First	LYear	LTeam	Lg	PEVA-B	YRS	PER	HR	RBI	H	AVE.
1	Hoover	Buster	1884	PHU	UA	8.132	1	8.132	0	0	100	0.364
2	Kienzle	Bill	1884	PHU	UA	4.253	1	4.253	0	0	76	0.254
3	McCormick	Jerry	1884	PHU	UA	3.702	1	3.702	0	0	84	0.285
4	Clements	Jack	1884	PHU	UA	2.903	1	2.903	3	0	50	0.282
5	Flynn	Joe	1884	PHU	UA	2.286	1	2.286	4	0	52	0.249

Philadelphia Keystones - Top Career Pitchers

Rank	Name	First	LYear	LTeam	Lg	PEVA-P	YRS	PER	W	L	SV	IP	ERA
1	Bakely	Jersey	1884	PHU	UA	3.380	1	3.380	14	25	0	344.7	4.47
2	Fisher	J.	1884	PHU	UA	0.919	1	0.919	1	7	0	70.7	3.57
3	Weaver	Sam	1884	PHU	UA	0.903	1	0.903	5	10	0	136.0	5.76
4	Gallagher	Bill	1884	PHU	UA	0.462	1	0.462	1	2	0	25.0	3.24
5	Maul	Al	1884	PHU	UA	0.200	1	0.200	0	1	0	8.0	4.50

PROVIDENCE GRAYS
Best Seasons and Careers of All-Time

Providence Grays - Best Position Player Years

Rank	Name	First	Year	Team	Lg	HR	RBI	AVG	Age	PEVA-B
1	Hines	Paul	1879	PRO	NL	2	52	0.357	24	43.731
2	Hines	Paul	1878	PRO	NL	4	50	0.358	23	38.405
3	York	Tom	1878	PRO	NL	1	26	0.309	28	27.661
4	Higham	Dick	1878	PRO	NL	1	29	0.320	27	27.094
5	O'Rourke	Jim	1879	PRO	NL	1	46	0.348	29	25.376
6	Hines	Paul	1880	PRO	NL	3	35	0.307	25	24.429
7	Hines	Paul	1884	PRO	NL	3	41	0.302	29	23.403
8	York	Tom	1879	PRO	NL	1	50	0.310	29	22.474
9	Brown	Lew	1878	PRO	NL	1	43	0.305	20	20.812
10	Hines	Paul	1882	PRO	NL	4	34	0.309	27	20.338
11	Wright	George	1879	PRO	NL	1	42	0.276	32	19.248
12	York	Tom	1881	PRO	NL	2	47	0.304	31	17.945
13	Farrell	Jack	1883	PRO	NL	3	61	0.305	26	16.797
14	Hines	Paul	1883	PRO	NL	4	45	0.299	28	16.189
15	Start	Joe	1882	PRO	NL	0	48	0.329	40	16.185
16	Gross	Emil	1880	PRO	NL	1	34	0.259	22	13.655
17	Carroll	Cliff	1884	PRO	NL	3	54	0.261	25	13.068
18	Denny	Jerry	1883	PRO	NL	8	55	0.275	24	13.004
19	Hines	Paul	1881	PRO	NL	2	31	0.285	26	12.117
20	Start	Joe	1879	PRO	NL	2	37	0.319	37	11.872

Providence Grays - Best Pitcher Years

Rank	Name	First	Year	Team	Lg	W	L	SV	IP	ERA	Age	PEVA-P
1	Radbourn	Charley	1883	PRO	NL	48	25	1	632.3	2.05	29	38.272
2	Radbourn	Charley	1884	PRO	NL	59	12	1	678.7	1.38	30	36.790
3	Sweeney	Charlie	1884	PRO	NL	17	8	1	221.0	1.55	21	27.423
4	Ward	John	1879	PRO	NL	47	19	1	587.0	2.15	19	24.362
5	Ward	John	1880	PRO	NL	39	24	1	595.0	1.74	20	19.056
6	Ward	John	1878	PRO	NL	22	13	0	334.0	1.51	18	14.937
7	Radbourn	Charley	1882	PRO	NL	33	20	0	474.0	2.09	28	13.913

Providence Grays - Top Career Batters

Rank	Name	First	LYear	LTeam	Lg	PEVA-B	YRS	PER	HR	RBI	H	AVE.
1	Hines	Paul	1885	PRO	NL	185.762	8	23.220	23	323	964	0.309
2	York	Tom	1882	PRO	NL	80.331	5	16.066	5	181	414	0.285
3	Start	Joe	1885	PRO	NL	70.375	7	10.054	5	271	741	0.297
4	Farrell	Jack	1885	PRO	NL	51.872	7	7.410	15	225	563	0.251
5	Denny	Jerry	1885	PRO	NL	40.825	5	8.165	20	204	446	0.248
6	Ward	John	1882	PRO	NL	33.736	5	6.747	4	175	386	0.246
7	Higham	Dick	1878	PRO	NL	27.094	1	27.094	1	29	90	0.320
8	O'Rourke	Jim	1879	PRO	NL	25.376	1	25.376	1	46	126	0.348
9	Brown	Lew	1881	PRO	NL	24.589	3	8.196	3	91	151	0.276
10	Carroll	Cliff	1885	PRO	NL	21.643	4	5.411	5	116	285	0.246
11	Wright	George	1882	PRO	NL	20.013	2	10.007	1	51	137	0.239
12	Gross	Emil	1881	PRO	NL	19.360	3	6.453	2	82	186	0.281

13	Irwin	Arthur	1885	PRO	NL	**18.954**	3	6.318	2	102	252	0.245
14	Radbourn	Charley	1885	PRO	NL	**17.537**	5	3.507	5	167	386	0.243
15	Gilligan	Barney	1885	PRO	NL	**16.917**	5	3.383	1	120	263	0.220
16	Radford	Paul	1885	PRO	NL	**11.392**	2	5.696	1	61	160	0.220

Providence Grays - Top Career Pitchers

Rank	Name	First	LYear	LTeam	Lg	PEVA-P	YRS	PER	W	L	SV	IP	ERA
1	Radbourn	Charley	1885	PRO	NL	**105.640**	5	21.128	193	89	2	2556.0	1.95
2	Ward	John	1882	PRO	NL	**68.865**	5	13.773	145	86	3	2124.0	1.99
3	Sweeney	Charlie	1884	PRO	NL	**13.469**	2	6.734	24	15	1	367.7	2.18
4	Shaw	Dupee	1885	PRO	NL	**6.378**	1	6.378	23	26	0	399.7	2.57
5	Bradley	George	1880	PRO	NL	**4.649**	1	4.649	13	8	1	196.0	1.38

PITTSBURGH REBELS
Best Seasons and Careers of All-Time

Pittsburgh Rebels - Best Position Player Years

Rank	Name	First	Year	Team	Lg	HR	RBI	AVG	Age	PEVA-B
1	Konetchy	Ed	1915	PTF	FL	10	93	0.314	30	19.572
2	Lennox	Ed	1914	PTF	FL	11	84	0.312	31	18.903
3	Oakes	Rebel	1914	PTF	FL	7	75	0.312	31	15.609
4	Kelly	Jim	1915	PTF	FL	4	50	0.294	31	11.361
5	Mowrey	Mike	1915	PTF	FL	1	49	0.280	31	11.159
6	Wickland	Al	1915	PTF	FL	1	30	0.301	27	11.088
7	Oakes	Rebel	1915	PTF	FL	0	82	0.278	32	10.565

Pittsburgh Rebels - Best Pitcher Years

Rank	Name	First	Year	Team	Lg	W	L	SV	IP	ERA	Age	PEVA-P
1	Allen	Frank	1915	PTF	FL	23	13	0	283.3	2.51	27	9.639
2	Knetzer	Elmer	1915	PTF	FL	18	14	3	279.0	2.58	30	6.974
3	Knetzer	Elmer	1914	PTF	FL	20	12	1	272.0	2.88	29	6.059
4	Rogge	Clint	1915	PTF	FL	17	11	0	254.3	2.55	26	5.847
5	Camnitz	Howie	1914	PTF	FL	14	19	1	262.0	3.23	33	4.541

Pittsburgh Rebels - Top Career Batters

Rank	Name	First	LYear	LTeam	Lg	PEVA-B	YRS	PER	HR	RBI	H	AVE.
1	Oakes	Rebel	1915	PTF	FL	26.174	2	13.087	7	157	339	0.295
2	Lennox	Ed	1915	PTF	FL	20.237	2	10.119	12	93	150	0.311
3	Konetchy	Ed	1915	PTF	FL	19.572	1	19.572	10	93	181	0.314
4	Kelly	Jim	1915	PTF	FL	11.361	1	11.361	4	50	154	0.294
5	Mowrey	Mike	1915	PTF	FL	11.159	1	11.159	1	49	146	0.280

Pittsburgh Rebels - Top Career Pitchers

Rank	Name	First	LYear	LTeam	Lg	PEVA-P	YRS	PER	W	L	SV	IP	ERA
1	Knetzer	Elmer	1915	PTF	FL	13.033	2	6.517	38	26	4	551.0	2.73
2	Allen	Frank	1915	PTF	FL	9.704	2	4.852	24	13	0	290.3	2.57
3	Barger	Cy	1915	PTF	FL	6.809	2	3.405	19	24	7	381.3	3.52
4	Rogge	Clint	1915	PTF	FL	5.847	1	5.847	17	11	0	254.3	2.55
5	Camnitz	Howie	1915	PTF	FL	4.741	2	2.371	14	19	1	282.0	3.32

PITTSBURGH BURGHERS
Best Seasons and Careers of All-Time

Pittsburgh Burghers - Best Position Player Years

Rank	Name	First	Year	Team	Lg	HR	RBI	AVG	Age	PEVA-B
1	Beckley	Jake	1890	PTP	PL	9	120	0.324	23	23.357
2	Fields	Jocko	1890	PTP	PL	9	86	0.281	26	13.610
3	Visner	Joe	1890	PTP	PL	3	71	0.267	31	12.981
4	Carroll	Fred	1890	PTP	PL	2	71	0.298	26	12.170
5	Hanlon	Ned	1890	PTP	PL	1	44	0.278	33	10.532

Pittsburgh Burghers - Best Pitcher Years

Rank	Name	First	Year	Team	Lg	W	L	SV	IP	ERA	Age	PEVA-P
1	Staley	Harry	1890	PTP	PL	21	25	0	387.7	3.23	24	10.092
2	Maul	Al	1890	PTP	PL	16	12	0	246.7	3.79	25	2.071
3	Galvin	Pud	1890	PTP	PL	12	13	0	217.0	4.35	34	1.564
4	Morris	Ed	1890	PTP	PL	8	7	0	144.3	4.86	28	0.778
5	Tener	John	1890	PTP	PL	3	11	0	117.0	7.31	27	0.631

Pittsburgh Burghers - Top Career Batters

Rank	Name	First	LYear	LTeam	Lg	PEVA-B	YRS	PER	HR	RBI	H	AVE.
1	Beckley	Jake	1890	PTP	PL	23.357	1	23.357	9	120	167	0.324
2	Fields	Jocko	1890	PTP	PL	13.610	1	13.610	9	86	148	0.281
3	Visner	Joe	1890	PTP	PL	12.981	1	12.981	3	71	139	0.267
4	Carroll	Fred	1890	PTP	PL	12.170	1	12.170	2	71	124	0.298
5	Hanlon	Ned	1890	PTP	PL	10.532	1	10.532	1	44	131	0.278

Pittsburgh Burghers - Top Career Pitchers

Rank	Name	First	LYear	LTeam	Lg	PEVA-P	YRS	PER	W	L	SV	IP	ERA
1	Staley	Harry	1890	PTP	PL	10.092	1	10.092	21	25	0	387.7	3.23
2	Maul	Al	1890	PTP	PL	2.071	1	2.071	16	12	0	246.7	3.79
3	Galvin	Pud	1890	PTP	PL	1.564	1	1.564	12	13	0	217.0	4.35
4	Morris	Ed	1890	PTP	PL	0.778	1	0.778	8	7	0	144.3	4.86
5	Tener	John	1890	PTP	PL	0.631	1	0.631	3	11	0	117.0	7.31

ROCKFORD FOREST CITYS
Best Seasons and Careers of All-Time

Rockford Forest Citys - Best Position Player Years

Rank	Name	First	Year	Team	Lg	HR	RBI	AVG	Age	PEVA-B
1	Anson	Cap	1871	RC1	NA	0	16	0.325	19	**5.003**
2	Stires	Gat	1871	RC1	NA	2	24	0.273	22	**3.837**
3	Hastings	Scott	1871	RC1	NA	0	20	0.254	24	**3.285**
4	Mack	Denny	1871	RC1	NA	0	17	0.246	20	**2.652**
5	Addy	Bob	1871	RC1	NA	0	13	0.271	26	**2.182**

Rockford Forest Citys - Best Pitcher Years

Rank	Name	First	Year	Team	Lg	W	L	SV	IP	ERA	Age	PEVA-P
1	Fisher	Cherokee	1871	RC1	NA	4	16	0	213.0	4.35	26	**2.834**
2	Mack	Denny	1871	RC1	NA	0	1	0	13.0	3.46	20	**0.200**

Rockford Forest Citys - Top Career Batters

Rank	Name	First	LYear	LTeam	Lg	PEVA-B	YRS	PER	HR	RBI	H	AVE.
1	Anson	Cap	1871	RC1	NA	**5.003**	1	5.003	0	16	39	0.325
2	Stires	Gat	1871	RC1	NA	**3.837**	1	3.837	2	24	30	0.273
3	Hastings	Scott	1871	RC1	NA	**3.285**	1	3.285	0	20	30	0.254
4	Mack	Denny	1871	RC1	NA	**2.652**	1	2.652	0	17	30	0.246
5	Addy	Bob	1871	RC1	NA	**2.182**	1	2.182	0	13	32	0.271

Rockford Forest Citys - Top Career Pitchers

Rank	Name	First	LYear	LTeam	Lg	PEVA-P	YRS	PER	W	L	SV	IP	ERA
1	Fisher	Cherokee	1871	RC1	NA	**2.834**	1	2.834	4	16	0	213.0	4.35
2	Mack	Denny	1871	RC1	NA	**0.200**	1	0.200	0	1	0	13.0	3.46

ROCHESTER BRONCOS
Best Seasons and Careers of All-Time

Rochester Broncos - Best Position Player Years

Rank	Name	First	Year	Team	Lg	HR	RBI	AVG	Age	PEVA-B
1	Knowles	Jimmy	1890	RC2	AA	5	84	0.281	34	10.628
2	Scheffler	Ted	1890	RC2	AA	3	34	0.245	26	9.074
3	Lyons	Harry	1890	RC2	AA	3	58	0.260	24	8.265
4	Griffin	Sandy	1890	RC2	AA	5	53	0.307	32	8.181
5	McGuire	Deacon	1890	RC2	AA	4	53	0.299	27	5.883

Rochester Broncos - Best Pitcher Years

Rank	Name	First	Year	Team	Lg	W	L	SV	IP	ERA	Age	PEVA-P
1	Barr	Bob	1890	RC2	AA	28	24	0	493.3	3.25	34	10.690
2	Calihan	Will	1890	RC2	AA	18	15	0	296.3	3.28	21	4.396
3	Titcomb	Cannonball	1890	RC2	AA	10	9	0	168.7	3.74	24	1.121
4	Miller	Bob	1890	RC2	AA	3	7	1	92.3	4.29	28	0.942
5	Fitzgerald	John	1890	RC2	AA	3	8	0	78.0	4.04	NA	0.825

Rochester Broncos - Top Career Batters

Rank	Name	First	LYear	LTeam	Lg	PEVA-B	YRS	PER	HR	RBI	H	AVE.
1	Knowles	Jimmy	1890	RC2	AA	10.628	1	10.628	5	84	138	0.281
2	Scheffler	Ted	1890	RC2	AA	9.074	1	9.074	3	34	109	0.245
3	Lyons	Harry	1890	RC2	AA	8.265	1	8.265	3	58	152	0.260
4	Griffin	Sandy	1890	RC2	AA	8.181	1	8.181	5	53	125	0.307
5	McGuire	Deacon	1890	RC2	AA	5.883	1	5.883	4	53	99	0.299

Rochester Broncos - Top Career Pitchers

Rank	Name	First	LYear	LTeam	Lg	PEVA-P	YRS	PER	W	L	SV	IP	ERA
1	Barr	Bob	1890	RC2	AA	10.690	1	10.690	28	24	0	493.3	3.25
2	Calihan	Will	1890	RC2	AA	4.396	1	4.396	18	15	0	296.3	3.28
3	Titcomb	Cannonball	1890	RC2	AA	1.121	1	1.121	10	9	0	168.7	3.74
4	Miller	Bob	1890	RC2	AA	0.942	1	0.942	3	7	1	92.3	4.29
5	Fitzgerald	John	1890	RC2	AA	0.825	1	0.825	3	8	0	78.0	4.04

RICHMOND VIRGINIANS
Best Seasons and Careers of All-Time

Richmond Virginians - Best Position Player Years

Rank	Name	First	Year	Team	Lg	HR	RBI	AVG	Age	PEVA-B
1	Mansell	Mike	1884	RIC	AA	0	0	0.301	26	2.362
2	Johnston	Dick	1884	RIC	AA	2	0	0.281	21	1.770
3	Nash	Billy	1884	RIC	AA	1	0	0.199	19	1.547
4	Glenn	Ed	1884	RIC	AA	1	0	0.246	24	1.121
5	Powell	Jim	1884	RIC	AA	0	0	0.245	25	1.058

Richmond Virginians - Best Pitcher Years

Rank	Name	First	Year	Team	Lg	W	L	SV	IP	ERA	Age	PEVA-P
1	Meegan	Pete	1884	RIC	AA	7	12	0	179.0	4.32	21	1.107
2	Dugan	Ed	1884	RIC	AA	5	14	0	166.3	4.49	20	0.933
3	Firth	Ted	1884	RIC	AA	0	1	0	9.0	8.00	29	0.200
4	Curry	Wes	1884	RIC	AA	0	2	0	16.0	5.06	24	0.200

Richmond Virginians - Top Career Batters

Rank	Name	First	LYear	LTeam	Lg	PEVA-B	YRS	PER	HR	RBI	H	AVE.
1	Johnston	Dick	1884	RIC	AA	1.770	1	1.770	2	0	41	0.281
2	Nash	Billy	1884	RIC	AA	1.547	1	1.547	1	0	33	0.199
3	Glenn	Ed	1884	RIC	AA	1.121	1	1.121	1	0	43	0.246
4	Powell	Jim	1884	RIC	AA	1.058	1	1.058	0	0	37	0.245
5	Mansell	Mike	1884	RIC	AA	0.943	1	0.943	0	0	34	0.301

Richmond Virginians - Top Career Pitchers

Rank	Name	First	LYear	LTeam	Lg	PEVA-P	YRS	PER	W	L	SV	IP	ERA
1	Meegan	Pete	1884	RIC	AA	1.107	1	1.107	7	12	0	179.0	4.32
2	Dugan	Ed	1884	RIC	AA	0.933	1	0.933	5	14	0	166.3	4.49
3	Firth	Ted	1884	RIC	AA	0.200	1	0.200	0	1	0	9.0	8.00
4	Curry	Wes	1884	RIC	AA	0.200	1	0.200	0	2	0	16.0	5.06

ST. LOUIS RED STOCKINGS
Best Seasons and Careers of All-Time

St. Louis Red Stockings - Best Position Player Years

Rank	Name	First	Year	Team	Lg	HR	RBI	AVG	Age	PEVA-B
1	Morgan	Pidgey	1875	SL1	NA	0	1	0.261	22	1.023
2	Hautz	Charlie	1875	SL1	NA	0	4	0.301	23	1.022
3	Redmon	Billy	1875	SL1	NA	0	1	0.195	NA	0.365
4	Croft	Art	1875	SL1	NA	0	2	0.200	20	0.228
5	McSorley	Trick	1875	SL1	NA	0	2	0.212	23	0.221

St. Louis Red Stockings - Best Pitcher Years

Rank	Name	First	Year	Team	Lg	W	L	SV	IP	ERA	Age	PEVA-P
1	Morgan	Pidgey	1875	SL1	NA	1	3	0	42.0	3.43	22	1.981
2	Blong	Joe	1875	SL1	NA	3	12	0	129.0	3.35	22	1.374

St. Louis Red Stockings - Top Career Batters

Rank	Name	First	LYear	LTeam	Lg	PEVA-B	YRS	PER	HR	RBI	H	AVE.
1	Morgan	Pidgey	1875	SL1	NA	1.023	1	1.023	0	1	18	0.261
2	Hautz	Charlie	1875	SL1	NA	1.022	1	1.022	0	4	25	0.301
3	Redmon	Billy	1875	SL1	NA	0.365	1	0.365	0	1	16	0.195
4	Croft	Art	1875	SL1	NA	0.228	1	0.228	0	2	15	0.200
5	McSorley	Trick	1875	SL1	NA	0.221	1	0.221	0	2	11	0.212

St. Louis Red Stockings - Top Career Pitchers

Rank	Name	First	LYear	LTeam	Lg	PEVA-P	YRS	PER	W	L	SV	IP	ERA
1	Morgan	Pidgey	1875	SL1	NA	1.981	1	1.981	1	3	0	42.0	3.43
2	Blong	Joe	1875	SL1	NA	1.374	1	1.374	3	12	0	129.0	3.35

ST. LOUIS BROWN STOCKINGS
(NATIONAL ASSOCIATION)
Best Seasons and Careers of All-Time

St. Louis Brown Stockings (National Association) - Best Position Player Years

Rank	Name	First	Year	Team	Lg	HR	RBI	AVG	Age	PEVA-B
1	Pike	Lip	1875	SL2	NA	0	44	0.346	30	23.989
2	Pearce	Dickey	1875	SL2	NA	0	29	0.248	39	7.012
3	Cuthbert	Ned	1875	SL2	NA	0	17	0.245	30	6.283
4	Battin	Joe	1875	SL2	NA	0	33	0.250	24	4.445
5	Dehlman	Herman	1875	SL2	NA	0	14	0.224	23	4.138

St. Louis Brown Stockings (National Association) - Best Pitcher Years

Rank	Name	First	Year	Team	Lg	W	L	SV	IP	ERA	Age	PEVA-P
1	Bradley	George	1875	SL2	NA	33	26	0	535.7	2.05	23	11.903
2	Galvin	Pud	1875	SL2	NA	4	2	1	62.0	2.18	19	2.934
3	Fleet	Frank	1875	SL2	NA	2	1	0	27.0	2.33	27	0.657
4	Pearce	Dickey	1875	SL2	NA	0	0	0	5.3	3.38	39	0.200

St. Louis Brown Stockings (National Association) - Top Career Batters

Rank	Name	First	LYear	LTeam	Lg	PEVA-B	YRS	PER	HR	RBI	H	AVE.
1	Pike	Lip	1875	SL2	NA	23.989	1	23.989	0	44	108	0.346
2	Pearce	Dickey	1875	SL2	NA	7.012	1	7.012	0	29	77	0.248
3	Cuthbert	Ned	1875	SL2	NA	6.283	1	6.283	0	17	78	0.245
4	Battin	Joe	1875	SL2	NA	4.445	1	4.445	0	33	71	0.250
5	Dehlman	Herman	1875	SL2	NA	4.138	1	4.138	0	14	57	0.224

St. Louis Brown Stockings (National Association) - Top Career Pitchers

Rank	Name	First	LYear	LTeam	Lg	PEVA-P	YRS	PER	W	L	SV	IP	ERA
1	Bradley	George	1875	SL2	NA	11.903	1	11.903	33	26	0	535.7	2.05
2	Galvin	Pud	1875	SL2	NA	2.934	1	2.934	4	2	1	62.0	2.18
3	Fleet	Frank	1875	SL2	NA	0.419	1	0.419	2	1	0	27.0	2.33
4	Pearce	Dickey	1875	SL2	NA	0.200	1	0.200	0	0	0	5.3	3.38

ST. LOUIS BROWN STOCKINGS
(NATIONAL LEAGUE)
Best Seasons and Careers of All-Time

St. Louis Brown Stockings (National League) - Best Position Player Years

Rank	Name	First	Year	Team	Lg	HR	RBI	AVG	Age	PEVA-B
1	Clapp	John	1877	SL3	NL	0	34	0.318	26	19.615
2	Pike	Lip	1876	SL3	NL	1	50	0.323	31	17.351
3	Clapp	John	1876	SL3	NL	0	29	0.305	25	13.420
4	Dorgan	Mike	1877	SL3	NL	0	23	0.308	24	13.349
5	Battin	Joe	1876	SL3	NL	0	46	0.300	25	10.703

St. Louis Brown Stockings (National League) - Best Pitcher Years

Rank	Name	First	Year	Team	Lg	W	L	SV	IP	ERA	Age	PEVA-P
1	Bradley	George	1876	SL3	NL	45	19	0	573.0	1.23	24	36.677
2	Nichols	Tricky	1877	SL3	NL	18	23	0	350.0	2.60	27	4.735
3	Blong	Joe	1877	SL3	NL	10	9	0	187.3	2.74	24	1.578
4	Blong	Joe	1876	SL3	NL	0	0	0	4.0	0.00	23	0.200
5	Battin	Joe	1877	SL3	NL	0	0	0	3.7	4.91	26	0.200

St. Louis Brown Stockings (National League) - Top Career Batters

Rank	Name	First	LYear	LTeam	Lg	PEVA-B	YRS	PER	HR	RBI	H	AVE.
1	Clapp	John	1877	SL3	NL	33.035	2	16.518	0	63	172	0.311
2	Pike	Lip	1876	SL3	NL	17.351	1	17.351	1	50	91	0.323
3	Battin	Joe	1877	SL3	NL	14.171	2	7.085	1	68	130	0.255
4	Dorgan	Mike	1877	SL3	NL	13.349	1	13.349	0	23	82	0.308
5	McGeary	Mike	1877	SL3	NL	10.093	2	5.046	0	50	137	0.257

St. Louis Brown Stockings (National League) - Top Career Pitchers

Rank	Name	First	LYear	LTeam	Lg	PEVA-P	YRS	PER	W	L	SV	IP	ERA
1	Bradley	George	1876	SL3	NL	36.677	1	36.677	45	19	0	573.0	1.23
2	Nichols	Tricky	1877	SL3	NL	4.735	1	4.735	18	23	0	350.0	2.60
3	Blong	Joe	1877	SL3	NL	1.778	2	0.889	10	9	0	191.3	2.68
4	Battin	Joe	1877	SL3	NL	0.200	1	0.200	0	0	0	3.7	4.91

ST. LOUIS MAROONS
Best Seasons and Careers of All-Time

St. Louis Maroons - Best Position Player Years

Rank	Name	First	Year	Team	Lg	HR	RBI	AVG	Age	PEVA-B
1	Dunlap	Fred	1884	SLU	UA	13	NA	0.412	25	37.571
2	Shaffer	Orator	1884	SLU	UA	2	NA	0.360	33	23.763
3	Glasscock	Jack	1886	SL5	NL	3	40	0.325	29	16.318
4	Glasscock	Jack	1885	SL5	NL	1	40	0.280	28	12.849
5	Rowe	Dave	1884	SLU	UA	4	NA	0.293	30	11.370
6	Gleason	Jack	1884	SLU	UA	4	NA	0.324	30	10.214

St. Louis Maroons - Best Pitcher Years

Rank	Name	First	Year	Team	Lg	W	L	SV	IP	ERA	Age	PEVA-P
1	Sweeney	Charlie	1884	SLU	UA	24	7	0	271.0	1.83	21	27.423
2	Taylor	Billy	1884	SLU	UA	25	4	4	263.0	1.68	29	16.180
3	Boyle	Henry	1884	SLU	UA	15	3	1	150.0	1.74	24	6.366
4	Healy	John	1886	SL5	NL	17	23	0	353.7	2.88	20	4.808
5	Boyle	Henry	1886	SL5	NL	9	15	0	210.0	1.76	26	4.806

St. Louis Maroons (SL5, SLU) - Top Career Batters

Rank	Name	First	LYear	LTeam	Lg	PEVA-B	YRS	PER	HR	RBI	H	AVE.
1	Dunlap	Fred	1886	SL5	NL	52.234	3	17.411	18	57	375	0.324
2	Glasscock	Jack	1886	SL5	NL	29.166	2	14.583	4	80	283	0.304
3	Shaffer	Orator	1885	SL5	NL	25.836	2	12.918	2	18	218	0.301
4	McKinnon	Alex	1886	SL5	NL	16.457	2	8.229	9	116	269	0.298
5	Rowe	Dave	1885	SL5	NL	11.570	2	5.785	4	3	152	0.278
6	Gleason	Jack	1885	SL5	NL	10.414	2	5.207	4	0	129	0.321

St. Louis Maroons (SL5, SLU) - Top Career Batters

Rank	Name	First	LYear	LTeam	Lg	PEVA-B	YRS	PER	HR	RBI	H	AVE.
1	Dunlap	Fred	1886	SL5	NL	52.234	3	17.411	18	57	375	0.324
2	Glasscock	Jack	1886	SL5	NL	29.166	2	14.583	4	80	283	0.304
3	Shaffer	Orator	1885	SL5	NL	25.836	2	12.918	2	18	218	0.301
4	McKinnon	Alex	1886	SL5	NL	16.457	2	8.229	9	116	269	0.298
5	Rowe	Dave	1885	SL5	NL	11.570	2	5.785	4	3	152	0.278
6	Gleason	Jack	1885	SL5	NL	10.414	2	5.207	4	0	129	0.321

St. Louis Maroons (SL5, SLU) - Top Career Pitchers

Rank	Name	First	LYear	LTeam	Lg	PEVA-P	YRS	PER	W	L	SV	IP	ERA
1	Sweeney	Charlie	1886	SL5	NL	17.594	3	5.865	40	34	0	639.0	3.07
2	Boyle	Henry	1886	SL5	NL	15.422	3	5.141	40	42	1	726.7	2.25
3	Taylor	Billy	1884	SLU	UA	8.136	1	8.136	25	4	4	263.0	1.68
4	Healy	John	1886	SL5	NL	6.032	2	3.016	18	30	0	419.7	2.90
5	Kirby	John	1886	SL5	NL	3.752	2	1.876	16	34	0	454.3	3.37

ST. LOUIS TERRIERS
Best Seasons and Careers of All-Time

St. Louis Terriers - Best Position Player Years

Rank	Name	First	Year	Team	Lg	HR	RBI	AVG	Age	PEVA-B
1	Tobin	Jack	1915	SLF	FL	6	51	0.294	23	15.463
2	Borton	Babe	1915	SLF	FL	3	83	0.286	27	15.217
3	Miller	Ward	1915	SLF	FL	1	63	0.306	31	14.797
4	Johnson	Ernie	1915	SLF	FL	7	67	0.240	27	8.859
5	Miller	Ward	1914	SLF	FL	4	50	0.294	30	8.829

St. Louis Terriers - Best Pitcher Years

Rank	Name	First	Year	Team	Lg	W	L	SV	IP	ERA	Age	PEVA-P
1	Davenport	Dave	1915	SLF	FL	22	18	1	392.7	2.20	25	21.910
2	Plank	Eddie	1915	SLF	FL	21	11	3	268.3	2.08	40	16.422
3	Crandall	Doc	1915	SLF	FL	21	15	1	312.7	2.59	28	8.983
4	Groom	Bob	1914	SLF	FL	13	20	1	280.7	3.24	30	4.791
5	Watson	Doc	1914	SLF	FL	3	4	0	56.0	1.93	28	4.762

St. Louis Terriers - Top Career Batters

Rank	Name	First	LYear	LTeam	Lg	PEVA-B	YRS	PER	HR	RBI	H	AVE.
1	Tobin	Jack	1915	SLF	FL	24.185	2	12.093	13	86	327	0.283
2	Miller	Ward	1915	SLF	FL	23.626	2	11.813	5	113	282	0.301
3	Borton	Babe	1915	SLF	FL	15.217	1	15.217	3	83	157	0.286
4	Hartley	Grover	1915	SLF	FL	10.126	2	5.063	2	75	169	0.279
5	Drake	Delos	1915	SLF	FL	8.980	2	4.490	4	83	220	0.257

St. Louis Terriers - Top Career Pitchers

Rank	Name	First	LYear	LTeam	Lg	PEVA-P	YRS	PER	W	L	SV	IP	ERA
1	Davenport	Dave	1915	SLF	FL	25.304	2	12.652	30	31	5	608.3	2.65
2	Plank	Eddie	1915	SLF	FL	16.422	1	16.422	21	11	3	268.3	2.08
3	Crandall	Doc	1915	SLF	FL	10.974	2	5.487	34	24	1	508.7	2.95
4	Groom	Bob	1915	SLF	FL	7.151	2	3.575	24	31	3	489.7	3.25
5	Watson	Doc	1915	SLF	FL	2.649	2	1.324	12	13	0	191.7	3.38

ST. PAUL APOSTLES
Best Seasons and Careers of All-Time

St. Paul Apostles - Best Position Player Years

Rank	Name	First	Year	Team	Lg	HR	RBI	AVG	Age	PEVA-B
1	Brown	Jim	1884	SPU	UA	0	NA	0.313	24	0.724
2	Tilley	John	1884	SPU	UA	0	NA	0.154	NA	0.260
3	Hengle	Moxie	1884	SPU	UA	0	NA	0.152	27	0.258
4	Ganzel	Charlie	1884	SPU	UA	0	NA	0.217	22	0.200
5	Dealy	Pat	1884	SPU	UA	0	NA	0.133	23	0.200

St. Paul Apostles - Best Pitcher Years

Rank	Name	First	Year	Team	Lg	W	L	SV	IP	ERA	Age	PEVA-P
1	Brown	Jim	1884	SPU	UA	1	4	0	36.0	3.75	24	0.944
2	Galvin	Lou	1884	SPU	UA	0	2	0	25.0	2.88	22	0.666
3	O'Brien	Billy	1884	SPU	UA	1	0	0	10.0	1.80	24	0.200

St. Paul Apostles - Top Career Batters

Rank	Name	First	LYear	LTeam	Lg	PEVA-B	YRS	PER	HR	RBI	H	AVE.
1	Barnes	Bill	1884	SPU	UA	0.200	1	0.200	0	0	6	0.200
2	Galvin	Lou	1884	SPU	UA	0.200	1	0.200	0	0	2	0.222
3	Carroll	Scrappy	1884	SPU	UA	0.200	1	0.200	0	0	3	0.097
4	Dealy	Pat	1884	SPU	UA	0.200	1	0.200	0	0	2	0.133
5	Dunn	Steve	1884	SPU	UA	0.200	1	0.200	0	0	8	0.250

St. Paul Apostles - Top Career Pitchers

Rank	Name	First	LYear	LTeam	Lg	PEVA-P	YRS	PER	W	L	SV	IP	ERA
1	Galvin	Lou	1884	SPU	UA	0.666	1	0.666	0	2	0	25.0	2.88
2	Brown	Jim	1884	SPU	UA	0.286	1	0.286	1	4	0	36.0	3.75
3	O'Brien	Billy	1884	SPU	UA	0.200	1	0.200	1	0	0	10.0	1.80

SYRACUSE STARS
Best Seasons and Careers of All-Time

Syracuse Stars - Best Position Player Years

Rank	Name	First	Year	Team	Lg	HR	RBI	AVG	Age	PEVA-B
1	Farrell	Jack	1879	SR1	NL	1	21	0.303	22	4.629
2	Purcell	Blondie	1879	SR1	NL	0	25	0.260	25	4.088
3	Dorgan	Mike	1879	SR1	NL	1	17	0.267	26	2.974
4	Richmond	John	1879	SR1	NL	1	23	0.213	25	2.060
5	Mansell	Mike	1879	SR1	NL	1	13	0.215	21	1.971

Syracuse Stars - Best Pitcher Years

Rank	Name	First	Year	Team	Lg	W	L	SV	IP	ERA	Age	PEVA-P
1	McCormick	Harry	1879	SR1	NL	18	33	0	457.3	2.99	24	3.295
2	Purcell	Blondie	1879	SR1	NL	4	15	0	179.7	3.76	25	0.775
3	Dorgan	Mike	1879	SR1	NL	0	0	0	12.0	2.25	26	0.200

Syracuse Stars - Top Career Batters

Rank	Name	First	LYear	LTeam	Lg	PEVA-B	YRS	PER	HR	RBI	H	AVE.
1	Farrell	Jack	1879	SR1	NL	3.821	1	3.821	1	21	73	0.303
2	Purcell	Blondie	1879	SR1	NL	3.463	1	3.463	0	25	72	0.260
3	Dorgan	Mike	1879	SR1	NL	2.974	1	2.974	1	17	72	0.267
4	Richmond	John	1879	SR1	NL	2.060	1	2.060	1	23	54	0.213
5	Mansell	Mike	1879	SR1	NL	1.971	1	1.971	1	13	52	0.215

Syracuse Stars - Top Career Pitchers

Rank	Name	First	LYear	LTeam	Lg	PEVA-P	YRS	PER	W	L	SV	IP	ERA
1	McCormick	Harry	1879	SR1	NL	3.295	1	3.295	18	33	0	457.3	2.99
2	Purcell	Blondie	1879	SR1	NL	0.704	1	0.704	4	15	0	179.7	3.76
3	Dorgan	Mike	1879	SR1	NL	0.200	1	0.200	0	0	0	12.0	2.25

SYRACUSE STARS
(AMERICAN ASSOCIATION)
Best Seasons and Careers of All-Time

Syracuse Stars (American Association) - Best Position Player Years

Rank	Name	First	Year	Team	Lg	HR	RBI	AVG	Age	PEVA-B
1	Childs	Cupid	1890	SR2	AA	2	89	0.345	23	24.650
2	Simon	Hank	1890	SR2	AA	2	23	0.301	28	9.569
3	McQuery	Mox	1890	SR2	AA	2	55	0.308	29	7.634
4	Wright	Rasty	1890	SR2	AA	0	27	0.305	27	7.468
5	Ely	Bones	1890	SR2	AA	0	64	0.262	27	6.237

Syracuse Stars (American Association) - Best Pitcher Years

Rank	Name	First	Year	Team	Lg	W	L	SV	IP	ERA	Age	PEVA-P
1	Casey	Dan	1890	SR2	AA	19	22	0	360.7	4.14	28	3.522
2	Keefe	John	1890	SR2	AA	17	24	0	352.3	4.32	23	3.209
3	McCullough	Charlie	1890	SR2	AA	1	2	0	26.0	7.27	24	1.280
4	Mars	Ed	1890	SR2	AA	9	5	0	121.3	4.67	24	0.971
5	Lincoln	Ezra	1890	SR2	AA	0	3	0	20.0	10.35	22	0.871

Syracuse Stars (American Association) - Top Career Batters

Rank	Name	First	LYear	LTeam	Lg	PEVA-B	YRS	PER	HR	RBI	H	AVE.
1	Childs	Cupid	1890	SR2	AA	24.650	1	24.650	2	89	170	0.345
2	McQuery	Mox	1890	SR2	AA	7.634	1	7.634	2	55	142	0.308
3	Wright	Rasty	1890	SR2	AA	6.613	1	6.613	0	27	106	0.305
4	Ely	Bones	1890	SR2	AA	6.237	1	6.237	0	64	130	0.262
5	O'Rourke	Tim	1890	SR2	AA	3.882	1	3.882	1	46	94	0.283

Syracuse Stars (American Association) - Top Career Pitchers

Rank	Name	First	LYear	LTeam	Lg	PEVA-P	YRS	PER	W	L	SV	IP	ERA
1	Casey	Dan	1890	SR2	AA	3.522	1	3.522	19	22	0	360.7	4.14
2	Keefe	John	1890	SR2	AA	3.209	1	3.209	17	24	0	352.3	4.32
3	Mars	Ed	1890	SR2	AA	0.971	1	0.971	9	5	0	121.3	4.67
4	Morrison	Mike	1890	SR2	AA	0.667	1	0.667	6	9	0	127.0	5.88
5	Sullivan	Bill	1890	SR2	AA	0.390	1	0.390	1	4	0	42.0	7.93

TOLEDO BLUE STOCKINGS
Best Seasons and Careers of All-Time

Toledo Blue Stockings - Best Position Player Years

Rank	Name	First	Year	Team	Lg	HR	RBI	AVG	Age	PEVA-B
1	Barkley	Sam	1884	TL1	AA	1	0	0.306	26	11.577
2	Welch	Curt	1884	TL1	AA	0	0	0.224	22	5.719
3	Miller	Joe	1884	TL1	AA	1	0	0.239	23	5.237
4	Mullane	Tony	1884	TL1	AA	3	0	0.276	25	4.851
5	Poorman	Tom	1884	TL1	AA	0	0	0.233	27	4.162

Toledo Blue Stockings - Best Pitcher Years

Rank	Name	First	Year	Team	Lg	W	L	SV	IP	ERA	Age	PEVA-P
1	Mullane	Tony	1884	TL1	AA	36	26	0	567.0	2.52	25	15.319
2	O'Day	Hank	1884	TL1	AA	9	28	1	326.7	3.75	22	2.252
3	Kent	Ed	1884	TL1	AA	0	1	0	9.0	6.00	25	0.200
4	Morton	Charlie	1884	TL1	AA	0	1	0	23.3	3.09	30	0.200
5	Brown	Ed	1884	TL1	AA	0	1	0	9.0	9.00	1884	0.200

Toledo Blue Stockings - Top Career Batters

Rank	Name	First	LYear	LTeam	Lg	PEVA-B	YRS	PER	HR	RBI	H	AVE.
1	Barkley	Sam	1884	TL1	AA	11.577	1	11.577	1	0	133	0.306
2	Welch	Curt	1884	TL1	AA	5.719	1	5.719	0	0	95	0.224
3	Miller	Joe	1884	TL1	AA	5.237	1	5.237	1	0	101	0.239
4	Mullane	Tony	1884	TL1	AA	4.851	1	4.851	3	0	97	0.276
5	Poorman	Tom	1884	TL1	AA	4.162	1	4.162	0	0	89	0.233

Toledo Blue Stockings - Top Career Pitchers

Rank	Name	First	LYear	LTeam	Lg	PEVA-P	YRS	PER	W	L	SV	IP	ERA
1	Mullane	Tony	1884	TL1	AA	15.319	1	15.319	36	26	0	567.0	2.52
2	O'Day	Hank	1884	TL1	AA	2.252	1	2.252	9	28	1	326.7	3.75
3	Brown	Ed	1884	TL1	AA	0.200	1	0.200	0	1	0	9.0	9.00
4	Kent	Ed	1884	TL1	AA	0.200	1	0.200	0	1	0	9.0	6.00
5	McSorley	Trick	1884	TL1	AA	0.200	1	0.200	0	0	0	2.0	4.50

TOLEDO MAUMEES
Best Seasons and Careers of All-Time

Toledo Maumees - Best Position Player Years

Rank	Name	First	Year	Team	Lg	HR	RBI	AVG	Age	PEVA-B
1	Swartwood	Ed	1890	TL2	AA	3	64	0.327	31	17.677
2	Werden	Perry	1890	TL2	AA	6	72	0.295	25	13.212
3	Nicholson	Parson	1890	TL2	AA	4	72	0.268	27	6.869
4	Scheibeck	Frank	1890	TL2	AA	1	49	0.241	25	6.814
5	Alvord	Billy	1890	TL2	AA	2	52	0.273	27	5.814

Toledo Maumees - Best Pitcher Years

Rank	Name	First	Year	Team	Lg	W	L	SV	IP	ERA	Age	PEVA-P
1	Healy	John	1890	TL2	AA	22	21	0	389.0	2.89	24	14.100
2	Smith	Fred	1890	TL2	AA	19	13	0	286.0	3.27	27	5.225
3	Cushman	Ed	1890	TL2	AA	17	21	1	315.7	4.19	38	3.263
4	Sprague	Charlie	1890	TL2	AA	9	5	0	122.7	3.89	26	1.399
5	O'Neil	Ed	1890	TL2	AA	0	2	0	16.0	7.88	31	0.747

Toledo Maumees - Top Career Batters

Rank	Name	First	LYear	LTeam	Lg	PEVA-B	YRS	PER	HR	RBI	H	AVE.
1	Swartwood	Ed	1890	TL2	AA	17.677	1	17.677	3	64	151	0.327
2	Werden	Perry	1890	TL2	AA	13.212	1	13.212	6	72	147	0.295
3	Nicholson	Parson	1890	TL2	AA	6.869	1	6.869	4	72	140	0.268
4	Scheibeck	Frank	1890	TL2	AA	6.814	1	6.814	1	49	117	0.241
5	Alvord	Billy	1890	TL2	AA	5.814	1	5.814	2	52	135	0.273

Toledo Maumees - Top Career Pitchers

Rank	Name	First	LYear	LTeam	Lg	PEVA-P	YRS	PER	W	L	SV	IP	ERA
1	Healy	John	1890	TL2	AA	14.100	1	14.100	22	21	0	389.0	2.89
2	Smith	Fred	1890	TL2	AA	5.225	1	5.225	19	13	0	286.0	3.27
3	Cushman	Ed	1890	TL2	AA	3.263	1	3.263	17	21	1	315.7	4.19
4	Sprague	Charlie	1890	TL2	AA	1.399	1	1.399	9	5	0	122.7	3.89
5	Doty	Babe	1890	TL2	AA	0.200	1	0.200	1	0	0	9.0	1.00

TROY TROJANS
Best Seasons and Careers of All-Time

Troy Trojans - Best Position Player Years

Rank	Name	First	Year	Team	Lg	HR	RBI	AVG	Age	PEVA-B
1	Connor	Roger	1880	TRN	NL	3	47	0.332	23	24.092
2	Connor	Roger	1882	TRN	NL	4	42	0.330	25	22.844
3	Ewing	Buck	1882	TRN	NL	2	29	0.271	23	11.039
4	Ferguson	Bob	1881	TRN	NL	1	35	0.283	36	9.032
5	Gillespie	Pete	1880	TRN	NL	2	24	0.243	29	8.975

Troy Trojans - Best Pitcher Years

Rank	Name	First	Year	Team	Lg	W	L	SV	IP	ERA	Age	PEVA-P
1	Welch	Mickey	1880	TRN	NL	34	30	0	574.0	2.54	21	9.344
2	Welch	Mickey	1881	TRN	NL	21	18	0	368.0	2.67	22	5.545
3	Goldsmith	Fred	1879	TRN	NL	2	4	0	63.0	1.57	23	4.900
4	Keefe	Tim	1882	TRN	NL	17	26	0	375.0	2.50	25	4.868
5	Keefe	Tim	1881	TRN	NL	18	27	0	402.0	3.25	24	4.088

Troy Trojans - Top Career Batters

Rank	Name	First	LYear	LTeam	Lg	PEVA-B	YRS	PER	HR	RBI	H	AVE.
1	Connor	Roger	1882	TRN	NL	54.729	3	18.243	9	120	335	0.317
2	Ferguson	Bob	1882	TRN	NL	24.842	4	6.211	1	93	296	0.266
3	Gillespie	Pete	1882	TRN	NL	23.856	3	7.952	4	98	262	0.264
4	Ewing	Buck	1882	TRN	NL	15.012	3	5.004	2	59	165	0.256
5	Cassidy	John	1882	TRN	NL	14.100	4	3.525	1	50	199	0.226
6	Caskin	Ed	1881	TRN	NL	11.572	3	3.857	0	70	206	0.237

Troy Trojans - Top Career Pitchers

Rank	Name	First	LYear	LTeam	Lg	PEVA-P	YRS	PER	W	L	SV	IP	ERA
1	Welch	Mickey	1882	TRN	NL	16.961	3	5.654	69	64	0	1223.0	2.79
2	Keefe	Tim	1882	TRN	NL	12.792	3	4.264	41	59	0	882.0	2.64
3	Goldsmith	Fred	1879	TRN	NL	4.900	1	4.900	2	4	0	63.0	1.57
4	Bradley	George	1879	TRN	NL	2.892	1	2.892	13	40	0	487.0	2.85
5	Salisbury	Harry	1879	TRN	NL	1.642	1	1.642	4	6	0	89.0	2.22

TROY HAYMAKERS
Best Seasons and Careers of All-Time

Troy Haymakers - Best Position Player Years

Rank	Name	First	Year	Team	Lg	HR	RBI	AVG	Age	PEVA-B
1	Force	Davy	1872	TRO	NA	0	16	0.408	23	**18.801**
2	King	Steve	1871	TRO	NA	0	34	0.396	29	**17.901**
3	Pike	Lip	1871	TRO	NA	4	39	0.377	26	**16.526**
4	Allison	Doug	1872	TRO	NA	0	20	0.304	26	**7.853**
5	York	Tom	1871	TRO	NA	2	23	0.255	21	**7.002**

Troy Haymakers - Best Pitcher Years

Rank	Name	First	Year	Team	Lg	W	L	SV	IP	ERA	Age	PEVA-P
1	Zettlein	George	1872	TRO	NA	14	8	0	187.7	2.54	28	**6.833**
2	McMullin	John	1871	TRO	NA	12	15	0	249.0	5.53	23	**6.373**
3	Martin	Phonney	1872	TRO	NA	1	2	0	37.3	5.79	27	**0.686**
4	Flowers	Dickie	1871	TRO	NA	0	0	0	1.0	0.00	21	**0.200**

Troy Haymakers - Top Career Batters

Rank	Name	First	LYear	LTeam	Lg	PEVA-B	YRS	PER	HR	RBI	H	AVE.
1	King	Steve	1872	TRO	NA	**19.998**	2	9.999	0	55	96	0.353
2	Pike	Lip	1871	TRO	NA	**16.526**	1	16.526	4	39	49	0.377
3	Force	Davy	1872	TRO	NA	**10.863**	1	10.863	0	16	53	0.408
4	York	Tom	1871	TRO	NA	**7.002**	1	7.002	2	23	37	0.255
5	Flynn	Clipper	1871	TRO	NA	**6.865**	1	6.865	0	27	48	0.338

Troy Haymakers - Top Career Pitchers

Rank	Name	First	LYear	LTeam	Lg	PEVA-P	YRS	PER	W	L	SV	IP	ERA
1	McMullin	John	1871	TRO	NA	**6.373**	1	6.373	12	15	0	249.0	5.53
2	Zettlein	George	1872	TRO	NA	**4.876**	1	4.876	14	8	0	187.7	2.54
3	Martin	Phonney	1872	TRO	NA	**0.209**	1	0.209	1	2	0	37.3	5.79
4	Flowers	Dickie	1871	TRO	NA	**0.200**	1	0.200	0	0	0	1.0	0.00

WILMINGTON QUICKSTEPS
Best Seasons and Careers of All-Time

Wilmington Quicksteps - Best Position Player Years

Rank	Name	First	Year	Team	Lg	HR	RBI	AVG	Age	PEVA-B
1	Burns	Oyster	1884	WIL	UA	0	NA	0.143	20	2.444
2	Lynch	Tom	1884	WIL	UA	0	NA	0.276	24	1.832
3	Casey	Dennis	1884	WIL	UA	0	NA	0.250	26	1.198
4	Benners	Ike	1884	WIL	UA	0	NA	0.045	28	1.111
5	Bastian	Charlie	1884	WIL	UA	2	NA	0.200	24	0.646

Wilmington Quicksteps - Best Pitcher Years

Rank	Name	First	Year	Team	Lg	W	L	SV	IP	ERA	Age	PEVA-P
1	Bakely	Jersey	1884	WIL	UA	0	2	0	17.0	4.24	20	3.870
2	Tenney	Fred	1884	WIL	UA	0	1	0	8.0	1.12	25	2.110
3	Murphy	John	1884	WIL	UA	0	6	0	48.0	3.00	NA	1.076
4	Nolan	The Only	1884	WIL	UA	1	4	0	40.0	2.92	27	0.999
5	McElroy	Jim	1884	WIL	UA	0	1	0	5.0	10.80	22	0.896

Wilmington Quicksteps - Top Career Batters

Rank	Name	First	LYear	LTeam	Lg	PEVA-B	YRS	PER	HR	RBI	H	AVE.
1	Lynch	Tom	1884	WIL	UA	1.002	1	1.002	0	0	16	0.276
2	Bastian	Charlie	1884	WIL	UA	0.366	1	0.366	2	0	12	0.200
3	Say	Jimmy	1884	WIL	UA	0.257	1	0.257	0	0	13	0.220
4	McCloskey	Bill	1884	WIL	UA	0.200	1	0.200	0	0	3	0.100
5	Casey	Dan	1884	WIL	UA	0.200	1	0.200	0	0	1	0.167

Wilmington Quicksteps - Top Career Pitchers

Rank	Name	First	LYear	LTeam	Lg	PEVA-P	YRS	PER	W	L	SV	IP	ERA
1	Nolan	The Only	1884	WIL	UA	0.999	1	0.999	1	4	0	40.0	2.93
2	Tenney	Fred	1884	WIL	UA	0.393	1	0.393	0	1	0	8.0	1.13
3	Murphy	John	1884	WIL	UA	0.323	1	0.323	0	6	0	48.0	3.00
4	Bastian	Charlie	1884	WIL	UA	0.200	1	0.200	0	0	0	6.0	3.00
5	Casey	Dan	1884	WIL	UA	0.200	1	0.200	1	1	0	18.0	1.00

WORCESTER RUBY LEGS
Best Seasons and Careers of All-Time

Worcester Ruby Legs - Best Position Player Years

Rank	Name	First	Year	Team	Lg	HR	RBI	AVG	Age	PEVA-B
1	Stovey	Harry	1880	WOR	NL	6	28	0.265	24	15.558
2	Stovey	Harry	1882	WOR	NL	5	26	0.289	26	15.306
3	Irwin	Arthur	1880	WOR	NL	1	35	0.259	22	11.326
4	Dickerson	Buttercup	1881	WOR	NL	1	31	0.316	23	10.689
5	Hotaling	Pete	1881	WOR	NL	1	35	0.309	25	9.080

Worcester Ruby Legs - Best Pitcher Years

Rank	Name	First	Year	Team	Lg	W	L	SV	IP	ERA	Age	PEVA-P
1	Richmond	Lee	1880	WOR	NL	32	32	3	590.7	2.15	23	13.353
2	Richmond	Lee	1881	WOR	NL	25	26	0	462.3	3.39	24	7.387
3	Richmond	Lee	1882	WOR	NL	14	33	0	411.0	3.74	25	3.698
4	Corey	Fred	1880	WOR	NL	8	9	2	148.3	2.43	25	1.403
5	Mountain	Frank	1882	WOR	NL	0	5	0	42.0	3.00	22	1.132
	Mountain	Frank	1882	WOR	NL	2	11	0	102.0	3.97	22	1.132

Note: Frank Mountain statistics reflect two stints with Worcester in 1882.

Worcester Ruby Legs - Top Career Batters

Rank	Name	First	LYear	LTeam	Lg	PEVA-B	YRS	PER	HR	RBI	H	AVE.
1	Stovey	Harry	1882	WOR	NL	36.781	3	12.260	13	84	290	0.275
2	Irwin	Arthur	1882	WOR	NL	17.577	3	5.859	1	89	219	0.246
3	Dickerson	Buttercup	1881	WOR	NL	12.548	2	6.274	1	51	155	0.310
4	Creamer	George	1882	WOR	NL	10.746	3	3.582	1	81	190	0.211
5	Richmond	Lee	1882	WOR	NL	9.356	3	3.119	2	90	197	0.250

Worcester Ruby Legs - Top Career Pitchers

Rank	Name	First	LYear	LTeam	Lg	PEVA-P	YRS	PER	W	L	SV	IP	ERA
1	Richmond	Lee	1882	WOR	NL	24.438	3	8.146	71	91	3	1464.0	2.99
2	Corey	Fred	1882	WOR	NL	2.878	3	0.959	15	37	2	476.0	3.27
3	Mountain	Frank	1882	WOR	NL	0.765	2	0.383	2	16	0	144.0	3.69
4	McCormick	Harry	1881	WOR	NL	0.459	1	0.459	1	8	0	78.3	3.56
5	Clarkson	John	1882	WOR	NL	0.200	1	0.200	1	2	0	24.0	4.50

WASHINGTON OLYMPICS
Best Seasons and Careers of All-Time

Washington Olympics - Best Position Player Years

Rank	Name	First	Year	Team	Lg	HR	RBI	AVG	Age	PEVA-B
1	Force	Davy	1871	WS3	NA	0	29	0.278	22	13.071
2	Waterman	Fred	1871	WS3	NA	0	17	0.316	26	13.059
3	Mills	Everett	1871	WS3	NA	1	24	0.274	26	7.910
4	Allison	Doug	1871	WS3	NA	2	27	0.331	25	7.859
5	Hall	George	1871	WS3	NA	2	17	0.294	22	7.458

Washington Olympics - Best Pitcher Years

Rank	Name	First	Year	Team	Lg	W	L	SV	IP	ERA	Age	PEVA-P
1	Brainard	Asa	1871	WS3	NA	12	15	0	264.0	4.50	30	7.299
2	Brainard	Asa	1872	WS3	NA	2	7	0	79.0	6.38	31	0.696
3	Stearns	Bill	1871	WS3	NA	2	0	0	18.0	2.50	18	0.200

Washington Olympics - Top Career Batters

Rank	Name	First	LYear	LTeam	Lg	PEVA-B	YRS	PER	HR	RBI	H	AVE.
1	Waterman	Fred	1872	WS3	NA	13.259	2	6.629	0	23	67	0.330
2	Force	Davy	1871	WS3	NA	13.071	1	13.071	0	29	45	0.278
3	Mills	Everett	1871	WS3	NA	7.910	1	7.910	1	24	43	0.274
4	Allison	Doug	1871	WS3	NA	7.859	1	7.859	2	27	44	0.331
5	Hall	George	1871	WS3	NA	7.458	1	7.458	2	17	40	0.294

Washington Olympics - Top Career Pitchers

Rank	Name	First	LYear	LTeam	Lg	PEVA-P	YRS	PER	W	L	SV	IP	ERA
1	Brainard	Asa	1872	WS3	NA	7.743	2	3.872	14	22	0	343.0	4.93
2	Stearns	Bill	1871	WS3	NA	0.200	1	0.200	2	0	0	18.0	2.50

WASHINGTON NATIONALS
(NATIONAL ASSOCIATION)
Best Seasons and Careers of All-Time

Washington Nationals (National Association) - Best Position Player Years

Rank	Name	First	Year	Team	Lg	HR	RBI	AVG	Age	PEVA-B
1	Hines	Paul	1872	WS4	NA	0	5	0.245	17	0.200
2	Bielaski	Oscar	1872	WS4	NA	0	3	0.196	25	0.200
3	Coughlin	Dennis	1872	WS4	NA	0	7	0.324	NA	0.200
4	Studley	Seem	1872	WS4	NA	0	2	0.095	NA	0.200
5	Hollingshead	Holly	1872	WS4	NA	0	6	0.341	19	0.200

Washington Nationals (National Association) - Best Pitcher Years

Rank	Name	First	Year	Team	Lg	W	L	SV	IP	ERA	Age	PEVA-P
1	Stearns	Bill	1872	WS4	NA	0	11	0	99.0	6.91	19	0.491

Washington Nationals (National Association) - Top Career Batters

Rank	Name	First	LYear	LTeam	Lg	PEVA-B	YRS	PER	HR	RBI	H	AVE.
1	Bielaski	Oscar	1872	WS4	NA	0.200	1	0.200	0	3	9	0.196
2	Coughlin	Dennis	1872	WS4	NA	0.200	1	0.200	0	7	12	0.324
3	Doyle	Joe	1872	WS4	NA	0.200	1	0.200	0	9	12	0.293
4	Lennon	Bill	1872	WS4	NA	0.200	1	0.200	0	6	12	0.222
5	Hines	Paul	1872	WS4	NA	0.200	1	0.200	0	5	12	0.245

Washington Nationals (National Association) - Top Career Pitchers

Rank	Name	First	LYear	LTeam	Lg	PEVA-P	YRS	PER	W	L	SV	IP	ERA
1	Stearns	Bill	1872	WS4	NA	0.668	1	0.668	0	11	0	99.0	6.91

WASHINGTON BLUE LEGS
Best Seasons and Careers of All-Time

Washington Blue Legs - Best Position Player Years

Rank	Name	First	Year	Team	Lg	HR	RBI	AVG	Age	PEVA-B
1	Hines	Paul	1873	WS5	NA	1	29	0.331	18	3.798
2	Beals	Tommy	1873	WS5	NA	0	24	0.272	23	2.452
3	Bielaski	Oscar	1873	WS5	NA	0	23	0.283	26	2.134
4	White	Warren	1873	WS5	NA	0	21	0.269	29	1.811
5	Glenn	John	1873	WS5	NA	1	21	0.265	23	1.739

Washington Blue Legs - Best Pitcher Years

Rank	Name	First	Year	Team	Lg	W	L	SV	IP	ERA	Age	PEVA-P
1	Stearns	Bill	1873	WS5	NA	7	25	0	283.0	4.55	20	2.029
2	Greason	John	1873	WS5	NA	1	6	0	63.0	5.43	22	0.482

Washington Blue Legs - Top Career Batters

Rank	Name	First	LYear	LTeam	Lg	PEVA-B	YRS	PER	HR	RBI	H	AVE.
1	Hines	Paul	1873	WS5	NA	3.798	1	3.798	1	29	60	0.331
2	Beals	Tommy	1873	WS5	NA	2.452	1	2.452	0	24	46	0.272
3	Bielaski	Oscar	1873	WS5	NA	2.134	1	2.134	0	23	49	0.283
4	White	Warren	1873	WS5	NA	1.811	1	1.811	0	21	43	0.269
5	Glenn	John	1873	WS5	NA	1.739	1	1.739	1	21	49	0.265

Washington Blue Legs - Top Career Pitchers

Rank	Name	First	LYear	LTeam	Lg	PEVA-P	YRS	PER	W	L	SV	IP	ERA
1	Stearns	Bill	1873	WS5	NA	2.029	1	2.029	7	25	0	283.0	4.55
2	Greason	John	1873	WS5	NA	0.482	1	0.482	1	6	0	63.0	5.43

WASHINGTON NATIONALS
(NATIONAL ASSOCIATION)
Best Seasons and Careers of All-Time

Washington Nationals (National Association) - Best Position Player Years

Rank	Name	First	Year	Team	Lg	HR	RBI	AVG	Age	PEVA-B
1	Allison	Art	1875	WS6	NA	0	3	0.214	26	**3.744**
2	Hollingshead	Holly	1875	WS6	NA	0	5	0.247	22	**0.719**
3	Stearns	Bill	1875	WS6	NA	0	7	0.256	22	**0.461**
4	Dailey	John	1875	WS6	NA	0	13	0.182	22	**0.445**
5	Ressler	Larry	1875	WS6	NA	0	5	0.194	27	**0.254**

Washington Nationals (National Association) - Best Pitcher Years

Rank	Name	First	Year	Team	Lg	W	L	SV	IP	ERA	Age	PEVA-P
1	Stearns	Bill	1875	WS6	NA	1	14	0	141.0	5.36	22	**1.014**
2	Parks	Bill	1875	WS6	NA	4	8	0	106.7	4.05	26	**0.671**
3	Witherow	Charles	1875	WS6	NA	0	1	0	1.0	18.00	23	**0.200**
4	Mason	Charlie	1875	WS6	NA	0	0	0	2.0	4.50	22	**0.200**

Washington Nationals (National Association) - Top Career Batters

Rank	Name	First	LYear	LTeam	Lg	PEVA-B	YRS	PER	HR	RBI	H	AVE.
1	Allison	Art	1875	WS6	NA	**1.461**	1	1.461	0	3	24	0.214
2	Hollingshead	Holly	1875	WS6	NA	**0.719**	1	0.719	0	5	20	0.247
3	Stearns	Bill	1875	WS6	NA	**0.461**	1	0.461	0	7	20	0.256
4	Dailey	John	1875	WS6	NA	**0.415**	1	0.415	0	13	20	0.182
5	Ressler	Larry	1875	WS6	NA	**0.254**	1	0.254	0	5	21	0.194

Washington Nationals (National Association) - Top Career Pitchers

Rank	Name	First	LYear	LTeam	Lg	PEVA-P	YRS	PER	W	L	SV	IP	ERA
1	Stearns	Bill	1875	WS6	NA	**1.014**	1	1.014	1	14	0	141.0	5.36
2	Parks	Bill	1875	WS6	NA	**0.639**	1	0.639	4	8	0	106.7	4.05
3	Mason	Charlie	1875	WS6	NA	**0.200**	1	0.200	0	0	0	2.0	4.50
4	Witherow	Charles	1875	WS6	NA	**0.200**	1	0.200	0	1	0	1.0	18.00

WASHINGTON NATIONALS
(AMERICAN ASSOCIATION)
Best Seasons and Careers of All-Time

Washington Nationals (American Association) - Best Position Player Years

Rank	Name	First	Year	Team	Lg	HR	RBI	AVG	Age	PEVA-B
1	Fennelly	Frank	1884	WS7	AA	2	0	0.292	24	16.134
2	Olin	Frank	1884	WS7	AA	0	0	0.386	24	2.457
3	Humphries	John	1884	WS7	AA	0	0	0.176	23	1.958
4	Hawkes	Thorny	1884	WS7	AA	0	0	0.278	32	1.209
5	Gladman	Buck	1884	WS7	AA	1	0	0.156	21	0.999

Washington Nationals (American Association) - Best Pitcher Years

Rank	Name	First	Year	Team	Lg	W	L	SV	IP	ERA	Age	PEVA-P
1	Barr	Bob	1884	WS7	AA	9	23	0	281.0	3.46	28	3.228
2	Hamill	John	1884	WS7	AA	2	17	0	156.7	4.48	24	0.855
3	Trumbull	Ed	1884	WS7	AA	1	9	0	84.0	4.71	24	0.622
4	Smith	Edgar (EE)	1884	WS7	AA	0	2	0	22.0	4.91	22	0.200

Washington Nationals (American Association) - Top Career Batters

Rank	Name	First	LYear	LTeam	Lg	PEVA-B	YRS	PER	HR	RBI	H	AVE.
1	Fennelly	Frank	1884	WS7	AA	10.940	1	10.940	2	0	75	0.292
2	Humphries	John	1884	WS7	AA	1.470	1	1.470	0	0	34	0.176
3	Hawkes	Thorny	1884	WS7	AA	1.209	1	1.209	0	0	42	0.278
4	Olin	Frank	1884	WS7	AA	1.179	1	1.179	0	0	32	0.386
5	Gladman	Buck	1884	WS7	AA	0.999	1	0.999	1	0	35	0.156

Washington Nationals (American Association) - Top Career Pitchers

Rank	Name	First	LYear	LTeam	Lg	PEVA-P	YRS	PER	W	L	SV	IP	ERA
1	Barr	Bob	1884	WS7	AA	2.196	1	2.196	9	23	0	281.0	3.46
2	Hamill	John	1884	WS7	AA	0.855	1	0.855	2	17	0	156.7	4.48
3	Trumbull	Ed	1884	WS7	AA	0.622	1	0.622	1	9	0	84.0	4.71
4	Smith	Edgar (EE)	1884	WS7	AA	0.200	1	0.200	0	2	0	22.0	4.91

WASHINGTON NATIONALS
(NATIONAL LEAGUE)
Best Seasons and Careers of All-Time

Washington Nationals (National League) - Best Position Player Years

Rank	Name	First	Year	Team	Lg	HR	RBI	AVG	Age	PEVA-B
1	Hoy	Dummy	1888	WS8	NL	2	29	0.274	26	15.180
2	Hines	Paul	1886	WS8	NL	9	56	0.312	31	12.931
3	Wilmot	Walt	1889	WS8	NL	9	57	0.289	26	12.119
4	Hines	Paul	1887	WS8	NL	10	72	0.308	32	9.751
5	Hoy	Dummy	1889	WS8	NL	0	39	0.274	27	9.367

Washington Nationals (National League) - Best Pitcher Years

Rank	Name	First	Year	Team	Lg	W	L	SV	IP	ERA	Age	PEVA-P
1	Whitney	Jim	1887	WS8	NL	24	21	0	404.7	3.22	30	15.607
2	O'Day	Hank	1888	WS8	NL	16	29	0	403.0	3.10	26	3.935
3	Shaw	Dupee	1886	WS8	NL	13	31	0	385.7	3.34	27	3.651
4	Whitney	Jim	1888	WS8	NL	18	21	0	325.0	3.05	31	3.090
5	Gilmore	Frank	1886	WS8	NL	4	4	0	75.0	2.52	22	2.525

Washington Nationals (National League) - Top Career Batters

Rank	Name	First	LYear	LTeam	Lg	PEVA-B	YRS	PER	HR	RBI	H	AVE.
1	Hoy	Dummy	1889	WS8	NL	24.547	2	12.273	2	68	277	0.274
2	Hines	Paul	1887	WS8	NL	22.682	2	11.341	19	128	299	0.310
3	Wilmot	Walt	1889	WS8	NL	17.800	2	8.900	13	100	231	0.255
4	O'Brien	Billy	1889	WS8	NL	11.475	3	3.825	28	139	245	0.248
5	Myers	Al	1889	WS8	NL	8.266	3	2.755	4	102	234	0.225

Washington Nationals (National League) - Top Career Pitchers

Rank	Name	First	LYear	LTeam	Lg	PEVA-P	YRS	PER	W	L	SV	IP	ERA
1	Whitney	Jim	1888	WS8	NL	18.697	2	9.349	42	42	0	729.7	3.15
2	O'Day	Hank	1889	WS8	NL	8.680	4	2.170	28	61	0	814.7	3.51
3	Gilmore	Frank	1888	WS8	NL	5.022	3	1.674	12	33	0	405.3	4.26
4	Shaw	Dupee	1888	WS8	NL	4.986	3	1.662	20	47	0	592.0	4.42
5	Keefe	George	1889	WS8	NL	3.108	4	0.777	14	29	0	383.3	4.53

WASHINGTON STATESMEN/SENATORS
Best Seasons and Careers of All-Time

Washington Statesmen/Senators - Best Position Player Years

Rank	Name	First	Year	Team	Lg	HR	RBI	AVG	Age	PEVA-B
1	Joyce	Bill	1896	WSN	NL	8	51	0.313	31	26.720
2	Freeman	Buck	1899	WSN	NL	25	122	0.318	28	20.576
3	Joyce	Bill	1895	WSN	NL	17	95	0.312	30	19.182
4	Selbach	Kip	1897	WSN	NL	5	59	0.313	25	17.820
5	McGuire	Deacon	1895	WSN	NL	10	97	0.336	32	17.188
6	Anderson	John	1898	WSN	NL	9	71	0.305	25	16.096
7	Hoy	Dummy	1892	WSN	NL	3	75	0.280	30	15.479
8	Joyce	Bill	1894	WSN	NL	17	89	0.355	29	15.302
9	Selbach	Kip	1896	WSN	NL	5	100	0.304	24	15.214
10	Selbach	Kip	1898	WSN	NL	3	60	0.303	26	14.725
11	Selbach	Kip	1895	WSN	NL	6	55	0.322	23	13.602
12	DeMontreville	Gene	1896	WSN	NL	8	77	0.343	23	12.897
13	McGuire	Deacon	1891	WS9	AA	3	66	0.303	28	11.914
14	DeMontreville	Gene	1897	WSN	NL	3	93	0.341	24	11.581
15	McGann	Dan	1899	WSN	NL	5	58	0.343	28	11.364
16	Abbey	Charlie	1894	WSN	NL	7	101	0.314	28	11.185

Washington Statesmen/Senators - Best Pitcher Years

Rank	Name	First	Year	Team	Lg	W	L	SV	IP	ERA	Age	PEVA-P
1	Mercer	Win	1897	WSN	NL	20	20	3	333.0	3.24	23	18.174
2	Mercer	Win	1896	WSN	NL	25	18	0	366.3	4.13	22	12.345
3	McJames	Doc	1897	WSN	NL	15	23	2	323.7	3.61	23	11.355
4	Mercer	Win	1894	WSN	NL	17	23	3	336.3	3.85	20	9.525
5	Killen	Frank	1892	WSN	NL	29	26	0	459.7	3.31	22	7.801

Washington Statesmen/Senators (WSN, WS9) - Top Career Batters

Rank	Name	First	LYear	LTeam	Lg	PEVA-B	YRS	PER	HR	RBI	H	AVE.
1	McGuire	Deacon	1899	WSN	NL	66.121	9	7.347	32	502	990	0.298
2	Selbach	Kip	1898	WSN	NL	65.794	5	13.159	26	345	736	0.310
3	Joyce	Bill	1896	WSN	NL	51.923	3	17.308	42	235	371	0.326
4	Abbey	Charlie	1897	WSN	NL	25.580	5	5.116	19	280	492	0.281
5	DeMontreville	Gene	1897	WSN	NL	24.679	3	8.226	11	179	386	0.337
6	Cartwright	Ed	1897	WSN	NL	24.186	4	6.046	16	273	472	0.295
7	Freeman	Buck	1899	WSN	NL	23.261	3	7.754	28	144	230	0.323
8	Hoy	Dummy	1893	WSN	NL	23.095	2	11.548	3	120	304	0.263
9	Farrell	Duke	1899	WSN	NL	19.711	5	3.942	6	212	377	0.301
10	Radford	Paul	1894	WSN	NL	16.461	3	5.487	3	120	314	0.242
11	Brown	Tom	1898	WSN	NL	16.340	4	4.085	9	122	306	0.280
12	Anderson	John	1898	WSN	NL	13.310	1	13.310	9	71	131	0.305
13	Larkin	Henry	1893	WSN	NL	12.679	2	6.340	12	169	231	0.295
14	Hassamaer	Bill	1895	WSN	NL	10.007	2	5.004	5	150	259	0.304

Washington Statesmen/Senators (WSN, WS9) - Top Career Pitchers

Rank	Name	First	LYear	LTeam	Lg	PEVA-P	YRS	PER	W	L	SV	IP	ERA
1	Mercer	Win	1899	WSN	NL	49.924	6	8.321	94	116	8	1766.3	4.11
2	McJames	Doc	1897	WSN	NL	16.405	3	5.468	28	44	3	621.0	3.86

3	Weyhing	Gus	1899	WSN	NL	**13.857**	2	6.928	32	47	0	695.7	4.53
4	Maul	Al	1897	WSN	NL	**11.712**	5	2.342	38	44	0	701.3	4.80
5	Killen	Frank	1899	WSN	NL	**10.502**	3	3.501	35	37	0	600.0	3.42

Note: Previous Names of Franchise: Washington Statesmen (WS9) 1899; Washington Senators (WSN) 1892-1899.

WASHINGTON NATIONALS
(UNION LEAGUE)
Best Seasons and Careers of All-Time

Washington Nationals (Union League) - Best Position Player Years

Rank	Name	First	Year	Team	Lg	HR	RBI	AVG	Age	PEVA-B
1	Moore	Harry	1884	WSU	UA	1	NA	0.336	NA	14.018
2	McCormick	Jerry	1884	WSU	UA	0	NA	0.217	NA	5.672
3	Baker	Phil	1884	WSU	UA	1	NA	0.288	28	5.563
4	Evers	Tom	1884	WSU	UA	0	NA	0.232	32	3.744
5	Wise	Bill	1884	WSU	UA	2	NA	0.233	23	2.817

Washington Nationals (Union League) - Best Pitcher Years

Rank	Name	First	Year	Team	Lg	W	L	SV	IP	ERA	Age	PEVA-P
1	Daily	Hugh	1884	WSU	UA	1	1	0	16.0	2.25	27	10.851
2	Wise	Bill	1884	WSU	UA	23	18	0	364.3	3.04	23	4.409
3	Geggus	Charlie	1884	WSU	UA	10	9	0	177.3	2.54	22	3.031
4	Voss	Alex	1884	WSU	UA	5	14	0	186.3	3.57	26	1.420
5	Powell	Abner	1884	WSU	UA	6	12	0	134.0	3.43	24	0.990

Washington Nationals (Union League) - Top Career Batters

Rank	Name	First	LYear	LTeam	Lg	PEVA-B	YRS	PER	HR	RBI	H	AVE.
1	Moore	Harry	1884	WSU	UA	14.018	1	14.018	1	0	155	0.336
2	Baker	Phil	1884	WSU	UA	5.563	1	5.563	1	0	107	0.288
3	Evers	Tom	1884	WSU	UA	3.744	1	3.744	0	0	99	0.232
4	Wise	Bill	1884	WSU	UA	2.817	1	2.817	2	0	79	0.233
5	Fulmer	Chris	1884	WSU	UA	2.425	1	2.425	0	0	50	0.276

Washington Nationals (Union League) - Top Career Pitchers

Rank	Name	First	LYear	LTeam	Lg	PEVA-P	YRS	PER	W	L	SV	IP	ERA
1	Wise	Bill	1884	WSU	UA	4.409	1	4.409	23	18	0	364.3	3.04
2	Geggus	Charlie	1884	WSU	UA	3.031	1	3.031	10	9	0	177.3	2.54
3	Voss	Alex	1884	WSU	UA	1.105	1	1.105	5	14	0	186.3	3.57
4	Powell	Abner	1884	WSU	UA	0.990	1	0.990	6	12	0	134.0	3.43
5	Lockwood	Milo	1884	WSU	UA	0.614	1	0.614	1	9	0	67.7	7.45

Note1: For players with more than one team during the year, actual stats reflect stint with team only, PEVA values reflect Total Year. Note2: Franchises with less than 5 players above 10.000 PEVA are listed with the five highest players. Note3: Age = Player age at end of year. Note4: LYEAR, LTEAM, LG reflects last year with team.

CHAPTER EIGHT

BEST POSTSEASONS EVER
BATTING/PITCHING (1871-2019)

PEVA Player Ratings Postseason Boxscore

PEVA	One Word	Description	Post PEVA
64.000	Maximum	Maximum Player Rating	6.400
32.000	Fantastic	MVP/Cy Young Award Candidate	3.200
20.000	Great	All-League	2.000
15.000	Very Good	All-Star Caliber	1.500
10.000	Good	Plus Starter	1.000
3.500	Average	Bench Player	0.350
0.200	Minimum	Minimum Player Rating	0.020

Ranked by Postseason PEVA Player Ratings, Postseason Grades reflect 10% of Regular Season Values

Players listed below reflect the Best Postseasons Ever for batters and pitchers. They include players from the three distinct eras of postseason professional Major League Baseball; the pre1900 era, noted by the Championship Series (CS) from 1884-1890 and 1892; the World Series (WS) only round postseasons between 1903 and 1968 (with no postseason held in 1904) between the National League regular season champ and the American League regular season champ; and the Multiple Round Playoffs (PL) beginning in 1969 through today, except for the strike season of 1994.

Best Batting Postseasons Ever
(Through 2019 Postseason)

Rank	Year	Name	First	Type	Team	Lg	G	HR	RBI	AVG	PA	RPR	FV	PEVA-B REG	PEVA-B POST
1	1956	Berra	Yogi	WS	NYA	AL	7	3	10	0.360	29	15	2.10	64.000	6.400
1	1932	Gehrig	Lou	WS	NYA	AL	4	3	8	0.529	20	17	1.08	64.000	6.400
1	1914	Gowdy	Hank	WS	BSN	NL	4	1	3	0.545	16	6	2.10	64.000	6.400
1	1989	Henderson	Rickey	PL	OAK	AL	9	3	8	0.441	44	20	1.31	64.000	6.400
5	1915	Hooper	Harry	WS	BOS	AL	5	2	3	0.350	23	7	1.12	62.837	6.284
6	1933	Ott	Mel	WS	NY1	NL	5	2	4	0.389	22	7	1.45	62.642	6.264
7	1967	Yastrzemski	Carl	WS	BOS	AL	7	3	5	0.400	30	9	1.70	62.624	6.262
8	2009	Rodriguez	Alex	PL	NYA	AL	15	6	18	0.365	68	33	1.57	62.492	6.249
9	1966	Robinson	Frank	WS	BAL	AL	4	2	3	0.286	16	7	1.49	62.344	6.234
10	1926	Ruth	Babe	WS	NYA	AL	7	4	5	0.300	31	11	1.47	62.088	6.209
11	1923	Ruth	Babe	WS	NYA	AL	6	3	3	0.368	27	11	1.23	61.557	6.156
12	1905	Bresnahan	Roger	WS	NY1	NL	5	0	1	0.313	22	4	1.91	61.259	6.126
13	1915	Lewis	Duffy	WS	BOS	AL	5	1	5	0.444	20	6	1.70	61.085	6.109
14	1911	Baker	Frank	WS	PHA	AL	6	2	5	0.375	25	12	1.49	60.480	6.048
15	1939	Keller	Charlie	WS	NYA	AL	4	3	6	0.438	17	14	1.37	60.460	6.046
16	2002	Bonds	Barry	PL	SFN	NL	17	8	16	0.356	74	34	1.22	60.380	6.038
17	1983	Matthews	Gary	PL	PHI	NL	9	4	9	0.333	34	14	1.70	60.342	6.034
18	1892	Duffy	Hugh	CS	BSN	NL	6	1	9	0.462	27	12	1.46	60.186	6.019
19	1927	Ruth	Babe	WS	NYA	AL	4	2	7	0.400	18	11	1.53	60.021	6.002
20	1960	Mantle	Mickey	WS	NYA	AL	7	3	11	0.400	33	19	1.52	59.978	5.998
21	1928	Ruth	Babe	WS	NYA	AL	4	3	4	0.625	17	13	1.53	59.503	5.950

Rank	Year	Name	First	Type	Team	Lg	G	HR	RBI	AVG	PA	RPR	FV	PEVA-B REG	PEVA-B POST
22	1928	Gehrig	Lou	WS	NYA	AL	4	4	9	0.545	17	14	1.30	57.470	5.747
23	1913	Collins	Eddie	WS	PHA	AL	5	0	3	0.421	22	8	1.50	56.762	5.676
24	1930	Simmons	Al	WS	PHA	AL	6	2	4	0.364	24	8	1.70	56.665	5.667
25	1931	Martin	Pepper	WS	SLN	NL	7	1	5	0.500	26	10	1.66	56.065	5.606
26	1967	Brock	Lou	WS	SLN	NL	7	1	3	0.414	31	11	1.54	56.032	5.603
27	1944	McQuinn	George	WS	SLA	AL	6	1	5	0.438	24	7	1.03	55.103	5.510
28	2013	Ortiz	David	PL	BOS	AL	16	5	13	0.353	68	25	1.09	54.190	5.438
29	1963	Skowron	Bill	WS	LAN	NL	4	1	3	0.385	14	5	1.40	54.172	5.417
30	2003	Rodriguez	Ivan	PL	FLO	NL	17	3	17	0.313	77	27	1.88	53.829	5.383
31	1931	Simmons	Al	WS	PHA	AL	7	2	8	0.333	30	12	1.70	53.555	5.356
32	1978	Jackson	Reggie	PL	NYA	AL	10	4	14	0.417	45	21	1.44	53.527	5.353
33	1977	Jackson	Reggie	PL	NYA	AL	11	5	9	0.306	42	20	1.69	53.085	5.309
34	1884	Gilligan	Barney	CS	PRO	NL	3	0	2	0.444	9	5	2.07	53.062	5.306
35	1952	Snider	Duke	WS	BRO	NL	7	4	8	0.345	31	13	1.65	52.801	5.280
36	1985	Brett	George	PL	KCA	AL	14	3	6	0.360	61	17	1.59	52.225	5.223
37	1950	DiMaggio	Joe	WS	NYA	AL	4	1	2	0.308	17	4	1.45	52.107	5.211
38	1913	Baker	Frank	WS	PHA	AL	5	1	7	0.450	21	9	1.27	51.709	5.171
39	1993	Molitor	Paul	PL	TOR	AL	12	3	13	0.447	55	30	1.17	51.398	5.140
40	1972	Bench	Johnny	PL	CIN	NL	12	2	3	0.293	48	10	2.00	50.909	5.091
41	1915	Luderus	Fred	WS	PHI	NL	5	1	6	0.438	18	7	1.12	50.662	5.066
42	1948	Elliott	Bob	WS	BSN	NL	6	2	5	0.333	23	9	1.19	50.216	5.022
43	1957	Aaron	Hank	WS	ML1	NL	7	3	7	0.393	29	12	1.44	50.155	5.016
44	2000	Piazza	Mike	PL	NYN	NL	14	4	8	0.302	62	19	2.09	49.615	4.961
45	1941	Keller	Charlie	WS	NYA	AL	5	0	5	0.389	21	10	1.55	49.450	4.945
46	1970	Robinson	Brooks	PL	BAL	AL	8	2	8	0.485	34	16	1.70	49.434	4.943
47	1962	Tresh	Tom	WS	NYA	AL	7	1	4	0.321	30	9	1.56	49.420	4.942
48	2012	Sandoval	Pablo	PL	SFN	NL	16	6	13	0.364	70	22	1.25	48.613	4.861
49	1930	Cochrane	Mickey	WS	PHA	AL	6	2	4	0.222	24	9	1.84	48.284	4.828
50	1990	Hatcher	Billy	PL	CIN	NL	8	1	4	0.519	31	12	1.70	48.270	4.827
51	1945	Greenberg	Hank	WS	DET	AL	7	2	7	0.304	31	14	1.13	48.038	4.804
52	1962	Hiller	Chuck	WS	SFN	NL	7	1	5	0.269	29	9	1.33	47.984	4.798
53	1953	Martin	Billy	WS	NYA	AL	6	2	8	0.500	25	13	1.41	47.498	4.750
54	1981	Garvey	Steve	PL	LAN	NL	16	3	6	0.359	66	15	1.40	47.466	4.747
55	2004	Beltran	Carlos	PL	HOU	NL	12	8	14	0.435	56	35	1.54	47.219	4.722
56	2000	Jeter	Derek	PL	NYA	AL	16	4	9	0.317	75	22	1.65	46.858	4.686
57	1936	Powell	Jake	WS	NYA	AL	6	1	5	0.455	26	13	1.48	46.763	4.676
58	1925	Harris	Joe	WS	WS1	AL	7	3	6	0.440	28	11	1.44	46.667	4.667
59	1984	Trammell	Alan	PL	DET	AL	8	3	9	0.419	37	16	1.40	46.577	4.658
60	1964	McCarver	Tim	WS	SLN	NL	7	1	5	0.478	29	9	2.07	46.461	4.646
61	1951	Dark	Alvin	WS	NY1	NL	6	1	4	0.417	26	9	1.41	45.968	4.597
62	1996	Williams	Bernie	PL	NYA	AL	15	6	15	0.345	69	29	1.64	44.716	4.472
63	1989	Clark	Will	PL	SFN	NL	9	2	8	0.472	39	18	1.40	44.640	4.464
64	1927	Koenig	Mark	WS	NYA	AL	4	0	2	0.500	18	7	1.60	44.321	4.432
65	1974	Garvey	Steve	PL	LAN	NL	9	2	6	0.385	40	12	1.19	44.304	4.430
66	1968	Brock	Lou	WS	SLN	NL	7	2	5	0.464	31	11	1.27	44.197	4.420
67	1998	Brosius	Scott	PL	NYA	AL	13	4	15	0.383	51	21	1.54	44.197	4.420
68	1920	Speaker	Tris	WS	CLE	AL	7	0	1	0.320	28	7	1.62	43.495	4.349
69	1990	Sabo	Chris	PL	CIN	NL	10	3	8	0.368	42	11	1.70	43.443	4.344
70	1981	Carter	Gary	PL	MON	NL	10	2	6	0.429	41	12	2.10	43.353	4.335

Rank	Year	Name	First	Type	Team	Lg	G	HR	RBI	AVG	PA	RPR	FV	PEVA-B REG	PEVA-B POST
71	1973	Staub	Rusty	PL	NYN	NL	11	4	11	0.341	46	16	1.43	43.309	4.331
72	1954	Thompson	Hank	WS	NY1	NL	4	0	2	0.364	18	8	1.70	43.225	4.322
73	1973	Campaneris	Bert	PL	OAK	AL	12	3	6	0.308	57	15	1.69	43.006	4.301
74	1976	Bench	Johnny	PL	CIN	NL	7	3	7	0.444	28	14	2.10	42.608	4.261
75	2017	Altuve	Jose	PL	HOU	SL	18	7	14	0.310	80	28	1.25	42.525	4.253
76	2016	Bryant	Kris	PL	CHN	NL	17	3	8	0.308	74	19	1.24	42.389	4.239
77	1886	O'Neill	Tip	WS	SL4	AA	6	2	5	0.400	24	9	1.59	42.090	4.209
78	1890	Wolf	Jimmy	WS	LS2	AA	7	0	8	0.360	28	12	1.37	41.638	4.164
79	1965	Fairly	Ron	WS	LAN	NL	7	2	6	0.379	29	13	1.44	41.621	4.162
80	2015	Murphy	David	PL	NYN	NL	14	7	11	0.328	64	24	1.09	41.550	4.155
81	2017	Springer	George	PL	HOU	AL	18	6	9	0.292	83	22	1.62	41.398	4.140
82	1970	Powell	Boog	PL	BAL	AL	8	3	11	0.355	36	19	1.30	40.833	4.083
83	1959	Kluszewski	Ted	WS	CHA	AL	6	3	10	0.391	25	15	1.40	40.658	4.066
84	1964	Mantle	Mickey	WS	NYA	AL	7	3	8	0.333	30	16	1.00	40.433	4.043
85	1971	Robertson	Bob	PL	PIT	NL	11	6	11	0.317	45	20	1.16	40.364	4.036
86	1979	Stargell	Willie	PL	PIT	NL	10	5	13	0.415	46	22	1.13	40.097	4.010
87	1945	Cavarretta	Phil	WS	CHN	NL	7	1	5	0.423	31	12	1.23	39.955	3.995
88	2011	Freese	David	PL	SLN	NL	18	5	21	0.397	71	33	1.35	39.910	3.991
89	1906	Rohe	George	WS	CHA	AL	6	0	4	0.333	25	6	1.47	39.810	3.981
90	2004	Pujols	Albert	PL	SLN	NL	15	6	14	0.414	67	29	1.40	39.515	3.951
91	1941	Gordon	Joe	WS	NYA	AL	5	1	5	0.500	21	7	1.14	39.391	3.939
92	1947	Lindell	Johnny	WS	NYA	AL	6	0	7	0.500	24	10	1.32	38.878	3.888
93	2005	Berkman	Lance	PL	HOU	NL	14	2	14	0.333	60	20	1.52	38.818	3.882
94	2007	Ramirez	Manny	PL	BOS	AL	14	4	16	0.348	63	27	1.61	38.517	3.852
95	2018	Pearce	Steve	PL	BOS	AL	13	4	11	0.289	47	23	1.23	38.424	3.842
96	2019	Rendon	Anthony	PL	WAS	NL	17	3	15	0.328	75	26	1.57	38.169	3.817
97	1885	Anson	Cap	WS	CHN	NL	7	0	0	0.423	28	8	1.31	38.108	3.811
98	1908	Schulte	Frank	WS	CHN	NL	5	0	2	0.389	22	6	1.70	38.101	3.810
99	1996	Lopez	Javy	PL	ATL	NL	15	3	8	0.365	61	20	2.10	38.068	3.807
100	1907	Steinfeldt	Harry	WS	CHN	NL	5	0	2	0.471	21	4	1.47	38.023	3.802
101	1884	Denny	Jerry	WS	PRO	NL	3	1	2	0.444	9	5	1.49	38.006	3.801
102	1938	Gordon	Joe	WS	NYA	AL	4	1	6	0.400	16	9	1.25	37.632	3.763
103	1984	Gibson	Kirk	PL	DET	AL	8	3	9	0.367	37	15	1.31	37.620	3.762
104	1939	Dickey	Bill	WS	NYA	AL	4	2	5	0.267	16	7	2.10	37.019	3.702
105	1972	Tenace	Gene	PL	OAK	AL	12	4	10	0.225	45	16	1.73	36.996	3.700
106	1952	Mantle	Mickey	WS	NYA	AL	7	2	3	0.345	32	8	1.52	36.978	3.698
107	1885	Kelly	King	WS	CHN	NL	7	0	0	0.346	28	9	1.45	36.670	3.667
108	2004	Ortiz	David	PL	BOS	AL	14	5	19	0.400	68	32	1.36	36.660	3.666
109	2016	Rizzo	Anthony	PL	CHN	NL	17	3	10	0.277	73	21	1.40	36.637	3.664
110	1993	Dykstra	Lenny	PL	PHI	NL	12	6	10	0.313	60	24	1.70	36.399	3.640
111	1922	Groh	Heinie	WS	NY1	NL	5	0	0	0.474	21	4	1.70	36.327	3.633
112	1979	Garner	Phil	PL	PIT	NL	10	1	6	0.472	41	14	1.42	36.032	3.603
113	1884	Hines	Paul	WS	PRO	NL	3	0	1	0.250	11	6	1.57	35.971	3.597
114	1949	Brown	Bobby	WS	NYA	AL	4	0	5	0.500	14	9	1.57	35.957	3.596
115	1946	York	Rudy	WS	BOS	AL	7	2	5	0.261	30	11	1.00	35.709	3.571
116	2011	Pujols	Albert	PL	SLN	NL	18	5	16	0.353	82	31	1.40	35.526	3.553
117	1997	Sheffield	Gary	PL	FLO	NL	16	3	7	0.320	71	20	1.43	35.476	3.548
118	1914	Evers	Johnny	WS	BSN	NL	4	0	2	0.438	18	4	1.44	34.849	3.485
119	2007	Ortiz	David	PL	BOS	AL	14	3	10	0.370	63	26	0.85	34.699	3.470

Rank	Year	Name	First	Type	Team	Lg	G	HR	RBI	AVG	PA	RPR	FV	PEVA-B REG	PEVA-B POST
120	2010	Cruz	Nelson	PL	TEX	AL	16	6	11	0.317	63	24	1.63	34.650	3.465
121	1916	Hooper	Harry	WS	BOS	AL	5	0	1	0.333	24	7	1.64	34.628	3.463
122	1972	Rose	Pete	PL	CIN	NL	12	1	4	0.313	54	8	1.69	34.616	3.462
123	1991	Puckett	Kirby	PL	MIN	AL	12	4	9	0.333	54	17	1.70	34.611	3.461
124	1935	Gehringer	Charlie	WS	DET	AL	6	0	4	0.375	27	8	1.50	34.526	3.453
125	1957	Mathews	Eddie	WS	ML1	NL	7	1	4	0.227	31	8	1.70	34.409	3.441
126	1913	Schang	Wally	WS	PHA	AL	4	1	7	0.357	16	9	1.64	34.310	3.431
127	1980	Aikens	Willie	PL	KCA	AL	9	4	10	0.387	37	15	1.06	34.232	3.423
128	1971	Clemente	Roberto	PL	PIT	NL	11	2	8	0.383	50	13	1.64	34.168	3.417
129	1976	Chambliss	Chris	PL	NYA	AL	9	2	9	0.432	39	15	1.15	34.099	3.410
130	1919	Jackson	Joe	WS	CHA	AL	8	1	6	0.375	33	11	1.50	34.072	3.407
131	1961	Skowron	Bill	WS	NYA	AL	5	1	5	0.353	20	8	1.40	33.875	3.387
132	1988	Hatcher	Mickey	PL	LAN	NL	11	2	8	0.300	44	17	1.17	33.856	3.386
133	1958	Bauer	Hank	WS	NYA	AL	7	4	8	0.323	31	14	1.39	33.818	3.382
134	1974	Wynn	Jimmy	PL	LAN	NL	9	1	4	0.192	40	9	1.49	33.753	3.375
135	1968	Kaline	Al	WS	DET	AL	7	2	8	0.379	30	14	1.56	33.588	3.359
136	2006	Molina	Yadier	PL	SLN	NL	16	2	8	0.358	59	13	1.80	33.577	3.358
137	1905	Donlin	Mike	WS	NY1	NL	5	0	1	0.263	22	5	1.60	33.566	3.357
138	1912	Herzog	Buck	WS	NY1	NL	8	0	5	0.400	34	11	1.37	33.397	3.340
139	2009	Ruiz	Carlos	PL	PHI	NL	15	2	9	0.341	57	17	2.10	33.283	3.328
140	1967	Maris	Roger	WS	SLN	NL	7	1	7	0.385	30	10	1.31	32.928	3.293
141	1924	Goslin	Goose	WS	WS1	AL	7	3	7	0.344	32	11	1.67	32.752	3.275
142	2007	Youkilis	Kevin	PL	BOS	AL	14	4	10	0.388	59	26	1.08	32.721	3.272
143	1910	Murphy	Danny	WS	PHA	AL	5	1	9	0.400	22	15	1.45	32.655	3.266
144	2010	Ross	Cody	PL	SFN	NL	15	5	10	0.294	59	21	1.52	32.642	3.264
145	1938	Crosetti	Frankie	WS	NYA	AL	4	1	6	0.250	19	7	1.75	32.496	3.250
146	2012	Beltran	Carlos	PL	SLN	NL	12	3	6	0.357	50	14	1.44	32.326	3.233
147	1958	Mantle	Mickey	WS	NYA	AL	7	2	3	0.250	31	7	1.51	31.869	3.187
148	1955	Snider	Duke	WS	BRO	NL	7	4	7	0.320	28	12	1.47	31.339	3.134
149	1955	Berra	Yogi	WS	NYA	AL	7	1	2	0.417	28	7	2.08	31.329	3.133
150	1921	Meusel	Irish	WS	NY1	NL	8	1	7	0.345	31	11	1.64	31.235	3.123

Best Pitching Postseasons Ever
(Through 2019 Postseason)

Rank	Year	Name	First	Type	Team	Lg	W	L	SV	IP	ERA	WHIP9	SO/W	PEVA-P REG	PEVA-P POST
1	2007	Beckett	Josh	PL	BOS	AL	4	0	0	30.0	1.20	6.30	17.50	64.000	6.400
2	1905	Mathewson	Christy	WS	NY1	NL	3	0	0	27.0	0.00	5.00	18.00	63.468	6.347
3	1961	Ford	Whitey	WS	NYA	AL	2	0	0	14.0	0.00	4.50	7.00	63.199	6.320
4	1884	Radbourn	Charley	CS	PRO	NL	3	0	0	22.0	0.00	4.50	17.00	61.571	6.157
5	1965	Koufax	Sandy	WS	LAN	NL	2	1	0	24.0	0.38	6.75	5.80	61.427	6.143
6	1951	Lopat	Ed	WS	NYA	AL	2	0	0	18.0	0.50	6.50	1.33	58.207	5.821
7	1967	Gibson	Bob	WS	SLN	NL	3	0	0	27.0	1.00	6.33	5.20	55.887	5.589
8	1988	Hershiser	Orel	PL	LAN	NL	3	0	1	42.7	1.05	8.02	2.46	55.625	5.562
9	1940	Newsom	Bobo	WS	DET	AL	2	1	0	26.0	1.38	7.62	4.25	55.224	5.522
10	2009	Lee	Cliff	PL	PHI	NL	4	0	0	40.3	1.56	7.36	5.50	55.124	5.512
11	1995	Hershiser	Orel	PL	CLE	AL	4	1	0	35.3	1.53	7.39	3.89	54.868	5.487
12	1926	Alexander	Pete	WS	SLN	NL	2	0	1	20.3	1.33	7.08	4.25	53.897	5.390
13	2008	Hamels	Cole	PL	PHI	NL	4	0	0	35.0	1.80	8.23	3.33	53.813	5.381
14	1920	Coveleski	Stan	WS	CLE	AL	3	0	0	27.0	0.67	5.67	4.00	52.358	5.236
15	1968	Gibson	Bob	WS	SLN	NL	2	1	0	27.0	1.67	7.33	8.75	51.441	5.144
16	2001	Schilling	Curt	PL	ARI	NL	4	0	0	48.3	1.12	5.77	9.33	50.112	5.011
17	1996	Smoltz	John	PL	ATL	NL	4	1	0	38.0	0.95	8.29	2.54	49.648	4.965
18	1930	Earnshaw	George	WS	PHA	AL	2	0	0	25.0	0.72	7.20	2.71	49.429	4.943
19	1926	Pennock	Herb	WS	NYA	AL	2	0	0	22.0	1.23	6.95	2.00	48.487	4.849
20	2014	Bumgarner	Madison	PL	SFN	NL	4	1	1	52.7	1.03	5.81	7.50	46.186	4.619
21	2005	Contreras	Jose	PL	CHA	AL	3	1	0	32.0	3.09	7.88	7.00	46.121	4.612
22	1955	Podres	Johnny	WS	BRO	NL	2	0	0	18.0	1.00	9.50	2.50	46.109	4.611
23	1892	Stivetts	Jack	CS	BSN	NL	2	0	0	29.0	0.93	8.69	2.43	45.255	4.525
24	1886	Clarkson	John	WS	CHN	NL	2	2	0	31.0	2.03	10.74	2.33	45.227	4.523
25	1996	Maddux	Greg	PL	ATL	NL	3	2	0	37.0	1.70	8.51	7.33	44.475	4.448
26	2019	Strasburg	Steven	PL	WAS	NL	5	0	0	36.3	1.98	8.42	11.75	42.938	4.294
27	1914	Rudolph	Dick	WS	BSN	NL	2	0	0	18.0	0.50	8.00	3.75	42.295	4.229
28	1888	Keefe	Tim	WS	NY1	NL	4	0	0	35.0	0.51	6.94	3.33	40.508	4.051
29	1979	McGregor	Scott	PL	BAL	AL	2	1	0	26.0	2.08	8.65	4.00	39.644	3.964
30	1968	Lolich	Mickey	WS	DET	AL	3	0	0	27.0	1.67	8.67	3.50	39.581	3.958
31	1989	Stewart	Dave	PL	OAK	AL	4	0	0	32.0	2.25	7.88	4.60	38.982	3.898
32	1950	Raschi	Vic	WS	NYA	AL	1	0	0	9.0	0.00	3.00	5.00	38.180	3.818
33	1933	Hubbell	Carl	WS	NY1	NL	2	0	0	20.0	0.00	8.55	2.50	37.790	3.779
34	1960	Ford	Whitey	WS	NYA	AL	2	0	0	18.0	0.00	6.50	4.00	37.723	3.772
35	1946	Brecheen	Harry	WS	SLN	NL	3	0	0	20.0	0.45	8.55	2.20	37.674	3.767
36	1935	Warneke	Lon	WS	CHN	NL	2	0	0	16.7	0.54	7.02	1.25	36.835	3.683
37	1908	Overall	Orval	WS	CHN	NL	2	0	0	18.3	0.98	6.87	2.14	36.550	3.655
38	1962	Terry	Ralph	WS	NYA	AL	2	1	0	25.0	1.80	6.84	8.00	36.062	3.606
39	2019	Cole	Gerrit	PL	HOU	AL	4	1	0	36.7	1.72	7.85	4.27	35.896	3.590
40	1927	Pennock	Herb	WS	NYA	AL	1	0	0	9.0	1.00	3.00	1.00	35.579	3.558
41	1925	Johnson	Walter	WS	WS1	AL	2	1	0	26.0	2.08	10.38	3.75	35.389	3.539
42	1957	Burdette	Lew	WS	ML1	NL	3	0	0	27.0	0.67	8.33	3.25	35.279	3.528
43	1934	Dean	Dizzy	WS	SLN	NL	2	1	0	26.0	1.73	8.65	3.40	34.494	3.449
44	1943	Chandler	Spud	WS	NYA	AL	2	0	0	18.0	0.50	10.00	3.33	34.346	3.435
45	1937	Gomez	Lefty	WS	NYA	AL	2	0	0	18.0	1.50	9.00	4.00	34.318	3.432
46	1921	Hoyt	Waite	WS	NYA	AL	2	1	0	27.0	0.00	9.67	1.64	34.000	3.400

Rank	Year	Name	First	Type	Team	Lg	W	L	SV	IP	ERA	WHIP9	SO/W	PEVA-P REG	PEVA-P POST
47	1972	Odom	Blue Moon	PL	OAK	AL	2	1	0	27.7	0.65	5.86	2.25	33.944	3.394
48	2006	Rogers	Kenny	PL	DET	AL	3	0	0	23.0	0.00	6.26	2.71	33.864	3.386
49	2001	Johnson	Randy	PL	ARI	NL	5	1	0	41.3	1.52	7.19	5.88	33.682	3.368
50	2011	Carpenter	Chris	PL	SLN	NL	4	0	0	36.0	3.25	10.50	1.91	33.636	3.364
51	1974	Sutton	Don	PL	LAN	NL	3	0	0	30.0	1.50	6.30	5.00	33.551	3.355
52	1916	Shore	Ernie	WS	BOS	AL	2	0	0	17.7	1.53	8.15	2.25	33.135	3.314
53	1956	Larsen	Don	WS	NYA	AL	1	0	0	10.7	0.00	4.22	1.75	32.383	3.238
54	1927	Moore	Wilcy	WS	NYA	AL	1	0	1	10.7	0.84	10.97	1.00	32.151	3.215
55	2004	Lowe	Derek	PL	BOS	AL	3	0	0	19.3	1.86	6.52	3.33	31.833	3.183
56	1928	Hoyt	Waite	WS	NYA	AL	2	0	0	18.0	1.50	10.00	2.33	31.657	3.166
57	1993	Schilling	Curt	PL	PHI	NL	1	1	0	31.3	2.59	9.77	2.80	31.541	3.154
58	2017	Verlander	Justin	PL	HOU	AL	4	1	0	36.7	2.21	7.36	4.75	31.480	3.148
59	1984	Morris	Jack	PL	DET	AL	3	0	0	25.0	1.80	7.92	4.25	31.473	3.147
60	1947	Casey	Hugh	WS	BRO	NL	2	0	1	10.3	0.87	5.23	3.00	31.376	3.138
61	1980	Carlton	Steve	PL	PHI	NL	3	0	0	27.3	2.30	13.83	1.35	31.348	3.135
62	1918	Vaughn	Hippo	WS	CHN	NL	1	2	0	27.0	1.00	7.33	3.40	31.062	3.106
63	1938	Ruffing	Red	WS	NYA	AL	2	0	0	18.0	1.50	9.50	5.50	30.831	3.083
64	1911	Bender	Chief	WS	PHA	AL	2	1	0	26.0	1.04	8.31	2.50	30.444	3.044
65	1959	Sherry	Larry	WS	LAN	NL	2	0	2	12.7	0.71	7.11	2.50	30.134	3.013
66	2000	Pettitte	Andy	PL	NYA	AL	2	0	0	31.7	2.84	13.64	2.25	29.942	2.994
67	1913	Plank	Eddie	WS	PHA	AL	1	1	0	19.0	0.95	5.68	2.33	29.594	2.959
68	1969	Cuellar	Mike	PL	BAL	AL	1	0	0	24.0	1.50	7.88	4.00	29.579	2.958
69	2003	Beckett	Josh	PL	FLO	NL	2	2	0	42.7	2.11	6.96	3.92	29.260	2.926
70	1949	Reynolds	Allie	WS	NYA	AL	1	0	1	12.3	0.00	4.38	3.50	29.198	2.920
71	1973	Matlack	Jon	PL	NYN	NL	2	2	0	25.7	1.40	7.01	2.50	29.076	2.908
72	2016	Kluber	Corey	PL	CLE	AL	4	1	0	34.3	1.83	9.44	4.38	28.808	2.881
73	1947	Shea	Spec	WS	NYA	AL	2	0	0	15.3	2.35	10.57	1.25	28.787	2.879
74	1999	Hernandez	Orlando	PL	NYA	AL	3	0	0	30.0	1.20	8.70	1.93	28.749	2.875
75	1952	Reynolds	Allie	WS	NYA	AL	2	1	1	20.3	1.77	7.97	3.00	28.711	2.871
76	1983	Boddicker	Mike	PL	BAL	AL	2	0	0	18.0	0.00	5.50	6.67	28.661	2.866
77	1990	Stewart	Dave	PL	OAK	AL	2	2	0	29.0	2.17	8.07	1.13	28.522	2.852
78	1958	Spahn	Warren	WS	ML1	NL	2	1	0	28.7	2.20	8.48	2.25	28.162	2.816
79	1975	Tiant	Luis	PL	BOS	AL	3	0	0	34.0	2.65	10.32	1.82	28.156	2.816
80	1981	Hooton	Burt	PL	LAN	NL	4	1	0	33.0	0.82	10.91	0.67	28.055	2.806
81	1978	John	Tommy	PL	LAN	NL	2	0	0	23.7	1.90	9.13	1.67	27.872	2.787
82	1970	Carroll	Clay	PL	CIN	NL	1	0	1	10.3	0.00	7.84	6.50	27.774	2.777
83	1948	Sain	Johnny	WS	BSN	NL	1	1	0	17.0	1.06	4.76	9.00	27.566	2.757
84	1964	Gibson	Bob	WS	SLN	NL	2	1	0	27.0	3.00	10.33	3.88	27.373	2.737
85	2010	Lee	Cliff	PL	TEX	AL	3	2	0	35.7	2.78	7.31	25.5	27.368	2.738
86	2014	Affeldt	Jeremy	PL	SFN	NL	2	0	0	11.7	0.00	5.40	1.00	27.314	2.731
87	1903	Phillippe	Deacon	WS	PIT	NL	3	2	0	44.0	3.07	8.39	7.33	27.165	2.717
88	1929	Ehmke	Howard	WS	PHA	AL	1	0	0	12.7	1.42	12.08	4.33	26.750	2.675
89	1997	Mussina	Mike	PL	BAL	AL	2	0	0	29.0	1.24	5.59	5.86	26.646	2.665
90	1921	Mays	Carl	WS	NYA	AL	1	2	0	26.0	1.73	6.92	9.00	26.608	2.661
91	1992	Smoltz	John	PL	ATL	NL	3	0	0	33.7	2.67	11.76	1.82	26.577	2.658
92	2000	Clemens	Roger	PL	NYA	AL	2	2	0	28.0	3.21	8.36	3.40	26.437	2.644
93	2007	Corpas	Manuel	PL	COL	NL	1	0	5	10.3	0.87	5.23	7.00	26.173	2.617
94	1981	Gossage	Rich	PL	NYA	AL	0	0	6	14.3	0.00	6.28	3.75	26.157	2.616

Rank	Year	Name	First	Type	Team	Lg	W	L	SV	IP	ERA	WHIP9	SO/W	PEVA-P REG	PEVA-P POST
95	2002	Rodriguez	Francisco	PL	ANA	AL	5	1	0	18.7	1.93	7.23	5.60	26.103	2.610
96	2012	Romo	Sergio	PL	SFN	NL	1	0	4	10.7	0.84	4.22	9.00	26.051	2.605
97	2003	Rivera	Mariano	PL	NYA	AL	1	0	5	16.0	0.56	3.94	14.0	25.887	2.589
98	1926	Haines	Jesse	WS	SLN	NL	2	0	0	16.7	1.08	11.88	0.56	25.770	2.577
99	2013	Lester	Jon	PL	BOS	AL	4	1	0	34.7	1.56	8.57	3.63	25.584	2.558
100	1989	Moore	Mike	PL	OAK	AL	3	0	0	20.0	1.35	7.65	2.60	25.568	2.557
101	1886	Caruthers	Bob	WS	SL4	AA	2	1	0	26.0	2.42	8.31	2.00	25.517	2.552
102	1969	McNally	Dave	PL	BAL	AL	1	1	0	27.0	1.67	8.00	2.40	25.500	2.550
103	1998	Rivera	Mariano	PL	NYA	AL	0	0	6	13.3	0.00	5.40	5.50	25.271	2.527
104	1955	Ford	Whitey	WS	NYA	AL	2	0	0	17.0	2.12	11.12	1.25	24.784	2.478
105	1976	Gullett	Don	PL	CIN	NL	2	0	0	15.3	1.17	7.63	1.33	24.696	2.470
106	1973	Hunter	Catfish	PL	OAK	AL	3	0	0	29.7	1.82	9.71	1.33	24.567	2.457
107	2000	Rivera	Mariano	PL	NYA	AL	0	0	6	15.7	1.72	6.32	10.00	24.541	2.454
108	2004	Lidge	Brad	PL	HOU	NL	1	0	3	12.3	0.73	5.84	6.67	24.475	2.448
109	1931	Grove	Lefty	WS	PHA	AL	2	1	0	26.0	2.42	10.38	8.00	24.472	2.447
110	1984	Lefferts	Craig	PL	SDN	NL	2	0	1	10.0	0.00	4.50	4.00	24.300	2.430
111	2010	Lincecum	Tim	PL	SFN	NL	4	1	0	37.0	2.43	8.27	4.78	24.090	2.410
112	2011	Motte	Jason	PL	SLN	AL	0	1	5	12.3	2.19	4.38	8.00	23.897	2.390
113	2012	Vogelsong	Ryan	PL	SFN	NL	3	9	9	24.7	1.09	9.49	2.10	23.830	2.383
114	2003	Pettitte	Andy	PL	NYA	AL	3	1	0	34.3	2.10	11.53	3.09	23.615	2.361
115	1924	Zachary	Tom	WS	WS1	AL	2	0	0	17.7	2.04	8.15	1.00	23.571	2.357
116	1913	Mathewson	Christy	WS	NY1	NL	1	1	0	19.0	0.95	7.58	3.50	23.479	2.348
117	2012	Verlander	Justin	PL	DET	NL	3	1	0	28.3	2.22	6.99	4.83	23.445	2.345
118	1936	Hubbell	Carl	WS	NY1	NL	1	1	0	16.0	2.25	9.56	5.00	23.424	2.342
119	2009	Sabathia	C.C.	PL	NYA	AL	3	1	0	36.3	1.98	9.17	3.56	23.401	2.340
120	1977	Lyle	Sparky	PL	NYA	AL	3	0	0	14.0	1.29	5.79	5.00	23.395	2.339
121	1978	Gossage	Rich	PL	NYA	AL	2	0	1	10.0	1.80	4.50	7.00	23.250	2.325
122	2014	Holland	Greg	PL	KCA	AL	0	0	7	11.0	0.82	7.36	3.00	23.181	2.318
123	1986	Hurst	Bruce	PL	BOS	AL	3	0	0	38.0	2.13	10.18	3.57	22.913	2.291
124	1990	Rijo	Jose	PL	CIN	NL	3	0	0	27.7	2.28	10.08	2.42	22.884	2.288
125	1985	Jackson	Danny	PL	KCA	AL	2	1	0	26.0	1.04	8.65	3.17	22.805	2.281
126	1909	Adams	Babe	WS	PIT	NL	3	0	0	27.0	1.33	8.00	1.83	22.779	2.278
127	1995	Glavine	Tom	PL	ATL	NL	2	0	0	28.0	1.61	8.04	2.11	22.722	2.272
128	1995	Maddux	Greg	PL	ATL	NL	3	1	0	38.0	2.84	9.95	2.71	22.691	2.269
129	1999	Rivera	Mariano	PL	NYA	AL	2	0	6	12.3	0.00	7.30	9.00	22.666	2.267
130	1990	Myers	Randy	PL	CIN	NL	0	0	4	8.7	0.00	7.27	3.33	22.617	2.262
131	1993	Guzman	Juan	PL	TOR	AL	2	1	0	25.0	2.88	12.60	1.24	22.557	2.256
132	1969	Taylor	Ron	PL	NYN	NL	1	0	2	5.67	0.00	6.35	7.00	22.515	2.252
133	1991	Morris	Jack	PL	MIN	AL	4	0	0	36.3	2.23	11.15	2.20	22.323	2.232
134	1926	Hoyt	Waite	WS	NYA	AL	1	1	0	15.0	1.20	12.00	10.00	22.143	2.214
135	1991	Avery	Steve	PL	ATL	NL	2	0	0	29.3	1.53	7.36	5.00	22.069	2.207
136	2015	Familia	Jeurys	PL	NYN	NL	0	0	5	14.7	0.61	4.29	4.50	22.045	2.204
137	1930	Grove	Lefty	WS	PHA	AL	2	1	0	19.0	1.42	8.53	3.33	22.025	2.203
138	1890	Lovett	Tom	WS	BRO	NL	2	2	0	35.0	2.83	9.00	2.33	21.922	2.192
139	2000	Stanton	Mike	PL	NYA	AL	3	0	0	8.7	1.04	6.23	10.00	21.856	2.186
140	2006	Carpenter	Chris	PL	SLN	NL	3	1	0	32.3	2.78	10.02	2.88	21.823	2.182
141	2016	Lester	Jon	PL	CHN	NL	3	1	0	35.7	2.02	8.33	5.00	21.784	2.178
142	2017	Estrada	Marco	PL	TOR	AL	2	1	0	19.3	2.33	6.98	15.00	21.755	2.176

Rank	Year	Name	First	Type	Team	Lg	W	L	SV	IP	ERA	WHIP9	SO/W	PEVA-P REG	PEVA-P POST
143	1950	Ford	Whitey	WS	NYA	AL	1	0	0	8.7	0.00	8.31	7.00	21.742	2.174
144	1903	Dinneen	Bill	WS	BOS	AL	3	1	0	35.0	2.06	9.51	3.50	21.732	2.173
145	1967	Lonborg	Jim	WS	BOS	AL	2	1	0	24.0	2.63	6.00	5.50	21.673	2.167
146	2018	Kelly	Joe	PL	LAN	NL	2	1	0	11.3	0.79	6.35	13.00	21.642	2.164
147	1982	Andujar	Joaquin	PL	SLN	NL	3	0	0	20.0	1.80	8.55	2.67	21.618	2.162
148	1960	Law	Vern	WS	PIT	NL	2	0	0	18.3	3.44	12.27	2.67	21.536	2.154
149	2013	Uehara	Koji	PL	BOS	AL	1	1	7	13.7	0.66	4.61	16.00	21.345	2.135
150	1887	Caruthers	Bob	WS	SL4	AA	4	4	0	71.0	2.15	9.63	1.58	21.267	2.127

Abbreviation Code: Type: CS (Championship Series) - Prior to 1900; WS - World Series Only; PL - 1969 to Present.

RPR - Run Production (Runs Scored plus Runs Batted In)
FV - Field Value, Defensive value for player during postseason. Maximum, average, and minimum values differ for each position. WHIP9 - Walks and Hits Per 9 Innings Pitched
SO/W - Strike Outs to Walks Ratio.

Note: Postseason PEVA-B (Batting) and PEVA-P (Pitching) currently valued at 10% of what would represent regular season PEVA values.

Total Postseason Rankings

To have a great postseason career, you have to have one thing. It's more than talent. It's more than being able to rise to the occasion. It's inherently a dependent function. You must play on winning teams, teams that make the playoffs, and teams that make it to the World Series. You can't be Ernie Banks. Not that a great player does not have an impact on making the postseason and that the even greater ones don't rise to that occasion. They do. But there are a whole lot of Yankees on these lists. They play in the World Series. They've won a whole lot of them. It's even harder to compare total postseason numbers, because of the expansion in the number of rounds and teams, yet it seems unfair to discount the additional rounds as well. For PEVA calculations, it adjusts for these things, but for the gross amount of Home Runs hit or Wins, the list includes all rounds; take all that into account as much as you'd like.

Listed below are PEVA postseason rankings and totals that reflect the 10% level. It includes a per season number that may even be better to use as a comparison. But the folks near the top are those that we relate to as great World Series players. They're in the lexicon of moments that play on and on in our minds when we recall October classics from the first in 1884 (okay, not too many recall that) through last year. We don't think there are many surprises on these lists.

Best Batting Postseason Careers
1884-2019

Rank	LPostYr	Name	First	PTeam	Post PEVA-B	Yrs	PerYr	HR	RBI	H	AB	AVG
1	1932	Ruth	Babe	NYA	28.065	10	2.806	15	33	42	129	0.326
2	1963	Berra	Yogi	NYA	22.935	14	1.638	12	39	71	259	0.274
3	1964	Mantle	Mickey	NYA	22.596	12	1.883	18	40	59	230	0.257
4	1938	Gehrig	Lou	NYA	22.452	7	3.207	10	35	43	119	0.361
5	2012	Jeter	Derek	NYA	19.177	16	1.199	20	61	200	650	0.308
6	1986	Jackson	Reggie	CAL	17.015	11	1.547	18	48	78	281	0.278
7	1951	DiMaggio	Joe	NYA	16.143	10	1.614	8	30	54	199	0.271
8	2006	Williams	Bernie	NYA	15.676	12	1.306	22	80	128	465	0.275
9	1922	Baker	Frank	NYA	15.186	6	2.531	3	18	33	91	0.363
10	1943	Dickey	Bill	NYA	14.432	8	1.804	5	24	37	145	0.255
11	1943	Keller	Charlie	NYA	13.928	4	3.482	5	18	22	72	0.306
12	1939	Simmons	Al	CIN	13.759	4	3.440	6	17	24	73	0.329
13	1984	Garvey	Steve	SDN	13.368	5	2.674	11	31	75	222	0.338
14	2016	Ortiz	David	BOS	13.248	9	1.472	17	61	88	304	0.289
15	1971	Robinson	Frank	BAL	13.183	5	2.637	10	19	30	126	0.238
16	1919	Collins	Eddie	CHA	13.154	6	2.192	0	11	42	128	0.328
17	2014	Pujols	Albert	LAA	12.942	8	1.618	19	54	90	279	0.323
18	2009	Ramirez	Manny	LAN	12.793	11	1.163	29	78	117	410	0.285
19	1963	Skowron	Bill	LAN	12.652	8	1.581	8	29	39	133	0.293
20	2017	Beltran	Carlos	HOU	12.241	7	1.749	16	42	66	215	0.307
21	1979	Bench	Johnny	CIN	12.180	6	2.030	10	20	45	169	0.266
22	1959	Snider	Duke	LAN	12.125	6	2.021	11	26	38	133	0.286
23	1918	Hooper	Harry	BOS	11.353	4	2.838	2	6	27	92	0.293
24	1983	Rose	Pete	PHI	10.690	8	1.336	5	22	86	268	0.321

Rank	LPostYr	Name	First	PTeam	Post PEVA-B	Yrs	PerYr	HR	RBI	H	AB	AVG
25	1968	Brock	Lou	SLN	10.684	3	3.561	4	13	34	87	0.391
26	1948	Gordon	Joe	CLE	10.642	6	1.774	4	16	25	103	0.243
27	1945	Greenberg	Hank	DET	10.574	4	2.644	5	22	27	85	0.318
28	1935	Cochrane	Mickey	DET	10.233	5	2.047	2	7	27	110	0.245
29	2011	Posada	Jorge	NYA	10.031	15	0.669	11	42	103	416	0.248
30	2000	Henderson	Rickey	SEA	9.648	8	1.206	5	20	63	222	0.284
31	2015	Rodriguez	Alex	NYA	9.582	12	0.798	13	41	72	278	0.259
32	2012	Jones	Chipper	ATL	9.494	12	0.791	13	47	97	338	0.287
33	2002	Justice	David	OAK	9.205	10	0.921	14	63	89	398	0.224
34	1985	Brett	George	KCA	9.179	7	1.311	10	23	56	166	0.337
35	1916	Lewis	Duffy	BOS	9.120	3	3.040	1	7	20	67	0.299
36	1934	Martin	Pepper	SLN	8.696	3	2.899	1	9	23	55	0.418
37	1975	Yastrzemski	Carl	BOS	8.599	2	4.299	4	11	24	65	0.369
38	1974	Robinson	Brooks	BAL	8.597	6	1.433	5	22	44	145	0.303
39	1967	Howard	Elston	BOS	8.580	10	0.858	5	19	42	171	0.246
40	1935	Goslin	Goose	DET	8.444	5	1.689	7	19	37	129	0.287
41	1968	Maris	Roger	SLN	8.404	7	1.201	6	18	33	152	0.217
42	1931	Foxx	Jimmie	PHA	8.127	3	2.709	4	11	22	64	0.344
43	1960	McDougald	Gil	NYA	8.052	8	1.007	7	24	45	190	0.237
44	1955	Rizzuto	Phil	NYA	8.046	9	0.894	2	8	45	183	0.246
45	2019	Springer	George	HOU	8.016	4	2.004	15	28	55	203	0.271
46	2001	O'Neill	Paul	NYA	7.977	8	0.997	11	39	85	299	0.284
47	1964	Tresh	Tom	NYA	7.954	3	2.651	4	13	18	65	0.277
48	1969	Aaron	Hank	ATL	7.915	3	2.638	6	16	25	69	0.362
49	1993	Molitor	Paul	TOR	7.901	3	2.634	6	22	43	117	0.368
50	2019	Turner	Justin	LAN	7.784	6	1.297	9	35	62	200	0.310
51	2014	Sandoval	Pablo	SFN	7.699	3	2.566	6	20	53	154	0.344
52	1888	O'Neill	Tip	SL4	7.688	4	1.922	5	25	35	146	0.240
53	2011	Berkman	Lance	SLN	7.672	5	1.534	9	41	59	186	0.317
54	1958	Bauer	Hank	NYA	7.612	9	0.846	7	24	46	188	0.245
55	2019	Altuve	Jose	HOU	7.580	4	1.895	13	29	60	207	0.290
56	2019	Freese	David	LAN	7.577	6	1.263	10	36	61	204	0.299
57	1978	McCarver	Tim	PHI	7.566	6	1.261	2	12	24	88	0.273
58	2019	Molina	Yadier	SLN	7.546	10	0.755	4	34	95	348	0.273
59	1953	Woodling	Gene	NYA	7.503	5	1.501	3	6	27	85	0.318
60	1920	Speaker	Tris	CLE	7.464	3	2.488	0	3	22	72	0.306
61	1984	Matthews	Gary	CHN	7.439	3	2.480	7	15	21	65	0.323
62	1937	Ott	Mel	NY1	7.438	3	2.479	4	10	18	61	0.295
63	2003	Bonds	Barry	SFN	7.351	7	1.050	9	24	37	151	0.245
64	1910	Schulte	Frank	CHN	7.318	4	1.829	0	9	26	81	0.321
65	1990	Henderson	Dave	OAK	7.314	4	1.829	7	20	36	121	0.298
66	1934	Frisch	Frankie	SLN	7.306	8	0.913	0	10	58	197	0.294
67	1978	Munson	Thurman	NYA	7.181	3	2.394	3	22	46	129	0.357
68	1923	Schang	Wally	NYA	7.147	6	1.191	1	9	27	94	0.287
69	1956	Martin	Billy	NYA	7.095	5	1.419	5	19	33	99	0.333
70	1974	Powell	Boog	BAL	7.086	6	1.181	6	18	33	126	0.262
71	1924	Gowdy	Hank	NY1	7.039	3	2.346	1	4	13	42	0.310
72	1956	Reese	Pee Wee	BRO	7.008	7	1.001	2	16	46	169	0.272
73	1993	Dykstra	Lenny	PHI	6.996	3	2.332	10	19	36	112	0.321

Rank	LPostYr	Name	First	PTeam	Post PEVA-B	Yrs	PerYr	HR	RBI	H	AB	AVG
74	1984	Cey	Ron	CHN	6.702	5	1.340	7	27	42	161	0.261
75	1914	Evers	Johnny	BSN	6.617	4	1.654	0	6	24	76	0.316
76	1943	Crosetti	Frankie	NYA	6.606	7	0.944	1	11	20	115	0.174
77	2017	Werth	Jason	WAS	6.590	9	0.732	15	30	57	227	0.251
78	2006	Rodriguez	Ivan	DET	6.542	5	1.308	4	25	39	153	0.255
79	2008	Edmonds	Jim	CHN	6.413	7	0.916	13	43	63	230	0.274
80	1932	Combs	Earle	NYA	6.372	4	1.593	1	9	21	60	0.350
81	2001	Brosius	Scott	NYA	6.362	4	1.590	8	30	48	196	0.245
82	2011	Jones	Andruw	NYA	6.340	11	0.576	10	34	65	238	0.273
83	1986	Lopes	Davey	HOU	6.276	6	1.046	6	22	43	181	0.238
84	1938	Lazzeri	Tony	CHN	6.270	7	0.896	4	19	28	107	0.262
85	1956	Campanella	Roy	BRO	6.262	5	1.252	4	12	27	114	0.237
86	1979	Stargell	Willie	PIT	6.202	6	1.034	7	20	37	133	0.278
87	1954	Dark	Alvin	NY1	6.189	3	2.063	1	4	21	65	0.323
88	1905	Bresnahan	Roger	NY1	6.126	1	6.126	0	1	5	16	0.313
89	1988	Carter	Gary	NYN	6.119	3	2.040	4	21	33	118	0.280
90	1958	Slaughter	Enos	NYA	6.070	5	1.214	3	8	23	79	0.291
91	2000	Clark	Will	SLN	6.039	5	1.208	5	16	39	117	0.333
92	1892	Duffy	Hugh	BSN	6.019	1	6.019	1	9	12	26	0.462
93	2005	Martinez	Tino	NYA	5.923	9	0.658	9	38	83	356	0.233
94	1959	Hodges	Gil	LAN	5.871	7	0.839	5	21	35	131	0.267
95	1942	Rolfe	Red	NYA	5.842	6	0.974	0	6	33	116	0.284
96	1997	McGriff	Fred	ATL	5.826	5	1.165	10	37	57	188	0.303
97	1947	McQuinn	George	NYA	5.746	2	2.873	1	6	10	39	0.256
98	1979	Campaneris	Bert	CAL	5.735	6	0.956	3	11	35	144	0.243
99	2009	Matsui	Hideki	NYA	5.722	6	0.954	10	39	64	205	0.312
100	2003	Lopez	Javy	ATL	5.705	9	0.634	10	28	57	205	0.278
101	2019	Cruz	Nelson	MIN	5.692	5	1.138	17	35	47	164	0.287
102	1981	Bando	Sal	ML4	5.692	6	0.949	5	13	39	159	0.245
103	1910	Steinfeldt	Harry	CHN	5.638	4	1.410	0	8	19	73	0.260
104	1964	Richardson	Bobby	NYA	5.602	7	0.800	1	15	40	131	0.305
105	2019	Bregman	Alex	HOU	5.532	3	1.844	10	27	37	160	0.231
106	1924	Meusel	Irish	NY1	5.522	4	1.381	3	17	24	87	0.276
107	1951	Brown	Bobby	NYA	5.513	4	1.378	0	9	18	41	0.439
108	1983	Baker	Dusty	LAN	5.415	4	1.354	5	21	42	149	0.282
109	1940	Gehringer	Charlie	DET	5.357	3	1.786	1	7	26	81	0.321
110	1983	Perez	Tony	PHI	5.320	6	0.887	6	25	41	172	0.238
111	1884	Gilligan	Barney	PRO	5.306	1	5.306	0	2	4	9	0.444
112	2006	Piazza	Mike	SDN	5.275	5	1.055	6	15	29	120	0.242
113	1945	Cavarretta	Phil	CHN	5.269	3	1.756	1	5	20	63	0.317
114	2018	Granderson	Curtis	MIL	5.255	8	0.657	9	30	47	210	0.224
115	1936	Koenig	Mark	NY1	5.253	5	1.051	0	5	18	76	0.237
116	1982	Tenace	Gene	SLN	5.219	6	0.870	4	14	18	114	0.158
117	1996	Murray	Eddie	BAL	5.157	4	1.289	9	25	41	159	0.258
118	2014	Cabrera	Miguel	DET	5.148	5	1.030	13	38	57	205	0.278
119	2007	Lofton	Kenny	CLE	5.105	11	0.464	7	34	97	392	0.247
120	1931	Dykes	Jimmie	PHA	5.091	3	1.697	1	11	17	59	0.288
121	1975	Rudi	Joe	OAK	5.075	5	1.015	3	15	37	140	0.264
122	1915	Luderus	Fred	PHI	5.066	1	5.066	1	6	7	16	0.438

Rank	LPostYr	Name	First	PTeam	Post PEVA-B	Yrs	PerYr	HR	RBI	H	AB	AVG
123	1990	Hatcher	Billy	CIN	5.031	2	2.515	2	6	21	52	0.404
124	1948	Elliott	Bob	BSN	5.022	1	5.022	2	5	7	21	0.333
125	1948	Sanders	Ray	BSN	5.016	4	1.254	2	3	11	40	0.275
126	1927	Groh	Heinie	PIT	5.007	5	1.001	0	4	19	72	0.264
127	1984	Nettles	Graig	SDN	5.000	7	0.714	5	27	41	182	0.225
128	2018	Murphy	David	CHN	4.982	4	1.246	8	19	30	97	0.309
129	1983	Morgan	Joe	PHI	4.968	7	0.710	5	13	33	181	0.182
130	1988	Gibson	Kirk	LAN	4.945	3	1.648	7	21	22	78	0.282
131	2008	Varitek	Jason	BOS	4.906	7	0.701	11	33	54	228	0.237
132	1927	Harris	Joe	PIT	4.864	2	2.432	3	7	14	40	0.350
133	1957	Coleman	Jerry	NYA	4.808	6	0.801	0	9	19	69	0.275
134	2018	Puig	Yasiel	LAN	4.807	6	0.801	5	23	51	182	0.280
135	1962	Hiller	Chuck	SFN	4.798	1	4.798	1	5	7	26	0.269
136	1969	Boyer	Clete	ATL	4.797	6	0.799	2	14	21	95	0.221
137	1944	Cooper	Walker	SLN	4.742	3	1.581	0	6	18	60	0.300
138	2019	Cain	Lorenzo	MIL	4.721	4	1.180	1	20	48	171	0.281
139	1938	Powell	Jake	NYA	4.716	3	1.572	1	5	10	23	0.435
140	2018	Bryant	Kris	CHN	4.716	4	1.179	6	16	35	145	0.241
141	1911	Murphy	Danny	PHA	4.696	3	1.565	1	12	18	59	0.305
142	1987	Trammell	Alan	DET	4.681	2	2.341	3	11	17	51	0.333
143	2016	Ruiz	Carlos	LAN	4.674	6	0.779	5	19	39	153	0.255
144	1919	Jackson	Joe	CHA	4.658	2	2.329	1	8	19	55	0.345
145	2005	Olerud	John	BOS	4.642	8	0.580	9	34	66	237	0.278
146	1990	Randolph	Willie	OAK	4.640	6	0.773	4	14	36	162	0.222
147	1983	Russell	Bill	LAN	4.625	5	0.925	0	18	57	194	0.294
148	2018	Holliday	Matt	COL	4.605	9	0.512	13	37	71	290	0.245
149	2006	Sheffield	Gary	NYA	4.602	6	0.767	6	19	40	161	0.248
150	1910	Chance	Frank	CHN	4.589	4	1.147	0	6	21	70	0.300

Abbreviation Code: LPostYr - Last Postseason Year; PTeam - Final Postseason Team.

Best Pitching Postseason Careers
1884-2019

Rank	LPostYr	Name	First	PTeam	Post PEVA-P	Yrs	PerYr	W	L	SV	IP	ERA
1	2011	Rivera	Mariano	NYA	18.838	16	1.177	8	1	42	141.0	0.70
2	1964	Ford	Whitey	NYA	18.789	11	1.708	10	8	0	146.0	2.71
3	1968	Gibson	Bob	SLN	13.470	3	4.490	7	2	0	81.0	1.89
4	2007	Schilling	Curt	BOS	12.460	5	2.492	11	2	0	133.3	2.23
5	1999	Hershiser	Orel	NYN	12.424	6	2.071	8	3	1	132.0	2.59
6	2009	Smoltz	John	SLN	12.303	14	0.879	15	4	4	209.0	2.67
7	2012	Pettitte	Andy	NYA	11.683	14	0.835	19	11	0	276.7	3.81
8	1913	Mathewson	Christy	NY1	11.260	4	2.815	5	5	0	101.7	0.97
9	2008	Maddux	Greg	LAN	10.679	13	0.821	11	14	1	198.0	3.27
10	1932	Pennock	Herb	NYA	9.987	5	1.997	5	0	3	55.3	1.95
11	2009	Beckett	Josh	BOS	9.779	4	2.445	7	3	0	93.7	3.07
12	1931	Hoyt	Waite	PHA	9.692	7	1.385	6	4	0	83.7	1.83
13	1993	Stewart	Dave	TOR	9.627	6	1.604	10	6	0	133.0	2.84
14	2019	Verlander	Justin	HOU	9.579	8	1.197	14	11	0	187.7	3.41

Rank	LPostYr	Name	First	PTeam	Post PEVA-P	Yrs	PerYr	W	L	SV	IP	ERA
15	1953	Reynolds	Allie	NYA	9.036	6	1.506	7	2	4	77.3	2.79
16	1966	Koufax	Sandy	LAN	9.019	4	2.255	4	3	0	57.0	0.95
17	2006	Glavine	Tom	NYN	8.977	12	0.748	14	16	0	218.3	3.42
18	1931	Earnshaw	George	PHA	8.877	3	2.959	4	3	0	62.7	1.58
19	2007	Clemens	Roger	NYA	8.507	12	0.709	12	8	0	199.0	3.75
20	2011	Lee	Cliff	PHI	8.366	3	2.789	7	3	0	82.0	2.52
21	1953	Raschi	Vic	NYA	8.348	6	1.391	5	3	0	60.3	2.24
22	2018	Lester	Jon	CHN	8.297	9	0.922	9	7	0	154.0	2.51
23	2018	Hamels	Cole	CHN	7.811	8	0.976	7	6	0	100.3	3.50
24	1942	Ruffing	Red	NYA	7.632	7	1.090	7	2	0	85.7	2.63
25	2012	Carpenter	Chris	SLN	7.464	5	1.493	10	4	0	108.0	3.00
26	1953	Lopat	Ed	NYA	7.252	5	1.450	4	1	0	52.0	2.60
27	2006	Johnson	Randy	NYA	7.168	9	0.796	9	10	0	146.3	3.32
28	1978	Hunter	Catfish	NYA	7.143	7	1.020	9	6	1	132.3	3.26
29	1937	Hubbell	Carl	NY1	7.005	3	2.335	4	2	0	50.3	1.79
30	1928	Alexander	Pete	SLN	6.974	3	2.325	3	2	1	43.0	3.56
31	1939	Gomez	Lefty	NYA	6.732	5	1.346	6	0	0	50.3	2.86
32	1974	McNally	Dave	BAL	6.716	6	1.119	7	4	0	90.3	2.49
33	2019	Wainwright	Adam	SLN	6.506	7	0.929	4	5	4	105.7	2.81
34	1929	Nehf	Art	CHN	6.409	5	1.282	4	4	0	79.0	2.16
35	1983	Palmer	Jim	BAL	6.291	8	0.786	8	3	0	124.3	2.61
36	1983	Carlton	Steve	PHI	6.267	8	0.783	6	6	0	99.3	3.26
37	1884	Radbourn	Charley	PRO	6.157	1	6.157	3	0	0	22.0	0.00
38	1986	Sutton	Don	CAL	6.128	5	1.226	6	4	0	100.3	3.68
39	1910	Overall	Orval	CHN	5.995	4	1.499	3	1	0	51.3	1.58
40	1931	Grove	Lefty	PHA	5.945	3	1.982	4	2	2	51.3	1.75
41	2016	Bumgarner	Madison	SFN	5.937	4	1.484	8	3	1	102.3	2.11
42	1914	Bender	Chief	PHA	5.878	5	1.176	6	4	0	85.0	2.44
43	1977	Gullett	Don	NYA	5.817	6	0.969	4	5	1	94.3	3.72
44	1992	Morris	Jack	TOR	5.807	4	1.452	7	4	0	92.3	3.80
45	1983	McGregor	Scott	BAL	5.717	2	2.859	3	3	0	49.7	1.63
46	2017	Lackey	John	CHN	5.674	10	0.567	8	6	0	144.0	3.44
47	1889	Caruthers	Bob	BR3	5.655	4	1.414	7	8	1	147.0	2.51
48	2005	Hernandez	Orlando	CHA	5.639	7	0.806	9	3	0	106.0	2.55
49	1947	Newsom	Bobo	NYA	5.542	2	2.771	2	2	0	28.3	2.86
50	2019	Strasburg	Steven	WAS	5.537	3	1.846	6	2	0	55.3	1.46
51	2007	Mussina	Mike	NYA	5.532	9	0.615	7	8	0	139.7	3.42
52	1925	Coveleski	Stan	WS1	5.366	2	2.683	3	2	0	41.3	1.74
53	1947	Chandler	Spud	NYA	5.323	4	1.331	2	2	1	33.3	1.62
54	1982	John	Tommy	CAL	5.281	5	1.056	6	3	0	88.3	2.65
55	2006	Wells	David	SDN	5.269	11	0.479	10	5	0	125.0	3.17
56	2011	Lidge	Brad	PHI	5.199	6	0.867	2	4	18	45.3	2.18
57	1963	Podres	Johnny	LAN	5.142	4	1.286	4	1	0	38.3	2.11
58	1984	Gossage	Rich	SDN	5.105	4	1.276	2	1	8	31.3	2.87
59	1974	Cuellar	Mike	BAL	5.041	5	1.008	4	4	0	85.3	2.85
60	1892	Clarkson	John	CL4	4.928	3	1.643	2	5	0	64.0	2.67
61	2010	Contreras	Jose	PHI	4.861	4	1.215	4	3	0	49.0	3.49
62	1925	Johnson	Walter	WS1	4.854	2	2.427	3	3	0	50.0	2.16
63	1922	Mays	Carl	NYA	4.808	4	1.202	3	4	1	57.3	2.35

Rank	LPostYr	Name	First	PTeam	Post PEVA-P	Yrs	PerYr	W	L	SV	IP	ERA
64	2019	Kershaw	Clayton	LAN	4.695	9	0.522	9	11	1	158.3	4.43
65	2012	Lowe	Derek	NYA	4.671	8	0.584	5	7	1	97.3	3.42
66	2019	Cole	Gerrit	HOU	4.572	4	1.143	6	4	0	65.7	2.60
67	1892	Stivetts	Jack	BSN	4.525	1	4.525	2	0	0	29.0	0.93
68	2009	Martinez	Pedro	PHI	4.457	5	0.891	6	4	0	96.3	3.46
69	2002	Stanton	Mike	NYA	4.452	11	0.405	5	2	1	55.7	2.10
70	1998	Eckersley	Dennis	BOS	4.450	7	0.636	1	3	15	36.0	3.00
71	1889	Keefe	Tim	NY1	4.408	3	1.469	4	3	1	61.0	2.66
72	1939	Pearson	Monte	NYA	4.383	4	1.096	4	0	0	35.7	1.01
73	1910	Brown	Mordecai	CHN	4.337	4	1.084	5	4	0	57.7	2.97
74	1958	Burdette	Lew	ML1	4.311	2	2.156	4	2	0	49.3	2.92
75	1972	Lolich	Mickey	DET	4.262	2	2.131	3	1	0	46.0	1.57
76	1932	Moore	Wilcy	NYA	4.254	2	2.127	2	0	1	16.0	0.56
77	1914	Rudolph	Dick	BSN	4.229	1	4.229	2	0	0	18.0	0.50
78	1935	Warneke	Lon	CHN	4.207	2	2.104	2	1	0	27.3	2.63
79	2014	Affeldt	Jeremy	SFN	4.138	4	1.035	2	0	0	31.3	0.86
80	1916	Shore	Ernie	BOS	4.137	2	2.069	3	1	0	34.7	1.82
81	1946	Brecheen	Harry	SLN	4.136	3	1.379	4	1	0	32.7	0.83
82	1981	Hooton	Burt	LAN	4.098	3	1.366	6	3	0	59.7	3.17
83	1993	Guzman	Juan	TOR	4.087	3	1.362	5	1	0	51.7	2.44
84	1964	Terry	Ralph	NYA	4.051	5	0.810	2	4	0	46.0	2.93
85	2001	Charlton	Norm	SEA	4.043	5	0.809	5	1	4	38.3	1.17
86	1975	Carroll	Clay	CIN	4.001	4	1.000	4	2	2	32.3	1.39
87	2019	Jansen	Kenley	LAN	3.899	7	0.557	1	1	16	49.3	2.01
88	1996	Avery	Steve	ATL	3.783	5	0.757	5	3	0	77.7	2.90
89	2012	Sabathia	C.C.	NYA	3.755	7	0.536	9	5	0	107.3	4.53
90	1962	Larsen	Don	SFN	3.719	5	0.744	4	2	0	36.0	2.75
91	1944	Cooper	Mort	SLN	3.704	3	1.235	2	3	0	45.0	3.00
92	2019	Romo	Sergio	MIN	3.677	5	0.735	3	1	4	25.3	3.55
93	2019	Tanaka	Masahiro	NYA	3.676	4	0.919	5	3	0	46.0	1.76
94	1914	Plank	Eddie	PHA	3.655	4	0.914	2	5	0	54.7	1.32
95	2019	Price	David	BOS	3.655	9	0.406	5	9	1	99.3	4.62
96	1975	Holtzman	Ken	OAK	3.644	4	0.911	6	4	0	70.3	2.30
97	2019	Scherzer	Max	WAS	3.636	7	0.519	7	5	0	112.0	3.38
98	1958	Spahn	Warren	ML1	3.636	3	1.212	4	3	0	56.0	3.05
99	2006	Rogers	Kenny	DET	3.626	4	0.907	3	3	0	43.3	4.15
100	2019	Miller	Andrew	SLN	3.586	6	0.598	2	1	1	38.0	0.95
101	1938	Dean	Dizzy	CHN	3.581	2	1.790	2	2	0	34.3	2.88
102	1987	Blyleven	Bert	MIN	3.560	3	1.187	5	1	0	47.3	2.47
103	1974	Odom	Blue Moon	OAK	3.504	3	1.168	3	1	0	42.0	1.07
104	2016	Estrada	Marco	TOR	3.450	3	1.150	3	3	0	47.7	2.64
105	1981	Guidry	Ron	NYA	3.408	4	0.852	5	2	0	62.7	3.02
106	1981	Fingers	Rollie	ML4	3.407	6	0.568	5	3	9	54.7	2.63
107	1987	Dayley	Ken	SLN	3.256	2	1.628	1	0	5	20.7	0.44
108	1947	Casey	Hugh	BRO	3.253	2	1.627	2	2	1	15.7	1.72
109	2009	Papelbon	Jonathan	BOS	3.235	4	0.809	2	1	7	27.0	1.00
110	2018	Davis	Wade	COL	3.228	6	0.538	4	0	8	40.0	1.80
111	1909	Phillippe	Deacon	PIT	3.206	2	1.603	3	2	0	50.0	2.70

Rank	LPostYr	Name	First	PTeam	Post PEVA-P	Yrs	PerYr	W	L	SV	IP	ERA
112	2011	Rodriguez	Francisco	MIL	3.203	6	0.534	5	4	3	36.7	2.95
113	1990	Boddicker	Mike	BOS	3.168	3	1.056	2	2	0	28.7	2.51
114	1934	Haines	Jesse	SLN	3.167	4	0.792	3	1	0	32.3	1.67
115	2014	Lincecum	Tim	SFN	3.139	3	1.046	5	2	0	56.3	2.40
116	1918	Vaughn	Hippo	CHN	3.106	1	3.106	1	2	0	27.0	1.00
117	1998	Myers	Randy	SDN	3.096	5	0.619	2	2	8	30.7	2.35
118	2011	Oswalt	Roy	PHI	3.095	4	0.774	5	2	0	72.3	3.73
119	2013	Garcia	Freddy	ATL	3.081	5	0.616	6	3	0	66.3	3.26
120	1923	Bush	Joe	NYA	3.043	5	0.609	2	5	1	60.7	2.67
121	1979	Seaver	Tom	CIN	3.033	3	1.011	3	3	0	61.7	2.77
122	1953	Sain	Johnny	NYA	3.018	4	0.755	2	2	0	30.7	2.64
123	1959	Sherry	Larry	LAN	3.013	1	3.013	2	0	2	12.7	0.71
124	1996	Jackson	Danny	SLN	2.994	5	0.599	4	3	0	57.3	3.30
125	1932	Pipgras	George	NYA	2.978	3	0.993	3	0	0	26.0	2.77
126	2019	Kluber	Corey	CLE	2.971	3	0.990	4	3	0	45.3	3.97
127	1988	Tudor	John	LAN	2.947	3	0.982	5	4	0	63.3	3.41
128	1909	Mullin	George	DET	2.924	3	0.975	3	3	0	58.0	1.86
129	1973	Matlack	Jon	NYN	2.908	1	2.908	2	2	0	25.7	1.40
130	2014	Vogelsong	Ryan	SFN	2.891	2	1.445	3	0	0	37.0	2.92
131	1947	Shea	Spec	NYA	2.879	1	2.879	2	0	0	15.3	2.35
132	1975	Tiant	Luis	BOS	2.836	2	1.418	3	0	0	34.7	2.86
133	1960	Labine	Clem	PIT	2.824	5	0.565	2	2	2	31.3	3.16
134	1928	Zachary	Tom	NYA	2.814	3	0.938	3	0	0	28.3	2.86
135	1997	Key	Jimmy	BAL	2.792	6	0.465	5	3	0	68.7	3.15
136	2019	Kelly	Joe	LAN	2.780	6	0.463	3	3	0	49.3	3.47
137	2012	Motte	Jason	SLN	2.778	3	0.926	1	1	8	21.7	2.08
138	2016	Lewis	Colby	TEX	2.762	3	0.921	4	1	0	52.0	3.12
139	1992	Moore	Mike	OAK	2.756	3	0.919	4	3	0	38.3	3.29
140	2001	Wohlers	Mark	NYA	2.756	7	0.394	1	2	9	38.3	2.35
141	2019	Greinke	Zach	HOU	2.748	6	0.458	3	6	0	92.0	4.21
142	2019	Osuna	Roberto	HOU	2.746	4	0.686	2	1	5	33.3	2.97
143	2015	Rosenthal	Trevor	SLN	2.734	4	0.683	1	0	7	26.0	0.69
144	1945	Derringer	Paul	CHN	2.730	4	0.683	2	4	0	52.7	3.42
145	2000	Cone	David	NYA	2.727	8	0.341	8	3	0	111.3	3.80
146	2018	Madson	Ryan	LAN	2.727	7	0.390	6	1	2	56.0	2.73
147	1954	Lemon	Bob	CLE	2.704	2	1.352	2	2	0	29.7	3.94
148	2001	Rocker	John	CLE	2.701	4	0.675	2	0	3	20.7	0.00
149	1929	Ehmke	Howard	PHA	2.675	1	2.675	1	0	0	12.7	1.42
150	2016	Casilla	Santiago	SFN	2.666	4	0.667	1	0	4	19.7	0.92

Abbreviation Code: LPostYr - Last Postseason Year; PTeam - Final Postseason Team.
Note: Postseason PEVA reflects 10% of regular PEVA values for the Regular Season.
Note: Statistics above reflect postseason stats only.

Hall of Fame - Position Rank

First Base

Rank	Name	LastName	HOF	PEVA TOTAL	YRS.	PER YR	HR	RBI	Ave.	W	SV	ERA
1	Lou	Gehrig	HOFP-1B	479.522	17	28.207	493	1995	0.340			
2	Cap	Anson	HOFP-1B	432.886	27	16.033	97	2076	0.333	0	1	4.50
3	Jimmie	Foxx	HOFP-1B	359.936	20	17.997	534	1922	0.325	1	0	1.52
4	Dan	Brouthers	HOFP-1B	348.085	19	18.320	106	1296	0.342	0	0	7.83
5	Roger	Connor	HOFP-1B	336.978	18	18.721	138	1322	0.317			
6	Eddie	Murray	HOFP-1B	324.361	21	15.446	504	1917	0.287			
7	Jeff	Bagwell	HOFP-1B	293.606	15	19.574	449	1529	0.297			
8	Harmon	Killebrew	HOFP-1B	270.652	22	12.302	573	1584	0.256			
9	Willie	McCovey	HOFP-1B	261.038	22	11.865	521	1555	0.270			
10	Jim	Thome	HOFP-1B	257.863	22	11.721	612	1699	0.276			
11	Willie	Stargell	HOFP-1B	241.847	21	11.517	475	1540	0.282			
12	Tony	Perez	HOFP-1B	215.659	23	9.376	379	1652	0.279			
13	Hank	Greenberg	HOFP-1B	215.163	13	16.551	331	1276	0.313			
14	Jake	Beckley	HOFP-1B	213.234	20	10.662	86	1575	0.308	0	0	6.75
15	Orlando	Cepeda	HOFP-1B	209.487	17	12.323	379	1365	0.297			
16	George	Sisler	HOFP-1B	197.119	15	13.141	102	1175	0.340	5	3	2.35
17	Johnny	Mize	HOFP-1B	191.547	15	12.770	359	1337	0.312			
18	Bill	Terry	HOFP-1B	157.226	14	11.230	154	1078	0.341			
19	Jim	Bottomley	HOFP-1B	145.525	16	9.095	219	1422	0.310			
20	Frank	Chance	HOFP-1B	108.846	17	6.403	20	596	0.296			
21	George	Kelly	HOFP-1B	93.677	16	5.855	148	1020	0.297	1	0	0.00

Second Base

Rank	Name	LastName	HOF	PEVA TOTAL	YRS.	PER YR	HR	RBI	Ave.	W	SV	ERA
1	Rogers	Hornsby	HOFP-2B	361.117	23	15.701	301	1584	0.358			
2	Eddie	Collins	HOFP-2B	349.132	25	13.965	47	1300	0.333			
3	Nap	Lajoie	HOFP-2B	337.934	21	16.092	83	1599	0.338			
4	Joe	Morgan	HOFP-2B	287.830	22	13.083	268	1133	0.271			
5	Charlie	Gehringer	HOFP-2B	233.202	19	12.274	184	1427	0.320			
6	Craig	Biggio	HOFP-2B	226.358	20	11.358	291	1175	0.281			
7	Rod	Carew	HOFP-2B	208.083	19	10.952	92	1015	0.328			
8	Roberto	Alomar	HOFP-2B	184.493	17	10.853	210	1134	0.300			
9	Ryne	Sandberg	HOFP-2B	177.295	16	11.081	282	1061	0.285			
10	Bid	McPhee	HOFP-2B	166.066	18	9.226	53	1067	0.271			
11	Bobby	Doerr	HOFP-2B	157.073	14	11.219	223	1247	0.288			
12	Nellie	Fox	HOFP-2B	155.463	19	8.182	35	790	0.288			
13	Jackie	Robinson	HOFP-2B	146.209	10	14.621	137	734	0.311			
14	Frankie	Frisch	HOFP-2B	141.796	19	7.463	105	1244	0.316			
15	Red	Schoendienst	HOFP-2B	131.155	19	6.903	84	773	0.289			
16	Billy	Herman	HOFP-2B	131.084	15	8.739	47	839	0.304			

17	Joe	Gordon	HOFP-2B	**127.893**	11	11.627	253	975	0.268		
18	Tony	Lazzeri	HOFP-2B	**126.796**	14	9.057	178	1191	0.292		
19	Johnny	Evers	HOFP-2B	**102.257**	18	5.681	12	538	0.270		
20	Bill	Mazeroski	HOFP-2B	**98.836**	17	5.814	138	853	0.260		

Third Base

Rank	Name	LastName	HOF	PEVA TOTAL	YRS.	PER YR	HR	RBI	Ave.	W	SV	ERA
1	Mike	Schmidt	HOFP-3B	**383.574**	18	21.310	548	1595	0.267			
2	Eddie	Mathews	HOFP-3B	**360.187**	17	21.187	512	1453	0.271			
3	George	Brett	HOFP-3B	**301.897**	21	14.376	317	1595	0.305			
4	Wade	Boggs	HOFP-3B	**293.035**	18	16.280	118	1014	0.328	0	0	3.86
5	Chipper	Jones	HOFP-3B	**277.793**	19	14.621	468	1623	0.303			
6	Deacon	White	HOFP-3B	**274.720**	20	13.736	23	977	0.312	0	1	7.20
7	Ron	Santo	HOFP-3B	**259.712**	15	17.314	342	1331	0.277			
8	Brooks	Robinson	HOFP-3B	**232.881**	23	10.125	268	1357	0.267			
9	Frank	Baker	HOFP-3B	**204.500**	13	15.731	96	987	0.307			
10	Jimmy	Collins	HOFP-3B	**167.223**	14	11.944	65	983	0.294			
11	Pie	Traynor	HOFP-3B	**141.423**	17	8.319	58	1273	0.320			
12	George	Kell	HOFP-3B	**134.828**	15	8.989	78	870	0.306			
13	Freddie	Lindstrom	HOFP-3B	**95.076**	13	7.314	103	779	0.311			

Shortstop

Rank	Name	LastName	HOF	PEVA TOTAL	YRS.	PER YR	HR	RBI	Ave.	W	SV	ERA
1	Honus	Wagner	HOFP-SS	**451.472**	21	21.499	101	1732	0.327	0	0	0.00
2	Cal	Ripken	HOFP-SS	**320.188**	21	15.247	431	1695	0.276			
3	Robin	Yount	HOFP-SS	**291.976**	20	14.599	251	1406	0.285			
4	Ernie	Banks	HOFP-SS	**264.788**	19	13.936	512	1636	0.274			
5	Derek	Jeter	HOFP-SS	**259.937**	20	12.977	260	1311	0.310			
6	George	Davis	HOFP-SS	**245.441**	20	12.272	73	1437	0.295	0	1	15.75
7	John	Ward	HOFP-SS	**212.855**	17	12.521	26	867	0.275	164	3	2.10
8	Luke	Appling	HOFP-SS	**210.671**	20	10.534	45	1116	0.310			
9	Joe	Cronin	HOFP-SS	**196.868**	20	9.843	170	1424	0.301			
10	Arky	Vaughan	HOFP-SS	**191.281**	14	13.663	96	926	0.318			
11	Alan	Trammel	HOFP-SS	**189.326**	20	9.466	185	1003	0.285			
12	Bobby	Wallace	HOFP-SS	**186.535**	25	7.461	34	1121	0.268	24	1	3.87
13	Lou	Boudreau	HOFP-SS	**168.772**	15	11.251	68	789	0.295			
14	Pee Wee	Reese	HOFP-SS	**166.690**	16	10.418	126	885	0.269			
15	Barry	Larkin	HOFP-SS	**165.994**	19	8.737	198	960	0.295			
16	Ozzie	Smith	HOFP-SS	**162.052**	19	8.529	28	793	0.262			
17	Joe	Sewell	HOFP-SS	**159.048**	14	11.361	49	1055	0.312			
18	Luis	Aparicio	HOFP-SS	**156.787**	18	8.710	83	791	0.262			
19	Hughie	Jennings	HOFP-SS	**152.306**	17	8.959	18	840	0.311			
20	Rabbit	Maranville	HOFP-SS	**148.551**	23	6.459	28	884	0.258			
21	Dave	Bancroft	HOFP-SS	**122.761**	16	7.673	32	591	0.279			
22	Joe	Tinker	HOFP-SS	**119.627**	15	7.975	31	782	0.262			
23	Phil	Rizzuto	HOFP-SS	**111.989**	13	8.615	38	563	0.273			
24	Travis	Jackson	HOFP-SS	**98.655**	15	6.577	135	929	0.291			

Catcher

Rank	Name	LastName	HOF	PEVA TOTAL	YRS.	PER YR	HR	RBI	Ave.	W	SV	ERA
1	Johnny	Bench	HOFP-C	256.662	17	15.098	389	1376	0.267			
2	Mike	Piazza	HOFP-C	255.854	18	14.214	427	1335	0.308			
3	Yogi	Berra	HOFP-C	251.624	19	13.243	358	1430	0.285			
4	Ted	Simmons	HOFP-C	239.551	21	11.407	248	1389	0.285			
5	Gary	Carter	HOFP-C	233.612	19	12.295	324	1225	0.262			
6	Carlton	Fisk	HOFP-C	214.953	24	8.956	376	1330	0.269			
7	Bill	Dickey	HOFP-C	202.680	17	11.922	202	1209	0.313			
8	Ivan	Rodriguez	HOFP-C	192.303	23	8.361	311	1332	0.296			
9	Mickey	Cochrane	HOFP-C	173.444	13	13.342	119	832	0.320			
10	Roy	Campanella	HOFP-C	162.658	10	16.266	242	856	0.276			
11	Gabby	Hartnett	HOFP-C	155.361	20	7.768	236	1179	0.297			
12	Buck	Ewing	HOFP-C	146.265	18	8.126	71	883	0.303	2	0	3.45
13	Ernie	Lombardi	HOFP-C	126.894	17	7.464	190	990	0.306			
14	Roger	Bresnahan	HOFP-C	120.459	17	7.086	26	530	0.279	4	0	3.93
15	Rick	Ferrell	HOFP-C	109.810	18	6.101	28	734	0.281			
16	Ray	Schalk	HOFP-C	102.242	18	5.680	11	594	0.253			

Outfielders - Right Field

Rank	Name	LastName	HOF	PEVA TOTAL	YRS.	PER YR	HR	RBI	Ave.	W	SV	ERA
1	Babe	Ruth	HOFP-RF	690.379	22	31.381	714	2217	0.342	94	4	2.28
2	Hank	Aaron	HOFP-RF	535.808	23	23.296	755	2297	0.305			
3	Frank	Robinson	HOFP-RF	411.403	21	19.591	586	1812	0.294			
4	Mel	Ott	HOFP-RF	369.518	22	16.796	511	1860	0.304			
5	Reggie	Jackson	HOFP-RF	301.318	21	14.348	563	1702	0.262			
6	Al	Kaline	HOFP-RF	297.259	22	13.512	399	1583	0.297			
7	Sam	Crawford	HOFP-RF	295.985	19	15.578	97	1525	0.309			
8	Roberto	Clemente	HOFP-RF	264.635	18	14.702	240	1305	0.317			
9	Harry	Heilmann	HOFP-RF	249.516	17	14.677	183	1539	0.342			
10	Paul	Waner	HOFP-RF	242.638	20	12.132	113	1309	0.333			
11	Tony	Gwynn	HOFP-RF	238.944	20	11.947	135	1138	0.338			
12	King	Kelly	HOFP-RF	235.100	16	14.694	69	950	0.308	2	0	4.14
13	Andre	Dawson	HOFP-RF	230.234	21	10.964	438	1591	0.279			
14	Vladimir	Guerrero	HOFP-RF	214.609	16	13.413	449	1496	0.318			
15	Willie	Keeler	HOFP-RF	220.111	19	11.585	33	810	0.341			
16	Sam	Thompson	HOFP-RF	206.207	15	13.747	127	1299	0.331			
17	Harry	Hooper	HOFP-RF	191.097	17	11.241	75	817	0.281	0	0	0.00
18	Sam	Rice	HOFP-RF	182.580	20	9.129	34	1078	0.322	1	0	2.52
19	Enos	Slaughter	HOFP-RF	180.421	19	9.496	169	1304	0.300			
20	Chuck	Klein	HOFP-RF	169.818	17	9.989	300	1201	0.320			
21	Ross	Youngs	HOFP-RF	110.998	10	11.100	42	592	0.322			
22	Tommy	McCarthy	HOFP-RF	100.436	13	7.726	44	735	0.292	0	0	4.93

Outfielders - Centerfield

Rank	Name	LastName	HOF	PEVA TOTAL	YRS.	PER YR	HR	RBI	Ave.	W	SV	ERA
1	Ty	Cobb	HOFP-CF	569.252	24	23.719	117	1937	0.366	0	1	3.60
2	Willie	Mays	HOFP-CF	520.998	22	23.682	660	1903	0.302			

Rank	Name	LastName	HOF	PEVA TOTAL	YRS.	PER YR	HR	RBI	Ave.	W	SV	ERA
3	Tris	Speaker	HOFP-CF	**479.576**	22	21.799	117	1529	0.345	0	0	9.00
4	Mickey	Mantle	HOFP-CF	**455.611**	18	25.312	536	1509	0.298			
5	Joe	DiMaggio	HOFP-CF	**297.630**	13	22.895	361	1537	0.325			
6	Ken	Griffey, Jr.	HOFP-CF	**286.056**	23	12.437	630	1836	0.284			
7	Duke	Snider	HOFP-CF	**253.177**	18	14.065	407	1333	0.295			
8	Billy	Hamilton	HOFP-CF	**231.802**	14	16.557	40	736	0.344			
9	Hugh	Duffy	HOFP-CF	**215.369**	17	12.669	106	1302	0.324			
10	Zack	Wheat	HOFP-CF	**213.678**	19	11.246	132	1248	0.317			
11	Elmer	Flick	HOFP-CF	**207.666**	13	15.974	48	756	0.313			
12	Richie	Ashburn	HOFP-CF	**207.541**	15	13.836	29	586	0.308			
13	Kirby	Puckett	HOFP-CF	**204.074**	12	17.006	207	1085	0.318			
14	Max	Carey	HOFP-CF	**194.330**	20	9.717	70	800	0.285			
15	Earl	Averill	HOFP-CF	**187.958**	13	14.458	238	1164	0.318			
16	Larry	Doby	HOFP-CF	**183.611**	13	14.124	253	970	0.283			
17	Edd	Roush	HOFP-CF	**173.402**	18	9.633	68	981	0.323			
18	Hack	Wilson	HOFP-CF	**149.587**	12	12.466	244	1063	0.307			
19	Earle	Combs	HOFP-CF	**131.405**	12	10.950	58	632	0.325			
20	Lloyd	Waner	HOFP-CF	**107.291**	18	5.961	27	598	0.316			

Outfielders - Left Field

Rank	Name	LastName	HOF	PEVA TOTAL	YRS.	PER YR	HR	RBI	Ave.	W	SV	ERA
1	Ted	Williams	HOFP-LF	**493.074**	19	25.951	521	1839	0.344	0	0	4.50
2	Stan	Musial	HOFP-LF	**481.184**	22	21.872	475	1951	0.331	0	0	-
3	Ed	Delahanty	HOFP-LF	**351.660**	16	21.979	101	1464	0.346			
4	Carl	Yastrzemski	HOFP-LF	**339.140**	23	14.745	452	1844	0.285			
5	Rickey	Henderson	HOFP-LF	**331.490**	25	13.260	297	1115	0.279			
6	Jim	O'Rourke	HOFP-LF	**329.815**	23	14.340	62	1203	0.311	0	2	4.12
7	Dave	Winfield	HOFP-LF	**327.768**	22	14.899	465	1833	0.283			
8	Jesse	Burkett	HOFP-LF	**276.693**	16	17.293	75	952	0.338	3	0	5.56
9	Billy	Williams	HOFP-LF	**275.510**	18	15.306	426	1475	0.290			
10	Fred	Clarke	HOFP-LF	**255.011**	21	12.143	67	1015	0.312			
11	Al	Simmons	HOFP-LF	**237.604**	20	11.880	307	1827	0.334			
12	Tim	Raines	HOFP-LF	**226.257**	24	9.427	170	980	0.294			
13	Joe	Kelley	HOFP-LF	**226.052**	17	13.297	65	1194	0.317			
14	Jim	Rice	HOFP-LF	**224.084**	16	14.005	382	1451	0.298			
15	Goose	Goslin	HOFP-LF	**220.227**	18	12.235	248	1609	0.316			
16	Ralph	Kiner	HOFP-LF	**208.610**	10	20.861	369	1015	0.279			
17	Joe	Medwick	HOFP-LF	**186.522**	17	10.972	205	1383	0.324			
18	Lou	Brock	HOFP-LF	**179.216**	19	9.432	149	900	0.293			
19	Kiki	Cuyler	HOFP-LF	**161.663**	18	8.981	128	1065	0.321			
20	Heinie	Manush	HOFP-LF	**156.227**	17	9.190	110	1183	0.330			
21	Chick	Hafey	HOFP-LF	**92.982**	13	7.152	164	833	0.317			
22	Monte	Irvin	HOFP-LF	**60.284**	8	7.535	99	443	0.293			

Designated Hitter

Rank	Name	LastName	HOF	PEVA TOTAL	YRS.	PER YR	HR	RBI	Ave.	W	SV	ERA
1	Frank	Thomas	HOFP-DH	**333.924**	19	17.575	521	1704	0.301			
2	Paul	Molitor	HOFP-DH	**242.403**	21	11.543	234	1307	0.306			
3	Edgar	Martinez	HOFP-DH	**225.436**	18	12.524	309	1261	0.312			

| 4 | Harold | Baines | HOFP-DH | 188.522 | 22 | 8.569 | 384 | 1628 | 0.289 | | |

Pitcher

Rank	Name	LastName	HOF	PEVA TOTAL	YRS.	PER YR	HR	RBI	Ave.	W	SV	ERA
1	Greg	Maddux	HOFP-P	594.209	23	25.835	5	84	0.171	355	0	3.16
2	Cy	Young	HOFP-P	505.634	22	22.983	18	290	0.210	511	17	2.63
3	Walter	Johnson	HOFP-P	488.778	21	23.275	24	255	0.235	417	34	2.17
4	Randy	Johnson	HOFP-P	408.708	22	18.578	1	40	0.125	303	2	3.29
5	Pete	Alexander	HOFP-P	387.680	20	19.384	11	163	0.209	373	32	2.56
6	Warren	Spahn	HOFP-P	372.497	21	17.738	35	189	0.194	363	29	3.09
7	Lefty	Grove	HOFP-P	342.629	17	20.155	15	121	0.148	300	55	3.06
8	Tom	Seaver	HOFP-P	336.144	20	16.807	12	86	0.154	311	1	2.86
9	Steve	Carlton	HOFP-P	328.713	24	13.696	13	140	0.201	329	2	3.22
10	Pedro	Martinez	HOFP-P	328.493	18	18.250	0	18	0.099	219	3	2.93
11	Tom	Glavine	HOFP-P	325.047	22	14.775	1	90	0.186	305	0	3.54
12	Kid	Nichols	HOFP-P	316.988	15	21.133	16	278	0.226	361	17	2.95
13	Robin	Roberts	HOFP-P	309.046	19	16.266	5	103	0.167	286	25	3.41
14	Roy	Halladay	HOFP-P	304.746	16	19.047	0	12	0.124	203	1	3.38
15	Carl	Hubbell	HOFP-P	302.043	16	18.878	4	101	0.191	253	33	2.98
16	John	Smoltz	HOFP-P	301.456	21	14.355	5	61	0.159	213	154	3.33
17	Christy	Mathewson	HOFP-P	293.500	17	17.265	7	165	0.215	373	28	2.13
18	Gaylord	Perry	HOFP-P	286.329	22	13.015	6	47	0.131	314	11	3.11
19	Mike	Mussina	HOFP-P	276.995	18	15.389	0	5	0.173	270	0	3.68
20	Bert	Blyleven	HOFP-P	271.050	22	12.320	0	25	0.131	287	250	3.31
21	Nolan	Ryan	HOFP-P	270.539	27	10.020	2	36	0.110	324	3	3.19
22	Phil	Niekro	HOFP-P	269.835	24	11.243	7	109	0.169	318	29	3.35
23	Don	Sutton	HOFP-P	266.168	23	11.573	0	64	0.144	324	5	3.26
24	Fergie	Jenkins	HOFP-P	250.825	19	13.201	13	85	0.165	284	7	3.34
25	Bob	Feller	HOFP-P	246.598	18	13.700	8	99	0.151	266	21	3.25
26	Mariano	Rivera	HOFP-P	245.654	19	12.929	0	1	0.000	82	652	2.21
27	Jim	Palmer	HOFP-P	240.182	19	12.641	3	41	0.174	268	4	2.86
28	Jim	Bunning	HOFP-P	232.753	17	13.691	7	75	0.167	224	16	3.27
29	Juan	Marichal	HOFP-P	231.781	16	14.486	4	75	0.165	243	2	2.89
30	Don	Drysdale	HOFP-P	231.166	14	16.512	29	113	0.186	209	6	2.95
31	Bob	Gibson	HOFP-P	227.176	17	13.363	24	144	0.206	251	6	2.91
32	Early	Wynn	HOFP-P	223.795	23	9.730	17	173	0.214	300	15	3.54
33	Hal	Newhouser	HOFP-P	219.148	17	12.891	2	81	0.201	207	26	3.06
34	Dennis	Eckersley	HOFP-P	217.107	24	9.046	3	12	0.133	197	390	3.50
35	Ed	Walsh	HOFP-P	214.819	14	15.344	3	68	0.193	195	34	1.82
36	Dazzy	Vance	HOFP-P	212.748	16	13.297	7	75	0.150	197	11	3.24
37	Amos	Rusie	HOFP-P	210.560	10	21.056	8	176	0.247	245	5	3.07
38	Sandy	Koufax	HOFP-P	206.787	12	17.232	2	28	0.097	165	9	2.76
39	Eppa	Rixey	HOFP-P	202.106	21	9.624	3	111	0.191	266	14	3.15
40	Whitey	Ford	HOFP-P	201.182	16	12.574	3	69	0.173	236	10	2.75
41	John	Clarkson	HOFP-P	197.394	12	16.449	24	232	0.219	328	5	2.81
42	Jack	Morris	HOFP-P	194.913	18	10.829	0	0	0.000	254	0	3.90
43	Burleigh	Grimes	HOFP-P	187.970	19	9.893	2	168	0.248	270	18	3.53
44	Ted	Lyons	HOFP-P	180.468	21	8.594	5	149	0.233	260	23	3.67
45	Tim	Keefe	HOFP-P	178.455	14	12.747	12	134	0.187	342	2	2.62
46	Red	Faber	HOFP-P	177.411	20	8.871	3	70	0.134	254	28	3.15

	Name	LastName	HOF	PEVA TOTAL	YRS.	PER YR	HR	RBI	Ave.	W	SV	ERA
47	Stan	Coveleski	HOFP-P	**176.253**	14	12.589	1	81	0.159	215	21	2.89
48	Joe	McGinnity	HOFP-P	**176.188**	10	17.619	0	90	0.194	246	24	2.66
49	Eddie	Plank	HOFP-P	**174.524**	17	10.266	3	122	0.206	326	23	2.35
50	Catfish	Hunter	HOFP-P	**172.508**	15	11.501	6	51	0.226	224	1	3.26
51	Bob	Lemon	HOFP-P	**171.875**	15	11.458	37	147	0.232	207	22	3.23
52	Mordecai	Brown	HOFP-P	**168.239**	14	12.017	2	74	0.206	239	49	2.06
53	Hoyt	Wilhelm	HOFP-P	**167.483**	21	7.975	1	21	0.088	143	227	2.52
54	Trevor	Hoffman	HOFP-P	**166.371**	18	9.243	0	5	0.118	61	601	2.87
55	Red	Ruffing	HOFP-P	**166.258**	22	7.557	36	273	0.269	273	16	3.80
56	Dizzy	Dean	HOFP-P	**163.005**	12	13.584	8	76	0.225	150	30	3.02
57	Vic	Willis	HOFP-P	**159.269**	13	12.251	1	84	0.166	249	11	2.63
58	Pud	Galvin	HOFP-P	**154.695**	15	10.313	5	220	0.201	364	2	2.86
59	Charley	Radbourn	HOFP-P	**153.761**	12	12.813	9	259	0.235	309	2	2.67
60	Waite	Hoyt	HOFP-P	**150.713**	21	7.177	0	100	0.198	237	52	3.59
61	Rich	Gossage	HOFP-P	**138.013**	22	6.273	0	2	0.106	124	310	3.01
62	Lefty	Gomez	HOFP-P	**135.569**	14	9.683	0	58	0.147	189	9	3.34
63	Rollie	Fingers	HOFP-P	**130.458**	17	7.674	2	9	0.172	114	341	2.90
64	Rube	Waddell	HOFP-P	**129.158**	13	9.935	4	83	0.161	193	5	2.16
65	Herb	Pennock	HOFP-P	**124.406**	22	5.655	4	103	0.191	240	32	3.60
66	Addie	Joss	HOFP-P	**121.462**	9	13.496	1	51	0.144	160	5	1.89
67	Jack	Chesbro	HOFP-P	**120.772**	11	10.979	5	82	0.197	198	5	2.68
68	Jesse	Haines	HOFP-P	**116.440**	19	6.128	3	79	0.186	210	10	3.64
69	Mickey	Welch	HOFP-P	**115.650**	13	8.896	12	202	0.224	307	4	2.71
70	Lee	Smith	HOFP-P	**113.816**	18	6.323	1	2	0.047	71	478	3.03
71	Chief	Bender	HOFP-P	**109.459**	16	6.841	6	116	0.212	212	34	2.46
72	Bruce	Sutter	HOFP-P	**108.819**	12	9.068	0	6	0.088	68	300	2.83
73	Rube	Marquard	HOFP-P	**104.505**	18	5.806	1	64	0.179	201	19	3.08

Executives and Managers

Rank	Name	LastName	HOF	PEVA TOTAL	YRS.	PER YR	HR	RBI	Ave.	W	SV	ERA
Executive												
1	Al	Spalding	HOFEP	**233.591**	8	29.199	2	327	0.313	253	11	2.14
2	George	Wright	HOFEP	**155.730**	12	12.978	11	330	0.302	0	0	1.80
3	Clark	Griffith	HOFEP	**135.858**	21	6.469	8	166	0.233	237	6	3.31
4	Charlie	Comiskey	HOFEP	**86.636**	13	6.664	29	883	0.264	0	0	0.73
5	Candy	Cummings	HOFEP	**78.342**	6	13.057	0	107	0.212	145	0	2.49
Manager												
1	Joe	Torre	HOFM	**214.765**	18	11.931	252	1185	0.297			
2	Miller	Huggins	HOFM	**110.533**	13	8.503	9	318	0.265			
3	Ned	Hanlon	HOFM	**110.182**	13	8.476	30	517	0.260			
4	John	McGraw	HOFM	**106.609**	16	6.663	13	462	0.334			
5	Al	Lopez	HOFM	**75.328**	19	3.965	51	652	0.261			

Note: Listed above, Top Five Executives and Managers in the Hall of Fame per Playing Career.

CHAPTER ELEVEN

BEST TEAMS OF ALL-TIME
(1871-2020)

Who were the best teams in history? That is not an easy calculation. Wins and losses only get you so far, although that is important, but it does not take into account the quality of the competition or league that year. Counting stats are unreliable when the game has changed so much over the various era. One thing to note right off the bat. We've segmented this into batting and pitching first off, which helps us understand just why the team was so great. And we'll note up front that it is much easier to compare a great Batting Team over the history of the game than a Pitching Team.

Why? Well, we have a theory, and it starts with the fact that nine players have batted throughout the game from 1871 to the present day, even if now one half, and more in 2020, of baseball has the designated hitter. And that has been consistent. With pitching, staffs have changed so much since the early days, and even over the last generation, that a team may have had only five pitchers prior to 1900, ten one generation ago, and twelve to fourteen now, even higher in 2020. And that seems to push the current teams on the pitching side of the Best Ever equation higher on the list than we wonder if accurate, and that's even after we adjust for era. It's probably better to think of Best Pitching by those eras, and that can extend to the Best Ever Total, too. Then there's those recent problems with very good teams that banged trash cans and stole signs, then won a World Series. Adjust as you must.

Best Batting Teams in History

Top 50 Best Batting Teams

RANK	YEAR	TEAM	NAME	TEAM	LG	TPEVA	HR	RBI	H	AB	RBI/AB	AVE
1	1875	Boston	Red Stockings	BS1	NA	196.454	15	565	1128	3515	0.161	0.321
2	1982	Milwaukee	Brewers	ML4	AL	179.546	216	843	1599	5733	0.147	0.279
3	1927	New York	Yankees	NYA	AL	171.098	158	908	1644	5354	0.170	0.307
4	1953	Brooklyn	Dodgers	BRO	NL	170.780	208	887	1529	5373	0.165	0.285
5	1931	New York	Yankees	NYA	AL	163.287	155	990	1667	5608	0.177	0.297
6	1884	Chicago	Cubs	CHN	NL	162.624	142	659	1176	4182	0.158	0.281
7	1972	Cincinnati	Reds	CIN	NL	158.351	124	650	1317	5241	0.124	0.251
8	1936	New York	Yankees	NYA	AL	157.153	182	997	1676	5591	0.178	0.300
9	1976	Cincinnati	Reds	CIN	NL	154.883	141	802	1599	5702	0.141	0.280
10	1982	California	Angels	CAL	AL	152.063	186	760	1518	5532	0.137	0.274
11	1879	Providence	Grays	PRO	NL	151.952	12	405	1003	3392	0.119	0.296
12	1984	Boston	Red Sox	BOS	AL	151.098	181	767	1598	5648	0.136	0.283
13	1937	New York	Yankees	NYA	AL	150.175	174	922	1554	5487	0.168	0.283
14	1952	New York	Yankees	NYA	AL	149.690	129	670	1411	5294	0.127	0.267
15	1933	New York	Yankees	NYA	AL	149.382	144	853	1495	5271	0.162	0.284
16	1873	Boston	Red Stockings	BS1	NA	149.027	12	489	930	2755	0.177	0.338
17	1960	New York	Yankees	NYA	AL	147.023	193	699	1377	5290	0.132	0.260
18	1896	Baltimore	Orioles	BLN	NL	146.373	23	854	1548	4719	0.181	0.328
19	1952	Brooklyn	Dodgers	BRO	NL	146.278	153	725	1380	5266	0.138	0.262
20	1939	New York	Yankees	NYA	AL	146.205	166	904	1521	5300	0.171	0.287
21	1891	Boston	Reds	BS2	AA	146.136	52	776	1341	4889	0.159	0.274
22	1951	Brooklyn	Dodgers	BRO	NL	144.929	184	794	1511	5492	0.145	0.275
23	1960	Milwaukee	Braves	ML1	NL	144.533	170	681	1393	5263	0.129	0.265

RANK	YEAR	TEAM	NAME	TEAM	LG	TPEVA	HR	RBI	H	AB	RBI/AB	AVE
24	1880	Chicago	Cubs	CHN	NL	143.676	4	378	876	3135	0.121	0.279
25	1952	Cleveland	Indians	CLE	AL	143.171	148	721	1399	5330	0.135	0.262
26	1897	Baltimore	Orioles	BLN	NL	142.379	19	821	1584	4872	0.169	0.325
27	1876	Chicago	Cubs	CHN	NL	141.360	8	441	926	2748	0.160	0.337
28	1929	Chicago	Cubs	CHN	NL	140.740	139	933	1655	5471	0.171	0.303
29	1965	Cincinnati	Reds	CIN	NL	140.392	183	776	1544	5658	0.137	0.273
30	1932	New York	Yankees	NYA	AL	139.838	160	954	1564	5476	0.174	0.286
31	1874	Boston	Red Stockings	BS1	NA	139.659	17	495	979	3130	0.158	0.313
32	2007	New York	Yankees	NYA	AL	139.536	201	929	1656	5717	0.162	0.290
33	1930	New York	Yankees	NYA	AL	139.300	152	986	1683	5447	0.181	0.309
34	1959	Milwaukee	Braves	ML1	NL	139.078	177	683	1426	5388	0.127	0.265
35	1944	St. Louis	Cardinals	SLN	NL	138.770	100	722	1507	5474	0.132	0.275
36	1970	San Fran.	Giants	SFN	NL	138.709	165	773	1460	5578	0.139	0.262
37	1892	Philadelphia	Phillies	PHI	NL	138.587	50	693	1420	5413	0.128	0.262
38	1961	New York	Yankees	NYA	AL	138.358	240	782	1461	5559	0.141	0.263
39	1972	Houston	Astros	HOU	NL	138.349	134	660	1359	5267	0.125	0.258
40	1970	Cincinnati	Reds	CIN	NL	137.134	191	726	1498	5540	0.131	0.270
41	2006	New York	Yankees	NYA	AL	136.941	210	902	1608	5651	0.160	0.285
42	1895	Philadelphia	Phillies	PHI	NL	136.760	61	930	1664	5037	0.185	0.330
43	1996	Seattle	Mariners	SEA	AL	135.872	245	954	1625	5668	0.168	0.287
44	1962	San Fran.	Giants	SFN	NL	135.504	204	807	1552	5588	0.144	0.278
45	1941	Boston	Red Sox	BOS	AL	134.850	124	804	1517	5359	0.150	0.283
46	1882	Chicago	Cubs	CHN	NL	134.682	15	451	892	3225	0.140	0.277
47	2017	Houston	Astros	HOU	AL	134.614	238	854	1581	5611	0.152	0.282
48	1933	Philadelphia	Athletics	PHA	AL	134.598	139	831	1519	5329	0.156	0.285
49	2000	San Francisco	Giants	SFN	NL	133.869	226	889	1535	5519	0.161	0.278
50	1926	New York	Yankees	NYA	AL	133.599	121	791	1507	5210	0.152	0.289

Best Pitching Teams in History

Top 50 Best Pitching Teams

RANK	YEAR	TEAM	NAME	TEAM	LG	PEVA	W	L	SV	ERA	Adj.F	ADJ. PEVA
1	1888	St. Louis	Browns	SL4	AA	70.183	92	43	0	2.09	2.378	166.887
2	2019	Houston	Astros	HOU	AL	175.535	107	55	47	3.66	0.930	163.248
3	1894	New York	Giants	NY1	NL	91.509	88	44	5	3.83	1.667	152.510
4	1993	Atlanta	Braves	ATL	NL	145.575	104	58	46	3.14	1.008	146.696
5	1925	Cincinnati	Reds	CIN	NL	123.561	80	73	12	3.37	1.184	146.284
6	1909	Chicago	Cubs	CHN	NL	84.728	104	49	11	1.74	1.637	138.669
7	1998	Atlanta	Braves	ATL	NL	135.255	106	56	45	3.25	1.008	136.296
8	1997	Atlanta	Braves	ATL	NL	135.166	101	61	37	3.18	1.008	136.207
9	1933	New York	Giants	NY1	NL	104.438	91	61	15	2.71	1.282	133.899
10	1996	Atlanta	Braves	ATL	NL	131.693	96	66	46	3.54	1.008	132.708
11	2017	Cleveland	Indians	CLE	AL	140.904	102	60	37	3.30	0.930	131.041
12	1940	Cincinnati	Reds	CIN	NL	106.689	100	53	11	3.05	1.225	130.704
13	1954	Cleveland	Indians	CLE	AL	110.051	111	43	36	2.78	1.185	130.455
14	1939	Cincinnati	Reds	CIN	NL	101.004	97	57	9	3.27	1.282	129.496

RANK	YEAR	TEAM	NAME	TEAM	LG	PEVA	W	L	SV	ERA	AVE	TOTAL PEVA
15	1879	Boston	Red Caps	BSN	NL	**43.543**	54	30	0	2.19	2.916	**126.967**
16	1910	Philadelphia	Athletics	PHA	AL	**80.273**	102	48	5	1.79	1.579	**126.722**
17	2011	Philadelphia	Phillies	PHI	NL	**135.613**	102	60	47	3.02	0.930	**126.120**
18	2016	Chicago	Cubs	CHN	NL	**135.090**	103	58	38	3.15	0.930	**125.634**
19	1970	Baltimore	Orioles	BAL	AL	**98.779**	108	54	31	3.15	1.265	**124.921**
20	1912	Washington	Senators	WS1	AL	**79.087**	91	61	7	2.69	1.579	**124.851**
21	2019	Los Angeles	Dodgers	LAN	NL	**133.495**	106	56	44	3.37	0.930	**124.151**
22	1960	Pittsburgh	Pirates	PIT	NL	**102.437**	95	59	33	3.49	1.210	**123.949**
23	1884	Providence	Grays	PRO	NL	**52.094**	84	28	2	1.61	2.378	**123.873**
24	2001	Arizona	Diamondbacks	ARI	NL	**122.915**	92	70	34	3.88	1.000	**122.915**
25	1916	Philadelphia	Phillies	PHI	NL	**77.739**	91	62	9	2.36	1.579	**122.722**
26	2006	Minnesota	Twins	MIN	AL	**122.308**	96	66	40	3.95	1.000	**122.308**
27	1899	Boston	Beaneaters	BSN	NL	**73.211**	95	57	4	3.26	1.667	**122.014**
28	1899	St. Louis	Cardinals	SLN	NL	**72.926**	83	67	1	3.36	1.667	**121.540**
29	1929	Philadelphia	Athletics	PHA	AL	**102.612**	104	46	24	3.44	1.184	**121.482**
30	1888	New York	Giants	NY1	NL	**50.949**	83	47	1	1.96	2.378	**121.149**
31	2002	Arizona	Diamondbacks	ARI	NL	**120.929**	98	64	40	3.93	1.000	**120.929**
32	2017	Washington	Nationals	LAN	NL	**129.903**	97	65	46	3.88	0.930	**120.810**
33	1877	Louisville	Grays	LS1	NL	**41.423**	35	25	0	2.25	2.916	**120.785**
34	2012	Cincinnati	Reds	CIN	NL	**129.337**	97	65	56	3.34	0.930	**120.283**
35	1898	Boston	Beaneaters	BSN	NL	**72.067**	102	47	8	2.98	1.667	**120.108**
36	1934	New York	Giants	NY1	NL	**93.679**	93	60	30	3.19	1.282	**120.105**
37	1942	St. Louis	Cardinals	SLN	NL	**97.724**	106	48	15	2.55	1.225	**119.721**
38	2009	St. Louis	Cardinals	SLN	NL	**119.214**	91	71	43	3.66	1.000	**119.214**
39	1963	Los Angeles	Dodgers	LAN	NL	**98.516**	99	63	29	2.85	1.210	**119.205**
40	2007	San Diego	Padres	SDN	NL	**118.019**	89	74	45	3.72	1.000	**118.019**
41	1897	Boston	Beaneaters	BSN	NL	**70.686**	93	39	7	3.65	1.667	**117.807**
42	1989	Kansas City	Royals	KCA	AL	**101.423**	92	70	38	3.55	1.161	**117.789**
43	1918	Washington	Senators	WS1	AL	**74.596**	72	56	8	2.14	1.579	**117.761**
44	1995	Atlanta	Braves	ATL	NL	**116.630**	90	54	34	3.44	1.008	**117.528**
45	1896	Cleveland	Spiders	CL4	NL	**69.941**	80	48	5	3.46	1.667	**116.564**
46	2017	Los Angeles	Dodgers	LAN	NL	**125.177**	104	58	51	3.38	0.930	**116.415**
47	1885	Chicago	Cubs	CHN	NL	**48.848**	87	25	4	2.23	2.378	**116.154**
48	1918	Chicago	Cubs	CHN	NL	**73.505**	84	45	8	2.18	1.579	**116.038**
49	1965	Los Angeles	Dodgers	LAN	NL	**95.781**	97	65	34	2.81	1.210	**115.895**
50	1899	Baltimore	Orioles	BLN	NL	**69.475**	86	61	4	3.31	1.667	**115.788**

Best Teams in Baseball History

Top 50 Best Teams

RANK	YEAR	TEAM	NAME	TEAM	LG	W	L	ERA	PITCHING APEVA	BATTING PEVA	AVE	TOTAL PEVA
1	1875	Boston	Red Stockings	BS1	NA	71	8	1.87	95.303	196.454	0.321	**291.757**
2	2019	Houston	Astros	HOU	AL	107	55	3.66	163.248	115.446	0.274	**278.694**
3	1927	New York	Yankees	NYA	AL	110	44	3.20	91.461	171.098	0.307	**262.559**
4	1888	St. Louis	Browns	SL4	AA	92	43	2.09	166.887	89.219	0.250	**256.105**
5	1937	New York	Yankees	NYA	AL	102	52	3.65	97.265	150.175	0.283	**247.440**
6	1879	Boston	Red Caps	BSN	NL	54	30	2.19	126.397	120.463	0.274	**247.430**
7	2019	Los Angeles	Dodgers	LAN	NL	106	56	3.37	124.151	117.840	0.257	**241.990**
8	1993	Atlanta	Braves	ATL	NL	104	58	3.14	146.696	91.119	0.262	**237.814**

RANK	YEAR	TEAM	NAME	TEAM	LG	W	L	ERA	PITCHING APEVA	BATTING PEVA	AVE	TOTAL PEVA
9	1982	Milwaukee	Brewers	ML4	AL	95	67	3.99	56.206	179.546	0.279	235.751
10	2016	Chicago	Cubs	CHN	NL	103	58	3.15	125.634	109.551	0.256	235.185
11	1970	Baltimore	Orioles	BAL	AL	108	54	3.15	124.921	109.557	0.257	234.469
12	1998	Atlanta	Braves	ATL	NL	106	56	3.25	136.296	97.085	0.272	233.381
13	1897	Boston	Beaneaters	BSN	NL	93	39	3.65	117.807	115.242	0.319	233.049
14	1929	Philadelphia	Athletics	PHA	AL	104	46	3.44	121.482	111.452	0.295	232.934
15	1969	Baltimore	Orioles	BAL	AL	109	53	2.83	112.071	120.746	0.265	232.817
16	1961	Detroit	Tigers	DET	AL	101	61	3.55	104.122	127.731	0.266	231.853
17	1885	Chicago	Cubs	CHN	NL	87	25	2.23	116.154	115.492	0.264	231.646
18	1952	Cleveland	Indians	CLE	AL	93	61	3.32	87.983	143.171	0.262	231.155
19	1960	Pittsburgh	Pirates	PIT	NL	95	59	3.49	123.949	106.827	0.276	230.776
20	1874	Boston	Red Stockings	BS1	NA	52	18	1.93	90.604	139.659	0.312	230.263
21	1951	Brooklyn	Dodgers	BRO	NL	97	60	3.88	84.481	144.929	0.275	229.410
22	1906	Chicago	Cubs	CHN	NL	115	36	1.75	112.971	116.156	0.262	229.127
23	1961	New York	Yankees	NYA	AL	109	53	3.46	90.467	138.358	0.263	228.825
24	1873	Boston	Red Stockings	BS1	NA	43	16	2.59	79.795	149.027	0.338	228.822
25	2006	New York	Yankees	NYA	AL	97	65	4.43	91.646	136.941	0.285	228.587
26	1976	Cincinnati	Reds	CIN	NL	102	60	3.51	72.093	154.883	0.280	226.976
27	1879	Providence	Grays	PRO	NL	59	25	2.18	74.762	151.952	0.296	226.714
28	1897	Baltimore	Orioles	BLN	NL	90	40	3.55	84.323	142.379	0.325	226.701
29	1951	New York	Giants	NY1	NL	98	59	3.48	112.119	112.435	0.260	224.553
30	2001	Seattle	Mariners	SEA	AL	116	46	3.54	112.961	110.086	0.288	223.047
31	1909	Pittsburgh	Pirates	PIT	NL	110	42	2.07	105.465	117.499	0.260	222.965
32	2009	St. Louis	Cardinals	SLN	NL	91	71	3.66	119.214	103.489	0.263	222.703
33	1876	Chicago	Cubs	CHN	NL	52	14	1.76	81.312	141.360	0.337	222.672
34	1982	Montreal	Expos	MON	NL	86	76	3.33	98.761	123.899	0.262	222.661
35	1898	Boston	Beaneaters	BSN	NL	102	47	2.98	120.108	102.448	0.290	222.556
36	1970	Cincinnati	Reds	CIN	NL	102	60	3.71	85.281	137.134	0.270	222.416
37	2006	Minnesota	Twins	MIN	AL	96	66	3.95	122.308	100.104	0.287	222.411
38	1990	Oakland	A's	OAK	AL	103	59	3.18	102.813	119.094	0.254	221.906
39	2009	New York	Yankees	NYA	AL	103	59	4.28	88.723	132.926	0.283	221.649
40	1912	Boston	Red Sox	BOS	AL	105	47	2.76	109.117	111.963	0.277	221.079
41	2017	Washington	Nationals	WAS	NL	97	65	3.88	120.810	100.121	0.266	220.931
42	1877	Boston	Red Caps	BSN	NL	42	18	2.15	99.869	121.014	0.296	220.883
43	1997	Atlanta	Braves	ATL	NL	101	61	3.18	136.207	84.566	0.270	220.774
44	1944	St. Louis	Cardinals	SLN	NL	105	49	2.67	81.874	138.770	0.275	220.644
45	1953	Brooklyn	Dodgers	BRO	NL	105	49	4.10	48.881	170.780	0.285	219.661
46	1918	Chicago	Cubs	CHN	NL	84	45	2.18	116.038	103.574	0.265	219.613
47	2016	Boston	Red Sox	BOS	AL	93	69	4.00	99.252	120.151	0.282	219.403
48	1939	Cincinnati	Reds	CIN	NL	97	57	3.27	129.496	89.704	0.278	219.200
49	2017	Los Angeles	Dodgers	LAN	NL	104	58	3.38	116.415	102.730	0.249	219.145
50	1948	Cleveland	Indians	CLE	AL	97	58	3.22	96.896	122.094	0.282	218.990

Note: APEVA = Adjusted Pitching PEVA for era pitched.

Note: Best teams lists only considers the Regular Season.

.

About Our Stats

Baseball has, like no other sport, been fascinated with the statistics of the game. It provides a basis for comparison, whether the era is pre-National League with leagues such as the National Association (yes, we include that league and others beyond the National and American) or today's game of the usual 162 games, or the most recent 60 game season. The statistics are part of the lore and fascination of the game. Now, determining and comparing a player from the distant past, or even one of the more modern era can be difficult, particularly with the changes in rules or the changes in season length. But, no matter the time period, the tenants of how a player should be judged within his era does not change. How does he compare to the average player of his year? How dominant was the player above that average? That's what we at statgeekbaseball has done. After five thousand hours of research, the Player Rating System we have developed, based around the stat we've named PEVA (Performance Evaluation) correlates that dynamic and with several unique concepts to keep it in line with how baseball itself values those players, have developed a system of comparison that can rank and list and compare those players of every era against each other. In this book, as well as on the website of statgeekbaseball.com, there's stats you can get nowhere else in the baseball world.

What stats are we talking about?

How about PEVA?

PEVA is the acronym for Stat Geek Baseball's Player Rating. This grade is given to each player and pitcher each season, rating their performance on a peer to peer review. Six components for pitchers and batters are melded together into the PEVA Rating, which ranges each year from 0.200 to 64.000. PEVA ratings are available for every pitcher and hitter in baseball history and are valid no matter whether you or your favorite played in the dead ball era, the Babe Ruth era, the steroid era, or today.

PEVA Player Ratings Boxscore

PEVA	One Word	Description
64.000	Maximum	Maximum Player Rating
32.000	Fantastic	MVP or Cy Young Award Candidate
20.000	Great	All-League
15.000	Very Good	All-Star Caliber
10.000	Good	Plus Starter
3.500	Average	Bench Player
0.200	Minimum	Minimum Player Rating

What are the PEVA Components?

What stats go into the PEVA components and how are they measured? PEVA components are measured on a comparative basis within the year in question, scaling the value between the Minimum, Average, and Maximum values for the year. The applicable stats are adjusted for Park Factors. There are exceptions to these rules, however, for components that test the boundaries of the maximum, for example, as well as for components that have more value and impact on other components. Yes, it's a bit complicated, some might say pedantic, but that's how things are measured in real baseball, too.

We won't even talk about the shift.

Position Player Components	Pitcher Components
Games Played	Games or Games Started
Plate Appearances	Wins or Saves or Wins plus Saves
Run Production (Runs Scored plus RBI)	Earned Run Average
On Base Percentage	WHIP9 (Walks & Hits Per 9 Innings Pitched)
Slugging Percentage	Innings Pitched
Field Value	Strikeout to Walk Ratio and Home Runs per 9 IP

Field Value – Position Values

Position	Maximum	Average	Minimum
1B	1.40	1.00	1.00
2B	1.50	1.10	1.00
3B	1.70	1.30	1.05
SS	1.75	1.35	1.10
OF	1.70	1.30	1.00
P	1.15	1.00	0.85
DH	0.85	0.85	0.85
C	2.10	1.70	1.55

Field Value – Position Components

Position	Component #1	#2	#3	#4
1B	Games/Innings	Fielding Pct.	Range Factor	
2B	Games/Innings	Fielding Pct.	Range Factor	
3B	Games/Innings	Fielding Pct.	Range Factor	
SS	Games/Innings	Fielding Pct.	Range Factor	
OF	Games/Innings	Fielding Pct.	Range Factor	Assists Per Game/9 IP
P	Innings Pitched	Fielding Pct.	Range Factor	CS% (2014)
DH	NA	NA	NA	
C	Games/Innings	Fielding Pct.	Range Factor	Caught Stealing Pct.

Notes: Games used in years when Innings Played not available or used,
i.e. Assists per Games used in years when Innings Played not available or used.
CS% for pitchers added in 2014. CS% for catchers not available prior to 1890.

We know the above explanation really does not go anywhere near explaining enough about the system, although you can argue whether that matters or not when viewing the Best Ever rankings in this book.

There's more at statgeekbaseball.com for those that are interested.

Definitions/Abbreviations
Regular Statistics

R = Runs	RBI = Runs Batted In
HR = Home Runs	RPR = Run Production: Runs Plus Runs Batted In
OBP = On-Base Percentage: Hits and Walks plus Hit By Pitch divided by the total of At Bats plus Walks plus Hit By Pitch plus Sacrifice Flies.	PA = Plate Appearances: At Bats, Walks, Hit By Pitch, Sacrifice Flies, Sacrifices, and Defensive Interference.
SLG = Slugging Percentage: Total Bases divided by At Bats.	OPS = On Base Plus Slugging: OBP plus SLG percentages.
AVE = Batting Average: Hits Divided by At Bats.	AB = At Bats
W = Wins L = Losses	IP = Innings Pitched
SV = Saves: Defined as a pitcher who a) finished a game & b) does not get the win and c) pitches at least one inning with a lead of no more than three runs or pitches with the tying run at bat, on base, or on deck, or pitches 3 innings with the lead.	ERA = Earned Run Average: The amount of earned runs divided by Innings Pitched times 9.
SO/W = Strikeout to Walk Ratio: Strikeouts divided by Walks	HR9IP = Home Runs per 9 IP: Home Runs divided by Innings Pitched multiplied by 9.
WHIP = Walks/Hits per Inning: Walks plus hits divided by Innings Pitched. WHIP9 = Walks/Hits per 9 Innings: Walks plus hits over 9 Innings Pitched	MLST = Major League Service Time: Years.days a player was on the Major League roster.

New Stats

PEVA-B = PEVA Batting Rating: Overall Player Rating for Batting	PEVA-P = PEVA Pitching Rating: Overall Player Rating for Pitching
PEVA-T = PEVA Total Rating: Overall Player Rating for Regular Season, including both Pitching and Batting.	FV = Field Value: Stat measuring a player's fielding value over the season compared to other players. Stats used within this value include Innings/Games Played, Fielding Percentage, Caught Stealing Percentage, Outfield Assists Per Game/9 IP, and Range Factor. The maximum, average, and minimum value for Field Value differs with each position. Maximums range from 2.10 for Catchers, 1.75 for Shortstops, 1.70 for OF/3B, 1.50 for 2B, and 1.40 for 1B.
EQ = Equivalent Years: Equivalent of Full Season Years by a Player based on Games, Plate Appearances, and IP compared to total # of games in a season.	Per EQ = Per Equivalent Years: PEVA divided by EQ Year
RAVE = PEVA Rolling Average: Rolling Average of PEVA values based on 50% of the most recent year, 30% of one year back, and 20% of two years prior.	

Made in the USA
Middletown, DE
22 July 2021